Windows® 2000 Server

On Site

Joli Ballew

President & CEO
Roland Elgey

Publisher
Steve Sayre

Associate Publisher
Katherine R. Hartlove

Acquisitions Editor
Charlotte Carpentier

Development Editor
Jessica Choi

Product Marketing Manager
Tracy Rooney

Project Editor
Dan Young

Technical Reviewer
André Paree-Huff

Production Coordinator
Carla Schuder

Cover Designer
Laura Wellander

Layout Designer
April E. Nielsen

CD-ROM Developer
Chris Nusbaum

Windows® 2000 Server On Site

The Coriolis Group, LLC
14455 N. Hayden Road
Suite 220
Scottsdale, Arizona 85260
www.coriolis.com

Library of Congress Cataloging-in-Publication Data

Ballew, Joli
    Windows 2000 server on site / Joli Ballew.
      p. cm.
    Includes index.
    ISBN 1-57610-883-X
    1. Microsoft Windows server. 2. Operating systems (Computers). I. Title.
QA76.76.063 B3595 2001
005.4'4769--dc21

2001042171
CIP

Printed in the United States of America
10 9 8 7 6 5 4 3 2 1

The Coriolis Group, LLC • 14455 North Hayden Road, Suite 220 • Scottsdale, Arizona 85260

A Note from Coriolis

Coriolis Technology Press was founded to create a very elite group of books: the ones you keep closest to your machine. In the real world, you have to choose the books you rely on every day *very* carefully, and we understand that.

To win a place for our books on that coveted shelf beside your PC, we guarantee several important qualities in every book we publish. These qualities are:

- *Technical accuracy*—It's no good if it doesn't work. Every Coriolis Technology Press book is reviewed by technical experts in the topic field, and is sent through several editing and proofreading passes in order to create the piece of work you now hold in your hands.

- *Innovative editorial design*—We've put years of research and refinement into the ways we present information in our books. Our books' editorial approach is uniquely designed to reflect the way people learn new technologies and search for solutions to technology problems.

- *Practical focus*—We put only pertinent information into our books and avoid any fluff. Every fact included between these two covers must serve the mission of the book as a whole.

- *Accessibility*—The information in a book is worthless unless you can find it quickly when you need it. We put a lot of effort into our indexes, and heavily cross-reference our chapters, to make it easy for you to move right to the information you need.

Here at The Coriolis Group we have been publishing and packaging books, technical journals, and training materials since 1989. We have put a lot of thought into our books; please write to us at **ctp@coriolis.com** and let us know what you think. We hope that you're happy with the book in your hands, and that in the future, when you reach for software development and networking information, you'll turn to one of our books first.

Coriolis Technology Press
The Coriolis Group
14455 N. Hayden Road
Suite 220
Scottsdale, Arizona
85260

Email: ctp@coriolis.com
Phone: (480) 483-0192
Toll free: (800) 410-0192

Look for these related books from The Coriolis Group:

Windows 2000 Server Architecture and Planning, 2nd Edition
by Morten Strunge Nielsen

Windows 2000 Registry Little Black Book, 2nd Edition
by Nathan Wallace and Anthony Sequeira

Windows 2000 Security Little Black Book
by Ian McLean

Windows Admin Scripting Little Black Book
by Jesse M. Torres

IIS 5 On Site
by Scott Reeves and Kalinda Reeves

Active Directory On Site
by Mark Wilkins

Active Directory Black Book
by Adam Wood

To Cosmo. For your unconditional love and support.
—Joli Ballew

&

About the Author

Joli Ballew (MCSE, MCT, A+) is a technology trainer, writer, and network consultant in the Dallas area. Some of her previous employment positions have included technical writing, educational content consulting, working as a PC technician, a network administrator, a high school algebra teacher, and an MCSE instructor at Eastfield Community College. She has written a book on Windows 2000 Professional for Syngress Media, and is currently writing a book on Windows 2000 Server for The Coriolis Group.

Joli attended high school at the Performing Arts Magnet in Dallas where she studied music and the arts and was a member of the National Honor Society. She attended college at the University of Texas at Arlington and graduated with a Bachelor's degree in Mathematics, with a minor in English, and the following year, earned her Texas Teaching Certificate from the State of Texas. After teaching math and algebra for ten years, she decided to change careers and enter the world of computing. She earned all of her certifications in 14 months, and entered the field of computer training and consulting soon thereafter. Joli spends her spare time golfing, surfing the net, and spending time with her wonderful family and friends.

Joli can be reached at **Jballew@swynk.com** and maintains a Web site at **www.swynk.com/friends/ballew**.

Acknowledgments

There are quite a few people that made this project a success. First, special thanks to Charlotte Carpentier, the acquisitions editor at Coriolis, for giving me this wonderful opportunity, and Dan Young, my project editor, who made it an enjoyable and successful project. Special kudos to Jessica also, for getting me off on the right foot and for always telling me how wonderful I was. Thanks to Catherine, who diligently and patiently corrected my grammar and never seemed to get tired of making everything right, and my editor Rick, for being so enthusiastic and encouraging. I would like to send a group thank you to everyone at Coriolis for their faith in my abilities and the incredible freedom I had with the creation of this book.

There are also many behind-the-scenes people I never had the opportunity to ever talk to or meet, including Carla Schuder, production coordinator; Laura Wellander, cover designer; April Nielsen, template designer; and Tracy Rooney, marketing specialist.

Finally, I'd like to thank Tom Shinder for being such a wonderful teacher and for always being available to give me advice and direction, and for giving me my first break in this business, and Mitch Tulloch, for his patience with my articles and for offering guidance when I needed it. I'd like to thank Ken Sagen for giving me my first writing opportunity and for all of his support. I'd also like to express my gratitude to James Truscott, my very first editor and also a good friend, for always being there to answer any questions I had. Finally, a very special thanks to my family and friends who put up with me over the past six months, including my parents, Cosmo, and my daughter Jennifer, and all of their support both emotionally and financially throughout this endeavor.

Contents at a Glance

Table of Contents

Chapter 2
Preparing for Windows 2000 Server 33

Part II   Planning for and Installing Windows 2000 Server

Part IV   Using Windows 2000 Server

Chapter 10
Using TCP/IP and DHCP 575

Introduction

Thanks for buying *Windows 2000 Server On Site*. I wrote this book because of a growing need, among system administrators, for a comprehensive text for migrating to or installing a Windows 2000 network. Although many books on this subject are available, none cover the requirements of installing Windows 2000 Server quite as completely as this one does.

In this book, I have tried to create a one-stop text for planning, installing, configuring, and implementing Windows 2000 Server on a new or existing network, and I have included multiple worksheets, tips, personal experiences, flowcharts, and more to help you with the tasks that await. All of the worksheets used throughout this book are also included on this book's companion CD-ROM. Those worksheets will prove invaluable when you're planning and implementing your move to Windows 2000 Server. Although this book was initially planned to serve as a guide to be read from start to finish, it is just as useful as a desktop reference that can be used by all levels of personnel in any organization using Windows 2000 Server.

With all the material in this book, you'll continue to pick it up day after day. Here's what you'll find:

- Detailed explanations for performing almost any imaginable task on your Windows 2000 server.

- Easy-to-navigate chapters and detailed information on all topics, including why certain implementations are best.

- Multiple worksheets available for printing from the CD-ROM, including worksheets for planning the migration, creating timelines, taking inventory, creating teams, defining the topology, installing servers, creating labs, testing the installation, configuring the installation, rolling out the installation, and training users.

- Detailed information on how to move your Windows NT network to Windows 2000 without worrying about data loss. This information includes instructions for performing the migration in two ways: upgrading the existing servers, or creating an entirely new domain and migrating the data.

- Entire chapters dedicated to installing and configuring Dynamic Host Configuration Protocol (DHCP), Domain Name System (DNS), and Dynamic DNS and implementing those features with Windows Internet Name Service (WINS) and legacy networks.

- References for planning domains, organizational units, and sites, plus detailed explanations for creating them.

- Information to help you plan for users and groups, use group policies, and use IPSec policies and Kerberos to secure the network.

Is This Book for You?

Windows 2000 Server On Site was written with the intermediate or advanced user in mind. Among the topics that are covered are:

- Planning for Windows 2000 servers on your network, including needs assessment, Active Directory, and the DNS namespace

- Installing Windows 2000 Server, including upgrades, remote installations, automated installations, and unattended installations

- Administering Windows 2000 Server, including implementing and managing Active Directory services and users and groups

- Optimizing Windows 2000 Server with the Performance console, disk monitoring, Event Viewer, and Backup and Restore utilities

- Installing, configuring, and administering advanced features available with Windows 2000 Server, including DHCP, DNS, WINS, and the Routing and Remote Access Service (RRAS)

How to Use This Book

This book is separated into four parts: "Windows 2000 Server in Your Organization," "Planning for and Installing Windows 2000 Server," "Administering and Optimizing Windows 2000 Server," and "Using Windows 2000 Server." If you are using this book as a guide for installing, configuring, and employing Windows 2000 servers on your network, the book is best read from start to finish. However, because it includes hundreds of hands-on, detailed descriptions of how tasks are performed using the operating system, this book can be used as a desktop reference for all administrators in the organization or by students or interns learning how to perform specific tasks.

The first two sections are written such that each chapter builds on the others. To use the book effectively for planning and installing a Windows 2000 Server network, you'll need to read these chapters sequentially. The last two sections assume that you have already installed Windows 2000 Server on your network, so these chapters do *not* have to be read sequentially. These chapters describe how to configure the server, how to optimize and monitor the server, and how to use such features as DNS, DHCP, and WINS on the network.

In the first section, "Windows 2000 Server in Your Organization," you'll be introduced to Windows 2000's features and benefits, its components, and Active Directory. By reading this chapter first, you'll be able to decide if you want to install Windows 2000 and if the added features warrant the move. You can also use the information in these chapters to justify your decisions to other company officials.

In the second section, "Planning for and Installing Windows 2000 Server," you'll begin the planning process with a myriad of worksheets and tips for making the process go smoothly. In the installation section, you'll learn how to install the operating system in all of the possible ways, including installing remotely, installing clean, performing upgrades, and installing by using automated or unattended utilities. You'll also learn how to migrate from a Windows NT Server network to a Windows 2000 network.

In the third section, "Administering and Optimizing Windows 2000 Server," you can begin skipping around, reading only the chapters that interest you or only the chapters that contain the information you need. Once the servers are up and running, you can do such tasks as optimizing Active Directory, setting up users and groups, optimizing disk performance, and using Event Viewer and the Performance console as you wish.

Finally, in the fourth section, "Using Windows 2000 Server," you'll learn how to plan for, install, configure, and implement DHCP, DNS, WINS, and RRAS. When these services are needed, use this section as a reference; it fully explains all concepts and procedures associated with each service.

In the appendices, you can find solutions to common problems and answers to frequently asked questions. Troubleshooting tips and tricks are also included.

On the CD-ROM, you can find blank worksheets for planning the migration, creating timelines, taking inventory, creating teams, defining the topology, installing servers, creating labs, testing and configuring the installation, rolling out the installation, and training users. These worksheets will walk you through the entire process of creating a Windows 2000 network or migrating from Windows NT, and they can be printed for everyone involved in the project. You'll find the worksheets to be one of the high points of the book, and you will use them many times and in many phases of the project.

The *On Site* Philosophy

Written by experienced professionals, books in The Coriolis Group's *On Site* series guide you through typical, day-to-day needs assessment, planning, deployment, configuration, and troubleshooting challenges. The *On Site* series uses real-world scenarios and indispensable illustrations to help you move flawlessly through system setup and any problems you may encounter along the way. The illustrations, including concise flowcharts with clear and logical steps, help professionals diagnose problems and assess needs to reduce total cost of ownership.

I welcome your feedback on this book. Please email The Coriolis Group at **ctp@coriolis.com**. Errata, updates, and more are available at **www.coriolis.com**.

Part I

Windows 2000 Server in Your Organization

Configuration
Deployment
Planning
Troubleshooting

Chapter 1

What Is Windows 2000 Server?

Windows 2000 Server is a multipurpose operating system, offered by Microsoft, that can be used to power client/server and peer-to-peer networks for companies of all sizes and types. This powerful operating system can be used as a file, print, or application server, a Web server, or a communications server. Windows 2000 Server is more reliable than all of the previous versions of Microsoft server products, and many improvements have been made since those versions. This reliability lowers a company's Total Cost of Ownership (TCO) by reducing costs associated with customer calls to the help desk, by offering new and improved wizards and help features, and by using the familiar Windows interface. Windows 2000 Server also reduces TCO by offering services that ease installations across your network while employing automated and unattended client installations, and by reducing the need for administrators to handle all problems by physically traveling to clients' computers.

In addition to increased reliability and lower TCO, there are other reasons why you should use Windows 2000 Server on your network. Windows 2000 Server offers full Internet and applications support, new Active Directory services, support for up to four processors using symmetric multiprocessing, and support for up to 4GB of random access memory (RAM). (Windows 2000 Advanced Server offers even more power, including support for up to eight processors and 64GB of memory.) The most notable enhancements of Windows 2000 Server, when compared to the older Windows NT 4 operating system, include Active Directory, IntelliMirror, and improvements in security.

In this chapter, you'll be introduced to Windows 2000 Server, including its features and benefits, its architecture, and its components. Understanding the features and benefits of Windows 2000 Server will help you decide not only if an upgrade is reasonable, but also if it is needed. Understanding the basics of Windows 2000 Server's architecture is also important, and it will be discussed briefly to give you a general idea of what makes this operating system tick. Finally, components will be discussed. Components include items such as Dynamic Host Configuration Protocol (DHCP), Domain Name System (DNS), management and monitoring tools, file and print access, Terminal Services, and more.

Overall, Windows 2000 Server is a great system, offering incredible security and reliability, and it can be an asset for just about any small- to medium-sized network. This chapter will help you understand more about this operating system and will, I hope, convince you to employ it on your network.

Features and Benefits

There are many reasons to upgrade your network to Windows 2000 products, and there are many benefits to using them instead of other operating systems. Listed next are the features and benefits of Windows 2000 Server, including its new features. There will be some overlap in the "Components" section of this chapter, where those features will be addressed in more detail.

Performance, Stability, and Reliability

When creating Windows 2000 Server, Microsoft took a good look at the pitfalls of the older NT system, including what caused it to crash, why it needed repair, and how its reliability could be improved. Windows 2000 Server was then created with many improvements over NT. One of those improvements was the need for fewer reboots.

In Windows NT Server, rebooting was a common occurrence. In Windows 2000 Server, however, rebooting isn't always necessary when an administrator needs to configure network addresses, install or remove plug-and-play devices, change protocol information or bindings, or do a host of other activities. The Task Manager can be used to end tasks without disrupting network services or causing a computer to need an otherwise unnecessary reboot.

System crashes are also lessened with a new feature known as System File Protection (SFP). Sometimes crashes occur because necessary files can't be found; this can happen when applications change specific .dll files to suit their own needs. When these files are changed, they can no longer be used by other programs. Windows 2000 eliminates these types of problems by preventing the applications from overwriting these files when they are installed, thus maintaining the integrity of these files for other applications and programs on the computer.

Lower TCO

As I mentioned earlier, TCO can be dramatically reduced after Windows 2000 Server is installed because this operating system can ease the burden on administrators in a number of areas. Multiple wizards are available to help administrators do just about anything they need to do. There are wizards for installing Active Directory, adding printers, performing backups, finding new hardware, connecting to the Internet, setting up routing and remote access, scheduling tasks, using remote installation services, installing clients' machines, importing certificates, and lots more. Using these wizards will lessen the amount of outside help administrators need when setting up these components.

Windows 2000 Server also reduces TCO by providing a utility to administer the network from one physical location, so you don't have to move from desk to desk and user to user. This central administration can also be expanded to include software installations on client machines, automatic or unattended installation of operating systems, and configuration of client computers. This reduced need to visit the desks of each client for every problem or installation can greatly reduce the cost involved in administering a network.

Active Directory

Active Directory has to be the most important improvement in Windows 2000 Server. Designed and employed correctly, Active Directory services can seem to make a network work on its own. Active Directory is a directory service that logically stores all objects in a network and makes those objects manageable from a single machine. Active Directory services store information about objects and make this information available to the users on the network. For example, users can traverse Active Directory looking for a printer that is on the third floor of their building and that can print envelopes. Active Directory can be used to search for specific objects, and it allows users to use a single logon to access resources anywhere on the network. (Of course, users also have to have the correct permissions to use the resources.)

Enhanced Installation Features

Many features are available to make Windows 2000 Server easier to install and deploy, and to reduce the costs associated with the installation of client machines on the network. This book focuses mainly on planning for, installing, and configuring Windows 2000 Server; however, understanding options for installing operating systems on clients is very important as well. The following list shows some of the enhanced features available in Windows 2000 Server:

- *Remote Installation Services (RIS)*—Allows a client to connect (with the appropriate hardware) to a RIS server to obtain an image of an installation; this image can be configured to produce clean installations for clients. For RIS to work properly, the service must run on Windows 2000 Server, have access to an Active Directory DHCP server and a DNS server, and perform only clean installations of Windows 2000 Professional on its clients.

- *Disk Imaging*—Is provided by the Microsoft System Preparation tool (Sysprep.exe) and can be used when multiple client installations are needed and those computers have the same hardware. This type of installation offers the clients new security IDs and is fully customizable; however, like RIS, it can perform only clean installations of Windows 2000 Professional.

- *Slipstreaming*—Allows Windows 2000 service packs to be installed only once, instead of the multiple times required by Windows NT. After new components are added to a system, the service pack does not have to be reinstalled. This saves time and money in a variety of ways.

- *Unattended installations and answer files*—Allow administrators to further define the remote installation process by creating an image that contains not only the operating system itself, but applications, device drivers, and service packs as well. This installation can be partially attended, fully attended, or fully unattended to account for multiple levels of groups in your organization. The Client Installation Wizard can be used on the client side to allow a user to select from a number of images, although this might not be a good idea for certain groups within an organization.

Internet Integration

Because the Internet is familiar to most users on a network and is fast becoming the preferred way to access information, Microsoft has incorporated this technology and theme into Windows 2000 Server. Active Directory is designed around the naming scheme that is familiar to users on the Internet, and this Internet integration trickles down to the clients even in the way they search their own network for information. For instance, a user in the **Ballew.com** company might have a resource named **Merritt.Accounting. Dallas.Ballew.com** and might access a printer called **Printer5.Accounting.Dallas. Ballew.com**. These names are like the names on the Internet, and the interface is the same. In fact, a browser like Internet Explorer can be used to traverse the local network. Access to the Internet might even seem local to the user.

Windows 2000 Server also includes Internet Information Services (IIS). IIS can be used to host Internet and intranet Web sites on network servers. IIS is a secure Web-server platform that can be used to integrate Active Server pages (.asp files), Windows Media Services, and Distributed Authoring and Versioning (DAV).

Improved Recovery Options

When servers are down and workers can't log on to the network to use data and resources, the company suffers. Windows 2000 offers new and improved options for recovery from boot problems; these options include safe mode, Last Known Good, the Recovery Console, and boot logging. These features make repairing a problematic server easier and more efficient.

- *Safe mode*—Only essential drivers are loaded. Often, a new driver will be installed on a computer, and when the computer is rebooted, it will blue-screen. Using safe mode allows the computer to boot without unnecessary drivers, and problems can then be addressed.

- *Last Known Good Configuration (LKGC)*—Allows the computer to boot to the state it was in the last time it booted successfully. Again, by starting the system with the LKGC, you can erase any device drivers, new adapters, and new services that were installed and that modified the Registry since the last boot.

- *Recovery Console*—A powerful tool that allows an administrator to log on to a machine and troubleshoot it when it won't boot with Safe mode. Troublesome drivers, a corrupt

Master Boot Record, Registry corruption, and many other catastrophic events can be repaired using this method. An administrator can use this tool to access root and system directories and to perform repairs.

- *Boot logging*—Can be used to debug boot errors. This log is written to the hard disk using a **bootlog** startup parameter. Figure 1.1 shows an example of a boot log. This portion of the log shows the drivers that have been loaded and indicates whether they were loaded successfully.

USB and Plug-and-Play Support

Universal Serial Bus (USB) and Plug-and-Play (PnP) technologies are also incorporated into Windows 2000 Server and are an important part of it. Windows NT 4 didn't provide any real support for PnP, and installing additional peripherals was usually trying. Windows 2000 Server solves this problem by offering a much easier way to install these components. A user can plug in a USB hub; that hub can contain a new CD burner, a ZIP drive, and even a printer, and then Windows will install those items, usually without user intervention. Each component will be discovered and installed one by one, and shortcuts will be placed on the desktop if they're needed. This support is a major improvement over NT, and USB is the wave of the (current) future.

Figure 1.1
Sample boot log.

Built-In Support for TCP/IP and IPX/SPX Protocols and Other Networking Services

Transmission Control Protocol/Internet Protocol (TCP/IP) is the protocol that is used to power the Internet, and Microsoft Windows 2000 products have full built-in support for it. An industry-supported suite of protocols, TCP/IP provides routable access to the Internet and all of its resources. Internetwork Packet Exchange/Sequenced Packet Exchange (IPX/SPX) is a protocol stack that is used primarily in Novell networks, is relatively small and fast, and is also fully supported.

Other networking services include dial-up services for mobile users; connectivity with Unix, Macintosh, and Novell servers and clients; and support for up to 256 simultaneous inbound connections to a Windows 2000 server.

New and Improved Security Features

Security is of critical importance to any network, although some networks need more protection than others do. Windows 2000 Server offers improved security, new technology, and auditing services for the network.

Public Key Infrastructure (PKI) allows a network to protect itself against unwanted attacks and lapses in security by using new authentication techniques based on the cryptography of user names and hostnames, thus ensuring that critical data cannot be stolen from the wire. *Cryptography* is a mathematical technique that allows the transmitted data to be encrypted on one end and decrypted on the other end to ensure that it cannot be interpreted by unwanted readers. *PKI* is a set of rules, policies, and standards that allow the verification of all parties in an electronic transaction. PKI consists of digital certificates, certification authorities, and various third party certificate signers.

Other security features include, but are not limited to, digital message signing, secret keys, data encryption, Microsoft Certificate Services, the ability to use smart cards and smart card logon, Microsoft Authenticode technology, fault tolerance, IP Security (IPSec) policies, and the Kerberos protocol. A Windows 2000 network is secure when these security features are implemented appropriately. Another security feature is *auditing*. An administrator can configure auditing to create logs of events, recording such things as who accesses certain files or folders, who logs on and off, who shuts down a computer, and who attempts to change groups, permissions, or Active Directory objects. Tracking events such as these can prove most valuable when there are security breaches on the network, and tracking which actions were performed by whom can be very useful.

COM+ and Component Services

The Component Object Model (COM+) provides an interface between objects on a network. COM+ technology was created to assist programmers in development of objects and application programs. Component Services, which are part of the software architecture, can process requests such as determining the type of certificate that a particular server issues, or intercepting system requests for the purpose of ensuring security. You can

1

think of COM+ Services as creating an interface between objects, the same way the clipboard can be used to move a particular piece of information from one program to another.

Terminal Services

The incorporation of Terminal Services into Windows 2000 Server is a great addition to the product. Many small- to medium-sized networks consist of workers using computers that are considered *thin clients*. These thin clients—which are sometimes called *terminal server clients*—can access applications stored on a server that they cannot host on their own computers. Terminal Services are used the way older mainframes were used: the client doesn't have any software or hardware, so to speak, and instead accesses everything from the terminal server. The terminal server has all of the programs and applications and provides storage for its users.

Using Terminal Services is a great way to run a network if all of your users need the same desktop, applications, and storage requirements and/or if tight security is a priority. The terminal server can be configured once, and all of the clients use that configuration. When software has to be upgraded, it is upgraded only one time on the terminal server. To maintain tight security on the network, everyone can have a restricted desktop and similar permissions to access resources. The TCO is also reduced because the client machines do not have to have large hard drives or lots of RAM or be independently maintained.

New Storage Enhancements

Another new feature in Windows 2000 Server is the ability to manage and allocate storage space on the server. Disk quotas can be used to limit the amount of space that clients can have on the server's hard disk. This limit can be configured in many different ways, but it is used to encourage users to clean out their files, erase old emails, and reduce the amount of unnecessary information they maintain in their folders.

Remote Storage is a utility that is used to monitor the disk space that is available on the company's server(s). This utility can be used to move data off the server if it has been successfully saved to another location. This movement takes place when the amount of available storage space drops below a specific level or threshold.

Improvements for Administration

Of all of the new offerings in Windows 2000 Server, some stand out and just make you want to say "Thanks!" Disk quota management is one such feature. With this feature, an administrator can limit the amount of disk space that users are allowed to have on the network server. This is done using a simple interface through group policy.

Other features include the services offered by Active Directory and the global catalog, the Distributed File System (DFS), automatic transitive trusts, and increased hardware support.

Wait, There's More!

Even more features are available in Windows 2000 Server, and although they are a little beyond the scope of this book, they deserve mentioning.

Windows 2000 Server incorporates support for growth when operating systems go to a 64-bit architecture (currently they are 32-bit), allowing upward compatibility, if you will. Windows also offers *Single Sign-On (SSO)*, which allows a user to have one set of credentials for logging on to a network; those credentials give the user access across multiple operating systems. Domains can now be partitioned to divide the responsibilities of managing a network without the need to create new domains each time. Using *organizational units*, an administrator can divvy up the duties of a single domain among multiple departments without the tedium of creating trusts or using additional hardware. *Scripts* can be used to automate tasks too complex for users to accomplish themselves. Scripts include logon, logoff, startup, and shutdown scripts, and these scripts can be DOS, .bat, .com, .exe, Visual Basic (VB), Java, or C++ scripts.

Networking features include *Dynamic DNS* or *DDNS*, which allows the integration of the DHCP server with the DNS server for automatic updating of IP addresses and domain names. *Rogue DHCP detection* is a new feature requiring that new DHCP servers be authorized and detected prior to integration on the network. This keeps unauthorized DHCP servers from becoming part of the network. *Automatic Private IP Addressing (APIPA)* is a feature that allows users on a network to communicate even if the DHCP server goes down. APIPA can be used for networks smaller than 200 or so clients in a small office. Because the IP addresses offered by APIPA are in the 169.254.y.z range, these clients will be able to see only those clients on their own subnet, and APIPA can be used only as a quick and nonpermanent fix when a DHCP server on the network goes down. *Network Address Translator (NAT)* works similarly to a proxy server, without the hassle. NAT is easy to use and configure and can offer a good firewall for a small network.

Components

When Windows 2000 Server is installed, many components are installed automatically during the setup of the server, while some components can be added after installation is complete. Because not all available components are needed in every circumstance, only some of the components are installed during installation. To see what services are installed on a Windows 2000 computer, simply open up My Computer and choose Add/Remove Programs. Keep in mind that the *components* that are installed are different from the *programs* that are installed. Figure 1.2 is an example of programs installed on a Windows 2000 computer. Figure 1.3 is an example of the components installed on a Windows 2000 computer.

Components, then, are additional utilities, programs, services, and support that you can add after basic installation to enhance what the server can do. For instance, to turn a specific network server into a machine that can support the creation, management, and configuration of Web sites, support File Transfer Protocol (FTP), and support Simple Mail Transfer Protocol (SMTP), you would choose to install Internet Information Services (IIS). IIS is

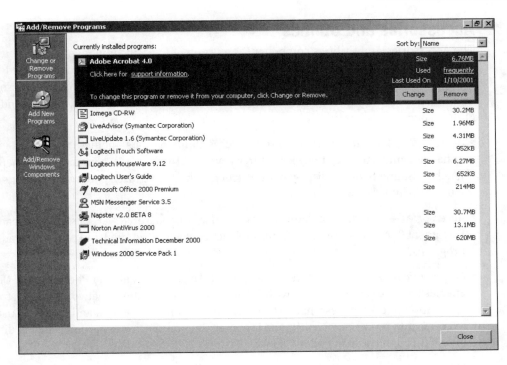

Figure 1.2
Currently installed programs.

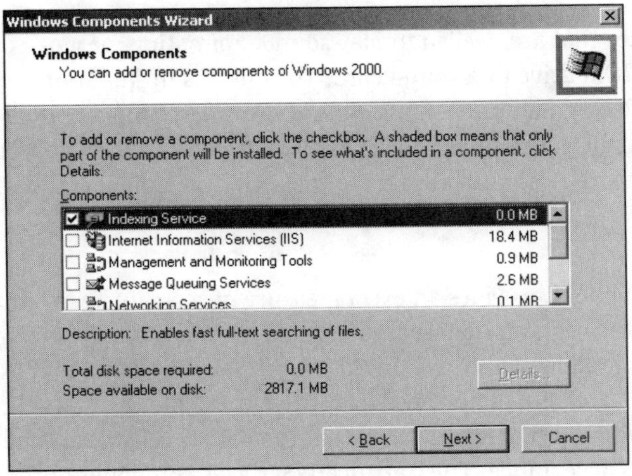

Figure 1.3
Currently installed components.

shown in Figure 1.3 as the second listed component. IIS is not currently installed on this machine.

Listed next are the available components for a Windows 2000 server. Each component is followed by a brief description of the service and its purpose.

Accessories and Utilities

The Accessories And Utilities component is a group of five subcomponents. These subcomponents can be further divided and installed or uninstalled through the Add/ Remove Programs icon in the Control Panel. The five subcomponents under Accessories And Utilities are the Accessibility Wizard, Accessories, Communications, Games, and Multimedia:

- *Accessibility Wizard*—Is used to provide accessibility options, including keyboard enhancements (such as sticky keys, filter keys, and toggle keys), sound enhancements (such as Sound Sentry), display options (such as high contrast), and mouse options (such as using mouse keys).

- *Accessories*—Include Calculator, Character Map, Clipboard Viewer, Desktop Wallpaper, Document Templates, Mouse Pointers, Object Packager, and the Paint and WordPad programs.

- *Communications*—Offers three services: Chat, HyperTerminal, and Phone Dialer. Chat enables a user to communicate with other users over a Windows network, similar to an application like MSN Messenger. HyperTerminal requires a modem and enables a user to connect to online services. Phone Dialer enables a user to use his computer to dial a phone through the installed modem.

- *Games*—Includes FreeCell, Minesweeper, Pinball, and Solitaire. You can uninstall the games from this dialog box. Be careful, however, that your boss's favorite game isn't FreeCell before you remove it.

- *Multimedia*—Offers services that are needed to play sound, animation, or video on a computer that uses a CD-ROM drive or a sound card. The options in this subcomponent include CD Player, Media Player, Sample Sounds, Sound Recorder, Utopia Sound Schemes, and Volume Control. If the server doesn't have a sound card or won't be used for multimedia purposes, there is no reason to leave these components installed.

Certificate Services

The Certificate Services component provides an extra measure of security by creating a reliable way to exchange information on nonsecure networks; this is done by providing a standard for establishing the validity of and creating trust between networks that exchange data. Certificates securely bind public keys to entities that hold the related private keys. These certificates are digitally signed and show that the data is reliable and has not been tampered with before its acceptance. The Certificate Services component provides a way to offer secure email, smart card authentication, and Web-based authentication. Installing Certificate Services allows an administrator to create a Certificate Authority on the server, issue digital certificates, and publish Web pages on the server. Figure 1.4 shows an example of a Certificate Authority warning.

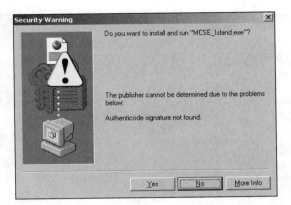

Figure 1.4
Example of Certificate Authority warning.

Indexing Service

The Indexing Service offers full-text searching of files. It is installed by default during the Windows 2000 Server setup but is set to manual startup. The Indexing Service is processor intensive, so before using this service, make sure that your server has the necessary resources.

Internet Information Services

Internet Information Services (IIS) is available for installation if your network needs to support Web site creation and management. The Details tab of the IIS dialog box lists a multitude of files required to make IIS run properly. These files should not be deleted or installed independently because all of them are needed. Some of these files include documentation, FrontPage 2000 extensions, Network News Transfer Protocol (NNTP) service, SMTP service, and Visual InterDev support.

Management And Monitoring Tools

To run a network efficiently and productively, you need tools for monitoring and management. The Management And Monitoring Tools component of Windows 2000 offers utilities that can improve performance and network capabilities. The three options available for installation or removal are:

- *Connection Manager Components*—Installs the Connection Manager Administration Kit and the Phone Book Service.

- *Network Monitor Tools*—Can be used to analyze packets of data that are transmitted across a network. Specifically, this analyzer is Microsoft Network Monitor, shown in Figure 1.5.

- *Simple Network Management Protocol (SNMP)*—Includes a service for creating "agents" that will monitor the activity of objects on the network and report problems to the computer that collects this information.

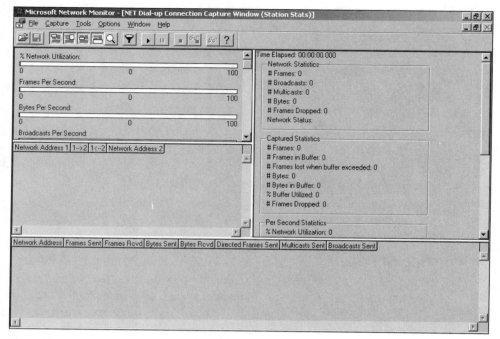

Figure 1.5
Microsoft Network Monitor.

Message Queuing

The Message Queuing component provides services associated with the transfer of information that distributed applications need to function reliably even if a computer is offline. This service also allows these applications to function reliably in heterogeneous networks, and it provides loosely knit communication services.

Networking Services

One of the main reasons to have and maintain a network is to relay information and data from one computer to another across data lines. The effectiveness of this communication defines how useful the network actually is. For information and communication to occur smoothly, many networking services work behind the scenes. Not all of the services listed here are necessarily needed on every network, but by understanding the fundamental purpose of each, you can decide if these services will be needed (or perhaps are currently needed) on your Windows 2000 network. The Networking Services component of Windows 2000 Server includes the following services:

- *COM Internet Services Proxy*—Is used when communications between distributed applications need to communicate through HTTP and IIS.

- *Domain Name System (DNS)*—Resolves hostnames to IP addresses for clients on the current network. DNS is what allows a user to type **www.microsoft.com** instead of the TCP/IP address, which would be difficult to remember.

- *Dynamic Host Configuration Protocol (DHCP)*—Allows the DHCP server to automatically assign its clients their TCP/IP addresses, so an administrator doesn't have to manually install the individual machines with those addresses.

- *Internet Authentication Service (IAS)*—Is used to authenticate dial-in users on a network. IAS also supports the RADIUS protocol (Remote Authentication Dial-In User Service), which is a security protocol widely used by Internet service providers (ISPs) and which is the most popular type of authentication to date.

- *Quality of Service (QoS) Admission Control*—Is new in Windows 2000 products and sets standards for the quality of data transmission. Using QoS services, you can specify the quality of each network connection for every subnet on the network.

- *Simple TCP/IP Services*—Provides support for such utilities as Quote Of The Day, Echo, Daytime Discard, and Character Generator.

- *Site Server Internet Locator Service (ILS) Service*—Can be used to keep user information current in network directories by scanning the TCP/IP stack and updating those directories. This service also provides support for telephony applications that allow users to access options such as caller ID, video conferencing, and faxing.

- *Windows Internet Naming Service (WINS)*—Is similar to DNS except that WINS is used to resolve NetBIOS names to IP addresses for clients on the network, and WINS is used mainly with down-level clients, such as Windows NT 4 and earlier. Again, this service allows a user to type a familiar name instead of a hard-to-remember IP address.

Other Network File And Print Services

Most networks are not created and formed solely by using Windows 2000 or NT products and operating systems. Networks are composed of many different users, computers, and operating systems. Some of the more common systems include the Macintosh OS and Unix. The Other Network File And Print Services component offers support for these operating systems.

Remote Installation Services (RIS)

RIS is an exceptional service that can be used to remotely install Windows 2000 Professional clients without having to physically visit each desk and install those clients manually. By using the Remote Installation Client Wizard, a DHCP server, a DNS server, and a RIS server, you can perform hundreds of remote installations quickly and efficiently across different physical locations.

Remote Storage

Remote Storage is another extremely useful service available in Windows 2000 Server. With Remote Storage, you can make a server's disk space more efficient by making magnetic tape devices and other removable media more accessible. Remote Storage can be configured to automatically move infrequently used data to these remote storage locations.

Script Debugger

This service simply lets an administrator view errors in script programs that run on a computer; this viewing helps you troubleshoot those errors.

Terminal Services and Terminal Services Licensing

Terminal Services allows a server to act as a mainframe, enabling thin clients to access the server for all their needs, including storage, data retrieval, and applications. This type of network lowers a company's TCO by reducing the costs associated with each workstation and by eliminating the need to upgrade software on each user's desktop. This is true because only the Terminal server has copies of the applications, so only one computer needs to be updated. Terminal Services can also be used to standardize a company's security, desktop, wallpaper, and so on, and it is helpful when security is a high priority. Backups can be managed from a central location as well.

Terminal Services Licensing is also handled here by allowing an administrator to register and track the number of users who employ your Terminal server. In order to use Terminal Services, you must also install the licensing application.

Windows Media Services

The Windows Media Services component enables you to stream multimedia content from the server to the network users. It also allows a network to use Advanced Streaming Format (ASF) over the Internet or a local intranet. Windows Media Services can be used to offer training programs or other network-wide broadcasts to all users on the network.

The Windows Media Administrator can be used to create and configure live unicast broadcasts, multicast broadcasts, PowerPoint presentations, and play-on-demand ASF files. Microsoft Windows Media Player and NetMeeting are both part of Windows Media Services and are shown in Figures 1.6 and 1.7.

Now that we've discussed the features and benefits of Windows 2000 Server and described its available components, you can see that there are many enhancements to the Windows NT operating system, and you should be seeing the advantages to choosing Windows 2000 as your operating system. In the next section, we'll discuss Active Directory, which is an integral part of Windows 2000 Server, and its features, benefits, and characteristics.

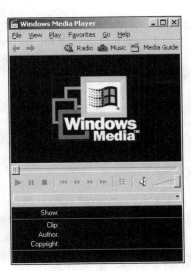

Figure 1.6
The Windows Media Player.

Figure 1.7
The NetMeeting interface.

Overview of Active Directory

Active Directory is the "glue" that holds all of the information, resources, objects, and users together on a network. Active Directory is what allows information to be readily available to users and clients, and it's a major part of what makes Windows 2000 Server such a successful operating system for networks.

Active Directory is just that: a directory. If you needed to find the phone number or address of an accountant in your area, you'd look up that information in a phone book. If you wanted to find out where in this book you could find information about DHCP, you'd use the index at the back of the book; the index is also a directory. If you were a user on a Windows 2000 network and you needed to access a printer that's in the accounting department of your office, you'd use Active Directory to find that information. Active Directory is a powerful tool for organizing, managing, administrating, and making available objects on a network. Objects can be thought of as anything that anyone in the network may need. An object could be a printer, a system resource, a user, or any number of other resources.

Active Directory is scalable; it is designed to be used effectively in a network that has one Windows 2000 server with five clients, two printers, and a small database, or in a network with 25 servers and millions of objects. Active Directory offers a hierarchical view of everything available on a network, and it is very secure. The interface will look familiar to administrators because its directory is designed around the namespace used on the Internet, using DNS names for clients and objects. Active Directory offers a single point of administration for all resources, including files, printers, hosts, databases, users, services, Web access, scanners, fax servers, print servers, and thousands of additional resources.

Having Active Directory installed is what makes a Windows 2000 Server a domain controller. Active Directory is not installed by default when Windows 2000 Server is installed. Figure 1.8 shows the Configure Your Server screen that is used to begin the process of installing Active Directory. Installing Active Directory will be covered in detail in Chapter 4.

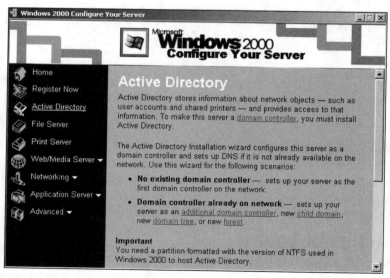

Figure 1.8
The Configure Your Server screen for installing Active Directory.

The following sections contain information on the features, benefits, and characteristics of Windows 2000 Server's Active Directory. These subjects, mentioned previously, will be explained in more depth here. Understanding the features of Active Directory will assist you tremendously when you're deciding if migrating to Windows 2000 Server is necessary for your environment. What might be more important is that understanding Active Directory will help you get a sense for how you will plan your Active Directory structure in Chapter 2.

Single Point of Administration

Active Directory offers the administrator a single point of administration. It can be accessed through the Active Directory Users And Computers MMC (Microsoft Management Console) snap-in. Active Directory can also be accessed from the Administrative Tools group in the Start menu. Once Active Directory is set up, users and resources can be easily configured, added, relocated, and removed through a single interface. Because Active Directory also stores information on the attributes of these users and resources, and maintains this information in logical organizational units, resources can be located and managed in a number of ways. Active Directory divides the network into two structure types: logical and physical.

To understand how the logical structure works, consider this example. Say that you want to locate all of the printers on the network that can print laser copies, so you perform a search for such attributes. You can further refine your search by searching for all laser printers that can print envelopes. If you needed to find these printers for replacement, the search would be very easy to initiate through Active Directory. In another example, to find a particular user, you could search for someone by name. This type of information in Active Directory is logical, meaning that the structure is designed logically around specific resources.

Another type of configuration that can be designed or accessed is for a physical division. Active Directory can be designed around a city, a state, a country, a building, or a site. Active Directory can be set up in such a way that Chicago is one division, Dallas is another, and San Francisco is another. Physical divisions can also be made by floors, departments, or countries. To find a list of printers that are in the Chicago office, for instance, you'd use a physical structure.

It's important to keep this in mind when you're designing an Active Directory structure for the first time. An appropriate amount of time should be spent on this decision because an incorrectly designed Active Directory structure could cause major headaches further down the road. (For instance, what if part of the structure is based on an office on the third floor, and at some point these users are moved to a different office on the fifth floor?)

Object Support

An *object* is a logical representation of a resource on a network. The object contains information about the resource it represents. An object's attributes include such information as where the object is located, what type of resource it is, what type of paper it can use if it's a printer, or how high a resolution it can use to scan documents if it's a scanner. Other objects might include information on a person, such as his or her name, email address, and phone number. Other types of objects, such as file shares, might include attributes concerning who owns the file, who can access the file, and whether it's a read-only file. Windows 2000 Server is capable of maintaining information on *more than a million objects.*

Building Blocks of the Active Directory Structure

Active Directory is simply an information bank of resources and objects on a network that allows the objects to be accessed in many different ways. The structure of Active Directory is built on four types of organizational building blocks. To effectively plan for Active Directory on your network, you'll need a thorough understanding of each of these units.

Domains in Windows 2000 Server are similar to Windows NT domains, but with the addition of Active Directory, each domain in a Windows 2000 network has its own Active Directory database and therefore creates a security boundary around itself. For other domains to be accessed, or for users in other domains to access resources in yours, appropriate trusts must be created. (Trusts will be detailed later.)

A domain consists of a Windows 2000 server acting as a domain controller, plus network resources, such as other computers, printers, and files. Unlike Windows NT, a Windows 2000 network has no primary or backup domain controllers; it has only member servers and domain controllers. Figure 1.9 shows an example of a Windows 2000 domain and its boundaries.

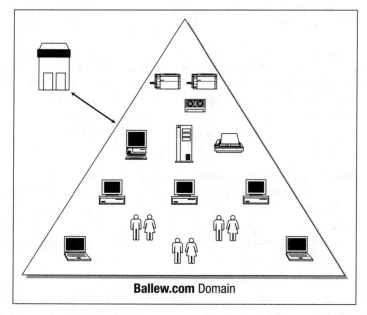

Ballew.com Domain

Figure 1.9
Contents of a Windows 2000 sample domain.

Because domains contain so many different items, there must exist a logical set of rules for grouping those resources and objects. The smallest type of logical unit for organizing the resources on a network is the *organizational unit (OU)*. An organizational unit can be thought of as a container that holds objects. The OU can be used to group objects together by department, location, function, type, or just about any other category you can think of. You can create an OU that contains objects in the Sales department, for instance. In turn, the Sales department can contain other OUs—perhaps a Users OU, a Printers OU, or a subdivision such as OUs based on laptop users versus desktop computer users. Each of these organizational units can then be independently managed by someone in that department. See Figure 1.10 for a graphical representation of organizational units.

One of the major considerations in planning an effective Active Directory involves determining what type of structure your company needs. Keep in mind the needs of your network as I continue explaining these terms.

A *tree* is an arrangement of one or more Windows 2000 domains that are connected by two-way transitive trusts, as is the case between parent and child domains.. The fictitious company shown in Figures 1.9 and 1.10, **Ballew.com**, has an Active Directory that consists of only one tree. **Ballew.com** is called the *root domain* and the first tree. In this case, **Ballew.com** is the domain name. Other domains can be added to this domain, forming child domains and a *domain tree*. In this book, I'll denote trees as triangles, as shown in Figure 1.11.

If **Ballew.com** grows and new domains are created, then the domain tree changes. For instance, if **Ballew.com** expands and new offices are created, the domain that currently consists of one tree and one domain can become a domain that contains a parent domain and additional child domains. Figure 1.12 shows an example of **Ballew.com** after such growth. **Ballew.com** still consists of only one tree.

Finally, *forests* are created from multiple trees. To understand forests, consider what might happen if **Ballew.com** acquired another company whose domain name was **Smith.com**. **Smith.com** is already established on the Internet, and it would be a bad business idea to change the name of **Smith.com** to anything else. Therefore, the merged corporation would consist of two trees, thus making a forest. Figure 1.13 shows this relationship more clearly.

Implicit Domain Trusts

In Windows NT, establishing trusts was quite a task. To create a two-way trust, an administrator had to establish two one-way trusts; transitive trusts were not supported. That meant that if you wanted domains A and B to trust each other, you had to configure domain A to trust domain B, and then configure domain B to trust domain A. If a third or fourth domain was involved, well, I think you get the idea.

Windows 2000 Server offers a better alternative to this. When a domain joins a tree, a two-way trust is created automatically between the adjoining domain and the parent

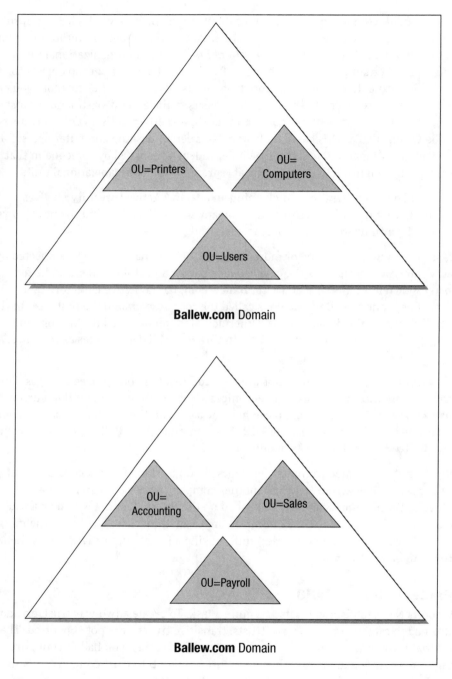

Ballew.com Domain

Ballew.com Domain

Figure 1.10
The organizational units.

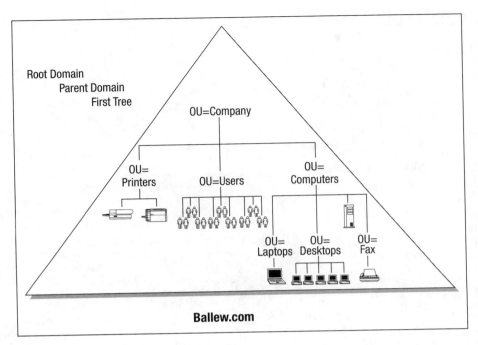

Figure 1.11
The **Ballew.com** domain.

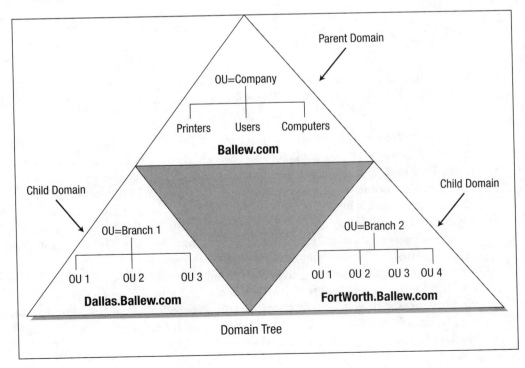

Figure 1.12
Ballew.com after adding child domains.

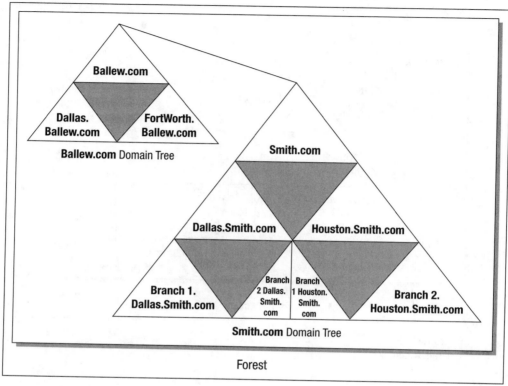

Figure 1.13
Forests.

domain. In addition, if two trees in a forest are associated, a two-way trust is created between the root domains of each. This automatic trust creation makes the administration and configuration of trusts almost plug and play.

Windows 2000 Server also offers *transitive trusts*. Transitive trusts work in the following manner: If domain A trusts domain B, and domain B trusts domain C, then domain A trusts domain C. This works out well most of the time, but in some instances, it won't. For example, consider the following sentences to understand why transitive trusts are not always appropriate. John trusts his accountant because his accountant has never made any mistakes doing John's books. The accountant trusts the IRS because the IRS has never made any mistakes concerning the accountant's company. Therefore, John should implicitly trust the IRS without question and at all times. Now consider the previous sentence: the result of the transitive trust. Should it really be true all the time? Maybe not. It is for this reason that transitive trusts can be disabled in a network under certain circumstances, although usually transitive trusts are welcomed by the administrator and used by default. See Figure 1.14 for an example of such a trust. (The double arrow represents a two-way transitive Kerberos trust.)

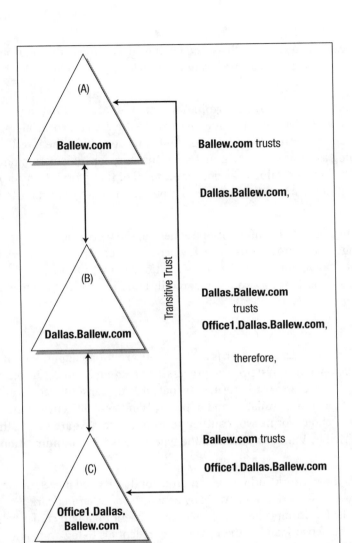

Ballew.com trusts

Dallas.Ballew.com,

Dallas.Ballew.com
trusts
Office1.Dallas.Ballew.com,

therefore,

Ballew.com trusts

Office1.Dallas.Ballew.com

Figure 1.14
Transitive trusts.

Flexible Querying Global Catalog

As you've already learned, each domain has an Active Directory, and it is the Active Directory that stores information about the objects in the domain. Consider two of the domains shown in Figure 1.12: **Dallas.Ballew.com** and **FortWorth.Ballew.com**. These two domains are separate and distinct, and each has its own characteristics. These two domains are also part of a domain tree and need to share information. The users in Dallas probably won't ever need all of the information in the Fort Worth office, but they might need information about users' email addresses, the types of printers or fax machines they have, which computers can use services such as NetMeeting, and various other attributes pertaining to the office's resources. Dallas users might also need to log on to the Fort Worth domain.

The global catalog meets these needs by performing two main functions. First, by providing information about Universal group membership to the domain controllers, the global catalog allows users in trusted domains to log on to any domain in the forest. Second, the global catalog allows users to search Active Directory for information on any object in the domain. The global catalog does not replicate all of the information across these domains; instead, it keeps information on certain objects that are important to the global community.

When the global catalog can't find the information requested, the global catalog sends a referral using the distinguished name for the object, whereby the user can then query the server in the appropriate domain for the required information. To make this referral service work properly, it's important that you plan carefully and fully understand how the global catalog works.

Security

Obviously, keeping the Active Directory secure is a major concern for an administrator and for the Windows 2000 operating system. The processes of logging on to get resources and obtaining the credentials necessary to traverse the network are certainly security-driven. Many network protocols are available, and in purely Windows 2000 environments, Kerberos is the protocol of choice for network authentication. Listed next are some other protocols that are supported by Windows 2000 and the type of network communication they are designed for:

- *Kerberos Version 5*—Is the network authentication protocol that is used by default on a computer with Windows 2000. Kerberos offers many benefits over other network authentication protocols. For instance, Kerberos allows the client to obtain credentials once from a server on the network and to then use those credentials to log on to any other server in the network. Kerberos also provides simplified trust management, offering two-way and transitive trusts between security authorities for available domains.

- *NT LAN Manager (NTLM)*—Was the authentication protocol of choice for a Windows NT network, which was based on a challenge/response technique. NTLM is currently used in a Windows 2000 network when users need to access resources on a Windows NT 4 server.

- *Internet Protocol Security (IPSec)*—Is an open standard for securing communications over the Internet. IPSec allows and ensures private and secure communications by using cryptographic services for its security abilities.

- *Public Key Infrastructure (PKI)*—Is a technique used to secure public and private access to resources on a network. PKI is used for such tasks as encrypting emails, protecting consumers' credit card numbers and other private information given on your Web site, encrypting NetMeeting calls to prevent eavesdropping, authenticating users, and signing electronic contracts.

- *Smart cards*—Offer another type of security and use a smart card reader. A smart card is essentially a computer on a credit card. The card can be swiped through a reader, and the user can be authenticated using the information on the card.

- *Secure Sockets Layer (SSL)*—Allows encryption for outbound connections and provides authentication and privacy by using public key technology. You might know about SSL already, having logged on to a Web server using **https** rather than **http** as part of the URL. Figure 1.15 shows a secure Web site using SSL and the **https://** convention. SSL ensures that the data transmitted to and from that site will be encrypted to provide security for the user.

- *Security features*—Are integrated in Active Directory. Each object, file, folder, user, computer, scanner, server, group, or printer on a network has permissions and rights that are assigned to it. The Active Directory stores this information as well as domain security policies. Domain security policies might contain restrictions—such as password restrictions or logon restrictions—that have system-wide effects. Figure 1.16 shows some of the restrictions that can be placed on users in the security policy held by Active Directory.

Extensibility of Schema

Active Directory can be extended, meaning that a programmer or administrator who has the proper training and skills can add new classes of objects to Active Directory or add new attributes to existing classes of objects. The schema itself has these attributes and classes defined in the Active Directory. Existing classes include User, Computer, Printer, and so on.

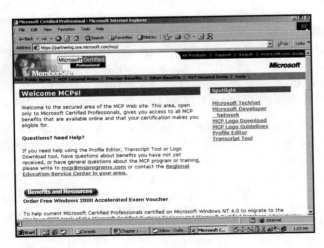

Figure 1.15
Sample site using https://.

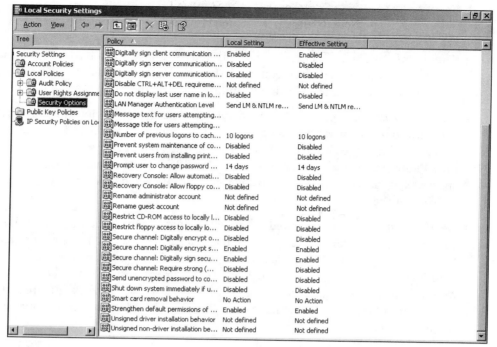

Figure 1.16
Security policies for the local machine.

Integration with DNS and LDAP

As we have seen, the Active Directory namespace is created and configured the same way that the names of Web sites are. In our example, we used two fictitious companies, **Ballew.com** and **Smith.com**. We further defined this namespace using **Dallas.Ballew.com** and **FortWorth.Ballew.com**. When a user types the name **Ballew.com** into a Web browser, the user is automatically taken to the appropriate Web site. That user does not have to type the IP address of that entity. DNS allows this to happen not only across the Internet but in an intranet as well. You can configure DNS on a Windows 2000 server simply by using the Administrative Tools menu and choosing DNS. From there, you can use the Configure DNS Server Wizard, shown in Figure 1.17, to turn the server into a DNS server.

Windows 2000, DNS, and DHCP can all work together to make the local intranet look and act like the Internet. DDNS can be used to incorporate these three concepts and services. DDNS allows DNS clients (your network clients) to dynamically record their computer names and addresses in the DNS database. If new clients or servers are added to the network, they also can automatically update the database files. This previously had to be done manually, so DDNS is a great new feature of Windows 2000. When DHCP is used to automatically assign TCP/IP addresses on a network, DDNS can also be used to keep the TCP/IP addresses and names of computers synchronized.

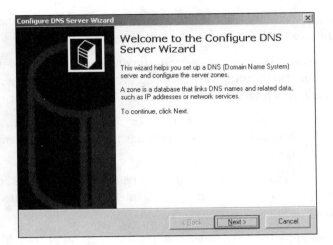

Figure 1.17
The Configure DNS Server Wizard.

Lightweight Directory Access Protocol (LDAP) is used to identify objects through Active Directory and to let users view and handle information in the Active Directory. LDAP is what allows a user to ask for specific components or objects on a network over a TCP connection. LDAP is designed around five models: Data, Organizational, Security, Functional, and Topological. These models define an object's attributes and class, how the objects are organized in the directory, how the objects are manipulated, where the supporting secure connections are, and how the information will be obtained for the clients. Because LDAP is an open standard, it can be integrated and used with other types of vendor directory services.

Replications

The Windows 2000 domain structure differs from Windows NT in many ways, but the biggest change is the move from having one primary domain controller (PDC) and a few backup domain controllers (BDCs) to having multiple domain controllers that eliminate PDCs and BDCs on the network. Every domain controller in a Windows 2000 network is either a domain controller or another type of server, such as application server, file and print server, or member server.

In a Windows NT domain, if the PDC went offline, one of the BDCs had to be promoted to a PDC to continue network operations. In a Windows 2000 network, every domain controller on the network has a copy of the Active Directory, promoting load balancing and fault tolerance across the network. Because of this, the Active Directory must be replicated often to keep all of the data up-to-date.

In addition to load balancing and fault tolerance, Active Directory replication has other benefits as well. Some of the other benefits include the following:

- Because replication occurs based on an object's globally unique identifier (GUID) and not on its distinguished name (DN), replication is more accurate. Active Directory can differentiate between deleted objects and new ones.

- Updates to the Active Directory database are based on values that have changed, and are not transmitted as the entire object. This minimizes conflicts that could arise when more than one change to an object is made.

- Replication can be configured to suit the needs of multiple types of data lines and links. Replication can also be designed to reduce traffic by using intelligent domain controller selection for clients on a network.

- Not all data is replicated among Active Directories connected through WAN links. The global catalog has millions of pieces of information, but it's configured to send across these lines only the information that is important to the network.

- Different types of replication can be chosen, including Pull, Store and Forward, and State-based. These different types of replication mean that multiple needs can be met, thereby reducing network load.

- Windows 2000 Server supports multi-master replication, a model that represents the concept of having multiple domain controllers instead of a PDC and multiple BDCs. In the multi-master replication model, replication traffic is not bothersome to clients on a network because replication can take place through a series of replications throughout the network and can occur at different intervals. If one server goes down, the others simply continue to offer network services, and this technology is transparent to the general user on a network.

Mixed Mode vs. Native Mode

When you're planning to incorporate Windows 2000 domain controllers on your network, you must decide if these servers will run in mixed mode or native mode. *Mixed-mode* domains are used when Windows 2000 Server domain controllers will coexist with Windows NT servers. Windows 2000 servers default to mixed-mode domains automatically when Windows 2000 Server is installed. Mixed mode is needed so that the down-level domain controllers (Windows NT 4 and 3.51) can use NTLM to be authenticated on the network. Mixed mode should be used when you have BDCs that cannot be upgraded for whatever reason, or when you want to try to maintain the down-level servers in case the migration to Windows 2000 must be reversed.

In native mode, all of the domain controllers on a network are running Windows 2000 Server. This is the goal, of course, so that everyone on your network can take advantage of the features of Windows 2000 Server. The following are some characteristics of native mode:

- After native mode is chosen, there is no option to revert to mixed mode.

- After native mode is chosen, there is no down-level support for replication to domain controllers other than Windows 2000 Server domain controllers.

- After native mode is chosen, no Windows NT 4 PDCs exist as domain controllers on the network.

- New group types—such as universal groups, domain local groups, and group nesting—are enabled.

- In native mode, groups can be converted from a distribution group to a security group and vice versa. In addition, global groups can be changed to universal groups, and domain local groups can be changed to universal groups. This cannot be achieved in mixed mode.

Tip: *Running DCPROMO to promote a Windows 2000 server to a domain controller and/or removing all Windows NT machines from a network does not automatically cause the mode to become native mode. The switch to native mode is performed through Windows 2000 Administration Tools.*

Summary

In this chapter, you were introduced to Windows 2000 Server, including its benefits, features, and components. One of the main improvements of Windows 2000 Server over its predecessors is the introduction of Active Directory. Active Directory is a directory service that is used to logically store all objects in a network, and make those objects manageable from a single machine. These services store information about objects and make this information available to the users on the network. Other very valuable tools include the ability to install Windows 2000 products in a variety of ways, including using RIS, disk imaging, unattended installations, and new plug and play capabilities.

There are other features of equal importance, including new security features such as PKI and Kerberos, as well as better encryption and an easy to use graphical interface. Administrative tools are easily configured and stored in management consoles, and there are utilities for disk management and performance enhancement.

After the features and benefits of Windows 2000 Server were discussed, Active Directory was introduced. Active Directory is what allows information to be readily available to users and clients, and a major part of what makes Windows 2000 Server such a successful operating system for networks. Some of Active Directory's features are: a single point of administration; support for millions of objects; new structures, including domains,

OUs, trees, and forests; and implicit domain trusts between parent and child domains. Other topics include replication, mixed mode vs. native mode, and how DNS and DHCP work together.

Moving Forward

This book is designed and written to help you decide how, when, where, why, and if you should migrate to Windows 2000 Server on your network. After reading this chapter, you should be ready to get started. Windows 2000 Server is a powerful, effective, portable, efficient, scalable, and reliable operating system, which can be used to enhance network operations in just about any organization.

The next chapter will offer information on the architecture of the system and what makes it work, help you assess the needs of your current network, and help you create a plan for your Active Directory structure. Even if you are completely sold on migration at this point, the needs of your organization might not support migration just yet. These issues will be addressed when you begin assessing the current situation of your organization.

Chapter 2

Preparing for Windows 2000 Server

Now that Windows 2000 Server's benefits, features, and characteristics have been discussed and the components of Active Directory have been defined, it's time to begin the process of taking inventory and establishing a plan of action. There are many questions to answer, decisions to make, and people to talk to before you create this plan, and justification for the project must be included as well. Just what will it take to get your organization prepared for the Windows 2000 servers you plan to install on your network? Can your organization afford it? Does your hardware support the new operating system? What about your employees—will they welcome the change? Who will be on the project committee and why? How long should the project last, and how will it affect your organization? These are just a few of the questions that need answers.

In this chapter, you'll learn first about how Windows 2000 Server works. The architecture of Windows 2000 Server—including user mode and kernel mode, Executive Services, the Object Manager, and the Hardware Abstraction Layer (HAL)—will be covered. Understanding the concepts presented in this section, including where and how Active Directory fits in, will prove to be most useful when you begin planning for the migration or installation of the servers.

The second section of this chapter will address the assessment process: how to take inventory of the organization's needs, estimate the cost, offer justification, define the scope of the project, and begin the initial planning stages. A basic outline of a project layout will be discussed, as well as some possible restructuring of the existing domain(s) and environment. This could be a good time to set some standards and do a makeover of the current design.

Finally, you'll learn more about Active Directory and create a plan for the namespace. Domains, trees, forests, and organizational units will be further detailed to help you and your organization make appropriate decisions. Planning the Active Directory structure well could be the most important part of planning because a poorly planned structure could certainly cause many headaches later. An incorrectly named domain, for instance, could require a new installation of servers on the network.

This is the most exciting and important part of the project. "Measure twice, cut once," they say, and that certainly holds true here. Allow plenty of time for this part of the project, and you'll be glad later that you did. We'll begin, then, with an overview of the architecture of Windows 2000 Server.

How Windows 2000 Works

The focus of this book isn't the architecture of Windows 2000 Server, but understanding how the operating system works certainly can't hurt. This section discusses the basic concepts associated with the layout of the operating system, what each component is responsible for, how Active Directory relates to this structure, and how the user mode and kernel mode interact. Knowing the basic infrastructure of the operating system (OS) will make the planning tasks more clear, and understanding how the OS works will help explain the need for hardware and software requirements, discussed later.

Overview

Windows 2000 Server is an operating system that is made up of components and managers that perform the tasks necessary to make the system function. Each of these components or managers works together to interface with all parts of the system, beginning with the user and going all the way down to the CPU. The server is designed to be preemptible and interruptible, meaning that the computer's operating system can work on more than one task at a time. This ability to preemptively multitask allows the computer to take control of the CPU without the permission of the application or the task itself.

Windows 2000 server machines can use up to four processors. Windows 2000 Advanced Server can use up to eight, and Windows 2000 Datacenter Server can use up 32 processors. The ability to use multiple processors is called *symmetric multiprocessing (SMP)*, and the processors' tasks can be distributed evenly across multiple processors in the machine. Also called *uniprocessing*, this distribution can drastically reduce the load on a single CPU, and because code that is being processed on one CPU will not affect the code being run on another, SMP can reduce problems associated with problematic applications. These include applications that cause a computer to hang, applications that don't play well with others, and programs written for specific company needs that are not guaranteed or signed by Microsoft to work properly. Even certain drivers can be problematic, causing a computer to freeze up when they malfunction.

The operating system itself is separated into two distinct layers: user mode and kernel mode. Figure 2.1 shows these two modes and their components.

User Mode

User mode is to the architecture of Windows 2000 Server as the graphical user interface (GUI) was to Windows 3.1. The GUI of Windows 3.1 allowed a user to perform commands on DOS without knowing any DOS commands. In Windows 2000 Server, user mode allows users and applications to interact with the kernel mode and the operating system

2

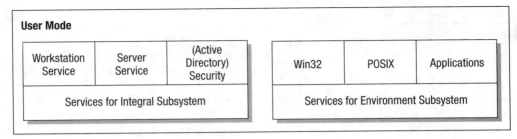

Figure 2.1
Windows 2000 architecture.

code without a user's intervention and without the user or the application knowing anything at all about the components of the kernel. User mode consists of two types of subsystems: integral subsystems and environmental subsystems.

Integral Subsystems

Integral subsystems perform functions necessary for the user to interact appropriately with the operating system. These functions include accepting user logon requests, providing the workstation and server services, and creating security tokens for users. The three integral subsystems are listed in Table 2.1.

Note: Active Directory is located in the security integral subsystem. This makes sense, of course, because we know that Active Directory is instrumental in securing the network and its resources.

Environment Subsystems

The environment subsystems, also located in user mode, allow users to run applications originally designed for other operating systems. Programmers of Windows 2000 Server wanted users to be able to run programs designed for MS-DOS, OS/2, and Windows 3.x, as well as newer 32-bit applications. Whereas the integral subsystems perform operating system functions, the environment subsystems deal more with allowing the application to interface with Executive Services. Table 2.2 lists the environment subsystems available in Windows 2000 Server.

Obviously, not all applications written for all other operating systems will be supported in Windows 2000 Server, even though a valiant attempt was made to make this happen.

Table 2.1   Integral subsystems.

Integral Subsystem	Purpose
Server service	Allows a Windows 2000 computer to act as a server and offer network resources to clients.
Workstation service	Allows a Windows 2000 computer to act as part of a network and access resources across the network.
Security subsystem	Accepts user logon requests and allows users to obtain logon authentication. The security subsystem creates security tokens and monitors users' rights and permissions. The security subsystem also tracks which resources are audited.

Table 2.2   Environment subsystems.

Environment Subsystem	Purpose
Windows 32-bit (Win32) subsystem	Provides a consistent user interface for all applications that are 32-bit, MS-DOS, or 16-bit, and provides a place for these applications to run. The Win32 subsystem controls all I/O (input/output) activities for these applications, including the use of keyboards and mice, plus all display output.
OS/2 subsystem	Provides the DLLs that contain the APIs (application programming interfaces) for OS/2 system applications.
POSIX (Portable Operating System Interface for Unix) subsystem	Ensures that POSIX-based applications can run successfully on Windows 2000 Server.

Problems might occur with some applications because the applications that run in the environment subsystem are constrained by strict limitations. Applications running in the environment subsystem:

- Do not have access to RAM and must use the hard disk as their virtual RAM resource.

- Run at a lower priority than processes running in kernel mode and thus have less access to the CPU.

- Must have no direct access to hardware or device drivers.

- Have no access to task-switching APIs.

- Are limited to an assigned address space.

User mode's integral and environment subsystems allow users to interface transparently with the operating system and to use applications designed for other operating systems. Besides user mode, Windows 2000 Server incorporates the kernel mode, discussed next.

Kernel Mode

Let's take another look at the architecture of Windows 2000 Server, shown in Figure 2.2. This time, notice how the user mode and the kernel mode are connected. It is the Executive Services that hold the two together and allow them to interface. In this section, I'll discuss the nine components of the Executive Services and explain how those services are used by the kernel to carry out the needs of the users and their applications. Following that, we'll examine the Object Manager and the Hardware Abstraction Layer.

Executive Services

Executive Services are used primarily to control system services and internal routines. System services are used by both the user mode and the Executive layer, while internal routines are available to only the components within the kernel mode. The managers and monitors discussed next all perform specific duties for the Executive layer. Understanding their functions will be instrumental in understanding not only how Windows 2000 Server

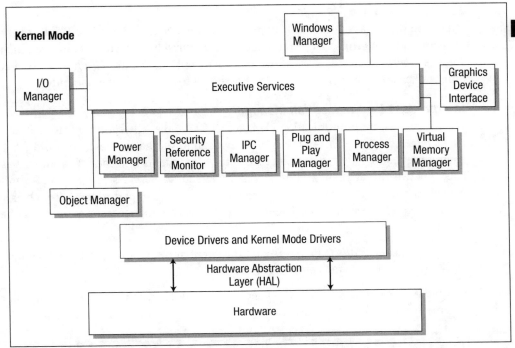

Figure 2.2
Windows 2000 Server architecture.

interacts with applications and users but also how it handles their requests. In some instances, I'll include examples of services to draw attention to how the user's request for services relates directly to the Executive Services themselves.

I/O Manager

The Input/Output (I/O) Manager receives and delivers input and output to and from different devices. For instance, the I/O Manager can receive requests to read and write from the user mode and translate those commands into Interrupt Request Packets (IRPs) for use by device drivers and the kernel mode. The I/O Manager is made up of the following three components:

- *File systems*—Accept input/output requests and translate them into calls that devices can understand. Redirectors and servers are considered file system drivers.

- *Device drivers*—Directly access the hardware being requested by the input/output call, and manipulate that hardware so that it can accept the request.

- *Cache Manager*—Improves I/O read tasks by placing disk reads in system RAM, and improves write tasks by cacheing write requests so they are performed in the background.

Security Reference Monitor

Every computer has a local security policy, and the Security Reference Monitor is responsible for enforcing this policy on the local computer. A local security policy can include rules related to auditing, user rights, or security options. Figure 2.3 shows a local computer policy and the user rights that are assigned to one particular computer.

Interprocess Communication Manager

The Interprocess Communication Manager (IPC) handles the communication between a user's request and the part of the system that can fulfill that request. For instance, the environment subsystem might place a call to write to a disk, so the IPC would act as a liaison between that client and the necessary Executive Services component. A similar type of communication exists when a client asks a server to perform a task such as saving a file or requesting some data. The IPC includes two components for performing these tasks:

- *Local procedure calls (LPCs)*—Used if the client and server (requester and component) are located on the same computer.

- *Remote procedure calls (RPCs)*—Used if the client and server (requester and component) are on different computers.

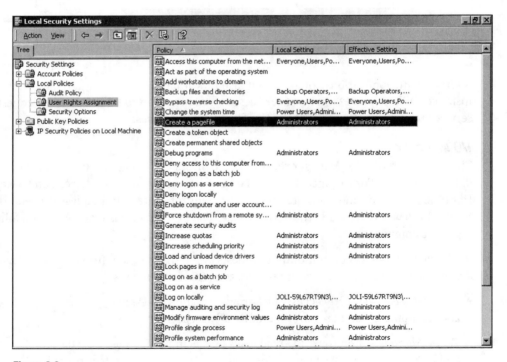

Figure 2.3
Local security policy and user rights.

2

Virtual Memory Manager

The Virtual Memory Manager (VMM) controls virtual memory. The Windows Virtual DOS Machine (NTVDM) is what allows the 16-bit, MS-DOS, and other legacy applications to run in their own address spaces. The ability to have private address spaces is a main factor in reducing blue screens in Windows 2000 products. Virtual memory also allows the use of page files, which let applications swap information out of and into RAM and physical disk storage, such as a hard drive. Figure 2.4 shows how the virtual memory settings can be changed through My Computer to control how much virtual memory is made available to the Virtual Memory Manager.

Process Manager

To understand what the Process Manager does, you first need to know what processes and threads are. A *process* is simply a program or a piece of a program. A *thread* contains specific commands inside a program. The Process Manager manages these processes and threads by creating and terminating them when necessary. The Process Manager can also elect to stop, resume, store, or retrieve threads and processes. Figure 2.5 shows the processes and threads running on a sample computer.

Plug And Play Manager

The Plug And Play Manager maintains control of all of the plug-and-play devices on a system. The Plug And Play Manager communicates with plug-and-play device drivers and can stop, pause, restart, eject, or otherwise interact with those devices. When you see the message shown in Figure 2.6, you have been in contact with the Plug And Play Manager.

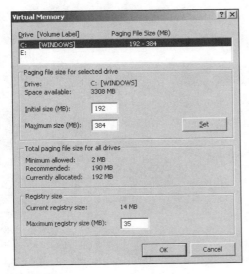

Figure 2.4
Virtual memory settings.

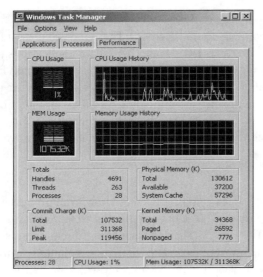

Figure 2.5
The Task Manager, showing threads and processes.

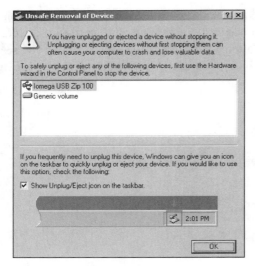

Figure 2.6
A Plug And Play Manager warning.

Power Manager

The Power Manager is responsible for managing and coordinating power events, such as shutting down a computer. When a computer is shut down, there might be more than just the computer itself that will be powered down. The Power Manager collects information on which devices need to be powered down, prioritizes and organizes that data, and sends the appropriate IRP calls to those devices. The next time you power off or on a computer, take note of the other devices that are awakening, such as printers, monitors, or other peripherals.

Windows Manager and Graphical Device Interface

These components together manage devices related to the display system. Both the Windows Manager and the Graphical Device Interface (GDI) use the Win32K.sys driver and perform functions related to controlling the display, sending data from the keyboard and mouse to the screen, and manipulating graphics.

Object Manager

Resources on a Windows 2000 computer are considered objects by the operating system and its components. An *object* is simply something that someone or some application may need to access. Objects are logical representations of users, printers, files, ports, processes, threads, directories, links, scanners, and various other resources. The Object Manager is designed to control the objects available on the computer or network. The Windows 2000 Object Manager can create, protect, and monitor these objects.

For example, for a file object called *Private*, the Object Manager knows the file's name and attributes and the actions that can be performed on that file. If the Object Manager knows that this file is a hidden file—with no rights for reading, copying, or deleting by members who request it—the file can be sufficiently protected.

HAL

The HAL is responsible for hiding the details related to accessing hardware. This means that the HAL communicates directly with the hardware and thus provides the kernel layer with a machine-independent interface. This is what enables Windows 2000 to work for Intel- and Alpha-based machines and for machines with multiple processors. For a computer with multiple processors, the kernel simply uses the interface provided by the HAL to work out the scheduling of the processors' activities.

The Assessment Process

If installing or migrating to Windows 2000 Server on your network were as simple as putting in the CD-ROM, accepting all of the defaults, and physically connecting the computer to your network, there wouldn't be any need for this book. Fortunately for me, and unfortunately for you, the process isn't nearly that simple. Moving toward Windows 2000 Server on your network is a complex process that involves much planning. The rest of this chapter is dedicated to preparing you for this transition.

Before you start any installations, all aspects and characteristics of the network must be documented, a plan must be put in place, decisions must be made concerning existing domains and standards, and hundreds of other concerns and needs must be addressed. Let's begin by reviewing what a good plan is and how it relates to this project, and then we'll begin to gather information.

Fundamental Project Methodology

There can be many ways to attack a large project, such as installing or migrating to Windows 2000 Server. In this book, we'll follow the project plan as outlined here:

1. Survey the current environment. Define the current domain structure, standards, hardware and software, critical applications, network topology, users' desktop environment, and security policies, including account policies, local policies, public key policies, and IP security policies. Decide if there are any problem applications that will cause the migration to fail. A full inventory should be done for all resources on the network.

2. Form a project committee that meets regularly. This committee will determine the scope of the project, the current environment, and the requirements for making the project successful. The committee will also be responsible for following the plan to its end and ensuring a successful rollout. This committee should also decide if moving to Windows 2000 Server is cost-effective and if any restructuring is needed for existing domains or standards.

3. Develop a plan for installing and using Windows 2000 Server on the network. This plan should address why moving to a Windows 2000 network is necessary and what administrators and executives want to accomplish through this migration or installation. Include a timeline, and discuss how much the migration is going to cost, who will design the Active Directory structure and namespace, how changes will affect the clients on the network, and how users will be trained to deal with these changes.

4. Decide how the plan will be carried out; document the timeline and assign tasks to certain people or departments. Many other issues will be at work when you're carrying out the plan. For instance, some servers will be offline during the upgrade, some network connectivity might be lost, and/or unforeseen problems might occur. If hardware and software need to be replaced, removed, or retired, these changes will need to be done before the current server is upgraded. If the domain structure or standards are changing, these changes should also be dealt with before installations are done. In this stage, you also need a plan for backing out of the changes if they go awry.

5. Test the migration or installation plan in a lab environment before making any solid changes to the network or its servers. After you've set up the test lab and configured it to emulate the current environment, including its applicable hardware and software, perform the test. At this time, any alterations to the plan must also be performed and retested. Document any changes as completely as possible, and verify those changes with all committee members.

6. Perform the rollout, keeping in mind the backout plan. Be sure to follow all precautions, including making full backups of data, keeping an existing BDC offline for redundancy, or even delaying the rollout if everything doesn't seem perfect.

Beginning the Assessment

Following this plan or a plan like this one will ensure that all aspects of the installation are covered and that the plan has been well thought out. In addition, distributing this plan and any applicable documentation created will ensure that all parties are fully informed of the decisions and changes.

We are going to focus now on the first four steps of the plan: gathering information about the current status of the network, forming the design team, developing a plan for the project, and deciding how that plan will be carried out. The last two stages of the project—testing and deploying—are subjects of other chapters. After reading the items that should be considered, you can begin to formulate a plan of action. Chapter 3 will offer checklists and worksheets for putting your ideas down on paper, and you may want to flip back and forth between the two chapters when making notes. You can also print blank worksheets and checklists from the CD-ROM accompanying this book. These printouts might be helpful while you're reading the following sections.

Surveying the Current Environment

Understanding fully the state of the current environment is crucial to a successful migration, upgrade, or installation of Windows 2000 servers on a network. This section addresses the issues that are important to the current state of the network and is a good place to begin in planning your project and assessing your needs.

Take Inventory

Take inventory. What a short and simple sentence. It certainly isn't a simple process, though, and might be impossible in very large networks. The first step in evaluating the current environment is to make a list of everything that exists on it. For Windows 2000 Server to function correctly on a network, all devices that will interact with the operating system should be checked against Microsoft's Hardware Compatibility List (HCL) to ensure that they will work properly. This is extremely important and will require the help and cooperation of other people. You may want to create a list of items that you believe to be on the network and send that list to each department head. Make sure that you include a deadline for receiving this information back, however, and that you follow up to make sure all departments have responded. A thorough checklist for inventory will be included in Chapter 3, but the following list can be used as a guide to help you begin thinking about the potential scope of starting this project.

Each department should inventory the following items:

- *Servers*—Name, type, location, memory, CPU, and all other pertinent information, including information on applications installed

- *Printers*—Name, type, location, and special attributes

- *Scanners*—Name, type, location, and special attributes

- *Applications*—Name, original platform (the operating system each application was designed for), and importance (whether each application is deemed a "critical" application by the department)

- *Card readers*—Name, type, location, and special attributes

- *Cameras*—Name, type, location, and special attributes

- *Tape devices*—Name, type, location, and special attributes

- *Desktop computers and laptops*—Name, type, location, memory, CPU, and all other pertinent information, including applications installed

- *Computer peripherals*—Manufacturer, name, and version number; peripherals can include:

  - Network interface cards (NICs)

  - Sound and video cards

  - Modems

  - Special monitors

  - DVD drives or CD-RW drives

  - USB devices

  - Special keyboards and mice

- *Other miscellaneous equipment*—Plotters, special DOS programs, or legacy devices that cannot be retired, as well as other potential problems

You can query the Device Manager to get most of this information. Figure 2.7 shows the Device Manager and its components.

Define the Current Domain Structure

Each company or organization has a unique structure. This structure—the way domains are currently configured—is important to document. If the current network consists of Windows NT 4 servers, the domain is single, master, or multi-master. The current domain structure will include information about the namespace as well. While you're reviewing the current domain structure, identify all of the PDCs, BDCs, member servers, application servers, file and print servers, and any other type of server on the network. Remember, Windows 2000 servers don't use PDCs and BDCs anymore, so getting all of the information possible about these machines is critical.

Tip: Defining the current domain structure and obtaining the information just mentioned can be combined with the previous section, on taking inventory, and with the following section, about defining a network topology. See Figure 2.9 for an example of a network topology that also contains information on domain servers.

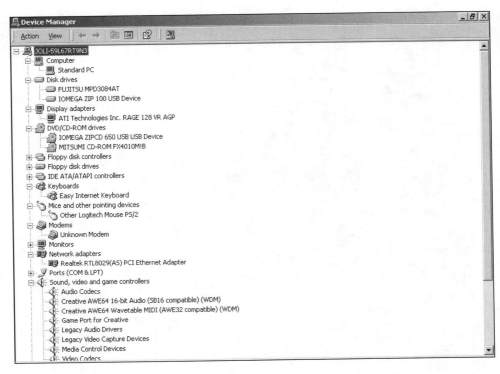

Figure 2.7
The Device Manager.

Each server, in turn, has a name, a location, crucial applications, users and groups, accounts, group memberships, and other attributes. Some of this information can be obtained through the Properties menu of the My Computer icon; Figure 2.8 shows a sample System Properties dialog box. Although this particular screenshot is from a Windows 2000 computer, an NT computer looks the same. The tabs in the System Properties dialog box provide information about the computer's domain, computer name, operating system, hardware, user profiles, and other items.

Define the Network Topology

After you have successfully completed the inventory and documented the necessary information about the servers on your current network, you need to document the topology of the network. Because Windows 2000 uses replication and Active Directory as a core component, and because the global catalog is important for sharing information, it is critical that you fully document the state of the network, as shown in Figure 2.9.

Your topology chart should show routed segments, subnets, and nonrouted segments, and it should indicate which protocols are used and how the DNS structure is defined. This chart could also include fast WAN links, the location of PDCs and BDCs, and current problem links.

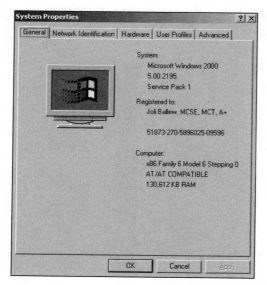

Figure 2.8
A computer's system properties.

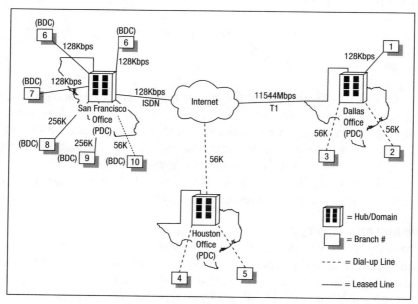

Figure 2.9
Sample topology.

The amount of detail included in the chart is completely up to the committee and the designer in charge of the migration or installation. Certainly a small network does not need a highly detailed chart. However, if the network consists of 5 domains in 5 countries, each domain has 15 branches, there are 25,000 users, and/or the locations are connected by slow links or span multiple continents, the need for a detailed topology map becomes much more obvious.

Define the Current Hardware, Software, and Critical Applications

Collect the new inventory lists from each department, any previous inventory lists, or any lists of your own, and compile a status report of the current hardware, software, and critical applications on the network. It is extremely important to obtain hardware and software information on the computers that will be affected by the installation of, or migration to, Windows 2000 Server on your domain controllers. Obtaining the other information will be useful when you migrate your workstations to Windows 2000 Professional and will ensure that existing components will work with the newer Windows 2000 servers. This information will also prove useful for determining if standards exist for hardware or software on the network, and the information can be used in the section "Define the Current Standards," coming up next.

Because we are concerned mainly with getting the Windows 2000 servers up and running, we'll concentrate on the servers at this time. Table 2.3 shows the essential hardware requirements as listed on Microsoft's Web site. Take a good look at the servers that you plan to upgrade or use for Windows 2000 servers, and make sure they meet the minimum requirements.

Warning! *Most problems with servers occur because there isn't enough memory to support the servers' applications and services. Make sure you allow for growth when choosing the computer that will function as a server. Another common problem occurs when the NIC isn't supported or when a driver is needed for a SCSI mass storage device.*

Of course, you'll need the usual mouse, keyboard, CD-ROM drive, network interface card (NIC), and so on when you're installing Windows 2000 Server. Be sure to check Microsoft's Web site for the latest information on which computers, hardware, software, and BIOS systems are supported.

Table 2.3   Hardware requirements for the server.

Component	Minimum	Recommended	Maximum
CPU	133 MHz Pentium compatible	Anything higher	n/a
RAM	128MB	256MB	4GB
Hard Disk	2GB, with1GB free space	Anything higher	n/a
Number of CPUs	1	n/a	4

Tip: *You can check hardware, software, and computer compatibility at **www.microsoft.com/windows2000/ upgrade/compat/default.asp** and BIOS compatibility at **www.microsoft.com/windows2000/upgrade/ compat/biosissue.asp**. Other helpful sites are included on this book's accompanying CD-ROM.*

Check the existing hardware against Microsoft's HCL at **www.microsoft.com/hcl/default. asp**. Here, you can search for specific devices by type and, with the inventory list in hand, verify which hardware devices will work, will need to be retired, or will need to be re-placed. Figure 2.10 shows an example of such a search. It is important to note in the example that not all devices are compatible.

Note: *If you see that a particular device isn't on the HCL, you might still be able to find a driver for the device on the manufacturer's Web site or on Web sites that offer drivers as products. To find such sites, just use your Web browser to search for "Windows 2000 drivers." It is my experience that, given enough time, you can find a suitable driver for almost any device.*

You can check existing applications and software at Microsoft's Web site as well. If you have a critical application that must be used, if it is not compatible with Windows 2000 Server, and if the manufacturer of that program cannot offer an upgrade to that applica-tion, then the decision to migrate might have to be delayed. However, to reduce TCO and

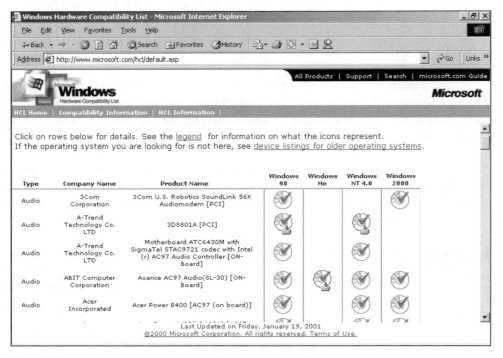

Figure 2.10
Part of the Microsoft Windows Hardware Compatibility List.

2

ease the administrative burden of maintaining this application, perhaps replacing it with another will be best. Obviously, this will incur costs, but if it is feasible to replace the program, move the data, and retrain the employees, it is well worth it in the end.

Microsoft maintains two databases of applications known to work with Windows; one database lists *certified* applications, and the other lists *compatible* applications. Figure 2.11 shows an example of applications that are certified for Windows 2000 Server. Certified applications are fully tested by Microsoft and an independent testing organization, and will run on Windows 2000 Server without any problem at all. The applications in this list do not represent all of the programs that will run on the server; rather, they are the ones that have been given Microsoft's highest certified ranking. Figure 2.12 shows the Web page where you can search for applications that are designated as compatible with Windows 2000 Server. Compatible applications are Microsoft's second highest ranking, which guarantees that the independent certified vendor has fully tested the application to run with Windows 2000 products and will provide Windows 2000-related support.

Tip: *To see if your applications are certified by Microsoft to run with Windows 2000 Server, go to* ***www.veritest.com/mslogos/windows2000/certification/ServerApps.asp***, *and to see if they are compatible, go to* ***www.microsoft.com/windows2000/upgrade/compat/search/software.asp***. *Other helpful sites are included on this book's CD-ROM.*

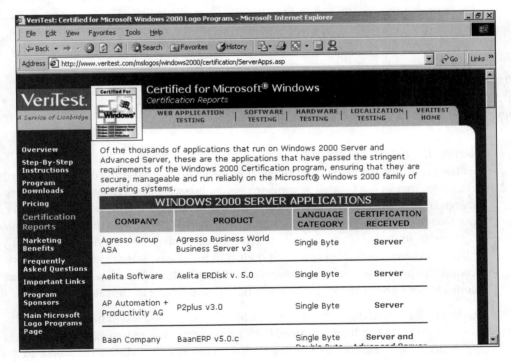

Figure 2.11
Certified application compatibility.

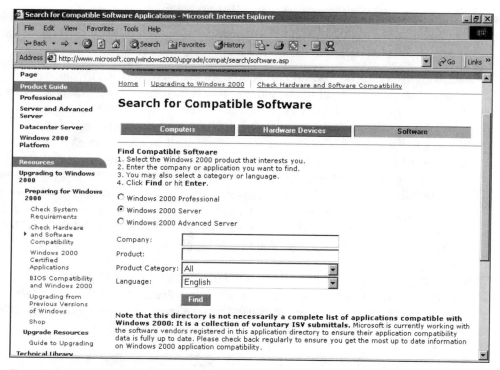

Figure 2.12
General application compatibility.

Tip: *Just because a particular application isn't on either one of these lists doesn't necessarily mean that the application won't work just fine on the server. Check the manufacturer's Web site for information on applications that are not found in Microsoft's lists.*

Define the Current Standards

As the inventory was being collected, you probably discovered some de facto standards—standards that weren't stated as company policy, but were adopted over time by users or management. The inventory may hold other surprises as well. For instance, you may find out that users in the graphics department have installed programs that you were unaware of. Even though this is against the written company policy, there is nothing currently in place to prevent users from installing their own programs. You can submit to the project committee any ideas you have concerning standardization. The more you standardize the components on your network, the fewer hassles you'll have in the future.

Consider standardizing as many items as possible. Standardization has many benefits, and a major one is the ability to reduce TCO for a company. For example, standardizing applications will require less training for the employees. This standardization also reduces the number of help desk calls, especially if users will not be allowed to install their own programs. This restriction will eliminate unnecessary errors due to incompatible applications or incorrect installations by clients. Networks characteristically start at one place and continually grow and mature, ending up in quite another place. Taking a step back and standardizing at this time can be a most useful and productive activity.

Following are some items you'll want to consider standardizing:

- *Hardware*—Use the inventory list created earlier to see what hardware the network consists of. Then use this list to set minimum hardware requirements for new computers and to bring the older computers into compliance if possible.

- *Applications*—The network uses certain applications that are critical to production. Those applications have already been checked (I hope) against the compatible-applications list at Microsoft. At this point in the planning, set some standards concerning these applications and future ones. For instance, don't allow users to install their own programs, and do standardize the basic word processing and spreadsheet programs used across the network. If a certified application like Microsoft Office can be used to replace 10 other word processing, spreadsheet, presentation, drawing, and graphics programs on your network, it will be worth it to make the transition to that now. Of course, there will be training and testing involved, but it would be wise to consider this when you're planning to migrate to or install Windows 2000 servers on your network.

- *Services*—What services are being used on the network by the servers and the clients? Are all of these services still necessary? Note which services will continue to be used, and delete any unnecessary services.

- *Naming schemes*—The network already has a naming scheme unless you are building a new network from scratch. Define the naming scheme and decide if changes need to be made. We'll address this issue more in "Planning the Active Directory Structure," next.

- *Users' desktops*—If users' desktops are standardized, it is important to note here. For instance, users in the accounting department may have a common look, while users in the graphics department have free rein. Define what, if any, standards exist for the users' environments.

- *Miscellaneous*—There are other standards besides these on a network. They can include standards for user account names, computer names, adapter cards, platforms, network protocols, backups, and documentation. Standards also include how service packs and updates are applied to machines.

Note: *I recently visited a company here in downtown Dallas that is involved in an upgrade to Windows 2000 servers and workstations. The company has more than 10,000 client computers and is standardizing the network prior to the upgrade. The company has decided to do the exact opposite of what I am suggesting. In fact, it plans to "unlock" the users' desktops and allow the users to install their own screensavers, use their own wallpaper, and perform tasks that they previously were not allowed to perform. I do not agree with this decision, although I am sure the users will be much happier. I believe that more problems will arise after this new, relaxed policy is put in place, and the support needed for these users will increase.*

Define the Security Policies

If an NT domain exists, there are policies in place for users on the network. Each of these policies needs to be defined, documented, and then assessed for changes necessary after the Windows 2000 Server installation. There are four types of policies mentioned here: account policies, local policies, public key policies, and IP Security policies. Following are some examples of each policy type:

- *Account policies:*

  - *Password policies*—Include password history, age, length, and complexity requirements.

  - *Account policy lockout*—Includes lockout duration, threshold, and lockout counters.

- *Local policies:*

  - Special keyboards and mice

  - *Audit policies*—Include auditing logon events, account management, directory service access, object access, policy changes, processes, privilege use, and system events.

  - *User rights assignment*—Includes adding workstations, creating pagefiles, denying local logons, loading and unloading device drivers, and debugging programs, to name a few.

  - *Security options*—Include requiring regular password changes, auditing events, automatically logging off, securing channels, and more.

- *Public key policies*—Include encrypted data recovery agents.

- *IP Security policies*—Include security for communication between clients and servers.

Important Reasons for Choosing Not to Migrate

Occasionally, after surveying the current environment, you'll need to ask if migrating to Windows 2000 Server is actually going to work. You may have come across some things during inventory that suggest you shouldn't. Here are some valid reasons to delay the installation of Windows 2000 servers on your network:

- If the hardware that you'll have to use isn't supported under Windows 2000 Server, and there is no way to upgrade or purchase newer machines, an upgrade is probably not warranted. The installation of Windows 2000 Server won't even continue if the minimum requirements aren't met.

- If the applications you need to use for the organization aren't compatible, certified, or otherwise in complete compliance with directives, upgrading may be impossible.

- If the network is generally unstable due to older legacy systems, inadequate wiring, or poorly configured users, groups, accounts, or namespaces, it is wise to delay the installation until these issues are resolved.

- If there isn't enough time to take inventory, form committees, draw the network topology, and check hardware and software compatibility, you should delay the migration. There is no point in doing the job without the required time and information available. Poor planning will certainly lead to frustration.

- Money is a big player in this decision. If there isn't enough money for new hardware, programs, people, training, licensing, or any other immediate costs to the company, the installation should be delayed.

Tip: *If the network is currently meeting all of the needs of the organization, there simply might not be any reason to upgrade at this time. I think everyone knows someone who still uses Windows 95; it meets their needs, they know how to email and print, and they simply don't want to move to Windows 98 (much less Windows ME!). If the move is unnecessary, calling off the migration might be the best thing.*

Forming the Project Committee

After you've assessed the network, considered the needs of the network, and decided to go ahead with the project of installing Windows 2000 Server on your domain controllers, it is time to begin forming a project team to handle the project. This team will be responsible for ensuring that the project gets off on the right foot, obtaining the necessary information from all of the departments in the organization, and following through on the plan of action it will design.

Consider the implications of changing the servers in your network. This change will affect all departments and almost every user on the network. To represent all of these people and departments, the committee that's chosen to lead this project must be diverse as well as responsible and enthusiastic. It isn't necessary to choose the smartest engineer to represent the engineering department; instead, choose someone who is enthusiastic about the migration and aware of the engineering department's needs and who can work well with others. For critical services, choose someone who is both reliable and knowledgeable and who has the necessary experience to fully understand the scope and purpose of the project.

To begin the formation of this project team, start by listing all of the departments in the organization. Then, list all of the services that the current servers on the network offer. These lists will give you a good idea of the project's scope and the committee's ideal make-up. An ideal committee should have a representative not only from each department but also for each service. The following list details most of the project team's responsibilities, and from this list, project leaders and team members can be chosen. We will use these lists again in Chapter 3 to begin selecting team members.

Responsibilities of team members will include the following tasks:

- Document the purpose and scope of moving to Windows 2000 Server.

- Determine how much the migration will cost the company, including downtime, training, new hardware, new software, licensing, increased payroll, and other pertinent issues.

- Develop a timeline for migration.

- Create the lab where the rollout will be tested.
- Plan the Active Directory namespace.
- Perform the inventory of the network.
- Plan how Active Directory will be replicated among the domain controllers.
- Plan how the global directory will be configured.
- Create standards from existing ones, or redefine the current standards.
- Make sure hardware and software are compatible and will work properly.
- Create policies or refine polices from existing ones. Design a model for security.
- Analyze the physical network (topology).
- Offer technical support.
- Design or redesign email and messaging.
- List deployment options and make appropriate decisions.
- Restructure domains or DNS namespaces.
- Coordinate training of users, clients, and network operators.

You'll need a representative to lead each of these tasks in the A Team (or core team, lead team, or other representative name). Depending on the size of the network, the A team may be as small as 5 people or as large as 25 or 30. Each member of this team will, in turn, have people who work on the project and report to him or her. For instance, determining the cost of this migration might be a daunting task for one person, so this task might be assigned to a small group of people. The A-team members should schedule meetings and should report their progress often to make sure everyone complies with the project's timeline.

Warning! *Watch out for the "too many chefs in the kitchen" syndrome. Don't let the base team's size get out of hand. There isn't any way to please everybody, and the more people you have on the base team, the harder it will be to come to a consensus on the issues regarding aspects of the project. On the other hand, the entire network needs to be represented because, for instance, the warehouse might use only legacy systems or proprietary applications.*

Formulating and Carrying Out the Plan

After the teams are formed and the tasks are laid out, creating the plan is the next task. At this stage, you should have enough information to be certain that Windows 2000 Server is right for your network, that the current environment can support the new operating system, and that the move is really necessary and cost-effective. The team members should now be gathering the required information and making the necessary decisions. In particular, these decisions will define the scope of the project, establish a timeline and milestones, determine what type of restructuring (if any) will need to be done to the

2

current domain structure and standards, determine the approximate cost involved in this move, and determine how the plan will be carried out across the organization.

Project Scope and Timeline

I've mainly been sticking to one theme in the discussions about planning, inventory, and standards because this book is generally concerned with network servers. After all, it is entitled *Windows 2000 Server On Site*. However, most migrations to Windows 2000 involve not only servers and domain controllers but also user workstations, and you might decide that the workstations shall also be part of the project. Although learning how to migrate clients isn't the goal of this book, you may well want to include that in the scope of your project.

In the example that follows, the main objective is considering the migration of the existing servers and/or the installation of new domain controllers. The scope consists of getting those installations done and getting the domain controllers back online for the network's current clients. In the real world, the server project might be designed for the A team, and the migrations of the workstations to Windows 2000 might be a project for the B team. These two teams would then coordinate their efforts.

Figure 2.13 shows a sample timeline, and Table 2.4 offers some sample milestones. Making sure that this timeline is followed is the responsibility of the project leader or project coordinator. Definite milestones should be in place for each phase, and the

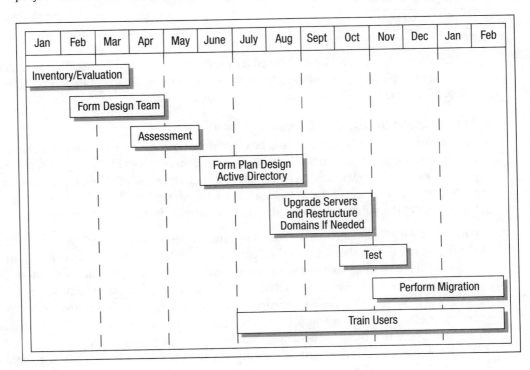

Figure 2.13
Sample timeline and milestone data sheet.

Table 2.4   Sample milestones.

Date	Milestone	Responsible Party
2/15	Inventories due	All department heads or department personnel
3/15	Assessment of needs due	All department heads or department personnel
3/31	Cost analysis due	Accounting representative
3/31	Project coordinator assigned	CEO, president, or lead administrator
4/30	Design team formed	Project leader, CEO, or lead administrator
5/10	Topology map and domain structure due	Project member
5/15	Design needs and assessment completed	Project team members
5/15	Standards defined	Project member
6/10	Training begun	Training department
7/1	Restructuring team formed, if needed	Project leader, CEO or lead administrator
10/30	Application, server, and hardware upgrades completed and restructuring completed	Technical team, support personnel, other network personnel
10/15	Lab completed	Project members (testing)
11/30	Testing completed	Project team members, network personnel
11/10	Server migration begun	Project team members or server operators
2/15	Migration completed	All members
2/28	Training completed	Training staff

responsible parties should be monitored for progress. In Chapter 3, checklists will assist you in creating a timeline that is right for your organization. Blank checklists can be printed from the CD-ROM accompanying this book.

Restructuring the Existing Domains

The existing domain structure should be clear at this point in the planning. Decisions are being made about scope, timeline, design team members, needs of the network, security policies, existing standards, and critical applications. Only one other major decision must be dealt with before any of these decisions are set in stone. The design team needs to take a long look at the current domain's structure and decide if it can be improved.

With Windows NT, domains were created to delegate responsibility, separate geographical divides, and deal with the limits of the Security Accounts Manager (SAM) database. In Windows 2000, those ideas and requirements have changed. In fact, Microsoft offers advice about the ideal number of domains in Windows 2000 and states that, basically, fewer is better. For instance, if a network currently has four domains in two countries, perhaps restructuring those domains to only one domain per country would be a better solution. Obviously, this restructuring would require a separate design team, timeline, set of requirements, and assessment, and could take an enormous amount of time to complete. But if it were necessary in your network, it would be well worth the effort.

When you're considering a restructuring of your current domains, consider the Active Directory design that you plan to use. We'll discuss planning for the Active Directory in the next section. After that planning, you'll need to decide if restructuring the current domains is necessary.

If any restructuring needs to be done, you have two options for it. Domains can be restructured before the upgrade or after. If you have a large network with many domains, and you plan to remove and restructure several of them, the best solution is to perform that restructure before the migration to Windows 2000 servers on the network. Combining domains can be a daunting task, requiring lots of planning, additional resources, and definite skill. Windows NT offers no direct way to move objects from domain A to domain B. You'll need the Windows NT Resource Kit or third-party tools for that. It is my opinion, then, that combining domains before an upgrade is the most difficult approach. If there are multiple domains to move, however, it is the best choice and it pays for itself in the end. To see the difficulty, consider the work involved in combining just two domains: migrating users and groups, updating rights and permissions, moving client computers, moving domain controllers, and updating group memberships, to name a few tasks.

Combining domains after an upgrade is much easier. It involves moving applications and services and then removing resource domains after the migration is complete. There are tools available to help with this and there are steps to follow that greatly simplify the process. This is a straightforward process if there aren't a large number of domains to move.

Restructuring the Existing Standards

One last thing to consider is the restructuring of existing standards. As I mentioned earlier, a network may have been born four years ago with standards in mind, but with the addition of more workstations, applications, users, departments, and peripherals, those standards may or may not exist anymore. Also, there may be standards that just grew out of habit, such as how to name new servers, what type of NICs to buy, what the new workstations will look like, or which applications are considered critical to the network. It would be a shame to spend another four years supporting a photo program that someone installed because it came with the new scanner, when Microsoft Photo Editor, which is certified by Microsoft, would work just as well or better. If it will work for your organization, moving the standard to certified applications will certainly be an improvement.

In addition, your network may have already been through four or five administrators since its creation. Perhaps Administrator Number Three is the one responsible for naming the BDC on the third floor "Spock," and maybe it was Administrator Number Four who purchased that new scanner and installed the proprietary scanner software on the network. If your network has evolved such that most of the original standards aren't standards anymore, this may be a good time to change. Standards can mean less technical support and lower TCO, and can offer new administrators a guide for buying hardware, software, and applications.

Cost Analysis

Although the tools and services available in Windows 2000 are aimed at reducing the TCO for a network or organization, the initial costs will be high. Approximating the costs involved in the transition, justifying those costs to superiors, and calculating the return on investment (ROI) are important tasks. Care must be taken at every step to ensure that the project is within budget constraints. A project team member should be assigned the task of following through on these issues.

Approximating the costs for a small network with only a few servers and a handful of workstations will be much easier than estimating the costs involved in migrating to Windows 2000 Server in a large network. There will, of course, be costs associated with new hardware and software, but there are also many areas where a migration may incur unexpected costs and require additional funding. Because there is no possible way to provide a generic cost analysis for you to base your specific plan on, I have included a comprehensive list of items that you might need to consider for your cost analysis:

- *Servers*—Purchasing new servers or upgrading existing ones

- *Workstations*—Purchasing new workstations or upgrading existing ones

- *Training*—Training staff, administration, end users, server operators, backup operators, print operators, and network administrators on new hardware, software, and/or standards

- *Network*—Adding bandwidth, subnets, sites, coverage, and capacity, and calculating increased usage during pilot runs and testing

- *Downtime*—Calculating costs associated with lost productivity during the transition when servers are offline due to upgrades or unforeseen problems

- *Lab*—Creating a lab to simulate the network (testing costs may be higher than expected if problems arise before the migration)

- *Software and applications*—Switching to certified applications or compatible applications, or deleting proprietary applications and replacing them with conventional ones

- *Licensing*—Purchasing the required licenses for the Windows 2000 products used

- *Salaries*—Calculating the salary costs for in-house design-team members and for any outside consultants hired to help with the initial implementation

- *Restructuring*—Calculating the additional costs associated with the restructuring (if you're restructuring current domains), including the costs of additional teams, resources, and time

- *Miscellaneous*—Amassing migration tools, rewriting custom scripts, migrating users and groups, and using any other specific network tools or configurations

2

Justifying the costs to superiors, then, must include information on how all of these initial costs are going to pay off in the future. To justify the cost of moving to Windows 2000 Server, you'll need to start by calculating what your organization spends currently in certain areas. For instance, if you currently spend $500,000 a year on help desk support for your network users, and you can document that moving to Windows 2000 Server will cut that in half, then this can be the justification. You can also consider the new features of Windows 2000 Server, along with enhancements from Windows NT. One of those enhancements is the Windows 2000 Server architecture itself and its ability to reduce blue screens, thus preventing downtime across the network. Another enhancement is the ability of Windows 2000 Server to delegate responsibility through organizational units in place of domain creation. Both of these features are valid points for justifying the cost.

To calculate the ROI, work with people in the financial and accounting departments, and find out if there is a method in place to create such a document. If no one in the organization can create such a document, you might need to bring in a consultant or a certified accountant. However it is achieved, make absolutely sure that there is enough money available to follow the plan to its end and that resources are available if unexpected problems occur.

Making the Plan Work

The project coordinator is responsible for making the plan work. It is a thankless job, though, and the project leader will need to be strong, smart, and ready to assume responsibility and take charge. As the design team is formed and the design team leaders begin to form their own teams, tasks will be assigned to certain people or departments. Be certain that the members of your team are enthusiastic about the upgrade or migration and that they are confident and competent in their fields.

There will be problems with the plan, and the team needs to be flexible. (If you've ever tried to do something as simple as replacing a NIC on a server, you know what I'm talking about. Nothing really ever goes the way you think it will.) Knowing from the onset that servers will be offline during the upgrade, that some network connectivity may be lost, and/or that unforeseen problems might occur will certainly help calm the crowd. The timeline needs to be studied for flaws before anything gets started. For instance, if hardware and software need to be replaced, removed, or retired, these changes will need to be ushered in before a server is upgraded. If the domain structure or standards are going to be changed, these changes should also be dealt with before installations. The Active Directory design should be fully planned and approved before *anything* is installed. You should also have a design for backing out of the changes if they go awry.

The plan to move to Windows 2000 Server must also be given adequate time to form, adapt, and grow. The sample timeline in this chapter proves this point. It is important that everyone on the team, in the organization, and on the board of directors is aware of how long such a move takes a company to complete. Make sure that the team has adequate preparation time and can fully test all operations before the network deployment, and that it is cost-effective and doable for the organization.

Planning the Active Directory Structure

Unbelievably, we're still not ready to install or upgrade a Windows 2000 server. We still need to plan the Active Directory structure. Planning the Active Directory structure is one of the most important phases of the project and should be a high priority for the project team. The person who is responsible for planning the Active Directory structure should be extremely comfortable with the current domain structure, topology, physical and logical boundaries, and current DNS structure of the network.

When you're defining the Active Directory structure, you need to address three distinct areas: planning the domain structure, planning the OU structure, and planning the site structure. This section of the chapter will focus on how these three structures can be designed, how they relate, and how they should, ideally, be created.

Note: Although I have tried to include the most important aspects of planning the Active Directory structure, keep in mind that entire books have been written simply on planning the domain structure, the OU structure, or the site structure. When you're choosing the members of your project team and, in particular, the person in charge of designing the namespace and Active Directory, make sure you have chosen someone who is capable and knowledgeable in this field.

Planning the Domain Structure

Most of the time, a Windows 2000 upgrade or migration is built from an existing Windows NT domain or domains. In some instances, the choice will be made to combine some of these domains or even delete them. The project team, along with management and administration, will decide if this is necessary. To make good initial decisions about how the Active Directory should be designed and, in particular, how the domain structure should be designed, it is important to be aware of the differences between Windows NT and Windows 2000. Even if the new Windows 2000 implementation isn't based on an existing domain, understanding how Windows 2000 is designed to work will help you plan the new domains.

Differences between Windows 2000 and Windows NT Domains

Table 2.5 lists the main differences between Windows NT and Windows 2000 as they apply to domain design.

Table 2.5   Design differences between Windows 2000 and Windows NT.

Windows 2000	Windows NT
The Active Directory database can include users, groups, computers, DNS records, Kerberos tickets, group policies, replication objects, and even phone numbers or Social Security numbers.	The SAM database usually contains information only on users, groups, and computers, plus some security information.
The namespace is hierarchical and can be extremely (almost infinitely) large.	The namespace is flat and is limited by size.

(continued)

Table 2.5 Design differences between Windows 2000 and Windows NT *(continued).*

Windows 2000	Windows NT
A search can be conducted for resources across domains because the domain structure is hierarchical.	A search for a resource in another domain requires manually browsing that domain, and a resource cannot be found from inside another domain.
The domain structure can be governed by the organization's composition and needs, and there is an unlimited number of ways to design domains.	The domain structure must conform to one of four types: single, master, or multi-master domain, or a complete trust model.
A single Active Directory can handle millions of objects.	Domains are limited to 40,000 objects.
Responsibility can be delegated within a domain. Therefore, fewer domains need to be created, thus reducing TCO and administrative tasks.	Delegating responsibility within a domain usually requires that another domain be created, thus raising TCO and creating multiple administrative tasks.
Domain controllers share the responsibility of the server duties in a multi-master domain model. If one server goes offline, fault tolerance is provided by the other servers.	Domain controllers consist of PDCs and BDCs. The BDC has only a read-only copy of the database information and must be manually promoted to a PDC when problems occur on the network.
The Active Directory schema (the set of rules that makes the database work) is extensible. This means that within the Active Directory structure, new attributes and information can be stored. For instance, you can add a user's phone number, Social Security number, or next of kin.	NT did not offer this type of manipulation.
Transitive trusts are automatically created between parent and child domains.	Trusts have to be manually created and maintained, and they can be quite cumbersome.

Planning the Active Directory Design

Knowing the differences in the structures will now allow you to effectively begin planning your Active Directory design. At this point, you should have a topology map in hand, have a firm grasp of the physical layout of the network (including its PDCs, BDCs, and member servers), and have a general idea of how you want the new, improved network to look. In addition, you should document information about the domains' organizational needs, requirements, and growth potential. You should also have a firm hold on what forests, trees, domains, and organizational units are. We'll start with the domain structure.

When you're designing the domain structure, start with one domain and then add domains if necessary. Single-domain structures are easier to plan, implement, and maintain. Also, because of the changes made in the design of Windows 2000 itself, a single-domain structure might be possible where it wasn't before the upgrade. Separate domains no longer need to be created for delegating responsibility or for accommodating different offices, such as Chicago, Dallas, and San Francisco offices. Similarly, separate domains do not need to be created for divisions, such as accounting, marketing, and sales. In these instances, a single domain may work just fine, with the divisions configured as organizational units (OUs). Figures 2.14 and 2.15 show examples of this.

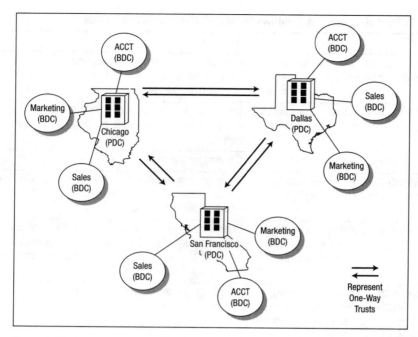

Figure 2.14
Domain configuration choice for an NT network with three domains.

There are reasons to have multiple domains, of course. The following list states some of those reasons. If your organization matches any of these criteria, then a multiple-domain structure is probably necessary. Here are the criteria to consider:

- The company needs to operate under a decentralized domain structure. *Decentralized* means that multiple administrators or administrative teams manage the network. These administrators or teams might be located in different geographical areas or perform differing and incompatible business functions.

- The company needs to increase the efficiency of necessary replication traffic. When a new domain is created, a new Active Directory is created as well. If Active Directory traffic is a problem across WAN links, or if the network has more than a million objects, traffic of this type could become unmanageable. Active Directory traffic between two domains is only the traffic created by the global catalog, versus the synchronization of domain controllers when a single domain is used.

- If the organization spans multiple countries, then multiple domains are probably needed. This type of organization will require decentralized management and thus multiple domains.

- If two companies merge, and each has existing and unchangeable domain names, multiple domains will be needed. For instance, if Smith.com and Jones.com merged, neither company would want to give up its name, and combining the two into one domain would be nearly impossible.

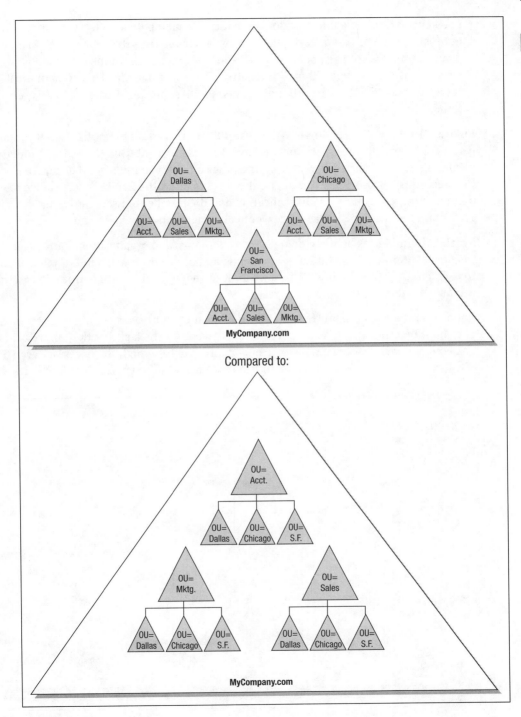

Figure 2.15
Single-domain configuration choices for a Windows 2000 network.

- Each entity requires a different domain policy. Domain policies affect an entire domain, not just a group or two of users. If company policy requires that a certain domain have a minimum password age or account lockouts after a certain number of bad logon attempts, then this policy stands as an attribute of that domain. This domain must stand on its own unless the other domain(s) in question can also adapt to this security standard.

Figure 2.15 showed how a single Windows 2000 domain could be configured. If you later discovered, through your planning and inventory assessment, that the Chicago office needed a security policy different from the other offices, you might well decide to place Chicago in its own domain. You might also need to allow the San Francisco office to maintain its own domain due to replication and the number of users in the organization. This being the case, the Dallas office would also maintain its own domain.

Recall the differences between domain trees, domains, and organizational units (see Chapter 1). Figures 2.15 and 2.16 show single and multiple domains in a single domain tree. To contrast this, Figure 2.17 shows multiple domains in multiple trees. Recall that two or more domain trees form a forest.

Notice that the two domain trees that form a forest do not have a common root domain. They have no other relationship to each other except for the fact that they are related due to a buyout, merge, or trust. This type of domain structure might be necessary even within a company. Consider an organization that makes different kinds of foods. The fact

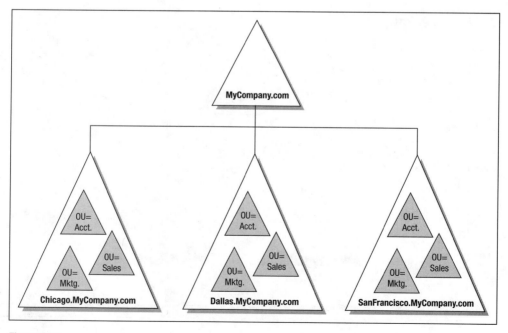

Figure 2.16
MyCompany.com with three domains.

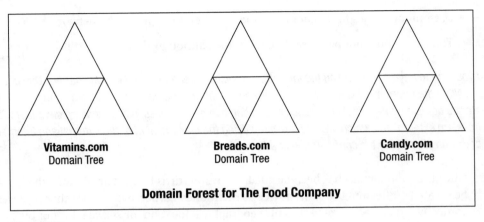

Domain Forest for The Food Company

Figure 2.17
Domain trees forming a forest.

that each division is owned by the same company is the only thing that relates the divisions. One division might make canned foods, one might make breads, and one might make candy. These divisions might go by different trade names and maintain separate identities. They might also each have a different type of consumer, require different strategies for marketing, and sell to different types of stores. And these divisions might each have their own Web sites and Internet names, making the flexibility of Windows 2000's disjointed naming conventions useful to them.

Planning a Domain Namespace

A *domain namespace* is what is used to locate objects on the network and to provide name resolution on the network. Planning a domain namespace starts with choosing a root domain name. If your organization already has a DNS domain name that is in use on the Internet, then you may want to use this name. If no such name exists, or this name is not the one you'd like to use, then the first step is to choose a name and register it with a domain name registrar, such as Network Solutions, Inc.

The name that is chosen should reflect adequately what the company is or does. For example, Microsoft uses the domain name **Microsoft.com**. The root domain should be simple to say, read, and type, and it should be available for registration. The name chosen should be a name that you can live with for the life of the company. For instance, you wouldn't want to choose the name **BigWidgets.com** because at some point the company might choose to make small- or medium-sized widgets.

As with anything, there are rules to follow when choosing a domain name. Following are the requirements for choosing a domain name:

• Use standard DNS and Unicode characters as defined in the RFC 1035. Valid characters are: A-Z, a-z, 0-9, and -.

- Use unique names for subdomains and all other domains on the network.

- The name must not be more than 63 letters, although shorter is better in most cases.

Tip: If you plan to have a Web site on the Internet, it is wise to create two root domain names. One of the names will be the Internet name, and the other will be the intranet name. These are also known as external and internal domain names. The advantages of creating two namespaces include making clear just what resources are external and which are internal, simplifying the management of the external and internal networks, and simplifying the configuration of a firewall.

Once the root domain has been decided, attention turns to any subdomains that need to be created. Following the same advice as mentioned earlier, pick names that represent the company, organization, department, geographical location, or service. Do not pick names that may change in a year or two. Bad examples of subdomains include **2000.corp.com**, **ThirdFloor.corp.com**, **BuildingOne.corp.com**, and so on. Good examples include **Chicago.corp.com**, **Sales.corp.com**, **Computers.corp.com**, and **Cannedfoods.com**.

Tip: This advice also holds true for naming domain controllers and workstations. It's better to name a computer DC1Dallas than to name it FirstFloorServer or TheEnterprise.

Finally, deciding a domain namespace becomes easier after the entire Active Directory structure has been decided. After forests, trees, domains, and organizational units have been determined, the namespace will most likely fall into place.

Warning! After the namespace has been decided, it will be most difficult to change. If changing the domain namespace is essential, it will most likely entail the reinstallation of all of the domain controllers on the network, as well as produce months of headaches for the administrators and the users.

Planning the OU Structure

An organizational unit is a container that holds resources. The OU is designed to be managed efficiently, accessed quickly, and administered with the least amount of effort possible. Planning an effective OU structure is just as important as creating a valid DNS namespace and will affect the organization just as much. A poorly designed OU structure can cause a network to be difficult to maintain and will not lend itself to logical management. In this section, we'll look at what makes a good OU structure and when to create an OU. Throughout, keep in mind how this structure can be used to share responsibilities among departments or divisions in your organization.

Note: Recall Table 2.4 and the following statements: In Windows NT, delegating responsibility within a domain usually required that another domain be created, raising TCO and creating multiple tasks for administrators. In Windows 2000, responsibility can be delegated within a domain. Therefore, fewer domains need to be created, reducing TCO and administrative tasks. It is the availability of the organizational unit that makes this possible.

An effective OU forms a meaningful, logical hierarchy that defines organizational structure and separates administrative tasks or services, defines the physical locations or functions of an organization, and/or delegates tasks of a network. If the OU successfully achieves these separations, then it is a good and carefully planned OU.

Choosing an OU Structure

Before deciding on a particular type of structure for your OUs, make a detailed list of each of the following: how the employees work and what jobs they perform (organizational structure), where the company and its branches are physically located, and what function(s) each department performs. Once these are documented, it will be easier to see which one is the most important or should have emphasis placed on it with OUs.

Tip: Create names for OUs that reflect their respective departments, locations, tasks, services, or functions. Be certain the names chosen will be useful for some time. The guidelines for creating domain names are applicable here as well.

OUs can be used to define the organizational structure of a network, as shown in Figure 2.18. This type of OU design separates the way people do their jobs in a particular setting. This example represents the customer service department of a major clothing store.

Figure 2.19 shows an example of OUs that represent different locations. In the case of a single domain with two or three physical locations, this may be a good choice.

Figure 2.20 shows an example of OUs created by function. This might be a good strategy for an organization whose main divisions are created not by location or job duty but by purpose.

Deciding When to Create an OU

You may now have a feel for how you see the Active Directory, its domains, and even its OUs on your new network. There are certainly a number of ways to create the network structure and organize its objects. However, when do you really need to create an organizational unit, and how do you keep from micromanaging the network? It is certainly very important to organize the resources in the network and to create an effective Active Directory structure, but when is enough, enough? Listed next are some reasons to create organizational units:

- To replace a resource domain in an older NT environment. Resource domains were used to delegate responsibility, and with Windows 2000, creating a domain for this purpose is no longer necessary.

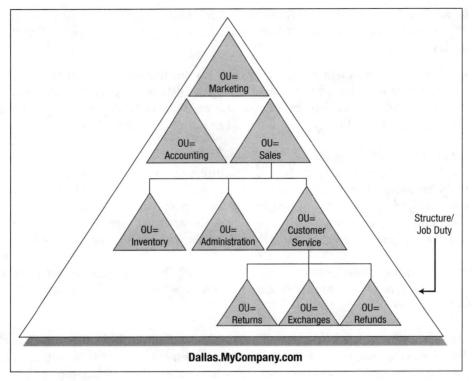

Figure 2.18
Organization unit designed by structure.

- To group users, computers, printers, scanners, file servers, fax machines, departments, locations, job functions, or any other object so that you can enable someone else to manage this group. For instance, you may hire technical support personnel, and delegate the responsibility of the printers, scanners, cameras, and plotters to this department or to the lead technical support administrator.

- To separate different types of users. For instance, the desktop users and the laptop users may have different rules for logging in or out and may need different group policies.

- To simplify administration of the network by creating OUs that can inherit the permissions of their parent OU.

- To simplify browsing the network for resources and to form a meaningful hierarchy. For example, if all of the printers were grouped together, then finding a particular printer on the network would be easier.

By creating the appropriate OU structure, you can increase the efficiency of the network. An appropriate OU structure will make managing the network easier because administration of the OUs can be shared. A good OU structure also allows the user to browse the network more efficiently. The ability to browse the network for resources and find them quickly reduces the bandwidth that is used as well as the time it takes to locate an object.

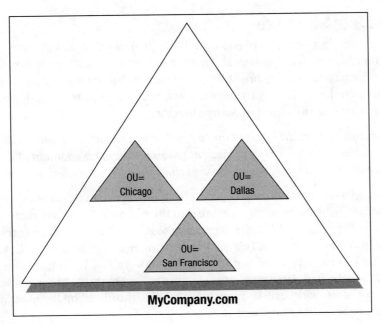

Figure 2.19
Organizational unit designed by location.

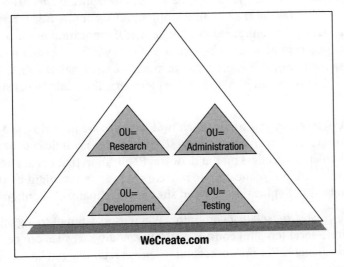

Figure 2.20
Organizational unit designed by function.

Finally, an appropriate OU structure makes securing the network more efficient. It is just as important to carefully design an effective OU structure as it is to design a proper Active Directory structure. Next, we'll discuss the last type of structure: site structure.

Planning the Site Structure

Site structure and domain structure are two completely different things. A *domain structure* is the representation of the logical environment, whereas a *site structure* is the representation of the physical environment. Both are part of the Active Directory and are represented there. In order to identify the physical organization of your network, you must construct at least one site object in Active Directory.

Note: *One domain can have multiple sites, and a single site can include multiple domains. Remember that site structure is a physical representation, and domain structure is a logical one. Both structures are represented in the Active Directory.*

Site structure is used to understand and map the physical network in terms of connectivity, bandwidth, and available links to physical areas of the network. A site is chosen based on its ability to offer high bandwidth to its clients and to offer good network connectivity. Sites should consist of one or more TCP/IP subnets that share a high bandwidth link, such as a fractional T1 line, Integrated Services Digital Network (ISDN), Digital Subscriber Line (DSL), or the like. Additional sites are created for areas that are separated from other areas of the network, usually by slow WAN links, thus needing logon services and replication to occur on their own subnet.

Adding Sites

Active Directory assumes there is enough available bandwidth to replicate effectively. If the domain is in a single building, and the building is appropriately configured for a LAN, then this network will generally be configured as a single site. If replication needs to take place over a slow 56K dial-up connection, the replication of data will be slow and irritating to the users. In these instances, it is appropriate to create new site objects. Listed next are reasons that additional sites should be added and benefits that these additional sites will offer:

- Additional sites can lessen replication traffic. Each time changes are made to the Active Directory of one domain controller in a tree or forest, that change is replicated, or copied, to the other domain controllers on the network. Replication that occurs in a single site is fast and efficient, but replication that occurs between sites might be slower due to distance or bandwidth. Replication between sites must be manually configured.

- Additional sites can be created to isolate logon traffic. When users attempt to log on, the workstation tries to find a local (on-site) domain controller. Additional sites can be created to separate these logons. For instance, bank teller workstations can be configured to obtain their logins from the first-floor domain controller, while the loan managers in the same building obtain their logins from the branch headquarters upstairs.

- Additional sites can also be used to ease administration by centralizing resources—such as printers, plotters, scanners, servers, and cameras—as well as their respective configuration information.

Designing the Site Structure

Designing the structure for a single site is very easy. As I mentioned previously, local area connections are usually fast, and there is no need to create any additional sites. If, however, you have decided that additional sites are needed, the following steps will assist you in that task:

Note: *You may be surprised by how many of these steps have already been completed, and you will further understand the importance of proper planning and documentation.*

1. Examine the physical environment, looking in particular at the topology map you created earlier. Refine that map to include not only the physical locations and speed of the data lines but also the TCP/IP subnets in each office and the status of the current network links. Although you may think that a particular ISDN line is handling the current traffic well, after reviewing the utilization of that line, you may well decide that it should be upgraded to a T1 or should not be used for replication during peak hours.

2. Determine which of those network areas defined in Step 1 need to be configured as sites. To do this, document the requirements of each specific area of the network, and determine if this area needs control over its logon process, if the network requires replication of the Active Directory, or if it needs to be separated to assist in resource management. If any of these are the case, then the site should be included as a site object.

3. Determine how all of the sites involved and configured will replicate their directories. A *site link object* will be used to hold the information required for scheduling these replications. Replication will most likely occur over different types of links, and consideration should be given to how often replication is necessary, or if it even *is* necessary. If a particular area of the network simply dials in to a server or connects via T1 or ISDN, that area might not have a domain controller. In this instance, replication would not be an issue.

4. Because the site link object contains the schedule for replication, each site link object needs to examined closely to determine how often replication should occur. Replication occurs every three hours by default, and I would suggest doing whatever possible to leave it that way. The availability of up-to-date information is very important to users on a network. However, it may not be cost-effective to maintain this replication schedule over expensive pay-as-you-go links. Prioritize the links that can perform the replication, using a default standard cost of 100 (the lower the cost, the higher the priority), and configure replication to occur over the least expensive link.

5. Create site bridges for redundancy. *Site bridges* are used to continue replication tasks even if a link goes down. Figure 2.21 shows an example of a redundant site bridge that can be used if the primary link between the two cities fails. This is a necessary precaution in the case of hospitals, banks, large corporations, and Internet companies, and it may or may not be needed in your particular organization.

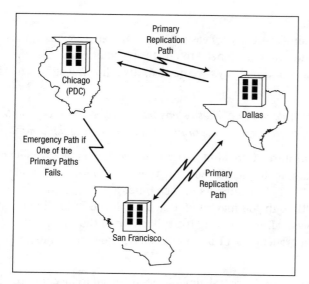

Figure 2.21
A site bridge.

Summary

This chapter included information on preparing for Windows 2000 Server, including the design of the operating system itself, as well as information to get you started with the planning process. The preparation and assessment process is a large project that includes finding out what the network is made of, including software, hardware, and applications. Assessing the network also entails understanding how the network is laid out, what users and administration expect to gain from installing Windows 2000 products, and whether the upgrade or migration is even feasible.

Discussed next were how plans could be developed and nurtured, including how to start, whom to involve, and what makes a plan work. Behind every completed and successful project is a good plan. In this chapter, the plan included surveying the current environment, forming a committee, using that committee to develop a plan and to decide how that plan would be carried out, and finally, testing and doing the rollout. You focused on the start of that plan here: assessing, forming the committee, and deciding on the plan.

Part of the assessment and planning phase includes how to create and organize the Active Directory, including the domain namespace, organizational units, and site structure. Domain namespace is the most important aspect of planning an Active Directory structure because the namespace cannot easily be changed. The namespace describes your organization and allows users to traverse the Active Directory efficiently to find data and objects. Planning for the organizational units was covered next, and you learned about multiple OUs and how these OUs can be configured. OUs can be separated by function, location, resource, or any other number of configurations. Site structure was covered next, and this included information on the physical layout of the network, how Active Directory uses that information to schedule replication, and how administrators can use site objects to control logons and optimize traffic on the network.

Moving Forward

The first two chapters have been full of information that you need to begin a migration to or, upgrade or installation of Windows 2000 servers on your network. Understanding what Windows 2000 is and how it works is necessary before starting any type of installation. Although it seems like a lot of information to take in, it will prove valuable once you start actually implementing these changes on the network.

We are now ready to begin putting our thoughts on paper. Whereas Chapter 2 has prepared us for Windows 2000, allowed us to get our thoughts together, and described how to get started, Chapter 3 will actually begin this process. It is in Chapter 3 that you will prepare for the first server installation. Chapter 3 and this book's CD-ROM include worksheets for organizing the data you will collect (or have already collected), including checklists for the following items and/or people:

- Inventory
- Domain structure
- Project team members
- Department heads
- Blank timeline
- Goals and milestones
- Topology
- Hardware
- Software
- Project team leader and administrations
- Testing
- Rollout
- Training

With the knowledge you have obtained concerning the Windows 2000 components and design, with a plan and a responsible committee in mind, you probably have a pretty good idea of where you want to go and how you want to integrate Windows 2000 on your network. That being the case, you are ready to begin.

Part II

Planning for and Installing Windows 2000 Server

Chapter 3

Installation Planning for Windows 2000 Server

Previously, I discussed Windows 2000 Server's features and characteristics, including its components, the addition and benefits of Active Directory, enhancements to the older Windows NT operating system, and the architecture of the operating system itself. In Chapter 2, you began formulating a plan that could be used for the migration of the existing servers on the network. This plan could also be used to add new Windows 2000 servers on the network and even to create a new network with only Windows 2000 servers. Also in Chapter 2, you created a general plan of action and began to think about how each section of the plan could be carried out. This chapter will help you gather your thoughts, form your committees, and prepare for the installation. By the time you get to Chapter 4, you will be ready to put in the Windows 2000 Server CD-ROM.

For this project to be successful, it's important that you leave adequate time for planning and for documenting the tasks that need to be completed. There must also be adequate resources for testing and deploying. For large organizations, these tasks can be quite daunting and can seem almost impossible to achieve with any degree of success. It may also seem unreasonable to get so many people or departments to work together. The goal of this chapter, then, is to offer worksheets and checklists for every step of the planning process, beginning with taking inventory and ending with rolling out the migration. These checklists will help you formulate views, create plans, and make sound decisions based on a proven planning methodology.

This chapter will enable you and others to share thoughts and information with other members of the project committee. Checklists are usually presented in the same order in which they should be used, allowing project members to make sure that they are address-ing all of the needs of the network and its users and that they are obtaining the required information in a timely manner. These checklists are also included in the CD-ROM that is shipped with this book, and the entire set should be printed and given to each committee member. With these checklists and worksheets in hand, each member can be fully aware of not only the tasks involved but also how his or her particular assignment relates to the project. Project leaders can also use these lists to show progress to the organization's administration, to justify costs, and to systematize the plan.

Chapter 3 is organized into the six parts of the plan that were discussed in Chapter 2. To refresh your memory, they are listed here:

1. Survey the current environment.

2. Form a project committee.

3. Develop a plan.

4. Decide how the plan will be carried out and what will make it work.

5. Test the plan.

6. Roll out the plan.

Note: There really isn't any way to shorten the planning process. I strongly suggest that you take as much time as is reasonably necessary to create the documents included in this chapter so that you can assess the current state of the network as completely as possible. Furthermore, developing a committee that can work well together is equally important.

Checklists for Surveying the Current Environment

Surveying the current environment isn't for the faint of heart. In a large organization, surveying the current environment could take almost as long as performing the rollout itself. This section's checklists will bring to light the magnitude of such an undertaking. As mentioned in Chapter 2, the tasks involved in understanding the current environment include many responsibilities, such as defining the current domain structure, defining company standards, and listing the hardware and software in use on all of the machines, to name just a few. The current domain structure will include the network topology and the physical layout of the network. Company standards can include the user's desktop environment and security policies, including account policies, local policies, public key policies, and IP security policies. Software inventory can include critical applications, general applications, and problem applications (applications that will cause the migration to fail or that will prevent deployment).

Even after this phase is complete, there are still issues that could cause the project to be postponed. A major roadblock could be cost, for instance. But accurately determining what is on the network will help you calculate the cost of any new hardware, software, resources, people, standards, and applications that will be needed.

Note: Although it would be impossible to create checklists that work for everyone, the lists that follow in this chapter will certainly give you a good start. For instance, in the first list, there are places for two servers, and your organization may have 1 or 50. From this book's CD-ROM, you can print the lists and manipulate them as you wish, suiting the needs of your environment. I would suggest (if no current inventory information exists) that one page be created for each server or workstation on the network. There are also many third-party tools to assist you in your inventory tasks. I found many such tools simply by typing "network inventory" into a search engine in my Web browser.

Inventory Checklists

Listed next are checklists for the hardware on your network, the software that is currently being used, and critical applications. The hardware list contains a place to note the computer's CPU, memory, storage, NIC, sound and video cards, modem, and special attributes. The software and critical applications checklists also offer places to document information with categories that are applicable. This data can be used to determine if the computer and its components meet minimum requirements. Keep in mind that meeting "minimum requirements" means that the item meets not just *Microsoft's* minimum requirements but also your *organization's* minimum requirements. For instance, an organization's requirement for an application might be not only that it is compatible with Microsoft 2000 Server but also that it is a Microsoft certified application. The completed lists can be used to compare what currently exists on the network to the standards that your organization has set for the network.

Note: *You can use the following lists most effectively by filling in the required information. Some of this information can be obtained through the Device Manager. If a driver is needed for a particular item, determine if a driver is available for Windows 2000, and put an asterisk beside the item if you know it is available. If you are unsure about driver availability, do not add an asterisk.*

Hardware

Hardware checklists are necessary for inventory and for comparison to minimum requirements. This seemingly simple first step can take an incredible amount of time if no inventory currently exists or if an older inventory is not accurate. Spend ample time now creating an accurate inventory, and the reward will pay off later tenfold.

The following samples are ones I have created to demonstrate how you might use the blank checklists in the CD-ROM to suit your specific needs. Included are checklists for hardware, such as servers and workstations, scanners, printers, cameras, and backup devices.

Sample computer checklist.

Item	Server 1	Server 2	WKST 1	WKST2
Name	Server_08	-	Laptop_24	-
Location	Chicago building, fourth floor	-	Chicago building, first floor	-
Type	AT/AT compatible	-	HP Pavilion N3390	-
CPU	PII	-	PIII	-
Memory	256-MB	-	PIII	-
Storage	35-GB	-	10-GB	-
NIC	3Com 905B*	-	None	-

(continued)

Sample computer checklist *(continued).*

Item	Server 1	Server 2	WKST 1	WKST2
Sound/Video	Creative AWE 64*	-	ESS Maestro	-
Modem	Unknown	-	ESS Es56CVM-PI	-
OS	Windows NT SP6	-	Win98/Win2000 dual boot	-
Special Attributes	RAS Server	-	Belongs to CEO	-
Domain	**Chicago.MyCompany.com**	-	**Chicago.MyCompany.com**	-
Other	n/a	-	n/a	-
Notes	n/a	-	Has two USB ports and one DVD-Rom	-

Again, if no inventory exists, it might be best to create a separate data sheet for each computer on the network. These sheets can then be transferred to a spreadsheet program for organization and safekeeping. I've shown two computers on the previous data sheet.

Note: You'll sometimes need to include other items on the checklist. For instance, BIOS and system drivers can be especially cranky about an upgrade to Windows 2000. If your machines are older, you may want to check their BIOS versions and system drivers (such as RAID or SCSI) for Windows 2000 compliance.

Sample printer checklist.

Item	Printer_01	Printer_02	Printer_03	Printer_04
Name	Printer_01	-	-	-
Location	Dallas Accounting	-	-	-
Type	HP OfficeJet 600 *	-	-	-
Memory	n/a	-	-	-
NIC	n/a	-	-	-
Modem	Phone port for fax	-	-	-
Domain	**Dallas.MyCompany.com**	-	-	-
Special attributes	Copies, faxes, prints; includes software for computer	-	-	-
Other	n/a	-	-	-
Notes	Local printer/fax for small office in accounting department	-	-	-

You can categorize printers by their type. Notice that Printer 01 in the previous sample can copy and fax as well as print. When you're taking inventory or asking others to do so, organize the printers into the following categories:

3

- Color laser
- Color ink jet
- Color LED
- Direct thermal
- Dot matrix
- Line
- Thermal
- Dye sublimation
- Monochrome laser
- Monochrome ink jet
- Miscellaneous

Sample scanner checklist.

Item	Scanner_01	Scanner_02	Scanner_03	Scanner_04
Name	Scan_Dal	-	-	-
Location	Dallas graphics department	-	-	-
Type	Epson Perfection 1200U Flatbed *	-	-	-
Pixels	Effective 10,200X14,040 at 1200 dpi	-	-	-
Optical resolution	1200 dpi	-	-	-
Speed	Color 6.5 msec/line; monochrome 2.2 msec/line	-	-	-
NIC	None; connected to local PC via USB port	-	-	-
Domain	**Dallas.MyCompany.com**	-	-	-
Special attributes	USB interface	-	-	-
Other	n/a	-	-	-
Notes	Works with Macintosh	-	-	-

Sample camera checklist.

Item	Camera_01	Camera_02
Name	Cosmo_01	-
Type	Ricoh RDC-5300	-
Memory	72MB with card	-

(continued)

Sample camera checklist *(continued)*.

Item	Camera_01	Camera_02
Pixels	2.3 mega pixels	-
Optical resolution	n/a	-
Domain	**Garland.Dallas.MyCompany.com**	-
Special attributes	USB and serial ports, JPEG file format	-
Other	Has rechargeable batteries and charger	-
Notes	Works with Windows 98 but unknown if Windows 2000 drivers are available	-

Sample backup device checklist.

Item	BU_01	BU_02
Name	BU-01	Zip_05
Location	San Francisco networking bldg. 7	San Francisco networking bldg. 7
Type	Quantum DLT 8000 *	Iomega Zip drive
Storage	40GB (80GB compressed)	250MB
Special attributes	n/a	External, portable
Domain	**SanFrancisco.MyCompany.com**	**SanFrancisco.MyCompany.com**
Other	Main backup	-
Notes	New	n/a

Sample miscellaneous device checklist.

Item	Device_01	Device_02	Device_03
Computer name	Workstation_01	Server_04	Workstations_01 to 25
Device type	Flat monitor	CD-ROM-RW	Card reader Smart Card reader
Model	NEC	Iomega Zip drive*	SecureTech-ST-100
Location	Dallas graphics	Dallas graphics	Dallas graphics
CPU	n/a	n/a	n/a
Memory	n/a	n/a	n/a
NIC	n/a	n/a	n/a
Modem	n/a	n/a	n/a
Domain	**Garland.Dallas.MyCompany.com**	**Garland.Dallas.MyCompany.com**	**Garland.Dallas.MyCompany.com**

(continued)

3

Item	Device_01	Device_02	Device_03
Storage	n/a	650MB	n/a
OS	Windows 98	Windows NT 4 SP 6	Windows 98, Windows ME
Special attributes	n/a	External	Small, one-hand operation 25 in use
Other	new	n/a	n/a
Notes	n/a	n/a	n/a

Sample miscellaneous device checklist *(continued).*

Before moving on to software inventory, note that not every device can be accounted for in these lists. You should also pass along a blank checklist where users or department personnel can list any other device that is not included here. For instance, you might have a SCSI hard drive that needs to be listed, RAID systems that should be detailed, and accessibility devices that may be used in special instances.

Software

Every computer has software installed on it, even if it is just the operating system. Most computers on a network will have many other applications on them as well. It is important to know just what applications are on each machine. The software checklist can be filled out by the same group of people that fills out the hardware checklist for the computers in the organization. The project team that will be formed later will make those decisions. The next objective is to introduce the checklists for collecting the appropriate data and assembling it in an organized manner.

Personal Experience

A few days ago, I was talking with a friend of mine, a representative from a company that provides upgrades to Windows 2000 for smaller networks here in Dallas. I asked how the upgrade process was going, and she said it would be going much better if the clients would cooperate with her inventory team. The problem, she says, is that when people find out there is going to be a change, they don't really want to share with anyone what they've installed on their computers, what peripherals they've got hiding in their desk drawers, or what they have on their hard drives. This lack of cooperation makes taking inventory of large networks frustrating and time-consuming. She also notes that equally difficult is finding items that are supposed to exist and don't. Perhaps these items were stolen, are being hidden, or became obsolete and were thrown out. She encourages all of the companies she works with to maintain proper inventories after they've been done successfully here. I would caution the inventory team to expect this, to be personable and nonthreatening, and to point out the good in the process. For larger organizations, instead of relying on the users to provide this information, you can use an inventory program such as SMS to do this work for you. An application such as this will take the guesswork out of taking inventory and will not involve the users at all. Using SMS or something similar may be an appropriate solution to solve the problem described above.

There are two ways to approach the task of obtaining information about applications in use. Either use a checklist that is based on what is installed on each computer, or use a checklist that asks about specific types of applications. Both lists are appropriate, but one may work better than the other in certain situations.

Note: Remember that blank checklists are on the CD-ROM that is included with this book, and they can be printed and manipulated for your convenience. Listed here are examples of how the checklists are laid out, as well as some sample checklists. These can be used to begin the software inventory.

Sample software checklist, organized by computer.

Computer(s)	Location	Application(s)	OS	Critical (?)	Problems
All workstations	Dallas	Internet Explorer	All	No	None
Workstation_04	Chicago	CorelDRAW	All	No	None
Server_02	San Francisco	Microsoft Exchange	All	Yes	No
Graphics department	Dallas	Proprietary graphics	Windows 98	No	Saves in proprietary file format not accessible by other programs
Warehouse_01 to 36	Chicago	Inventory! Version 2	Windows 98	Yes	Inventory! Version 2 does not work with Windows ME or Windows 2000

Sample software checklist, organized by software type.

Application Name	Type	OS	Location	Critical (?)	Problems
Internet Explorer	Web browser	All	All	No	None
CorelDRAW	Illustration	All	Dallas and Chicago only	No	No
Microsoft Exchange	Email	All	Chicago, Dallas, San Francisco	Yes	No
Inventory! Version 2	Inventory	Windows 9x	Chicago warehouse	Yes	Computers cannot be upgraded because there is no Inventory! program that can be used for Windows ME or 2000

Critical and Problem Applications

Before a checklist can be completed for applications critical to the network, the characteristics for a critical application must be defined. Although one department may see an application as a critical one, it may not really be critical to the organization at all. For instance, if the graphics department uses a program for its design work, the graphics department may deem that application "critical" because it's the application that has been used for the last four years. However, this particular program may not meet the company's new standards for applications because its file format cannot be opened easily by other programs. The administration may see fit to replace this program with a different one, such as Adobe Photoshop, Paint Shop Pro, Corel PHOTO-PAINT, or something similar. Perhaps a new standard forces the application to be certified by Microsoft. If such a program can be replaced, even if it requires retraining and the movement or conversion of data, it isn't really a critical application to the network.

Sample critical application checklist.

Item	Application_01	Application_02	Application_03
Application name	Inventory! Version 2	-	-
Department	Warehouse	-	-
Location	Chicago	-	-
Originally designed for what OS	Was written specifically for our warehousing and inventory needs	-	-
Why the application is deemed critical	No newer version available	-	-
Problems	Cost to change programs at this time is too expensive	-	-
Suggestions for replacement	None	-	-
Notes	Vendor plans to release newer version in the future	-	-

Sample problem application checklist.

Item	Application_01	Application_02	Application_03
Application name	Proprietary graphics	-	-
Department	Graphics	-	-
Location	Dallas	-	-
Originally designed for what OS	Windows 98	-	-
Why application is deemed a problem	Saves files in proprietary file format	-	-
Problems	Files cannot be opened by other programs	-	-
Suggestions for replacement	CorelDRAW	-	-

Table Note: Program is well accepted by users, and will require training to replace

Tip: It would be well worth your while to insist that proprietary applications, noncertified applications, and/or problem applications be retired or replaced on the network. The time and effort spent maintaining these programs and working around their problems isn't usually worth the time and cost involved in keeping them. Consider an application like Inventory!, used in a warehousing department. Inventory! will continue to be a problem application for some time. The computers in that department will not be upgraded until another *version is created, and this same problem will most likely come up again during the next operating system change. Although it may cost quite a bit of money right now to move the data, revamp the inventory system, and retrain users, I believe you can tell that the trade-off will be well worth it in the future.*

Current Topology

The current environment not only consists of the networks' existing hardware, software, and critical applications, but also includes many other qualities. Topology is one of them. *Topology* is how the network is laid out, including nodes and network lines, the speeds of those lines, and the physical location of servers and workstations. To plan effectively for Active Directory replication, data transfer, and hundreds of other issues relevant to the upgrade, you'll need to draw an accurate topology map. The next checklist offers a place to organize data that needs to be obtained to draw an accurate map of the network. Figure 3.1 shows a sample topology map that can be used as a base to sketch your

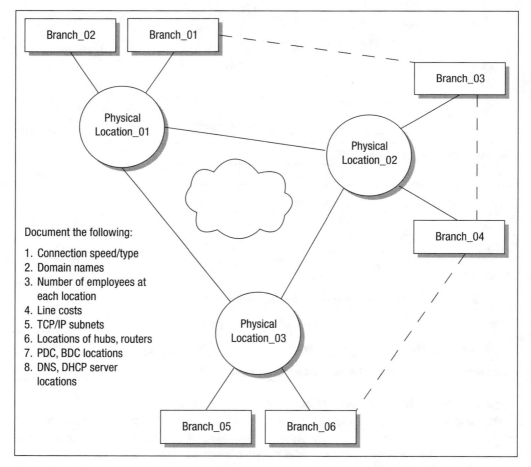

Figure 3.1
Sample topology map.

network. A topology map does not have to be a complicated drawing, but it must include the general layout of the organization. Remember that this map will be used to create Active Directory replication plans and perhaps to restructure the domains as well.

Topology checklist.

Information to Collect	Domain Information	Notes
Physical location 1		
Physical location 2		
Physical location 3		
Physical location 4		
Physical location 1, branch offices/divisions		
Physical location 2, branch offices/divisions		
Physical location 3, branch offices/divisions		
Physical location 4, branch offices/divisions		
Speed of links connecting offices		
Speed of links in each office		
TCP/IP subnets in each office		
Location of domain controllers		
Location of backup domain controllers		
Physical links between sites		
Domain names		
Number of employees in location 1		
Number of employees in location 2		
Number of employees in location 3		
Number of employees in location 4		
Number of employees in each branch		
Links that are the most expensive to maintain		
Links that are the least expensive to maintain		
Other		

Current Domain Structure

Using the topology map that was drawn in the previous section, add the PDCs, BDCs, member servers, file and print servers, fax servers, email servers, and workstations to each node. Figure 3.2 shows a blown-up view of the Dallas office; following that are checklists for assessing the domain structure of the network.

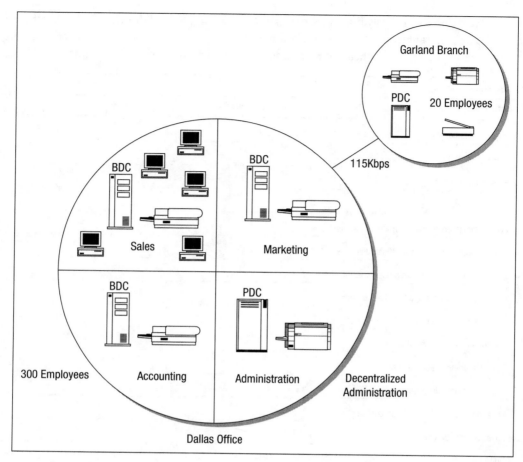

Figure 3.2
Sample domain structure.

Choosing your domain model.			
Domain Model	**Names of Domains**	**Names of Resource Domains**	**Locations**
Single domain			
Single master domain			
Multi-master domain			
Complete trust domain			
Notes			

Choosing your administrative structure.

Administrative Model	Number of Administrators	Company Size	Division	Department	Management of Resources
Centralized					
Decentralized					
Hybrid					
Notes					

Important questions about the domain structure.

Question	Notes
Is the current domain structure working?	
What improvements can be made to the current domain structure?	
Does the current domain structure need to be changed?	
If domains could be consolidated, which ones could you remove or combine?	
Do domains need to be added?	
Will your plan for Active Directory match the current structure?	
Are there any applications on any PDCs or BDCs that will not be upgraded?	
If you plan to do some restructuring, what extra costs will be involved?	
Will the current physical network hold up under the increased bandwidth requirements for Active Directory?	
Does the company plan to merge with another company?	
Does the company plan to upgrade the current PDCs?	
Does the company plan to re-create the domain and install clean copies of Windows 2000 Server?	
Will restructuring the domain improve or hamper network performance?	
Other?	

Current Standards

There are probably standards in place for network hardware, software, services, naming conventions, desktop requirements, platforms, backups, documentation, and updates, even though the standards may not be evident or documented in company policy. Sometimes these standards were put in place when the network was created, and sometimes they are simply born out of habit. These standards need to be determined and documented. By looking for patterns in the inventory and topology lists, and by answering pertinent questions, you can determine the standards.

Determining current standards.		
Item	**Current Standard, If Any**	**Suggestion for New Standard**
Hardware, including CPU, RAM, HDD		
NIC		
BIOS, including APM/ACPI/Windows compliance		
SCSI, RAID, USB system drivers		
Web browsers		
Office applications		
Graphics programs		
Virus programs		
Updates, including service packs, hot fixes, and application upgrades		
Computer names		
Account names		
Email names		
User names		
Protocols, including TCP/IP, IPX/SPX, NetBEUI		
Permissions		
Rights		
Group creation		
Domain creation		
Computers and laptop brand names		
Printers		
Scanners		
Cameras		
Connections and data links		
User desktops		
Other		

Note: While observing a large company's upgrade in progress, I noticed that the actual upgrade wasn't scheduled until 18 months after the initial planning began. I asked the project team members what they'd be doing during that 18 months. They said that they

3

were devoting the first nine months of the upgrade process to assessing and creating standards on the network. They wanted to get rid of noncertified applications, create disk quotas for all of the users, give some responsibility for backing up data to the users themselves, limit the desktop configurations to reduce problems, and do a host of other activities. Although it would take nine months and require extensive training for the users, the team members said that in the end, this process would lessen the company's TCO.

Current Security Policy

Every network has a security policy, even if it is a network of five users and the policy is simply knowing the password to the resource. Usually, though, the network is much larger than that, and the security policy is much more detailed. There are many ways to secure a network and/or a local machine, and security can be achieved by configuring account policies, local policies, public key policies, and IP security policies. Other security measures include access control, virus protection, encryption, digital certificates, back-ups, disaster recovery, and more. It is important to make note of the security measures in place on your network. The following checklists will assist in obtaining and documenting this information.

Note: Administrative tasks involved in securing a Windows 2000 network just got easier. Included in Windows 2000 Server is the Security Configuration And Analysis tool, which offers an organized way to refer to security needs. Another option is to use the security templates available as a snap-in through the MMC.

Account policies: password policy.				
Location/Group	**History**	**Maximum Age**	**Minimum Age**	**Minimum Length**
Location 1				
Location 2				
Location 3				
Location 4				
Branch 1				
Branch 2				
Branch 3				
Branch 4				
Specific users				
User_01				
User_02				

(continued)

Account policies: password policy *(continued).*

Location/Group	History	Maximum Age	Minimum Age	Minimum Length
User_03				
Specific groups				
Sales				
Management				
Administration				
Power Users				
Server Operators				
Other				
Temp_01				
Temp_02				

Account policies: account lockout policy.

Location/group	Duration	Threshold	Reset Counter after ___ Tries
Location 1			
Location 2			
Location 3			
Location 4			
Branch 1			
Branch 2			
Branch 3			
Branch 4			
Specific users			
User_01			
User_02			
User_03			
Specific groups			
Sales			
Management			
Administration			

(continued)

Account policies: account lockout policy *(continued)*.

Location/group	Duration	Threshold	Reset Counter after ___ Tries
Power Users			
Server Operators			
Other			
Temp_01			
Temp_02			

Local policies: audit policies.

Location/group Policy Change	Logon Privilege Use	Management Process Tracking	Directory Service Access System Events	Object Access
Location 1				
Location 2				
Location 3				
Location 4				
Branch 1				
Branch 2				
Branch 3				
Branch 4				
Specific users				
User_01				
User_02				
User_03				
Specific groups				
Sales				
Management				
Administration				
Power Users				
Server Operators				
Other				
Temp_01				
Temp_02				

Local policies: user rights assignment.

Location/Group Restore Files and Directories	Add Workstations Other Specifically Defined Rights	Backup Files and Folders	Shut Down the System	Increase Quotas
Location 1				
Location 2				
Location 3				
Location 4				
Branch 1				
Branch 2				
Branch 3				
Branch 4				
Specific users				
User_01				
User_02				
User_03				
Specific groups				
Sales				
Management				
Administration				
Power Users				
Server Operators				
Other				
Temp_01				
Temp_02				

Local policies: security options.

Location/Group	Rename Accounts	Disable CTRL-ALT-DEL	Install Drivers	Access to Peripherals	Other
Location 1					
Location 2					
Location 3					

(continued)

Local policies: security options *(continued)*.

Location/Group	Rename Accounts	Disable CTRL-ALT-DEL	Install Drivers	Access to Peripherals	Other
Location 4					
Branch 1					
Branch 2					
Branch 3					
Branch 4					
Specific users					
User_01					
User_02					
User_03					
Specific groups					
Sales					
Management					
Administration					
Power Users					
Server Operators					
Other					
Temp_01					
Temp_02					

Miscellaneous policies.

Question	Notes
Any policies for encryption and decryption of data?	
Will IP security policies be used across the network?	
Will the network be able to support Kerberos network-wide in the future?	
Will smart cards be used?	
Will Encrypting File System (EFS) be used network-wide?	
What is currently being audited?	
What groups exist and what is their level of access to resources?	

(continued)

Miscellaneous policies *(continued)*.	
Question	**Notes**
How are the servers secured?	
How will the new domain controllers be secured?	
What is the policy for backup tapes?	
Where are extra copies of backups stored off site?	
How are backups implemented?	
What is the schedule for backups, and will this policy need to be changed?	
Will your network administrator use Windows security templates?	
How will Public Key Infrastructure (PKI) be used?	
How will Certificate Authorities be used?	
How will Web servers employ certificates?	
How will trusts be managed and by whom?	
Other	

Logon security.			
Location/Group	**Message Text**	**Logon Locally (Allow/Deny)**	**Automatic Logoff If Time Expires (Yes/No)**
Location 1			
Location 2			
Location 3			
Location 4			
Branch 1			
Branch 2			
Branch 3			
Branch 4			
Specific users			
User_01			
User_02			
User_03			
Specific groups			

(continued)

3

Logon security *(continued)*.

Location/Group	Message Text	Logon Locally (Allow/Deny)	Automatic Logoff If Time Expires (Yes/No)
Sales			
Management			
Administration			
Power Users			
Server Operators			
Other			
Temp_01			
Temp_02			

Desktop lockdown.

Location/Group	Hide Icons	Disable Control Panel, Registry Editor, Add/Remove Programs/Screensaver/Wallpaper	Password Protect Screensaver	Other?
Location 1				
Location 2				
Location 3				
Location 4				
Branch 1				
Branch 2				
Branch 3				
Branch 4				
Specific users				
User_01				
User_02				
User_03				
Specific groups				
Sales				
Management				
Administration				

(continued)

Desktop lockdown *(continued)*.

Location/Group	Hide Icons	Disable Control Panel, Registry Editor, Add/Remove Programs/Screensaver/Wallpaper	Password Protect Screensaver	Other?
Power Users				
Server Operators				
Other				
Temp_01				
Temp_02				

Almost all of these checklists will be filled out by the members of the project team or their staffs. Forming this project committee is another task that must be completed. The next section contains checklists for forming the committee. While the committee is being formed, some of the inventory processing can be taking place. At the first meeting of the project team, print a copy of all of the checklists for each team member.

Checklists for Forming a Project Committee

The project committee (a.k.a. the project team, the A team, the base team, or the design team) must be formed with care. Team members must be able to meet often and work together well.

The team will be responsible for determining not only how large the project is but also if the current environment can support Windows 2000 Server. In addition, the team will decide the requirements for making the project successful and will follow the plan to its end. And what's more, this committee should also decide if moving to Windows 2000 Server is cost-effective and if any restructuring is needed for existing domains or standards.

This section's checklists will guide you through this part of the process, beginning with selecting the members, organizing the team members and documentation, determining the job assignments, and creating a meeting schedule. The rest of this chapter focuses on team members' jobs: developing the plan, making the plan work, testing, and rollout.

Note: These lists are for direction only and cannot be expected to meet the needs of every organization. I hope that these lists will help you form an effective and complete team and that all aspects of the project will be covered.

Selecting Members

Forming the team and selecting members isn't a quick and easy 1-2-3 process where you simply ask who wants to join in. In fact, in large organizations, it may take three months just to select the project leader. Once the project leader is chosen, the team will be formed. The formation of the team can also be a lengthy process, which, depending on the size of the company, can take upwards of three to four months.

The following list contains facets of Windows 2000 Server planning and installation that must have people associated with them. Some of these people may have to be brought in as consultants, and some can be chosen from the company as is. Make sure that there are people on the team who are knowledgeable in the fields listed.

3

Warning! *Although it seems that knowledge in a particular field may be the most important trait of a possible candidate, if the most knowledgeable person is hard to get along with, generally causes rifts between other members, is absent from work a lot, or is on the verge of retirement, it may be a bad idea to choose this candidate. Keep in mind that the people you choose for this committee will be working closely together for quite a long period of time, and sometimes character is more important than knowledge.*

Member selection worksheet.

Role	Possible Candidate	Notes
Project leader		
Enterprise administration		
Network administration		
Domain administration		
Security advisor or expert		
DNS administrator		
DHCP administrator		
Technical support representative		
Management representative		
Email and messaging expert or administrator		
Engineering representative		
Development representative		
Manufacturing representative		
Sales representative		
Accounting representative		
Production representative		
Warehouse representative		
Field representative		
Telecommunications administrator or expert		
Protocol expert		

(continued)

Member selection worksheet *(continued).*

Role	Possible Candidate	Notes
Alternate OS expert		
Web design administrator		
Training administrator or coordinator		
Backup and recovery administrator or expert		
Proprietary internal company projects or applications expert		
Remote Access Service (RAS)		
Other		

Tip: *You might not need all of these members, and you might need some who aren't listed here. The important thing to remember is to have a representative from every department and an expert for each service on the network.*

Listing Project Team Members

After you've compiled a list of possible candidates and notes for each of the roles listed in the previous section, you are ready to compile a list of project team members. If your organization is small, the team may contain only a few members. However, if the organization is large, it may contain 25 or more people. List the people you've chosen in the following worksheet, and give a copy of the list to everyone on the team. After this list is created, you'll be ready to delegate assignments for the members.

Project team member list.

Member Name	Department	Location	Expertise	Possible Assignment	Notes
Member_01					
Member_02					
Member_03					

Sample project team member list.

Member Name	Department	Location	Expertise	Possible Assignment	Notes
John Doe	Domain administration	Chicago	DNS	Active Directory design	Lead administrator
Bob Smith	Mail and messaging	Dallas	Exchange 2000		Mail and messaging
Sally Jones	Enterprise administration	Chicago	Planning and strategy		Migration issues

Note: *You may be figuring out that this team can get large; in fact, if it is too large, it will become ineffective. If this becomes the case when forming your team, suggest that the team be broken up into an A team and a B team, or a core team and subteams. This could help in organizing the people and resources involved.*

Listing Job Assignments

So far in this section, you've looked at member roles and possible team members to fill those roles. After members are chosen, the project leader or perhaps a core team needs to decide how certain tasks will be performed and by whom. The following checklist should be filled out completely and thoroughly, and then should be dutifully checked throughout the project for completeness and for changes to the plan. Many of the tasks listed here can be completed with the help of other checklists in this chapter. The notes made in this checklist can also be used to help develop a timeline for the project later.

Responsibilities of team members.		
Task	**Team Member Responsible**	**Approximate Time for Completing Task**
Document the purpose and scope		
Document reasons for moving to Windows 2000		
Determine the cost of the project and justify its expense		
Perform the inventory of the network		
Make sure hardware and software are compatible and will work properly		
Choose which services to employ		
Design and implement DNS		
Design and implement DHCP		
Design a group policy		
Work on protocol configuration		
Develop a timeline for migration		
Plan the Active Directory namespace		
Plan the Active Directory design (trees and forests)		
Plan how Active Directory will be replicated among the domain controllers		
Plan how the global catalog will be configured		
Create standards or redefine the current standards		
Create policies or refine existing policies		
Design a model for security		
Choose the upgrade method		

(continued)

Responsibilities of team members *(continued)*.		
Task	**Team Member Responsible**	**Approximate Time for Completing Task**
Perform a physical network analysis (topology)		
Provide technical support for team members and users		
Design the migration plan		
Create the lab where the rollout will be tested		
Design or redesign email and messaging		
List deployment options and make appropriate decisions		
Restructure domains		
Restructure DNS namespaces		
Coordinate training efforts for users, clients, and network operators		
Design sites		
Design OUs		
Design domains		
Handle internal issues		
Create a pilot plan		
Other		

Creating a Meeting Schedule

Creating a meeting schedule is listed here for the sake of reminding you that your team must meet regularly in order to communicate effectively. If team members are in physically different locations, however, this can be expensive or downright impossible. There should be a schedule in place, and this schedule should be based on the timeline and milestones as well as on necessity. When you're creating a meeting schedule, make sure that all of the meetings are necessary, that they occur often enough, and that they each have a planned agenda.

Note: I am following a company through an upgrade at this time, and its core team meets every Friday around 11:00. If the meeting runs late, it's continued over lunch. Apparently, this plan works because the team members are relaxed on Friday and they have an entire week's worth of information. That information includes how their department is progressing in completing tasks, and what, if any, problems are arising. This schedule also gives each team member a chance to ask questions and share concerns. The fact that the meeting sometimes spills over into lunch doesn't seem to bother the majority of the team members.

Checklists for Developing the Plan

This section includes checklists and worksheets for developing the plan. With the design team in place, and members knowing their assignments, it comes down to actually completing those assigned tasks. Some of the tasks that were assigned, such as taking inventory, have already been addressed in previous sections. Most of the other immediate tasks will be addressed here.

This section will cover checklists for creating a document that contains the purpose and scope of the project, making sure the computers and equipment on the network meet minimum requirements and are on Microsoft's Hardware Compatibility List (HCL), and making sure that upgrade paths are correct. A timeline and milestone worksheet, along with instructions for properly preparing users for the change, will be included. Finally, I'll discuss issues concerning restructuring, cost analysis, and Active Directory design.

The Purpose and Scope

Defining the purpose and scope of the project is an important first step. Defining why you want to install Windows 2000 on the network (the purpose) and how large or small the implementation will be (scope) are necessary to keep the project focused and on track.

By defining the *purpose* of the project, you can document why the company will benefit from Windows 2000, what its advantages are over the current OS, and how it will reduce the company's TCO. Defining the purpose is necessary to justify the costs and the migration to higher-ups.

Included in the *scope* of the project are which services you plan to employ and how you plan to carry out the migration. The design team might decide that the PDCs and BDCs will be migrated first, and then the file and print servers, and finally the mail and messaging servers. Deciding on a scope allows the team to form a basis for the order of the migration.

The services worksheet gives you a place to make notes on how certain services will be used after the migration to Windows 2000 Server. This worksheet might be helpful in defining the purpose of the migration and will need to be taken into account when figuring out the scope.

Purpose worksheet.
Information to Include in the Purpose Report
Why upgrade to Windows 2000?
Why upgrade now instead of later?
Why can't you wait until the next version of Windows Server is released?
How will Active Directory be used to improve network performance?

(continued)

Purpose worksheet *(continued).*

Information to Include in the Purpose Report

How will the new trust configuration ease the administrator's workload?

How will OUs be used to improve the network?

How will trees be used to improve the network?

How will forests improve the network?

What advantages does Windows 2000 offer over the current operating system?

What current problems can be solved by installing Windows 2000 Server on the network?

What can the company expect to gain from this upgrade?

What features of Windows 2000 Server could potentially harm the network?

How will the upgrade affect the TCO of the company?

How will the new security features of Windows 2000 work?

Other

Scope worksheet.

Information to Include in the Report

When will the migration pay for itself?

Who will be affected by the project?

How long will it take?

What should be the first server upgraded? Why?

How will the BDCs be upgraded? Why?

How long will it take to complete the project?

Include the timeline.

How will the data be backed up during the migration?

How will restructuring of domains be handled?

How will restructuring of standards be handled?

In what order will the servers be migrated?

How will users be trained?

How much downtime is expected?

In what order will team members perform their assigned tasks?

Other

Note: Scope *can mean two things. The scope can address the questions "what?" and "why?" as in "Why should I install Windows 2000 Server?", or it can address how large a project will be, as in "How are you going to install Windows 2000 Server?" I have tried to include both types of questions in the checklist. Before handing in a document concerning the scope of a project, make sure you understand the requestor's definition of the word.*

3

Services worksheet.
How Will the Following Windows 2000 Services Be Used on the Network?
Active Directory and replication
Global catalog
IntelliMirror
Remote Installation Services (RIS)
Encrypted File System (EFS)
Security protocols such as L2TP, EAP, and IPSec
Kerberos
Transitive trusts
Security Configuration Editor
Security Configuration Manager
Windows NT LAN Manager (NTLM)
Delegation of responsibility
Public key cryptography
Certificate Services
Smart cards
Disk quotas
Dynamic disks, Remote Storage Service, Distributed File System (DFS)
Dynamic DNS
WINS
DHCP
Quality of service
Protocol support
Group policy
Other
In-house applications

Hardware Compatibility List and Minimum Hardware and Software Requirements

This section's checklists will help you figure out if the hardware and software on your servers meets the minimum requirements—so you can decide what needs to be purchased, replaced, or retired or what can be used as is—and if the equipment you have is on Microsoft's HCL (Hardware Compatibility List). As mentioned earlier, the HCL can be found at **www.microsoft.com/hcl/default.asp**. This link can be accessed from the CD-ROM that is included with this book.

Another important question that needs to be addressed is whether the hardware and software meet not only Microsoft's minimum requirements but also the new or existing standards on the network. If Microsoft states that the minimum requirement for RAM on a server machine is 256MB, and the OS can be installed on as little as 128MB, your current machines may meet minimum requirements. However, if the standards put in place during the transition state that every server machine should have 512MB of RAM, then you might not have met minimum requirements for your network. For software, the applications may be compatible but not certified, and your network standard may require them to be certified. In those instances, even though the software may be considered compatible, it may not meet your network's new minimum requirements. The following checklists will help you organize this information.

Listed in the next table are the Microsoft standards for server software. You can use this list to fill out the required information for the checklists that follow. In those checklists, compile information previously acquired from the inventory lists, and simply note yes or no in the spaces. If the item does not meet minimum requirements, make a note of why. From these worksheets, you can determine what hardware or software should be replaced, retired, or upgraded.

Microsoft standards for software.

Hardware	Minimum Requirements	Suggested Requirements	Maximum Requirements
CPU	133MHz Pentium compatible	133MHz or higher	n/a
RAM	128MB	256MB	4GB
Hard disk space	2GB with 1GB free (more for network installation)	More than 2GB	n/a
Number of CPUs	1	n/a	4
BIOS	Must be compatible	Supports ACPI (Advanced Configuration and Power Interface)	n/a

*Note: These requirements came directly from Microsoft's Web site at **www.microsoft.com/ windows2000/upgrade/upgradereqs/default.asp**. You will see many different versions of the minimum requirements from different books and publishers. Check Microsoft's site for changes to these minimum requirements before starting an installation.*

Sample checklist for Microsoft standards for server hardware.				
Server_01	**Meets Minimum (Yes/No)**	**Meets Suggested (Yes/No)**	**On HCL**	**Notes**
CPU	Yes	Yes	Yes	
RAM	Yes	No (only 128MB)	Yes	Can be upgraded to 256 MB
Hard disk space	Yes	Yes	Yes	
Number of CPUs	Yes	Yes	Yes	
BIOS	No	No (upgrade available)	Yes, after upgrade	
NIC	Is on HCL	-	-	
Modem	Is on HCL	-	-	
Other	n/a	-	-	

Sample organizational standards for server hardware.			
Hardware	**Minimum Requirements**	**Suggested Requirements**	**On MS HCL**
CPU	PII	PIII or higher	Yes
RAM	256	512	Yes
Hard disk space	10GB	25GB	Yes
Number of CPUs	1	1–4	Yes
BIOS	ACPI compatible	ACPI compatible	Yes
NIC	10/100Mbps	100 Mbps	Yes
Modem	56K	Use DSL/ISDN	Yes
Other	n/a	-	-

Warning! *There may not be enough money available to replace or upgrade everything that you think should be replaced or upgraded. When you're creating the list of questionable server hardware, or any similar list for that matter, keep in mind that you may have to solve these problems by switching one machine with another, upgrading with spare parts from another machine, or using a computer from a test lab. Most likely, you'll lease the computers you need. Purchasing all new computers, upgrading to the IT department's ideal standards, or retiring questionable hardware doesn't always go the way you would like.*

Sample list of questionable server hardware currently being used.					
Hardware	**Retire**	**Replace**	**Upgrade**	**Reasons**	**Solution**
Server_01	No	No	Yes	Upgrade is possible	Upgrade BIOS; add 128MB of RAM
NIC_01 to NIC_20	Yes	Yes	No	NICs are problematic and do not have drivers for Windows 2000	Replace these 20 NICs

Microsoft Standards for Server Software

Microsoft has four levels of software applications. Microsoft has been working with independent software vendors (ISVs) and has developed a register of Windows 2000 applications. This is a work in progress, of course, and will continually be added to and altered. Not all applications will be listed here, but it is a good place to begin to check for software compatibility. To access this information, simply go to **www.microsoft.com/windows2000/upgrade/compat/search/software.asp**. The four types of certifications are:

1. *Certified*—The highest ranking. Ensures that the application has passed rigorous testing and will work without problems in Windows 2000.

2. *Compatible*—The software vendor states the application is compatible with Windows 2000 and offers product support for Windows 2000 users.

3. *Planned*—The software vendor will offer a compatible version soon.

4. *Caution*—Be careful; there will most likely be problems.

Please note that not all applications can be found here. Even if the application you are searching for isn't listed, it may well be compatible. Your next step is to check the manufacturer's Web site.

Sample list of organizational standards for server software.

Software	Minimum Requirements	Suggested Requirements	Certification Level	Notes
Office applications	MS Office	MS Office	Certified	Part of new standard
Email application	Outlook Express	Outlook	Certified	Part of new standard
Graphics application	Must be compatible	Written for Windows 2000	Compatible	None
Printer/scanner/fax software	Must function	Upgrade driver	Planned	New driver not available now, but will be soon

Sample list of questionable server software.

Software	Retire	Replace	Upgrade	Reasons
Graphics application	Yes	Yes	No	No upgrade in the works, move to CorelDRAW
Printer/scanner/fax	No	No	No	Cannot afford to replace—will wait for new driver
Inventory!	No	No	Yes	Inventory! has been upgraded from *Caution* to *Planned*
Outlook Express	No	Yes	Yes	Replace with Outlook's complete version

Upgrade Paths

The following checklist is provided to help you determine if the current operating system on your servers can be directly upgraded or if other actions need to be taken. Making the decision to upgrade or to install cleanly is addressed in the next chapter, and the necessary checklists will be included there. Decision Tree 3.1 is included following Table 3.1, to assist in choosing the correct upgrade paths for your specific server and operating system.

Tip: In my experience, if a computer is running an operating system that is more than two operating system versions behind (for example, a Windows 3.1 machine that needs to become a Windows 98 machine), it is generally better to perform a clean install and start over. If you have a Windows NT 3.5 Server on your network, and you plan to upgrade it to Windows 2000 by first upgrading to Windows NT 4 SP 4, I'd say you'd be better off just installing that server clean. In many instances, if the computer is that far behind, it may not be upgradeable. In that instance, other solutions will need to be found.

Table 3.1   Upgrade paths for Windows 2000 Server.

Current OS	Upgrade Is Possible	More Information
Windows 3.1	No	Perform a clean install if the computer is compatible
Windows 95	No	Upgrade to Windows 2000 Professional instead, or perform a clean install
Windows 98	No	Upgrade to Windows 2000 Professional instead, or perform a clean install
Windows NT Workstation 3.51	No	Upgrade to Windows 2000 Professional instead, or perform a clean install
Windows NT Workstation 4	No	Upgrade to Windows 2000 Professional instead, or perform a clean install
Windows NT Server 3.5	No	Upgrade to Windows NT 4 SP 4 first, then to Windows 2000 Server, or perform a clean install
Windows NT Server 3.51	Yes	Chapter 4 or Microsoft's Web site (links are on the CD-ROM)
Windows NT Server 4	Yes	Chapter 4 or Microsoft's Web site (links are on the CD-ROM)
Windows NT Server 3.51 with Citrix software	No	Perform a clean install
Windows NT 4 Server Enterprise	Yes	Chapter 4 or Microsoft's Web site (links are on the CD-ROM)
Windows NT 4 Terminal Server	Yes	Chapter 4 or Microsoft's Web site (links are on the CD-ROM)
Back Office Small Business Server	No	Perform a clean install

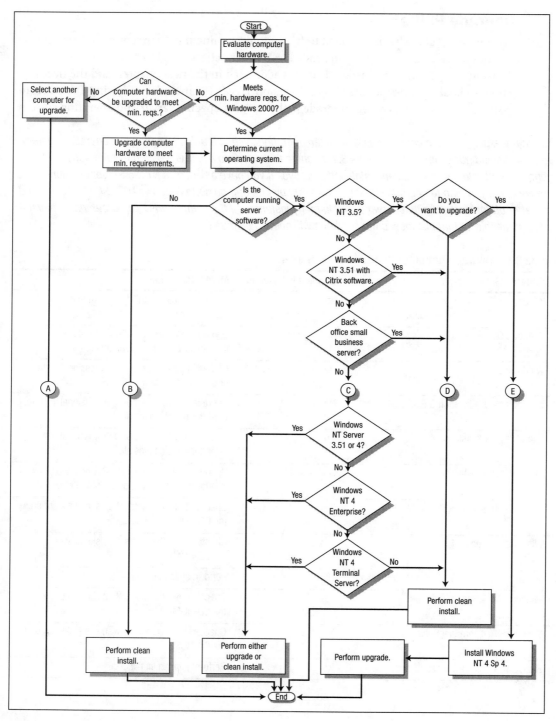

Decision Tree 3.1
Upgrading your server.

The Timeline

Creating a timeline is addressed when the project team is ready to start the process of moving to Windows 2000 Server. At this point in the process, enough information has been gathered to decide on what the phases of the project will be, how much time some of the phases will take, who will be involved, and how the plan will be carried out. Gather all of the previously filled-out worksheets, sit down with the core members of the project team, get lots of blank paper and, ideally, a large white board with plenty of markers and erasers, and begin.

Listed next are the checklists and worksheets that you should have in hand before beginning this task:

- Hardware inventory checklists, including:
  - Computers
  - Printers
  - Scanners
  - Cameras
  - Backup devices
  - Card readers
  - Other forms of storage
  - Other forms of communications
  - Miscellaneous devices
- Software inventory checklists, including information on:
  - Computers
  - General applications
  - Critical applications
  - Problem applications
- Topology maps
- Domain structure worksheets and checklists for each physical location on the network
- Current standards
- Current security policies
- List of project team members
- List of project team job assignments

- Meeting schedule
- Purpose and scope of the project (with approval, hopefully)
- Checklists for servers (created in the last section), including information on:
  - Problem servers
  - Possible upgrades
  - What needs to be retired
  - What needs to be replaced
  - What needs to be upgraded
  - Justification for retirement, replacement, or upgrade
- Checklists for software (created in the last section), including information on:
  - Problem applications
  - Application ratings
  - Nonrated applications

With all of this information on the table, it is time to begin creating the timeline. The team members are responsible for adhering to this timeline as closely as possible. Although there is virtue in trying to remain flexible, it is better to set deadlines and do your best to meet them. Here is an example of a timeline that you can use as an outline. You may also want to review Figure 2.13 (in Chapter 2).

Tip: *Many applications on the market today are created specifically for the purpose of creating timelines and managing projects. You might choose to use a GANNT chart from Microsoft Project or a similar application instead of creating your own or using the one here.*

Sample timeline.

Jan.	Mar.	May	Jul.	Sept.	Nov.	Jan.	Mar.	May	Jul.	Sept.	Nov.
Inventory/evaluation	Continue										
		Select project leader									
					Select team members for project committee						
					Create a timeline/plan			Continue			
		Assess the needs of the network			Continue			Continue			
					Define the network's security, standards, structure					Continue	
					Create new standards			Continue			

(continued)

Sample timeline (continued).

Jan.	Mar.	May	Jul.	Sept.	Nov.	Jan.	Mar.	May	Jul.	Sept.	Nov.
				Design Active Directory		Continue					
									Test	Test	
										Begin upgrades	
		Continue									
		Complete migration									
					Train users				Continue	Continue	
		Continue									

The Milestones

Milestones are significant events that coincide with completing certain goals. For instance, the event associated with selecting a project leader is a milestone, while the date of May 15 is considered a deadline. By creating milestones along with deadlines, a sense of achievement is born out of events. To create milestones for your project, then, will require that a timeline is completed and agreed upon by committee members, department leaders, the CEO, and any other VIP who has a hand in accepting the plan. Following is a sample milestone worksheet.

Note: The following timeline is intended to show a sample milestones worksheet. The dates associated with these milestones may or may not suit your needs and are not intended to suggest how long any particular task should take. Your timeline and milestone worksheet may include other sections as well, such as implementing DHCP where static TCP/IP addressing was previously used. This is only an example, and does not include all or even half of the tasks involved in the project.

Sample milestones worksheet.

Date	Task	Responsible Parties
January 15	Inventory checklists distributed	Department heads
March 10	Basic inventory checklists completed	Department heads and department personnel
May 15	Project leader selected	CEO/senior network administrator/enterprise administrator
February 20	Needs assessment from departments completed	Department heads
April 15	Project team chosen	Project leader/CEO/network administrator
April 25	First project team meeting	All project team members
June 30	Complete inventory completed	Project team members and subordinates
July 30	Current state of network analyzed	Security, standards, topology team members

(continued)

Sample milestones worksheet *(continued).*

Date	Task	Responsible Parties
August 1	User training begins	Training team
August 27	Standardization agreement completed	Project team
September 30	Active Directory design completed	Project team members
August 10	Testing lab set up	Testing team member
January 1	First domain controller upgraded	Project team member
July 30	Migration completed	

Training

User training can be arranged in a variety of ways. Training can be done internally (by a staff of in-house trainers) or can be outsourced to one of the hundreds of companies that perform such duties. If the organization is small, it may be even wiser simply to send the users to classes at a local junior college. Other options include Web-based training, self-training, or informal "just-in-time" training (simply allowing the experienced user to call the help desk when problems arise). Either way, it *is* necessary to train the majority of users on the network changes, and doing so effectively will reduce headaches further down the road.

To decide which training option is right for you, answer the questions below and make notes about each one. After a decision has been made on the type of training that will be implemented, create a timeline documenting how and when each group of users will obtain this training. The main points in this section are that *all users get the training they need* and that the training is *documented appropriately*.

Training worksheet.

Questions/Attributes of Organization	Possible Suggestion for Training/Notes
Does the organization currently have a training department?	In-house
If a training department exists, are those trainers properly educated?	Classes off site for trainers
Are there more than 500 people who need to be trained?	Compare costs of all training options
Are there between 25 and 500 people who need training?	Compare costs of all training options
Are there fewer than 25 people who need to be trained?	Classes off site may be cheapest
Will any user's critical application be retired or replaced?	Depends on number of users
Will any user(s) need to be trained on new hardware?	Depends on number of users
Are version upgrades needed for Web browsers or email?	Consider relying on help desk for information

(continued)

Training worksheet *(continued)*.	
Questions/Attributes of Organization	**Possible Suggestion for Training/Notes**
Can the training be done via the Internet?	Consider available bandwidth
How many departments need to be trained?	
How long will it take to train users?	
How much will training cost if done in-house?	
How much will training cost if done through outsourcing?	
How effective will each type of training be for your particular users?	
How will new employees be trained?	
What differences in training will be used for novice, intermediate, and advanced users?	
Who will assemble the training teams or choose a training site?	
Who will develop the training plan?	
How will success be measured after training is completed?	
How will ongoing training needs be addressed?	
Other?	

Standards Restructuring

By now, you and your project team should have a good idea of the current standards on the network, including standards for hardware, software, applications, computers, naming schemes, the users' desktops, security issues, and more. You should also know just how those standards are working for the company and if they are effective. Most likely, after taking a long look at the current standards, you'll see many ways to make improvements. Because you are already aware of the status of the network, including these standards, let's focus here on improving those standards to make the network more efficient.

Creating standards and maintaining them are two completely different things. Up to this point, you've documented the current standard, and you now plan to improve on that standard. Once improvements have been chosen, however, there is more work involved in documenting the new standard, bringing the existing environment up to the new standard, maintaining the standard, and continually reviewing and updating the standard as necessary. The following lists offer a variety of ways that your current standard could be improved, and after working through these checklists, you may decide to implement some of these changes. Remember, though, that changing the existing standards costs money, requires training, and affects the future of the network.

Note: Throughout the migration planning for the servers, it is wise to look also at the clients. It's likely that once the servers are moved to Windows 2000, the clients will be moved as well. Gathering information about how the user desktop should look after clients are migrated will assist in properly creating the migration plan now.

Improving hardware standards.	
Possible Improvement	**Notes/Ideas**
Remove/replace/upgrade legacy computers	
Remove/replace/upgrade legacy software	
Remove/replace/upgrade legacy hardware	
Raise minimum RAM on domain controllers to:	
Raise minimum HDD space on domain controllers to:	
Raise fault tolerance level on all domain controllers by:	
Raise minimum RAM on servers to:	
Raise minimum HDD space on servers to:	
Raise fault tolerance level on all servers by:	
New computers that are purchased or leased must meet minimum stated requirements for the NIC type and minimum speed for servers:	
Minimum requirements for Web servers (RAM, CPU, NIC, speed)	
All wiring should be Cat 5 or higher	
Data line speed to remote branches should be raised to:	
Replace dial-up connections with ISDN, DSL, T1	
Create a formal process for requesting changes to the standard	
Other	

Improving applications and software standards.	
Possible Improvement	**Notes/Ideas**
Get rid of older DOS programs	
Replace or remove problem applications	
Remove 16-bit applications and replace them with newer applications	
Remove any programs that directly access hardware	
Remove any programs that rely on the FAT file system	

(continued)

3

Improving applications and software standards *(continued)*.	
Possible Improvement	**Notes/Ideas**
Replace applications that require specific drivers or are not written for the Win32 API	
Replace software that saves files in proprietary file formats that can't be converted to more common formats	
Replace or remove software that comes with printers, scanners, and cameras that is proprietary or not needed	
Critical applications that are not compatible or certified will be retired or replaced by:	
New applications will be compatible	
New applications must be certified	
Users will not be allowed to install programs themselves	
Existing office applications will be standardized	
Existing Web browsers will be standardized	
Existing email applications will be standardized	
Do not install multiple applications for the same purpose; choose only one and remove the rest	
Create a formal process for requesting changes to the standard	
Other	

Improving services standards.	
Possible Improvement	**Notes/Ideas**
Remove WINS and NetBIOS	
Upgrade, replace, or retire NetBIOS applications	
Implement DNS or DDNS	
Implement DHCP	
Upgrade down-level clients	
Improve fault tolerance for DNS and DHCP servers by:	
Use group policies for simplifying administration	
Use Remote Installation Services (RIS) for multiple installations	
Implement IntelliMirror	
Implement auditing	
Create a formal process for requesting changes to the standard	
Other	

Improving naming schemes.

Possible Improvement	Notes/Ideas
Domain names should describe physical location or other descriptive characteristic	
Domain names should be DNS-compliant	
Computer names should be DNS-compliant	
Computer names should be descriptive and representative	
Printer names should represent location and/or type	
Directory shares should have representative names and follow specific naming guidelines	
User names should follow a pattern, such as last name and first initial, or first name and last initial	
Configure namespaces to flow in a hierarchical manner, such as **jballew.garland.dallas.mycompany.com** or **jballew@mycompany.com**	
Server names should be descriptive and meaningful	
Plan the naming scheme so that it suits your Active Directory needs	
Make DNS names available for registration on the Internet	
Decide if the existing namespace should apply to both internal and external namespaces	
Make sure the naming scheme will not need to be changed in the foreseeable future	
Create a formal process for requesting changes to the standard	
Other	

Improving the user's desktop (or, for that matter, the server).

Possible Improvement	Notes/Ideas
See if the existing standard can be tightened and made more secure without offending users	
Give novice users a highly restrictive desktop	
Give intermediate users a secure desktop	
Give advanced users fewer restrictions on their desktops	
Consider restrictions on Control Panel, folder redirection, scripts, and Windows components	
Make the backup to the servers automated, using logoff or logon scripts	

(continued)

Improving the user's desktop (or, for that matter, the server) *(continued)*.

Possible Improvement	Notes/Ideas
Deny users the ability to install programs	
Limit disk space available to users on the local machines as well as on the servers	
Convert file systems to NTFS during migration	
Move to certified applications for user applications	
Install a virus-checking program on all computers, configure it so it cannot be disabled, and make sure updates are done automatically	
Consider offering a standard set of screen savers and wallpaper if a high level of control is warranted, and/or train users on the benefits of password-protecting their screen savers	
Prevent users from uninstalling business applications	
Prevent users from editing the Registry	
Decide if users will be able to install printers or other peripherals	
Decide if Internet access will be restricted	
Other	

Maintaining the standards.

Possible Improvement	Notes/Ideas
Have monthly checks to update inventory	
Use updated inventory list to check purchases or installations against standards	
Keep the users' desktops as secure as possible, preventing the removal or addition of programs	
Occasionally review the standard for effectiveness	
Track changes to the computing atmosphere, including the addition of computers, software, peripherals, and so on	
If possible, create a formal process for changing computers or policies, and have a committee keep track of and approve or disapprove requested changes	
Monitor the network and look for changes that do not fit into the standard	
Choose specific vendors for hardware and stick with them if possible	
Other	

Improving security standards.	
Possible Improvement	**Notes/Ideas**
Use Kerberos authentication across the network as soon as possible	
Decide how NTLM will be phased out	
Implement smart cards for highly secure desktops or departments	
Decide how data will be encrypted when it is "on the wire"	
Determine if the password policy can be strengthened	
Determine if the account policy can be strengthened	
Determine if logons can be strengthened	
Determine if users' permissions and rights can be more restrictive	
Move all desktops and servers to NTFS when possible	
Decide how EFS will be used	
Look into how Certificate Services can improve the network	
Look into how group policies can be used to enhance security	
Use IntelliMirror for immediate restorations of destroyed systems	
Create a formal process for requesting changes to the standard	
Other	

Improving miscellaneous standards.	
Possible Improvement	**Notes/Ideas**
Bind only necessary protocols, and remove the rest	
Use Windows 2000 to deploy service packs and machine updates via the network	
Automate backups of servers	
Automate backups of user data	
Create an organized way to keep inventory up-to-date and to document changes	
If possible, avoid upgrades, opting for clean installs instead	
Use Microsoft certified applications whenever possible	
Use one of the twelve security templates for basic security needs	
Make servers physically accessible to only a limited number of users	
Require training for all users periodically and on a scheduled basis	
Create a formal process for requesting changes to the standard	
Other	

If you've decided to change the standard, you'll need to form another team to deal with this part of the project. Changing the standard includes justifying the expense of such a change, getting the approval of the changes by the CEO or other VIP, determining which exact standards will be implemented, deciding how those changes will be implemented, anticipating how the network environment will change, and deciding how the plan will be followed, maintained, and updated.

The changes will be well worth it in the end because any improvement that can further secure a network or simplify administration is a move in the right direction. Changing the standard during an upgrade of this magnitude will also be better accepted than changing the standards unexpectedly later. It is much easier to lock down a desktop if that change in standard is integrated with a new desktop operating system. Now is a good time to incorporate new standards and tighter security requirements.

Cost Analysis

As you've probably guessed, an upgrade of this type can be quite expensive. Consider the costs that would be associated with a network as small as 1 PDC, 1 BDC, 10 workstations, and 15 users. You will need to consider the hardware upgrade or replacement costs, the training, the downtime, the consultant's fees, the planning fees and time, additional bandwidth requirements, testing labs, licensing fees, restructuring, and so on. Even for a small network, the costs could be astronomical. Now multiply your estimate by a really large number. This is proof that the cost of upgrading a large network can be frightening.

To assist in calculating, documenting, and justifying this expense to senior administrators, use the following checklists. Again, you'll need all of your previous checklists and worksheets on the table, a large white board, a calculator, and lots of patience. While forming this cost analysis, you may want to maintain an alternate cost analysis as well. For instance, you may benefit from having an analysis for minimum requirements, another one for suggested requirements, and one for optimal performance. To justify the cost of items such as RAM chips, new applications, and other upgrade needs, you should prepare these documents carefully.

Note: There are many ways to save money while working on this project. Instead of purchasing new computers, consider leasing them, and instead of buying upgrade parts, perhaps they can be taken from an existing machine. You can also cut costs by using the machines that are purchased for the test lab during or after deployment to help justify and share some of the expenses.

Hardware Needs: Domain Controllers and Servers

Basically, four types of domain controllers and servers need to be considered when you're calculating cost: those that exist on the network and can be used as is; those that exist on the network and can be used if more RAM, a faster CPU, or more hard drive space is added; those that will be removed through restructuring and reused;

and those that need to be purchased. The first type of computer—the one that can be used as is—isn't going to incur hardware costs. The second type—the computer that needs more RAM, a faster CPU, a new NIC, or more hard drive space—will most likely have upgrade costs associated with it. The third type of computer—the one that will be reused—also doesn't incur hardware costs. And the fourth type—computers that need to be purchased—will definitely need to be considered closely. You should already have checklists filled out for these servers and know what each server needs or doesn't need. That information can be transferred here for a basic cost analysis.

Calculating hardware costs for domain controllers and servers.

Server Name	Upgrade Estimate	Purchasing Estimate	Notes
Sample_01	RAM and HDD=$_____	-	-
Sample_02	New system board and CPU=$_____	-	-
Sample_03	-	$_____	-
Sample_04	Unknown, system isn't working	$_____	System is under warranty and can be repaired
Totals			

Hardware Needs: Workstations and Peripherals

If the current migration plan includes upgrading the workstations on the network to Windows 2000 Professional in the near future, the cost analysis for these upgrades should also be included. Although this book's focus is not on migrating client computers, the plan is basically the same. If your next project includes migrating all of the Windows NT Workstation machines to Windows 2000 Professional, this book and your experience may be all you need. Here is a sample of a worksheet that can be used to calculate the costs of upgrading or replacing workstations on the network.

Calculating hardware costs for workstations and peripherals.

Server Name	Upgrade Estimate	Purchasing Estimate	Notes
Sample_01	RAM and HDD=$_____	-	-
Sample_02	New system board and CPU=$_____	-	For about the same price, the system can be replaced
Sample_03	-	$_____	-
Sample_04	NIC $_____	-	-
Totals			

Software Needs

Previously, you created a checklist that included creating software standards that were to be incorporated on the network. Some of the standards were minimum standards, and some were suggested standards. You also compiled lists of problem software and critical applications. Those checklists can now be used to obtain a cost analysis for each application that will be used on the network.

Tip: As I mentioned previously, it would be wise to keep two or three cost analyses running because the costs associated with upgrading to suggested standards or requirements might not be feasible, and upgrading to minimum requirements might be the only option.

Calculating software and application costs.

Software Name	Upgrade	Replacement	Licensing	Use As Is	Notes
Sample Graphics	Cannot be upgraded	$	n/a	$	
Printer/fax/scanner software	None available	$	$	-	
Inventory!	$	$	$	Yes	Will upgrade when new version is released
Email Plus	$	$	$	No	Install Outlook Express on clients' Outlook on Servers
Web Browser 101	$	$	$	No	Install Internet Explorer
Windows 2000 Server	$	$	Licensing costs only		
Windows 2000 Professional	$	$	Licensing costs only		

Training Needs

From the training worksheets created earlier, you should have decided how each department would be trained and chosen a type of training for them. I hope you also included a cost comparison that can be used here to calculate a basic layout of the charges. There should also be information concerning ongoing training costs, including training for new employees.

Note: This list might seem oversimplified for some people and might include too much information for others. It is simply meant to remind you of all of the people who need to be trained and to give you an opportunity to determine how much each type of training may cost for each department.

Training costs.			
Department/Group Web-based	In-House	Classroom	Outsourcing
Network administration			
End users			
Novice users			
Intermediate users			
Advanced users			
Power users			
Seasonal workers			
Part-time workers			
Server operators			
Print operators			
Backup operators			
Engineering			
Accounting			
Sales			
Marketing			
Other departments			
Help desk			
Training department			
New employees			
Ongoing training			
Lab costs			
Lost productivity while users are being trained			
Documentation for trainees			
Other			

Warning! *If you plan to train users in-house, there will be costs involved in setting up the labs for training these employees. And for all training, there will be costs associated with lost productivity due to the employees' absences from the office. These costs, and not just the actual cost of training the employees, need to be figured into the scheme of things as well.*

Network Needs

There will be costs associated with the network, and because it would be difficult to create a checklist that would apply to even a minority of existing networks, I've included a list of questions instead. Answering these questions can help you determine what costs may be associated with the purchase, configuration, or restructuring of the network. The needs of the network are always changing, and with the inclusion of Windows 2000 and Active Directory on the network, those needs are many.

Network needs cost assessment.	
Question/Consideration	**Notes**
What additional bandwidth will be required?	
Will new subnets be created?	
How many sites will there be?	
Will network coverage increase?	
Will domains be restructured?	
Will deleting domains have any effect on network performance?	
How many domains will be deleted?	
Will adding domains help in any way?	
How many domains will be added?	
What effect will the additional domains have on network performance?	
What locations and departments will need replication of Active Directory?	
Where are the global catalog servers located?	
Which links will replication occur over?	
How much will those replication links cost each month?	
What is the replication schedule for primary links? Secondary links?	
How fast are the remote links?	
How often do remote links need to be used during normal business hours?	
How fast is the company growing?	
Will there be redundant, fault-tolerant links?	
If the speed of remote links is improved, what are the associated costs?	
How will DHCP be used and how will it affect network performance?	
How will DDNS be used and how will it affect network performance?	

(continued)

Network needs cost assessment *(continued)*.	
Question/Consideration	Notes
How much increased bandwidth will be needed during the pilot?	
What is the expected downtime, and how much productivity will be lost during the upgrade?	
How much restructuring is planned?	
Have you obtained a cost analysis of the domain restructuring plan from the restructuring team?	
Other	

The Testing Lab

Creating a lab for testing the upgrade or migration may be done without incurring any costs at all, except for time and personnel. It may be possible to use existing equipment for all of the testing. Another scenario for creating the testing lab may include purchasing new equipment, using it in the lab, and then rolling it out with the migration. Finally, additional equipment may be needed simply to supply the lab with needed inventory.

Whichever method is chosen, those costs need to be documented and justified. Preferably, the lab costs will be minimal and will already be included in additional purchases, planned purchases, or existing equipment.

Testing lab costs.		
Component	Why It Is Needed	Anticipated Cost
Lab site (room, building)		
Lab wiring and appropriate electrical outlets		
Computers that emulate the current environment		
Other hardware that emulates the current environment		
Software that emulates the current environment		
Software that will be installed		
Cost of building the lab (manual labor)		
Hubs and routers of the same version and from the same vendor		
Lab must be isolated		
Lab must be secure		
Lab must be expandable		

(continued)

Testing lab costs *(continued)*.

Component	Why It Is Needed	Anticipated Cost
Lab must be capable of handling the proposed migration		
Multiple labs may be needed for international differences or other reasons		
Lab personnel must be paid		
Other		

Salaries

Salary calculations for this project should include money given to additional people who were hired solely for the project, including consultants, outsourcing companies, and researchers. Other salary costs may be incurred for raises or promotions for the people on the project committee. Each cost analysis will be different for every organization, and calculating these extra salaries should be straightforward.

Salary worksheet.

Personnel (Name, Company)	Raise (If Applicable)	Salary (If Applicable)	Fee (If Applicable)
Admin_01, in-house			
Admin_02, in-house			
Consultant_01, company name			
Other			

Active Directory Planning

Designing the Active Directory structure is probably the most important task in the planning of the Windows 2000 migration. A poorly designed Active Directory structure can severely affect how successfully the network functions. Before you install Active Directory on a server (thus making it a domain controller), it is important to have a properly thought-out Active Directory design.

This section includes checklists for planning the Active Directory structure. It is important to have a properly designed namespace and a plan for the number of organizational units (OUs), sites, and domains and their respective configurations. During the planning of Active Directory, you may also decide that some domain restructuring needs to be done. Because of the amount of information that needs to be collected, separate checklists are offered relating to designing the namespace, restructuring the domains, and designing the structure of Active Directory, including trees, OUs, and forests. It is important that all of these decisions be made before you install any domain controllers on the network because during the installation of Active Directory, you will be asked questions about the design plan.

While installing Active Directory, you will be asked to make the following decisions or otherwise have the following information:

- Will this domain controller be added to an existing domain?

- Will this domain controller be the first domain controller in a new domain?

- Do you want to create a new child domain or a new domain tree?

- Do you want to install a DNS server?

- What is the full DNS name of the new domain?

- How will database and database log files be configured?

- Do you want to create or join a forest?

Designing the Namespace

There are two types of namespace designs: DNS namespaces and domain namespaces. This section is mainly concerned with the domain namespace and planning for Active Directory. In starting this process, begin planning with one domain, and add domains if necessary. Of course, if the network already contains multiple domains, this may not be possible. The following checklists will assist you in making the right decisions for the Active Directory structure for your particular network.

Note: Again, these checklists are included to get you started on the right track; they can by no means reflect all of the necessary decisions that may need to be made on your specific network. However, the lists are a great place to start documenting information and justifying the reasons behind the decisions you and your team will make.

Namespace design.	
Information to Collect	**Notes**
How will the domain(s) be partitioned?	
What is the logical structure of the organization?	
What is the physical structure of the organization?	
What administrative requirements, including delegation of responsibility, will affect the namespace?	
Does the organization have a central IT group?	
Do all entities trust each other?	
Are the organizational units inside the organization autonomous?	
How many forests are needed?	
How many trees are needed?	

(continued)

Namespace design *(continued)*.	
Information to Collect	**Notes**
How are the current divisions, departments, accounts, users, and computers named?	
What changes might occur over the next 10 years that might affect the chosen name and namespace design?	
Are external and internal domain names the same?	
Can external and internal domain names be different if they are the same now?	
The namespace should be hierarchical and easily understandable	
Names should be descriptive and remain static	
Has your organization chosen a registered DNS domain name for use on the Internet?	
How will the namespace design affect email addresses?	
Limit the number of domain levels to three or four	
Other	

Note: Make sure you not only design the namespace effectively, but that you follow a few rules as well. Use standard DNS and Unicode characters as defined in RFC 1035, use unique names for subdomains and all other domains on the network, use root domain names that are no more than 63 letters (although the shorter the better in most cases), and make sure the root domain reflects the organization's structure.

Designing the Domain Structure

By now, the network environment, including the current domain structure, should be clear to everyone involved in the project. After deciding if new standards will be put in place and what this project might cost, you need to decide if the domain should be left the way it is currently configured or if the domain should be restructured. The following checklist will ask you to document and find answers to relevant questions.

Note: If your organization consists of only one or two domains, and those domains have different physical or functional boundaries, it isn't likely that you'd need to restructure the existing domain(s). Restructuring domains is time-consuming and costly and is not a decision that should be made lightly, or unnecessarily.

Using the existing domain structure.	
Existing Domain Structure	**Notes**
Only one domain currently exists	
Domains delegate administrative tasks appropriately	

(continued)

Using the existing domain structure *(continued).*	
Existing Domain Structure	**Notes**
Domains represent distinct physical boundaries	
Replication of Active Directory needs to be isolated in current domains	
Current SAM databases are not near the Windows NT 40MB limit	
Microsoft states that a key element in creating an ideal domain model is to have fewer domains	
The current domain model will work for the transition into a new Active Directory design	
Domains meet administrative needs	
Domains meet organizational needs	
Domains meet technical needs	
Account domains can be new Windows 2000 domains, and resource domains can be OUs	
The organization is not expanding to other physical locations at this time	
The current administrative model (decentralized, centralized, or hybrid) will be maintained	
The DNS servers function effectively and support the DNS requirements of Active Directory	
Other	

Restructuring the Domain

There are many reasons for restructuring a domain, as I mentioned briefly in Chapter 2. The following checklists will help you determine if you need to add any domains, delete domains, or even combine domains. By answering the questions in each section, you'll be able to decide if restructuring is needed. This restructuring of domains can be done before or after the migration to Windows 2000, and that decision can be made after the Active Directory design has been completed.

Note: *There will be more talk about restructuring later in the chapter. This section will help you decide and justify if you need to restructure; the next mention of migration methods will offer a checklist to make sure you are going about it correctly.*

Adding domains.	
Information to Collect	**Notes**
Does the company need to operate under a decentralized domain structure?	
Are administrators located in different geographical locations?	

(continued)

3

Adding domains *(continued)*.	
Information to Collect	**Notes**
Are administrators required to perform differing and incompatible business functions?	
Does the efficiency of necessary replication traffic need to be increased?	
Are network links between physical locations slow?	
Is decentralized administration of resources needed?	
Do international differences exist?	
Does the network have more than a million objects?	
Does the organization span multiple countries?	
Will two or more companies merge, or have they merged already?	
Do merging companies have existing and unchangeable domain names?	
Will any entities require a different domain policy?	
Should a specific domain stand on its own due to its security standard?	
Other	

Deleting domains.	
Information to Collect	**Notes**
Do you need a more centralized domain structure?	
Is the domain needed to handle replication traffic?	
Are there international differences between the domains in question?	
Have two or more geographical locations merged?	
Have domain business functions merged?	
Can delegation of responsibility be controlled through OUs instead of through domains?	
Are the links between two sites faster than before, and do you now need multiple domains to support replication?	
Can domain policies between two domains be combined?	
Can security standards be combined or agreed upon between domains?	
Can domains that existed for administrative purposes use OUs instead?	
Can resources at a particular site be managed through Active Directory and no longer require their own domains?	

(continued)

Deleting domains *(continued)*.	
Information to Collect	**Notes**
What is the recovery plan when domains are deleted?	
How will resources be moved into OUs?	
How will groups be migrated?	
How will users be migrated?	
How will accounts be migrated?	
How will member servers be moved to the new domain?	
How will workstations be moved to new domains?	
Are there administrators in your organization who can perform the migration of users, groups, and accounts?	
Does anyone in the organization have any experience with Windows 2000 migrations?	
Other	

Combining domains.	
Information to Collect	**Notes**
What domains will be eliminated?	
Why will those particular domains be eliminated?	
What domains will take over the duties of the eliminated domains?	
What size will the combined domains be?	
What is the speed of each data link between the current domains?	
How will combining domains affect the speed of those links?	
Can delegation of responsibility still be achieved?	
Do you need a more centralized domain structure?	
Is the domain needed to handle replication traffic?	
Are there international differences between the domains in question?	
Have two or more geographical locations merged?	
Have domain business functions merged?	
Can delegation of responsibility be controlled through OUs instead of through domains?	

(continued)

Combining domains *(continued)*.	
Information to Collect	**Notes**
Are the links between two sites faster than before, and do you now need multiple domains to support replication?	
Can domain policies between two domains be combined?	
Can security standards be combined or agreed upon between domains?	
Can domains that existed for administrative purposes use OUs instead?	
Can resources at a particular site be managed through Active Directory and no longer require their own domains?	
Are there administrators in your organization who can perform the migration of users, groups, and accounts?	
Does anyone in the organization have any experience with Windows 2000 migrations?	
Is there a single country that uses more that one language?	
Other	

Designing the Organizational Structure

The purpose behind creating trees, forests, and OUs, thus forming an organizational structure, is to *arrange* what exists on the network and make those resources easily accessible to users. You can organize resources in the company by network structure, by location, by functional unit, by job function, or in hundreds of other ways.

To create an organizational structure that is effective on your network, you'll need to take into account what is important to users, what needs to be administered, what tasks can be delegated, and how you want users to see things on the network through Active Directory. The following checklists will assist you in making the right decisions regarding the organizational units, trees, and forests in your organization. First, you'll look at the organizational unit, followed by trees, and finally, forests.

Note: *If no organizational units are created, then resources on the network will simply be displayed as a single list and will not be separated by location, function, or capability. The same is true for all users in the domain.*

Creating meaningful organizational units.	
When to Create an OU	**Notes**
To replace a resource domain in an older NT environment	
To delegate responsibility	
To group users together	

(continued)

Creating meaningful organizational units *(continued)*.

When to Create an OU	Notes
To separate users by job function	
To separate users by location	
To separate users by ability	
To separate users by group policy requirements	
To separate departments	
To separate departments by location	
To separate departments by function	
To group computers (servers, domain controllers, workstations)	
To separate computers by type (desktop, laptop, remote, dial-in, mobile)	
To group file servers	
To group application and print servers	
To separate DNS, WINS, and DHCP servers	
To group printers, scanners, cameras, and graphics tablets	
To group digital phones	
To group applications	
To group company projects	
To simplify administration of permissions	
To simplify browsing of the network	
To control how objects in the domain are viewed	

Creating effective organizational units.

Tips for Creating a More Effective OU	Notes
To keep searches from taking an inordinate amount of time, do not configure "deep" OU structures	
To avoid difficulties related to reconfiguring the OU structure, create OU names that are not likely to change	
To decide on the best OU configuration for your organization, list the benefits of creating OUs based on structure	
To decide on the best OU configuration for your organization, list the benefits of creating OUs based on function	

(continued)

3

Creating effective organizational units *(continued)*.	
Tips for Creating a More Effective OU	**Notes**
To decide on the best OU configuration for your organization, list the benefits of creating OUs based on location	
Other	

Tip: It is better to create fewer trees and have more organizational units than to create lots of trees and have fewer organizational units.

Creating meaningful and effective trees.	
When to Create a Tree	**Notes**
You have one or more domains with a contiguous namespace	
You need to create a hierarchy of domains	
You want the units to be configured through transitive trusts	
You want a single logon process for the trees	
You want a common schema	
You want a common global catalog	
You want to enable new domain controllers to join trees easily	
You want to be able to remove domains easily from trees	
You want to define a security boundary	
You see that a division in the organization has a registered DNS name and DNS servers	
Other	

Tip: The following checklist for creating a forest offers information concerning when a single forest should be formed. It is best to have only one forest in an organization. Creating additional forests without the proper justification is discouraged. Additional forests are sometimes needed, however, and require much more administration and management than single forest structures do.

Creating meaningful and effective forests.	
When to Create a Single Forest	**Notes**
The structure needs to be simple to maintain	
The structure needs to be easy to configure	
You want to have only one domain	

(continued)

Creating meaningful and effective forests *(continued)*.	
When to Create a Single Forest	**Notes**
You want users to see only a single directory in the global catalog	
Users do not need to be aware of the current domain structure	
When new domains are added, you do not want to have to configure additional trusts	
All configuration changes to Active Directory should have to be done only once	
Other	
When to Create Multiple Forests	**Notes**
Divisions do not trust each other	
Divisions need to remain autonomous	
A policy concerning changes to the forest cannot be agreed upon by the divisions involved	
The schemas for each division must be separately maintained	
You need to configure the trusts explicitly between domains	
Users do not need to have a contiguous view of the directory	
There are no plans to combine two or more forests into a single forest in the near future	
Other	

Designing the Site Structure

As you know, domain structure and site structure are completely different things. Defining sites on your network allows you to define how replication will take place in Active Directory. Sites are generally used to gain control over user logons, make finding resources easier, and reduce replication traffic in a domain.

Creating sites and site objects.	
Consider Creating a Site If You Need to:	**Notes**
Lessen replication traffic	
Control replication traffic	
Isolate logon traffic	
Ease administration by centralizing resources	
Organize resources by closeness	
Separate one site into two because of a slow connection	
Other	

(continued)

3

Creating sites and site objects *(continued)*.	
Sites Should Have:	**Notes**
Uniformly good network access	
High bandwidth, as in a LAN	
Inexpensive bandwidth, as in a LAN	
Their own domain controllers	
A global catalog	
An association with at least one subnet	
An association with at least one site link	
A connection to all other sites via routing links for message queuing	
Other	

Checklists for Making the Plan Work

The project manager and his or her core team have multiple tasks to complete, deadlines to meet, and many people to organize. A project of this magnitude requires a level of organization that doesn't come easily to everyone. Ideally, every core team member has adequate skills in this area. If not, the previous checklists and worksheets should help each team get set up nicely with the proper papers and document and organize its ideas.

In the following section, the focus will be on documenting progress, anticipating problems, meeting deadlines, and making the plan work. Each checklist in this chapter can be assigned to a particular group or person, as indicated next. The way you use these lists is up to you, and they can be changed to meet the needs of your organization simply by moving around the tasks and responsible parties.

I'll also assume at this point that you've decided whether you want to restructure or upgrade your existing domains. With that in mind, I've provided checklists that address making either of the in-place upgrading or restructuring choices work. Knowing what is involved in the migration may bring new concerns or issues to light.

Note: If you haven't decided if you will restructure the domains or simply upgrade the domain controllers, working through the lists at the end of this section will help you make that decision.

Worksheets for Project Team Leaders

As you are aware, the project team is at the heart of the migration project. The project team is responsible for keeping the project on track and fulfilling promises. Project team leaders are in charge of making everything go the way it is planned. The project leader has duties of his or her own, but generally doles out jobs and makes sure they get done in a timely fashion. The project leader also makes important decisions concerning the plan and its deployment based on the gathered information. The following checklist can be used by the project team for just that purpose.

Making the plan work.	
Suggestion	**Notes**
Assign tasks to responsible parties, such as department heads, division heads, administrators, and core team members	
Hold weekly meetings to judge progress	
Reward successes and note failures	
Be available to answer questions	
Be flexible, expect setbacks, and be prepared	
Document thoroughly	
Stay within budget	
Be certain that responsible parties have adequate knowledge and enthusiasm	
Maintain progress lists	
Inform administrators and other teams of changes to the proposed plan	
Other	

Documenting progress.			
Checklists, Planning, and Documentation	**Assigned to**	**Date Assigned**	**Date Achieved**
Computer inventory	(Suggestion: department head)		
Printer/fax inventory	(Suggestion: department head)		
Scanner/camera/miscellaneous inventory	(Suggestion: division head)		
General software			
Problem applications			
Critical applications	(Suggestion: division head)		
Current network topology	(Suggestion: senior network administrator)		
Current domain structure			
Current standards			
Current security			

(continued)

Documenting progress *(continued).*

Checklists, Planning, and Documentation	Assigned to	Date Assigned	Date Achieved
Purpose of project			
Scope of project			
Definition of services			
Timeline			
Standards of restructuring			
Cost analysis			
Active Directory planning			
Server documentation, including HCL information, minimum requirements, and organizational standards comparisons			
DNS design			
DHCP design			
Protocol configuration			
Global directory			
New standards			
Design of the migration plan			
Creation of a test lab			
Choice of deployment options			
Other			

Anticipating problems.

Possible Problem	Possible Solution
Inventory efforts fail or are incomplete	
Network clients are not cooperating with data gathering	
Current topology, domain structure, or DNS design requires major restructuring	
Server is offline longer than expected during the upgrade	
Network connectivity is lost	
Hardware and software that need to be replaced, removed, or retired are more expensive than was originally planned for	
Domain restructuring fails	

(continued)

Anticipating problems *(continued)*.	
Possible Problem	**Possible Solution**
Backup and recovery plan fails	
Deadlines are missed	
Project team members quit or retire	
Administration changes approval levels	
Other	

Worksheets for Department Heads, Administrators, or Division Heads

Making the plan work.	
Suggestion	**Notes**
Delegate your tasks to responsible parties	
Make sure responsible parties are knowledgeable and enthusiastic	
Oversee their progress	
Hold weekly meetings to judge progress	
Hold parties responsible for their actions	
Reward successes; note failures	
Be available to answer questions	
Be flexible, expect setbacks, and be prepared	
Document thoroughly	
Stay within budget	
Follow up on user training	
Other	

Documenting progress.			
Checklists, Planning, and Documentation	**Assigned to**	**Date Assigned**	**Date Achieved**
Hardware inventory			
Software inventory			
Task_03			
Task_04			
Task_05			

3

Anticipating problems.	
Possible Problem	**Possible Solution**
Tasks take longer than expected	
Subordinates "drop the ball"	
Task completion uncovers hidden costs related to hardware or software	
Users fight the upgrade or change	
Accurate inventory is not possible	
Responsible parties transfer, quit, or retire	
The plan changes midstream	
Critical applications can't be upgraded	
Costs skyrocket	
Other	

Training Worksheets

Training the users plays an important role in any successful rollout. The following worksheets can be used to keep track of the planning stages, document who has been trained, and resolve training problems.

Making the plan work.				
Group Deemed Successful	**Training Choice**	**Cost**	**Start Date**	**End Date**
Group_01				
Group_02				
Group_03				
Group_04				

Documenting progress.			
Milestone	**Date Planned**	**Date Achieved**	**Within Budget**
Network administrators trained			
Administration trained			
Department_01 trained			
Department_02 trained			
Group_01 trained			

(continued)

Documenting progress *(continued)*.

Milestone	Date Planned	Date Achieved	Within Budget
Group_02 trained			
Novice users trained			
Intermediate users trained			
Advanced users trained			
Other			

Anticipating problems.

Possible Problem	Possible Solution
Clients are not taking training seriously	
Clients are upset about the upgrade	
Clients do not agree with the changes and do not want to comply	
The current in-house training department isn't large enough for the project	
It is taking longer than expected to train users	
Advanced users are not learning anything during the training	
The scheduled off-site classes were cancelled	
The Web-based classes are too slow and are frustrating for the clients	
The cost of training is too high	
Other	

Migration Methods Decision Worksheets

Making this plan work also includes understanding what options are available for the migration of the network servers and which options you plan to use. This section will cover the two methods that you can use, along with the advantages and disadvantages of each, so that you can select the appropriate method for your organization. Ideally, you've made a decision regarding the restructuring of domains. If so, then these checklists will justify that choice and give you a place to jot down ideas. If you have not made a final decision on this point, this section will make sure that you have all of the information you need to make an appropriate choice. These choices need to be finalized before you move on to the testing phase of the project.

Note: The company I've been visiting and keeping notes on currently has seven domains. The company is migrating to Windows 2000 Server and Professional across the board. Even though team members are only in the standardizing phase of the project, they have already decided that most of the domains will be consolidated. It is important to note that they knew this before changing any standards because domain consolidation will affect how standards are applied. Although the following checklists are located here in the chapter, a major restructuring of current domains will be dealt with by other teams and project committees.

The two methods to be discussed here are the upgrade method and the restructuring method. The upgrade method involves upgrading existing PDCs first, upgrading the BDCs next, and upgrading the remaining servers last. The restructuring method involves installing new servers in new domains and then migrating the existing servers in stages. In larger organizations, both methods may be employed. The advantages and disadvantages of each method will be discussed next, and worksheets for each method will be provided.

The Upgrade Method

As I mentioned in the previous section, the upgrade method is used when the PDC is upgraded to Windows 2000 Server. This type of migration is the least expensive way to move to Windows 2000 Server on the network because the upgrade is performed on each of the domain controllers one at a time. Many times, no new equipment is needed, and restructuring the domain isn't an issue. Unfortunately, this type of migration also carries the highest risk. Upgrading servers (PDCs, specifically) is risky because the upgrade isn't reversible. There is no Uninstall option for Windows 2000. An NT machine can be recovered from backup, but it isn't easy if many servers are involved or if there are complications with the BDCs. In fact, in larger organizations, it may simply be impossible.

Upgrading is a good choice for smaller organizations using single domains that do not require restructuring. It is cheaper and faster than other migration types. The users, groups, and computer accounts will be upgraded as well, and the new Windows 2000 server will default to mixed mode to support down-level clients. This type of migration also retains many of the system settings, preferences, and, in most instances, applications.

The current domain model's integrity is also maintained. In fact, it isn't possible to modify the domain structure while performing this type of migration. A Windows NT 4 PDC cannot "join" a Windows 2000 domain. This rigidity is, of course, a disadvantage of upgrading versus domain consolidation. Other disadvantages include its high risk factor.

The following worksheet can be used to justify your choice for using the upgrade method, to make notes to see if the upgrade method will work for your organization, and to make sure that you have thought of all of the issues involved in upgrading in this manner.

Note: The upgrade method for migrating Windows NT to Windows 2000 works similarly to upgrading a Windows NT 3.51 computer to Windows NT 4. The settings are all intact, the applications work, and the users and groups are still available. It is this characteristic that makes it the easiest way to upgrade. Remember, though, that there is no Uninstall or Revert feature in Windows 2000 Server.

Upgrading a domain by using the upgrade method (in-place upgrade).	
Concern/Issue/Characteristic	**Notes**
The company has only one domain	
The company is small	
There are autonomous domains that can use this method	
There are resource domains that will use this method	
The PDCs on the network will be Windows 2000 domain controllers in the new domain	
The users, local groups, global groups, and computer accounts need to be preserved	
Support is needed for down-level Windows NT Server clients	
You need to maintain the current domain model	
You need to maintain the current administrative model	
System settings should be retained	
Preferences need to be retained on the servers	
Security settings should be retained	
Applications should not have to be reinstalled after the migration	
The upgrade should be easy and fast	
The upgrade should be inexpensive	
No new hardware can be purchased (and the current PDC can handle Windows 2000)	
Very little flexibility is needed for domains and the upgrade	
The risk of upgrade failure should be calculated	
You need to create good backups	
You need to maintain a mixed-mode configuration because some of the BDCs cannot be upgraded or made into member servers	
You can still restructure after this upgrade, using Windows 2000 features and tools	
Structural change is not the main reason for upgrading	
The existing domain is in good condition and will easily upgrade	
All applications, including critical ones, are compatible with Windows 2000	
Recovering from a failed Windows 2000 Server installation is achievable through either backup tapes or some other third-party tool	
The users and groups on the existing PDC will be migrated to the Windows 2000 domain immediately but downtime must be expected if problems occur	
The organization has a small or understaffed IT department	
Other	

The Domain Consolidation Method

The domain consolidation method is much different from the upgrade method. Whereas the upgrade method destroyed the original Windows NT domain one piece at a time, the domain consolidation method creates a new domain and leaves the existing Windows NT domain or domains intact. Once the new domain is created and complies with the company's standards and requirements for namespaces, the resources on the Windows NT domain can be migrated. This method allows the existing Windows NT domain to continue to function, and the migration can be completed a piece at a time. This method also creates a safety net in case the migration fails at some point due to a flaw in the plan or in case a critical application fails.

The domain consolidation method is used when the existing domain structure will be changed dramatically, when a phased-in approach is needed for the migration, or when the company is very large (6,000+ users). Besides the ability to create a safety net and to phase in the migration, this method also offers other advantages. The domain consolidation method enables the domain administrator to completely reconfigure the domains with little fear of failure and without having to rush or worry about downtime.

Of course, this method does have disadvantages, the main one being cost. As you can probably tell, the creation of a separate Windows 2000 domain will have its expenses initially. Technically, there will be two domains for every one, depending on the domain structure, during the migration. This cost can be lessened, however, by leasing the required machines, by using the newly purchased machines for the new domains, or by reallocating existing resources.

Another obvious disadvantage is that there will, in essence, be two sets of administrators and management for the migration team. Unfortunately for the existing network administrators, that usually translates to more work for them and hardly any extra help. When you do (or did) the original cost analysis, the improved salaries for these people or salaries for part-time help should have been calculated.

The following worksheet can be used to justify your choice for using the domain consolidation method, to make notes to see if this method will work for your organization, and to make sure that you have thought of all of the issues involved in upgrading in this manner.

Note: *I'll emphasize once more the importance of a properly planned network infrastructure. Your network may have been "born" five years ago, and over the past five years, it may have gone through eight or ten network administrators as it grew and evolved. If the current PDC in the Chicago building is named* Best_Server *and the current PDC in the Dallas office is called* Spock, *starting over with a new naming convention would be nice, even though it may be costly.*

The price for starting over? Perhaps in the thousands. Having a new standard in place so this type of thing doesn't ever happen again? Priceless.

Upgrading a domain by using the domain consolidation method (restructuring).	
Concern/Issue/Characteristic	**Notes**
Additional hardware costs are required	
Additional management costs are required	
Sufficient IT staff is available	
There is a large user population	
This method requires a phased-in migration	
The existing domains need to be restructured	
Domains need to be combined	
Domains need to be deleted	
Domains need to be added	
You want or need to start the network from scratch	
You would like to reconfigure user accounts or groups	
The current network design is flawed	
The current domain design is flawed	
You need a low-risk option for the upgrade	
You need the ability to revert to Windows NT domains	
Small- to medium-sized companies may not be able to afford the cost	
All Windows NT BDCs will need to be upgraded, decommissioned, or retired	
The namespace needs to be redesigned	
Downtime needs to be minimized	
Multiple domains exist	
Costs are justified	
Two or more companies are merging	
Other	

Checklists for Testing the Plan

Before you make any solid changes to the network or its servers, it is vital that the plan is fully tested. If the network is small, this testing may consist of using a spare room to set up a lab for testing the upgrades and applications; if the network is large, much more will be required. There will be different lab setups for migrations that use the upgrade plan and for migrations that use the domain restructuring plan. This section sums up what should be accomplished during the testing phase of the project.

You should treat the testing lab the way you would treat the actual deployment. The test lab should be set up and configured to emulate the current environment, including its applicable hardware and software, and the changes that you want to perform on the network should be performed in this lab. These tests will undoubtedly bring about changes to the plan or uncover flaws in the design. Therefore, any alterations to the plan must be performed and retested. You must be sure to document any changes as completely as possible and to verify those changes with all committee members.

If you think you're ready to test your plan, then you should feel that the plan is generally ready for the rollout. If there are any issues that haven't been resolved, such as a fully planned Active Directory structure, then the planning isn't complete and you are not ready to test the plan. Testing the plan and testing applications or NICs are two different things. Plenty of things need to be tested in the lab before you attempt any upgrade or conduct a pilot. The following checklists and worksheets attempt to address these things, although your network probably has its own special needs and issues. Use these checklists carefully, making the appropriate changes when they are needed, and the rollout will (keep your fingers crossed) go smoothly.

Tip: *From the beginning of the project, you will want to have a small lab set up that can be used to test critical applications on a Windows 2000 machine. This lab can also be used to test NICs, modems, sound cards, and their respective drivers for compatibility. You'll need the test results to complete the migration plan.*

Creating the test lab.	
Component/Requirement	**Notes**
State the scope and purpose of the lab	
Draw the physical structure of the lab	
Obtain approval and funding	
Obtain the required hardware and software	
Build the network	
Make sure the lab reflects the existing network realistically	
Make sure all hardware (including hubs and routers) and software resemble the network as closely as possible, and are, preferably, the same version, and are from the same vendor.	
Make sure the lab is capable of reflecting the proposed network	
Test the lab before performing any installations	
Install the server software (in this case, Windows NT)	
Make sure the lab is isolated from the current network	

(continued)

Creating the test lab *(continued).*

Component/Requirement	Notes
Determine if multiple labs are needed for multiple locations, applications, or scenarios	
Determine where the lab should be located	
Make the lab expandable	
Ensure that the lab is physically secure	
Other	

Determining what will be tested.

Component/Requirement	Notes
Backout plan	
Windows 2000 services and features	
Hardware and software compatibility	
Critical applications	
Performance testing	
Traffic patterns and potential bottlenecks	
Bandwidth performance	
Interoperability with other operating systems, such as Novell NetWare, Unix, or the Macintosh OS	
In-house applications	
Logon and logoff scripts	
In-house scripts	
Drivers for hardware, including printers, scanners, and smart cards	
Service pack deployments	
Desktop configurations	
Security settings	
Services and configurations	
Migration of accounts and groups	
Mixed-domain issues (Windows 2000 coexisting with Windows NT servers and BDCs)	
Fault tolerance techniques currently used	
Terminal Services, SMS, SNMP, Back Office	

(continued)

3

Determining what will be tested *(continued).*

Component/Requirement	Notes
Authentication	
Network connectivity	
DNS	
DHCP	
Dial-up service, RAS, VPN (Virtual Private Network)	
IP addressing	
Trusts	
Other	

Problems encountered during testing.

Problem	Solution	Notes
There are flaws in the domain design		
There are flaws in the namespace design		
There are performance problems		
The backout plan fails		
Bottlenecks occur		
Critical applications do not work properly		
Peripherals do not have appropriate drivers		
Scripts no longer work		
In-house applications don't work		
There are bandwidth problems due to replication of Active Directory over slow links		
RAID systems don't work correctly		
Required services fail		
Account and group migration fails		
The DNS namespace won't work with Active Directory		
DHCP and DDNS don't work		
The Remote Access Service fails		
Trusts have complications		

(continued)

Problems encountered during testing *(continued)*.		
Problem	Solution	Notes
Hardware needs to be expanded with more RAM, a faster CPU, or more HDD space		
The lab isn't scalable		
Domains can't be configured as requested		
The lab doesn't reflect all of the needs on the network		
Network communications fail (too slow, timeout, unavailable)		
The scope changes		
The cost increases		
Users have trouble learning new tasks		
Feedback from users isn't as positive as was hoped for by the test group		
Other		

Keep in mind that testing is simply part of the project and that the sole purpose of the testing process is to find problems with the plan. Do not be discouraged by what you find out while testing. Almost all network problems have solutions, and it is better to find out those problems in a test lab, rather than finding out when you get a call from the CEO of the company telling you that you're fired. The information you obtain through this testing process will make the deployment and rollout of Windows 2000 Server much more pleasant and productive.

Checklists for the Pilot and Rollout

Once you have completed the planning, assessment, inventory, and testing processes, you can begin focusing on the deployment of Windows 2000 Server. If problems were uncovered during the testing process, those problems should have been dealt with and resolved successfully. Before the actual deployment, you will probably choose to perform a pilot of the rollout. A pilot allows a small portion of the network to test the migration plan by being the first group to receive the new operating system. By piloting the migration in a small area, you can discover and solve unknown problems before affecting the entire network. The pilot is simply an extension of the test lab environment, using real people and network computers.

The Pilot

You should pilot the migration plan before full-scale deployment. Listed next are some of the things you should look for during the pilot, followed by tips that can make the pilot more successful.

3

Performing the pilot.

What to Look for During the Pilot	Notes
How long did the installation take?	
Did the installation take longer than planned?	
How many people did the installation require?	
Does the current staff have the necessary skills to perform the rollout successfully?	
What tools were needed?	
What tools were needed that were not anticipated?	
Will the deployment schedule still work?	
Did you meet the requirements for a successful deployment?	
Has the level of risk changed from previous estimates?	
Will the backup plan work?	
How is the user feedback? Positive? Negative?	
Does the migration plan need to be changed?	
Does the system work properly and as planned?	
Does the system meet the business needs and goals of the upgrade?	
How is the support staff working out? Is the staff large enough to handle the increased workload?	
Other	

Making the pilot successful.

Tips	Comments/Notes
Start small and involve only a few users	
Back up everything	
Do not add any new applications or services at this time	
Verify that hardware in pilot sites has been upgraded and meets minimum requirements	
Prepare the users with training and encouragement	
Keep users informed of changes to be performed and when these should happen	
Back up user data	
Document all problems and resolve them—both in the test lab and at the pilot site	

(continued)

Making the pilot successful *(continued)*.	
Tips	**Comments/Notes**
Select multiple pilot sites if multiple pilots are needed due to differences in migration techniques and applications	
Encourage users to report problems, even if they think a problem is their fault	
Evaluate the success of the pilot and make appropriate changes to the plan	
Other	

Note: *The following information is included to offer administrators a place to make notes concerning in-place upgrades and domain restructuring during the pilot. If the PDC will simply be upgraded to a Windows 2000 domain controller, the in-place upgrade checklist may prove helpful. If there is to be some piloting for a domain consolidation, then the domain consolidation worksheet may prove useful.*

Upgrading a domain by using the upgrade method (in-place upgrade).	
Concern/Issue/Characteristic	**Notes**
Back up all domain controllers	
Test the backups	
Test the recovery plan	
Schedule the downtime of servers for nonpeak usage	
Move a BDC off the network for backup	
Test Active Directory	
Test DNS	
Test the domain model after the upgrade	
Test applications	
Test connectivity	
Determine if user accounts can migrate successfully	
Determine if groups can migrate successfully	
Determine if computer accounts can migrate successfully	
Determine if the services will work well	
Determine if trusts have been configured correctly	
Other	

3

Upgrading a domain by using the domain consolidation method (restructuring).	
Concern/Issue/Characteristic	**Notes**
Back up all domain controllers	
Test the backups	
Test the recovery plan	
Schedule downtime of servers for nonpeak usage	
Test the domain model after the upgrade	
Test additional domains	
Test applications	
Test connectivity	
Determine if user accounts will migrate successfully	
Determine if groups will migrate successfully	
Determine if computer accounts will migrate successfully	
Determine if the services will work well	
Test Active Directory	
Test DNS	
Determine if trusts are configured correctly	
Determine if down-level servers are available	
Other	

Rollout Checklists and Worksheets

Once the pilot has proved successful for representative groups on the network, you may feel ready to begin the full-scale deployment plans. The object of the game is to perform the migration of servers throughout the network with as little interruption to users as possible. The winner is whoever can achieve this successfully.

Network downtime during the migration is directly related to lost productivity, which translates to lost revenue and increased costs. If the plan has been correctly planned, tested, and piloted, problems and costs related to lost productivity should be minimal.

While minimizing downtime for users is a good way to measure success, there are many other ways to make the deployment successful. The following list includes points to focus on during the rollout. Making sure that consideration has been given to all of these points will help make the rollout smooth and efficient.

Communicate to Users

One sure way to mess up a Windows 2000 deployment is to keep your users in the dark about when changes will be made, what changes will be made, and why those changes will be made. Average users will generally balk at a new technology if they feel uninformed or anxious about the changes. To make sure that this lack of communication doesn't harm your installation, consider keeping the following people informed of the changes that will occur on the network:

- End users

- Administration

- Project teams

- Other

Note: There may be others in the network who should be kept apprised of changes and impending plans during the migration, and you will most likely have different levels of information for each group. For instance, power users will require a different level of information than administrators will, and administrators will require a different level than end users will. Be careful not to give too much or too little information to the groups who require it.

Train Users and Administrative Staff

User training has most likely already begun by the time the migration starts taking place. In most cases, training end users begins when new standards are put in place, when changes are made to users' desktops, or when retrieving data from the servers is modified. In contrast, training for the IT staff may have started months before any migration; in fact, some of the administrators may be obtaining certifications and/or specialized skills from outside the organization. Training for the project teams, CEO, power users, server operators, and so on will also differ. These training plans have already been made, and training should already be taking place.

I'm emphasizing training because it is important that the end users feel qualified to handle the changes, that the project team members have enough training and skills to make the proper decisions, and that the deployment team has the proper skills and abilities to perform the tasks ahead. If any of these groups are not properly trained, the migration will most likely go askew.

*Note: Many employers insist that their network administrators have an MCSE (Microsoft Certified Systems Engineer) certificate. This training is available from Microsoft and is meant to guarantee that holders of such a certificate are properly trained to perform network administration tasks. See **www.microsoft.comtrainingandservices/default.asp** for details.*

3

Training checklists.	
Training Concern	**Notes**
End users have been properly trained	
End users are enthusiastic about (or at least accepting of) the change	
Anxious end users should be retrained	
Management has been properly trained	
Management is enthusiastic about (or at least accepting of) the change	
Anxious members of management should be retrained	
Network administration (IT) members have the proper credentials	
Network administration (IT) members are enthusiastic	
Network administration (IT) members are trained in the new operating system	
Server operators, backup operators, printer operators, and other IT members are appropriately trained	
Technical support staff is ready and appropriately trained	
In-house trainers are prepared to continually train new users and retrain existing ones	
Other	

You may discover, after training a particular group, that many of the members of that group seem uncomfortable with or uneasy about the new technology. To keep the project on track and maintain the user's support, it is necessary that these users feel comfortable with their training. You may need to consider how users will be retrained if they do not adequately understand the material the first time through.

Have a Backup Plan

There cannot be enough emphasis placed on the importance of having a backup plan. In the test lab, when changes were made to the servers, the backup plan should have been thoroughly tested before any pilot. During the pilot, the backup plan may have been needed and called upon. During the actual large-scale migration, it is imperative that the plan be useful. The following list contains some of the ways you can ensure that a backup plan is created, documented, tested, and maintained.

Backup utility worksheet.	
Backup Type	**Notes**
Tape drives	
Zip drives	
External hard disks	

(continued)

Backup utility worksheet *(continued)*.	
Backup Type	**Notes**
Rewriteable CD-ROMs	
Mirrored volumes	
Striped volumes	
Leaving a BDC off the network	
Windows 2000 backup utility	
Off-site storage of backup tapes	
Backup Wizard	
Media pools	
Other	

You'll need to create a document that outlines the steps that the backup plan will take in case of emergencies. It should fully spell out what will be needed to restore the network to its premigration state. The backup plan and any applicable tapes or copies of data should be stored off site until the migration is deemed a success. In addition, throughout the migration process, backups should be made at various stages in case a particular phase of the migration goes awry.

Phase In the Rollout

When deciding on a type of migration, you may have chosen the domain restructuring method instead of the upgrade method because you wanted not only to control how the migration was phased in but also to create a safety net in case the project failed. There are many good reasons to phase in a migration to Windows 2000, some of which are listed next:

- The pilot can be phase I.

- Risk is reduced due to the safety net.

- Disruption is minimized.

- The migration can be phased in during nonpeak hours.

- You can rework the plan if problems arise.

What is most important when you're using the phase-in approach is to make sure that you can recover from disaster if necessary. In addition, you'll want to remain flexible in case problems arise and the plan needs to be changed. For instance, if you find out that the desktop lockdown is generally hurting morale and making the users angry, you may consider rethinking those decisions. Leaving yourself and the plan open for changes is one of the great things about phasing in a migration.

Summary

By completing the tasks put forth in this chapter, you have come one step closer to migrating to Windows 2000 Server on your network, and you have learned about many of the necessary steps involved in such a project. If you are the administrator of a small organization, you may be just about ready to get started. In a larger operation, however, you may need to spend another few months planning, gathering information, conducting meetings, and assessing the needs of the network.

The first step in network assessment is to take inventory. Taking inventory is extremely important to the migration or upgrade because an accurate inventory will prevent problems due to incompatibility or lack of resources later. Inventory lists can also be used to compare the current state of a computer to the current minimum standards on the network. Complete inventory lists will also be invaluable to future network administrators.

This chapter also discussed the current state of the network, including the network's topology, domain structure, and administrative structure. Understanding the topology helps you plan because the topology map offers information concerning the speed of data lines, the lines' locations and costs, and the location of PDCs and BDCs.

After looking at both the current inventory and the current state of the network, you looked at current standards. Although the current standards may not be stated in company policy, standards do exist nonetheless.

Another task was to create the project committee, whose members are not only competent in their fields but also easy to get along with and fairly flexible. Job assignments were doled out, and a timeline, a meeting schedule, and other committee tasks were created.

One of the largest jobs is to analyze the cost of the entire project. The cost analysis worksheets can be used not only to define the cost but also to justify the cost of the project to your management or administration. There are ways to cut costs, including using parts from other machines to upgrade, retiring programs that are proprietary, and reconsidering organizational standards.

Finally, you learned how to plan an effective Active Directory structure, including namespace design, domain design, and structure design.

Once you have successfully completed all of the worksheets and checklists that pertain to your organization, you will be ready to install Windows 2000 Server.

Moving Forward

The next chapter will include information on installation methods, including automated and unattended installations, as well as on the installation process itself. Chapter 4 will walk you through installing and upgrading to Windows 2000 Server. Also discussed is when to install a clean copy of Windows 2000 Server and when an upgrade is appropriate. By now, you've probably already decided how you want to handle that, though.

After the Windows 2000 Server installation is completed, attention will turn to the installation of Active Directory. The installation of Active Directory will change the server into a domain controller. When this phase is completed, you will learn how to set up each component area and migrate existing information to the new domain controller.

If you would like to obtain additional information concerning the topics presented in this chapter, you can find a myriad of information at Microsoft's Web site. Many helpful Web addresses are included on this book's CD-ROM, and one site of particular interest is **www.microsoft.com/technet/win2000/dguide/home.asp**. Here you can read Microsoft's *Windows 2000 Server Deployment and Planning Guide*, which includes chapters such as "Planning for Deployment" and "Building a Windows 2000 Test Lab." Another helpful site is **www.microsoft.com/technet/win2000/reskits.asp**, where you can browse for information on topics such as "Active Directory Replication" and "Windows 2000 DNS."

Chapter 4

Installing Windows 2000 Server and Active Directory

The goal of this book is to help readers successfully install Windows 2000 Server on a computer and incorporate that computer into a network. As you have seen previously, this is a fairly straightforward task for a small workgroup or home business, but for a larger organization with an existing network, this seemingly simple assignment quickly becomes a yearlong project.

The previous chapters prepared you for this installation by offering checklists and worksheets for any size organization and by explaining the components available in Windows 2000 Server. After preparing the physical network, preparing the organization, and testing the deployment plan fully, you are finally ready to proceed with the installations.

This chapter consists of two main sections: "Windows 2000 Server Installation" and "Active Directory Installation." In the first section, you'll learn about the different ways that the operating system can be installed, including clean installations, upgrades, installations from a network, automated installations, and unattended installations. You'll also decide which file system to use and which components to install. After discussing these issues, this chapter will lead you through these installation methods. In this chapter's second section, you'll learn how to use the Active Directory Installation Wizard to install Active Directory, thus turning the Windows 2000 server into a domain controller. This section will also explain how to demote a domain controller to a member server.

By the end of this chapter, you will have successfully installed a Windows 2000 server and converted it to a domain controller. If this is the first installation you will perform, it should be carried out in your organization's test environment, as part of the finalization of the plan and deployment for Windows 2000 Server on your network.

Before you install Windows 2000 Server, you'll need to decide which installation method to use, which file system to use, and which components to install.

Installation Methods

Windows 2000 Server can be installed in many ways. Certainly you can just pop in the CD-ROM, but how much fun is that? There are other ways to install the operating system besides the boring old CD-ROM routine. This section discusses all of the installation options and provides step-by-step instructions for installing a clean copy of Windows 2000

Server, performing an upgrade, reinstalling Windows 2000 Server, and performing an unattended installation.

Clean Installations vs. Upgrades

If a new computer has been purchased for the sole purpose of installing Windows 2000 Server on it, it's obvious that you'll do a clean installation. If the network already has a computer that serves as a PDC, BDC, or member server in an NT domain, the choice may not be so clear. While planning your installations and working through the checklists, especially the migration methods decision worksheets at the end of Chapter 3, you probably decided which machines will be upgraded (if any) and which will receive a clean installation. You made these decisions based on how you wanted the domain to look after the upgrade(s) and on how you wanted to migrate to Windows 2000 products. Some networks will both upgrade existing machines and do clean installations on new ones. For instance, one subnet may be a newly created branch in an existing organization, while the corporate offices may have existed for 15 years.

Tip: Although both types of installations will be discussed here, I strongly suggest that you perform a clean installation of Windows 2000 Server whenever possible. Installations sometimes go awry, and troubleshooting a failed installation is much easier for a clean one than for an upgrade. Also, leftover driver files, partial data files, half-removed applications, shortcuts that don't work, and many other annoying remnants of an old operating system can not only cause problems but also continue to hang around for the next three years like a dark cloud.

Upgrading allows Windows 2000 Server to be installed on a machine that is currently running Windows NT Server 3.51, Windows NT Server 4, or Windows NT Terminal Server. Upgrading maintains current settings on the server. Installing "clean," by contrast, is a process that installs a new copy of Windows 2000 Server on a machine, does not maintain any previous settings or applications, and leaves no remnants of the previous server version behind. Technically, the hard drive is formatted during a clean installation, thus wiping the hard drive of any data before installing the new OS. To give you an opportunity to double-check your decision, the following checklist is provided.

Deciding on an upgrade or a clean installation.	
Guideline	**Notes**
Perform a clean installation if the current machine is running Windows 9x, Windows NT Server 3.5, Windows NT Workstation 3.51 or 4, or any non-Windows OS.	
If you want to have a dual-boot system, perform a clean installation.	
To maintain user settings, applications, and data, perform an upgrade.	
Perform a clean installation if no OS currently exists on the machine.	
If you're using the domain consolidation method of migration, do a clean installation.	
If you're using the upgrade migration method, simply upgrade the current domain controllers.	

Installing from a Network

If you are planning to install multiple Windows 2000 servers, you can make the installation files available from a network server by creating a shared distribution folder and making it available to clients on the network. Distribution folders are created for unattended installations as well. When you do a network installation, the client must be able to connect to the server that contains the installation files. The client can be just about any type of computer. A client can use Windows NT Server, Windows 9x, or any other operating system (even MS-DOS) that will allow it to reach the shared distribution folder. When the connection between the two is established, the options to upgrade or install will be offered. On Windows NT 3.51 (or higher) servers, both installing and upgrading will be available as installation methods. If the connecting computer uses anything other than Windows NT 3.51 or higher, then only the installation option will be available. Figure 4.1 shows a distribution folder on a Windows 2000 server, and Figure 4.2 shows how that folder looks to a Windows 2000 Professional client.

Automated Installations

Automated installations are convenient when there are many installations of Windows 2000 to be completed. In the real world, automated installations are more commonly used for installing client machines such as Windows 2000 Professional, but if you need to install multiple Windows 2000 Server machines, automated installations can be used for that purpose as well.

All installations require the administrator or other authorized employee to answer questions about the installation. These questions ask for information such as user name, computer name, time zone, password, license information, network information, and workgroup or domain identification. Automating an installation is done by creating an

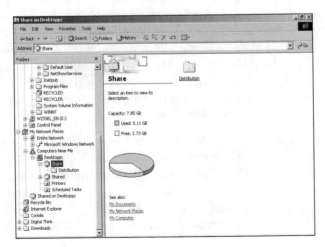

Figure 4.1
Distribution folder on a server.

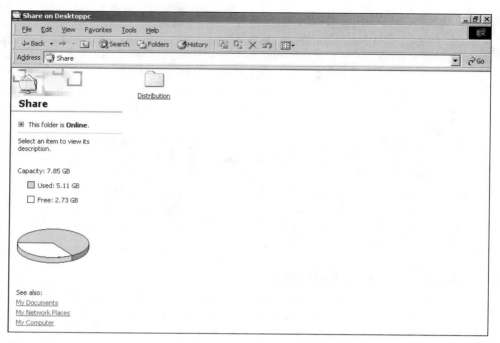

Figure 4.2
Distribution folder as seen by a client.

answer file that can answer these questions with or without user input. Automated installations can be timesaving in many ways. You can make several different installations available for clients to choose from—for instance, one for the sales department, one for the research department, and another for the marketing department. In addition, automated installations can be created to be unattended. You can probably see how useful this can be, especially if the clients are not computer savvy. Both of these methods reduce the cost and time usually associated with having a single administrator physically attend to the installation of machines throughout the network. The answer file that must be used with automated installations can either be created by using the Setup Manager or be created manually by editing the sample file included with Windows 2000 Server. Later in the chapter, I will walk you through the creation of an answer file.

To use the automated installation capabilities of Windows 2000 Server, you need distribution files along with the answer file. The distribution files include the contents of the I386 folder from the Windows 2000 Server CD-ROM, as well as other files that will be discussed later. Some of the installations that can be automated include not only those for the operating system but also those for applications, service packs, and language support. Automated installations can also be used for performing unattended installations.

Unattended Installations

Unattended installations are a type of automated installation in which the answer file has the answer to every question that the operating system asks tß the installer. By creating the answer file with all of the answers, you can configure the installation to allow (or require) no input whatsoever from its users. This type of installation can be useful when multiple servers need to be installed but it is necessary to keep the installations highly secure and free of user errors.

The automated and unattended installations can be achieved in several ways: by using a bootable CD-ROM; by using Winnt.exe, Winnt32.exe, and appropriate switches; by using the System Preparation tool (Sysprep.exe) to create an image; or by using Systems Management Server (SMS). Each of these methods requires a different type of installation preparation, and some of these methods require answer files or uniqueness database files. How these files are configured and how the installations are carried out will be discussed in more depth later in this chapter.

Selecting a File System

When installing Windows 2000 Server on a new machine or a newly formatted hard drive, you will be asked to decide on a file system for the new server. Windows 2000 supports FAT16 (16-bit file allocation table), FAT32 (32-bit file allocation table), and New Technology File System (NTFS). The version of NTFS that is supported in Windows 2000 Server is NTFS version 5. NTFS 5 offers the most features and is an improvement over Windows NT 4 NTFS.

The ability of Windows 2000 Server to support all three file systems—FAT16, FAT32, and NTFS—is a new feature of the operating system. Before the release of Windows 2000 products, no operating system offered this range of support. Windows 9x products supported FAT16 and FAT32, and Windows NT Server products supported FAT16 and NTFS. The ability to support all three file systems allows Windows 2000 to be compatible with more than one operating system.

FAT16 and FAT32

FAT16 and FAT32 systems are typically used with Windows 2000 Server if there is a need to dual-boot, switching between Windows 2000 Server and another operating system such as Windows 98. FAT16 and FAT32 are also used if the Setup program determines that the hard drive on which Windows 2000 will be installed is small. If the hard drive is smaller than 2,048MB, then the drive is automatically formatted as FAT16. If the hard drive is larger than 2GB, then the drive is formatted as FAT32. Choosing FAT16 or FAT32 as the file system isn't the best option, though. In most instances, you should choose NTFS.

FAT16 and FAT32 were the file systems used by early DOS and Windows computers. FAT stands for *file allocation table*, and it is this table that keeps track of which files are on the disk and where they are located. The FAT contains links that point to the locations of files, and it keeps track of information such as a file's size, the file's attributes, the last time the file was modified, and the location of the first piece of data in the file. Data that is stored in more than a single cluster on a hard drive contains another pointer to the location of the second part (or more) of the file.

When FAT16 was first created, it was used mainly for small drives that contained very little data by today's standards. When hard drives became larger, however, there was a lot of wasted space due to the FAT's cluster size configuration. When Windows 95 OSR2 was released, FAT32 was released as well. FAT32 made the cluster size more efficient by supporting 32-bit entries instead of 16-bit entries. FAT file systems become fragmented when files or applications are saved and then deleted, and new files and applications take their place. As the new files are saved to the hard disk, they are saved in non-continuous sectors, thus causing the drive to become fragmented.

If you need to have a compatible file system or to dual-boot with DOS-based operating systems, then you need to use the FAT file system for the boot partition. If not, it's better to choose NTFS (discussed next). Figure 4.3 shows a laptop computer that dual-boots with Windows 98 and Windows 2000 Server. Notice the three partitions: 1, 2, and 3. On this computer, partition 1 is simply MS-DOS, partition 2 is FAT32 and contains Windows 98, and partition 3 contains Windows 2000 Server and is NTFS. Because **FDISK** is a DOS command, NTFS isn't specified at the MS-DOS command prompt because DOS doesn't know anything about NTFS. The computer in Figure 4.3 has been booted to Windows 98 and thus cannot access the NTFS partition.

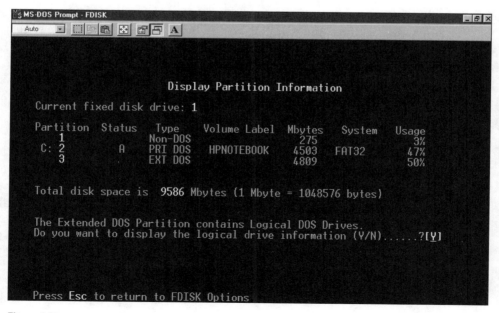

Figure 4.3
The results of the **FDISK** command, showing a computer's partitions and file systems.

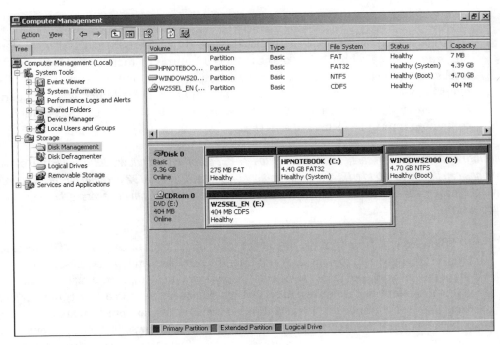

Figure 4.4
File systems as seen through Windows 2000 Server's Computer Management utility.

Contrast what is shown in Figure 4.3 with what is shown in Figure 4.4. Figure 4.4 displays the file systems on the same computer through Windows 2000 Server's Computer Management utility. Here you can see that Windows 2000 Server sees the other partitions and recognizes their file systems.

One problem with FAT16 and FAT32 is that they are not secure. The partitions in the previous example can be booted too easily with a floppy disk. It is discouraged to have the setup shown in this example because Microsoft does not recommend dual-booting a Windows 2000 server.

Note: *Even though this type of configuration is discouraged, it is sometimes necessary. The computer in the previous example can act as an additional server for my small network (Windows 2000 Server side), or it can perform duties that no other computer in my network can (Windows 98 side). All of the computers on my network are configured as Windows 2000 Professional machines, but to send photos from my digital camera via email, I can use only Windows 98 because there aren't any Windows 2000 drivers available for it. There is also no need for a high degree of security on this network, and the laptop needs to act as both a server and a client when I take it to consulting gigs. As you can see, there are circumstances when you might need a setup like this.*

NTFS

NTFS (New Technology File System) has the same basic capabilities of FAT file systems but is much more robust. Some of the advanced features include file-level and directory-level security, local security, disk compression, disk quotas, and encryption. NTFS also offers higher levels of security and better scalability to larger volumes. NTFS supports Active Directory services, and if Active Directory needs to be installed, the partition containing it must be formatted as NTFS.

Warning! A FAT16 partition cannot be converted to a FAT32 partition in Windows 2000, but FAT16 or FAT32 partitions can be converted to NTFS partitions without data loss. After a FAT32 partition has been converted to NTFS, however, the conversion cannot be reversed. Well, technically, it can be reversed, but you'll lose all of your data.

NTFS file-level permissions are one of the main advantages of choosing NTFS instead of FAT. NTFS allows you to control access to all files, folders, and directories, whether the client is accessing the file or folder over the network or sitting at the machine locally. NTFS also offers disk compression so that more data can be stored on a computer's hard drive than could be normally. NTFS compression and FAT compression are completely different, though; before you upgrade any version of Windows 2000 on a computer, make sure that no existing data is compressed. Windows 2000 NTFS compression doesn't recognize Windows 9x FAT compression.

Another NTFS feature is the ability to control disk usage on a per-user basis by using disk quotas. Disk quotas can be configured by right-clicking on the partition and choosing Properties. Figure 4.5 shows the dialog box.

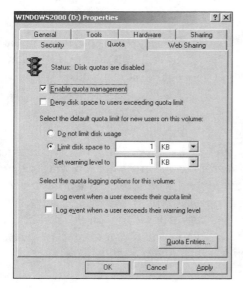

Figure 4.5
The Quota tab of the Properties dialog box for a partition.

Finally, encryption can be configured to allow users to encrypt file data on the physical disk. Encryption increases security and offers additional protection from data loss through malicious intent.

Warning! *The same file cannot be both encrypted and compressed. One or the other must be chosen.*

FAT vs. NTFS

Tables 4.1 and 4.2 summarize the advantages and disadvantages of the FAT and NTFS systems. Use this information to help you decide which file system you require. Keep in mind that some characteristics can be both an advantage and a disadvantage, depending on the circumstances. You should use the FAT file system if you need to dual boot or if the partition size is less than 2GB. Remember though, NTFS is the best choice in almost all other circumstances.

Table 4.1   FAT advantages and disadvantages.

Advantage	Disadvantage
-	Maximum partition size is 4GB
-	Inherently causes disk defragmentation
-	Allows only folder level permissions, not file level
-	Wastes drive space due to cluster size limitations
Can be converted later to NTFS	-
FAT32 is recognized by Windows 95 OSR2, Windows 98, and Windows 2000	-
FAT is recognized by MS-DOS, Windows 3.1, Windows 9x, Windows NT, Windows 2000, and OS/2	-
Write the advantages and disadvantages that affect your organization here:	

Table 4.2   NTFS advantages and disadvantages.

Advantage	Disadvantage
-	Only Windows NT and Windows 2000 can read NTFS drives
-	Cannot be converted back to FAT without data loss (Although third party tools now exist that can convert NTFS to FAT without data loss, nothing similar ships with Windows 2000.)
Maximum partition size is 16 exabytes	-
Writes data to disks intelligently, reducing physical distances between data files and reducing fragmentation	-

(continued)

Table 4.2   NTFS advantages and disadvantages *(continued).*

Advantage	Disadvantage
Has disk-logging features that make recovery easier	-
Allows compression of data	-
Allows encryption of data	-
Allows file-level permissions as well as folder-level permissions	-

Choosing Which Components to Install

Before the installation process begins, you will need to decide which components need to be installed on the server or domain controller you are configuring. For instance, if you intend for your domain controller to act as a DHCP server, then you'll need to install the necessary components, including network services, DHCP, DNS, or WINS, depending on the particular state of the network and the duties of the server. In this section, you'll learn what components are available for installation and why you'd want to include them in your installation. After making these final decisions, you'll be ready to install your first Windows 2000 server.

Figure 4.6 shows the Windows Components Wizard as seen through the Add/Remove Programs icon in the Control Panel. In Chapter 1, you learned what each of these components is for. In this section, you'll learn under what circumstances you should install them. You should never choose to simply install every one of these components *just in case* you may need them at some point. A single server or domain controller rarely needs to have all of these components installed. Furthermore, these components do not have to be installed during the Windows 2000 Server installation; they can also be installed later.

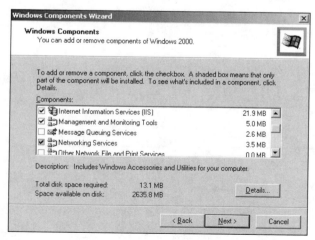

Figure 4.6
The Windows Components Wizard.

Tip: Personally, if I were installing just a single server, I would wait until after the basic installation was complete before installing additional components. This way, if there were any troubleshooting chores to be done, it would be a very straightforward process. However, if multiple servers were being installed in an automated or unattended fashion, this would not be the best scenario.

When to Install Accessories and Utilities

Many of the options in this section will install automatically if no changes are made during the installation and if the default settings are accepted while you're installing the new operating system. To select a component to install, check the box by its name.

- *Install the Accessibility Wizard*—If any users who will access this server have any vision, hearing, or mobility limitations. The Accessibility Wizard can be used to configure items that address such issues. If you are sure that this feature is unnecessary at this time, and you need to save 0.4MB of space, uncheck this box.

Tip: I suggest that you accept the defaults here and install these components. You can never predict what will happen, who may be hired, or why these services may be needed in the future.

- *Install Accessories and its related components*—If you need access on this server to the calculator, the character map, the clipboard viewer, desktop wallpaper, document templates, mouse pointers, the Object Packager, the Paint program, and/or WordPad. As you can probably tell from this list, many of these components really aren't necessary on most servers. Although choosing not to install the desktop wallpaper saves only 0.5MB of space, it could theoretically prevent an unnecessary load on the CPU caused by an operator who wasn't intending to cause one. Other unnecessary items might include the mouse pointers, document templates, or the calculator. For a server that will be used for presentations or other public tasks, it is probably best just to accept the defaults.

- *Install Communications and its related components*—If this server will be connecting to other computers and online services. Communications include Chat, HyperTerminal, and Phone Dialer. These components allow you to speak with other Windows users over the network.

- *Install Games*—If the IT administrator or CEO loves playing Solitaire, FreeCell, Minesweeper, or Pinball. Do not install any games if it is against stated company policy or if it will ultimately distract the administrator of this machine.

Tip: Be careful when making this decision. I can tell you from experience that if the clients on the network have been playing Solitaire on their coffee breaks for the past three years, and all of a sudden Solitaire isn't available, things can turn a little ugly. It is always easier to give than to take away, so make sure you understand the makeup of the network before unplugging any of the users' favorite games.

Personal Experience

I went to work for a start-up company a year or so ago, and we were planning to teach MCSE classes to aspiring computer experts. After we purchased the classroom servers and workstations and set up the network, everything looked good. However, we quickly found out that the server would not only be used for administering the classroom network but would also be used for multimedia presentations, for working through the CD-ROMs that came with the books, and for accessing resources on the Internet. We discovered that although we'd really built some awesome workstations, we'd failed to put sound cards in the servers. We didn't think about needing a sound card in a server. What is the moral of the story? Make sure you know exactly what your server will be used for and that it has the appropriate hardware as well as installed components.

- *Install Multimedia and related components*—If this server will need to play sounds, animations, or videos and has the necessary hardware to do this. There is no need to install the Multimedia sound components on a server that doesn't have a sound card or speakers. However, if this machine will be used to handle multimedia broadcasts to the network or to stage multimedia presentations, this component will certainly be necessary.

When to Install Certificate Services

In the real world, certificates, such as birth certificates, guarantee a person's identity to others. Birth certificates are agreed upon by the public to be a valid form of identification for individuals, even when they're visiting different countries. The computing world also uses certificates for identification. Certificates in this context are used to identify a computer's identity and are sometimes referred to as *digital certificates*. A digital certificate, which is used in public key encryption, is a set of data that completely identifies an entity, much like a birth certificate would when combined with a Social Security card and a driver's license.

Certificates are assigned by a valid Certificate Authority. The Certificate Authority is a trusted third party that verifies that people and things are who they say they are. If you want to create your own certificates instead of relying on a third-party Certificate Authority, you'll need to install Certificate Services. Microsoft's Certificate Services allow an organization to create, issue, renew, and rescind certificates within the company. Certificate Services can be used to manage certificates as well, including viewing them, backing them up, restoring them, setting policies, and stopping or starting the Certificate Authority service.

Install Certificate Services if:

- You want to create, issue, renew, and rescind your own certificates instead of relying on a third party to do this for the organization.

- You want to write standards for certificate policies instead of accepting third-party standards.

4

- You need to manage certificates from various transports, such as HTTP, Remote Procedure Calls, or another custom transport.

- You plan to use smart card authentication.

- You need certificates to secure email and to provide authentication for Web clients.

When to Install the Indexing Service

The Indexing Service is used to facilitate automatic indexing of all file names and corresponding file contents on the server and to permit speedy searches for any file name or text string matching the contents of those files. The Indexing Service is installed by default with Windows 2000 Server, but it isn't started unless specifically configured to do so. Under Services, it is set to Manual by default; to make the Indexing Service work automatically, change the setting to Automatic. The Indexing Service is CPU-intensive and should be used with caution.

Install the Indexing Service if any of the following are true:

- IIS (Internet Information Services) will be used and the search function is needed.

- The server has plenty of resources to handle the load on the CPU and has enough RAM to run such a CPU-intensive program.

- There is a need for quick searches for file names or text strings.

- Users need to search for files based on their properties.

When to Install Internet Information Services

IIS (Internet Information Services) and COM+ Services work together to allow an organization to build Web applications, offer Web support, offer FrontPage support, handle Web transactions, and support Active Server pages. IIS can also be used to support database transactions and to post receipts. If you install IIS and its program files, additional support will be provided for File Transfer Protocol (FTP) Server, Hypertext Transfer Protocol (HTTP), FrontPage Server extensions, Internet Services Manager and HTML, Network News Transfer Protocol (NNTP), Simple Message Transfer Protocol (SMTP), Visual InterDev RAD Remote Deployment Support, and World Wide Web Server.

Install IIS if:

- Your organization needs to maintain its own Web site.

- You need to authenticate visitors to your Web site.

- You need support for Web services using HTTP, FTP, NNTP, or SMTP.

- You want to support programmability through Web-standard Common Gateway Interface (CGI) and Internet Server API (ISAPI) applications as well as Active Server pages.

- The server needs to provide authentication and secure communications.

Note: IIS is installed by default in all clean installations of Windows 2000 Server. In upgrades, the Setup program tries to detect other versions of IIS that exist on the computer that is to be upgraded. If Setup finds a previous version of IIS, Peer Web Services, or Personal Web Manager, IIS 5 is installed automatically. IIS is not installed if the older services aren't detected during the upgrade.

When to Install Management and Monitoring Tools

These management and monitoring tools can be used to improve network performance. The Management And Monitoring Tools component includes the following tools:

- Connection Manager Components
- Directory Service Management Tool
- Network Monitor (a packet analyzer)
- Simple Network Management Protocol (SNMP)
- Support for client dialing
- Support for updating client phone books
- Support for migrating from Novell Directory Services (NDS) to Active Directory

You should consider installing Management and Monitoring Tools if you need to perform any of the following tasks:

- Centrally managing a network
- Migrating NDS data to Active Directory
- Offering phone and fax support
- Monitoring the network by using a packet analyzer (Network Monitor)

When to Install Message Queuing Service

Message Queuing offers reliable network communication services for use by distributed applications. The Message Queuing service allows these applications to function even if a computer is temporarily offline. Message Queuing can provide guaranteed message delivery, security of transfer, efficient routing, and priority-based messaging. Software developers and system administrators use Message Queuing for many complex tasks. Some of the tasks that can be performed using Message Queuing are listed next.

Consider installing this feature if your administrators need to do any of the following tasks:

- Configuring routing links
- Changing site gates for a routing link

4

- Using MSMQ (Microsoft Message Queuing) components such as MSMQ Exchange Connector

- Setting permissions or managing queued objects

- Auditing access to routing links

- Managing queues on other computers

- Performing other tasks similar to the ones in this list

When to Install Networking Services

Any time a server will connect to a network in any way (which is the purpose, isn't it?), the Networking Services component needs to be installed. This component has many subcomponents, and not every one needs to be installed on every server. The Networking Services component provides specific, network-related services and protocols, including the following:

- COM Internet Services Proxy

- Domain Name System (DNS)

- Dynamic Host Configuration Protocol (DHCP)

- Internet Authentication Service (IAS)

- QoS Admission Control Service

- Simple TCP/IP Services

- Site Server ILS Service

- Windows Internet Naming Service (WINS)

You should install all or part of Networking Services if the server you are configuring and installing will include any of the services listed in Table 4.3 or will act as a DNS, WINS, IIS, or DHCP server for the network. Table 4.3 shows the server task and the component that should be installed to achieve that goal.

Table 4.3   Networking Services components.

Server Purpose or Task	Networking Component to Install
Automatically assign TCP/IP addresses to clients	DHCP
Resolve fully qualified domain names (FQDNs) to TCP/IP addresses	DNS
Resolve TCP/IP addresses to FQDNs	DNS
Resolve NetBIOS names to TCP/IP addresses for clients	WINS
Support Web hosting	All IIS components, TCP/IP, Indexing Service

(continued)

Table 4.3   Networking Services components *(continued)*.

Server Purpose or Task	Networking Component to Install
Enable Distributed Component Object Model to use HTTP to traverse the Internet	COM Internet Services Proxy
Support caller ID, conference calling, video conferencing, faxing	Site Server ILS Service
Keep clients updated with current user information	Site Server ILS Service
Allow dial-up and VPN (Virtual Private Network) clients to become authenticated on the network	Internet Authentication Service
Specify the quality of the connection for every subnet on the network	QoS Admission Control Service
Specify which applications get what amount of bandwidth	QoS Admission Control Service
Support Character Generator, Daytime Discard, Echo, and Quote of the Day	Simple TCP/IP Services
Communicate over the Internet or within a network	Simple TCP/IP Services

When to Install Other Network File and Print Services

The Other Network File and Print Services component exists so that networked computers that do not use Windows products can access shared files and folders on the Windows 2000 server. Specifically, this component is installed to offer support for Macintosh and Unix computers on the network.

Install this component if:

- You have Macintosh clients on the network who need to access files on a Windows 2000 server.

- You have Macintosh clients on the network who need to send their print jobs to a print spooler on a server running Windows 2000 Server.

- You have Unix clients on the network who need access to printers available to this Windows 2000 server.

When to Install Remote Installation Services

The Remote Installation Services (RIS) component is used to remotely install Windows 2000 Professional on client computers that are remote-boot-enabled. To set up a RIS server, you'll also need a separate partition for the installation files, DHCP, DNS, and Active Directory.

Warning! Remote Installation Services cannot be used to install Windows 2000 Server products.

RIS should be installed if this server will be used to install Windows 2000 Professional to remote clients on the network.

Note: I won't be discussing RIS in this book because RIS can be used only to remotely install Windows 2000 Professional. However, if you plan to use a server for remote installations of clients, then you'll need to install RIS.

4

When to Install Remote Storage

Remote storage consists of additional media, such as magnetic tape devices, that the server uses to accumulate and store data. Most servers have these additional devices and use them either for additional storage space or for backups. The Remote Storage component offers services that can be used to access infrequently used data that is saved on these media.

You should consider installing Remote Storage if any of the following scenarios are characteristic of your environment:

- Magnetic tapes are used by the server for extra storage.

- These magnetic tapes hold infrequently used data.

- The server will be a file server.

- The file server will be expanded with media such as magnetic tape.

- Information should be retrieved automatically from tape when a request is made for it.

When to Install Script Debugger

Script Debugger is installed automatically during the Windows 2000 Server installation. This component is used to identify errors in script programs that run on the server. These scripts may be written in VBScript, JavaScript, or other scripting languages. Script Debugger offers client and server tools for finding and solving script errors.

When to Install Terminal Services

Terminal Services are not installed by default with Windows 2000 Server. Terminal Services is a utility that allows the Windows 2000 server to act as a mainframe for "thin" clients. The server can be configured to hold all applications and data, while the clients are configured to log on to this server and use its resources. Because a client can access the applications on the server, no applications need to be installed on their machines. In addition, data is stored on the server instead of one of the client machines, making backups more efficient and secure.

You should install Terminal Services if:

- Clients will log on to the server and will be "thin" clients.

- The server will hold all applications for the clients or be an application server.

- The server will hold all data for the clients.

- Client installation disks for Terminal Services need to be created.

- Clients have minimal disk space, memory, and other resources.

- The network needs to provide centralized security and support.

- Windows CE machines need server support.

When to Install Terminal Services Licensing

Terminal Services Licensing must be installed if Terminal Services is installed on the server and configured to run in Administration mode. Terminal Services Licensing provides the ability to register and track the number of clients using Terminal Services, and it offers a 90-day client license for the initial installation.

When to Install Windows Media Services

The Windows Media Services component provides support for delivering streaming video to users on your local intranet or on the public Internet. Media Services includes Windows Media Tools, Windows Media Player, and utilities such as NetShow.

Media Services can be used to produce and transmit streaming media presentations over any type of line: dial-up lines, leased lines, or LAN lines. There is no minimum speed for line type, although performance may suffer over low-bandwidth lines. Windows Media Services includes the following features:

- Microsoft PowerPoint 2000 Presentation Broadcasting, which can be used to create, schedule, and broadcast live PowerPoint presentations

- Windows 2000 Load Simulator, which can be used to calculate and tune the network load for highest obtainable scalability

- Windows Media Rights Manager, which can be used to encrypt content and thereby reduce unauthorized access to presentations

- Windows Media Pay-Per-View Solutions, which can be used to configure streaming videos as pay-per-view, allowing companies to charge for each viewing

- High-quality sound, wide bandwidth, and high-quality video

- Support for more than 4,000 concurrent client connections

- Load balancing techniques

- Integration with other Microsoft products, such as Office and Internet Explorer

You should consider installing all of the Media Services if you plan to offer any type of streaming video to your users. Streaming video applications include the following:

- *Training*—Users can receive training through Web-based tutorials, intranet-based tutorials, or third-party tutorials. These types of training can lower training costs by making it easier to update the material presented and by reducing required travel time.

- *Missed meetings or presentations*—Windows Media Services can be used to capture meetings and presentations and replay them for people who missed them.

- *Web services*—Streaming video looks great on a Web site and can be used to sell services, attract clients, or encourage purchases.

- *Shows*—Streaming video presentations are impressive, and they can be broadcast in lobbies or other areas of the building where potential customers gather.

Tip: Install only the components that are necessary, so you don't bog down the system with unused components.

Now that you know what each component is used for, you can decide what type of server you are installing and make the appropriate choices. If the server you plan to install first is going to be a "plain-Jane" domain controller, there is no need to install Certificate Services, games, or Windows Media Services. However, if this server will be a Web server, a DHCP server, or a DNS server, the installation parameters obviously change.

The Installation Process

As I mentioned earlier, there are several ways to install Windows 2000 Server. This section focuses on four installation methods: a clean installation using the CD-ROM; an upgrade of a Windows NT Server machine; a simple reinstallation of Windows 2000 Server; and an unattended, automated installation.

Performing a clean installation from the CD-ROM is the easiest way to install Windows 2000 Server, and a clean installation can be performed on almost any machine. You can start the installation by placing the CD-ROM in the CD-ROM drive and waiting for AutoRun to begin the procedure. If the CD-ROM doesn't start automatically, click on the CD-ROM icon in the Control Panel to open the installation options screen. You can also use Explorer to see the contents of the CD-ROM. Figure 4.7 shows the options screen.

If you choose the first option, Install Windows 2000, the installation procedure will begin. Selecting Install Add-On Components will open the Windows Components Wizard

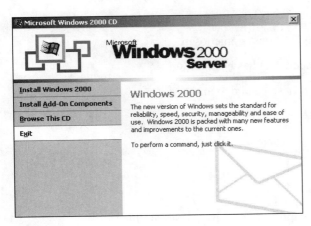

Figure 4.7
The options screen.

discussed in the previous section. Selecting Browse This CD-ROM will display the choices needed to create boot disks, copy the I386 folder to a distribution folder, copy applicable files to a separate partition on a RIS server, install support tools, choose Setup, or read information on installing Windows 2000 Server. Finally, selecting Exit will close the options screen.

As you can tell, there is more to this CD-ROM than just installing the server software; there are many other tools and utilities that may be useful later. Some of the tools, such as Sysprep and the Setup Manager, are necessary for creating answer files and carrying out automated and unattended installations. You will install these tools when you begin an unattended and automated installation later in the chapter.

With all of the information gathered, and knowledge of the different types of installations available, it is time now to actually do some installing.

Performing a Clean Installation

This section takes you through the procedures required to carry out a clean Windows 2000 Server installation from the CD-ROM. The installation will take about two hours. No user settings will be maintained, and the hard drive will be formatted during the installation.

If this is a new computer, a computer that has a newly formatted hard drive, or a computer that has an operating system already on it, you'll need to check some items before starting the installation. Make sure that the following statements are true or that decisions have been made regarding them:

- Minimum hardware requirements have been met.

- Hardware is on Microsoft's HCL.

- Hard drive partitions have been decided.

- The file system (preferably NTFS) has been chosen.

- The licensing mode (described later) has been chosen.

- Domain or workgroup names have been documented.

- Services you want to install have been decided.

- Data has been backed up if applicable.

- Drives have been uncompressed.

- Disk mirroring is disabled.

- UPS (uninterruptible power supply) devices have been disabled.

- All Read me files for applications and drivers on the machine have been read.

- Viruses have been found (if applicable) and then removed.

- Virus-checking software has been disabled.

- The BIOS manufacturer has been checked, and the most current BIOS revision has been downloaded and applied.

Finally, it is good practice to check the system by using the **/checkupgradeonly** switch of the winnt32 command before starting any installation. This command switch can be used to test the system for compatibility before you perform the installation. With all of the planning you did in Chapter 3, you should be aware of almost any problem that could arise. However, running D:\I386\Winnt32.exe /checkupgradeonly (where D: represents the CD-ROM drive) will certainly not hurt and will notify you if any previously undetected problems are found. Figure 4.8 shows a successful upgrade check.

After these tasks are complete, and you are positive you are ready to begin the installation, follow the steps listed next to install a clean copy of Windows 2000 Server on a computer. This section describes installing the software on a computer with a single drive with a single partition, by using the installation CD-ROM:

1. Restart the computer and press the appropriate key to enter the computer's BIOS setup options. It may be a dark blue screen (depending on the BIOS), and it can be accessed by pressing the F2 key or the Delete key or a combination of two or more keys. The appropriate key combination will be displayed at the bottom of the screen when the computer boots. Listing 4.1 shows a sample BIOS screen.

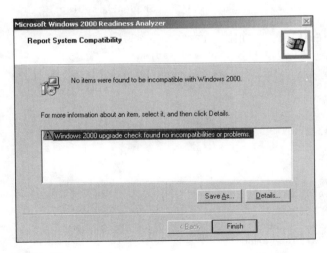

Figure 4.8
The Microsoft Windows 2000 Readiness Analyzer dialog box, reporting that an upgrade check found no incompatibilities.

Listing 4.1   A sample BIOS screen.

```
CMOS SETUP UTILITY
AWARD SOFTWARE, INC.
STANDARD CMOS SETUP       INTEGRATED PERIPHERALS
BIOS FEATURES SETUP       SUPERVISOR PASSWORD
CHIPSET FEATURES SETUP      USER PASSWORD
POWER MANAGEMENT SETUP      IDE HDD AUTO DETECTION
PNP/PCI CONFIGURATION      SAVE & EXIT SETUP
LOAD BIOS DEFAULTS        EXIT WITHOUT SAVING
LOAD SETUP DEFAULTS
ESC : Quit       ¨ ≠ Æ Ø : Select Item
F10 : Save & Exit Setup      (Shift) F2 : Change Color
Virus Protection, Boot Sequence…….
```

Once there, configure the BIOS to boot directly from the CD-ROM drive. In this example, the boot sequence can be configured under the BIOS Features Setup. You might not have mouse support on this screen, and if this is the case, you can use the arrow keys. Listing 4.2 shows the boot sequence configured as CDROM, C, A.

Listing 4.2   A sample BIOS boot sequence configuration screen.

```
Rom PCI/ISA BIOS
BIOS FEATURES SETUP
AWARE SOFTWARE, INC.
Virus Warning  :Enabled      Video BIOS Shadow:Enabled
CPU Internal Cache     :Enabled      C8000-CBFFF Shadow:Disabled
External Cache     :Enabled      CC000-CFFFF Shadow:Disabled
CPU L2 Cache ECC Checking     :Enabled      D0000-D3FFFF Shadow:Disabled
               D4000-D7FFFF Shadow:Disabled
Quick Power On Self Test     :Enabled      D8000-DBFFFF Shadow:Disabled
Boot Sequence  :CDROM, C, A      DC000-DFFFF Shadow:Disabled
Swap Floppy Drive     :Disabled
Boot Up Floppy Seek     :Enabled
Boot Up NumLock Status      :On
Gate A20 Option     :Fast
Typematic Rate Setting     :Enabled
Typematic Rate (Chars/Sec)     :30
Typematic Delay (Msec)     :250
Security Options     :Setup
PCI/VGA palette Snoop     :Disabled
OS Select for DRAM > 64 MB     :non-OS2
Report No FDD For WIN95     :No     ESC:Quit      ¨ ≠ Æ Ø : Select Item
               F1:Help     PU/PD/+/_:Modify
               F5:Old Values     (Shift)F2:Color
               F6:Load BIOS Defaults
               F7:Load Setup Defaults
```

2. Restart the computer, and as it begins the boot process, place the Windows 2000 Server CD-ROM into the CD-ROM drive.

3. When you see the instruction "Press any key to boot from CD," press any key. If you don't press a key, you'll have to start over. If this message doesn't appear, and the computer instead boots to the hard drive or looks for a floppy disk in drive A:, the computer might not be capable of booting from the CD-ROM. If this is the case, you'll need to create a set of boot disks. The sidebar explains how to make boot disks. If your computer isn't capable of booting from the CD-ROM drive, you'll need to follow the instructions there.

Note: *With Windows NT Server, you made boot disks by using the /OX switch. This switch is no longer available in Windows 2000, and it has been replaced with the **makeboot** command.*

If you are installing by using the four boot disks instead of the Windows 2000 Server CD-ROM, you will be prompted to insert disks 2, 3, and 4 during this part of the process. Simply follow the instructions to insert the disks, and after all four disks have been loaded, installation will continue as shown in Step 4.

4. Setup will now begin initializing. This part of setup takes place without user intervention and loads drivers, dynamic volume support, the Hardware Abstraction Layer (HAL), the ACPI bus driver, Partition Manager, host adapters, and other required components. If you watch closely, you can see what is being loaded onto the system as it is flashed on the bottom of the installation screen. After these components are loaded, the text portion of setup begins.

5. As the text-mode setup begins, you will see the message "Setup is Starting Windows 2000" at the bottom of the screen. You will be asked to choose one of the three following options:

Creating Boot Disks

A set of boot disks is made up of four disks. Boot disks must be created if you are installing Windows 2000 Server on a computer that does not have an operating system on it and/or that cannot boot from the CD-ROM drive. Two different sets of boot disks can be made. One set is for 16-bit operating systems such as Windows 3x or Windows 9x, and the other set is for 32-bit systems such as Windows NT and Windows 2000.

To make boot disks for 16-bit operating systems, simply browse the Windows 2000 CD-ROM, choose the BOOTDISK folder, and click on MAKEBOOT. For 32-bit systems, browse the Windows 2000 CD-ROM, choose the BOOTDISK folder, and click on MAKEBT32. You can also create boot disk sets by choosing Start|Run and typing either "[CD_ROMdrive_letter]:\bootdisk\makebt32.exe" or "[CD_ROMdrive_letter]:\bootdisk\makeboot.exe" in the Open box.

- Press Enter to set up Windows 2000.

- Press R to repair or recover a Windows 2000 Server installation.

- Press F3 to close the Setup program.

6. You will be performing a clean installation of Windows 2000 Server, so press Enter.

7. The text-mode portion of the installation continues, and the next panel displayed contains the licensing terms. If you want to continue the installation, read the terms and press F8; if you do not want to continue the installation or do not agree with the terms after reading them, press Escape.

8. If you press F8 to agree with the terms of the licensing agreement, the next screen will show information about the current configuration of the hard disk(s).

To continue from this screen, press C.

If the computer has an operating system installed on it that Windows 2000 Server recognizes, it will show information about the current hard disk configuration on your particular computer. A computer that has a previous operating system on it may have multiple partitions and volumes, whereas a computer that hasn't had an operating system installed on it may show one large drive with no partitions or volumes at all. In either circumstance, you need to have *some* unpartitioned space that can be highlighted and used for creating a new partition. Figure 4.9 shows an example of unpartitioned space on a computer.

You need some unpartitioned space for installing Windows 2000 Server. In a clean installation, however, you need only be concerned with two things: deleting all of the existing partitions, and then creating a new partition for the Windows 2000 Server

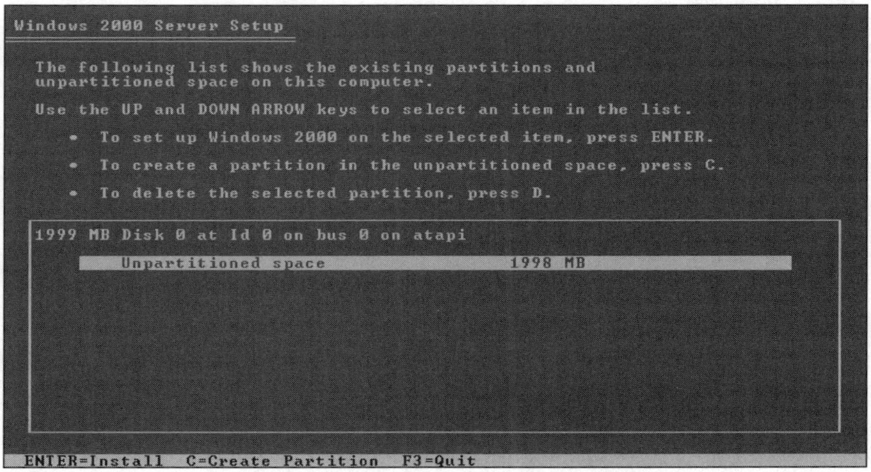

Figure 4.9
Unpartitioned space on a new computer.

Choosing the Installation Partition Size

The boot partition must be at least 671MB for all of the operating system files to install properly. Microsoft recommends that it be at least 2GB so you'll have a place to install the tools and any future service packs.

installation. Deleting the partitions will erase all of the data on them and create the necessary unpartitioned space. To delete partitions and create a new one, follow the steps listed next.

To configure the hard disks, look at all of the existing partitions and volumes (if applicable). Select each partition one at a time and press D to delete it. Figure 4.10 shows the screen you will see after pressing D while a partition is highlighted. (If you have previously formatted and repartitioned the hard disk with a third-party tool or a DOS disk, this isn't necessary.)

To delete this partition, you'll have to press L to confirm your choice. This necessary precaution gives you the opportunity to back out of this decision because deleting the partition causes all data on that partition to be lost.

To create a partition, highlight the unpartitioned space, as shown in Figure 4.9, and press C. Figure 4.11 shows the screen for creating a partition.

If you are comfortable with the requirements for partition sizes, feel free to change them to suit your needs. If you want to create other partitions at this time, you can do that also. However, Microsoft suggests that you create and size only the

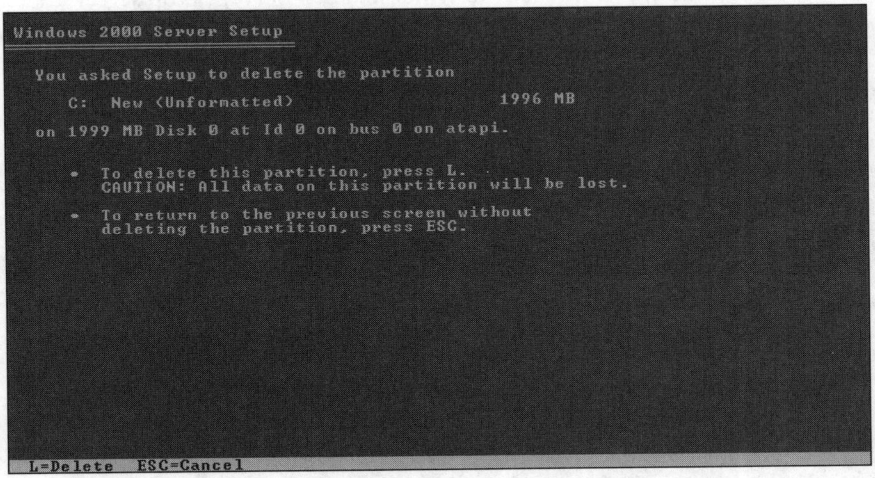

Figure 4.10
Deleting partitions and confirming the deletion.

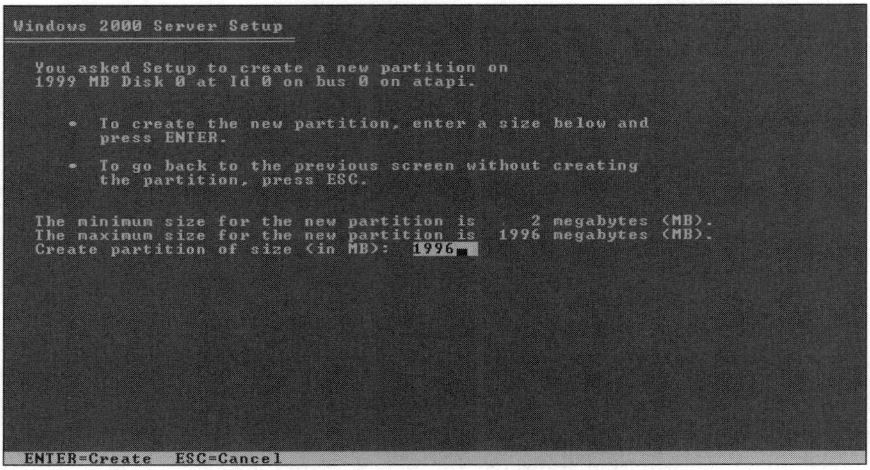

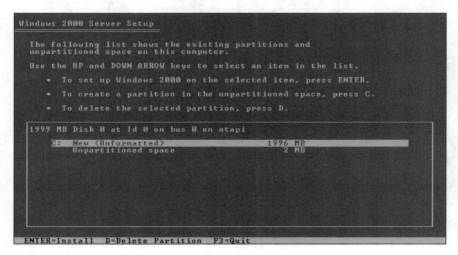

Figure 4.11
Creating partitions.

installation partition during setup, and then, after setup is complete, use the Disk Management tool to partition any remaining space on the hard drive.

9. After you've deleted all partitions and created one partition, the configuration screen should show only (new) unpartitioned space. Figure 4.12 shows an example of a new, unformatted 1,996MB partition. At this point, all other partitions should be deleted, and the screen should look similar to the one in this figure. (If they aren't, return to Step 8 and try again.)

10. After pressing Enter, you will see the Windows 2000 Server Setup screen that asks you to decide which file system you want to use (see Figure 4.13). If you are unsure,

Figure 4.12
A new, unformatted partition.

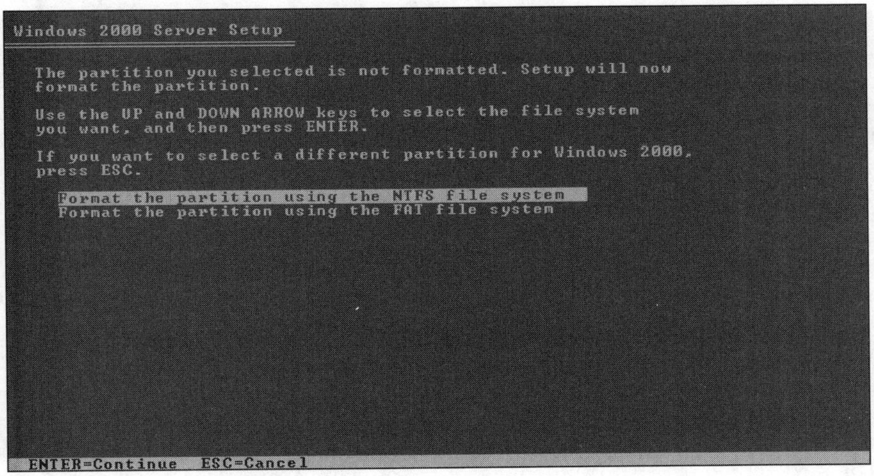

Figure 4.13
FAT or NTFS?

choose FAT. It is possible to change from FAT to NTFS without any complications, but it is not possible to change from NTFS to FAT without data loss. If the computer is going to be a domain controller, though, it will have to be NTFS. You may as well make that decision now, if you are sure it will be a domain controller.

11. There is no turning back after this point, so make sure that you are ready to install. When you choose a file system and press Enter, the drive is formatted. Formatting erases everything on the drive, and when the format is completed, there will be no way to retrieve any data that wasn't backed up.

   You will see a yellow progress bar during the formatting process, and this phase could take a long time if the drive is large.

12. When formatting is finished, Windows 2000 Server Setup checks the physical hard disk for errors and begins copying files from the CD-ROM to the folders on the local drive.

   At the end of this copy process, the system reboots. (When you see the yellow bar turn red, the countdown to reboot has begun.)

13. This ends the text mode portion of setup. GUI-mode setup begins with the Starting Windows screen. The screen will be black and will show a white progress bar at the bottom.

   Next is the Windows 2000 Server Setup screen. You have to press Next to continue, or wait 15 seconds.

   During this part of setup, Windows 2000 Server Setup looks for hardware on the system and installs devices and their drivers. NTFS folder and file permissions for the operating system files are also configured at this point. This may take quite a bit of time—perhaps between 3 and 30 minutes—depending on what the Setup program finds to install. There may be some flickering as Setup detects monitors and display adapters, and this is quite normal. Figure 4.14 shows this phase.

Note: I installed this version of Windows 2000 Server to a virtual machine on a computer that was running Windows 2000 Professional. This part of the installation took approximately one hour under these circumstances.

14. After all of the devices have been found and accepted, you'll begin seeing screens and dialog boxes that look familiar. These dialog boxes are similar to the ones seen in a Windows 9x or Windows NT installation. The first of these pages is the Regional Settings screen. From this screen, you can configure options for the system locale, user locale, and keyboard layout. You can change the options for locales or keyboards by choosing Customize.

15. The next screen is titled Personalize Your Software. You'll need to enter information such as the user name, the organization name, and possibly the product key. Then choose Next.

Tip: Don't panic if the product key you entered doesn't work the first time. It is easy to mix up the number one with the letter I, or the number zero with the letter O. If you receive an error, simply try again. The installation won't abort if an invalid number is typed in.

16. The licensing mode screen is next. There are two modes: Per Seat and Per Server. Choose the option that is right for your organization, and choose Next. See Figure 4.15. (See the sidebar for more information on licensing options.)

17. Setup will now give you a place to enter the computer name and the administrator password. The computer name can be as long as 63 characters and should consist of

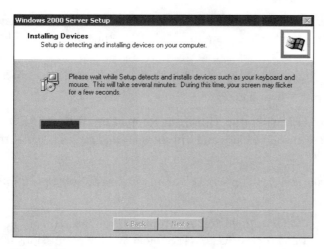

Figure 4.14
Installing devices.

4

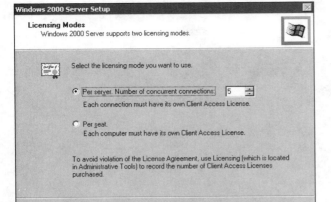

Figure 4.15
Licensing modes.

only characters that are made from the letters A-Z or a-z, and the numbers 0-9. You can also use hyphens (-) and underscores (_), although the underscore is discouraged. (See the error message in Figure 4.16.) The computer name will be shown as all capital letters, no matter how you type it in, and Setup will suggest a computer name that it finds appropriate based on previous information you have given it. See Figure 4.17 for an appropriate computer name that does not generate errors.

Licensing Mode Options

Windows 2000 Server offers two licensing modes: Per Seat and Per Server. In Per Seat mode, licenses are assigned to every computer that requires access to the Windows 2000 server. In Per Server mode, licenses are assigned to every server.

Per Seat licensing is the best choice if the network is large and if many computers will be accessing many different servers. In Per Seat licensing, each client computer is given a Client Access License (CAL), which gives that computer the right to access information and resources on a particular Windows 2000 server.

Per Server licensing is the best choice if the company or network is small and has only one computer running Windows 2000 Server. Per Server licensing allows the administrator to set a maximum number of concurrent connections, rejecting connections that would cause the number of licenses to go over the limit. In Per Server licensing, CALs are assigned to the server instead of to the client. The server must have as many CALs as it has clients who will access the server concurrently.

If you are still unsure which mode to choose, select the Per Server mode. Microsoft allows an organization to change, one time, from Per Server to Per Seat at no cost. This is done through the Licensing icon in the Control Panel. However, there is no conversion from Per Seat to Per Server available.

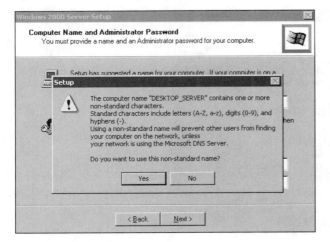

Figure 4.16
Warning for an invalid computer name.

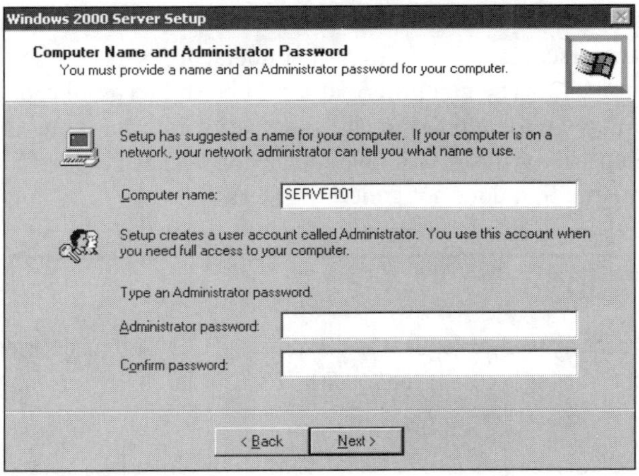

Figure 4.17
Example of a valid computer name.

An administrator password will also be needed. Passwords are case sensitive and should be complex. Microsoft recommends a combination of upper- and lowercase letters as well as numbers and symbols. A good password for the administrator account would be something like PL*ki09D. Password-breaking programs can easily figure out passwords that consist of real words, common names, or number combinations such as a birthday or the like, so a complex password is definitely needed. Choose Next to continue.

Warning! *Although I hate to suggest that you write down the password and put it in a safe place before continuing, I must. It will do you no good at all to create a great password and then not be able to remember it for logging on. If you can't remember the password, and you can't log on, you will most likely be faced with reinstalling the software.*

18. The Windows 2000 Components screen is next. Here you can select which services should be installed on this computer. A box that is shaded with a checkmark in it means that some of the components are to be installed and some are not. To see more about a particular component, highlight it and select Details from the dialog box. After making all of these selections, click on Next.

19. Setup has already figured out whether or not you have a modem; if you do, you'll need to type in some information regarding the dialing properties of your network. This information includes the area code and whether or not you need to dial another number to reach an outside line (nine, for instance). You also need to specify tone or pulse dialing. If the computer you are installing on doesn't have a modem, this screen will not be shown.

20. On the next screen, check the current time, date, and time zone, and make any necessary changes. Click on Next.

21. The next screen is the Network Settings screen. Network Settings will automatically detect any network adapter cards installed in the computer. This detection may take a few minutes. Once the card is recognized, choose Custom Settings to examine what Setup has found. Choosing Custom Settings allows you to manually configure networking components as well.

Note: *You will not see the following options if there isn't a network card that can be identified by Windows 2000 Setup. However, after installation is complete, all of the network settings can be configured through My Computer properties and Local Area Connection.*

Accepting the Typical Settings will set up the computer with the TCP/IP protocol with automatic addressing, Client For Microsoft Networks, and File And Print Sharing For Microsoft Networks. This configuration may work fine for some networking situations and servers, but choosing Custom Settings gives you extra flexibility during the installation.

Tip: *I suggest that whenever a Custom choice is offered, you should always explore the settings instead of simply accepting the defaults. Even if the settings will work fine, it is best to see what is being installed and retain the option of changing them if they aren't suitable.*

22. After you choose to explore the Custom Settings, the Local Area Connection Properties screen is shown. (You can view the same screen after installation is complete by

right-clicking on My Network Places and choosing Properties.) This screen shows the components that can be installed and/or configured: Gateway And Client Services For NetWare, Client For Microsoft Networks, Network Load Balancing, File And Printer Sharing For Microsoft Networks, Network Monitor Driver, and Internet Protocol (TCP/IP). You can also configure the network interface card itself by choosing Configure from the dialog box.

You may want to configure some of the components just listed during installation. For instance, you can highlight Internet Protocol (TCP/IP), choose Properties, and configure the server to obtain an IP address automatically, use a specific IP address, obtain a DNS server address automatically, or use a specific DNS server address. Figure 4.18 shows this dialog box. Choosing the Advanced tab from that screen offers even more configuration options, including WINS addresses and IP Security.

You might also want to change the properties for the File And Printer Sharing For Microsoft Networks feature. By highlighting this feature and choosing Properties, you can change the optimization from the default of Maximize Data Throughput For File Sharing to any of the other choices: Minimize Memory Used, Balance, or Maximize Data Throughput For Network Applications. This Properties box can also be used to make browser broadcasts to LAN Manager 2.x clients.

23. If this server is the first server installed on the network, the server should be assigned a static TCP/IP address. Look again at the Internet Protocol (TCP/IP) Properties page as shown in Figure 4.18. If you are going to assign a static address, you'll also need a subnet mask and a default gateway. If the server isn't the first server on the network,

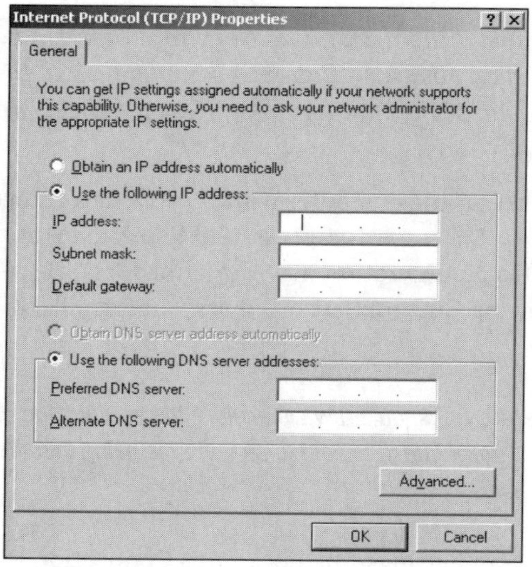

Figure 4.18
TCP/IP Properties.

you may want to either assign it a static address or allow it to obtain an address automatically from a DHCP server. You may also want to configure the DNS server if one is available; if there isn't, these settings can be assigned later through My Network Places|Properties|Local Area Connection|Properties.

24. The next screen enables you to join either a workgroup or a domain. If this computer is a member of a domain, you'll choose Domain. In a small network with only a few users, you may consider joining (or creating) a workgroup. However, because workgroups don't take advantage of all of the security features available to domains, including authentication features, workgroups are rarely configured. If you know the name of the domain and are a member of it, go ahead and complete the network identifications. If you are not configuring networking at this time, Figure 4.19 shows these installation options. To configure these options after installation is complete; right-click on My Computer, choose Properties, and then choose Network Identification.

To specify a domain, you must type a valid domain name that exists on the network. You will also need a user account and a password that has permissions to join a domain. If no network exists, as in this example, enter a name for a workgroup and click on Next.

Note: This section deals with installing a clean copy of Windows 2000 Server on a machine that may or may not have had an operating system on it already. Because I want to demonstrate the easiest installation option for a Windows 2000 server, in this example, I will choose to join a workgroup. After the installation is complete, I will demonstrate how to install Active Directory on this machine to create a new domain for this server. See the section "Active Directory Installation" later in this chapter to see how this server will start a new domain on a new network.

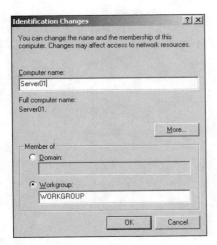

Figure 4.19
Workgroup or domain.

25. The final stage of Setup installs the components you have chosen and configures the server for use. The Performing Final Tasks screen shows the progress for completing the last few tasks, including installing Start menu items, registering components, saving settings, and removing temporary files. This could take quite a bit of time if the computer is slow.

26. When the final tasks are completed, a message screen appears, informing you that Setup is complete and that you should remove the CD-ROM and any floppies and click on Finish to restart the computer.

27. Windows 2000 Server will now start for the first time. Once the system has restarted and this bootup is completed, press Ctrl+Alt+Del at the logon screen to log on to the computer. Log on using the Administrator account and the password you created.

28. The first time Windows 2000 starts, you will see the Configure Your Server screen, as shown in Figure 4.20. From here, you can perform the tasks listed next:

    • Register the copy of Windows 2000 that was just installed.

    • Install Active Directory.

    • Make the server a file server.

    • Make the server a print server.

    • Make the server a Web or media server.

    • Configure DHCP, DNS, or Remote Access and Routing.

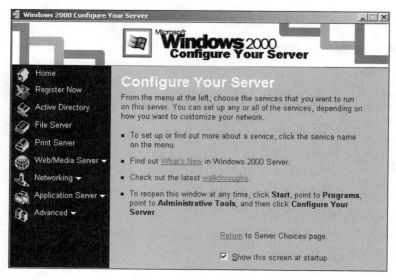

Figure 4.20
The Configure Your Server screen.

- Configure Component Services, Terminal Services, Database Server, or Email Server.

- Configure Message Queuing, use Support Tools, or install optional components.

Upgrading a Windows NT Server

Installing Windows 2000 over Windows NT Server is much more automated than installing Windows 2000 cleanly is. This is because Windows 2000 can determine such things as regional settings, keyboard settings, and file system configuration from the previous operating system configuration. Upgrading is a good choice if you want to keep your existing users, settings, groups, rights, and permissions, and if all of the current computer hardware and software is supported. You also need to make sure that the current system is one that can be upgraded successfully. To refresh your memory, the following NT systems can be upgraded:

- Windows NT Server 3.51

- Windows NT Server 4

- Windows NT 4 Server Enterprise Edition

- Windows NT 4 Terminal Server

In this section, I will demonstrate the process of installing Windows 2000 Server as an upgrade from a Windows NT 4 Server. Before starting this procedure, you might want to put the Windows 2000 CD-ROM into the CD-ROM drive and type d:\i386\winnt32.exe / checkupgradeonly where d: is the drive letter of the CD-ROM. This command will verify that the system's hardware is supported and that the system can be upgraded.

In addition, make sure the following items have been checked, planned for, or achieved:

- Minimum hardware requirements for Windows 2000 Server have been met.

- Hardware is still on Microsoft's HCL.

- Hard drive partitions will remain the same during the upgrade.

- The file system will or will not be upgraded from FAT, or NTFS will continue to be used.

- Licensing mode will still work as planned.

- Domain or workgroup names have not changed.

- Services will remain the same.

- Data has been backed up.

- Drives have been uncompressed (unless the drives were compressed with the NTFS compression utility).

- Disk mirroring is disabled.

- UPS (uninterruptible power supply) devices have been disabled.

- All Read me files for applications and drivers on the machine have been read.

- Viruses have been found (if applicable) and then removed.

- Virus-checking software has been disabled.

- The BIOS manufacturer has been checked, and the most current BIOS revision has been downloaded and applied.

- New TCP/IP information has been attained if the server currently has TCP/IP installed on it and the information will change.

With these tasks behind you, you can begin the upgrade.

Note: This upgrade demonstration was performed on a Windows NT machine that was not connected to a TCP/IP network. I chose this type of installation so that you could see the most basic screens associated with an NT upgrade. When installing on a network server, you may need to answer a few questions concerning current TCP/IP settings and changes to those settings, depending on your specific configuration.

1. To upgrade a Windows NT Server machine to Windows 2000 Server, you need to boot the system to the current operating system. The upgrade cannot be carried out if the system is booted from the CD-ROM drive or boot floppies. The system must be booted fully so that the upgrade process can determine how the current operating system is set up, which user settings have been configured, which users and groups have been configured, and how regional settings, keyboard layout, and time and date are set. If the computer is booted from the CD-ROM drive, the choice to upgrade will not be shown.

2. After the computer has booted successfully, do any of the following: begin the installation from the CD-ROM; run Winnt32.exe, with switches if appropriate, from the command line; or choose a distribution folder over a network. After the installation has begun, choose Upgrade Windows 2000 from the Welcome screen. You will then see Figure 4.21.

3. The next screen is the licensing screen. Accept the agreement by placing a dot in the button to accept. If you choose not to accept this agreement, the installation will abort.

4. The next screen lets you choose to upgrade the drive to NTFS (see Figure 4.22); you will see this screen only if the current server's file system is FAT. Most likely, if you are upgrading a Windows NT server, the file system isn't FAT but is already NTFS.

5. The next screen is the loading information screen. This process is usually brief.

6. The next screen offers the Directory of Applications for Windows 2000 and asks if you'd like to get the most recent information about Windows 2000 compatible and

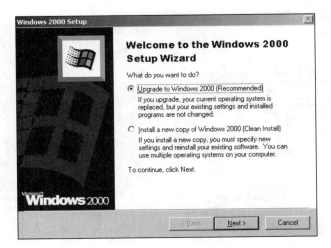

Figure 4.21
Choosing to upgrade.

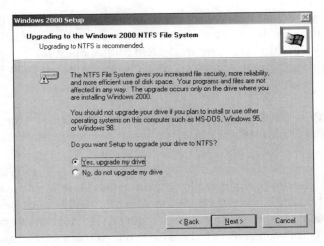

Figure 4.22
Upgrading the drive to NTFS (optional).

certified applications. If you want to do that, click on the Directory Of Applications button; if you don't, choose Next. See Figure 4.23. If you choose to see the Directory of Applications, you will automatically be connected to the Internet and the appropriate Microsoft Web site. (Of course, this happens only if you have a connection to the Internet through this computer. If no such connection exists, you will see the Connect To The Internet Wizard.)

7. The next part of the process involves the Copying Installation Files screen. During this part of the installation, Setup copies all of the installation files to the hard drive. The system restarts and Setup continues.

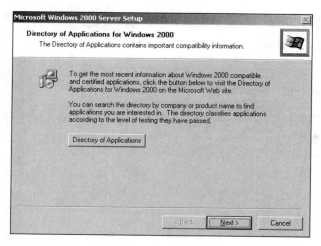

Figure 4.23
You can view the Directory of Applications.

8. You may see a screen that lists incompatible hardware or software currently on the machine. If so, you will need to decide if you want to continue with the installation or abort it. The Windows 2000 Setup screen reports system compatibility. If this screen is shown, the hardware or software may not work properly once Windows 2000 Server is installed.

Tip: *If you used the **/checkupgradeonly** switch of the **winnt32** command before installation, then you are already aware of any problems. In addition, inconsistencies should have already been uncovered by someone on the planning committee.*

9. The Setup program searches for previous versions of Windows, checks the drive for errors, and begins deleting and copying the necessary files. During this time, you may see an error message stating that there isn't enough room on the hard drive to save the files or that the BIOS isn't compatible. If there isn't enough room on the hard drive to save the installation files, you probably should rethink your planning and installation strategy for this computer. If the BIOS isn't compatible, you may want to contact the person responsible for checking this computer and verifying that it was ready for the upgrade. Either way, you'll have to fix these problems before the installation can be carried out.

10. Setup initializes. The system restarts. This is only one of two necessary reboots during an upgrade.

11. If the file system needs to be converted from FAT to NTFS, that conversion takes place now. Figure 4.24 shows what this process looks like. The black screen shows the progress of the conversion.

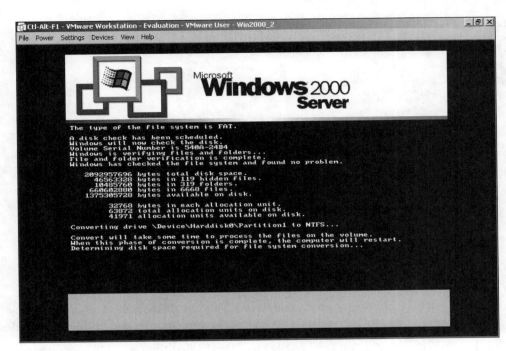

Figure 4.24
Conversion from FAT to NTFS.

12. After a successful conversion, the system starts Windows and begins installing devices. Devices can be keyboards, mice, or items used on the computer. This part of the process is similar to a clean installation, except that less user input is required because the existing computer and user settings will be retained.

13. Windows 2000 Server Upgrade begins configuring network settings. For an upgrade, these settings may be the same as for the previous installation and will not need to be changed. Depending on the current configuration, you may be asked for additional information, or network settings configuration may simply finish and installation will continue.Be sure to have current TCP/IP configuration information on hand just in case.

14. Setup again begins copying files and installing components. Components can include Internet Information Services, Indexing Service, Other Network File And Print Services, Remote Installation Services, Terminal Services, Windows Media Services, and any other applicable components that were used in the previous operating system setup.

15. The Setup program begins completing its final tasks, including installing Start menu items, registering components, saving settings, and removing temporary files.

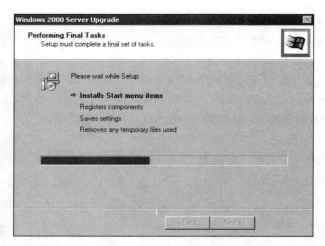

Figure 4.25
Final tasks.

Figure 4.25 shows the applicable screen. This could take quite a bit of time—anywhere from 3 to 30 minutes—depending on the computer and installed components.

16. The computer restarts and finally boots for the first time as a Windows 2000 server.

Notice that there were no screens for changing regional settings, changing the date and time, joining domains or workgroups, or configuring services. This is understandable because an upgrade is being performed and not a clean installation. The upgrade uses the information regarding domains, workgroups, date, time, user settings, and the like when it is installing. Upgrades are faster than clean installations for this reason.

Reinstalling Windows 2000 Server

There will be instances when you cannot repair a Windows 2000 server or domain controller and the only option is to reinstall. This is a last-ditch effort, however, and should be done only if all other avenues and troubleshooting methods have been exhausted. Reinstalling Windows 2000 Server is exactly like installing a copy of Windows 2000 Server for the first time.

Tip: Before reinstalling, look at the appendixes for other troubleshooting options.

There are three types of reinstallations. Either the computer is a standalone server and not a member of any domain, is a member server and belongs to a domain, or is a domain controller in a domain. To reinstall a standalone server that is *not* a member of any domain, simply follow the directions discussed earlier for installing Windows 2000 Server.

4

If you need to reinstall Windows 2000 Server on a computer that is a member of a domain but is not a domain controller, certain precautions need to be taken before the reinstallation. To reinstall Windows 2000 Server in this scenario, follow these steps:

1. First log in as a domain administrator, and delete the computer account for this computer. This can be done through Start|Programs|Administrative Tools|Active Directory Users And Computers. Double-click on Domain Controllers; then highlight the computer in question and either right-click and choose Delete, or choose Action| Delete. See Figure 4.26.

2. Create a new account for the computer. This is achieved through Start|Programs| Administrative Tools|Active Directory Users And Computers. Highlight Domain Controllers, and from the Action menu, choose New|Computer. You will see the dialog box shown in Figure 4.27.

   Once the new account is created, you will see it in the Active Directory Users And Computers screen immediately.

   This action must be taken because the computer account is used to identify the computer on the network, and a password is assigned to it. (This is not the

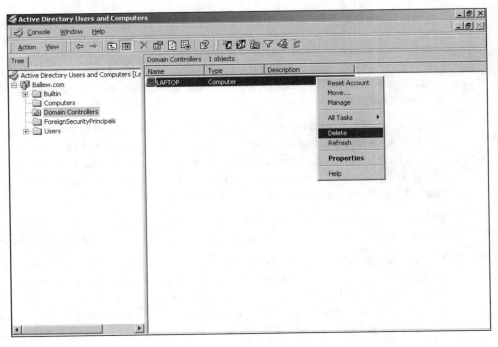

Figure 4.26
Deleting a computer account.

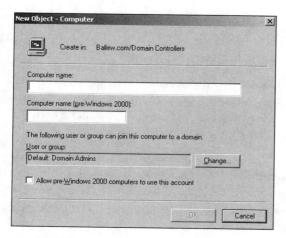

Figure 4.27
Creating a computer account.

administrator's password; this is a computer account password that users never see.)
The password is changed occasionally to ensure that it is secure, and this password is
used to authenticate a computer when it logs on to the network. The computer
password makes sure that the computer is really who it says it is, and not an imitator.
If you do not delete the computer account that belongs to this computer, then after
Windows 2000 Server has been reinstalled on it, the computer account password for
the new installation will not match the computer account password for the domain
controller. You will not be able to log on to the domain because the domain controller on the network will think that this computer is an impostor.

3. Place the Windows Server CD-ROM into the CD-ROM drive and begin the installation.
   The first screen you will see will be the upgrade screen. Setup notices that you
   already have something installed on the machine and suggests that you upgrade to
   Windows 2000 Server instead of performing a clean installation. For this scenario, I'd
   suggest the default option, Upgrade To Windows 2000.

4. The next screen is the licensing screen that you should already be familiar with.
   Accept the agreement by placing a dot in the button to accept and choosing Next.

5. The next screen, shown earlier in the chapter, enables you to view the Directory of
   Applications for Windows 2000, and it asks if you'd like to get the most recent
   information about Windows 2000 compatible and certified applications. If you want
   to do that, click on the Directory Of Applications button; if you don't, choose Next. If
   you click on the Directory Of Applications button, you will be automatically logged
   on to the Internet and will be taken to the appropriate Microsoft Web site. If you do
   not have a current connection to the Internet, the Connect To The Internet Wizard

appears. (Of course, this happens only if you have a modem or other connection device in the computer.)

6. The next screen is the Copying Installation Files screen. Wait for the files to be copied, and the installation will continue on its own.

7. From here, the installation is similar to the installation described earlier for upgrading a Windows NT 4 Server to Windows 2000 Server.

8. After the files have been copied to the hard drive, the system restarts and Setup continues.

9. Because this is a reinstallation of Windows 2000 Server, you should not see a screen that lists incompatible hardware or software currently on the machine. The first time Windows was installed, these problems, if any, should have been corrected. If there is still any incompatibility, the Windows 2000 Setup screen will report it. If this screen is shown, the hardware or software may not work properly once Windows 2000 Server is installed.

Tip: *If you used the **/checkupgradeonly** switch of the **winnt32** command before installation, then you are already aware of any problems.*

10. The Setup program continues the installation in a manner similar to an upgrade, copying files, initializing setup, installing devices, configuring network settings, and so on.

11. The Setup program completes its final tasks, including installing Start menu items, registering components, saving settings, and removing temporary files. This part of the installation should take less time the second time around than it did the first.

Notice that there were no screens for changing regional settings, changing date and time, joining domains or workgroups, or configuring services. This is understandable because you are performing a reinstallation of the operating system and not a clean installation. The reinstallation is very similar to an upgrade in this regard, using the information regarding domains, workgroups, date, time, user settings, and the like when it is installing. Reinstallations are faster than clean installations for this reason.

If you need to reinstall Windows 2000 Server on a computer that is a member of a domain and is a domain controller, certain precautions need to be taken before the reinstallation. To reinstall Windows 2000 Server in this scenario, follow these steps:

1. When you're reinstalling a Windows 2000 server that is not only a member of a domain but also a domain controller, you must make sure that the data on the domain controller is backed up before starting any reinstallation. If the reinstallation is the result of a computer that won't boot or otherwise has had a fatal error, you will have to rely on your backup tapes for this.

2. If you have another domain controller on the network, some of the worry about reinstalling the domain controller is lessened. If this is the only domain controller on the network, it may be quite scary. You will need to begin by protecting the client's logon data.

   As with the previous scenario that described the computer account and password issues arising from reinstalling a member server in a domain, the same types of issues arise here. When a domain controller is reinstalled on the network, and even if it is given the same name it had before the installation, users on the network will not recognize it for the same reason that the member server couldn't be recognized in the earlier example. Windows 2000 uses security identifiers (SIDs) to verify that a computer is who it claims to be. The new domain controller will have a different SID than the last one, even if it is named the same. For this reason, the following steps must be performed so that users on the network will be able to locate the server after reinstallation.

3. The clients in the domain need to be moved to another domain, a fake domain, or a workgroup while the server is being reinstalled. From Active Directory Users And Computers, you can move the users to another workgroup or domain.

4. Reinstall the server, following the steps listed earlier.

5. Now make those clients members of the new domain.

When it comes to reinstalling domain controllers, a few other issues need to be addressed. One issue is the global catalog. If the server that is to be reinstalled is responsible for the global catalog, then some other domain controller will need to be responsible for it during the installation. In order for users to log on to the domain in a multidomain setup while this computer is offline, a computer that contains the global catalog must be available.

Preparing for an Unattended Installation

Besides manually installing Windows 2000 Server, you can install it in an automated fashion. I'll first address preparing for an unattended installation by creating an answer file and a uniqueness database file (UDF), and then discuss how those unattended installations can be carried out using the **winnt** and **winnt32** commands. Following that, I'll discuss other automated installations that may or may not be unattended, including bootable CD-ROM installations and Systems Management Server. Finally, I'll discuss using Sysprep (the System Preparation tool) for disk cloning, including creating an image, installing applications, and running Sysprep.

Unattended installations are used when Windows 2000 Server needs to be installed on similar servers and the installation needs to be done with little or no user intervention. If the unattended installation—including the answer file, the UDF, and the distribution folders—is configured correctly, the installation can be performed without a single keystroke from the client after installation has begun.

The answer file plays a big role in the unattended installation, providing the answers to the questions normally asked of the client. The answer file holds information such as user name, computer name, time zone, platform, user interaction level, and administrator password. Because the syntax required in the answer file is, well, syntax, a wizard is available for creating the answer file. The answer file usually has a .txt extension. An answer file can be configured to point to a specific distribution folder that holds the I386 files and related information, or it can be configured to point to a CD-ROM drive. If the installation answer file is to be used with a CD-ROM, the file name must be winnt.sif.

Note: *If you prefer, you can create the answer file from scratch by using Notepad, or you can modify the sample answer file located on the installation CD-ROM. To me, that seems a little unnecessary for a simple answer file, and I prefer the Setup Manager Wizard.*

UDFs are used when more than one computer is to be installed and machine-specific information needs to be entered. This data might be multiple user names or computer names, and it is used with the answer file to provide the ability to install more than one machine at a time. The UDF has a .udf extension.

Distribution folders are created so that a machine will have access to the installation files, necessary drivers, and other files associated with a network installation. The distribution folder also should contain any OEM files, mass storage device drivers and HALs, System 32 files, and any miscellaneous files necessary for a proper installation of the operating system.

The easiest way to create the answer file and the UDF, and to point to a distribution folder, is to begin with the Setup Manager Wizard. The Setup Manager Wizard is not installed by default on your Windows 2000 server, so it must be extracted from the Windows 2000 Server CD-ROM.

To extract the Setup Manager Wizard from the Windows 2000 Server CD-ROM, follow these steps:

1. Use Windows Explorer to find C:\, the directory root, on the Windows 2000 server that will be used for creating the answer files. Create a folder named Deploy.

2. Use Windows Explorer to locate the \Support\Tools folder on the Windows 2000 Server CD-ROM. This folder will contain the files 2000rkst, deploy, setup, sreadme, and support. Select the Deploy folder.

3. The Deploy folder contains 7 files. Select all of them and choose to extract the files. (These files can be opened with an unzip utility as well.)

4. Browse to the C:\Program Files\Deploy folder created in Step 1, and choose Extract or OK. Close out the CD-ROM and all of the open windows.

5. Browse to the new folder and make sure all files are available.

Congratulations. You have successfully extracted the tools required for running the Setup Manager Wizard for creating answer files and perhaps even the Sysprep utility that you will use if you need to create a disk image in the next section.

Now you are ready to create an answer file for your first unattended installation. The Setup Manager Wizard can be used to create answer files not only for fully unattended installations but also for partially unattended installations. Determine the type of installation you need to provide, and then continue with the following steps:

1. Start the Setup Manager Wizard by clicking on the Setupmgr icon in the Deploy folder under Program Files.

2. The Setup Manager Wizard starts. Notice the information on the Welcome screen. The Setup Manager Wizard helps you to create an answer file and a distribution folder so that automatic installations can be performed on the network. The automatic installations can take on many forms, as will be discussed later.

3. The next screen asks what kind of answer file you'd like to create. There are three options: Create A New Answer File, Create An Answer File That Duplicates This Computer's Configuration, and Modify An Existing Answer File. If you are creating a new answer file, accept the defaults and choose Next. See Figure 4.28.

4. The Product To Install screen is next. Here you can choose to create an answer file for a Windows 2000 Server unattended installation, a Sysprep installation (cloning), or a Remote Installation Services (RIS) installation. (RIS installations are used to install only Windows 2000 Professional, not Windows 2000 Server, and are not addressed in this book. Sysprep will be discussed in the next section.) Choose Windows 2000 Unattended Installation and choose Next.

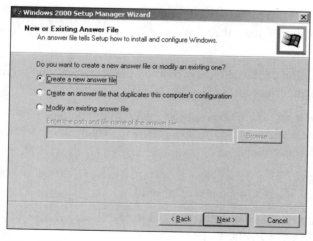

Figure 4.28
New or Existing Answer File.

4

5. Choose Windows 2000 Server (Windows 2000 Professional is the default) from the platform screen, and choose Next.

6. The next screen asks for input regarding the interaction level of the user. There are five choices:

   - *Provide Defaults*—Sets all of the answers to the default answers for installations, and prompts the user to review them. If the user wants, he or she can change any of the answers that are supplied.

   - *Fully Automated*—Does not ask the user for any input or allow the user to make any changes to the answers provided. This is the option you will pick for an unattended installation.

   - *Hide Pages*—Is used when some of the answers will be provided in an answer file; hides the pages for which all answers have been provided. Pages for which only some of the answers have been provided, or pages for which none of the answers have been provided, will be shown to the user. The user will be able to change the values on any of the pages he or she sees, even if those answers have been specified.

   - *Read Only*—Is used to display the pages that contain at least one missing value, and when you want the user to interact with Setup only to supply the answers to the unanswered questions. The user will not be able to change the settings for any other answers, even if they are on the same page as the one shown. (Choose this option if specific users need to input only their time zone and screen resolution, and nothing else.)

   - *GUI Attended*—Automates only the text-mode portion of Setup, and requires user input for all of the GUI-mode portion.

7. To continue using the Windows 2000 Setup Manager Wizard, you must accept the terms of the license agreement as documented in the Microsoft End User License Agreement.

8. The next screen is the Customize The Software screen, used to enter a computer name and an organization name. If you want the name and organization to be specified in the answer file, put that information here; if you leave it blank, these fields will not be specified in the answer file.

9. If you chose to create an answer file for Windows 2000 Server, you will see a licensing mode screen that asks if you want to configure the mode as Per Seat or Per Server. Make the appropriate selection and choose Next.

10. The Computer Names screen shown in Figure 4.29 allows you to type the names of the destination computers that will use this installation and answer file. When more than one computer is listed, a uniqueness database file is automatically created. You can also choose to allow the Windows 2000 Setup Manager Wizard to assign names based on the organization's name if you don't want to create the names yourself.

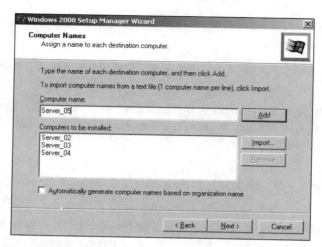

Figure 4.29
Assigning computer names.

11. The Administrator Password screen is next; this prompts you for password information for the target server. You can also configure the computer to automatically log on as Administrator when the computer boots up for any number of times you specify for up to the first 99 times. You may not want to do this if security is a high priority in your organization. Because all of the servers that are being installed using this answer file will have the same password, it may also be wise to visit these computers and change those passwords after the installation, or to at least send an email to the administrator at the site, reminding him to change it himself. You may even consider leaving the passwords blank initially to avoid confusion.

12. The Display Settings dialog box is next. This offers the opportunity to change the default settings for colors, screen area, and refresh frequency from the default of 16 colors, 640×480, and 60Hz to something more appropriate for your server. Be careful when changing the colors and screen area on a whim, however, because some of the target machines may not have a high-tech video card that can handle 32-bit color. Decide if changing these values is necessary, and then click on Next.

13. The Network Settings screen is offered next with two options: Typical Settings or Custom Settings. Choose Typical Settings if you want the machines to be configured as Microsoft Networking Clients and to have TCP/IP configured to use a DHCP server. Choose Custom Settings if you want to change these settings, configure the client with additional network adapters, or set properties for Client For Microsoft Networks, Other File And Printer Sharing for Microsoft Networks, or Internet Protocol TCP/IP. It is best to choose Custom Settings so that you can see what would be installed by default. If you decide to change any of these settings, that's fine, and if not, choose Next from each page shown.

4

14. In the Workgroup Or Domain screen, you can configure how the computer(s) who will use this answer file will participate on the network. If the target computer will join a workgroup, type the workgroup name and choose Next. If the target computer will join a domain, type the domain name and create a computer account in the domain, if necessary. Figure 4.30 shows how I will configure my answer file.

15. Choose the appropriate time zone in the Time Zone dialog box that is displayed, and click on Next. Remember, the time zone chosen is for the target computer.

16. At this point, you have created a basic answer file that can be used to install Windows 2000 Server. If you choose not to edit the additional settings, the Setup Manager Wizard skips the next seven screens and goes directly to creating the distribution folder. If you edit the additional settings, you can change telephony settings, regional settings, language settings, browser and shell settings, installation folder settings, printer installation settings, and commands to run settings. For the purpose of instruction, I will walk you through the editing process with the additional settings. If you choose not to do this, you can skip to Step 24.

17. You will see the seven screens discussed next only if you have chosen to edit the additional settings that will be applied to the answer file. The first screen is the Telephony screen, where you can enter the country and region where the target computer will be installed, the area code, and a number needed to access an outside line, and select tone or pulse dialing. If you leave these options blank, there will be no answer file key for this setting.

18. The Regional Settings screen is next. You can use the default regional settings for this computer, or you can specify new regional settings to be used in the answer file for the target computers. This option will come in handy if you are creating an answer file in your U.S. office for a server in the Italy office.

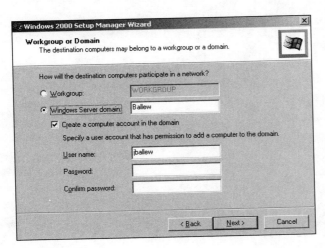

Figure 4.30
Choosing a workgroup or domain.

19. The Languages screen allows you to add languages for the target computer. After choosing the languages needed, click on Next.

20. The Browser And Shell Settings page, shown in Figure 4.31, offers choices regarding the Internet and browser setting for the target machines:

   • *Use Default Internet Explorer Settings*—Applies the default settings in the answer file.

   • *Use An Autoconfiguration Script Created By The Internet Explorer Administration Kit To Configure Your Browser*—Allows you to specify an installation (.ins) file and to use an autoconfig script.

   • *Individually Specify Proxy And Default Home Page Settings*—Allows you to set a proxy server and its address and port number, and/or specify a home page and favorites for the browser. Figure 4.31 shows the Browser And Shell Settings page, and Figure 4.32 shows the default home page for the configuration I am setting up.

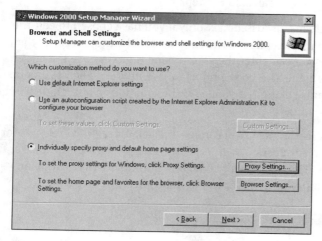

Figure 4.31
Browser and shell settings.

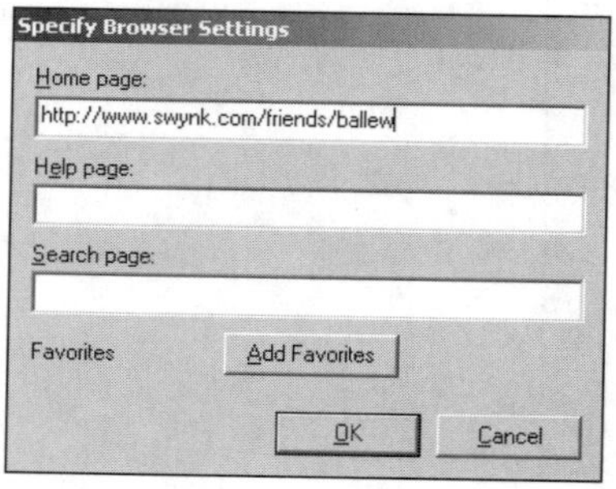

Figure 4.32
Home page settings.

4

21. The next page is the Installation Folder page. Here, you can accept the default installation folder, Winnt, or specify your own. You can also have Setup create a unique name for you.

22. The Install Printer screen is next. This allows you to specify a printer to which the target computer will connect after the installation is complete. The first time a user logs on, if the user has the right to install printers, the printers that are named here will be configured.

23. The Run Once page is next, and this is the final screen shown during this phase. If any commands need to be run after installation is complete—for instance, to install drivers or other software programs—those commands can be typed here. The commands can be listed and then moved up or down so they can be run in the proper order. Disk Defragmenter is a popular command. After you have filled in any necessary commands, click on Next. Figure 4.33 shows the Run Once screen.

24. After all of the additional settings have been configured, the next screen that appears is the Distribution Folder page. If you choose the option Yes, Create Or Modify A Distribution Folder, other screens will follow for configuring such a folder. If you choose No, This Answer File Will Be Used To Install From A CD-ROM, then some of the screens described next will not be shown. In this example, a distribution folder needs to be created because of the language files I have chosen. If a distribution folder is needed for your particular installation, and you choose this option, a warning will be shown.

25. On the Distribution Folder Name page, displayed next, you can create a new distribution folder or modify an existing one. You can also specify how the share name will look to clients. I have changed the default name to the distribution folder that suits my needs and have renamed the distribution folder D:\Distribution2.

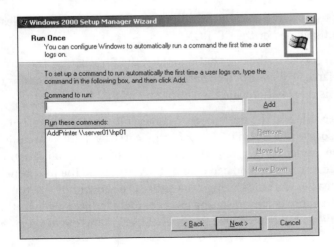

Figure 4.33
The Run Once screen.

26. The next two screens ask for information regarding mass storage drivers and new Hardware Abstraction Layers. In the Additional Mass Storage Drivers screen, you can specify additional drivers that would normally be installed by using the F6 key at the beginning of the installation. The HAL screen can be used to specify a new HAL to replace the old one on a target machine.

27. If you need to run additional commands at the end of Setup, you can specify those commands on the Additional Commands screen, shown next. The commands will run after installation is complete, but before any user logs on, so make sure these commands can run under these circumstances.

28. The OEM branding screen is shown next. This offers a place for an organization to enter a path to a log or background to run while Windows 2000 Server is setting up and installing. The background must be 16 colors and 640×480 resolution.

29. Using the Additional Files And Folders screen, shown next, you can add additional files and folders to be copied to the target computers during the installation. By choosing Add Files, you can choose data, programs, and any other files that need to be placed on the target computers during installation.

30. You're almost finished. The next screen tells you that the answer file was successfully created; this screen also offers a default name and location for the unattend.txt file that will be used. You can accept this name or type a new one. The Setup Manager Wizard also states that a .udf file may have been created, or there might be a .bat script to help with the installation. Click on Next.

31. The Setup Manager Wizard is now ready to copy the Windows 2000 Server Setup files to the distribution folder that was specified earlier. You will need to select the location of the setup files by choosing either Copy From The CD-ROM or Copy The Files From This Location. My files are on the CD-ROM, so I will accept the defaults.

32. The next screen shows the progress associated with the copying of the needed files from either the location specified or the CD-ROM.

33. After the files have been copied to the distribution folder, the Completing The Windows 2000 Setup Manager Wizard screen appears, summarizing the locations of the files. Write down this information, and then click on Finish.

Now take a look at the answer file and the uniqueness database files that were created on my computer during this process (see Listing 4.3 and Listing 4.4). If you look carefully, you can see that some of the header names are the same as some of the configuration changes that were made. Because of this, you can change the answer file the next time you want to create one, instead of working through the entire process with the Setup Manager Wizard. Some of the more common setting changes include specifying whether to install Windows 2000 Server or Windows 2000 Professional, changing the destination computer name, changing the product ID, changing the names of workgroups or domains, and changing network configurations such as TCP/IP addressing or network adapter information.

Listing 4.3   Sample of an unattend.txt file.

```
;SetupMgrTag
[Data]
    AutoPartition=1
    MsDosInitiated="0"
    UnattendedInstall="Yes"

[Unattended]
    UnattendMode=FullUnattended
    OemSkipEula=Yes
    OemPreinstall=Yes
    TargetPath=\WINNT

[GuiUnattended]
    AdminPassword=*
    OEMSkipRegional=1
    TimeZone=20
    OemSkipWelcome=1

[UserData]
    FullName=User_Name
    OrgName=Organization_Name
    ComputerName=*

[Display]
    BitsPerPel=4
    Xresolution=640
    YResolution=480
    Vrefresh=60

[LicenseFilePrintData]
    AutoMode=PerServer
    AutoUsers=5

[TapiLocation]
    CountryCode=1
    Dialing=Tone
    AreaCode=972

[RegionalSettings]
    LanguageGroup=1
    Language=00000409
```

```
[SetupMgr]
    ComputerName0=Server_02
    ComputerName1=Server_03
    ComputerName2=Server_04
    ComputerName3=Server_05
    DistFolder=D:\Distribution3
    DistShare=win2000dist2

[Branding]
    BrandIEUsingUnattended=Yes

[URL]
    Home_Page=http://www.swynk.com/friends/ballew

[Proxy]
    Proxy_Enable=0
    Use_Same_Proxy=1

[GuiRunOnce]
    Command0="rundll32 printui.dll,PrintUIEntry /in /n \\server01\hp01"

[Identification]
    JoinDomain=Ballew
    DomainAdmin=jballew

[Networking]
    InstallDefaultComponents=No

[NetAdapters]
    Adapter1=params.Adapter1

[params.Adapter1]
    INFID=*

[NetClients]
    MS_MSClient=params.MS_MSClient

[NetServices]
    MS_SERVER=params.MS_SERVER

[NetProtocols]
    MS_TCPIP=params.MS_TCPIP

[params.MS_TCPIP]
    DNS=Yes
    UseDomainNameDevolution=No
    EnableLMHosts=Yes
    AdapterSections=params.MS_TCPIP.Adapter1
```

4

```
[params.MS_TCPIP.Adapter1]
    SpecificTo=Adapter1
    DHCP=Yes
    WINS=No
    NetBIOSOptions=0
```

Perhaps you can tell from this example that many very specific changes can be made in this file so that it can be used again in another circumstance. In addition, the file can be edited in Notepad, and the file can be created from scratch by a seasoned administrator. Listing 4.4 shows a sample UDF.

Listing 4.4   Sample uniqueness database file.

```
;SetupMgrTag
[UniqueIds]
    Server_02=UserData
    Server_03=UserData
    Server_04=UserData
    Server_05=UserData

[Server_02:UserData]
    ComputerName=Server_02

[Server_03:UserData]
    ComputerName=Server_03

[Server_04:UserData]
    ComputerName=Server_04

[Server_05:UserData]
    ComputerName=Server_05
```

You can see that the UDF looks like you'd expect it to, with the names of the computers listed in the different sections. To read additional information on the subject of manually editing an answer file, or to obtain more information on UDFs, look for the Unattend.doc file and the Readme.txt file in the Deploy.cab folder. There are literally hundreds of parameters that can be set. Some of the parameters are obvious, such as computer name or time zone, and some are a bit more obscure. Table 4.4 lists some of the more obscure parameters that can be set by editing the answer file manually.

Many more parameters can be set in the answer file. The important thing isn't to know what all these parameters are and to use them in every answer file; you just need to be aware that they exist and are available if you need them.

Now that the answer file and the UDFs have been created, you can begin the unattended installation. There are two ways to perform an unattended installation of Windows 2000

Table 4.4   Examples of answer file parameters.

Answer File Parameters	Values	Notes
DriverSigningPolicy	Ignore|Warn|Block	Default is Warn; specifies how signed drivers are processed during setup.
FileSystem	ConvertNTFS|LeaveAlone	Specifies whether or not the partition should be upgraded.
Repartition	Yes|No	Specifies whether the partitions on the first drive should be deleted and reformatted as NTFS.
AutoLogon	Yes|No	Specifies whether the administrator can automatically log on after the installation is complete.
ProfilesDir	Path to the profile folder is the value	Specifies the location of Windows 2000 profiles.
Boot16	Yes|No	Enables MS-DOS boot mode; the default is no.
MigrateDefaultUser	Yes|No	Moves user information from Windows 9X clients to the new account.
FreeCell	On|Off (default is On)	Installs FreeCell.

Server. The first is to use **winnt /u:*answer file***, and the second is to use **winnt32 /unattend:*answerfile***. The answer file is the file created by the Setup Manager Wizard as described in this section. The next section will guide you through such an installation and describe the important points along the way.

Using **Winnt** and **Winnt32** to Perform an Unattended Installation

To perform an unattended installation of Windows 2000 Server, you need to use one of two commands. For machines that currently run Windows 3.x or MS-DOS, use the **winnt.exe** command followed by the appropriate switches. For machines that run Windows 9x or Windows NT, use the **winnt32.exe** command and the appropriate switches. Unattended installations do not use the Setup icon that is used to begin an attended installation of Windows 2000 Server.

Table 4.5 shows switches that can be used with **Winnt.exe**.

*Tip: The most common syntax used with **winnt** is: winnt [/s:sourcepath] [/t:drive] [/u:answer_file].*

Table 4.6 shows the switches available for use with the **Winnt32.exe** command.

*Tip: The most common syntax used with **winnt32** command is: winnt32 [/s:sourcepath] [/tempdrive: drive] [/unattend [num]:answer_file].*

For both the **Winnt** and **Winnt32** commands, the **/udf:id[,*UDF_file*]** switch must be used if an automated installation of Windows 2000 Server will also incorporate a UDF along with the answer file. For example, to use a UDF with a Winnt32 installation, you could

Table 4.5 Switches for Winnt.exe.

Switch	Purpose
/s[:sourcepath]	States the location of the Windows 2000 installation files.
/t[:tempdrive]	Creates temporary files when Windows 2000 is installing. This switch is used to state where those temporary files should be stored and where Windows 2000 will be installed.
/u[:answer file]	Used when an unattended setup will be employed, and requires the /s switch to point to the source files for installation. The answer file is needed to input the information that a user would normally enter during the installation.
/udf:id[,UDF_file]	UDF information overrides information in an answer file.
/r[:folder]	Used to specify additional folders to be installed with the installation folder. After installation is complete, the folder remains on the client hard drive.
/rx[:folder]	Used to specify additional folders that need to be copied during the installation.
/e	Tells Setup to execute a command when the GUI-mode portion of Setup is complete.
/a	Used to enable Accessibility options.

Table 4.6 Switches for Winnt32.exe.

Switch	Purpose
/s:sourcepath	Specifies where the installation files are located. This switch can be used to specify multiple servers from which to copy files.
/tempdrive:drive letter	Creates temporary files when Windows 2000 is installing. This switch is used to state where those temporary files should be stored and where Windows 2000 will be installed.
/Unattend or /u	Used when performing unattended installations that are upgrades. User settings are saved, and no client involvement is needed during the installation.
/unattend[num][:answer_file]	Used for clean installations. The answer file is needed to enter the information that a user would normally type during the installation. The num value is the number of seconds after installation is completed that the computer is rebooted.
/copydir:folder_name	Used to create additional folders within the folders where Windows 2000 Server is being installed. For instance, if a folder called Private_apps is in the source folder, it can be copied along with the installation files to the target computer by including the switch /copydir: Private_apps.
/copysource:folder_name	Used to create additional temporary folders within the folders where Windows 2000 Server is being installed. For instance, if a folder called Private_apps is in the source folder, it can be copied along with the installation files to the target computer by including the switch /copyfolder:Private_apps. This is essentially the same command as copydir, except that /copysource folders are deleted when Setup finishes running.
/cmd:command_line	Used to run a specific command before Setup completes the installation of Windows 2000 Server. During setup, the computer reboots three times. This command switch allows a command to be run from the command line after the second reboot but before a complete installation.

(continued)

Table 4.6 Switches for Winnt32.exe *(continued).*

Switch	Purpose
/debug[level][:filename]	Used to create a debug log file of the Windows 2000 Server installation. By default, a debug log file is saved to %systemroot%\Winnt32.log, and it includes warnings and errors. To change the location of the log file or the information it records, change the parameters with this syntax: /debug4:c:\debuglog. In this example, the log will be saved to the file debuglog, and it will record not only errors and warnings but also detailed information about the errors. The levels are 1:warnings, 2:errors, 3:information, and 4:detailed information.
/udf:id[,UDF_file]	Used as an identifier by Setup to specify how a uniqueness database file will alter an answer file. The UDF overrides any value in the generic answer file, and the id identifies which values are to be used for a specific installation.
/syspart:drive_letter	Used if the computer currently runs Windows NT 3.51, Windows NT 4, or Windows 2000. Must always be combined with the /tempdrive parameter. The /syspart switch tells Setup that it can copy the startup files to a hard drive, make the disk active, and then install the disk into a different computer. When that computer boots, it continues with the next stage of setup. The /syspart switch is used when the source and reference computers do not have similar hardware, eliminating the file-copy phase from the target computer task list.
/checkupgradeonly	Used to check a system for compatibility with Windows 2000 Server. The file is saved in the Winnt32.log file for Windows NT Server 3.51 or higher, and in the Upgrade.txt files for Windows 9x machines.
/cmdcons	Used to install the Recovery Console during installation. Once the Recovery Console is installed, an entry is placed in the boot.ini file, and the Recovery Console becomes an option when the system is booted.
/m:folder_name	Instructs the Setup program to look in a different area first for the setup files and, if found, to install the operating system from there. If they are not found at this location, the default location will be used.
/makelocalsource	Copies the installation files to the hard drive permanently. Might be used when the installation files will be needed later and the CD-ROM is not available to the client.
/noreboot	Causes the computer to wait for an administrator to reboot the computer after the first part of the installation process. This may be necessary if a command needs to be run at that time.

use the following syntax: **winnt32 /unattend:***unattend.txt***/udf:server02,unattend.udf**. If only the uniqueness ID is specified on the command line, the UDF will need to be placed on a floppy disk and given to the client to insert when prompted. Otherwise, the UDF can be obtained from the network share. In other circumstances, a batch file can be created to start the installation and to use the answer file and .udf file created earlier. I will demonstrate using the answer file on a floppy disk along with the CD-ROM in a later section.

When both an answer file and a UDF are used, the UDF overrides the key values in the answer file. Table 4.7 illustrates the different combinations of UDFs and answer files that can occur, along with the outcomes of such scenarios.

In addition to answer files and UDFs, other methods can be used for automating installations, and many people may find these other options a little simpler to deploy and control. The syntax required in the command lines, the distribution folder creation, and the

Table 4.7 **Answer file and UDF file outcomes.**

UDF Key Specified	Answer File Key Specified	Key Used
No	Yes	Answer file
Yes	No	UDF
Yes	Yes	UDF
Specified with no value	No	User may be prompted

creation of answer files and UDFs may be a little more than some administrators bargained for. If this particular type of installation doesn't work for your specific needs, there are other ways to install remote machines.

The next section will focus on some of these other options, including using a CD-ROM and answer file for unattended installations, using Systems Management Server, and using Sysprep for an unattended installation that uses an image of a computer (also called *cloning*, *ghosting*, or *disk duplicating*).

Other Options for Automated Installations

This section covers two types of automated installations: the bootable CD-ROM installation and the Systems Management Server (SMS) installation. One of the easiest ways, in my opinion, to learn how the answer file works or to test an answer file is to use the answer file with a CD-ROM installation.

The bootable CD-ROM installation method can be used if the following conditions are met:

- The computer's BIOS allows the computer to boot from the CD-ROM drive and supports the El Torito Bootable CD-ROM format (no emulation mode).

- The installation is a clean installation, not an upgrade.

- The answer file contains a [Data] section.

- The answer file is named Winnt.sif, not unattend.txt or any other name.

- Winnt.sif is on a floppy disk.

- The computer's BIOS is set to boot in this order: network adapter, CD-ROM, HDD, floppy disk.

- No UDF is needed.

When you are sure that the previous criteria have been met, you can install with this method. To install using a bootable CD-ROM and an answer file, perform the following steps:

1. Place the Windows 2000 Server CD-ROM into the CD-ROM drive, and reboot the computer.

2. The computer will boot from the CD-ROM.

3. When the Windows 2000 Setup screen is displayed, insert the floppy disk with the file winnt.sif into the floppy drive.

4. The floppy disk will be read. When that's done, remove the disk.

5. The Windows 2000 Setup program will continue and will use the answers in the winnt.sif file for the answers to setup questions.

The installation may require input from the user, depending on what type of answer file was created. Remember, there were five options to choose from when creating the answer file. The first option, Provide Defaults, prompts the user to review the answers and allows the user to change any of the supplied answers. The second, Fully Automated, does not ask the user for any input or allow the user to change the answers provided. The third option, Hide Pages, is used when some of the answers will be provided in an answer file, but you want to hide the pages for which all answers have been provided. This option allows the user to change the values on any of the pages shown, even if some of the answers on that page have been specified. The fourth option, Read Only, is used to display the pages that contain at least one missing value and when you want the user to interact with Setup only to supply the answers to the unanswered questions. The user will not be able to change the settings for any other answers, even if they are on the same page as the one shown. The last option, GUI Attended, automates only the text-mode portion of setup and requires user input for all of the GUI-mode portion. Therefore, the bootable CD-ROM method can be used for various types of attended or unattended installations.

Another method for automating installations is to use Microsoft's Systems Management Server. SMS can be used to automate many tasks usually associated with network administration. Some of these tasks include keeping track of hardware and software inventory, installing and distributing software, creating organizational reports, and uncovering network problems by using available network diagnostic tools.

Using the utilities available in SMS, an organization can streamline installations and distributions of software and operating systems from a central location for clients who are geographically dispersed across great physical distances. SMS can also be used to automate unattended operating system installations. Using SMS, an administrator can create *packages*, or collections, to distribute operating system upgrades or software installations. These packages can be deployed via Web sites, networks, or disks, and can be used with systems as diverse as Windows NT, Windows 2000, Windows 9x, and Windows 3x.

For SMS to work for your organization, the following must be true:

- Clients must be running Windows NT, Windows 2000, Windows 9x, or Windows 3x.

- Clients must be running the SMS client agent.

- Enough bandwidth must be available to support network installation.

- Clients must need only an upgrade and not a clean installation.

- Hardware must be on the new OS's HCL.

- A Systems Management Server must be in use on the network.

Using Sysprep to Perform an Automated Installation

It is often necessary to install Windows 2000 Server on multiple computers that have identical hardware and configuration requirements. Perhaps you purchased some identical computers and want to install Windows 2000 Server on all of them as quickly as possible. To facilitate this installation, you can use the Sysprep tool available with Windows 2000 Server. The Sysprep tool is not installed by default when Windows 2000 Server is installed, but it can be installed from the CD-ROM under Support\Tools. If you participated in the section on creating unattended answer files, then those tools are already available to you. If you did not participate in that exercise, you can obtain these tools by performing the steps listed next.

Warning! Sysprep.exe supports only Windows 2000 Professional and Windows 2000 Server. The server needs to be configured as a standalone server. Sysprep can be used only for clean installations, not for upgrades.

To extract the Sysprep tool from the Windows 2000 Server CD-ROM, follow these steps:

1. Use Windows Explorer to create a new folder called Sysprep in the root directory on the Windows 2000 Server machine.

2. Locate the \Support\Tools folder on the Windows 2000 Server CD-ROM. This folder will contain the files 2000rkst, deploy, setup, sreadme, and support. Choose the Deploy folder.

3. The Deploy folder contains seven files. Select sysprep.exe and setupcl.exe, and extract the files. (You can also select all of the files and extract them if necessary.)

4. Save the file to the Sysprep folder created earlier. Close out the CD-ROM and all of the open windows.

5. Browse to the new folder and make sure all files are available.

The Sysprep utility can be used to prepare a hard disk for a disk image of the Windows 2000 Server installation for multiple computers that have identical or similar hardware configurations. Similar hardware configurations include having the same mass storage devices and HALs. In addition to preparing an image of a Windows 2000 Server installation, Sysprep can also be used to include applications, desktop settings, or other user-specific configuration options. In this section, I will walk you through the process of creating a Sysprep image. This process includes preparing a reference computer, running the Sysprep tool, using a third-party tool to create an image, testing the image, and deploying the image to new or existing machines in the organization.

The first step in using Sysprep for creating disk images on a computer is to prepare the reference computer for replication. This computer will be used to create the images to be deployed on the other computers, and it will contain the operating system, applications, and user settings. To configure a reference computer, perform the following steps:

1. Install Windows 2000 Server on a clean computer, one whose hard disk has been formatted before the installation. Leave the administrator password blank and join a domain during this installation.

2. Log on as Administrator, and configure the settings that will be used for all of the computers to be cloned. These settings include desktop appearance, installation of drivers, and installation of necessary applications. Remember that any changes made to this image will be copied to other computers, so do not make changes that will not be useful to the other servers.

3. Install applications that will be used by the other servers. Do not install unnecessary applications (those that will not be used by all servers that are being installed).

4. Test all of the applications and settings that have been installed and configured. Consider how awful a deployment of 1,000 Windows 2000 servers would be if the Microsoft Office installation were not tested before image deployment, and all 1,000 servers had to have Office reinstalled! After an image has been copied to other media, it cannot be changed.

Warning! When you create an image and modify the desktop when you're logged on as an administrator, then the desktop settings will apply only to users who log on to the machine as administrators. To make sure that all users who log on to this computer receive the same desktop settings, copy the administrator profile to the default profile before copying the image.

You can further prepare the image for deployment by creating an answer file for the users who will install this image. To create this answer file, run the Setup Manager Wizard as described in the section "Preparing for an Unattended Installation," but instead of choosing Windows Unattended Installation in Step 4 in that section, choose Sysprep Install. The Setup Manager Wizard will walk you through a process similar to the one described earlier, and an answer file will be created.

Creating the answer file for a disk duplication is similar to creating the answer file for the unattended installation described earlier. The answer file for a disk duplication can be configured to fully automate the installation of the image or to allow user input. You can also edit this file in the same way you edit the unattend.txt file—by using Notepad or by running the Setup Manager Wizard again. In this instance, however, the answer file must be named sysprep.inf and must be stored in the Sysprep folder on the system partition (the Sysprep folder created earlier). If the sysprep.inf file is located here, it will be used; if it isn't placed here, no answer file will be used during the installation.

The second step in using Sysprep to create an image involves running the Sysprep utility. To run the Sysprep utility, follow these steps:

1. Restart the computer and log on as administrator. This ensures that all settings have been saved to the Registry and that the computer doesn't have any unnecessary programs running.

2. Use Windows Explorer to locate the Sysprep folder in the root directory; then double-click on the Sysprep icon. Alternatively, to use the switches listed next, run Sysprep from the command line.

   The following switches are available from the command line:

   - **-quiet**—Instructs Sysprep to run without displaying any messages on the screen. If the **–quiet** switch is used, you will not see the warning that the utility might modify some of the system's security settings.

   - **-pnp**—Instructs Sysprep to detect devices the next time the computer restarts. This switch works well if the target computers have the same mass storage devices and HALs but have dissimilar plug-and-play devices, such as network adapters, modems, or sound and video cards.

   - **-reboot**—Instructs Sysprep to restart the computer automatically after the image has been installed to the hard drive and then to start the Mini-Setup Wizard described later.

   - **-nosidgen**—Runs Sysprep without generating a SID.

   When Sysprep has started, a warning will appear that states, "Please note that the execution of this application may modify some of the security parameters of the system. Please press Cancel unless you are preparing this installation for duplication. After running this application, your computer will automatically shut down."

Warning! *This is serious business. If you run Sysprep on a computer that has a myriad of personal settings, they'll all be removed and the system will shut down automatically. This is why it is best to run Sysprep on a newly installed system, where there are no important settings to be lost.*

3. When Sysprep is finished running, the system is shut down and is ready to be imaged. If the hard disk were to be physically cloned, the hard disk would be removed and physically copied. Other cloning techniques include using any compatible third-party cloning tool, such as Symantic Ghost or PowerQuest Drive Image Pro. Follow the manufacturer's instructions for completing this step.

4. After the computer is cloned and restarted, the Mini-Setup Wizard starts. The first screen shown is the license screen. To continue, read the license information and choose Next.

Creating an Image

Because the actual creation of the image will be done by a third-party tool, I can't walk you through this step. Generally, though, to create an image for installation, you'll do the following.

- Read any pamphlets, instructions, or readme files that were shipped with the third-party disk imaging utility.

- If the third-party application came with a floppy disk for the reference computer, you will most likely need to insert the floppy disk into the floppy disk drive and restart the computer.

- Follow the on-screen instructions to create the image.

- Use the image on a new or existing computer, and test the operating system and its applications and/or user settings.

- If the image test is successful, then copy the image to a compact disk, network share, or Web site for access by clients.

Note: If an answer file is used, only the pages that need answers will be shown to the user. I will list all possible screens here.

5. The next screen is the Regional Settings screen. Make the appropriate choices and choose Next.

6. The next screen is the Personalize Your Software screen. Fill in the name and organization parameters, and choose Next.

7. The next screen is the licensing mode screen. Make the appropriate choices and choose Next. This isn't the same screen that asks you to agree to the licensing terms; instead, this screen asks if you want to configure the answer file to choose Per Seat or Per Server for the target computers. (These licensing modes were explained earlier, in the sidebar called "Licensing Mode Options.")

8. The next screen is the Computer Name And Administrator Password page shown earlier in this chapter. The name of the computer must be unique, and the password should be complex. Make sure you write down or remember the password so you can log on later. Confirm the password and choose Next.

9. Configure the date and time, the networking settings, and the workgroup or computer domain names, and then choose Finish. Some of these settings may occur automatically. The computer will restart.

Before deploying this image to hundreds or thousands of networked computers, fully test the image of the first computer cloned. It would be best to test everything installed on this first (test) computer. The following list reviews a few of the items that should definitely be considered:

4

- Verify that the operating system starts successfully with no service warnings or display problems.

- Verify that all applications work properly. For programs with multiple applications, such as Microsoft Office, test all components. These components may include Excel, PowerPoint, Access, and others, and must be fully tested from a client's point of view. For instance, does Excel still work properly with the company's database?

- Verify that Internet settings for the browsers are set appropriately.

- Verify that users can connect using all methods necessary, such as dial-up, VPN, or RAS.

- Run Chkdsk to make sure that there are no corrupt files, and run Disk Defragmenter.

- Verify that Device Manager sees all required hardware.

- Verify that all devices work properly, including the sound, video, and mass storage devices.

When you are positive that all of the applications work and that the image is ready for full-scale deployment, you can continue with the installations.

Deploying the image is the last step in using Sysprep for image duplication. The same disk duplicating or image creating software that was used to create the image can be used to deploy it. Deploying the image is also referred to as *restoring the image*.

To restore an image, follow these steps:

1. The destination computer needs to be started. The computer can be started in many ways, the first of which is similar to the bootable CD-ROM method described earlier. If the image created with a third-party tool was saved to a CD-ROM, that image can be used to boot a computer and begin the installation.

   The destination computer can also be started from a floppy disk. The floppy disk must contain either the driver files for the CD-ROM (so that the computer can use a CD-ROM that contains the image) or information that points to a distribution folder (on the network) containing the image. The second type of floppy disk may be a network client system disk or a script that runs a batch file for connecting to the share.

2. Once the destination computer has accessed the installation files, either on a share or from a CD-ROM, installation begins. This step may also require help from the third-party disk imaging application that was used previously.

3. The next time the destination computer is restarted, the Mini-Setup Wizard will gather the required information from either the user or an answer file and will complete the installation.

4. All previous information or data on the hard drive will be replaced with the new image because Sysprep can be used for only clean installations. The Sysprep folder will be removed.

Sysprep, although it has limits, is an extremely fast and powerful way to install multiple Windows 2000 machines. However, because of its limitations—requiring identical mass storage devices and HALs, among other things—it isn't always suitable. Therefore, there is one other installation method I'd like to discuss, and that method is the use of the **Winnt32** command's **/syspart** switch.

Using the /syspart Switch to Install Windows 2000 Server

The **/syspart** switch can be used with the Winnt32.exe installation technique when clean installations (not upgrades) of Windows 2000 Server are needed and the reference computer and the target computers do *not* have identical hardware. Syspart can be used on computers that have different HALs, have different mass storage devices, or are dissimilar in other ways that can affect installation.

As I mentioned earlier (see Table 4.6), the **/syspart** switch can be used if the reference computer currently runs Windows NT 3.51, Windows NT 4, or Windows 2000. This switch must always be combined with the **/tempdrive** parameter. The **/syspart** switch tells Setup that it can copy the startup files to a hard drive, make the disk active, and then install the disk into a different computer. When that computer boots, it continues with the next stage of setup. The syntax for the switch is **/syspart:drive_letter**.

Technically, you use Winnt32 with the **/syspart** switch on a reference computer to complete the first stage of installation. Reducing the time it takes to install a target computer, this technique completes the file-copy phase of setup on the reference computer and eliminates the file-copy step on the target computer.

To function properly, the **/syspart** switch has certain requirements, including having two separate physical disks. One hard disk must be available on the reference computer, and another hard disk with a primary partition must exist either on the reference PC, the target PC, or another computer on the network. The target hard disk cannot have any operating system on it. The **/syspart** switch can then be used to generate a working set of files that contain the required configuration information and applicable drivers and driver support for the dissimilar hardware on the target computer. These files can then be used on systems that are not alike so that the hardware can be properly detected and configured for the new target computer's operating system.

To use the **/syspart** switch, follow these steps:

1. Start both the reference computer and the target computer.

2. From the target computer, connect to the distribution folder on the reference computer.

3. From a command prompt, begin Setup, using the **Winnt32** command with the appropriate switches.

4. Sample syntax is as follows: **winnt32 /unattend:*unattend.txt* /s:*install_source* / syspart:*target_installation* /tempdrive:*target_installation* /noreboot**.

Note: *By adding the switch* ***/noreboot*** *to the end of this line, you prevent the computer from rebooting after the file-copy phase of the installation.*

5. The target computer will then have a file structure that contains files and folders named Folder Settings, ntdetect.com, txtsetup.sif, and boot.ini, to name a few.

The switches and file names listed in Step 4 have certain characteristics, limitations, and parameters associated with them. To fully understand the syntax of the **Winnt32** command, you should understand what each of the terms implies.

As you already are aware, the **unattend.txt** parameter refers to the answer file that is used if the installation is to be unattended. The ***install_source*** parameter specifies where Setup can find the Windows 2000 Server files. You can specify up to eight source file locations to speed up the file-copy process. The **/syspart** and **/tempdrive** parameters both point to the same primary partition on the target computer's hard disk. This partition will be made active during the installation. The **/noreboot** switch prevents the computer from rebooting after the file-copy phase of the installation is over.

Active Directory Installation

Installing Active Directory—thus promoting a Windows 2000 server to a domain controller—is much easier than installing the operating system itself. In fact, installing Active Directory can take fewer than 30 minutes. Before installing Active Directory, make sure you have the information available that you gathered previously in Chapter 3.

While installing Active Directory, you will be asked to make the following decisions or otherwise have the following information:

- Will this domain controller be added to an existing domain?
- Will this domain controller be the first domain controller in a new domain?
- Do you want to create a new child domain or a new domain tree?
- Do you want to install a DNS server?
- What is the full DNS name of the new domain?
- Where will the database and database log files be created?
- Do you want to create or join a forest?
- Where will the shared system volume be created?

With this information at hand, you can start the Active Directory Installation Wizard.

Using the Active Directory Installation Wizard

After the Windows 2000 server has been installed, you can upgrade it to a domain controller by running the Active Directory Installation Wizard. You can reach this wizard by choosing Start|Programs|Administrative Tools|Configure Your Server. From this screen, you have many choices:

- You can choose Active Directory from the left side of the screen and choose Start The Active Directory Installation Wizard to install Active Directory Services.

- You can promote a Windows 2000 server to a domain controller by typing **dcpromo.exe** at the **Run** command.

- For a newly installed server, you can choose Active Directory from the Home screen that appears automatically the first time the server is booted up.

In this example, I will show you how to install Active Directory from the Active Directory Installation Wizard in Configure Your Server.

The Active Directory Installation Wizard can be used to do the following tasks:

- Add a domain controller to an existing domain.

- Create the first domain controller in a new domain.

- Create a new child domain.

- Create a new domain tree.

To use the Active Directory Installation Wizard, perform the following steps:

1. Log on to the server as an administrator with the correct password.

2. If this is a new server that has just been installed, you will see the Configure Your Server screen. Choose Active Directory from the left side of the screen, and notice the options.

3. Scroll down to the bottom of the Active Directory screen and choose Start The Active Directory Installation Wizard. Starting the wizard will display the screen shown in Figure 4.34.

Figure 4.34
Welcome to the Active Directory Installation Wizard.

4. The next screen asks you to decide on the domain controller type. You can make this server a domain controller for a new domain, or you can make this server an additional domain controller for an existing domain. Because this is the first domain controller in *my* domain, I will choose the first option. You need to select the option that will work on your network. If you are choosing to restructure the domain, you may want to select the first option.

   Notice the warnings that are written in this dialog box. Making this server a domain controller will delete all of the local accounts and all cryptographic keys on this server. All encrypted data should be decrypted before you continue, or the data will be permanently inaccessible.

5. The next screen asks you to decide if this Active Directory installation will create a new domain tree or a new child domain. In keeping with the idea that this is the first domain controller in a new domain, I will choose Create A New Domain Tree. If you are joining an existing domain, choose Create A New Child Domain In An Existing Domain Tree.

6. The next screen also offers two more options: you can create a new forest of domain trees, or place this new domain tree in an existing forest. If this domain controller is the first domain controller in a new domain, or if you want this domain controller to be independent of other domains, choose the first option. If you want the user in the new domain tree to have access to resources in existing domain trees or vice versa, choose the second option.

7. If you have chosen to create a new domain, as I have, you will see the screen shown in Figure 4.35. This screen asks for the full DNS name for the new domain. If your organization has a DNS name that is registered with the Internet, you can use that name. I will type in **Ballew.com**. The Active Directory Installation Wizard will take a little time to think about that choice and will then return with a suggestion for the domain NetBIOS name.

Note: Problems encountered during installation usually have to do with DNS issues. Chapter 11 discusses DNS, and Appendix A covers the most common installation problems. If you are having problems with this part of the installation, you can access these references.

8. The NetBIOS Domain Name screen, displayed next, offers suggestions for the new domain's NetBIOS name for the network. These are usually just the first fifteen characters of the DNS name, unless those characters are already in use. Either accept the suggestion, or change it to something else.

9. The Active Directory Installation Wizard next presents the Database And Log Locations screen. The wizard recommends a database location and a log location and suggests that these two items are configured on two separate hard disks. If you have two hard disks, make the appropriate changes, or if only one hard disk is configured on the machine, accept the defaults.

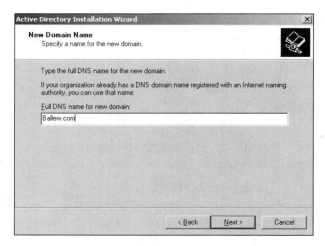

Figure 4.35
Specifying a new domain name.

10. The next dialog box asks you to specify the folder to be shared as the system volume. The *system volume* stores the server's copy of the domain's public files and holds the data that is replicated to all domain controllers in the domain. The volume must be located on an NTFS 5 volume. If the defaults are acceptable, choose Next.

11. If no DNS server exists in the new domain, a warning message will appear. It states that the wizard cannot contact the DNS server that is used to resolve the name that you have chosen for the domain, so the wizard cannot determine if this DNS server supports dynamic updates. The wizard asks that you either install DNS on this computer or type the name of a DNS server that can handle this request. Choose OK to continue.

12. The Configure DNS dialog box is next. Here you can install and configure a DNS server for the new domain, or install and configure a DNS server later. Depending on your specific needs, choose the appropriate option. For the sake of offering an example, I will choose to install a DNS server on this computer (recommended).

13. The next step is to select default permissions for user and group objects. There are two options. The first option (the default) configures permissions to be compatible with pre-Windows 2000 servers such as Windows NT Server 4. The second option configures permissions for Windows 2000 servers only. This is the most secure choice, but all of the servers must be running Windows 2000 for this option to work effectively. I will choose the first option, in case I need to add Windows NT machines later. The choice can always be changed later.

14. The Active Directory Installation Wizard continues with the Directory Services Restore Mode Administrator Password screen. This screen prompts you to specify an administrator password to use if the computer ever needs to be started with

4

the Directory Services Restore Mode. Type and confirm the passwords and choose Next. (Make sure you write this information down and put it in a safe place if you ever need it.)

15. Finally, the Summary screen appears with the information that you have entered during this installation. Check each entry carefully, and when you are positive that all of the information is correct, choose Next. Make sure the new domain name is spelled correctly, and the locations of the log files, database files, and Sysvol folder are correct. Check permissions and the information regarding DNS. See Figure 4.36.

16. The installation of Active Directory will begin. During the installation, watch the screen. If you watch closely, you may see a few of the following things happening:

- Installing Active Directory
- Configuring the Sysvol directory
- Configuring log files and database files
- Creating partitions
- Creating directory service objects
- Configuring security principals
- Configuring NETLOGON services
- Configuring LSA policy information
- Setting the DNS computer name root
- Setting security

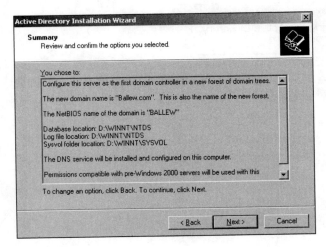

Figure 4.36
Summary screen.

- Securing classes in the Registry

- Securing program files

- Securing Winnt and Winnt\system32

- Configuring Lan Manager Server

- Configuring DNS service on this computer

- Updating shortcuts for Active Directory

17. The final screen of the Active Directory Installation Wizard appears. It states that (in this case) Active Directory is now installed on this computer for the domain <name> and that the sites are managed with the Active Directory Sites And Services administrative tool. See Figure 4.37. Choose Finish.

18. Restart the computer, and log on to the new domain by using the administrator name and password.

19. You can use the Configure Your Server screen again to begin the configuration of users and groups and to add computers to your new domain.

With Active Directory successfully installed, you have completed the installation of a domain controller for your network. If this installation has been completed in a test environment, continue to check the operating system installation fully before deploying it across the network. If this is your first installation, congratulations. If you had any problems along the way, check out the troubleshooting appendix included at the end of this book. In the next section, you will learn how to demote a domain controller, using techniques similar to those used to create a domain controller.

Figure 4.37
Finishing the Active Directory Installation Wizard.

4

Demoting a Domain Controller

You might need to demote a domain controller if it is no longer needed or if it needs to be returned to a member server state. When a domain controller is demoted, if it is not the last domain controller in the domain, it replicates itself and its data to another Active Directory server before demotion. Once demoted, it will no longer have any Active Directory information, and it will use the Security Accounts Manager (SAM) for its local security. If the server is a global catalog server, you will need to manually choose another server for that role later. Other problems may arise when demoting domain controllers depending on what masters roles they are responsible for. If the domain controller is the PDC emulator, there will be problems with down level clients because the emulator is responsible for processing password changes from clients on the network and then updating them to the BDCs. Even if there are no BDCs on the network, the emulator still acts as a primary replication tool for getting those changes to other domain controllers. Delayed updates of user passwords can cause a user to be unable to access a resource.

If the domain controller acting as a schema master or domain naming master is demoted, the users on the network won't be affected. Schema and Domain Naming masters are used by administrators to modify the schema or add or remove domains. If the computer acts as a Relative ID master, the same is true. Users on the network will not be affected since relative IDs are handed out when administrators run out of identifiers for the objects they create. Finally, because the Infrastructure master is used for updating group-to-user references, immediate notice by the users on the network is unlikely. To demote a domain controller to a member server, follow these steps:

1. Boot the Windows 2000 domain controller, using the administrator logon and password.

2. (Optional) Choose Start|Programs|Administrative Tools|Configure Your Server. The Configure Your Server screen should look familiar if you've installed Active Directory or booted a new Windows 2000 server. From this dialog box, choose Active Directory. Notice the dialog box's cautionary statement: "Running the Active Directory Installation Wizard will demote this server to be a member server or stand-alone server, depending on what type of domain controller this is. Before you proceed, be sure that there are no dependent servers connected to this server."

3. Choose Start|Run and enter **dcpromo** in the Open box.

4. The Welcome screen of the Active Directory Installation Wizard appears. It reminds you that this computer is already a domain controller, and if you continue, you will remove Active Directory services from this machine. Because this is what you intend to achieve, click on Next.

5. If the computer is a global catalog server, you will see an information box. It gives advice regarding global catalogs. Click on OK.

6. The next dialog box removes Active Directory from the domain controller, thus converting it to a member server or standalone server. If this server is the last domain controller in the domain, check the box that signifies that. See Figure 4.38.

   The yellow triangle indicates a warning, which states that removing Active Directory from the last domain controller in the domain means that computers in this domain will no longer be able to log on, all user accounts will be deleted, all cryptographic keys will be deleted, and all encrypted data will be permanently inaccessible if not decrypted before continuing. If this is what you want to do, choose Next.

7. The next dialog box is the Network Credentials screen. Type the user name and password of an administrator, and choose Next. Make sure the domain name is correct if more than one domain exists.

8. Type an administrator password and confirm that password in the next dialog box.

9. The next screen is shown in Figure 4.39. This is the Summary screen, which verifies that you really do want to remove Active Directory from this computer, that the domain is correct, and that you understand that after you choose Next, the computer will no longer be a domain controller. If you want to demote this server, choose OK. If you are performing this simply as an exercise, now is the time to back out by choosing Cancel.

10. If you chose Next from the last screen, the process of demoting the domain controller begins. Some of the services and configuration changes that occur include stopping the services NetLogon, RPCLocator, IsmServ, kdc, TrkSvr, and w32time, and demoting the SAM database and LSA.

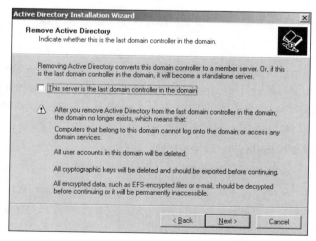

Figure 4.38
Removing Active Directory.

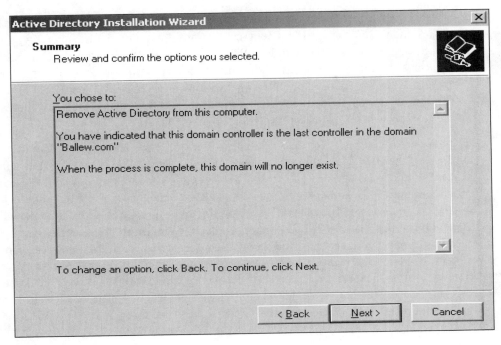

Figure 4.39
Summary screen.

11. The final screen states that the Active Directory Installation Wizard has finished running and that Active Directory has been removed from the computer. Click on Finish to finish.

The domain controller is now either a standalone server or a member server, with no trace of Active Directory on it at all. To promote this server to a domain controller again, run DCPROMO, as shown earlier in this chapter.

Summary

In this chapter, you learned about the different types of installations available to you in Windows 2000 Server. Five types of installations were discussed: clean installations, upgrades, reinstallations, automated installations, and unattended installations. You also learned to how install Active Directory and how to change a standalone or networked server to a domain controller.

Clean installations are used when a computer has been purchased specifically for a server installation or when an existing operating system will be completely erased before the installation of Windows 2000 Server. Because they are easier to troubleshoot than are upgrades, automated installations, or unattended installations, clean installations offer a good place to begin when you're learning the installation process. Clean installations are also best if the current operating system is more than two versions behind Windows 2000 (as with Windows NT Server 3.5). Clean installations are required if the operating system cannot be upgraded (as with a Windows 98 or Windows NT Workstation machine). Clean installations should also be chosen if the current domain structure will be changed, if domains need to be renamed, or a plan for backing out is required. Clean installations can be configured as separate domains during the transition to Windows 2000 on a network, so they can provide necessary fault tolerance in case of failure.

Upgrades are much easier to perform than clean installations because upgrades use the settings on the current machine for a base. Therefore, upgrading is the best choice if a current Windows NT server needs to run Windows 2000 Server, but user settings, computer configurations, and other components on the current machine should not be lost during the installation. Upgrades allow a machine to be quickly moved into Windows 2000 without the hassle of reinstalling programs, reconfiguring groups and users, reconfiguring security settings, and doing other necessary procedures. However, some systems can't handle the upgrade process because some do not have the necessary hardware, or applications on the server are not compatible with Windows 2000 Server. If this is the case, the upgrade could fail or otherwise not work efficiently. With either an upgrade or a clean installation, reliable backups should be made before any operating system change.

Reinstalling Windows 2000 Server is much faster than either of the two previous types of installations. Reinstalling should be performed only as a last resort to troubleshooting.

Automated and unattended installations are available when there are client computers that need Windows 2000 Server installed on them, but the administrator can't (or doesn't want to) visit all of the client machines. Automated installations can be performed over a network by using a distribution folder, through bootable CD-ROMs, or by using Winnt or Winnt32 at a command line. Those installations can be configured to be fully unattended by using answer files and uniqueness database files along with other techniques.

Answer files and uniqueness database files can provide answers to the questions that are asked of the client during a Windows 2000 installation. These answer files can provide all of the answers or only some of them. Providing all of the answers results in an unattended installation, and by adding a uniqueness database file, you can install many machines in this fashion at the same time. Automated installations—either fully unattended or partially unattended—make being a network administrator much easier. Tasks usually completed by attending to every desktop in the organization can be achieved much faster using these techniques.

After you complete the basic installation of Windows 2000 Server, you turn that stand-alone server into a domain controller by running the Active Directory Installation Wizard. Active Directory, which is the heart of Windows 2000 Server, offers users the ability to log on and browse for resources throughout domains and the forest. A good Active Directory configuration depends on proper planning before installing Active Directory. Make sure you have made all of the necessary decisions concerning domains, DNS, and computer names and passwords before beginning this task.

Finally, demoting a domain controller to a standalone server was discussed. Demoting a domain controller from the network can have very drastic consequences and should be done with care. Make sure there is a global catalog available to users should they need one, especially if the machine in question has the only global catalog on the network.

Moving Forward

In the next two chapters, you will continue to learn about Active Directory. In Chapter 5, I will introduce some Active Directory components, such as the global catalog, replication, operations masters roles, joined domains, trusts, mixed mode, and native mode. I'll also discuss how to create organizational units and sites in the Active Directory console. Understanding these concepts is important for creating an effective Active Directory structure.

In Chapter 5, you will also learn how existing resources can be migrated to the new domain controllers. Some of these resources include domain controller data, users and groups, client computers, and physical resources. This migration affects domains in transition, and it is useful when there are more than one or two domain controllers on the network.

Chapter 5

Setting Up Windows 2000 Server

Now that you've installed Windows 2000 Server and made it a domain controller, it is time to learn how to make Active Directory work as effectively as possible for your organization. This chapter consists of two main parts: "Setting Up Active Directory Components" and "Migrating Existing Information." After working through these two sections, you will be able to configure the global catalog and understand how replication works, configure the Flexible Single Master Operations (FSMO) roles, and understand how trusts are used. You'll also be able to migrate the data and resources from older domain controllers on the network to the new Active Directory domain controllers. You'll learn about the tools that ship with Windows 2000 Server (Netdom, ClonePrincipal, and MoveTree) and the Active Directory Migration Tool (ADMT).

Active Directory Components

The Active Directory database is the heart of Windows 2000 Server. For the server to work efficiently on the network, use bandwidth appropriately, and allow users to access data and objects resourcefully, Active Directory and its components must be configured properly. Some of the components you will learn about in this section include the global catalog, operations masters, trust relationships, mixed mode and native mode, and organizational units and sites.

By now, you should understand the basic units of Active Directory—including forests, trees, domains, organizational units, sites, and domain controllers—and how they are configured and used on a network. This knowledge provides a basis for understanding how the global catalog works to replicate information and make it available to users. Furthermore, understanding what type of information is held in the global catalog and how that data is replicated can help you determine how the domain controllers and their global catalogs should be placed on the network.

This section also addresses operations master roles. In all domains, there are five operations master roles: schema master, domain naming master, RID (relative ID) master, primary domain controller (PDC) emulator, and infrastructure master. It is important to understand how these roles are configured by default, what each role is responsible for, and how these roles can be configured if a change is needed. When more than one domain controller exists on a network or when there is a lot of growth on the network, you might need to assign these roles to domain controllers other than the default controller.

You'll also learn how trust relationships are used in mixed-mode domains and native-mode domains and how to change from one mode to the other. When Windows 2000 Server is installed, it defaults to mixed mode so that the new server can communicate with and replicate to down-level clients (Windows NT domain controllers). You can change a domain to native mode when there are no Windows NT servers in the domain or when all have been upgraded. Changing from mixed mode to native mode offers many improvements, but the change is not reversible. Once a domain has been declared a native-mode domain, no Windows NT servers can be added.

Finally, you will learn to create organizational units by using the Active Directory Users And Computers console, and create sites by using the Active Directory Sites And Services console.

Understanding and Configuring the Global Catalog and Replication

A Windows 2000 Server global catalog contains information about a domain. The global catalog, which includes information about objects contained in a tree or a forest, is created automatically on the first Windows 2000 domain controller installed in a forest. The global catalog contains information on every object in its own domain, as well as some information for every object in all of the other domains in the forest. The information stored for other domains in the forest includes user names, logon names, and email addresses. Whatever is the most common information accessed by users from other domains can be configured for access by the global catalog.

The global catalog has two main functions: allowing users to log on to the network, and allowing users to find Active Directory information for objects in the forest. The global catalog enables network logons by providing universal group association information to a domain controller when a client begins the logon process. For global catalogs to receive new information about users, objects, passwords, or any other additions to the network, replication must take place among the domain controllers. Replication ensures that the information obtained from the Active Directory database is current and valuable to the client.

To understand how replication works, you need first to understand what information is replicated and why. The following two sections will discuss the global catalog's directory partitions and how information is replicated throughout the domains and forests.

Global Catalog Directory Partitions

The global catalog has three sections, called *directory partitions*. Each partition contains information about objects that are in the forest, tree, or domain, and each partition contains a different type of information: schema, configuration, or domain data.

The first directory partition contains schema information. The *schema* is a set of policies, rules, and definitions regarding the contents of Active Directory. The schema is *extensible;* you can tailor it to meet the needs of any network by adding attributes to existing classes or by adding new classes and properties. The information in the schema is universal to all domains in the domain or forest.

Warning! Changing or modifying the schema should be done with care. Changes made to the schemas are irreversible, and mistakes will easily and quickly be replicated to all of the domain controllers on the network. If you decide to modify the schema's attributes, first remove the domain controller from the domain, make the appropriate changes, and test it fully; then reintroduce the domain controller back into the domain. Otherwise, you may be looking at the reinstallation of all of the domain controllers in the forest (as well as a new job).

The second directory partition contains configuration information, such as how domains are structured and how the Active Directories are configured for replication. The information in the configuration partition is universal to all domains in the domain or forest.

The third directory partition contains the domain data. *Domain data* is a good name for this partition because it contains information about all of the objects in its domain. The information in the domain data partition is specific to this domain, and thus is not replicated to other domains in the forest. However, some information regarding domain-specific objects must be replicated so that clients in other domains can locate resources across domains. Therefore, some information about each of these objects is replicated and saved in the global catalog. How these replications take place is the subject of the next section.

Replication

These three groups of information—schema, configuration, and domain data—are replicated differently by domain controllers and global catalogs. To explain which replicates what, I have summarized the information in Table 5.1.

All replication between sites can be automatically configured by the domain controllers on the network, or manually configured by administrators on the network. Active Directory is smart enough to take information—such as which protocol you are using, how fast the link is, how much the link costs to maintain, and how often you'd like to replicate—and configure the replication activities for you. Doing so can greatly increase replication

Table 5.1 Storing and replicating information.

Global Catalogs Store and Replicate:	Domain Controllers Store and Replicate:
Schema for the forest	Schema for the domain tree and forest
Configuration for all domains in a forest	Configuration for all domains in the domain tree or forest
Directory objects and all of their properties for the global catalog's own domain	Directory objects for the domain controller's own domain and partial information about those objects for the global catalog

efficiency on the network, as well as lower bandwidth costs by reducing the amount of time spent replicating. Why replicate at 8:00 A.M., when everyone is also trying to log on, when you can schedule replication for 11:00 A.M., when everyone is taking a coffee break? Similarly, why allow replication to occur over a 56K line when a T1 line is available? Configuring replication between sites efficiently and effectively may take a few tries. However, configuring this replication to work the best it possibly can will certainly have big payoffs for the network.

Replication within sites occurs automatically among domain controllers using a circular structure, a ring topology if you will. (Of course, the entire discussion in this section assumes that you have more than one domain controller and that replication is needed.) Active Directory configures replication so that it has a backup plan if there are three or more domain controllers. Active Directory also enables an emergency route to be configured. Figure 5.1 shows an example of the circular replication strategy and how a failure of a single domain controller will not affect the replication of the other domain controllers on the network. This secondary link for replication will also be used if a domain controller is removed intentionally from a domain.

Replication of the Active Directory database and the global catalog is achieved through physical network connections using a LAN or WAN and Ethernet, cable, ISDN, DSL, T1, dial-up, or any other connectivity method that is necessary to promote communication. There are, of course, best practices for placing global catalogs and domain controllers on the network to maximize efficiency across a network and to make replication more efficient, and some of those practices are introduced next.

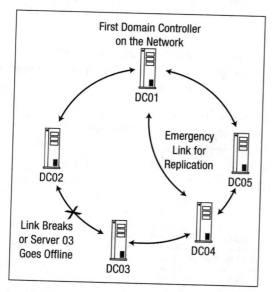

Figure 5.1
Secondary replication.

Placement of the global catalog and the Active Directory domain controller is the topic of more than a few rather large books, and there is no set of rules governing how the network should be configured. Each organization has a different domain structure, organizational unit structure, and site structure, and the topic of global catalog server placement is a large one. There are plenty of books on this subject, as well as white papers from Microsoft, that can assist you in these decisions. If you'd like to access those papers, just go to Microsoft's Web site and search for global directory help, or look at some of the links included on this book's CD-ROM. Because this decision is so specific to each organization, I'll simply include some best practices and some suggestions for making good decisions. When you're deciding where to place the domain controllers that contain global catalogs, consider the helpful hints listed here:

- The first domain controller in a forest will be configured as the global catalog server.

- Only global catalogs can resolve user principle names (UPNs) (for instance, **jballew@swynk.com**).

- Users must have fast, reliable service from the global catalog servers.

- Sites that have poor connectivity to the other sites on the network should have their own global catalog servers.

- In a native-mode domain, users will not be able to log in with anything other than cached credentials if a global catalog server can't be found. Therefore, having one global catalog per site may be the best option.

- Global catalogs increase replication traffic.

- Active Directory Schema snap-in, checking the box Replicate This Attribute In The Global Catalog, will cause a full-scale synchronization of all global catalogs in the forest. This can cause loads of network traffic, so consider this carefully before choosing this option.

- You can turn off the global catalog logon authentication requirement of domain controllers, thereby eliminating the need for a global server placement.

Understanding and Configuring the Operations Master Roles

By now, you know that the Active Directory database is replicated, at predetermined intervals and when certain data changes, to all other Active Directory domain controllers on the network. You also know that this is different from older replication strategies. In a Windows 2000 domain, every domain controller has a writable copy of Active Directory, and when changes are made on one domain controller, those changes are automatically replicated to the others. All domain controllers can write data to Active Directory and replicate that data. This feature is called *multi-master replication*, and it is different from the way Windows NT Server replicated information. In Windows NT, a PDC had the only writable copy of replication data, and BDCs had read-only copies. Changes could not be made directly from the BDCs, instead changes made on BDCs were effected from the PDC.

Windows 2000, however, makes all Active Directory domain controllers equals (or peers), thus opening up the possibility that an object can be changed on two domain controllers at the same time, causing a conflict of information. Because of these potential conflicts, and the need to have some control over specific operations, Microsoft created the Flexible Single Master Operations (FSMO) roles.

Windows 2000 Server provides five FSMO roles. Two of them apply to forests, and three of them are domain-specific. In this section, you'll learn about the five roles, including how to determine which roles are assigned to which computers, how to decide if the locations of those roles need to be changed, and how to change the roles.

Forest Roles

There are two forest FSMO roles: the schema master and the domain naming master. These two roles can exist on any domain controller on the network, and they can exist together on a single machine. Only one schema master can exist per forest.

The *schema master* is what holds a writable copy of the schema. Because the schema is extensible and can be edited, this information must be stored in a central location, available to all domains in the forest. Suppose that, as an administrator, you would like the user properties that are replicated through the global catalog to contain more than just the user name, address, phone number, and email address. You would like to add something a little less common, like the client's company tax ID number or the client's mother's maiden name. This can be achieved through the Schema Manager MMC snap-in.

Warning! Changes to the schema will be replicated throughout the network. Microsoft recommends that you don't modify the schema at all, but if you must, then take the domain controller offline first, just in case the schema change isn't successful. Changes to the schema cannot be reversed, so take special precautions when making any alterations.

The *domain naming master* is the single place to make changes such as adding or deleting domains in the forest. As with the schema master, there can be only one domain naming master in any forest at any time. You will not be able to run DCPROMO on a server and make it a domain controller if the domain naming master cannot be located and one is supposed to exist on the network.

Both the schema master and the domain naming master should be configured on the same machine. If you have a single domain and domain controller, these two forest roles and the three domain roles will reside on the single domain controller.

The failure of the schema master will not be noticed by the organization's general population because the only time the schema master will be accessed is when an administrator needs to modify the schema. Likewise, the failure of the domain naming master will also go unnoticed until a domain needs to be added or removed.

5

Domain Roles

Besides the two forest FSMO roles, there are three domain FSMO roles: the PDC emulator, the relative ID (RID) master, and the infrastructure master. Each of these three roles exists in every domain in the forest and resides on a domain controller.

Of all of the FSMO roles, the *PDC emulator* is the most visible to users and administrators, and the failure of the PDC emulator server will definitely affect clients on the network. Every domain has exactly one PDC emulator, and that emulator is used mainly to act as a Windows NT PDC when Windows NT BDCs or down level clients are on the network. Technically, the PDC emulator is the entity responsible for replicating updates to the existing BDCs. The PDC emulator also handles password changes and is the primary password authority on the network.

For instance, say User A changes his password when he arrives at work Monday morning. In a Windows NT network, if that user tried to access a resource that had not been informed of the new password due to replication delays, User A would not be able to access that resource until some time later. With the PDC emulator, password changes are sent immediately to all other domain controllers, thus mostly eliminating this problem. Even if the problem still arises due to slow WAN links or other problems, a password that fails is passed to the PDC emulator to see if it can be verified there prior to being rejected.

Another job of the PDC emulator is account lockout processing. Locking out an account due to an unacceptable number of logons is an important and time-sensitive task, similar to getting a password change out to other domain controllers quickly. In this instance, you would want to use a PDC emulator on a domain controller that is available and has a high priority over others.

One last note concerning the PDC emulator—it is still used even if the domain is completely rid of Windows NT PDCs and BDCs. Password changes are still given preferential treatment by the PDC emulator; group policy objects are still processed by the PDC emulator; and account lockouts are still handled by the PDC emulator.

Tip: *The PDC emulator should have a good connection or be on the same machine as the global catalog if possible.*

RID masters are used for assigning unique identifiers to objects within a domain. Every object in a domain has two identifiers: the security ID (SID) and the relative ID (RID). The RID master assigns relative IDs to the domain controllers on the network so that they can assign relative IDs to the objects that they create. If the RID master is unavailable, users won't notice. Administrators may not notice either. Each domain controller has a set of RIDs, and the domain controller contacts the RID master only if more RIDs are needed.

The *infrastructure master* is responsible for updating group member lists when group members are renamed or moved. The infrastructure master becomes involved only if a user from one domain is added or moved to a group in another domain. In a single-domain structure, the infrastructure master doesn't really do anything. However, in a multiple-domain structure, it does have duties. Because of the nature of those duties, the infrastructure master and the global catalog should not reside on the same computer.

With all of these roles fresh in your mind, you can probably see that some configurations might be better than others when you're creating multiple domains and configuring their masters. If you want or need to, you can transfer these master roles to other machines, or you can seize the role of the master.

Transferring Roles

When Windows 2000 Server installs, it configures the operations masters automatically. The operations masters are configured on a specific machine in many ways. One way is to use the Active Directory Users And Computers snap-in. From this console, you can also change the operations masters. To see the domain masters on your computer, follow these steps:

1. Choose Start|Programs|Administrative Tools|Active Directory Users And Computers.

2. Right-click on the domain icon, and choose Operations Masters from the pop-up menu. You will see the screen shown in Figure 5.2, which shows the tabs for RID, PDC, and infrastructure masters.

Knowing when to change or transfer a FSMO role from its default setting can be difficult. In a small network with only one domain controller, this issue will never come up. Even if

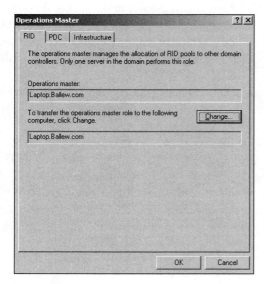

Figure 5.2
The Operations Master dialog box.

you add two or three domain controllers, the default settings and configurations will work just fine in almost any circumstance. However, as the network grows, you may need to alter how the operations masters are set.

To understand fully, let's review the basics. When the first domain controller in a forest is installed, it contains all five masters. The first child domain to this domain is assigned a RID master, a PDC emulator, and an infrastructure master. The schema master and the domain naming master remain with the first domain controller installed. With the addition of multiple domains, the structure becomes more complex. In these situations, you may want to consider the following helpful hints:

5

- If the operations masters are not all on the same computer, make sure the computers that contain them are connected and are direct replication partners.

- If more than one domain controller exists on a network, make sure that at least one of the other domain controllers is capable of either taking over or seizing the operations master roles if needed.

- If the load from the RID master and the PDC emulator is too much for the domain controller, either those roles can be separated, or you can install more global catalog servers.

- Do not put the global catalog and the infrastructure master on the same computer unless there is only one domain controller on the network. The reasoning behind this is included in the following sidebar.

- Make sure that the schema master and the domain naming master are on the same computer, preferably one that is a global catalog server.

- If the PDC emulator can be placed on its own machine, do so. The load may be heavy for its tasks.

- Make sure that all servers with FSMO roles have good network connectivity.

If you have decided to transfer an operations master role, this is what you can do: In a forest, the schema master role and the domain naming master role can be moved. In a domain, the

Infrastructure Masters and Global Catalogs

To understand why an infrastructure master should not be placed on the same computer as the global catalog, you'll need to look deeper into what both of these entities do. When an object is relocated to a new domain, the security identifier and the distinguished name both change. One of the infrastructure master's jobs is to periodically check references to membership for objects in its domain that are not held on its domain controller. In order for the infrastructure master to get information about objects that are not in its domain, it queries the global catalog server (which should be on another domain controller). The problem with both entities being on the same domain controller is that the infrastructure master will never be updated.

RID master, the PDC emulator, and the infrastructure master roles can be moved. Remember, any changes should conform to the previous guidelines, and changes to the default configuration aren't usually necessary. The adage "If it ain't broke, don't fix it" may be worth saying a few times before starting this procedure.

To change the schema master role assignment, you first need to install the Active Directory Schema snap-in. Installing the Active Directory Schema snap-in for the first time on a domain controller requires that you also install the Adminpak.msi administration tools. In this example, you will first install these tools from the Windows 2000 CD-Rom, and then install the Active Directory Schema snap-in. If the snap-in ever needs to be added to another console, only the snap-in needs to be added, not the tools.

1. Log on to the server in question as an administrator.

2. From the Control Panel, choose Add/Remove Programs. Click on Add New Programs, browse to the I386 folder, and choose Adminpak.msi. Click on Finish. You will see the Windows Installer window, followed by the Windows 2000 Administration Tools Setup Wizard.

Warning! *You will not be able to install the Active Directory Schema snap-in by browsing the CD-ROM.*

3. Choose Next, and choose to install all of the administrative tools. You will see an installation progress screen similar to many you've seen before, and the tools will be installed.

4. Choose Start|Run, and type "mmc".

5. When the Microsoft Management Console appears, maximize the window and choose Console|Add/Remove Snap-In, as shown in Figure 5.3.

6. On the Standalone Tab of the Add/Remove Snap-In dialog box, shown in Figure 5.4, choose Add.

7. In the Add Standalone Snap-In dialog box, shown in Figure 5.5, select Active Directory Schema and choose Add. Then choose Close. The Active Directory Schema snap-in will appear in the Add/Remove Snap-In dialog box. Choose OK from this dialog box.

To change the schema master role assignment follow these steps:

1. In the Active Directory Schema console, right-click on Active Directory Schema in the left pane, and choose Change Domain Controller.

2. Either choose to let Active Directory specify any domain controller, or click on Specify Name and type the name of the new domain controller that will take over this role. Choose OK.

3. Now, right-click on Active Directory Schema again, and choose Operations Master. You will see the dialog box shown in Figure 5.6.

4. Close the Change Schema Master dialog box.

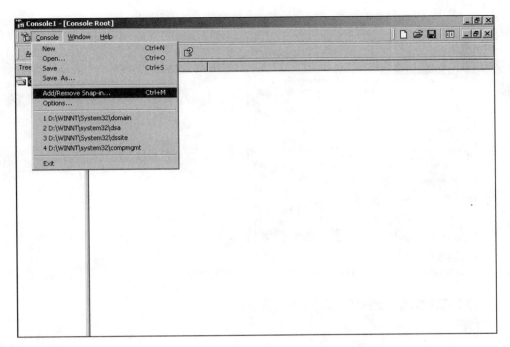

Figure 5.3
The Microsoft Management Console.

Figure 5.4
The Add/Remove Snap-In dialog box.

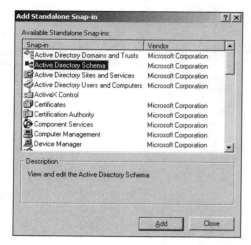

Figure 5.5
Adding the Active Directory Schema snap-in.

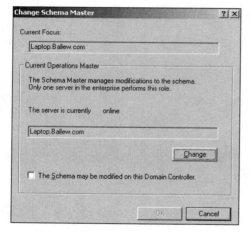

Figure 5.6
The Change Schema Master dialog box.

With the completion of this step, you have successfully changed the schema master from the present domain controller to another domain controller on the network. Because you want the schema master and the domain naming master to be on the same computer, you might want to transfer the domain naming master role assignment next.

To transfer the domain naming master role to another domain controller, follow these steps:

1. Choose Start|Programs|Administrative Tools|Active Directory Domains And Trusts.

2. Right-click on the domain controller that will become the new domain naming master, and choose Connect To Domain. See Figure 5.7.

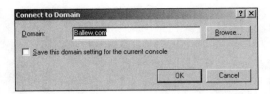

5

Figure 5.7
The Connect to Domain dialog box.

3. In the dialog box offered, type the domain name or browse to the appropriate domain. Click on OK.

4. Right-click on Active Directory Domains And Trusts, and choose Operations Master. See Figure 5.8.

5. Click on Change and then on OK.

You have successfully changed the domain naming master role on this computer. These two examples depend on the fact that there is more than one domain controller in the forest. If there is only one domain controller, there isn't any other computer to transfer the role to.

To transfer the RID master, the PDC emulator, and/or the infrastructure master role assignments, follow these steps:

1. Choose Start|Programs|Administrative Tools|Active Directory Users And Computers.

2. In the left pane, right-click on the domain name that will become the new RID master, PDC emulator, or infrastructure master, and select Connect To Domain. See Figure 5.7, shown earlier.

3. Either select the domain or browse to the desired domain.

4. In the left pane, right-click on Active Directory Users And Computers, and choose Operations Masters. See Figure 5.9.

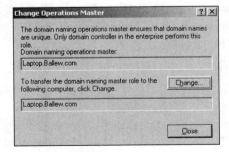

Figure 5.8
The Change Operations Master dialog box.

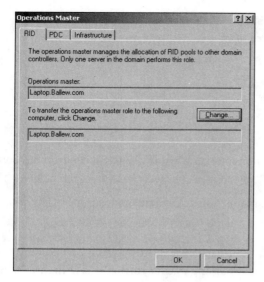

Figure 5.9
The Operations Master dialog box.

5. From the Operations Master dialog box, you can change any of the domain operations masters. Select the appropriate tab, and choose Change. (Again, this depends on the fact that you have another domain controller that can take over the role.)

6. Click on OK in the Change dialog box.

If the domain controller containing these masters isn't available, a role can also be *seized*. A domain controller should be seized in only the most drastic cases of failure. After a domain controller's schema master, domain naming master, or RID master has been seized, the original server where the masters roles were located cannot be reintroduced.

Understanding and Establishing Trust Relationships

You learned a little about trusts in Chapter 2 when you began planning the Active Directory structure for your network. In this section, we'll go into more depth on the subject of trusts, and I'll discuss the differences between Windows NT Server 4 trusts and Windows 2000 trusts, transitive trusts, and nontransitive trusts.

Differences between Windows 2000 and Windows NT

Trusts are established between domains and forests mainly so that users in those domains and forests can access the resources they need, in their own domain or others, to do their jobs. In Windows NT Server domains, these trusts had to be created and managed manually. Furthermore, if domain A was configured to trust domain B, that didn't also imply that domain B would trust domain A. Not only that, but if three or more domains were configured, six or more trusts had to be configured as well. Imagine how many trusts would have to be configured if there were more than three domains. In larger and older Windows NT networks, there was sometimes a need to hire one person just to manage those trusts.

With Windows 2000, however, all of that has changed. Microsoft heard the cries of administrators everywhere and changed how trusts would be created by default and managed by administrators. By making trusts automatic and transitive, these changes drastically reduced the need to hire a trust administrator, thus reducing the total cost of ownership (TCO). This has been a huge improvement and yet another reason to move to Windows 2000 servers throughout a network.

Kerberos Transitive Trusts

In Windows 2000 Server, two-way, transitive trusts are created automatically when a parent domain adds a child domain. There is no need at this point to configure any type of trust manually. The parent domain trusts the child domain, so the child domain trusts the parent domain. When a third domain is added into the mix, transitive trusts are configured automatically. Transitive trusts work like this: If domain A trusts domain B, and domain B trusts domain C, then domain A trusts domain C. Decision Tree 5.1 shows this relationship. Again, no manual trusts need to be configured by the administrator. When the domain configuration belongs to a large forest containing many trees, the advantages are multiplied. In a forest, a transitive trust relationship is established between the root domains of each tree in that forest. That means that every domain in a Windows 2000 forest can automatically share resources with every other domain in a Windows 2000 forest (providing that appropriate permissions and rights are configured). Compare this model to the older Windows NT model, in which domains had to be manually configured to trust each other, and you will easily see the advantages.

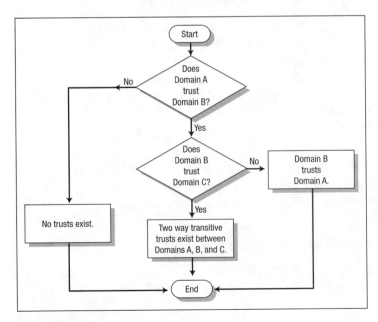

Decision Tree 5.1
Transitive trusts.

In addition to these automatic trusts being created throughout a forest, you know that every forest contains only one schema, one configuration, and one global catalog. Putting the information together—including what you know about the global catalog, its placement, and domain operations masters—you can see how the global catalog is used to keep information current and available to all of the users in a forest. This is done through replication of the Active Directory database and the global catalog between domains.

Nontransitive Trusts

There is some resemblance to Windows NT domain trusts when the network structure contains more than one forest. Trusts between forests in Windows 2000 must be explicitly created in the same manner that trusts were created between domains in Windows NT. Trusts between forests are one-way and nontransitive, and they can be thought of the same way that NT domains were: as resource domains and account domains. It is important to note that this relationship is necessary between forests and is not simply an oversight. Consider the relationship between two separate entities, **Ballew.com** and **Smith.com**. There should not be any type of automatic trust between these two organizations unless it is specifically created by the two companies. If **Ballew.com** and **Smith.com** decide to merge and form a single company, then an explicit trust between the two entities will be needed. Thus, nontransitive trusts need to be created if a trust is needed between domains in different forests.

Kerberos and Windows NT LAN Manager

Authentication within Windows 2000 domains can be negotiated with either the Kerberos authentication protocol or the Windows NT LAN Manager (NTLM) authentication protocol. Kerberos is the preferred protocol on Windows 2000 networks and is used by Windows 2000 clients for authentication on the network. NTLM exists to authenticate down-level Windows NT clients. This authentication will be needed during a Windows NT-to-Windows 2000 migration and if Windows NT machines must be used on the network even after the migration is complete.

Kerberos is the best protocol choice for many reasons, including the following:

- Whereas NTLM is fundamentally proprietary, Kerberos is platform-independent.

- Authentication is faster because a Kerberos server can authenticate the user request without having to contact any other server. NTLM servers must contact a domain controller, slowing down the process.

- Kerberos trusts are transitive, and NTLM trusts are one-way.

- A Kerberos server creates a ticket when a user is authenticated, and that ticket is used by the server to authenticate the user at other resources. NTLM clients must be authenticated at each resource.

- Authentication traffic is encrypted with improved symmetric cryptography. NTLM clients cannot take advantage of these new techniques.

There is another instance in which nontransitive trusts need to be created. Thus far, the discussion regarding transitive and nontransitive trusts has focused on Windows 2000 domains and forests. What happens when the domain mode is mixed, meaning that there are some Windows 2000 Server domains and some Windows NT Server domains? In this instance, the Windows NT Server domains are treated as foreign domains, just as **Ballew.com** would see **Smith.com**. Nontransitive trusts will need to be created and managed manually in these instances.

Manually Creating Trusts in Windows 2000 Server

To manually create a trust on your Windows 2000 server, follow these steps:

1. Choose Start|Programs|Administrative Tools|Active Directory Domains And Trusts.

2. Right-click on the domain for which you want to add a trust relationship, and choose Properties. The Properties dialog box is shown in Figure 5.10.

3. Choose the Trusts tab. Under Domains Trusted By This Domain, choose Add. By typing in a trusted domain and password, you will enable this domain to offer its resources to other domains. See Figure 5.11. Confirm the password and choose OK.

4. To enable users in this domain to access another domain's resources, you'll need to do something similar to Step 3. You should be back on the Trusts tab in the domain's Properties dialog box. Under Domains That Trust This Domain, choose Add. The dialog box will look the same as Figure 5.11, except that it will say Add Trusting Domain instead of Add Trusted Domain. You'll need to type in a password, confirm it, and choose OK.

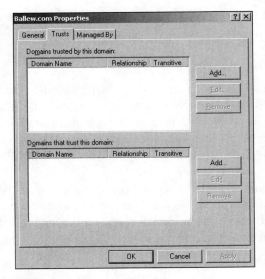

Figure 5.10
The Properties dialog box for a domain.

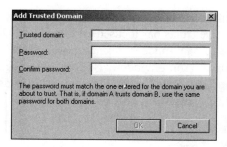

Figure 5.11
The Add Trusted Domain dialog box.

5. Now, browse through the listed domains in your network to choose the appropriate domain for the required trust relationships.

6. For the domain that you have chosen to offer resources to, or get resources from, you must perform the same tasks. Both domains must choose to trust for the configuration to be complete. This procedure is very similar to the procedure used to create trusts for Windows NT domains.

Trusts play an important part in justifying a move to Windows 2000 Server domains. Having transitive trusts available by default can lessen the TCO of trust tasks immediately, and Kerberos security is also a big seller in the justification department.

In this section, you learned about transitive trusts, nontransitive trusts, the difference between the two, and how to create trusts manually. Transitive trusts are fully appreciated only in Windows 2000 domains that have no Windows NT domain controllers on them. In keeping with this theme, the next section discusses the difference between mixed mode and native mode and the advantages of moving to an all-Windows-2000 domain.

Converting Domains to Native Mode

Windows 2000 networks can support two modes: mixed mode and native mode. Mixed mode is chosen by default when a Windows 2000 server is installed as a domain controller. Mixed-mode networks consist of both Windows 2000 domain controllers and Windows NT domain controllers. Mixed-mode networks are necessary for authentication and replication when an existing Windows NT domain is being migrated to a Windows 2000 domain. Mixed-mode domains can be changed to native mode through the Active Directory Users And Computers console; however, once the change has been made from mixed to native, it cannot be reversed. This section addresses the differences between mixed mode and native mode and walks you through the process of changing the mode. Table 5.2 shows the differences between mixed mode and native mode.

When you are positive that all of the Windows NT servers on your network have been upgraded or removed, and when you are sure that no other Windows NT domain controllers will need to be added, you can make the change from mixed mode to native mode on

Table 5.2   Characteristics of domain modes.

Mixed Mode	Native Mode
Supports Windows NT domain controllers on the network	Supports only Windows 2000 domain controllers on the network
Is the installation default	Must be manually upgraded
Can add Windows NT domain controllers to the network	Cannot add Windows NT domain controllers to the network
Does not support universal groups	Supports universal groups
Group nesting is limited	Full group nesting is supported
Group conversions are not supported	Groups can be changed
Can change to native mode	Cannot change to mixed mode
Supports down-level replication	(There is no need for this type of replication)
Uses both Kerberos and NTLM authentication	Uses only Kerberos authentication
Can use nontransitive trusts	Uses Kerberos trusts exclusively

5

your Windows 2000 servers. The process is a simple yet powerful change. To change modes and thus take full advantage of native-mode features and improvements, follow these steps:

1. Choose Start|Programs|Administrative Tools|Active Directory Users And Computers.

2. Right-click on the domain that you're upgrading to native mode, and choose Properties.

3. Select Change Mode.

4. The next box is a warning that asks, "Are you sure you want to change this domain to native mode? After this operation is completed, the domain cannot be reset to mixed mode."

5. If you choose Yes, the computer will restart and the changes will be made. If you choose No, the Properties dialog box will remain open. Either close the Properties dialog box, or reboot the computer. Figure 5.12 shows what the General tab of the domain properties box shows after this procedure has been completed. As you can see, there is no option for reverting to mixed mode.

Although changing a computer to native mode is a simple task, that decision isn't to be made lightly. You must be positive that you are ready to commit to Windows 2000 domain controllers (and beyond), that there are no remaining Windows NT domain controllers on the network, and that there will be absolutely no need to install any down-level domain controllers in the future. The second part of this chapter will be dedicated to migrating the information from existing down-level clients. If you've moved on to native mode, then this information won't pertain to you in the context in which it's offered. In most instances, however, the network remains in mixed mode and there are resources to migrate.

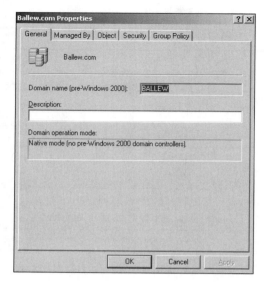

Figure 5.12
Native mode.

Before you migrate the data from other down-level machines, upgrade, or otherwise restructure the domains, you need to create some organizational units in Active Directory. The next two sections will assist you in creating organizational units and sites.

Creating Organizational Units

By now, you should know how you want to organize your organizational units, what you want to name them, and how they will be configured on the network. The information included in the following section is added here so that you can review briefly what you want to gain from an OU and how you should organize the structure.

Organizational Units Review

The purpose of creating OUs is to arrange network resources so that they can be accessed easily by the users in the domain or forest. You can organize resources in the company by network structure, by location, by functional unit, by job function, or in hundreds of other ways. In the previous example, I created my organizational units on the company's functional units: Sales, Marketing, and Accounting. Figure 5.13 shows the Sales OU and its contents.

Here is a review of OUs and how and when they should be created:

- OUs should offer a logical group structure that is easily understood by clients and that makes browsing the network simple and straightforward.

- OUs can be used to delegate responsibility.

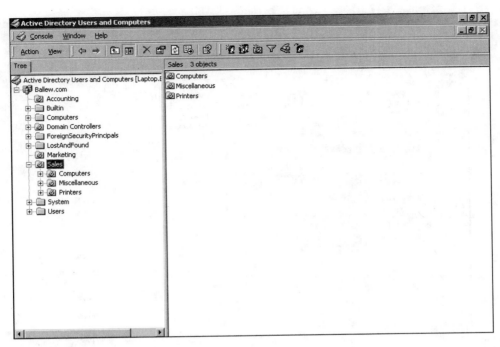

Figure 5.13
Organizational units by department and objects.

- OUs can be used to group users, physical resources (such as computers or printers), physical locations, or departments (to name a few).

- OUs can be used to replace older Windows NT resource domains.

- OUs can be configured in place of trees in some instances.

Physically creating an OU is very easy; it is the planning involved that is difficult. To create an OU, follow these steps:

1. Log on with administrator credentials.

2. Choose Start|Programs|Administrative Tools|Active Directory Users And Computers. Right-click on the domain in which you would like to create an OU. From the pop-up menu, choose New|Organizational Unit, as shown in Figure 5.14.

3. The next dialog box asks for the name of the new OU, as shown in Figure 5.15. Type the name and choose OK.

4. To create an OU within the OU just created, right-click on the new OU and repeat the process starting in the middle of Step 2. In Figure 5.16, I have created three OUs: Sales, Marketing, and Accounting. By right-clicking on Sales, I can repeat the process. By right-clicking on Marketing, I can also repeat the process. The final OU structure that I will use for the Sales OU is shown in Figure 5.17.

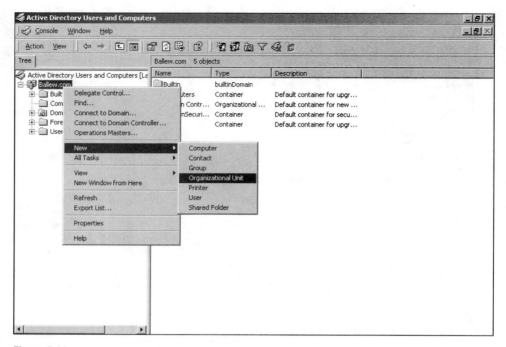

Figure 5.14
Creating an OU.

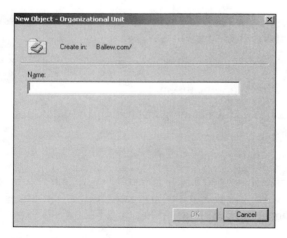

Figure 5.15
The New Object – Organizational Unit dialog box.

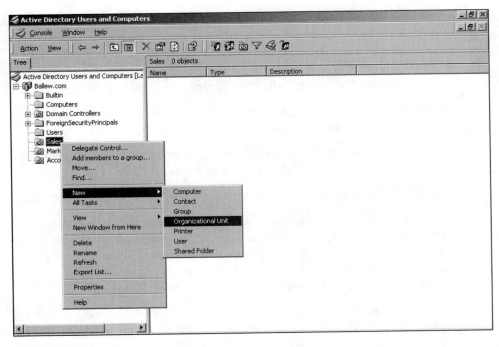

Figure 5.16
Creating OUs inside an OU.

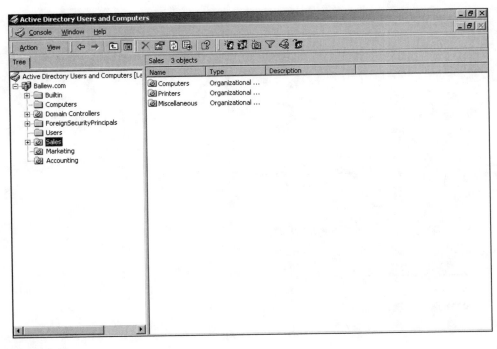

Figure 5.17
Final Sales OU structure.

After you create an OU, you can set its properties by right-clicking on the domain and choosing the Properties option. To set an OU's properties, follow these steps:

1. Log on to the server with administrator credentials.

2. Choose Start|Programs|Administrative Tools|Active Directory Users And Computers.

3. Right-click on the OU that you want to set the properties for, and choose Properties. The Properties dialog box for a Sales OU is shown in Figure 5.18.

4. The Properties dialog box contains three tabs. Use the General tab to enter the general description of the OU and the location information.

5. Use the Managed By tab to enter information about the person who manages this OU.

   The Managed By tab has an option: Change. When selected opens another dialog box. From this dialog box, you can select a person to manage the OU and avoid having to type the required information. If information is entered in the name box, the options to View or Clear are available. Figure 5.19 shows the Managed By tab after the option to Change has been chosen and a user, Joli A. Ballew, has been added.

6. Use the Group Policy tab to document the OU's group policy links or block policy inheritance. On this tab, you can change the current group policy object links and change their priorities. You can also add links, edit links, and delete links.

7. Choose Apply or Close.

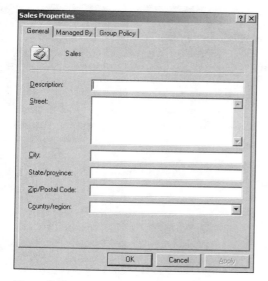

Figure 5.18
Properties for a Sales OU.

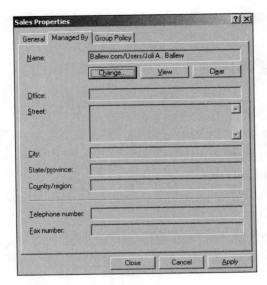

Figure 5.19
The Managed By tab of the Properties dialog box for an OU.

You should fill in all of the applicable data when configuring an OU's properties. Active Directory and the Indexing Service can use the information for searching for objects and resources within the forest.

To view the default Active Directory permissions for an OU, follow these steps:

1. Log on to the server with administrator credentials.

2. Choose Start|Programs|Administrative Tools|Active Directory Users And Computers.

3. Choose View|Advanced Features from the menu at the top of the Active Directory Users And Computers console.

4. Right-click on the OU in question, and choose Properties. The Properties dialog box looks different from the one shown in the previous example. Along with the usual three tabs—General, Managed By, and Group Policy—there are two extra tabs: Object and Security.

5. Choose the Security tab, shown in Figure 5.20.

6. Choose Advanced to see the Access Control Settings dialog box, which has Permissions, Auditing, and Owner tabs. Figure 5.21 shows this dialog box.

7. From here, you can click on any name, select View/Edit and see the Advanced Permissions Assignment dialog. You can also add or remove groups or users from this page.

Now that you have learned how to create organizational units, it is time to discuss how to create sites. The next section discusses site structure and creation.

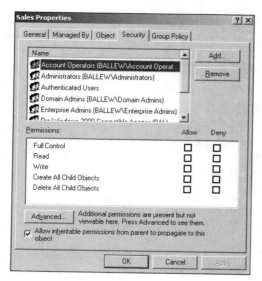

Figure 5.20
The Security tab of the Properties dialog box for an OU.

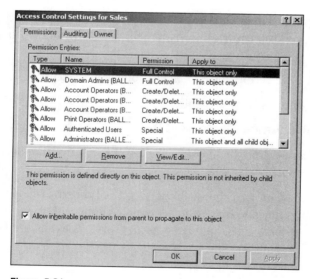

Figure 5.21
Setting permissions, auditing, and owner properties for an OU.

Creating Sites

In Chapter 3, you made decisions regarding the site structure of your network based on the physical topology of your organization and on the speed of the connections between domain controllers. If those decisions have been approved, you are now ready to complete the tasks associated with creating those sites on the domain controllers in your network.

In this section, I'll review what sites are and what roles they play in the overall replication strategy on the network. I'll also discuss how replication takes place in single domains and across domains, what site link bridges are, and how to configure them. The concepts discussed here can be used to either validate your decisions or help you complete the task of making them. I'll also explain how to create sites, configure replication strategies, create site links and bridges, and configure site connections.

Sites and Subnets

The Internet is technically one large network that is made up of millions of smaller ones. These smaller networks may be companies, hospitals, government offices, educational institutions, or any other number of things. Some of these smaller networks incorporate themselves with the Internet and some are independent of it. Intranets can be divided into smaller entities for the purposes of replicating data, reducing network traffic, delegating responsibility, or maintaining independence from other parts of the network. These smallest of networks are a type of subnetwork, or subnet. *Subnets* can separate a network into physical entities. Separating the network into subnets reduces network traffic by transforming one large network into smaller ones. Figure 5.22 shows this concept.

Note: In Chapter 10, I will discuss subnets further, and there are many books available on the subject of TCP/IP and subnets if more information is needed.

In an organization using a TCP/IP network, computers and resources are placed in sites based on their location in a particular subnet. Sites are made up of groups of computers that reside in one or more IP subnets. These computers are well connected by fast data lines, usually by a LAN. If a site contains more than one IP subnet, those subnets should also be connected by fast links; otherwise, performance on the network will suffer.

Sites work like this: When a client requests information from a domain controller, that request is forwarded to a domain controller within the client's site. This is an important concept to understand because it explains why the computers within a site should be well connected. With the domain controller and the client at the same site, service is guaranteed to be fast and efficient, and requests for service go immediately to a domain controller that is close and available. The request does not have to travel (or should not have to travel) to another LAN. This technique allows network traffic among slow sites to be reduced and thus localizes the traffic that is generated.

Note: It is always more convenient to have the requestor and the entity that can fulfill the request at the same site.

When Active Directory is installed on the first domain controller in a domain, one site is automatically created. It is named Default-First-Site-Name, which can be renamed, and it is created in the Sites container in the Active Directory Sites And Services console. The first domain controller should be installed in this site. Additional domain controllers can be installed in this site or any other as long as the IP address of the domain controller belongs in the site's subnet. For instance, a domain controller that is physically in subnet 2

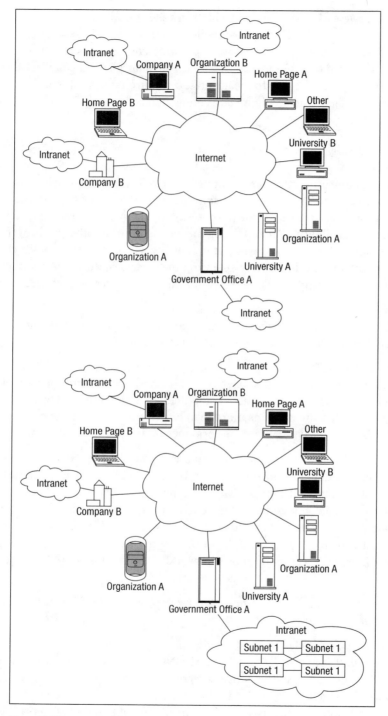

Figure 5.22
Networks and subnets.

cannot be installed in the site that represents subnet 1. In the Default-First-Site-Name site, there are three items: a Servers folder, a place to configure licensing properties, and NTDS site settings.

Intrasite Replication

Sites are created for reasons other than moving data efficiently from the client to the server. Domain controllers in a site also need to replicate information often. It is this replication that ensures that the data received from the domain controllers and Active Directory is as up-to-date as possible.

Intrasite replication occurs more often than intersite replication (replication between sites) does. Within a site, data needs to be replicated quickly among all of the domain controllers. Information from other sites usually isn't accessed as often as information within a site, and thus, the replication of data within a site needs to occur more often than replication from one site to another. Domain controllers that are contained in the same site replicate pretty much whenever they need to. In fact, when a domain controller has any change at all, it notifies all of the other domain controllers in the site that are its replication partners. At that time, the partners ask for the information, and it is sent. Can you imagine the mess this would cause if the links between the replication partners were slow or expensive? This is the reason that sites should be created from subnets that are configured with good, fast links and reliable data lines.

Site membership for domain controllers is determined by its IP subnet, as you know. Site membership for client computers is not. Client computers choose a site every time they connect to the network, and their sites can change under certain circumstances. A domain controller's site will not change, however, unless the domain controller's Server object is intentionally moved to another site by an administrator on the network.

Site Links

If two or more sites are created, then links must be established between them so that clients can connect and replications can be performed. These site links are created manually in the Active Directory Sites And Services console. Because sites are usually separate physical entities connected by slower links than are used within a site, a schedule for replication of Active Directory components should be defined and configured.

When Active Directory is installed on the first domain controller in a domain, one site link is automatically created. It is named DefaultIPSiteLink, which can be renamed, and it is created in the IP container in the Active Directory Sites And Services console. Additional site links need to be created separately. In addition to creating site links between sites, you may consider creating fault-tolerant links among multiple sites in case a particular link fails. You might even consider creating a site link bridge (although this is optional), which I'll discuss later.

Replication along the site links occurs using one of two protocols. The most common protocol for replication is the IP replication protocol. This protocol is used over TCP/IP only, and it is the most reliable and manageable choice available at this time. The second protocol, Simple Mail Transfer Protocol (SMTP), is used mainly when the links between the sites are slow or unreliable. The IP replication protocol uses remote procedure calls (RPCs) for all replication tasks. RPCs allow requests to be made from other computers on the network without any of those computers having to understand the details of that communication. The IP replication protocol use synchronous transmission strategies and can be configured to use schedules during their replication tasks. SMTP, on the other hand, uses asynchronous transmission strategies and usually ignores any schedule that is configured for replication. SMTP is not used within the site for replication, but it can be chosen for replication between sites if the links are unreliable.

Using SMTP for replication poses other problems for administrators, though. For instance, to use SMTP for replication over site links, you have to install the Certification Authority (CA) from Add/Remove Programs in the Control Panel. To guarantee that the replication updates are not only valid but also secure, the SMTP messages must be signed by the CA. IP replication does not require a Certificate Authority and thus is easier to use and configure.

Intersite Replication

Configuring replication within a site isn't any big deal. Replication occurs when it occurs, and the products associated with Windows 2000 expect sites to have the appropriate bandwidth to handle the replications. Replication as it occurs *between* sites is a much bigger fish. In fact, configuring intersite replication can make or break network communications efficiency and data availability. By default, replication occurs every three hours between sites in a Windows 2000 domain, but that attribute can be changed, as can other attributes of intersite replication. Later in this section, you will learn how to perform this on your domain controller; here, I will discuss the attributes available for configuration.

Site links always have costs associated with them. In the Site Link Properties dialog box, you need to decide on a site's cost and relate it to the arbitrary value of 100. Based on these values, the domain controller can decide which link to use and when. For instance, three available links might connect Site1 to Site4; one link may be a T1 line, another link might be a DSL line, and a third, dial-up. If the T1 line is the preferred line, you may assign it the default value of 100, while the DSL line may get a 120, and dial-up a 140. In the algorithm that is used to select a link for replication, the lowest number gets the highest priority. This way, the T1 line is used if it is available, then the DSL, and finally the dial-up. With this type of configuration, the most cost-effective site link can be used.

Site link replication frequency can also be changed from the default of three hours to anywhere from 15 minutes to once a week. If the replication is scheduled for once a week, though, and that site link is unavailable at that time, no replication will occur. It is best to find some happy medium where the cost of replication, the traffic that it generates, and the usefulness of the data will all be weighed.

Site Link Bridges

Bridging links is a way to form transitive relationships between site links. If Site1 and Site2 are connected by a link, and Site2 and Site3 are connected by a link, then Site1 and Site3 are connected by an implied transitive link. Decision Tree 5.2 shows this relationship. By creating a site link bridge, you are basically telling Active Directory Sites And Services that you'd like it to consider all possible links to and from sites when transferring information. I will discuss the steps involved in creating site link bridges later in this section.

Procedures

The purpose of this section was to discuss sites and how they could be configured for optimal efficiency on a network. In this last part of the section, I will include steps for completing the tasks discussed, including renaming a site, creating a site, creating a subnet, creating a site link, configuring a site link's attributes (such as cost, replication frequency, availability, and schedules), creating site link bridges, and manually forcing replication over a site.

To rename a site, follow these steps:

1. Choose Start|Programs|Administrative Tools|Active Directory Sites And Services.

2. Double-click on the Sites folder.

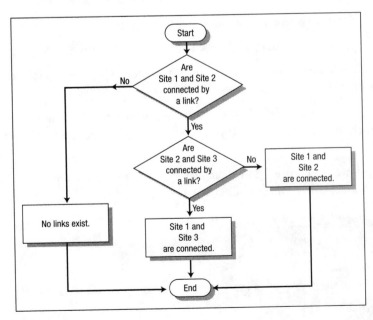

Decision Tree 5.2
Site link bridges.

3. Right-click on the site that needs to be renamed, and choose Rename. (I've created three sites: Dallas, Garland, and Fort-Worth for reference later.)

4. Type the new name of the site, and choose OK.

Warning! *There are rules associated with naming sites. The name must be 63 characters or fewer, can contain only the letters a-z or A-Z and the numbers 0-9, and hyphens (-). The name cannot contain blank spaces or periods and cannot consist only of numbers.*

To create a site, follow these steps:

1. Choose Start|Programs|Administrative Tools|Active Directory Sites And Services.

2. Right-click on the Sites folder, and choose New Site.

3. Type the name of the new site, highlight the site link object in the dialog box, and choose OK. Notice the message shown in Figure 5.23.

   To finish configuring the new site, you must also link the site with a site link, add subnets for the site in the subnets container, install domain controllers in the new site, and select the licensing for the new site. Make a note of these requirements and choose OK.

4. Notice the new sites listed in the Active Directory Sites And Services console.

To create a site link for the new site, follow these steps:

1. Choose Start|Programs|Administrative Tools|Active Directory Sites And Services.

2. Expand or double-click on the Inter-Site Transports folder to see the two folders under it: IP and SMTP.

3. If you plan to configure this site link by using IP (recommended, if possible), right-click on IP and choose New|Site Link. If you need to use SMTP, do the same thing for the SMTP folder.

4. The dialog box shown in Figure 5.24 will appear. Name the site link, and select two or more sites to connect using this link. Choose OK.

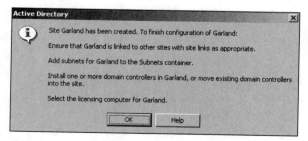

Figure 5.23
Other tasks to complete for site creation.

5

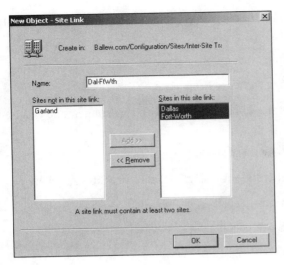

Figure 5.24
The New Object – Site Link dialog box.

5. Double-click on the folder to see the new site link.

To create a subnet and associate it with a site, follow these steps:

1. Choose Start|Programs|Administrative Tools|Active Directory Sites And Services.

2. Double-click on the Sites folder, and then right-click on the Subnets folder. Choose New|Subnet. Figure 5.25 shows this dialog box.

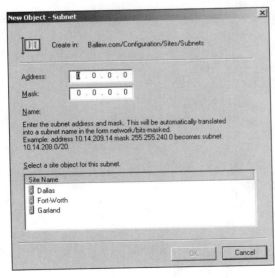

Figure 5.25
The New Object – Subnet dialog box.

3. Enter the subnet address and the subnet mask, and select the sites that will participate in this subnet. Choose OK.

4. Double-click on the Subnets folder again to see the new subnet.

5. Right-click on the new subnet and choose Properties.

6. On the Subnet tab, choose the site to be associated with this subnet, and choose OK. See Figure 5.26.

To select a site licensing server, follow these steps:

1. Choose Start|Programs|Administrative Tools|Active Directory Sites And Services.

2. Double-click on the site that needs licensing configured.

3. Right-click on Licensing Site Settings and choose Properties.

4. Select Change on the Licensing Settings tab.

5. You will be presented with a Select Computer dialog box that lists the computers on your network. Select the computer that you want to serve as the site licensing server, and choose OK.

Note: This computer does not have to be a domain controller, but if the licensing server and the domain controller are at the same site, management will be easier.

6. Choose OK.

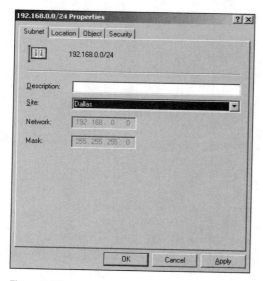

Figure 5.26
Subnet properties.

To configure site link cost, replication intervals, and replication schedules, follow these steps:

1. Choose Start|Programs|Administrative Tools|Active Directory Sites And Services.

2. Expand or double-click on the Inter-Site Transports folder to see the two folders under it: IP and SMTP.

3. Double-click either the IP folder or the SMTP folder, and then select the site that you need to configure. Either double-click on that site or right-click and choose Properties. You will see the dialog box shown in Figure 5.27. Notice the cost (100) and replication interval (180 minutes) on the General tab.

4. Make the appropriate changes, and then choose Change Schedule.

5. The next screen should look familiar to many Windows NT administrators. From this screen, you can configure when replication is available and when it is not. Make the appropriate schedule changes and choose OK.

6. To ignore any schedules, right-click on either IP or SMTP and choose Properties. Place a check in the Ignore Schedules box. (You can also see that Bridge All Site Links can be checked or unchecked.)

To create a site link bridge, follow these steps:

1. Choose Start|Programs|Administrative Tools|Active Directory Sites And Services.

2. Expand or double-click on the Inter-Site Transports folder to see the two folders under it: IP and SMTP.

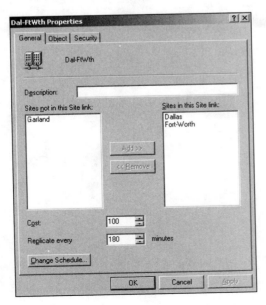

Figure 5.27
Site cost link and replication.

3. Right-click on the appropriate folder and choose New|Site Link Bridge.

4. Type a name for the site link bridge. Choose two or more sites to connect, and choose Add. Choose OK.

Warning! *Just as checking the Ignore Schedules box will void any schedules previously defined, checking the Bridge All Site Links box will also void whatever is configured here.*

Forcing replication is sometimes necessary when you're configuring sites and transports. To manually force replication over a connection, follow these steps:

1. Choose Start|Programs|Administrative Tools|Active Directory Sites And Services.

2. Select the site that you need to manually replicate, and double-click on it.

3. Select the Servers folder, located either underneath or in the right pane, and double-click on it.

4. Select the domain controller and double-click on it.

5. Double-click on NTDS Settings, right-click on the connection, and choose Replicate Now. (You can also select New Active Directory Domain Controller, New Connection, or Properties to make additional configuration changes.) Figure 5.28 shows the Replicate Now choice.

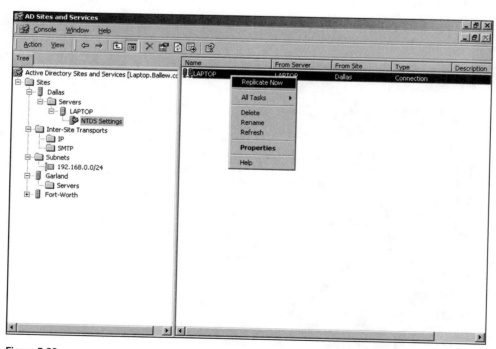

Figure 5.28
Forcing replication.

That just about does it for site configuration. As usual, planning for sites is a much more difficult task than actually creating them is. With that done, however, you can move on to the next phase. Now that you understand how to create OUs and sites, you can begin thinking about moving some data and resources. The next section focuses on migrating resources, users, groups, servers, and so on from what's left of the previous domain structure to the new Windows 2000 domain structure. There may be a few instances when these steps aren't necessary, but in most cases, there are resources to move.

Migrating Existing Information

There are two migration methods: domain restructuring, and upgrading. Most likely, a migration will include both of these methods to ensure success. A migration plan can include one or the other or a combination of both.

Note: Although upgrading a PDC to a Windows 2000 domain controller isn't technically a migration of data because the data isn't really moved, I'll use this term for consistency with previous chapters. Migrating information through upgrading is sometimes referred to as an intra-forest migration or an inter-forest migration.

With the domain restructuring method, domain controllers are built from scratch, and then information is migrated to them from other machines on the network. The older machines are eventually retired, reformatted, reused, or replaced. The previous sections dealt with readying a Windows 2000 server for such a migration. You learned how to install a clean version of Windows 2000 Server, how to make it a domain controller by installing Active Directory, and how to configure the domain controller effectively by creating organizational units and sites and configuring the domains to replicate efficiently. If you are preparing to migrate the existing data on the network, then you are nearly ready to proceed.

With the upgrade method, a Windows NT server is simply upgraded to Windows 2000. Although this destroys the existing domain structure and the PDCs and BDCs one by one, it is the fastest and least expensive way to perform a migration. For each PDC that is upgraded, group settings, users, accounts, and the like are kept in their original form for reuse after the Windows 2000 server is booted the first time.

In either instance, the domains can be kept in mixed mode while the migration is taking place. Maintaining mixed-mode status enables the existing down-level clients to replicate and communicate with the Windows 2000 servers.

Note: Even if your migration plan is based on the domain restructuring method, you should read the next section regarding the upgrade method. The domain restructuring method you have in mind may include combining some of the resource domains to become their own domain, or you may simply want to turn an existing resource domain into an organizational unit in Active Directory. Either way, the process described in the next section is likely what you will use to migrate resource domains.

The Upgrade Method

If you have decided to use the upgrade method for migrating your Windows NT network to a Windows 2000 network, there are certain guidelines that you can follow to ensure that you don't cause any problems during the transformation. For instance, you can't upgrade a BDC unless the PDC has already been upgraded; therefore, it makes sense to count on upgrading the PDCs first. In addition, you shouldn't install the first Windows 2000 domain controller in native mode while other Windows NT domain controllers exist on the network. Doing so would not allow you to access those domain controllers from the new native mode domain. Other, less obvious, migration suggestions can also be offered, including Microsoft's suggestion that you upgrade the account domains before upgrading the resource domains. This makes the migration go more smoothly for everyone. There aren't any rules set in stone concerning the migration of clients or member servers, although it *is* best to get both the PDCs and BDCs upgraded first.

The following guidelines are provided to assist you in migrating your Windows NT network to Windows 2000 by upgrading the current domain controllers on the network. Before popping in that CD-ROM and choosing Upgrade, however, make sure that the upgrade plan has been fully tested in a lab environment and that all problems have been worked out. In addition, read the following suggestions for creating a backup plan and providing for some redundancy during the migration.

There is the slim chance that the upgrade of a PDC will fail. To recover from such a disaster, you'll need to have a backup plan in place:

1. Before migrating any PDC in a domain, create a fully synchronized BDC and take it offline. This strategy keeps corrupt data from replicating to every BDC in the domain and offers a place to begin recovery of the domain if it's needed. Make sure you fully test this BDC before upgrading the PDC.

2. The recovery plan should also include decisions concerning when the migration is pronounced a failure or success. There should be a "no turning back" point figured in somewhere as well.

3. If any domains contain only a PDC and no BDCs, create one BDC for backup. Then if the PDC goes down during the upgrade, the BDC can be promoted.

4. There should be adequate backup on tape as well as on other devices. The domain, as it existed before the upgrade, should be recoverable up to the point decided on in Step 2.

As I mentioned previously, you'll need to start by upgrading the PDC that will be the first Windows 2000 domain controller on the network. Using what you know about root domains, operations masters roles, and minimum requirements for the operating system, either choose an existing machine or purchase one that can be used for this purpose. I'll assume you have chosen an appropriate machine and that it has Windows NT installed on it. I'll further assume that it is a PDC on the network. Remember, you'll need to begin with the account domains.

To upgrade the PDC that will be the first Windows 2000 domain controller, follow these steps:

1. Force a full synchronization of the PDCs and BDCs currently installed on the network so that all of the domain controllers are up-to-date. (This is preferably done in the late afternoon or at night, or at any other appropriate time when users are not on the network.)

2. Follow the guidelines from Chapter 4 to upgrade the Windows NT PDC to Windows 2000 Server.

3. Once Windows 2000 has been installed, it will see that the previous computer's role was a PDC, and it will prompt you to install Active Directory.

4. During the Active Directory installation, make sure that you spell the domain name correctly and that you do each step carefully so no mistakes are made that can't be undone.

5. During the upgrade, the Windows NT Security Accounts Manager (SAM) database is copied into Active Directory. The SAM database includes information on users, local and group accounts, computer accounts, security principals, and existing trusts. As new Windows 2000 domain controllers are added, transitive relationships are formed between them, but the Windows NT domain controllers on the network will retain their existing one-way trusts.

After the domain PDC has been upgraded to a Windows 2000 server, fully test the connectivity between all other domain controllers and clients. Make sure that the applications and services are working and that there are no surprises that didn't get uncovered during testing. (Hopefully, this exact procedure has already been performed in the test lab, and if so, these precautions are unnecessary.) When you are sure that the PDC upgrade was successful, you can begin the upgrade of the BDCs:

1. Force synchronization again. The Windows 2000 server will be using the PDC emulator to act as a PDC, so it will be able to perform this synchronization.

2. Upgrade the BDC by using the Upgrade option during the initial installation phase.

3. The information on the BDCs—including any local accounts, services that the BDC is responsible for, groups, and so on—will be moved to the new Windows 2000 domain. As the rest of the BDCs are upgraded, eventually all information will be moved.

With the successful upgrade of all of the PDCs and BDCs in the domain, the domain is now a Windows 2000 domain, and it can be changed from mixed mode to native mode. In addition, any redundant or unnecessary BDCs that are now Windows 2000 servers can be removed or replaced. The structure of the Windows 2000 domain allows domain controllers to be peers, not primary and backup domain controllers as in Windows NT, so only as many domain controllers as are needed should remain on the network.

Warning! *During the migration process or indefinitely thereafter, you may be running a domain that is considered a mixed environment, where you have Windows NT BDCs alongside Windows 2000 domain controllers or clients. The LAN Manager Replication Service is not supported in Windows 2000. To get around this, you'll have to create a bridge between the LAN Manager Replication Service and the File Replication Service so they both can function. To achieve this, you'll need to configure a Windows 2000 domain controller to copy the necessary files to a Windows NT export directory. This can be achieved through a batch file (script) called* L-bridge.cmd. *You can view a sample* L-bridge.cmd *file on the Windows 2000 Resource Kit CD-ROM.*

Mixed Mode or Native Mode?

If the network that you are upgrading is small, or if all of the Windows NT machines on the network have been upgraded and are functioning correctly, you may decide to change from mixed mode to native mode. This is a good time to review some characteristics of each.

Warning! *Remember that a domain can be moved from mixed mode to native mode easily, but the reverse is not true. You cannot move from native mode to mixed mode without data loss and disruption on the network.*

Reasons to remain in mixed mode include the following:

- NT domain controllers need to exist in the domain.

- Critical applications exist that can be run only on Windows NT Server BDCs.

- Organizational branches or other physical entities exist that should not be given a domain controller that has an Active Directory that can be written to. In this case, a BDC may be needed.

- The recovery plan requires that BDCs exist on the network for a certain amount of time after the initial migration is complete. These BDCs can be used as backups if the migration fails.

- Even in mixed mode, the following Windows 2000 features can be used:

  - Transitive trusts for Kerberos authentication for Windows 2000 servers and Windows 2000 Professional clients

  - Organizational units

  - IntelliMirror (can be used by Windows 2000 Professional clients)

  - Windows Installer

  - 64-bit memory architecture

  - Kerberos authentication for Windows 2000 servers

  - Microsoft Management Console

  - Group policy for Windows 2000 Professional clients

- Security configuration and analysis
- Active Directory multi-master replication

Reasons to move to native mode include the following:

- Active Directory takes over all searches and related queries, whereas in a mixed-mode domain, the browsing service was used.
- Groups—specifically, universal and domain local groups—are available.
- The size of the SAM database is no longer an issue with the increased scalability of Active Directory.
- Migration tools can now be used.
- Group nesting is now available.
- Transitive trusts can be used throughout the domain.
- Windows NT member servers can still exist on the network.

Tip: *The upgrade method detailed in this section can also be used for migrating resource domains to organizational units or to other domains.*

In the next section, you will learn the steps involved in a domain restructuring type of migration. This type of migration is more complex and time-consuming than upgrading, but it provides an opportunity to start from scratch and migrate in the new Windows 2000 servers with multiple places for redundancy. This migration is safer but more expensive than the upgrade just discussed.

The Domain Restructuring Method

You can use the domain restructuring method in many circumstances. In particular, the domain restructuring may take place instead of an upgrade, before an upgrade, or after an upgrade. In this section, I'll concentrate on the domain restructuring that would take place instead of an upgrade. All these methods can be combined with the upgrade method to complete all migration tasks necessary.

In this section, you'll learn about migrating account domains, migrating resource domains, and using the tools required to make the migration successful. Migrating users and resources will also be addressed, along with moving member servers and workstations.

Migrating Account Domains

As I mentioned earlier, the migration sequence is important to a successful plan. Account domains should be migrated before resource domains. Information in the account domains will most likely be migrated using migration tools and the restructuring method, whereas information in resource domains may be upgraded using a combination of restructuring, migration tools, and upgrading.

Note: Keep in mind that the restructuring method is used to guarantee that the Windows NT network will be available while the Windows 2000 network is being built and configured. The new Windows 2000 forest is kept independent of the Windows NT network for several reasons: testing, disaster recovery, and backup. Moving account domains is the first step in migrating the data, but because of the nature of the migration, both networks should remain available until the migration is complete and working smoothly.

To migrate Windows NT account domains to Windows 2000 domains, follow these steps:

1. Purchase or lease a new computer, or reformat an existing one, that can be used as the first domain controller in a new Windows 2000 environment. This computer must be able to perform the duties of a root domain controller. Install Windows 2000 Server and Active Directory on it.

2. Depending on the size of the domain, install other necessary domain controllers in the same manner. Decide which of these computers will perform the roles of global catalog server, operations masters, and replica domain controllers.

3. After Steps 1 and 2 are complete, you should have built a Windows 2000 forest with multiple domain controllers. These computers should be in top shape and should not have any domain information on them other than domain name, forest name, DNS name, and so on. No account or user information will be on these computers at this time. Test the connectivity between these domain controllers, and then make sure there are no problems with replication, DNS, service warnings, performance, or event or application logs.

4. Establish trusts between the new domain and the old one. You can use the Netdom utility to find out what trusts currently exist and to create trusts that are needed for the migration.

5. Migrate information concerning users, computers, and groups to the new Windows 2000 domain. This can be done in a number of ways, using a number of tools available in Windows 2000. Many third-party tools can also assist you. The easiest way to perform the task of cloning the information is to use ClonePrincipal, discussed in the "Migration Tools" section later in this chapter.

6. After all of the information in the account domains has been moved successfully and has been fully tested, take the old Windows NT account domain offline. You can decommission this domain by first removing the BDCs and then removing the PDCs. You should keep the PDC in a safe place for a reasonable amount of time in case it is needed for disaster recovery.

7. Look for other problems, and solve them. For instance, look for duplicate accounts, and delete them. This is a common problem.

8. At this point, you can begin migrating workstations and member servers into this domain if you'd like. During the planning and inventory phases, you completed worksheets and checklists regarding the client machines, and you should know if the

workstations are capable of handling the move. After thoroughly testing the new domain structure and moving accounts and data, you can begin this migration task.

Well, that certainly sounds simple enough. Unfortunately, it is not achieved overnight. Although you may be able to get Windows 2000 installed on the domain controllers without much ado, moving the accounts from the Windows NT domain to the new one is rather tedious. In the next section, I'll discuss the process for migrating resource domains into organizational units, and then I'll introduce some of the migration tools that come with Windows 2000 Server. Decision Tree 5.3 shows these steps visually.

Migrating Resource Domains

Once the account domains are moved to the new Windows 2000 domain, you can begin moving the resource domains. These resource domains can be moved, restructured, or upgraded in any order, but you will probably want to migrate the resource domains that contain applications first, and upgrade the domains that contain mostly workstations last. These resource domains may become a new domain, or they may be configured as organizational units. In keeping with the idea that less is better, in the steps that follow, I'll discuss making a resource domain a new organizational unit. Following that, I will address the steps involved in simply upgrading a Windows NT resource domain to a Windows 2000 domain.

To transform a Windows NT resource domain into an organizational unit in a Windows 2000 domain, thus eliminating the need to maintain trusts and additional domains, follow these steps:

1. Choose an application server or member server in the resource domain that needs to be migrated. The application server chosen should be using shared local groups in the current domain, and I'm assuming that the domain probably contains other workstations or member servers.

2. Because the resource domain will be moving into the new forest, appropriate trusts will need to be configured. Because there should now be Windows 2000 account domains, older Windows NT domains, and this resource domain, the procedure is a little more complicated than in the previous example. Use Netdom again to establish which trusts exist between the resource domain and the account domains in the new forest and to create additional trusts as needed.

3. Because the resource domain uses shared local groups and their reach goes only as far as the domain controllers in their domain, you'll need to clone the information and then migrate it. This will allow users to access the resources during the migration and after, if it fails. You can read about cloning options in the section titled "Migration Tools" later in this chapter.

4. After the information is cloned, you'll need to do something about the PDC in the resource domain. The PDC needs to have Windows 2000 Server installed, and the machine should be configured as a domain controller. You can do this by following the steps in the previous section on upgrading domains.

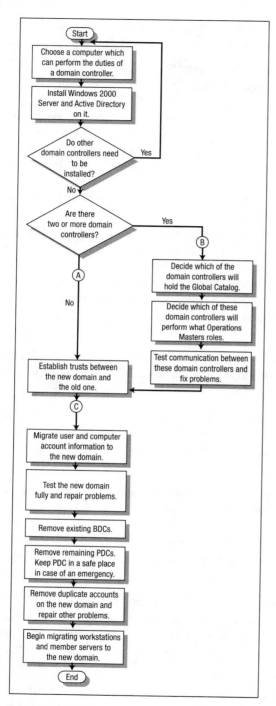

Decision Tree 5.3
Migrating account domains.

5

5. When the PDC is a Windows 2000 domain controller in the resource domain, the BDCs on the network can be upgraded as well. During the upgrade of the BDCs, install them as member servers. The resource domain will now take the shape of a Windows 2000 domain with one domain controller and several member servers.

Tip: If the PDC can't be upgraded, there are other ways to turn a BDC into a Windows 2000 member server. If you can't upgrade the PDC first, then each BDC will need to be taken offline and upgraded to a PDC separately; then Windows 2000 will need to be installed; Active Directory will need to be installed; and then the computer can be made into a member server from there.

6. The computers can now be moved to the new domain's organizational unit configured to house these resources. You'll need to create computer accounts for the new computers, which can be member servers, workstations, or former BDCs.

7. Once the new Windows 2000 domain is functioning and users are successfully migrated and accessing the resources within the new organizational unit, the old NT domain can be taken offline. You may want to keep the PDC in a closet for a few months, just in case something goes awry.

Note: Personally, I'd say this is the best way to move a resource domain in most situations. Any time domains can be restructured so that there are fewer of them than before, this is usually a good move. It lessens administrative tasks immensely, while allowing the OU to be controlled within a domain.

To upgrade a Windows NT resource domain to become a new Windows 2000 domain, the steps are similar. You can use the upgrade method described in the previous sections to upgrade the PDCs and BDCs to Windows 2000 machines, and make the first domain controller installed the root domain controller of the new domain. It really isn't much different from simply upgrading a Windows NT domain to a Windows 2000 domain. To review the procedure for upgrading a Windows NT domain, refer to the section titled "The Upgrade Method."

Migration Tools

Windows 2000 Server offers many tools for migrating information from Windows NT domains to Windows 2000 domains or from one Windows 2000 domain to another. Three tools ship with the operating system: ClonePrincipal, Netdom, and MoveTree. A fourth tool, ADMT, is available from Microsoft's Web site as a download. There are many third-party tools as well. I'll stay away from the third-party tools, except to state their advantages, but I'll discuss ClonePrincipal, Netdom, MoveTree, and ADMT in depth.

Tip: The tools shipped with Windows 2000 Server aren't going to be the best currently available. Although they may work well for smaller organizations, larger organizations are going to need additional help. Before choosing a tool for migrating resources, consider what is currently available from other vendors.

Netdom is a command-line tool that is used to manage and re-create trusts and to move computer accounts between domains. Because ClonePrincipal can move only user and group accounts, Netdom is often used with ClonePrincipal for completing migration tasks. The command-line syntax for using Netdom is:

```
C:\Netdom <type command here> [/d:domain] object [/options]
```

Netdom commands are listed in Table 5.3.

For more information on the additional switches listed for each command, read the help file that is in the Support\Tools folder on the Windows 2000 CD-ROM. In a nutshell, Netdom can be used to complete the following tasks:

- Join Windows 2000 computers to Windows NT or 2000 domains, specify the OU for the new account, and generate a password so the computer can join.

- Manage computer accounts belonging to a domain, including clients and servers, and move clients of the domain from this domain to another. Netdom can also maintain the security descriptor during and after the move to the new domain, specify an OU for the new account if it is added, and query computer accounts.

- Establish and detail trusts between Windows NT domains and Windows 2000 domains.

- Verify and reset secure channels for domain clients and servers, BDCs, and other domain replicas.

To install Netdom, install the Support Tools that are located in the Support\Tools folder on the Windows 2000 Server CD-ROM. Simply double-click on the Setup icon in the Support\Tools folder.

Table 5.3 Netdom commands.

Command	Purpose	Additional Switches
Add	To add computer accounts to a domain	/OU:Path
Join	To join a workstation or member server to a domain	/OU:Path, /Reboot[:time in seconds]
Move	To move workstations or member servers to a new domain	/OU:Path, /Reboot[:time in seconds]
Query	To obtain trust and membership information from a domain	/Verify, /Reset, /Direct
Remove	To remove a workstation or member server from a domain	None
Rename	To rename Windows NT BDCs	None
Reset	To reset passwords used for group memberships	None
Time	To synchronize the time within a domain	/Verify
Trust	To verify, establish, or create a trust relationship for a domain	/Verify, /Add, /Remove, /Twoway, /Kerberos, /Flush
Verify	To verify passwords between a client and its domain	None

5

MoveTree is another command-line utility provided in the Support\Tools folder on the Windows 2000 Server CD-ROM. MoveTree can be used to move users, groups, and organizational units between domains. It is not as powerful as the other tools available, and it cannot be used to move users or groups within a domain. MoveTree enables the SID history, is scriptable, and provides passwords, but it doesn't have any additional features that the other tools provide, such as the ability to migrate computers and trusts. If you'd like to learn more about the MoveTree command, see the information available in the Support\Tools folder on the Windows 2000 Server CD-ROM.

The ClonePrincipal migration tool can be used to clone user and group accounts in a Microsoft Windows NT domain and move them to a Windows 2000 domain or forest being created by domain restructuring methods. ClonePrincipal is also located in the Support\Tools folder on the Windows 2000 Server CD-ROM, and it can be installed by double-clicking on its Setup icon.

ClonePrincipal consists of Visual Basic scripts that can be customized to support many migration scenarios. Seven files make up ClonePrincipal; five are .vbs files and two are .dll files. These files are used to perform the tasks associated with migrating user and group accounts, including copying the security ID (SID) of a source principal to the SID History of the target object, copying the properties of that object, creating the target object if necessary, cloning global and local groups, and cloning user accounts. Copying the SID of a resource, migrating that SID to the new domain, and then placing that SID in the resource's SID history list are very important parts of migrating resources. With the SID in the history list, the account will be able to access resources with the new account because the SID automatically changes when it is moved to a new domain. Access tokens created at logon are given out based on the user's primary SID as well as on the user's SID history.

In order to use ClonePrincipal for migration tasks, certain requirements must be met. The new domain, to which resources will be moved, must be running Windows 2000. This makes sense because the migration of domains should be taking place from other Windows 2000 domains to another Windows 2000 domain or from an older Windows NT domain to a Windows 2000 domain. The new domain also must be running in native mode. This means no BDCs.

Fewer restrictions are placed on the domains to be moved, however. These domains can be running Windows NT 4 SP 4 or later or Windows 2000 in mixed or native mode, as long as the destination and source domains' forests are different. For objects that will be moved using ClonePrincipal, they must be users, global groups, local groups, shared local groups, domain local groups, or universal groups. In addition, trusts must be configured between two domains. The person using ClonePrincipal to carry out these migrations must be an administrator, and a local group called **<srcDomainName>$$$** must be created so that the source domain name is stated.

Note: <srcDomainName> is the name of the domain, and must be followed by three dollar signs as shown above.

For more information on the syntax of ClonePrincipal, on altering the .vbs files, and on additional requirements for using ClonePrincipal, open the Support\Tools folder on the Windows 2000 Server CD-ROM and look for the file w2rksupp.chm. This file contains information about the Windows 2000 Support Tools, describing the required files, the syntax, and other procedural issues, and offering illustrations and examples for using these tools.

ADMT, or Active Directory Migration Tool, is also available to help administrators migrate users and resources. I like ADMT better than the other tools simply because it has a nice graphical user interface that is easier to use than command-line utilities and their switches or than altering Visual Basic files. ADMT supports Windows-2000-to-Windows-2000 domain migrations as well as Windows-NT-to-Windows-2000 domain migrations. What makes ADMT popular is that it can be used within the same forest or between forests. ADMT is offered as a snap-in through the Microsoft Management Console and can be downloaded from the Microsoft Web site free of charge. In addition, ADMT provides wizards for guiding you through the services used most often.

ADMT must meet only one configuration requirement, and that is that the target computer is running Windows 2000 Server. The source computer needs to be running Windows 2000 or Windows NT 4. You should use ADMT if any of the following needs must be met:

- Local groups need to be cloned, their SID history needs to be updated, or they need to maintain membership associations.

- Trusts need to be migrated.

- Wizards and graphical user interfaces are needed.

- Security translations must be performed.

- Users, groups, or computers need to be migrated from a Windows NT 4 domain or a Windows 2000 domain.

- Migrations need to occur between or within domains.

- SID history needs to be enabled for all resources migrated.

- User profiles and service accounts need to be migrated.

- Access control lists need to be updated.

- A current Active Directory domain needs to be restructured.

- Resource domains need to be consolidated into organizational units.

- Users, passwords, computers, groups, and so on need to be handled in a specified manner that you want to configure.

- Passwords can be preserved.

ADMT can be downloaded from this page of the Microsoft Web site: **http://www.microsoft. com/windows2000/downloads/deployment/admt/default.asp**. Install ADMT by running admt.exe. The benefits of ADMT are listed on this Web page as well, and I suspect that the benefits list will grow often with the addition of new services. Besides the obvious benefit of having a wizard guide you through the migration process and perform the tasks mentioned previously, the benefits of ADMT include the following:

5

- ADMT is all you need to begin the migration; no additional programs are required for the source domain computers.

- You can choose from many options when creating a migration strategy. Some of these options include leaving user accounts active in both domains, copying user profiles, determining what to do if there is a conflict when migrating computer accounts, setting user password requirements, and choosing objects that will be translated.

- In every instance, the migration can be tested without actually performing the migration or making any changes at all to the domains. There are two options in each wizard's dialog box: Test The Migration Settings And Migrate Later and Migrate Now. There is also an option to Undo the last thing migrated.

- Groups can be restructured before the migration.

ADMT was released after Windows 2000 Server was, and that's why you have to download ADMT from Microsoft's Web site instead of finding it on the CD-ROM with the rest of the tools. It is a good tool for small- to medium-sized businesses, but it may not have enough power to get a large organization migrated without problems. For that, you might need to use third-party tools.

Third-Party Tools

Sometimes you'll need a third-party migration tool. Third-party vendors who produce and sell such tools do so with all organizations in mind, large or small, and where all types of configurations can be dealt with. Third-party vendors offer amenities such as better management capabilities, better reporting, and improved post-migration cleanup.

Although ADMT offers the ability to test the migration before deploying it across the network, third-party vendors can offer testing with better reports than those provided by ADMT. In addition, these vendors can provide tools needed by larger businesses, including project worksheets, security tools, rollback tools, and scripting support.

Using ADMT

I think that ADMT is Microsoft's best tool for assisting with the migration of Windows NT networks to 2000, so I'd like to introduce some of its wizards. To obtain ADMT, download it from Microsoft's Web site; then install it by using admt.exe, as mentioned earlier. Then you can begin using it to migrate users, groups, and computers, between or inside domains, and to migrate trusts. ADMT provides seven wizards: the User Account Migration Wizard, the Computer Migration Wizard, the Group Account Migration Wizard, the Service Account Migration Wizard, the Group Mapping And Merging Wizard, the Trust

Migration Wizard, and the Reporting Wizard. In this section, I'll cover the User Account Migration, Computer Migration, and Group Account Migration Wizards. The wizards that are not addressed are used and configured in the same manner as these three, with only a few changes in the order and content of the dialog boxes.

ADMT takes only a few minutes to download, and it installs easily. The entire process took me approximately seven minutes from start to finish. I created a shortcut on the desktop and clicked on it, and it immediately opened in a Microsoft Management Console. From there, you can start any wizard by choosing Action and selecting the proper wizard from the drop-down menu.

The User Account Migration Wizard can be used to migrate user accounts from Windows NT 4 domains to Active Directory. To migrate users from an existing domain to a new one, follow these steps:

1. Open ADMT by choosing Start|Programs|Administrative Tools|ADMT. From the Action menu, choose User Account Migration Wizard.

2. The first page is the Welcome page. To continue, choose Next.

3. The next page, Test Or Make Changes, is shown in Figure 5.29. This page provides a good way to test a migration of users without actually making any changes to the network. Place a dot in the appropriate radio button and choose Next.

4. The Domain Selection page asks for the source and target domain names. You can choose the names of the domains from the drop-down list. See Figure 5.30.

5. The next page asks which accounts you'd like to migrate and offers a list of all the available accounts. Select the accounts you'd like to migrate, and choose Add. Then choose OK.

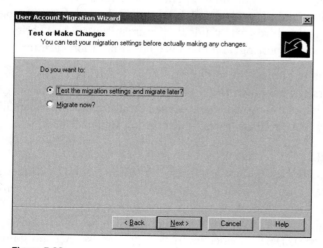

Figure 5.29
Test or Make Changes.

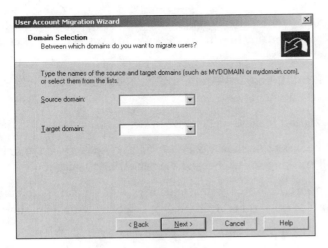

Figure 5.30
Domain Selection.

6. The Organizational Unit Selection page allows you to select the OU to which these accounts should be migrated. Browse to select the correct OU, and choose Next.

7. The Password Options page allows you to select how passwords for the user accounts should be dealt with. You can choose Complex Passwords or Same As User Name. You can also browse to the location of the password file. Make the appropriate selections and choose Next.

8. The Account Transition Options page allows you to select how migrated accounts should be configured, including disabling source accounts, disabling target accounts, or leaving both accounts open. You can also migrate the users' SIDs to the new domain. (I'd select Leave Both Accounts Open for fault tolerance.)

9. To enable the SID history, you must provide the appropriate administrator password and credentials on the User Account page.

10. The User Options page allows you to migrate user groups, profiles, and security settings. You can translate roaming profiles, update user rights, migrate associated user groups, and rename accounts.

11. The User Account Migration Wizard continues with a page for dealing with naming conflicts that may arise during the migration. There are choices for ignoring conflicting accounts by not migrating them, replacing the duplicated accounts, or renaming conflicting accounts. Make the appropriate choices and choose Next.

12. The Service Account Information page can be used to migrate service accounts for this user, if necessary. Make your choices and choose Next.

13. The User Account Migration Wizard ends with a short message concerning these service accounts, followed by a summary page. From this page, you can Refresh, View Log, Skip, or Close.

The Group Account Migration Wizard is used to migrate group accounts from Windows NT 4 domains or Windows 2000 domains to Active Directory. To use the Group Account Migration Wizard, follow these steps:

1. Open ADMT by choosing Start|Programs|Administrative Tools|ADMT. From the Action menu, choose Group Account Migration Wizard.

2. The welcome page will appear; to continue, choose Next.

3. Use the Test Or Make Changes page, shown in Figure 5.29 earlier, to test a migration of users without actually making any changes to the network.

4. The Domain Selection page asks for the source and target domain names. You can choose the names of the domains from the drop-down list. See Figure 5.30, shown earlier.

5. On the Group Selection page, you should see at least one shared local group. Select the group and choose Add, and then Next.

6. Following this, you'll be asked to name a target container. You can browse to this container in the window offered. Select a container, and choose OK.

7. The Organizational Unit Selection page allows you to select the OU to which these accounts should be migrated. Browse to select the correct OU, and choose Next.

8. Unlike the User Account Migration Wizard, the Group Account Migration Wizard does not have a Password Options page. The next page is Group Options. On this page, settings can be configured that pertain to updating user rights, copying group members, migrating group SIDs, and renaming accounts.

9. To enable the SID history, you must provide the appropriate administrator password and credentials on the User Account page. Choose Next.

10. The Group Account Migration Wizard continues with a page for dealing with naming conflicts that may arise during the migration. There are choices for ignoring conflicting accounts by not migrating them, replacing the duplicated accounts, or renaming conflicting accounts. Make the appropriate choices and choose Next.

11. The Group Account Migration Wizard closes with a summary screen and options to Refresh, View Log, Stop, or Close.

If you'd like to verify that a new SID history has been created for an object, follow these steps:

1. Using the Windows 2000 Support Tools|Tools|Active Directory Administration Tool, open ldp.exe.

2. Choose Connection|Connect|OK.

3. Choose Connection|Bind|OK.

4. Choose View|Tree.

5. Expand the tree to see the group with the added sIDHistory attribute.

The Computer Migration Wizard can be used to migrate computers from a Windows NT 4 or Windows 2000 domain to Active Directory.

1. Open ADMT by choosing Start|Programs|Administrative Tools|ADMT. From the Action menu, choose Computer Migration Wizard.

2. On the Welcome page, choose Next.

3. Use the Test Or Make Changes page, shown in Figure 5.29 earlier, to test a migration of computers without actually making any changes to the network.

4. The Domain Selection page asks for the source and target domain names. You can choose the names of the domains from the drop-down list. See Figure 5.30, shown earlier.

5. On the Computer Selection page, choose the computers to migrate, choose Add, then choose Next.

6. The Organizational Unit Selection page allows you to select the OU to which these computers should be migrated. Browse to select the correct OU, and choose Next.

7. The Translate Objects page is next. On this page, you can specify what you'd like to translate: files and folders, local groups, printers, Registry, shares, user profiles, and user rights.

8. To enable the translation of objects chosen, you must provide an account and password with the appropriate permissions. Type the required information and choose Next.

9. The Computer Options page offers the following configurations: Minutes Before Computers Restart After Wizard Completion (five minutes is the default), Do Not Rename Computers, or Rename Computers With This Prefix Or Suffix. Make the appropriate choices and choose Next. Remember that the computer to be rebooted is a remote computer, so be sure that the necessary configurations are in order.

10. The Computer Migration Wizard continues with a page for dealing with naming conflicts that may arise during the migration. There are choices for ignoring conflicting accounts by not migrating them, replacing the duplicated accounts, or renaming conflicting accounts. Make the appropriate choices and choose Next.

11. The Completing The Computer Migration Wizard screen is next, followed by a summary screen similar to other screens seen earlier.

The four wizards not addressed—the Reporting Wizard, the Group Mapping And Merging Wizard, the Trust Migration Wizard, and the Service Account Migration Wizard—are used in a similar manner. The Reporting Wizard can be used to create reports containing information about your migration. The Group Mapping And Merging Wizard is used to prepare Windows NT 4 or Windows 2000 groups for migration to Active Directory. These two wizards can be used before you actually complete any migration. The Service Account Migration Wizard can be used to migrate service accounts from Windows NT 4 or Windows 2000 domains to Active Directory. The Trust Migration Wizard is used to migrate trust information from Windows NT 4 or Windows 2000 domains to Active Directory.

Post-Migration Issues

After most of the migration tasks have been completed, and while the new domains are being tested, you'll need to do a little housekeeping before deeming the transition a success. There are obvious problems with messy SID history lists, re-creating group policies that weren't migrated, dealing with encrypted files that weren't migrated, and other similar tasks, but the real success of this migration is that the network functions as it's supposed to.

Several Active Directory Support Tools can be used to monitor, maintain, and troubleshoot the Active Directory. One of these tools, Ldp.exe, was already introduced when you migrated group accounts by using ADMT earlier. To troubleshoot problems that may arise after objects and resources have been migrated, you may need to employ some of these extra tools. Many changes were made to Active Directory during the migration of data, and those changes may have caused problems with Active Directory after the migration was completed. In this section, I will introduce the following tools: Ldp.exe, Replmon.exe, Repadmin.exe, and Nltest.exe. All of these tools can be found on the Windows 2000 Server CD-ROM under Support\Tools, and there are help files associated with them if you need more information.

Note: *You most likely have these tools installed from previous examples. If not, choose Add/Remove Programs from Control Panel, select Add New Programs, from a CD-ROM or Floppy, and browse the Windows 2000 Server CD-ROM for Support\Tools\Setup.*

Ldp.exe was mentioned earlier as a way to check the SID history of objects. Ldp.exe can be used to perform LDAP actions such as bind, search, connect, modify, add, and delete, and to view attributes of objects that are stored in Active Directory. Choosing Replication from the Browse|Replication menu allows you to view information about objects that were replicated between domain controllers. This information includes the Attribute ID, Update Sequence Numbers, the GUID of the originating domain controller, and date and time stamps. Ldp.exe can be used to determine if objects have been replicated successfully. To read more about Ldp.exe, browse the Windows 2000 Support Tools for the Ldp.doc file.

Replmon.exe is a graphical tool that can be used to monitor and view the status of Active Directory replication and to synchronize domain controllers, just to name a couple of its best qualities. Replmon.exe can also be used to perform the following tasks:

- Identify failed replication partners.

- Show replication status history.

- Generate status reports.

- Trigger replication.

- Display changes that have not yet been replicated.

5

Repadmin.exe can be used to diagnose replication problems between domain controllers by allowing the administrator to view the replication topology being used on the network. Repadmin.exe can also be used to manually force replication among domain controllers in a domain. To read more about Repadmin.exe and to see examples or syntax, browse to the Repadmin.exe help file in the Windows 2000 Support Tools.

One last tool, Nltest.exe, can also be used to troubleshoot problems in Active Directory. Nltest.exe is used mainly when trust relationships need to be tested or when you're checking on the status of a trust. Nltest is a command-line tool. It can also be used to force a shutdown or to get a list of domain controllers in a domain. To learn more about Nltest, read the help file associated with it in the Windows 2000 Support Tools on the Windows 2000 Server CD-ROM.

Many problems can arise during the post-migration phase of this project. If you used ADMT for migration, then you may also need to use the Support Tools available on the Windows 2000 Server CD-ROM to troubleshoot them. Because the Active Directory has had numerous changes made to it, many of those problems will show themselves through Active Directory. Understanding what tools are available for troubleshooting such problems is important. When you're browsing through the Support\Tools folder, notice the other tools available.

Summary

In this chapter, you learned the many aspects involved in setting up Windows 2000 Server. You learned about the global catalog and replication, operations masters, trust relationships, and the different modes available in a Windows 2000 network, and you learned how to create organizational units and sites. You also learned how the upgrade method can be used to change a Windows NT 4 domain to a Windows 2000 domain, and what tools are available for migrating data when the domain restructuring method is used.

In a Windows 2000 domain, the global catalog is used for two main purposes: it allows clients to log on to the network, and it allows clients to find resources in the domain and forest. The global catalog contains all of the information about resources within its own domain, and some information about resources outside of its domain. To keep the global catalog current, it is replicated among all of the domains in a forest.

The global catalog is made up of three partitions: schema, configuration, and domain data. Each of these partitions contains information about objects that are in the forest, tree, or domain. These three partitions are replicated differently in domains and forests, depending on the information to be replicated. All replication between sites can be automatically configured by the domain controllers on the network or manually configured by administrators on the network.

There are five operations master roles in Windows 2000 Server. Two of these roles are specific to a forest, and three are specific to a domain. The two forest operations masters are the schema master and the domain naming master. The schema master is what holds a writable copy of the schema, and the domain naming master is the single place to make changes such as adding or deleting domains in the forest. There can be only one domain naming master and one schema master in any forest at any time. The three domain operations masters are the PDC emulator, the RID master, and the infrastructure master. The PDC emulator is used mainly to act as a Windows NT PDC when there are Windows NT BDCs on the network. The RID master assigns unique identifiers for objects within a domain. The infrastructure master updates group member lists when group members are renamed or moved. These five roles can be moved from one domain controller to another, and transferring them may make improvements across the network.

You learned about the differences between Windows NT trusts and Windows 2000 trusts, and with the addition of Kerberos transitive trusts, these trusts became easier to manage. In a Windows 2000 Server domain, trusts are created automatically when a parent domain adds a child domain. In a forest, a transitive trust relationship is established between the root domains of each tree in that forest. Trusts between forests must be explicitly created in the same manner that trusts were created between domains in Windows NT.

The differences between mixed-mode and native-mode domains were described. Mixed mode is chosen by default when a Windows 2000 server is installed as a domain controller. Mixed-mode networks—which consist of both Windows 2000 domain controllers and Windows NT domain controllers—are necessary for authentication and replication when an existing Windows NT domain is being migrated to a Windows 2000 domain. Mixed-mode domains can be changed to native mode after all of the Windows NT domain controllers have been removed.

You also learned how to create organizational units and sites. The purpose of creating OUs is to arrange network resources so that they can be easily accessed by the users in the domain or forest. OUs can be created through Active Directory Users And Computers, accessed through Administrative Tools.

Sites are made up of groups of computers that reside in one or more IP subnets. Computers and resources in an organization using a TCP/IP network are placed in sites based on their location in a particular subnet. When two or more sites exist, site links must be configured. Sites, site links, and site link bridges are created through the Active Directory Sites And Services console.

This chapter discussed more about the upgrade and domain restructuring methods, and you learned how data, resources, and other objects on the network are migrated once the upgrade or domain restructuring begins. Using the upgrade method, you first upgrade the PDC that would be the first Windows 2000 domain controller on the network, and you then upgrade the BDCs. It is important to back up all of the data before the installations,

5

and you can force synchronization if necessary. You learned how to migrate account domains and then resource domains, and how to make those resource domains become organizational units in the new domain structure. You also took another look at mixed mode versus native mode, and made decisions accordingly.

In the domain restructuring method, a Windows 2000 domain is built, and you use various tools to migrate information from the Windows NT domain to the Windows 2000 domain. The tools available on the Windows 2000 Server CD-ROM include ClonePrincipal, Netdom, and MoveTree; ADMT can be downloaded from the Microsoft Web site.

Netdom is a command-line tool that is used to manage and re-create trusts and to move computer accounts between domains. MoveTree is a command-line utility used to move users, groups, and organizational units between domains. It is not as powerful as the other tools available, and it cannot be used to move users or groups within a domain. ClonePrincipal is used to clone user and group accounts that currently exist in a Microsoft Windows NT domain and move them to a Windows 2000 domain or forest being created by domain restructuring methods. ClonePrincipal consists of Visual Basic scripts that can be customized to support many migration scenarios. The Active Directory Migration Tool (ADMT) is a good tool for small- to medium-sized businesses. It is all you need to begin the migration; no additional programs are required for the source domain computers. ADMT provides seven wizards, which can be used to simplify the migration tasks.

Finally, some Active Directory troubleshooting tools were introduced in case problems arose during the migration. These tools are Ldp.exe, Replmon.exe, Repadmin.exe, and Nltest.exe. All of these tools can be found on the Windows 2000 Server CD-ROM under Support\Tools.

Moving Forward

Now that you have learned what components are available for configuration through Active Directory, it is time to move on to the actual administration of a network using Active Directory. In Chapter 6, you'll learn more about what's available from Active Directory, including tools and services, and you'll learn how to secure Active Directory using NTFS permissions.

Chapter 6 will introduce the Active Directory consoles, including the Domains And Trusts console, the Users And Computers console, and the Sites And Services console. Chapter 6 will also discuss the Microsoft Management Console and its available snap-ins, and it will cover preconfigured and custom MMCs.

Chapter 6 will also explain how to do certain tasks in Active Directory, including publishing resources, assigning permissions, finding and moving objects, and sharing folders. This will be followed by an introduction to NTFS permissions and to securing your network's Active Directory resources. After all of the Active Directory consoles have been introduced, an MMC has been configured, and NTFS permissions have been set, you'll be ready to plan and create user and group accounts for the network.

Part III

Administering and Optimizing Windows 2000 Server

Configuration
Deployment
Planning
Troubleshooting

Chapter 6

Using Active Directory Services and Securing Resources

A ctive Directory is a powerful and flexible administrative tool that can be used to simplify administration and management tasks. There are many duties that you, as a network administrator, will need to attend to regularly. The consoles available through Active Directory and the Microsoft Management Console (MMC) make these tasks easier to manage and perform. In this chapter, you will learn about many of the Active Directory Administrative Tools, including the Domains And Trusts console, the Users And Computers console, the Sites And Services console, and the Microsoft Management Console. The first three consoles mentioned are accessed through Administrative Tools in Active Directory itself, and the MMC is a separate utility. In addition to these consoles, many tools are available from the Windows 2000 Server CD-ROM. In the last chapter, you tinkered a little with some of these consoles and tools, and in this chapter, you'll learn even more.

After you have familiarized yourself with the available consoles and support tools, you'll learn how to use these consoles to perform such tasks as publishing Active Directory resources, creating explicit trusts, assigning permissions for resources, finding and moving Active Directory objects, and adding shared folders. After learning these skills, you will learn how to secure resources on the network by using group policies and New Technology File System (NTFS) permissions. Group policies can be configured with the help of the Active Directory Users And Computers console and the Active Directory Sites And Services console.

After you have secured the user's environment using group policies, you'll learn about NTFS permissions. A thorough understanding of how NTFS permissions work and how they are configured will prove most useful in fully securing the Active Directory and its resources. I'll discuss assigning "regular" NTFS permissions as well as "special" ones in this section. During the discussion on NTFS permissions, you'll learn about Share permissions as well, including how they are assigned and what their limitations are.

Active Directory Administration Tools

In this section, you will learn about two types of management tools: the Active Directory consoles available through Administrative Tools, and the Microsoft Management Console, available by typing "mmc" at the **Run** command. You can make shortcuts on the desktop for these utilities. For the Active Directory consoles, drag them from the Start menu; for MMC, first create and save the console that you want, and then drag it from the Start menu to the desktop.

In the first section, I'll introduce each of the consoles and their purpose, describe the graphical interface, point out the main configuration choices, and describe the tasks that can be achieved using each. After you're familiar with the consoles and how they can be used for managing Active Directory tasks, you will learn how to do some of those tasks in the following sections. Those tasks include the following:

- Restricting access to author mode in an MMC

- Restricting access to certain snap-ins

- Configuring a saved MMC to hide features and menus

- Reordering columns and changing views

Introduction to Active Directory Consoles

You can open the three Active Directory consoles by choosing Start|Programs|Administrative Tools and then the Active Directory console you want. These tools are invaluable for configuring and managing the Active Directory services. The first console up for discussion is the Active Directory Domains And Trusts console.

The Active Directory Domains And Trusts Console

The Active Directory Domains And Trusts console helps you manage trusts between domains in a Windows 2000 network, in either mixed mode or native mode. The domain trusts that can be handled here can be in the same forest or in different ones, and can be configured for full or partial Kerberos v5 environments.

To refresh your memory, in Windows 2000, trusts are created automatically when child domains are added to parent domains, and those trusts are transitive. This means that if domain A trusts domain B, and domain B trusts domain C, then domain A trusts domain C automatically. In addition, domain B trusts domain A, and domain C trusts B and A by default.

It seems as though this doesn't leave much reason to hire an administrator for creating these trusts, as Windows NT networks did. However, you'll still need to manage trusts because not all trusts are between Windows 2000 domains, and not all trusts created automatically are desired. If Windows NT domain controllers exist on a network, or if there is more than one forest in the organization, those trust relationships will need to be explicitly created and managed, just as with Windows NT trusts.

In the Active Directory Domains And Trusts console, you can perform the following tasks:

- Create explicit domain trusts from Windows NT domains or other forests.

- Verify or revoke a trust.

- Identify the domain naming master and/or transfer the role.

- Add user principal name (UPN) suffixes (the name after the @ symbol, as in **Ballew** or **Smith**).

- Obtain information regarding domain management.

- Connect to another domain controller.

- See the properties of the domain, including its description, and view trusts currently configured.

Figure 6.1 shows the Active Directory Domains And Trusts console. When the domain name is highlighted in the tree pane, the Action menu allows you to access the Manage, Export List, Properties, and Help commands. When Active Directory Domains And Trusts is highlighted, the Action menu allows you to access the Connect To Domain Controller, Operations Master, Refresh, Export List, Properties, and Help commands.

The Active Directory Users And Computers Console

The Active Directory Users And Computers console is the tool you'll use most often when administering Active Directory. This console is used for handling administrative tasks related to users, groups, computers, and organizational units. By default, the Active

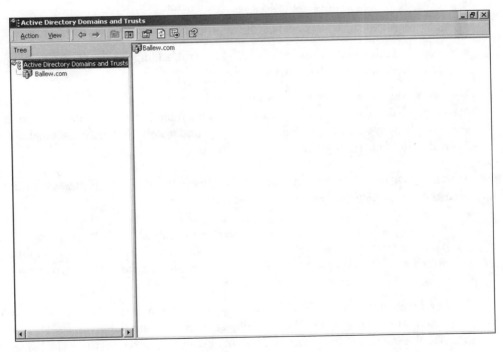

Figure 6.1
The Active Directory Domains And Trusts console.

Directory Users And Computers console works with the domain with which your computer is connected. In the example seen in this chapter, that domain will be the domain Ballew (**Ballew.com**).

You can use the Users And Computers console to do various tasks:

- Access information about users, groups, and computers in the current domain.
- Access information about users, groups, and computers in any other domain as long as the correct permissions are available.
- View advanced options and obtain information about objects from a trusted domain.
- Delete or recover orphaned objects.
- Find accounts and shared resources anywhere in the forest.
- Find users, computers, and printers anywhere in the forest.
- Create, view, delete, move, and edit computer accounts.
- Create, view, delete, move, and edit user accounts.
- Create, view, delete, move, and edit security and distribution groups.
- Create, view, delete, move, and edit published resources.
- Manage domain controllers by delegating control and viewing properties.
- Manage organizational units by delegating control, adding members, and moving, finding, renaming, and deleting OUs.

The Users And Computers console is shown in Figure 6.2. The built-in user groups have been expanded, and you can take note of additional folders that have been created. In the previous chapter, I created the Sales, Marketing, and Accounting organizational units, but the rest of the folders shown are created by default.

Tip: *If you are looking at the Active Directory Users And Computers console on your domain controller and you can't see all of these groups, choose View/Advanced Features.*

Although the built-in groups—Account Operators, Administrators, Backup Operators, Guests, Print Operators, Replicator, Server Operators, and Users—may look familiar, perhaps some of the other folders that you see in Figure 6.2 don't. For introductory purposes, some of the available folders and their purposes are described next.

The ForeignSecurityPrincipals folder contains information about objects that are stored in an external trusted domain. When an object from an external domain is added to a group in the existing domain, Active Directory creates these security principal objects to allow these foreign security principals to become a part of domain local groups.

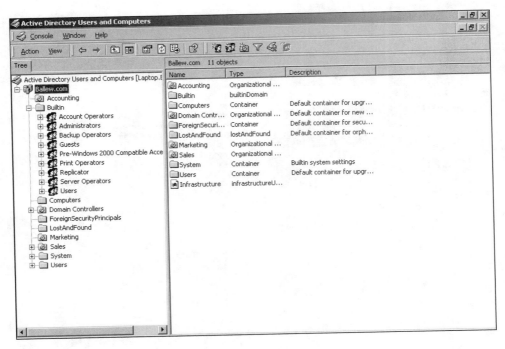

Figure 6.2
The Active Directory Users And Computers console.

The LostAndFound folder holds objects that have been orphaned, such as resources that belonged to accounts that were deleted or moved. If a group or account is deleted, and that group or account contained resources, those resources have no place to go and thus have no way to be located. The LostAndFound folder holds these objects until an administrator can delete or recover and move them.

The System folder contains built-in system settings, such as default domain policy, file replication service, IP security policies, and Winsock services.

Finally, look at Figure 6.3. Shown in this figure is the "meat and potatoes" of this utility, allowing an administrator to create new computers, contacts, groups, organizational units, printers, users, and shared folders. After any of these items are created, they can be managed as well from this console.

Figure 6.4 continues with this visual introduction to Users And Computers by showing you an example of tasks that can be performed on a single user account. After right-clicking on a user name, you will see the following options:

- *Copy*—Allows an administrator to copy the user account and use it as a template for another account. The copied account will maintain almost all of the settings as the original account, but the user names will be left blank for the new account.

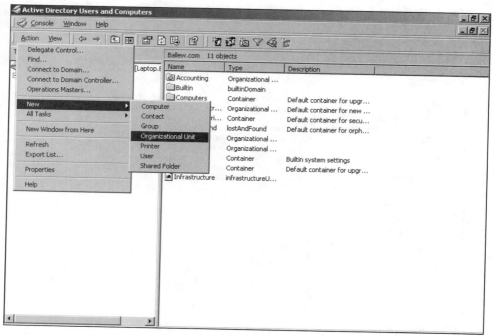

Figure 6.3
Creating new objects.

- *Add members to a group*—Allows an administrator to add that user to another group.

- *Name mappings*—Allows an administrator to see the certificates issued to the users and the Kerberos principal name of the user.

- *Disable account*—Allows an administrator to disable an account, and is sometimes used in place of deleting the account when an employee leaves or will be replaced.

- *Reset password*—Allows an administrator to reset a password on an account for security reasons, or if the account has been locked out due to account lockout policies.

- *Move*—Allows an administrator to move the account to another organizational unit or container.

- *Open home page*—Allows an administrator to open the user's home page.

- *Send mail*—Allows an administrator to send an email to the user. (An email must be configured in the user's properties.)

- *Find*—Allows a user to find users, contacts, and groups by typing a name or description of the object the user is looking for.

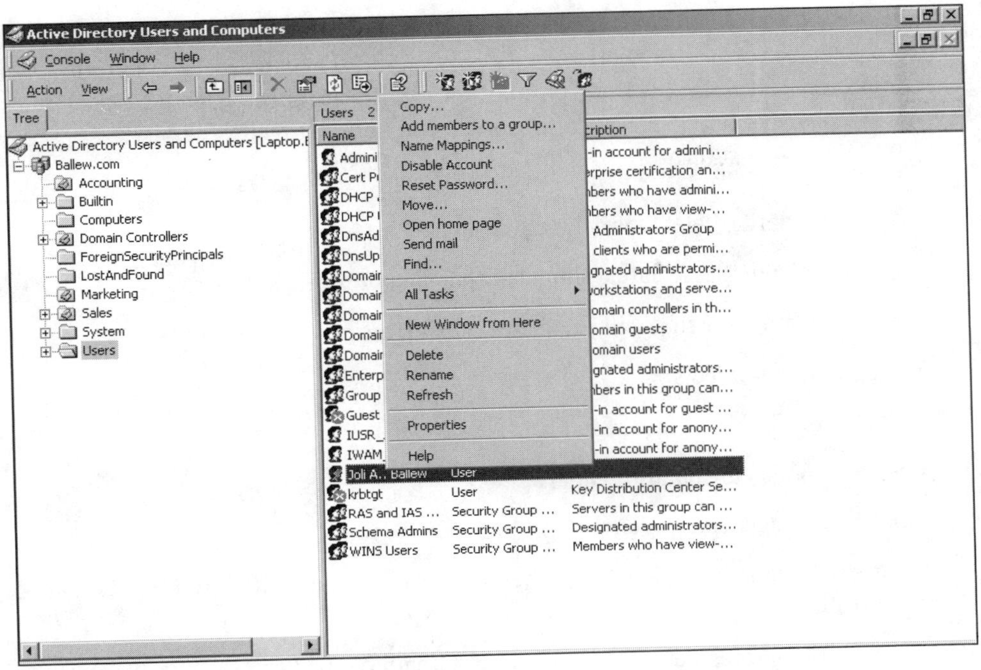

Figure 6.4
Active Directory Users and Computers tasks.

- *Delete*—Allows an administrator to delete an account. Once deleted, the accounts SID is destroyed and the account cannot be recreated using the same SID.

- *Rename*—Allows an administrator to rename an account.

- *Refresh*—Allows an administrator to refresh the console after changes have been made.

- *Properties*—Allows an administrator to view the properties of the user.

- *Help*—Allows an administrator to get help from Windows 2000 on topics related to the Microsoft Management Console.

From here, many alterations can be made to this specific user account. The same options exist for computers, domain controllers, printers, and other resources. It should be apparent now that administrators can use the Active Directory Users And Computers console to perform almost any task regarding users, groups, and resources within a domain or forest.

The Active Directory Sites And Services Console

The purpose of the Active Directory Sites And Services console is to enable administrators to give information to Active Directory concerning how the network is physically arranged. In the Sites And Services console, you can add sites and give the attributes of that site so that Active Directory can decide how replication will take place among domain controllers across the network. As you know, sites are created based on groups of computers—either in the same physical locations or connected by fast links—that will need authentication, replication, and other Active Directory services.

You can use the Sites And Services console to do various tasks:

- Create, rename, delete, or delegate control of a site.
- Create a subnet, associate a subnet with a site, or delete subnets.
- Select a computer that will perform licensing tasks.
- Create server objects.
- Enable or disable a global catalog.
- Select a policy for handling queries.
- Select a bridgehead server.
- Move a domain controller to another site, or remove a malfunctioning domain controller.
- Connect to a forest, domain, or another domain controller.
- Check how replication is configured.
- Configure security permissions for certificate templates.
- Create and delete site links.
- Create and delete site link bridges.
- Configure site link replication, cost, and frequency.
- Ignore schedules previously configured for replication.
- Bridge site links or add a site to a site link.
- Add or configure connections manually.
- Force replication over a specific link.

The Active Directory Sites And Services console is shown in Figure 6.5.

By right-clicking on Active Directory Sites And Services in the left pane, or by highlighting Active Directory Sites And Services and choosing the Action menu, you can see the following choices: Connect To A Forest, Connect To A Domain Controller, Refresh, Export List, and more. By right-clicking on a particular site, you can perform such tasks as delegating control, creating a new site, refreshing the view, exporting a list, and viewing properties. From the New menu for a site, you can configure licensing settings, site settings, and Servers containers. By right-clicking on a particular subnet, you can choose

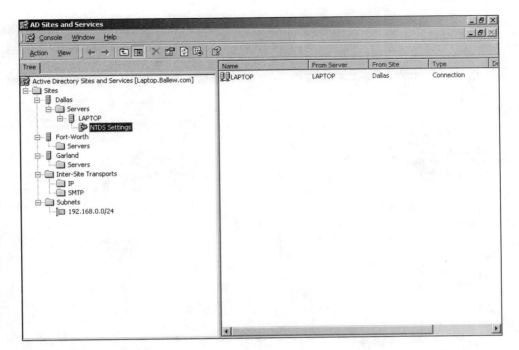

Figure 6.5
The Active Directory Sites And Services console.

to refresh, rename, or delete it. By right-clicking on IP or SMTP, you can create a new site link, create a new site link bridge, delete an object, refresh the view, and look at the properties of the object. See Figure 6.6 for an example of site options.

The three Active Directory consoles that have been introduced in this chapter can be used to perform just about any task you'll need to do in the Active Directory. Before moving on to the Microsoft Management Console and creating custom consoles similar to these, I'd like to talk more about the support tools that are available from the Windows 2000 Server CD-ROM. You learned a little about these tools in the last chapter, following the discussion about migration and some of the problems that can follow such an extreme movement of data. In the next section, we'll discuss the other tools as well, including some that are installed through Windows 2000 Support Tools, and how they can be used to assist in troubleshooting Active Directory and further managing it.

Windows 2000 Support Tools
If you install the Windows 2000 Support Tools from the Windows 2000 Server CD-ROM, the Start menu will offer access to those tools, as shown in Figure 6.7. These tools include Active Directory Administration Tool, Active Directory Replication Monitor, ADSI Edit, Application Compatibility Tool, Dependency Walker, DiskProbe, Global Flags Editor, Process Viewer, Security Administration Tools, SNMP Query Utility, and Windiff. In this

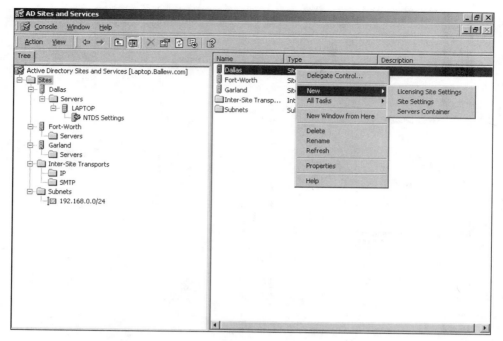

Figure 6.6
The Sites context menu.

section, I'd like to go into more depth concerning some of the tools that are designed to work with and for the Active Directory.

Many command-line tools are available to help you manage Active Directory. These command-line utilities include Acldiag.exe, Dfsutil.exe, Dnscmd.exe, Dsacls.exe, Dsastat. exe, Movetree.exe, Netdom.exe, Nltest.exe, Repadmin.exe, Sdcheck.exe, Showaccs.exe, and Sidwalk.exe. There are also two GUI tools: Replmon.exe and Ldp.exe. Finally, two tools are available that can be run in the Microsoft Management Console: the Security Migration Editor and ADSI Edit.

Before you go any farther, you should install the Windows 2000 Support Tools from the CD-ROM if you haven't already done so. To install the Windows 2000 Support Tools, log on as administrator and follow these steps:

1. Browse the Windows 2000 Server CD-ROM and click on the Support folder.

2. Click on the Tools folder.

3. Choose 2000RKST or Setup.exe.

4. The first page of the Windows 2000 Support Tools Setup Wizard appears; choose Next.

6

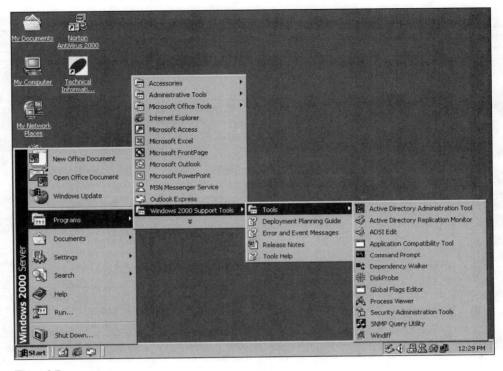

Figure 6.7
Windows 2000 Support Tools.

5. Follow the installation instructions that appear on the screen, and make the appropriate choices. Choose Custom installation to modify where or how the files will be installed.

6. Check the installation by choosing Start|Programs|Windows 2000 Support Tools|Tools.

If you've already installed the other tools in this folder, you should now have all of the tools mentioned previously installed on your computer. We'll discuss the command-line tools first, followed by the GUI tools, and finally the Microsoft Management Console tools: Security Migration Editor and ADSI Edit.

Table 6.1 describes the remaining command-line tools not previously examined.

There are also two GUI tools: Replmon.exe and Ldp.exe. Both were introduced in the last chapter, and they can be used to perform many tasks associated with Active Directory troubleshooting. The first tool, Replmon.exe, can be used to force replication events, show how replication takes place, supervise replication status, and more. The second tool, Ldp.exe, is used to allow Lightweight Directory Access Protocol to be used with Active Directory. Because these tools have already been discussed, I'll move on to the tools available in the MMC.

Table 6.1   Command-line tools.

Tool	Purpose
Acldiag.exe	ACL stands for *access control list* which is used by Windows 2000 to determine which users have access to which objects. Use the Acldiag.exe tool to determine what rights a user has been granted or denied and to reset the ACLs to their default state.
Dfsutil.exe	DFS is the Distributed File System, which allows users to use the network server as part of their own system. DFS allows users to access and process data on the server. Dfsutil.exe checks the configuration of the DFS servers, displays the physical layout, and manages the system.
Dnscmd.exe	DNS is the Domain Name System, which translates domain names into TCP/IP addresses for client queries. Clients do not have to know the TCP/IP address to access the Web site or server. Use the Dnscmd.exe utility to check and manage these DNS records.
Dsacls.exe	Use this utility to modify or view the ACLs in the Active Directory.
Dsastat.exe	This is a diagnostic tool for Active Directory. Use this tool for troubleshooting naming problems on domain controllers.
Sdcheck.exe	This is another diagnostic tool for Active Directory, used for checking ACLs. Use this utility to determine if ACL replication and inheritance are being performed correctly.
Showaccs.exe	Use this tool to inspect and modify ACL entries and to deal with access control policies. This tool can be used to examine ACLs on file and print shares, the registry and file system, and to view group membership.
Sidwalk.exe	Use this tool to inspect and modify ACL entries and to deal with access control policies. Using this tool, you can set ACLs on objects that have been moved, orphaned, or deleted.

Two tools are available that can be run in the Microsoft Management Console: the Security Migration Editor and ADSI Edit. ADSI Edit can be used to view, modify, delete, and set ACLs on the objects that are stored in Active Directory. This tool can also be used to view, modify, delete, and move those objects. Because ADSI Edit attempts to open and load in the current domain, problems may occur if the client isn't logged onto the required domain when ADSI Edit is launched. Therefore, it is best to use ADSI Edit as a snap-in to an MMC console. You'll learn how to install snap-ins in the next section. For the purposes of this section, you can open ADSI Edit by choosing Start|Programs| Windows 2000 Support Tools|Tools|ADSI Edit. The ADSI Edit console is shown in Figure 6.8. (I've expanded the Domain, Configuration, and Schema containers.)

By right-clicking on the objects, you can perform different tasks for the Domain Naming Context (DNS), the Configuration container, and the schema. In addition, the Canonical Names (CN) and OUs can also be modified. You can change the settings of the containers, add objects, rename objects, move objects, update the schema, and make new connections. ADSI Edit is a powerful support tool included with Windows 2000 Server Support Tools.

The Security Migration Editor can be used to edit mappings among previous and existing Security IDs. The Security Migration Editor can be accessed through Start|Programs|

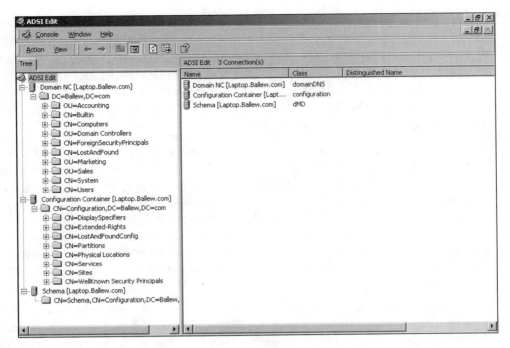

Figure 6.8
ADSI Edit.

Windows 2000 Support Tools|Tools|Security Administration Tools. Using this utility, you can create new account mappings and find tools that can help you migrate Windows NT domains to Windows 2000 domains.

To learn more about these tools, see the help files located on the Windows 2000 Server CD-ROM. Appendix B lists more troubleshooting tools, and this book's CD-ROM contains links to various parts of Microsoft's Web site.

Next, you'll learn about the Microsoft Management Console and how to configure it to suit your specific needs. Preconfigured consoles will be discussed, as well as how to create your own custom consoles.

Introduction to MMC

Using the Microsoft Management Console for the administration of a Windows 2000 network can greatly enhance your efficiency in handling those management tasks. Using MMC, you can create consoles that have all of the most-used tools for your specific administrative needs; these consoles can be used to manage the software, hardware, and other components of your network. The tools that you need to accomplish these tasks can be snapped-in to the console and thus made available from a central location.

MMC Characteristics

It is assumed that the MMC will be configured to host the tools you use most often to do your job, such as the Active Directory Users And Computers console. You can add that console to an MMC and access it from a shortcut on the desktop. In addition, you can place other tools in this console. To fully explain the MMC and how consoles are created, I'll discuss some of the characteristics of the MMC, then preconfigured consoles, followed by creating custom consoles, and finally, using those consoles.

Microsoft Management Consoles can be run by Windows 2000 Server, Advanced Server, and Professional, as well as by Windows NT and Windows 9x. *Snap-ins* are components (programs, basically) that can be added to a console for the purpose of performing some administrative task. *Extension snap-ins* can be added to increase the functionality of an existing snap-in. Figure 6.9 shows a list of snap-ins available from a Windows 2000 Server machine that has the Support Tools installed. If you remember, the Active Directory Schema snap-in was installed in a previous chapter. Besides the snap-ins seen in Figure 6.9, you can add other items, such as ActiveX controls, Web page links, folders, and tasks.

The Microsoft Management Console can be run in several modes. In some instances, you will need to, or want someone else to, actually create a new console. In this instance, the MMC will need to be used in author mode. In other instances, you will only need to, or want someone else to, use an existing console to perform administrative duties. In this instance, the MMC will need to be run in user mode.

Author mode can be assigned to a console so that the user can add and remove snap-ins to the console, create new windows and taskpad views, add items to the Favorites list, and view all parts of the console tree. Author mode gives the user full control over the console. In addition, you can type "mmc /a" at the **Run** command to start an existing

Figure 6.9
Available snap-ins.

console or a new console in author mode. Author mode is probably unnecessary for most users of a console because the console they'll be using has already been configured.

Tip: Because the /a switch can be employed by users to invoke author mode, you will want to configure user profile settings or group policy settings to prevent this.

6

User mode has three configurations: full access, limited access with multiple windows, and limited access with a single window. You will want to configure the user mode to suit the needs of your clients. The Full Access option allows users to do just about anything to or with the console except for adding or removing snap-ins or changing the console's properties. Users can move between snap-ins, open new windows, and access all parts of the console tree. In contrast, the Limited Access, Multiple Windows option allows the clients to view multiple windows in the console, but does not allow them to open new windows or access every part of the console tree. The Limited Access, Single Window option is the most restrictive. In this mode, users cannot open new windows, gain access to all parts of the console tree, or view multiple windows.

You can change the user mode by opening the Microsoft Management Console and choosing Console|Options. In the Options dialog box, you can see the name of the console, change the icon, change the user mode, enable context menus on the console taskpads, specify whether console changes should be saved, and specify whether users can customize the views. Figure 6.10 shows this dialog box.

You can restrict access to author mode in the MMC through the Group Policy snap-in. Through this utility, access to snap-ins can be limited as well. You can restrict access to

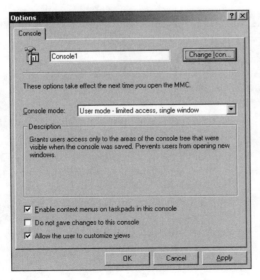

Figure 6.10
Console Options.

certain snap-ins or to a certain domain, or a combination of both. To set restrictions by using the Group Policy snap-in, you must be an administrator or have equivalent rights. For information on setting group policies, see "Using the MMC" later in this chapter.

The MMC consists of two panes, a left pane and a right pane, similar to the Active Directory consoles seen earlier. The left pane contains two tabs: the Tree tab and the Favorites tab. The Tree tab shows what items are available from this console, and the Favorites tab can be used to save shortcuts to items that are used often by the client. This tab can be used to create a Favorites list for a particular user. You can also create a custom view to hide the Tree tab.

Preconfigured MMCs

The preconfigured consoles that are available in Windows 2000 can be found by choosing Start|Programs|Administrative Tools or by right-clicking on My Computer and choosing Manage. Preconfigured consoles differ depending on the operating system being used and on the resources and components that have been installed. Some of the preconfigured MMCs on Windows 2000 servers, as well as applications that have a similar interface and are used like an MMC, include the following:

- Component Services
- Computer Management
- Distributed File System
- Local Security Policy
- Services
- Active Directory Domains And Trusts, Sites And Services, and Users And Computers
- Certification Authority
- Event Viewer
- Remote Storage
- Telephony
- Terminal Services Licensing
- Terminal Services Manager
- Active Directory Migration Tool
- Security Administration Tools
- Internet Authentication Service
- Internet Services Manager

To see how one of these preconfigured consoles works, open a console by choosing Start|Programs|Administrative Tools|Local Security Policy. As you can see from Figure 6.11, it appears similar in use and function to the other consoles shown earlier.

The Local Security Policy console contains a Tree pane, a Details pane, an Action menu, and a View menu. The objects in this console can be manipulated and modified as in any console. This console is in user mode; there is no menu bar with Console, Window, and Help, as you will see in the custom MMCs in the next section. It is in the Console menu that snap-ins can be added or removed. Because this is a preconfigured console, it doesn't need options to add or remove snap-ins.

These preconfigured consoles may be all an administrator of a small network needs to sufficiently manage a network. If they aren't, custom consoles can be built, as described in the following section.

Custom MMCs

Custom consoles can be created to assist an administrator in managing many tasks through one easy-to-use interface. For instance, if an administrator constantly uses Active Directory Users And Computers, Certificates, Certification Authority, and Remote Storage, then a custom Microsoft Management Console can be configured that contains all

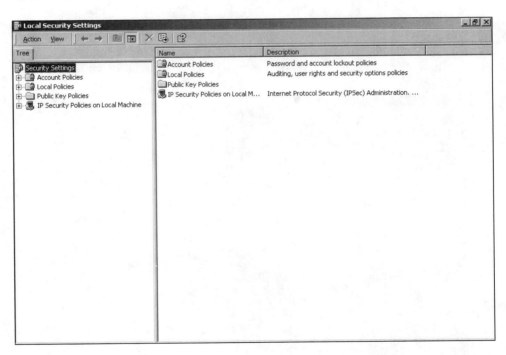

Figure 6.11
The Local Security Policy console.

four of these snap-ins. Having all these applications in one place saves the administrator time because he or she won't have to continually transfer back and forth between them.

Another reason for creating custom consoles is that they can be distributed among clients who use the consoles to do their jobs. An administrator can create a console that contains only the snap-ins that a particular user needs to perform his duties, put that console in user mode, and make the location of applications easier for the user to find and manage. In addition, consoles can be configured for distribution to entire groups of workers.

Note: MMCs are saved as .msc files.

Creating Custom MMCs

In this section, you'll learn how to create a custom MMC, including installing snap-ins and extensions, and you will explore the available menus and their offerings.

To create a custom MMC:

1. Choose Start|Run, type "mmc", and choose OK.

2. Maximize both of the windows by choosing the Maximize button in each console: the MMC and the Root.

3. Choose Console|Add/Remove Snap-in. The Add/Remove Snap-in dialog box will appear, and it is shown in Figure 6.12.

4. On the Standalone tab, choose Add. You will see the same dialog box shown in Figure 6.9, and shown again here for reference as Figure 6.13, which shows the

Figure 6.12
The Add/Remove Snap-in dialog box.

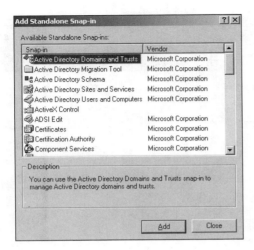

Figure 6.13
The Add Standalone Snap-in dialog box.

snap-ins available on my Windows 2000 Server computer; the snap-ins available on other computers may differ, depending on installed components.

5. Although you are free to select a snap-in of your choice, for now, select Group Policy. Later this chapter will discuss how to restrict author mode in the MMC by using the Group Policy snap-in, so you'll need to install it. Choose Add.

6. Because Group Policy was selected, a prompt appears and asks for the group policy object. The default is the Local Computer, which I will choose. (Most snap-ins do not ask for additional information.) Choose Close.

7. The Add/Remove Snap-in dialog now contains the snap-in you've chosen. It should be listed only once. If you choose Add again before choosing Close, it will be listed twice. If this is the case, simply select the repeated snap-in and choose Remove.

8. Now look at the Extensions tab again. Notice that the Group Policy snap-in now has several extensions available. All of the extensions are installed by default, or if you'd like to customize the extensions, simply uncheck the box and select the ones you'd like to keep.

9. Select the Standalone tab again and choose OK.

10. Figure 6.14 shows the new MMC console with some of the trees expanded. There is one main tree, Local Computer Policy, and two subtrees, Computer Configuration and User Configuration. Each of these subtrees has other folders, as shown in Figure 6.14.

11. To add another snap-in, choose Console|Add/Remove Snap-in. The Add/Remove Snap-in dialog box will appear (see Figure 6.12). Choose Add.

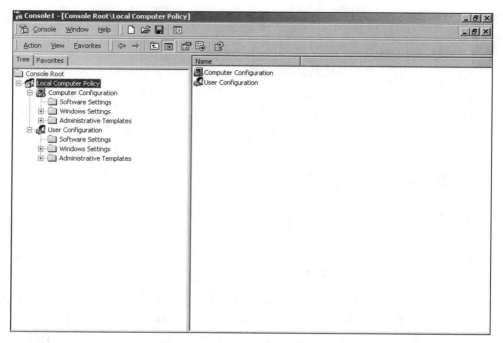

Figure 6.14
Local Computer Policy.

12. This time, select Event Viewer, and choose Add.

13. A dialog box appears, and you must choose how this snap-in will be used. It will manage either the local computer or another computer. Select the local computer (the default); then choose Finish, followed by Close.

14. The Add/Remove Snap-in box should now contain two snap-ins. Choose OK.

15. Expand Event Viewer (local) in the left pane of the MMC. Notice the options:

   - Application

   - Directory Service

   - DNS Server

   - File Replication Service

   - Security

   - System

16. Click on Application under the Event Viewer (Local) tree. Notice, in the details pane, the log that is kept regarding application events. Figures 6.15 and 6.16 show some errors in the application and system logs.

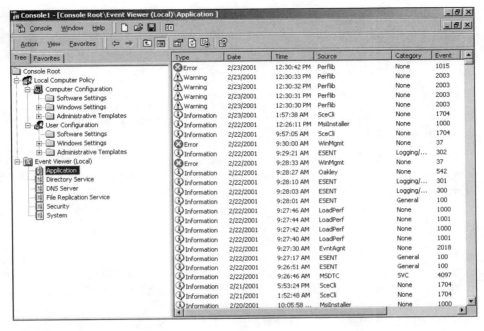

Figure 6.15

The application log.

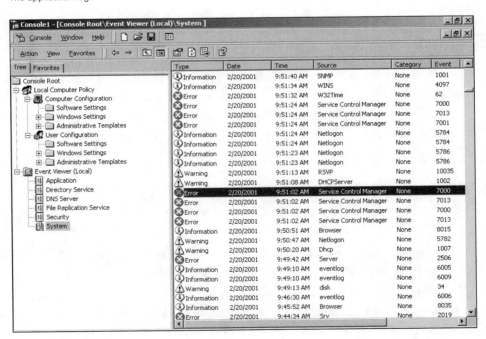

Figure 6.16

The system log.

17. By double-clicking on the events logged in the Event Viewer, you can determine why a certain error, warning, or information note was logged. In the System log shown in Figure 6.16, some of these errors occurred due to logon failures.

18. To save the console for later use, choose Console|Save As, type a name for the console, and choose Save.

19. To see the console, choose Start|Programs|Administrative Tools and the name of the console.

Now that you've explored the Microsoft Management Consoles, configured your own custom management console, and saved that console to Administrative Tools, it is time to learn how to use a few of the available snap-ins. In the next section, I'll start with setting group policies to prevent console users from opening the saved consoles in author mode.

Using the MMC

In this section, you'll learn how to use the Microsoft Management Console to perform certain tasks, including restricting access to author mode in an MMC, restricting access to certain snap-ins, and configuring a saved MMC to hide features and menus, and to reorder columns. These are some of the more common tasks associated with administrators and their consoles. Once you've manipulated the management consoles, you'll perform some of the tasks associated with MMCs and Active Directory.

The first step in securing a custom console involves setting group policies so that users will not be able to enter author mode simply by opening the console from the Run line with the **/a** switch, which enables them to add or remove snap-ins and have full control over them. Once a console is set and distributed, it will not need to be modified by its users. To secure the custom consoles through group policies, and to restrict access to author mode, follow these steps:

1. Open the console that contains the Group Policy snap-in that you added earlier. (Choose Start|Programs|Administrative Tools|<*console name*>.)

2. Click on Local Computer Policy and then on User Configuration.

3. Click on Administrative Templates and then Windows Components.

4. Click on Microsoft Management Console. See Figure 6.17 to see the entire tree and the location of this item.

5. In the details pane, double-click on Restrict The User From Entering Author Mode. In the dialog box that appears, select Enabled. Choose OK.

You can also restrict access to certain snap-ins as well. To restrict access to a specified list of snap-ins, follow these steps (after the restriction has been enabled, you will configure which snap-ins are permitted and which are not):

1. Open the console that contains the Group Policy snap-in that you added earlier.

2. Click on Local Computer Policy and then User Configuration.

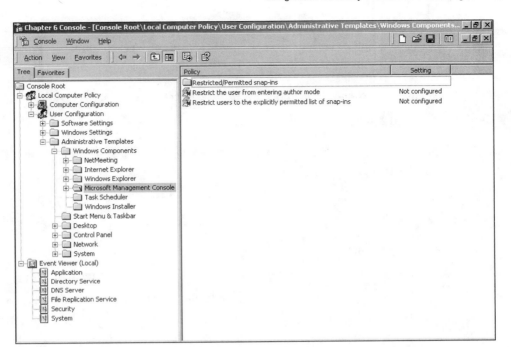

Figure 6.17
The console tree.

3. Click on Administrative Templates and then Windows Components.

4. Click on Microsoft Management Console. See Figure 6.17 to see the entire tree and the location of this item.

5. In the details pane, double-click on Restrict Users To The Explicitly Permitted List Of Snap-Ins. In the dialog box that appears, select Enabled. Choose OK.

   To set the list of snap-ins that are either available or restricted, select the folder named Restricted/Permitted Snap-ins in the details pane.

6. In the details pane, you will see all of the available snap-ins. By default, they are Not Configured. Right-click or double-click on any of the snap-ins in the list and choose either to enable or to disable the snap-in. The choices made here will be noted in the group policy for all users who access this console.

Note: For more details on group policies, see "Administering Active Directory Services," next.

You may also want to configure a saved MMC to hide features and menus and to reorder columns. This can be done through the View menu of an opened console:

1. Open the console that contains the Group Policy snap-in that you added earlier.

2. Choose View|Customize.

3. From the Customize dialog box, you can choose to view or hide the following items simply by placing or removing a checkmark in the box by each item:

- Console Tree
- Standard Menus—Action and View
- Standard Toolbar
- Status Bar
- Description Bar
- Taskpad Navigation Tabs
- Snap-in Menus
- Snap-in Toolbars

4. By choosing View|Choose Columns, you can hide or display columns.

5. From the Favorites menu, you can choose to add or organize favorites for a console.

Finally, one last task should be addressed. From the Help menu, you can choose Help Topics, Microsoft On The Web, and About Microsoft Management Console. The Help Topics tab is extremely useful and includes information about the MMC, group policies, Internet Explorer maintenance, Remote Installation Services, Event Viewer, Internet Protocol Security, and security settings. All of these items are very important to making the consoles function efficiently.

Administering Active Directory Services

Now that you are familiar with the Active Directory consoles, the Microsoft Management Console, and how to use them, we can discuss certain tasks. In this section, you'll learn how to set up explicit trust relationships between domains, publish Active Directory resources, assign permissions, find and move objects, and add shared folders, and how to perform similar tasks in the other consoles. Using the consoles available to you through Active Directory and the MMC is the first step in learning to manage the Active Directory and its resources. After explaining how to perform certain tasks in these consoles, I'll focus on how to secure resources.

Preparation

Because you will be using mainly the three Active Directory consoles mentioned earlier for most of your initial Active Directory tasks, it may be helpful to place all three of those consoles in one custom MMC. From this one MMC, you can then access all of the consoles you need without having to switch back and forth between them. To set up a custom MMC with these three consoles, follow these steps:

1. Choose Start|Run and enter "mmc".

2. Maximize the consoles, and choose Console|Add/Remove Snap-in.

3. Choose Add, and then select the three Active Directory consoles: Domains And Trusts, Users And Computers, and Sites And Services. Choose OK.

4. Save the console.

Setting Up Explicit Trust Relationships

Setting up an explicit trust relationship is necessary when network domains are Windows NT 4 domains or when there is more than one forest that needs to be networked. Although transitive trusts are created automatically between Windows 2000 parent and child domains, these bidirectional trusts are not created for Windows NT domains and therefore must be created manually. You were introduced to the basics of creating trusts in Chapter 5, and in this section, you'll learn even more.

Follow the next two procedures to create an explicit bidirectional trust relationship between two domains and to remove trusts relationships from domains. For the purpose of making the explanation clear, Domain A will be the resource domain, or trusting domain, and Domain B will be the administration domain, or trusted domain. The first few steps will explain how to set up a trust from Domain A to Domain B. (The terms *trusted* and *trusting* are leftover from Windows NT, and are useful for comparison here.) Start by creating the two-way explicit trust relationship:

1. Log on to Domain B as an administrator, and start the Active Directory Domains And Trusts console.

2. Connect to a domain controller by right-clicking on Active Directory Domains And Trusts and choosing Connect To Domain. Choose the domain controller you want to connect to, or type in the name of the domain controller, and choose OK.

3. In the details pane, right-click on the domain for which you want to configure a trust, and choose Properties.

4. Select the Trusts tab. In the Domains Trusted By This Domain list, add the names of the domains that are trusted. To do this, choose Add, followed by the domain name and administrator password.

5. In the Domains That Trust This Domain list, add the names of the domains that you want to trust Domain B, followed by the appropriate password.

6. Domain A should be listed in the Trusting Domains box. The Transitive column states that Domain A either does or does not have a transitive relationship with Domain B. If a transitive relationship exists, both would be Windows 2000 domains; if one domain or forest is not a Windows 2000 domain, no transitive relationship will exist.

7. Now log on to Domain A as a member of the domain administrative group. Perform the same steps described in this explanation to add Domain B to the Domains Trusted By This Domain list.

8. Now, a one-way trust relationship has been created from Domain A to Domain B. To make the trust relationship two-way, you must perform the previous steps on the

opposite domain controllers. For instance, log on to Domain A, activate Domains And Trusts, and repeat the procedure. Once that is complete, the domains will trust each other, and users can log on from either domain and connect to resources on the other.

9. If any other domains need to be involved in these trust relationships, the tasks multiply. Adding a third domain into the mix will involve explicitly creating trusts between Domains C and B, Domains C and A, and back again. This is why the transitive automatic trusts in Windows 2000 are so helpful, and why the ultimate goal is to remove any and all Windows NT domains during the migration.

To remove a trust relationship, follow these steps:

1. Make sure that no users are logged on or accessing resources in the domain for which the trust is to be removed.

2. From the trusted domain, open the Active Directory Domains And Trusts console, select the domain for which the trust is to be removed, right-click, and choose Properties. Select the Trusts tab.

3. In the same manner as adding a trust, select the trust to be removed, and choose Remove.

4. Once the trust has been removed from this domain, log on to the trusting domain, and perform the same steps again.

Publishing Active Directory Resources

Resources in Active Directory consist of users, computers, folders, network services, printers, and files. Publishing these resources in Active Directory makes it easier for users to find the resources across the network. In this section, you'll learn how to publish resources by using the custom MMC that you created earlier. To publish resources, including shared folders, follow these steps:

1. If a Windows NT printer needs to be shared, open Active Directory Users And Computers, and right-click on the domain name. Choose New|Printer and enter the network path.

2. To publish a computer, open Active Directory Users And Computers, and right-click on the domain name. Choose New|Computer and enter the network path.

3. To publish a contact, group, OU, user, or shared folder, open Active Directory Users And Computers, and right-click on the domain name. Choose New|<resource> and choose OK.

As I mentioned earlier, network services can also be published in Active Directory. Publishing services allows administrators to locate information and manage their services by using the Active Directory console instead of by searching for the computers that run these services. The ability to use Active Directory to search for the service makes managing the services more efficient.

Note: *It makes sense that services would be published under the Sites And Services console. However, to view the services, you must choose View\Show Services Node.*

To publish a service, follow these steps:

1. Log on to the domain controller as an administrator.

2. Open Active Directory Sites And Services, and choose View\Show Services Node.

3. In the details pane, open the Services folder.

4. Four folders contain services: NetServices, Public Key Services, RRAS, and Windows NT. Double-click on the folder that contains the service that you want to publish. For instance, to publish Windows NT Directory Services, open the Windows NT folder.

5. Right-click on the service to publish, and choose Properties.

6. Select the Security tab and set the permissions appropriately. See Figure 6.18 for the Directory Service Properties service in the Windows NT folder.

7. Choose OK. The service is published.

Note: *If you are not sure how to set these permissions, they will be addressed next. In addition, you'll learn about group policies and NTFS permissions later in this chapter.*

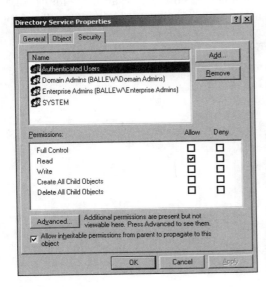

Figure 6.18
Directory Service Properties.

Understanding and Assigning Active Directory Permissions

Active Directory is used to group and make available objects and resources for the users on the network. It is important that these resources are protected with the appropriate permissions for access control and that security is configured appropriately. Active Directory permissions, which are similar to the NTFS permissions you'll learn about later, are used to define who can access what in the Active Directory database.

On a Windows 2000 network, every object that is stored in Active Directory has an access control list associated with it. This list contains information about the permissions that have been assigned to an object and determines whether a user can access the object. There are different levels of permissions for objects, and there are different permissions that can be set for different objects. For instance, the Guest user account has an option to set logon hours and dial-in permissions, but a services resource object doesn't. When an object is created, the owner of that object sets permissions so that others on the network can access it.

To understand which permissions are available to set and how these permissions are configured, look at the Active Directory Users And Computers console. Select an object, such as a computer or user, right-click on it and choose Properties, and then select the Security tab in the Properties dialog box. Figure 6.19 shows the Security tab for a user, and Figure 6.20 shows the Security tab for a computer. You can see that the permissions seem to be the same.

Depending on the object accessed, different permissions will be available for configuration. If you scroll down through each of these Permissions list boxes, you will see the

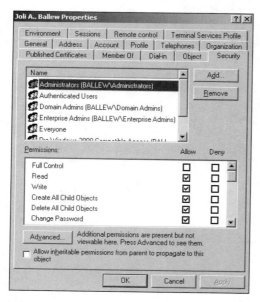

Figure 6.19
Security tab for a user.

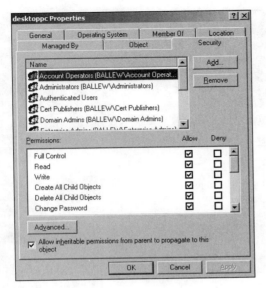

Figure 6.20
Security tab for a computer.

different permissions. In Figures 6.21 and 6.22, you can see how the permissions differ for the user and computer objects.

Almost every object in Active Directory contains standard permissions, and they are described in Table 6.2.

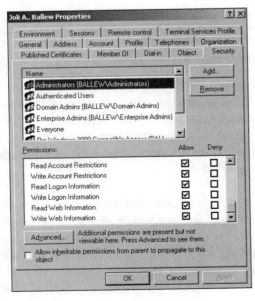

Figure 6.21
User permissions continued.

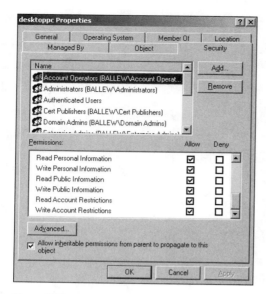

Figure 6.22
Computer permissions continued.

Table 6.2   Standard permissions.

Permission	Purpose
Full Control	Allows the user to modify permissions, take ownership, view objects and their attributes, modify object attributes, and add or remove child objects from an organizational unit.
Read	Allows the user to view objects and their attributes.
Write	Allows the user to modify the object's attributes.
Create All Child Objects	Allows the user to add a child object to an organizational unit.
Delete All Child Objects	Allows the user to remove a child object from an organizational unit.

Warning! *If a user belongs to one group with the NTFS Read permission, and that user is assigned to another group that has the NTFS Full Control permission, that user's effective permissions are Full Control (the most lenient of the two). When share permissions are added in, the effective permissions become more complex. When assigning permissions, make sure that you remain aware of a user's group membership and effective permissions. There'll be more information on permissions later.*

As you can see from Figures 6.19 through 6.22, all of the available permissions can be allowed or denied. Although I wouldn't recommend assigning permissions by denying access for particular users, it can be done. For managing access to objects, there are easier and more efficient ways, including managing group membership and simply not assigning permission, and those ways will be discussed later. Once the Deny permission has been assigned, no other permission will override it. Even if the user is a member of three groups, all with Full Control permissions to an object, one Deny permission will prevent the user from accessing the resource.

To change the permission for a particular object, follow these steps:

1. Open Active Directory Users And Computers.

2. Choose View|Advanced Features and make sure that command has a checkmark by it.

3. Select an object, such as a printer, computer, or user, and right-click on it.

4. Choose Properties, and select the Security tab.

5. To add a new permission, choose Add, and select the account or group to which the new permission will be assigned. To change existing permissions, highlight the group or user in the Name list box, and modify the permissions in the Permissions list box. As you highlight different groups or users, you'll notice that the default permissions differ. For instance, some groups have no permissions assigned, and other groups have all permissions allowed or a combination of denied and allowed.

6. Select the appropriate permissions by choosing Allow or Deny, or select the Advanced button to see more choices.

7. On the Advanced tab, you can select permissions such as List Contents, Delete Subtree, Modify Owner, and more.

8. Choose OK three times to close the dialog boxes.

You can also enable or disable permission inheritance between parent and child objects by placing or removing the checkmark in the Allow Inheritable Permissions checkbox in these Properties dialog boxes.

Before moving on to finding and moving Active Directory objects, right-click on a previously created organizational unit. Choose Properties from the context menu, and look at the Security and Group Policy tabs. From here, you can create a new group policy object, add a group policy object link, edit a group policy object, enable No Override, delete the group policy object, and see the object's properties. You can also block policy inheritance from here. These items are shown in Figure 6.23.

You'll learn more about group policy objects later in this section.

Finding Active Directory Objects

Sometimes you will need to search for certain Active Directory objects. To do this, use the **Find** command. (Open Active Directory Users And Computers, right-click on the domain to search, and choose Find.) The Find dialog box, in its simplest form, is shown in Figure 6.24.

Notice that there are menu-bar options: File, Edit, View, and Help. And there are drop-down list boxes for Find and In. The Find list offers the following choices: Users,

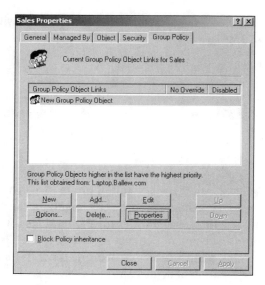

Figure 6.23
OU properties.

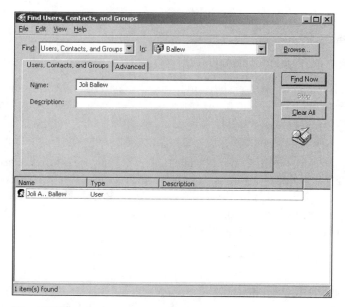

Figure 6.24
The Find dialog box.

Contacts, and Groups (shown in Figure 6.24); Computers; Printers; Shared Folders; Organizational Units; Custom Search; and Remote Installation Clients. The In list contains the names of domains and the Entire Directory option. The Browse button lets you surf the entire directory.

The Advanced button allows you to search by field. The field choices begin with a User, Group, or Contact, and each of those items contains fields specific to it. For instance, the User field can be searched for an item relating to the user's country, home address, division, first name, email address, job title, last name, logon name, department, and more. You can even search for a user based on her middle name.

When the object is located, it is listed in the Name box, as shown in Figure 6.24. You can double-click on the item to see its properties. The Find feature makes finding resources and objects easy and effective. In addition, the File menu can be used to perform certain tasks related to this object. In the example showing the user name, I can use the File menu to rename or delete the highlighted object (a user, group, or contact), add members, reset passwords, send mail, open the user's home page, and more. The Find feature is the perfect solution for finding and managing objects for which you can't remember the name or objects located in a certain building or city.

Moving Active Directory Objects

Sometimes you'll need to move Active Directory objects within a domain, and sometimes you'll need to move them between domains. For instance, an employee in Domain A may be moved from the Sales OU to the Marketing OU because of a recent promotion, or a printer or computer may be moved from one domain to another because of restructuring among domains. Moving Active Directory objects within a domain is one of the easier tasks associated with Active Directory administration. To move objects within a domain, follow these steps:

1. Open Active Directory Users And Computers, and highlight the object you need to move.

2. Right-click on the object and choose Move. (You can highlight more than one object if you need to move multiple items.)

3. From the resulting dialog box, select the OU or container that the object will be moved into, and choose OK.

4. The resulting permissions may change for the object. Permissions that the object inherited from its former parent object will disappear, and the object will inherit the permissions of the OU or container it is subsequently placed in. If any permissions were directly assigned to the object in the manner listed in the previous section, those permissions will remain.

Moving objects or resources from one domain to another is the same as migrating the information, described in Chapter 5. The domain restructuring techniques detailed in that chapter can be used for moving resources from one domain to another.

Using Task Scheduler

You can configure Task Scheduler through the Microsoft Management Console to schedule programs or batch files to run at specified times or intervals or to run only once. These programs can be maintenance utilities, scripts, or even specific documents that need to be opened at a specific time. The tasks that are created while you're configuring Task Scheduler are saved as scheduled tasks in the Control Panel. You can also configure Task Scheduler to perform tasks on a remote computer by using My Network Places to browse to that computer. Task Scheduler can be used to automate many of the administrator's common tasks. Task Scheduler is mentioned in this section because it can be used to perform certain tasks related to the network and Active Directory. Task Scheduler can be configured to start many programs associated with Active Directory, including consoles, and it can be used to open consoles, perform disk cleanup, run Network Monitor, and perform many other administrative tasks automatically. Understanding how to use Task Scheduler can reduce the tasks that must be completed manually by administrators.

To configure Task Scheduler to perform local tasks, follow these steps:

1. Open Task Scheduler through the Control Panel by clicking on the Scheduled Tasks icon.

2. Double-click on Add Scheduled Task.

3. The Schedule Task Wizard appears. Read the information and choose Next.

4. Figure 6.25 shows the application choice page. Select a program that you would like to schedule, and choose Next. This application can be configured for the local machine, or you can browse the network for a remote machine. (I'll choose Outlook Express, and I'll configure it to run every morning at 8:00 on the local machine.) Choose Next.

5. The next page asks how often you want to run this task. You can run the task daily, weekly, monthly, one time only, when the computer starts, or when you log on. Make the choice that suits your needs, and choose Next.

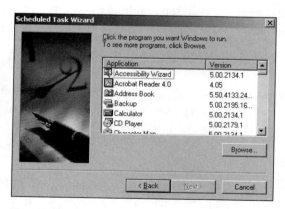

Figure 6.25
Choosing a scheduled task.

6. On the next page, you specify the time and days for the task to run. The choices are start time, every day, weekdays only, every *<number>* of days, and the start date. Make the appropriate choices, and choose Next.

7. The next page asks for a user name and password that have the rights associated with the task that is to be performed. For instance, if the task is Solitaire, any user account will do, but if the task to be scheduled requires administrator privileges, then an administrator password will be required. Type the correct password and choose Next.

8. The next page should inform you that you have successfully scheduled a task. You can also specify that you want to open advanced properties; check the box as shown in Figure 6.26. Then choose Finish.

9. From the dialog box that appears next, you can enable or disable the task, change the schedule or duration, and change the settings associated with the task. Notice what options are available, make any necessary changes, and choose OK. The task will appear in the Scheduled Tasks folder. To see the configuration screen (shown in Figure 6.26) again, simply open the task through this folder.

Note: Disk Defragmenter cannot be scheduled with Task Scheduler in Windows 2000. However, you can get around this limitation by purchasing DiskKeeper or by download-ing applicable .vbs files from the Internet.

Although there are many other tasks that can be performed using the consoles introduced in this chapter, the tasks are performed in a manner similar to what has already been described. For instance, adding a shared folder to an organizational unit is achieved through the same menu as adding a new computer, contact, user, or group to that OU. Delegating control of a particular OU or object is also achieved by right-clicking on the OU to be administered. Instead of repeating the steps for these types of tasks, I'll let you explore those menus on your own, and I'll move on to securing the resources that have been added to the network through Active Directory.

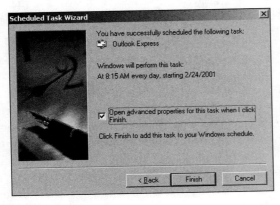

Figure 6.26
A successfully scheduled task.

Securing the Active Directory, the users, and the network is an ongoing process. You should continually monitor the network, and reconfigure security selections as needed. In the next section, I'll discuss two types of security. The first, group policies, can be configured through the Active Directory consoles previously introduced, and these policies are used to secure the client's environment. The second, NTFS permissions, can be configured for Active Directory files and folders on NTFS volumes. There are many options available for configuring a group policy for users on the network, as well as many different combinations of NTFS permissions, account permissions, and other group permissions. The rest of the chapter will deal with how group policies and NTFS permissions can be used to secure resources on a Windows 2000 network.

Securing the Network by Using Group Policies and NTFS Permissions

The remaining pages in this chapter are devoted to securing the Active Directory database and its resources by using group policies to restrict and protect users, and by using NTFS file and folder permissions to protect resources. Group Policy is a Microsoft Management Console snap-in that is used for restricting or defining the user's desktop. By using the snap-in to create a group policy object (GPO), an administrator can effectively design how the desktop will look to all users in a domain, OU, or site. The GPO is simply a collection of policy settings that define the user's desktop. Different group policy objects can be created for different groups.

NTFS permissions offer another type of security. Permissions, in their simplest form, determine who can access an object and who can't. In addition, NTFS permissions can be used to specify what users who access a resource can or can't do *to* it. For instance, perhaps a user has permissions to access a file, read that file, and even write to that file, but not to delete or move the file. This level of security can enable an administrator to fully protect resources. NTFS permissions are available only on NTFS volumes, and these permissions are effective if the user is accessing the resource across the network or sitting at the machine locally. The ability to use NTFS to assign permissions that prohibit local access, and to assign permissions to both files and folders, is available only on NTFS volumes.

Exploring Group Policies

In this section, you'll learn about group policies. First I'll explain why group policies are used, what benefits they offer to both users and administrators, and how they are structured. Then I'll describe how policies are applied when there are multiple policies, or when there are multiple child and parent container policies, and what the options are for configuring inheritance. These options include blocking the policy inheritance, disallowing any overrides of policies, and disabling or deleting a group policy. Finally, I'll describe how to create a group policy object, how to use the Group Policy snap-in, and how to edit group policy objects, and I will include other group policy management tasks that are performed regularly. Throughout this section, tips and notes will assist you in creating the best policy for your network, and available policy options will be described.

Understanding Group Policies

Group policies are used for the main purpose of securing the user's desktop. Applying a group policy is the best way to ensure that a user's environment is secure and to enable a corporate or company-wide desktop policy. Group policies are configured using the Group Policy snap-in with a Microsoft Management Console, and they are *linked* to domains, sites, or organizational units. The security design that is configured and linked to a particular area will affect all users in the unit.

6

When Computer Configuration settings are set, all users who log on to a specific computer will obtain those settings. This occurs because the settings are initialized when the computer boots. In contrast, when User Configuration settings are set, all users have a profile of sorts that follows them around and applies to them no matter where they log on or which computer they log on to. The User Configuration settings are applied when the user logs on. When these policies conflict, the user settings win out because they are applied last. There will be more discussion on how group policies are processed later in this section.

Group policies can also be configured for the purpose of enhancing the user's environment. A group policy can specify which programs will appear on the Start menu, can automate certain tasks or programs when a user logs on or off, and can make or distribute applications, shortcuts, and other network utilities so that they are more readily available to the user. Group policies can also be used to restrict access to certain files or folders, perform maintenance tasks for Internet Explorer, configure RIS, or configure automatic installations of applications that users cannot uninstall. Because only administrators can change the group policies that are configured, they remain very secure on the network.

Group policy objects (GPOs) hold group policy settings. Many types of group policies can be configured, and group policy snap-ins can be used to extend the group policy namespace under the User Configuration or Computer Configuration nodes, or both. You can access the settings for these policy types through the Group Policy snap-in in the MMC. A few of the different types of group policies are as follows:

- *Folder Redirection*—Allows the administrator to redirect a folder from a client's user profile to a specified location on the network for centralized management. The folders that can be redirected to these network shares include Application Data, Desktop, My Documents, My Pictures, and Start Menu.

By redirecting folders—such as the My Documents folder or the My Pictures folder—from their default locations to a network share, you can make those folders available to the user from any machine on the network. In addition, if the My Documents folder is redirected to a network share, the data in that folder can be backed up and managed by an administrator. Because users do not always back up their data regularly, this redirection can prove useful in reducing data loss and TCO. Finally, if the user's data is on a network share, the user can then take advantage of the offline files and folders utilities to access that information even when he or she is away from the office.

- *Administrative Templates*—Administrative templates come in two flavors: templates for computers and templates for users. The templates for computers are Registry-based policies that are used to require certain Registry settings that establish the behavior and appearance of the desktop, including components, applications, and settings for printers, disk quotas, and file protection. The templates for users also contain settings for the Start menu, taskbar, and desktop. There are more than 400 settings available for the user's environment.

- *Security Settings*—These policies can be set to limit user access to resources such as files and folders. Under Security Settings, an administrator can configure account policies, local policies, public key policies, and IPSec (IP Security) policies.

- *Account policies*—Include password policies, lockout policies, and Kerberos policies. Local policies include audit policies, user rights, and other security options. Public key and IPSec policies include additional policies you can configure. As with all of these policies, security policies can be configured for a domain, an OU, a site, or a group of users or computers.

- *Scripts*—Scripts are batch (.bat) and command (.cmd) files that are used to automate tasks that are run when the computer is started up or shut down or when a user logs on or logs off. Scripts have many configuration choices, including whether the scripts should be run synchronously or asynchronously, whether they are visible or hidden, and what the maximum timeout period for a script can be. Multiple scripts are run from the top of a list to the bottom, and the order in which the scripts are run can be changed. Scripts can be written as .vbs or .js files, or with a Windows Scripting Host, in addition to being written as batch files or command files.

- *Default setting*—For processing scripts is to do so asynchronously and hidden. This means that the scripts will be processed while the logon process is completed and the desktop is loaded, and the user will not see the script running in any visible window. This is usually fine, but errors can occur if the user attempts to use an application that is currently being manipulated by a script or is otherwise unavailable because of it.

- *Synchronous processes*—Makes sure that the desktop does not load until after the script is finished running. This certainly eliminates the potential for the error just described but can cause unnecessary wait times for clients when they're trying to log on. Users cannot log on until the scripts have finished running.

- *Software Settings*—Administrators can use the Software Settings policies to manage and configure software installations automatically for clients across the network. Software can be either published or assigned. When application installations are automatic, tasks usually associated with physically visiting every machine can be reduced dramatically.

When applications are assigned, the applications or upgrades occur automatically on client machines and connect the users to the application installation program. Here, the user has no choice in whether the application is installed. Users cannot delete these applications once they are installed.

Conversely, publishing applications allows the users to decide if they want to install the application. Users can also remove the applications. These applications are installed through the user's Add/Remove Programs icon in the Control Panel.

Both assigning applications and publishing applications require the use of .msi files. These Microsoft Installer files are used with application files and a shared folder for distribution via Software Settings.

Group policies can be very useful to an organization, especially if the administrator is capable of using all of the policy's features. Besides the obvious usefulness of having a tool available for easily creating a desktop policy for the entire domain, OU, or site, the benefits of using the other features are just as great. It's very convenient to be able to install upgrades or applications automatically, use logon and logoff scripts to back up data or clean drives, manage password and account policies, redirect folders, and make RIS work more efficiently for Windows 2000 Professional installations—all from one central location.

The users in an organization will benefit as well from these group policies. You may not want your users to watch scripts run, interact with installations, or back up their own data. The environment may need to be tightly controlled and handled with strict desktop, account, and other policies. There are certainly instances when folder redirection can benefit a company. On the other hand, companies with more loosely knit environments may want their users to watch scripts run, interact with installations, and back up their own data. They may also want users to have very few desktop restrictions and possibly even to have no password or account restrictions at all. Whatever the case or the environment's needs, the appropriate policies can be set using the six policies mentioned here.

Group Policy Structure

To use a group policy effectively and to take advantage of *all* of the available components, the network must consist of Windows 2000 domain controllers using Active Directory and Windows 2000 clients. Though that is most likely the goal in the end, it is even more reason to get rid of those old NT machines as quickly as possible. In this section, I'll discuss how a group policy is structured and how the policies are contained, and I'll go into more detail concerning GPOs.

A group policy is made up of objects, containers, and templates. The group policy objects store their information in containers and templates. As you know already, GPOs contain the policies that have been defined using the Group Policy snap-in. The group policy object's properties are stored in a Group Policy container (GPC) in Active Directory. The GPC contains information on both the users and computers. The GPC also contains the following information:

- *Version*—Provides the number of times the GPO has been changed or updated, and ensures that the information in the Group Policy template is up-to-date.

- *Status*—Tells whether the GPO is enabled or disabled.

- *Functionality version*—Tells the version of the utility that was used to create the GPO.

- *File system path*—Tells where the Sysvol folder is stored.

- *List of components*—Lists which extensions have a setting configured in the GPO.

Group Policy templates (GPTs) also store information in Active Directory and are located in the Sysvol folder on a domain controller. The GPT is a container as well, and it stores information about security settings, applications for software installation, administrative templates, and script file locations. GPTs are created automatically when a group policy object is created, and they are named based on the GUID of the GPO they are associated with. Listing 6.1 provides an example of a GptTmpl template that contains information on security settings.

Listing 6.1   GptTmpl template on a domain controller from the Sysvol folder.

```
[Unicode]
Unicode=yes
[System Access]
MinimumPasswordAge = 0
MaximumPasswordAge = 42
MinimumPasswordLength = 0
PasswordComplexity = 0
PasswordHistorySize = 1
LockoutBadCount = 0
RequireLogonToChangePassword = 0
ForceLogoffWhenHourExpire = 0
ClearTextPassword = 0
[Kerberos Policy]
MaxTicketAge = 10
MaxRenewAge = 7
MaxServiceAge = 600
MaxClockSkew = 5
TicketValidateClient = 1
[Version]
signature="$CHICAGO$"
Revision=1
```

In each Group Policy Template folder is a file called GPT.ini. The GPT.ini file specifies the version number of the utility that was used to create the GPO, specifies whether the user or computer portions are enabled or disabled, and specifies whether any extensions contain data for users or computers in the GPO. To view the files, templates, GPOs, and other related group policy folders on your Windows 2000 domain controller, follow these steps:

1. Use Windows Explorer and click on the domain controller's root drive (C:\ or D:\).

2. Expand the Winnt folder.

3. Expand the Sysvol folder.

4. Expand the domain folder and the second Sysvol folder.

   Under the domain folder are two folders: Policies and Scripts. Under the second Sysvol folder are the domain names. Under this domain name are two folders: Policies and Scripts.

5. The Scripts folders will be empty if no scripts are currently configured on your computer. However, both of the Policies folders will contain additional folders. Click on the first folder listed under either Policies folder, and explore the Adm, User, and Machine folders. You can open most of these files by using Notepad if you want to read their contents.

6. Some of these folders will be empty, and some will contain policies. Continue to open and explore the folders to get an idea of how they are structured and what they contain. When you're finished, close all of these windows.

Warning! *Don't edit these policies in Notepad or from Windows Explorer. The purpose of the preceding example was to show where the policies are stored and how they are structured in the operating system. To modify any group policies, use the Group Policy snap-in or right-click on the domain name in Active Directory Users And Computers and choose Properties. The policy is on the Group Policy tab.*

Listing 6.2 provides an excerpt from a policy folder on a Windows 2000 domain controller for **Ballew.com**. The policy folder is stored in the Winnt\SYSVOL\sysvol\Ballew.com\ Policies\<policy name>\Adm\conf folder in the root volume of the domain controller. The folder "conf" contains information about the setting for using conferencing applications.

Listing 6.2 Excerpt from an Adm file in the Sysvol folder of a domain controller.

```
CATEGORY !!WindowsComponents
CATEGORY !!NetMeeting

App Sharing
CATEGORY !!AppSharing
POLICY !!DisableAppSharing
KEYNAME "Software\Policies\Microsoft\Conferencing"
EXPLAIN !!DisableAppSharing_Help
VALUENAME "NoAppSharing"
END POLICY
POLICY !!PreventSharing
KEYNAME "Software\Policies\Microsoft\Conferencing"
EXPLAIN !!PreventSharing_Help
VALUENAME "NoSharing"
END POLICY
POLICY !!PreventSharingDesktop
KEYNAME "Software\Policies\Microsoft\Conferencing"
EXPLAIN !!PreventSharingDesktop_Help
```

```
VALUENAME "NoSharingDesktop"
END POLICY
POLICY !!PreventSharingCMDPrompt
KEYNAME "Software\Policies\Microsoft\Conferencing"
EXPLAIN !!PreventSharingCMDPrompt_Help
VALUENAME "NoSharingDosWindows"
END POLICY
POLICY !!PreventSharingExplorer
KEYNAME "Software\Policies\Microsoft\Conferencing"
EXPLAIN !!PreventSharingExplorer_Help
VALUENAME "NoSharingExplorer"
END POLICY
POLICY !!PreventGrantingControl
KEYNAME "Software\Policies\Microsoft\Conferencing"
EXPLAIN !!PreventGrantingControl_Help
VALUENAME "NoAllowControl"
END POLICY
```

As you can probably see after reading this section and looking at the examples, there are many ways to configure group policies, and there are literally thousands of combinations of policies and settings. As you know, these policies can be set for users or computers and at the site level, OU level, or domain level. So what happens when there are multiple policies? In what order are they initialized, and how can you figure out which policy will be applied if multiple policies exist? This is the subject of the next section.

Order of Policy Inheritance

As mentioned previously, policies can be set at the local level, domain level, site level, and OU level. These policies can also be set for users or for groups. This flexibility can create a conflict between different policies, so there have to be rules in place for the order of policy operations. All Windows 2000 domains will use the same rules for policy inheritance.

Note: *Get out of your head any thoughts about how Windows NT dealt with system policies. Windows NT system policies were applied to users, groups, and computers, whereas Windows 2000 group policies are applied to local machines, sites, domains, and OUs.*

Group policies are processed in the following order:

1. The computer is booted, and any local computer settings configured to take effect before logons are applied.

2. When the computer logs on to the network, the group policies are applied. The first policies applied to the computer are the Computer Configuration settings.

3. The Computer Configuration settings occur synchronously unless otherwise configured. The user's desktop begins to load, and the logon process continues. GPOs are processed in a certain order: local GPO, site GPO, domain GPO, and OU GPO. Any exceptions are dealt with also.

4. After Computer Configuration settings run, the startup scripts are run. Again, this process is hidden and synchronous by default. The scripts run in a preconfigured order and have a default timeout of 10 minutes. If there is a problem with a script, there may be a delay in the logon procedures.

5. At this time, the user is prompted to press Ctrl+Alt+Del and log on.

6. The user is authenticated, and the user's profile is loaded.

Note: *The user profile is not part of a group policy. A user profile is created through the Active Directory Users And Computers console to provide a desktop environment that contains the user's personal data, folders, Start menu parameters, and application settings. User profiles can be local, roaming, or mandatory, and they can be configured to affect the appearance of the user's desktop no matter what computer the user logs onto. User profiles are stored in the C:\Documents And Settings\<user logon name> folder.*

The way the user profile is used is governed by the group policy settings that are in effect for the user. Sometimes there is no user profile or no group policy.

7. User Configuration settings are processed in the following order: local GPO, site GPO, domain GPO, and OU GPO. Again, the process is hidden from the user and performed synchronously by default.

8. Logon scripts run. Logon scripts and startup scripts are not the same. Remember, there are four kinds of scripts: logon, logoff, startup, and shutdown. These scripts are hidden and run simultaneously.

9. The user is logged on and can begin using the network. The desktop appears as configured in the group policy.

In Step 3 and Step 7, it was noted that the group policies are processed in the following order: local GPO, site GPO, domain GPO, and OU GPO. Here is more detail about this order of operations:

- *Local GPO*—Can be found on every Windows 2000 computer. The local GPO is configured for a computer even if it doesn't belong to any network and isn't part of any Active Directory domain. Local GPOs are the least powerful GPOs and are overridden by every other GPO that can be created. In a non-networked environment, local GPOs can be very powerful, but for the discussion at hand, they are the lowest in the group policy hierarchy and are thus loaded first.

- *Site GPOs*—Are the next powerful group in the processing sequence. Site GPOs are linked to sites to make the settings apply to them. A site GPO overrides a local GPO. Your domain may or may not have GPOs linked to sites; if it doesn't, this part of the processing is not applicable.

- *Domain GPOs*—Are the third GPO processed. They override any site and local GPOs that have been configured. If more than one domain GPO exists for a network, those policies are processed in the order specified by the administrator of that domain. Domain GPOs override site and local GPOs.

- *Organizational unit GPOs*—Are processed last. It is likely that more than one OU GPO exists; when that happens, these GPOs are processed in the following order:

  - The OU GPO that is set for the OU root is processed first. This is the parent OU.

  - Any GPOs belonging to child OUs are processed next.

  - Following that, "grandchild" OUs are processed, and so on.

  - Last, any GPOs that are configured for users or computers are processed.

If no GPOs exist, there is no overwriting of the previous GPO. If multiple GPOs exist for one OU, then those policies are processed in an order specified by the administrator.

To make sure that you understand the process, look again at the order in which OU GPOs are processed. If there is a policy for the parent OU and a policy for a child OU, then a client in the child OU will receive the policy that was processed last — the one for the child OU. If a client in the child OU also has a policy for the users in that child OU, then the users will receive this policy. I'll say that it is *writing over* the previous policy. The last policy to have its say always wins.

The same is true of the GPO processing for a local policy, site policy, domain policy, and OU policy. If a client is a member of an OU, that client may also be a member of a site and is definitely a member of a domain. When the policies for this client are processed, the client receives the policy that is processed last. If a GPO exists for the site, the domain, and the OU, the client will receive the policy that is configured for the OU. In contrast, if no policy exists for the OU, but policies exist for the site and domain, the domain policy will win out because it is the last to be processed in the list.

As with anything else, though, there are exceptions to the rules. The order in which these policies are processed cannot be changed, but the *way* in which they are processed can be.

Sometimes a higher authority will need to enforce certain policies. For instance, the issue of backing up data may need to be addressed. There are ways that administrators of higher-level units can enforce policies if they need to. The ways that you can change group policy default behavior are described next.

First, any client who does not log on to the domain will not receive domain-level GPOs. Members of workgroups receive only local GPOs. You must keep this in mind and create local policies if users will not log on to the network every day.

Second, the *Block Policy Inheritance* option can be configured. In a domain or an OU only, administrators of OUs or nested OUs can block policy inheritance from the other levels processed before them. Because policies are inherited and are changed by the lower level only if there is a conflict, some inherited policies may be undesirable even though they do not conflict with an existing policy. If this is the case, administrators can block all policy inheritance from these upper levels. This setting can be configured in the Group Policy Editor, as described later in this section.

Third, the No Override option can be configured. *No Override* allows administrators at the higher levels to make sure that their policies are enforced at the lower levels. For instance, if members of a certain department are ignoring the company's backup policy and creating their own, the administrator at the higher level can set No Override to correct the situation.

Note: *If both No Override and Block Policy Inheritance are set, the No Override option will win. This makes sense, of course because the higher-level policy should be in control in the end.*

Finally, the Loopback setting can be configured. The *Loopback* setting is an advanced setting usually reserved for environments such as classrooms or kiosks, where the environment must be carefully controlled. Consider the following situation: In a library at a local college, both students and faculty can use the computers for research. However, when the faculty members log on, you want them to perform only the tasks that are available in the library; you don't want them to come into the library and log on to a computer to receive the same rights they would receive it they logged on at their desks. You want the library to be secure; you don't want students looking over a faculty member's shoulder and seeing something he shouldn't. To address problems like this, the Loopback setting was created. The Loopback policy setting allows an administrator to attach a set of user restrictions to the user portion of a GPO that holds the computer objects.

There are two settings for Loopback: Replace and Merge. Replace simply ignores the user's own GPO list and replaces it with the GPO for the computer that he is currently logged onto. In Merge mode, the user's policies are applied first, the new GPO is applied second, and the user's own GPO policies are overridden if necessary.

In the next section, I'll discuss some group policy design tips, and then you'll be ready to learn how to manually configure group policies.

Group Policy Design Tips

There are many ways to enhance your group policy or otherwise make it more efficient. Because all organizations contain diverse components, structures, and functions, the way group policies are configured is different for everyone. In this section, I'll discuss some of the ways that you can create an effective group policy. These tips will be mostly generic so they can be applied to the majority of organizations and networks.

Your group policy should reflect the organization of your company in general. If the company is centralized or decentralized, the group policy you configure should reflect that. If the company is separated into independent units, then those units should be able to create their own policies; in contrast, if a company is managed by a single domain with a single administrator, its group policies should probably have the same centralized configuration. If the company is divided into OUs that reflect job function, physical location, or department, the group policies would be more efficient if those entities had a hand in creating and managing their OU policies. In summary, make sure that the group policies that are configured reflect the organizational structure of the company. This makes for a more meaningful group policy and one that is easier to manage as well.

Listed next are some other ways to enhance group policies; some of these ways may apply to your particular situation, and some may not. By considering all of these guidelines, you can configure GPOs that are right for your network:

- Consider having the least number of GPOs possible. Remember, GPOs that affect users must be processed during user logon, and an inordinate number of policies can slow down this process.

- If your organizational units for users and computers are separate units, GPO administration can be greatly simplified. This is because users and computers are generally managed separately, Loopback settings can be used, and either the computer portion or the user portion of the GPO can be disabled to reduce processing time.

- Because group policies and scripts are processed synchronously by default, logon performance may be enhanced by changing this. Asynchronous processing allows users to log on before the scripts have finished running. Although this may enhance performance in some areas, there may be problems running certain applications if the scripts or policies are still loading after logon.

- Although Block Policy Inheritance and No Override can be used to solve problems related to policy processing, they should be used carefully. Having too many of these types of overrides configured can greatly hamper troubleshooting efforts when things go wrong with the policies.

- Loopback processing should be used only in kiosks, reception areas, labs, classrooms, libraries, and the like. It is a special type of processing for group policies for special circumstances. It should not be used as general procedure.

- For centralized group policy configurations, control of the policies should not be delegated to other users unnecessarily. If decentralized administration is used, consider delegating some of the tasks and management.

- Although you can apply a GPO to multiple OUs, doing so can cause the structure to be difficult to manage and maintain.

- When you're configuring GPOs, try to avoid creating policies that traverse domains in a single Active Directory container. Processing group policies is slow enough without adding more time to it for crossing domain boundaries.

- Avoid using legacy scripts during logon.

If you plan to design a group policy, you should plan for it carefully, the way you planned for Active Directory and the domain structure. Many items can be configured for users, and before deciding on a group policy for your OU, site, or domain, make sure you know

Table 6.3   Group policy configuration components.

Component	Configuration Options	Notes
Control Panel	Hide, display, or disable Control Panel icons, including Add/Remove Programs, System, Users And Passwords, Scheduled Tasks, and more.	-
Desktop	Hide desktop icons such as My Network Places, My Computer, The Recycle Bin, and more. Restrict what can be added or deleted on the desktop. In addition, the Start menu can be defined and configured, and the taskbar controlled.	-
Folder Redirection	Redirect folders that are normally stored on a user's hard drive—including the folder containing the user profile—to network shares.	-
Network	Configure settings for DNS, SNMP, offline files and folders, and hidden shares.	-
Printers	Priority, logging, and printer settings can be controlled.	-
Scripts	Scripts can be defined for logging on and off, starting up, and shutting down.	-
Security	Account policies, local policies, and public key policies can be configured. From earlier discussions, recall that these relate to passwords, account lockout, and the like.	-
Software Installation	Applications can be published or assigned so that users can choose to install them or so that they are installed automatically. Also, published applications can be repaired, removed, or updated.	-
System	Regulate disk quotas and scripts.	-

6

everything that can be configured. Table 6.3 provides one last look at group policies and what is available for configuration. When looking at this list, note by each item what you'd like to see regarding the group policy for your department or area.

Finally, with the concepts of group policy discussed, inheritance of polices fully understood, and design tips considered, you are ready to move on to performing some of these tasks. This section continues with more on group policies, including how to create GPOs, how to use the Group Policy snap-in, how to edit GPOs, and how to configure No Override and Block Policy Inheritance.

Creating a Group Policy Object

The first task to be learned when administering group policies is how to create a group policy object. The following steps describe how to create a GPO at the domain level:

1. Log on with administrator's credentials.

2. Choose Start|Programs|Administrative Tools|Active Directory Users And Computers, or open the management console that contains this snap-in.

3. Select the domain from the console tree, right-click, and choose Properties.

4. The Properties dialog box appears. It contains five tabs: General, Managed By, Object, Security, and Group Policy. Select the Group Policy tab.

5. Choose Add, and then, in the Add dialog box, select the All tab.

6. You can see that there is a default domain policy that can be used and edited. For the purpose of this exercise, you will create your own; later, you'll learn how to edit a GPO. Next to Look In drop-down list box, there are three icons; click on the second icon. Figure 6.27 shows this icon.

7. Name the policy and choose OK. The new policy now appears in the Properties dialog box for the domain. Choose Close.

Editing Group Policy Objects

Group policies can be edited through the Group Policy snap-in or through the dialog boxes presented in the previous example. In this section, you'll learn how to edit these polices by choosing the policy from the domain's Properties dialog.

1. Log on with administrator's credentials.

2. Choose Start|Programs|Administrative Tools|Active Directory Users And Computers, or open the management console that contains this snap-in.

3. Select the domain from the console tree, right-click, and choose Properties.

4. The Properties dialog box appears. It contains five tabs: General, Managed By, Object, Security, and Group Policy. Select the Group Policy tab.

5. Select the GPO that was just created, and choose Edit. A new window will open, with sections called Computer Configuration and User Configuration.

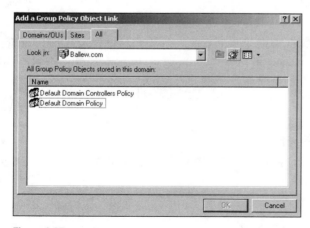

Figure 6.27
The New Group Policy Object icon.

Both sections contain three folders: Software Settings, Windows Settings, and Administrative Templates. As you know, the Software Settings folder can be used to configure automatic software installation by either publishing or assigning those applications to users or computers. The Software Settings folder contains a Software Installation folder. By right clicking on the Software Installation folder, an administrator can modify how the user will interact with these installations; the administrator can choose either Basic or Maximum, and can configure other options concerning how new packages will be used, such as publishing or assigning them. There may be other folders here as well, depending on other factors, including what programs from other vendors have been installed on the server.

Under the folder Computer Configuration/Windows Settings, there are two folders: Scripts and Security Settings. Recall that these folders contain information and policies that apply to anyone who logs on to this computer. In contrast, the User Configuration/ Windows Settings folder offers the Scripts and Security Settings folders, as well as Internet Explorer Maintenance, Remote Installation Services, and Folder Redirection. These settings apply to users no matter which computer they log on to.

Finally, Administrative Templates is available from both the Computer Configuration and User Configuration folders. In Computer Configuration, there are four folders: Windows Components, System, Network, and Printers. In User Configuration, there are folders for Windows Components, Start Menu and Taskbar, Desktop, Control Panel, Network, and System.

Through this myriad of options, you can set group policies to meet any organizational need. Next, I will describe how to change some of the settings for the group policy you just created.

Understanding and Configuring Group Policy Options

The following steps assume that either you are inside a console that contains the Group Policy snap-in, or you have opened the Group Policy console from the Properties page of the domain, as described earlier. Figure 6.28 shows the appropriate console.

To edit Computer Configuration policies that deal with the local security of the computer, including policies for passwords, accounts, audits, user rights, and security, perform the following steps:

1. Click on the Computer Configuration folder and then on Windows Settings.

2. Choose or expand Security Settings.

3. Click on Account Policies to change the password policy, account lockout policy, or Kerberos policy.

   - Password policies can be set here for password history, age, length, complexity, and encryption.

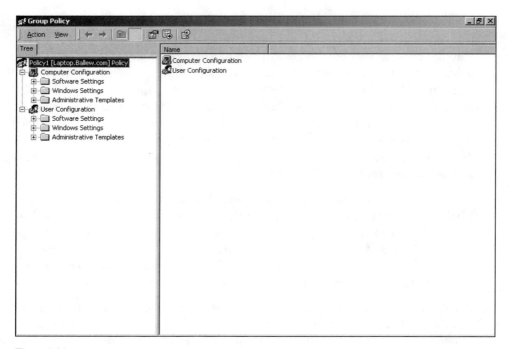

Figure 6.28
The Group Policy console.

- Account lockout policies can be set here for account lockout duration, threshold, and lockout reset counters. To change a policy, simply double-click on it and check the required boxes.

- Audit policies can be set by choosing the Local Policies folder and selecting Audit Policies. Auditing can be set for logon events, account management, directory service access, object access, policy change, privilege use, process tracking, and system events. To change a policy, simply double-click on it and check the required boxes.

- User rights assignments can be set by choosing the Local Policies folder and User Rights Assignments. Rights can be set for a number of events, such as accessing this computer from the network, acting as part of the operating system, adding workstations to a domain, backing up files and directories, changing the system time, creating a pagefile, debugging programs, and many more. To change a policy, simply double-click on it and check the required boxes.

4. Click on Local Policies to change the settings for auditing, user rights, and security options.

- Auditing can be set for logon events, account management, directory service access, object access, policy change, privilege use, process tracking, and system events. To change a policy, simply double-click on it and check the required boxes.

- User rights can be set for a number of events, such as accessing this computer from the network, acting as part of the operating system, adding workstations to a domain, backing up files and directories, changing the system time, creating a pagefile, debugging programs, and many more. To change a policy, simply double-click on it and check the required boxes.

- Security options can be set for many things, including setting additional restrictions for anonymous connections, allowing server operators to schedule tasks, automatically logging off users when their logon time expires, preventing users from installing printer drivers, and disabling the Ctrl+Alt+Del requirement for logon. To change a policy, simply double-click on it and check the required boxes.

5. Click on Event Log to configure settings for such parameters as maximum application log size, maximum security log size, maximum system log size, and guest account restrictions, plus how logs will be retained. To change a policy, simply double-click on it and check the required boxes.

To edit Computer Configuration policies that deal with Internet Explorer, NetMeeting, Task Scheduler, or Windows Installer for the local computer, perform the following steps:

1. Under the folder Computer Configuration, choose Administrative Templates.

2. Open Windows Components. There are four folders: NetMeeting, Internet Explorer, Task Scheduler, and Windows Installer.

3. For NetMeeting, to disable remote desktop sharing, simply double-click on the folder and check the required boxes.

4. For Internet Explorer, to use only machine settings, disable a user's ability to change policies, disable a user's ability to add or delete sites, make the proxy settings per machine rather than per user, disable automatic installation of Internet Explorer components, disable periodic checks for Internet Explorer updates, disable software update shell notifications, or disable showing the splash screen, simply double-click on the folder and check the required boxes.

5. For Task Scheduler, to hide property pages, prevent task run or end, disable drag-and-drop, disable new task creation, disable task deletion, disable advanced menus, or prohibit browsing, simply double-click on the folder and check the required boxes.

6. For Windows Installer, to disable the program, disable rollback, disable patching, enable browsing, or set other related Windows Installer functions, simply double-click on the folder and check the required boxes.

To edit Computer Configuration policies that deal with disk quotas for the local computer, perform the following steps:

1. Under the folder Computer Configuration, choose the System Folder.

2. There are five folders: Logon, Disk Quotas, DNS Client, Group Policy, and Windows File Protection. Select Disk Quotas.

3. There are six available configuration choices:

   - Enable Disk Quotas—Enables quotas for all NTFS volumes on the computer. Users will be unable to change this setting.

   - Enforce Disk Quota Limit—Denies disk space to users who exceed their disk quota limit.

   - Default Quota Limit And Warning Level—Allows an administrator to specify a quota limit and a warning level for users who first exceed their limit.

   - Log Event When Quota Limit Exceeded—Generates an event log entry when a user exceeds his or her quota limit.

   - Log Event When Quota Warning Level Exceeded—Generates an event log entry when the warning level has been exceeded.

   - Apply Policy To Removable Media—Allows an administrator to apply these disk quota policies to removable media as well.

To edit User Configuration policies that deal with Internet Explorer, perform the following steps:

1. Under the User Configuration folder, choose Administrative Templates.

2. Choose Windows Components|Internet Explorer.

3. Under this folder are five more folders: Internet Control Panel, Offline Pages, Browser Menus, Toolbars, Persistence Behavior, and Administrator Approved Controls.

4. Internet Control Panel allows an administrator to enable or disable the General page, Security page, Content page, Connections page, Programs page, and Advanced page.(See the sidebar for a description of the items that can be configured in Internet Control Panel.)

5. The Offline Pages folder in Administrative Templates/Internet Explorer allows an administrator to enable settings that restrict the user's ability to add or remove channels; add, edit, disable, or remove schedules for offline pages; configure offline page hit logging; download site subscription content; create or edit schedule groups; or set subscription limits.

6. The Browser Menus folder allows an administrator to enable or disable the following menu options from Internet Explorer: Save As, New, Open, Save As Web Page

Internet Control Panel Settings

In Internet Control Panel, there are six settings that can be configured for users. If a setting is disabled or not set, the user can perform the actions listed. If the setting is enabled, however, the user cannot perform the listed actions.

- When the General page is enabled, users cannot set their home page, cache, history, or Web page appearance.

- When the Security page is enabled, users cannot set their own security zones, including how download and user authentication are handled.

- When the Content page is enabled, users cannot see or change ratings, certificates, AutoComplete, Wallet, or Profile Assistant settings.

- When the Connections page is enabled, users cannot see or change connection and proxy settings.

- When the Programs page is enabled, users cannot see or change default settings for Internet programs.

- When the Advanced page is enabled, users cannot see or change advanced settings such as security, multimedia, and printing.

Complete, Source, Full Screen, Favorites, Tools, Help, Save The Program To Disk, and Context. You can also configure the browser menus so that the user cannot close the browser or the Explorer windows.

7. The Toolbars folder allows an administrator to disable the option to customize the browser toolbar buttons, disable the option to customize browser toolbars, and configure toolbar buttons. From the Configure Toolbar Buttons Properties dialog box, you can disable all of the buttons, such as Back, Forward, Stop, Refresh, Home, Search, History, Favorites, Full Screen, and Tools.

8. The Persistence Behavior folder allows an administrator to set file-size limits for the local machine zone, the intranet zone, the trusted sites zone, the Internet zone, and the restricted sites zone.

9. Last, the Administrator Approved Controls folder allows an administrator to restrict a user's access to the following Internet Explorer items: Media Player, menu controls, Microsoft Agent, Chat, survey control, Shockwave Flash, Netshow file transfer control, DHTML edit control, Microsoft Scriptlet component, Carpoint, Investor, and MSNBC.

As with all of the previous configuration changes, to enable, disable, or choose not to configure a certain restriction, simply double-click on the item in question and make the appropriate changes.

To edit User Configuration settings that deal with folder redirection, perform the following steps:

1. Make sure you are editing the group policy through Active Directory Users And Computers. If you are editing the policy you created earlier, you will be able to see a folder called Folder Redirection under the User Configuration/Windows Settings folder.

2. Under Folder Redirection, there are four folders: Application Data, Desktop, My Documents, and Start Menu. By default, these folders are empty. To configure folder redirection for these areas, right-click on the folder in question, and choose Properties. From these menus, an administrator can perform tasks related to redirecting folders for users and groups and can configure settings for these redirections.

3. For practice, you can choose the My Pictures folder under the My Documents folder, right-click, and choose Properties.

4. In the Setting box, choose one of the three choices other than No Administrative Policy Specified: Follow the My Documents folder; Basic—Redirect everyone's folder to the same location; or Advanced—Specify locations for various user groups. The last choice has more configuration options, so this example will use that choice.

5. After you choose the Advanced setting, there will be a place to add groups of users. Choose Add to open the Specify Group and Location dialog box, shown in Figure 6.29.

6. Browse and select the group that will have its My Pictures folders redirected. Choose OK.

7. You will be returned to the Specify Group And Location dialog box, where you will then browse to the target folder location. Select the location where the files will be redirected, and choose OK. Figure 6.29 shows a partially completed dialog box.

   As with all of the previous configuration changes, to enable, disable, or choose not to configure a certain restriction, simply double-click on the item in question and make the appropriate changes.

8. Choose OK. To edit, remove, or add groups to this folder redirection, simply right-click on the folder again, choose Properties, and select the appropriate tabs or buttons. On the Settings tab, you can configure the following options:

   • Grant the user exclusive rights to <folder>.

   • Move the contents of <folder> to a new location.

   • Leave the folder in the new location when the policy is removed, or redirect the folder back to the local user profile's location when the policy is removed.

Figure 6.29
The Specify Group And Location dialog box.

To edit User Configuration settings that deal with the desktop and Control Panel, perform the following steps:

Note: *This same procedure can be used to configure any setting in Group Policy.*

1. Located under User Configuration/Administrative Templates are six folders, two of which are called Desktop and Control Panel. To configure settings or restrictions for the desktop, open the Desktop folder; for Control Panel, open the Control Panel folder.

2. The Desktop folder contains two folders—Active Directory and Active Desktop—as well as 10 settings that can be disabled, enabled, or not configured. As with the other settings, the default is Not Configured. To change any of the settings, double-click on the setting and make the appropriate choices.

The settings that can be configured using Desktop Settings are:

- Hide all icons on the Desktop

- Remove the My Documents icon from the desktop or from the Start Menu

- Hide the My Network Places icon from the desktop

- Hide the Internet Explorer icon from the desktop

- Do not add shares of recently opened documents to My Network Places

- Prohibit user from changing the path of the My Documents folder

- Disable adding, dragging, dropping, and closing the Taskbar's toolbars

- Disable adjusting desktop toolbars

- Don't save settings at exit

These are very useful settings for locking down user desktops. You may decide to activate some of these settings on your network for the purpose of disabling certain icons in Control Panel for users or making sure that no changes are saved after logoff.

The Active Desktop folder contains settings for enabling or disabling Active Desktop; disabling items; prohibiting changes such as adding, deleting, editing, or closing items; and enabling or setting restrictions on wallpaper choices by users. These configurations might be useful when a high level of security is needed but Active Desktop still needs to be enabled. Administrators can allow Active Desktop to be used, but limit actions that can be performed by users.

The Active Directory folder contains three settings: setting the maximum size of Active Directory searches; enabling filtering in the Find box; and hiding the Active Directory folder. The Active Directory folder displays the objects that are in Active Directory in the user's browse window. By enabling this policy, an administrator can configure the user's desktop so that the folder doesn't appear in the My Network Places folder. Settings for maximum size of Active Directory searches can be configured so that only a specified, limited number of results are returned when a user searches Active Directory for objects.

The Control Panel folder under Administrative Templates contains four folders and three settings. The three items that can be configured for the Control Panel in this folder are Disable Control Panel, Hide Specified Control Panel Applets, and Show Only Specified Control Panel Applets. Having the ability to disable Control Panel or hide some or all of its applets can be very useful in high-security environments or in situations when the users will not need access to these items.

Under the Add/Remove Programs folder, an administrator can completely disable the Add/Remove Programs icon or set other less restrictive configurations. The other configuration options are:

- Hide Change or Remove Programs page

- Hide Add New Programs page

- Hide Add/Remove Windows Components page

- Hide the Add a program from CD-ROM or floppy disk options

- Hide Add programs from Microsoft option

- Hide the Add programs from your network option

- Go directly to the Components wizard

- Disable Support Information

- Specify default category for Add New Programs

Under the Display folder, there are additional options that deal with the user's display settings. You can disable the Display icon in the Control Panel or hide any of the following tabs: Background, Appearance, Settings, and Screen Saver. You can also disable the option to change wallpaper, activate a screen saver, password-protect the screen saver, and set how long to wait before a screen saver appears. Most organizations don't impose every one of these restrictions, but the needs or mandates of some organizations require they use a specific wallpaper or password-protect the screensaver for security. Banks are a good example of an organization that would impose these limits.

In the Printers folder, you can set options for disabling the deletion or addition of printers, browsing to printers, setting a default path to a network printer, and browsing a common Web site to find a printer, and finally Regional options can be restricted so that new languages cannot be specified.

As with all of the previous configuration changes, to enable, disable, or choose not to configure a certain restriction, simply double-click on the item in question and make the appropriate changes.

There are other folders available for configuration through this console. The Offline Files folder allows users to save or cache information stored on a server to their local computers so they can use the information later. This is a good setting to configure for laptop users, who may need to access information on the server, cache that information, and use the information while away from the office. Besides disabling offline files completely, you can set the following options:

- Disable user configuration of offline files

- Synchronize all offline files before the user logs off

- Action on server disconnect (specifies how the offline folders respond if the server suddenly becomes unavailable)

- Disable offline files and folder completely

- Prevent use of offline files folder

- Administratively assign offline files

- Disable reminder balloons, balloon frequency, and lifetime

- Set an event logging level for corrupt data, server offline, net stop and start, and server available for reconnection

The Network And Dial-Up folder also offers various configuration options, including prohibiting such actions as deleting RAS connections, changing TCP/IP settings, sharing connections, viewing status statistics for active connections, using the Network Connection Wizard, and enabling, changing properties for, or disabling a LAN connection. Figure 6.30 shows the networking and dial-up connections that can be configured here.

Keep in mind that there are literally hundreds of options and combinations for how these configurations can be set for users and computers. Now that you've been introduced to

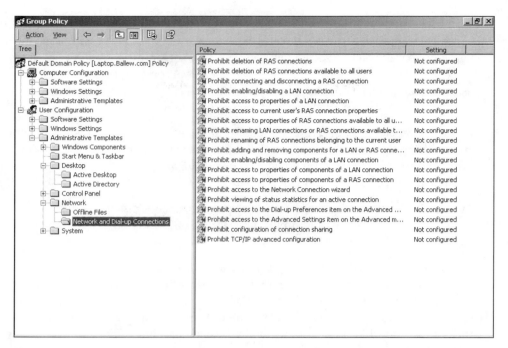

Figure 6.30
Network And Dial-Up Connections.

the most commonly used settings, you can figure out on your own how to change the others. To explore others not shown in the previous examples, click on System Folders, Remote Installation Services, and Software Settings.

Configure Block Policy Inheritance and No Override

As I mentioned earlier, using group policies to enhance network security is a great way to start securing the network. However, using group policies between units such as domains, sites, or OUs might require some tweaking. In these instances, you'll probably need to block policy inheritance or configure the No Override option. To enable these settings, follow these steps:

1. Open Active Directory Users And Computers, and highlight the domain name you are working with.

2. Right-click on the domain name and choose Properties.

3. Select the Group Policy tab.

4. To block policy inheritance, place a checkmark in the Block Policy Inheritance checkbox.

5. To enable No Override, right-click on the appropriate policy and choose No Override from the context menu.

6. If both are chosen, the No Override setting will win.

Using the Group Policy Snap-In for Internet Explorer Maintenance

There is one last item in the Group Policy snap-in that I'd like to introduce. In an MMC that contains the Group Policy snap-in, select the User Configuration/Windows Settings/ Internet Explorer Maintenance folder. In that folder are five additional folders: Browser User Interface, Connections, URLs, Security, and Programs. These folders offer an administrator more ways to secure and configure Internet Explorer settings for the users on the network.

The Browser User Interface folder contains folders that can be used to customize Internet Explorer settings, such as the toolbars and background bitmaps. Administrators can customize the toolbars to show a company name or company logo. For instance, if I type in "Ballew.com" and choose a background bitmap, Internet Explorer or Outlook Express can be configured to look completely different from its default. Figure 6.31 shows how the settings can be configured.

You can also configure animated bitmaps through the second available folder. These bitmaps will take the place of the animated Internet Explorer logo at the top of the toolbar. You can use a bitmap of your company logo or any other animated logo. In addition, custom logos can be configured in the Custom Logo folder.

Finally, the Browser Toolbar Buttons folder can be used to create toolbar buttons that perform specific tasks, similar to macros in Microsoft Office programs. For instance, you can create a toolbar button that runs a script, such as running a virus check or backing

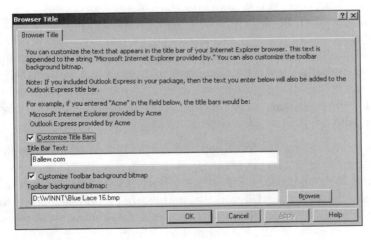

Figure 6.31
Internet Explorer settings.

up the user's address book. To create this button, open the Browser Toolbar Buttons folder, choose Add, type the toolbar caption, select the colors, and type the path to the script or batch file that should be run. Choose OK twice to apply the button.

Besides group policies, there are other ways to secure Active Directory and the network. In the next section, you'll learn about NTFS permissions, including how they are used and applied to secure files and folders on the network and how they are calculated when combined with other permissions, rights, or settings.

Introduction to NTFS and Share Permissions

NTFS permissions are rules associated with users and resources; these rules determine which users can gain access to any given resource and which users cannot. In the following sections, you'll learn about NTFS permissions and how to assign them to protect resources on the network.

This section is organized into two main parts: "Introduction to NTFS Permissions" and "Assigning NTFS Permissions." In the first section, you'll learn what NTFS permissions are and how they work, what Share permissions are, and how to plan for the creation of NTFS permissions. Then I'll discuss the different types of permissions: folder permissions, file permissions, and special permissions. You'll learn how these permissions are inherited, what happens when there are multiple permissions that seem to conflict, and what occurs when the files and folders are moved among different volumes. In the second section, you'll learn how to perform these tasks in Windows 2000 Server, including assigning regular NTFS permissions, special NTFS permissions, and Share permissions.

How NTFS Permissions Work

Every file, folder, or other resource or object on an NTFS volume has an access control list (ACL) associated with it. This list is used to keep track of which users and groups can access the file or folder and to what degree. ACLs contain access control entries (ACEs). ACEs contain information about a specific user's permissions. If a user wants to access a file and read it, there must be an ACE in the ACL for that user. If no ACE exists for that user, or if the entry doesn't match what the user wants to do, then that particular type of access is denied. If a user has Read permission in the ACE but not Write permission, the user can only read the file. Every time a user tries to access a file, folder, or other resource on the network, the ACL and ACEs are checked.

NTFS permissions can be used only on NTFS volumes and are not available for configuration on FAT or FAT32 volumes. NTFS permissions not only affect resources over a network, but also protect resources locally. Files and folders can have dissimilar permissions assigned as well. The ability of NTFS permissions to work locally and to allow the administrator to place permissions on files as well as on folders is another good reason to use the NTFS file system instead of FAT. FAT permissions, known as Share permissions, do not allow this type of configuration.

Note: *If you select Sharing after right-clicking on a folder in an NTFS volume, you'll see four tabs: General, Web Sharing, Sharing, and Security. If you select Sharing after right-clicking on a folder in a FAT or FAT32 volume, you'll see only two: General and Sharing. This is, of course, because there isn't any way to create NTFS permissions on a FAT or FAT32 volume; thus, there are no tabs called Web Sharing or Security.*

How Share Permissions Work

Share permissions will not be discussed at length here, but the characteristics of shares should be mentioned briefly. You can create shared folders simply by right-clicking on an object or resource and choosing the Sharing option. Shared folder permissions are used on FAT volumes the same way that NTFS permissions are used on NTFS volumes. The purpose of setting a Share permission on an object in a FAT volume is to secure the object.

Share permissions can be placed only on folders, not on files, and because of this, there are fewer security options available for shares, and there is less control over files in shared folders. Users who are not supposed to access the share can do so if they are sitting at the machine where the share resides, and as you know, this is not the case with NTFS permissions. Three permissions can be associated with a share: Read, Change, and Full Control. Full Control is the default permission and is assigned to the Everyone group. Full Control allows the user to read and write to the file, and to change the permissions and take ownership if the share is on an NTFS volume. The Read permission allows a user to look at the files in the folder, see the file's attributes, and run programs. The Change permission allows a user to read and modify the files in the folder and to add or delete files and folders.

Share permissions are applied cumulatively. This means that if a user is a member of three groups such that one group has the Read permission, one has the Write permission, and one has the Full Control permission, then the user has the cumulative permission of Full Control. Deny overrides all permissions, however, and is available for configuration as well. If a user has both Share and NTFS permissions, figuring out the resulting permission is a little more difficult. You'll learn about multiple permissions in the section called "When Multiple Permissions Exist," later in the chapter.

Warning! *If a user has been assigned a Share permission on a FAT volume, then that user has all he needs to access that resource. However, if a user is assigned a Share permission for a resource that resides on an NTFS volume, then that user must also have the appropriate NTFS permissions.*

Planning for NTFS Permissions

As with any component of Windows 2000, whether it is installation, data migration, group policies, or NTFS permissions, appropriate steps must be taken in the planning stages to ensure that deployment is done correctly. When you're planning for the creation of NTFS permissions, consider the following suggestions:

- Give groups of users the minimal amount of access that they need to do their jobs. For example, if a user needs only to read information from the company's database, don't give that user permission to write to or otherwise modify the database. It is much easier to give additional permissions to users than it is to take them away.

- If users or groups of users need to modify data contained in the folders they have access to, give those users Read and Execute permissions instead of Full Control or Modify. This goes along with the previous suggestion of not giving the users more control than they need. Read and Execute allow the users to do the work they need to do without giving them the ability to delete folders or files accidentally or to change ownership or permissions for those files.

- Because it is easier to keep track of permissions when they are assigned to folders rather than files, try to organize your folders and files into manageable units. For instance, create some folders to be home folders, some to be program folders, and some to be data folders.

- Permissions should be assigned to groups, not to individual accounts. Assigning permissions to individuals may be acceptable for small organizations with only a few users, but it will quickly become a nightmare when the organization grows. When planning for permission assignments, think big. Pretend your organization is made up of a million users; create groups that represent what access they will need for certain resources; and then assign those groups permissions.

- Don't overuse the Deny permission; in the end, it will complicate permissions trouble-shooting.

- Consider using the standard templates that ship with Windows 2000 for securing operating-system-specific files and folders such as NTLDR and NTDETECT.com. There are nine templates available and four levels of security for those templates. These templates are available for workstations, servers, and domain controllers.

Types of NTFS Permissions

This section discusses three types of permissions: folder permissions, which apply to NTFS folders; file permissions, which apply to NTFS files; and special permissions, which can be assigned to any NTFS object through the Advanced button in the Security tab of the object's Properties dialog.

Folder Permissions

There are six standard folder permissions: List Folder Contents, Read, Read And Execute, Write, Modify, and Full Control. Each of these permissions is described next.

The List Folder Contents permission is the most restrictive of all of the standard permissions; it only allows a user to view the folder's contents. This includes viewing the names of the folders, subfolders, and files in a specific folder. A user with this permission can only see what is in the folder, and cannot perform any function on it, such as changing attributes or modifying the folder.

The Read permission is the second most restrictive permission. It can be assigned so that a user has permission only to read the folder's contents, the permissions associated with the folder, and the folder's attributes. (Folder attributes are read-only, archive, hidden, and system.) A user with the Read permission can see what is in the folder, and see its attributes, but cannot perform any functions on it.

The Read And Execute permission is next in line in the hierarchy. This permission allows a user to do everything included in the List Folder Contents and Read permissions as well as to traverse the folder. *Traverse the folder* means that the user can pass through the files and folders located here to reach other files and folder, even if the user doesn't have any permissions associated with those folders.

The Write permission is more lenient, allowing a user to view the attributes of the folder, see who is the owner of the folder, view the permissions for the folder, change the folder's attributes, and create new files and subfolders inside the folder.

The Modify permission is pretty much what it sounds like: Users with this permission can modify folders. Modifying means that the user can create files and folders, write data, delete, and read the permissions of a file or folder. Users also have the ability to traverse the folder, execute files, list folder contents, read data, read the attributes, and synchronize the folder.

Finally, the Full Control permission allows a user to perform all of the actions available to all other permissions—including reading, writing, traversing, and listing folder contents—as well as to change the folder's ownership properties, delete files and folders, and delete subfolders.

Within the Properties dialog box of a folder on an NTFS volume are the four tabs mentioned earlier: General, Web Sharing, Sharing, and Security. Figure 6.32 shows the Security tab. Notice that you can choose to deny access to a folder by checking the Deny checkbox for the permissions you want to deny. You can either deny each permission separately or deny Full Control. If you deny Full Control, all boxes in the Deny column are checked automatically.

Tip: You may want to deny access to, or otherwise secure, such folders as %systemroot%, %systemroot%\System32, and other system folders.

File Permissions

There are five standard file permissions: Read, Read And Execute, Write, Modify, and Full Control. Each of these permissions is detailed next.

The Read permission is the most restrictive permission. It can be assigned so that a user only has permission to read the folder's contents, the permissions associated with the file, and the file's attributes. (Folder attributes are read-only, archive, hidden, and system.) A user with the Read permission can see what is in the file, and see its attributes, but cannot perform any functions on it.

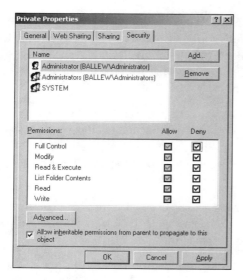

Figure 6.32
The Security tab.

The Read And Execute permission is next in line in the hierarchy. This permission allows a user to do everything included in the Read permission, plus execute the file.

The Write permission is more lenient, allowing a user to view the attributes of the folder, see who is the owner of the folder, view the permissions for the folder, change the folder's attributes, and create new files and subfolders inside the folder. The user can also over-write data in the file.

The Modify permission is pretty much what it sounds like: Users with this permission can edit files. Users with the modify permission for files can traverse the folder to execute a file, list folder contents, read data, read attributes, create files, write data to the file, delete the file, and synchronize the file.

Finally, the Full Control permission allows a user to perform all of the actions available to all other permissions as well as to change the folder's ownership properties, delete files and folders, and delete subfolders.

Special Permissions

Special permissions can be set on both files and folders in an NTFS volume. You can see the special permissions by right-clicking on a folder, choosing Sharing from the context menu, choosing the Security tab, and then choosing Advanced. From there, choosing the View/Edit button opens the Permission Entry dialog box shown in Figure 6.33.

The Traverse Folder/Execute File permission allows a user to move through folders that he or she does not have permission to access, in order to reach other folders in the path. This permission applies only to folders, not to the files in the folders. However, because the Everyone group is assigned the Bypass Traverse Checking right, which also allows this

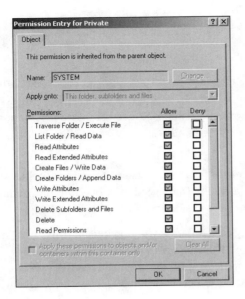

Figure 6.33
The Permission Entry dialog box.

behavior, the Traverse Folder permission takes effect only when the group or user is not granted this right by default. The Execute File permission allows a user to run program files within the folder.

The List Folder/Read Data permission contains two permissions as well. The List Folder permission allows a user to view the folder's contents (including the names of the folders, subfolders, and files in it). A user with this permission can see what is in the folder but cannot perform any function on it, such as changing attributes or modifying the folder. The Read Data permission allows the user to read the files contained in the folders.

The Read Attributes permission allows the user to view the attributes of a file or folder but does not allow the user to change those attributes. File and folder attributes can be hidden, read-only, archive, or system, or something otherwise defined by the NTFS.

The Read Extended Attributes permission allows a user to view the extended attributes of a file or folder but does not allow the user to change those attributes. Attributes are defined by NTFS or other programs and can vary from folder to folder.

The Create Files/Write Data permission allows a user either to create files within a folder or to write data to existing files. Creating files within a folder applies to folders only. Writing data to files applies to files only. If you allow a user to write data to a file, then you are allowing that user to modify the data in that file. Be careful which users have this permission, and for what files.

The Create Folders/Append Data permission is similar to the Create Files/Write Data permission. The Create Folders permission allows a user to create a folder within another folder, and this applies to folders only. The Append Data permission allows a user to add information to a file, but does not allow the user to change, delete, or overwrite any data already in the file. Append Data applies only to files.

The Write Attributes and Write Extended Attributes permissions allow a user to change the attributes of a file or folder. These permissions are similar to the Read Attributes and Read Extended Attributes permissions described earlier. Because the Write permission allows a user to remove attributes (such as hidden and read-only) from files and folders, this permission should be used with extreme caution.

The Delete Subfolders And Files permission simply allows a user to delete subfolders and files within a given folder. As you will see later, the Delete Subfolders And Files permission is given by default only when the user has the standard Full Control permission.

The Delete permission isn't quite as closely controlled as the previous permission. The Delete permission is given by default in both the standard Full Control and Modify permissions, and it allows a user to delete a file or folder. If the user has the Delete Subfolders And Files permission on the parent folder, this Delete permission does not have to be given as well.

The Read Permissions special permission allows a user to see which permissions have been given to a file or folder. The user cannot change those permissions without having the Change Permissions permission.

The Change Permissions special permission allows a user to change all permissions applied to a file or folder. This permission is useful when you want an administrator to be able to change the permissions of a folder but not to have the ability to delete the file or folder.

The Take Ownership permission allows a user to take ownership of a specific file or folder. By default, only users with the Full Control standard permission can take ownership of a file or folder. You may want a user to have this ability but not to have Full Control. One note about taking ownership: Ownership can only be taken, not given. You cannot create a file and then pass ownership to another party. This makes sense, of course, because there would multiple problems associated with users becoming owners of files or folders they didn't create. (Think about inappropriate email, files, viruses, and so on.)

Finally, the Synchronize permission is available for multithreaded, multiprocess applications and programs. It can be used to allow the threads of a program to wait for synchronization from other threads to enhance performance for those applications.

Because the standard permissions are really just a mix of special permissions, it is important to know which special permissions are included in their respective standard permissions. As you would imagine, the Full Control standard permission includes all fourteen permissions listed previously, whereas the Read permission includes only five. To fully understand what exactly is being applied when you're setting standard NTFS permissions for a file or folder, review Table 6.4.

Table 6.4 The relationship between standard and special permissions.

Special Permission	Full Control	Modify	Read And Execute	List Folder Contents	Read	Write
Traverse Folder/Execute File	X	X	X	X	-	-
List Folder/Read Data	X	X	X	X	X	-
Read Attributes	X	X	X	X	X	-
Read Extended Attributes	X	X	X	X	X	-
Create Files/Write Data	X	X	-	-	-	X
Create Folders/Append Data	X	X	-	-	-	X
Write Attributes	X	X	-	-	-	X
Write Extended Attributes	X	X	-	-	-	X
Delete Subfolders And Files	X	-	-	-	-	
Delete	X	X	-	-	-	-
Read Permissions	X	X	X	X	X	X
Change Permissions	X	-	-	-	-	-
Take Ownership	X	-	-	-	-	-
Synchronize	X	X	X	X	X	X

6

Note: When you're looking over Table 6.4, notice that List Folder Contents and Read And Execute are composed of the same special permissions. However, these standard permissions are not the same. The difference between them has to do with how their permissions are inherited. The List Folder Contents permissions are inherited only by folders, whereas the Read And Execute permissions are inherited by both files and folders.

Warning! Although these special permissions can be used to meet almost any specific type of security need, stay with the standard permissions when possible. There will be times when you'll need to troubleshoot permissions problems, and it will be a hard enough task without having to keep track of hundreds of special permissions assigned to users and groups on the network.

Characteristics of NTFS Permissions

As you can probably tell by now, in any given instance, multiple permissions can exist. Besides just having conflicting permissions for files or folders, or for parent and child folders, you can also end up with a user having some NTFS permissions and some Share permissions. Even more complicated than that is if a user has several NTFS permissions because of his or her membership in multiple groups, combined with several Share permissions. Determining which permissions are applied to a particular user can become quite a complicated task. In addition to sorting through all of these scenarios, what happens when permission inheritance is included in the mix, or if files or folders are moved from an NTFS partition to a FAT partition? In this section, you'll learn about these permission conflicts and scenarios, and how they are all sorted through, to understand what *effective* permissions are eventually assigned to any user or group in the organization.

When Multiple Permissions Exist

As I mentioned earlier, every object on a network—whether it is a file, folder, or other resource—contains an ACL. This ACL contains an ACE for every entity on the network that has permission to access the object. One ACL might contain hundreds of ACEs. When a user, group, application, or other entity tries to access an object, the ACEs are checked to determine what access that entity will be granted. Based on the permissions listed for a particular user or entity, access is either granted or denied.

What happens if there is more than one entry for the requestor? Consider this scenario: Mary Anne is a member of the Printers group, the Sales group, and the Marketing group. All members of the Printers group are given the NTFS Read permission for File A. All members of the Sales group are given the NTFS Modify permission for File A. All members of the Marketing group are given the NTFS Full Control permission for File A. In addition, Mary Anne has three Share permissions for File A from other group memberships. Two Read permissions and one Change permission have been assigned. What do you think Mary Anne's *effective* permissions are? (That's what you'll learn next.) Effective permissions are defined by what Mary Anne can actually do with File A. Although it seems complex and perhaps even contrived, it is a very real situation.

To understand how these permissions are calculated, consider what happens when only NTFS permissions are assigned. NTFS permissions are cumulative. That means that if a user belongs to three groups, their permissions are combined to define their effective permissions. In the previous example, if you ignore the Share permissions, Mary Anne's NTFS permissions from the three groups are Read, Modify, and Full Control. Her effective, collective, cumulative permission is Full Control. You can think of it as being the least restrictive or as being a combination of all of the permissions.

Share permissions work the same way. Mary Anne has three Share permissions: one Read, one Change, and another Read. Because Share permissions are also cumulative, Mary Anne can change File A. (Change includes Read.)

In the previous scenario, Mary Anne has both NTFS and Share permissions. To complete the task of defining the effective permissions, you'll need to calculate the effective NTFS permission and the effective Share permission, which we've already done. The least restrictive NTFS permission is Full Control, and the least restrictive Share permission is Change. To calculate what Mary Anne can actually do with the file requires taking the *more* restrictive of the two permissions. In this case, the most restrictive permission between Full Control and Change is Change. Change is Mary Anne's effective permission for File A.

You can throw a wrench into this by adding a Deny permission for one of the groups or for Mary Anne's user account. If any one of the groups that Mary Anne belongs to is denied access to File A, she will not be able to access the file.

Look at one more example. Bob has the NTFS permissions Full Control, Write, and Read, and he has the Share permissions Change and Read for File A. Bob has also been demoted recently, and he is now a member of a group that has been denied access to File A. Before Bob was demoted, his effective NTFS permission was Full Control, the least restrictive of all of his NTFS permissions, and his effective Share permission was Change, the least restrictive of his Share permissions, thus giving him the effective permission of Change, the most restrictive of the two. However, because Bob is now a member of a group that has been denied access to File A, all bets are off. Bob can no longer access File A because Deny overrides everything. (See the sidebar "Understanding the File Delete Child Hidden Permission" for more information on the Deny permission.)

Tip: *The Deny permission should not be used for generally denying access to objects. It would complicate permissions managements. The best time to use the Deny permission is when a user is part of a group, needs to remain part of the group, but needs also to be denied access to a certain object such as a file or folder.*

Multiple permissions may also exist between files and folders, or permissions may be set for files and not for their containing folders. For instance, a user might have the Read permission for a folder and have the Full Control permission for a file inside that folder. The user will be able to access the file and have full control of it. File permissions override folder permissions. Alternately, an administrator can set permissions for a certain file without having to assign additional permissions for the folder that it is contained in. If a user has access to a file but not to the folder, the user can still access the file.

Understanding the File Delete Child Hidden Permission

When discussing permissions, there are two little problems with using the phrase "Deny always means Deny." You are probably aware of the first problem: User A has a Share permission of Deny, sits down at the computer where the file is stored locally, and gets access. This happens because Shares can apply permissions only across a network and not locally. Beyond this, however, is one other way a user can get past a Deny permission.

In Windows 2000, as noted in Microsoft's article numbered Q152763, the hidden permission called File Delete Child (FDC) is supported on all NTFS volumes. In the article, Microsoft states, "Users who have full control on a volume or directory also have the FDC permission. This permission allows a user to delete files at the root level where they have full control, even if they do not have permissions on the specific file itself." Microsoft did this to maintain POSIX compliance. For more information on how to disable the FDC permission, you can read the article or obtain more information from the CD-ROM that is included with this book.

Warning! If you give a user permission to access a file, but not to access the folder, the user must know the full Universal Naming Convention (UNC) path or local path to the file to access it. If a user doesn't have access to the folder, he or she won't be able to see the folder while browsing, and therefore won't be able to access the file.

Inheritance and NTFS Permissions

NTFS permissions can be inherited, and they are, by default, inherited from parent folders to child folders. As an example, if Folder A is assigned the permission Modify, then by default all subfolders and files in that folder have the Modify permission assigned. This is the default status because it is usually what is needed by organizations for their users.

Under certain circumstances, inheritance might need to be disabled. Disabling inheritance is a simple process. You right-click on the folder, choose Properties, select the Security tab, and remove the check in the box that says, "Allow inheritable permissions from parent to propagate to this object." Once this box is cleared, you will be asked to decide between three options: Copy, Remove, or Cancel.

If you decide to disallow inheritable permissions from the parent, then you'll need to decide which permissions should be assigned to the object. Choosing Copy will copy previously inherited permissions to the object from the parent folder and will then deny any other inheritance of permissions from that folder.

If you choose Remove, the inherited permissions are removed and the object will keep only the permission clearly specified for the object. If you choose Remove, you'll need to manually add users, computers, and groups, and set their permissions.

If you decide against either choice, you can choose Cancel to return to the Security tab options. In any case, the decision to allow inheritable permissions is made by the administrator of the object.

When Files or Folders Are Moved

Finally, copying or moving files and folders among FAT and NTFS volumes can cause permissions to change. Files and folders can be copied or moved within a single NTFS volume, between NTFS volumes, or to non-NTFS volumes. In this section, you'll learn what happens in all of these instances.

When a file or folder is copied from one NTFS volume or partition to another, or within the same volume, Windows 2000 thinks of it as a new file—a new addition to the volume. Therefore, it inherits the permissions of the folder or volume in which it is placed.

Note: You must have permission to write to the destination folder in order to copy a file there.

When a file or folder is moved from one NTFS volume to a different NTFS volume, the file or folder inherits the permissions of the folder in which it was placed, the same way a copy works between volumes. Again, this occurs because when a file or folder is moved to a new volume, Windows 2000 thinks of it as a new file, a new addition to the volume.

The only time a file or folder retains its permissions is when it is moved within the same NTFS volume or partition. If a file or folder is moved from one area to another on the same volume, Windows 2000 knows that you are not creating a new file but simply moving an existing one. Because of this, permissions are retained.

If a file or folder is either copied or moved from an NTFS volume to a non-NTFS volume (a FAT or FAT32 volume), all NTFS permissions are lost. This occurs because FAT does not recognize NTFS permissions and thus cannot maintain them.

Helpful Hints

Now that you know all about NTFS permissions—including how NTFS permissions work, what types of permissions exist, and how those permissions are applied—you can better appreciate the following suggestions for applying NTFS permissions. Although these suggestions won't be appropriate for all situations, they do represent techniques proven to work for many different types of organizations. Before we move on to assigning permissions in the next section, let's review the following points:

- Assign permissions to groups and not to individual users' resources. It is inefficient to manage objects or users when groups are more easily managed.

- Set permissions on directories such as \Winnt, \Winnt\System 32, and \root, as well as others, so that the necessary precautions are taken to allow administrators access to these folders but to disallow those who shouldn't have access.

- Begin assigning permissions for users in the most restrictive way possible. Don't give users Write permission if they need only the Read permission.

- Assign permissions at the folder level, and try to stick with the standard permissions. Assigning file-level permissions and special permissions complicates troubleshooting and maintenance.

- When configuring permissions, try to assign the Allow permission and not the Deny permission. If you don't want a particular user or group to have access to something, simply don't assign permissions to them for that resource. It is more effective to *not allow* access than to *deny* access.

- Use descriptive names when sharing files and folders. Make access to these shared resources easy and straightforward.

- For folders that are considered *public* folders, make sure that users have at least Read and Write permissions so that users can read the files and add their own files to the folder. Of course, the owner of the file or folder should have Full Control.

- For executable files such as applications and programs, users will need the Read and Execute permissions. The administrators should have the Change permission as well. If you set permissions in this way, users can access and execute the programs but cannot delete any program files or otherwise damage the application. This is a major concern in many organizations, and access to program and application files should be restricted.

- For any files that the user creates, he or she should have Full Control over those files. The user will need to be able to delete, modify, and create new files in folders that belong to the user.

Assigning NTFS Permissions

In this section, I'll walk you through many of the most common tasks associated with managing NTFS permissions, including assigning NTFS permissions to users and objects, modifying the permissions once assigned, and assigning special NTFS permissions. I'll also explain how to deny access, set file attributes, take ownership of a file or folder, and test those permissions once they are configured. I'll begin with the most basic NTFS task, granting standard permissions.

Exploring Standard NTFS Permissions on a Folder

To view, set, or change standard permissions, follow these steps:

1. Log on as an administrator.

2. Use Windows Explorer to find a folder in the root directory for which you'd like to set permissions.

3. Right-click on the folder, and choose Properties from the context menu.

4. Select the Security tab.

   Here you will see the six standard permissions: Full Control, Modify, Read And Execute, List Folder Contents, Read, and Write. Notice that the Allow checkboxes are all checked and grayed out. By default, a folder inherits permissions from its parent folder, and in this case the parent folder is the root directory, which is shared by default to the Everyone group, which is given Full Control. If you were to "unshare" the root folder, these permissions would be different. Likewise, if you were sharing a folder whose parent folder isn't the root directory, these boxes might not be checked.

5. To change or set permissions for this folder, simply check the appropriate boxes.

Exploring Special Permissions

To view, set, or change special permissions, follow these steps:

1. Log on as an administrator.

2. Use Windows Explorer to find a folder for which you'd like to grant special permissions.

3. Right-click on the folder, and choose Properties.

4. Select the Security tab.

5. Here you will see the six standard permissions. To see the advanced, or special, permissions, choose the Advanced button.

6. In the Permissions Entries box, there are four headings: Type, Name, Permission, and Apply To. The Type heading has a key with the word Allow or Deny beside it, as shown in Figure 6.34. Notice that the dialog box's title bar says "Access Control Settings." The ACE is either Allow or Deny, and is shown under the Type heading.

7. To view the settings for an entry, highlight the entry and choose the View/Edit button. Choose Cancel to return to the main screen.

8. Notice the two boxes that can be checked at the bottom of the Access Control Settings screen. You can check or uncheck these boxes as needed: Allow Inheritable Permissions From Parent To Propagate To This Object; and Reset Permissions On All Child Objects And Enable Propagation Of Inheritable Permissions.

Modifying Permissions

You can change any of the standard or special permissions from Allow to Deny simply by checking the appropriate boxes. However, there are more complicated tasks that can be performed, including adding users or groups and assigning them permissions, or modifying special permissions by removing all existing permissions and starting over. In this example, you'll learn how to perform these tasks.

To modify permissions, follow these steps:

1. Log on as an administrator.

2. Use Windows Explorer to find a folder for which you'd like to grant or modify permissions.

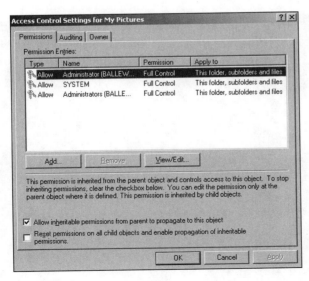

Figure 6.34
Access control settings.

3. Right-click on the folder, and choose Properties.

4. Select the Security tab.

5. To add a new group or user to the Name box, thus enabling that user access to this folder, choose the Add button.

6. In the Select Users, Computers, Or Groups dialog box, select a group. I will choose Users. Choose OK.

7. Highlight the Users group in the Properties box. Notice that the default permissions for users are Read, Read And Execute, and List Folder Contents. If you want to modify the permissions for all of the users in your organization, you can do so here.

8. With the Users group still highlighted, click on the Advanced tab. Click on the Users group again and choose the View/Edit button. Figure 6.35 shows what the permissions look like.

9. In the Name box, you can change whom you'd like to assign permissions for, and in the Apply Onto box, you can change what these permissions will apply to. There are six choices for permission application: This Folder Only; This Folder, Subfolders, And Files; This Folder And Subfolders; This Folder And Files; Subfolders And Files Only; Subfolders Only; and Files Only. These options allow an administrator to completely define who can have access to what.

10. If you want to assign permissions based on the default permissions already assigned, you can do so simply by checking the appropriate Allow or Deny box. However, you

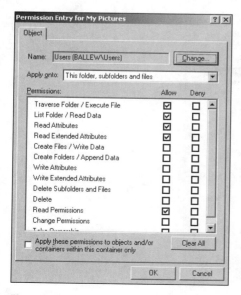

Figure 6.35
The Permission Entry dialog box.

can also choose the Clear All button to start from scratch. This is akin to starting over completely and is comparable to removing the ACE permission setting.

11. Finally, you can check the box Apply These Permissions To Objects And/Or Containers Within This Container Only. Choose Cancel, or set new permissions and choose OK, to return to the previous screen.

12. To remove the Users group just added, choose the Remove button in the Access Control Settings dialog box. Groups can also be removed from the Properties page.

13. One last note: In the Properties page, uncheck the box Allow Inheritable Permissions From Parent To Propagate To This Object, and look at the Security dialog box that appears. You can copy or remove the existing permissions, or cancel to return to the previous screen. For the sake of performing the exercise, choose Remove. Notice that all explicitly named groups or users are removed. In my case, only the Everyone group remains. This occurs because the Everyone group is not explicitly named, but is inherited from the parent directory. (Your results may differ, depending on the state of your existing folders and permissions.) Choose Cancel.

Setting File Attributes

To change a file or folder's attributes, use Windows Explorer to find the file or folder, right-click on it, and choose Properties. Select the General tab. From this screen, you can see what attributes have been assigned to the object, and change them as necessary. Figure 6.36 shows an example.

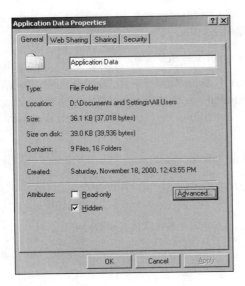

Figure 6.36
Changing file attributes.

Taking Ownership of a File or Folder

A user can take ownership of a file or folder if any of the following conditions is true:

- The user is an administrator.

- The user has the special permission of Take Ownership.

- The user has Full Control of the object.

If any of the three criteria are met, you can follow these steps to take ownership.

1. Use Windows Explorer to locate the file or folder, and highlight it.

2. Right-click on the file or folder and choose Properties.

3. Choose the Security tab then the advanced button, and then the Owner tab.

4. If the folder you are taking ownership of has files and subfolders, you can also check the box Replace Owner On Subcontainers And Objects.

Testing Permissions

Because of the sheer number of permissions that can be assigned to a single person or group, you may want to test some of the permissions as you set them to make sure that access is truly denied or allowed, or to see if any other special permissions are working properly. In this section, I'll show you how to test permissions after setting them.

For the sake of the exercise, I'll create a folder called "Test" in the root directory of the hard drive, and assign NTFS permissions to it for certain users. Follow along:

1. Use Windows Explorer to go to the root directory. In the right pane, right-click and choose New|Folder. Name the folder Test.

2. Right-click on the folder and choose Properties. Select the Security tab.

3. Uncheck the box Allow Inheritable Permissions From Parent To Propagate To This Object, and choose Remove from the dialog box that appears. Doing so removes all inherited permissions from this folder and allows you to explicitly set permissions for this object.

4. Choose Add. Select two groups: Users and Administrators. Choose OK.

5. Highlight the Administrators group and give that group Full Control of the Test folder.

6. Highlight the Users group and uncheck all of the boxes except Read.

7. Select the Advanced button, and highlight the Users group again. Choose the View/ Edit button.

8. Notice the items not checked in the Allow permissions entry list.

9. Choose OK three times.

To test your permissions, perform the following steps:

1. Log on first as an administrator, and go to Step 2. Then return to Step 1 but log on as a member of the Users group.

2. For each of these logons, try to perform the following tasks. When you're logged on as an administrator, these tasks should be performed easily. When you're logged on as a user, any task that doesn't have to do with the Read permission cannot be performed. Try these tasks:

   - Modify the folder.

   - Write to the folder.

   - Delete a file in the folder.

   - Add information to the end of a file in the folder (append).

   - See or modify the attributes of the folder.

   - Change the permissions on the folder.

   - Take ownership of the folder.

Assigning Share Permissions

Although this last part of the chapter focused mainly on NTFS permissions, Share permissions are often used on NTFS computers. In this last section, I'll walk you through many of the most common tasks associated with managing Share permissions, including sharing a folder and assigning permissions, and modifying permissions on shared folders.

Sharing a Folder

Sharing folders is easy, but assigning the appropriate permissions and understanding how those permissions work with NTFS permissions is a little more complex.

To share a folder or stop sharing a folder, follow these steps:

1. Use Windows Explorer to find the folder to be shared.

2. Right-click on the folder and choose Sharing from the context menu.

3. In the dialog box, select the Sharing tab if it isn't chosen already, and select the radio button Share This Folder. By default, the option Do Not Share This Folder is chosen.

4. The name of the folder is automatically placed in the Share Name box.

5. In the Comment box, write a comment about the folder if you'd like; it isn't required.

6. To specify how many users you'd like to give access to this folder, choose either Maximum Allowed or Allow _____ Users. The maximum number of users is 10.

7. By default, the Everyone group has Full Control of this folder.

8. To stop sharing a folder, remove the dot in the radio button for sharing, and place it instead in the Do Not Share This Folder option.

Assigning Share Permissions

Because the Everyone group has Full Control permission to all shared folders by default, you might decide that this isn't the permission you want for users on your shared folder. If you want to assign or modify the permissions, follow these steps:

1. Right-click on the shared folder and choose Sharing.

2. From the Sharing tab, choose Permissions.

3. Select the Everyone group and choose Remove.

4. Choose Add.

5. In the dialog box that appears next, select the groups or users whom you would like to be able to access this folder. For the sake of example, I'll choose Users and Administrators. Choose OK.

6. Choose OK twice.

Modifying Share Permissions

To modify Share permissions, follow these steps:

1. Right-click on the shared folder and choose Sharing.

2. From the Sharing tab, choose Permissions.

3. Select the Everyone group and choose Remove.

4. Highlight the user or group that you added in the previous exercise, and look at the share permissions in the box below. In my example, both the Administrators and the Users groups are given only the Read permission. (In the Look In box, you can choose a different domain or look through the entire directory.)

5. To give the selected user or group full control, check the Full Control permission's Allow box. If you'd like a user or group to have the Change permission, place a check in the Allow box next to the Change permission. To leave the permissions as they are—to allow the users and administrators to only Read this folder—simply choose OK.

6. Choose OK twice.

Note: *If you right-click on a file, you won't see the Sharing option. Shares work only for folders and not for files. To assign permissions to files, you'll need to assign NTFS permissions.*

Connecting to a Shared Folder

Once a folder is shared, a client will need to access that folder. Although this can be done in a number of ways, I prefer to locate a share by using the Add Network Place Wizard:

1. Log on to the network, and make sure you are connected to the domain where the share can be located.

2. Open My Network Places, and choose Add Network Place.

3. Choose Browse.

4. Browse to the domain that contains the share, and then to the share itself.

5. Choose Finish to accept the name of the share as it will appear to you, or enter a new name.

Summary

In this chapter, you learned about many of the Active Directory Administrative Tools, including the Domains And Trusts console, the Users And Computers console, the Sites And Services console, and the Microsoft Management Console. The first three consoles mentioned are accessed through Administrative Tools in Active Directory itself, whereas the MMC is a separate utility.

You can use the Active Directory consoles to do many tasks, including publishing Active Directory resources, creating explicit trusts, assigning permissions for resources, finding and moving Active Directory objects, and adding shared folders. The Microsoft Management Console can be configured to contain these consoles, or the MMC can be configured to hold other often-used interfaces. In this chapter, you learned about both preconfigured MMCs and custom MMCs.

Windows 2000 Support Tools were also introduced, including the Active Directory Administration Tool, Active Directory Replication Monitor, ADSI Edit, the Application Compatibility Tool, Security Administration Tools, and several command-line utilities. These tools can be obtained from the Windows 2000 Server CD-ROM or from Microsoft's Web site, or they are included by default during the installation of Windows 2000 Server. They can be used to simplify tasks associated with migrations, security, and installations, to name only a few of their purposes.

You also learned how to secure resources on the network by using group policies and NTFS permissions. Group policies are configured with the help of the Active Directory Users And Computers console and the Active Directory Sites And Services console.

Following that, you learned about NTFS permissions. Having a thorough understanding of how NTFS permissions work and how they are configured is most useful in fully securing the Active Directory and its resources. Permissions, in their simplest form, determine who can access an object and who can't. NTFS permissions can be used to specify what users who access a resource can or can't do *to* it.

The section on NTFS permissions discussed the order of inheritance, what happens when multiple permissions exist, and how permissions are changed when files and folders are copied or moved. Finally, tasks associated with NTFS and Share permissions were detailed, including creating objects, assigning permissions to those objects, setting file attributes, taking ownership, and testing permissions after they are assigned.

Moving Forward

In the next chapter, user and group accounts will be introduced. User accounts will be introduced first, including how to plan, create, and maintain the accounts. Profiles and home directories for users will also be introduced. The second part of the chapter will focus on group accounts and will begin with planning and creating those accounts. Additionally, built-in, special, and predefined groups will be discussed. After users and groups have been set up successfully, you'll be ready to tackle optimizing and configuring network services.

Chapter 7

Administering Windows 2000 Server

The administration of Windows 2000 Server will continue with the creation, management, and configuration of user and group accounts. For a user to have access to network resources, the user must be assigned a user account. You could create a user account for each person who needs access to a resource, and you could then manage those accounts independently. However, there is a more efficient way to manage these accounts and to incorporate all that Windows 2000 has to offer. Accounts are better managed through groups.

In this chapter, you'll learn about user and group accounts. You'll discover how users and groups can be combined and configured to manage the user accounts in the organization. In the first section, you'll be introduced to the built-in user accounts, Administrator and Guest, as well as to domain user accounts and local user accounts.

Following that, you'll learn how to plan for your user accounts. You'll need to go back over some of the previous plans made for naming conventions, including what you decided on for email account names, domain names, and OUs. You can base your naming scheme for user accounts on a previous plan if you'd like, or you can choose any of the other naming schemes that will be introduced. Other issues that will be considered include setting password rules and account lockout rules, among others, although you may have already set these up through group policies.

Once the planning phase is complete, you'll be ready to create these accounts by using the Active Directory Users And Computers console. In this console, you can perform such tasks as creating the local and domain user accounts, entering contact information, creating profile paths, setting restrictions, setting security, deleting user accounts, copying user accounts, creating home folders, and disabling user accounts. All of these tasks will be detailed in this chapter.

The next section introduces domain local, global, and universal groups. These groups should be used to make the management of users and resources efficient, to apply group policy settings, or to otherwise separate and administer resources. There are two kinds of groups: security and distribution. *Security groups* can be used to assemble resources into manageable units and to assign permissions to resources through those units.

Distribution groups are created solely for the purpose of email distribution. Windows 2000 Server comes with many groups already defined, and each of these groups will be discussed.

Next, group accounts will be discussed, including how group accounts should be used and the best ways to incorporate them. Design strategies for group accounts will be offered, and I'll discuss the special-identity groups that are created by the system for classifying which users are on the network and using resources at any given time. User rights will be discussed, a description of each user right will be given, and this discussion will include reasons to modify or not modify the default user rights.

Finally, delegating responsibility will be discussed. You can delegate the authority to create new users and groups to other members of the network after a general plan has been established. The delegation of responsibility can take place at the OU level, the domain level, or the site level. Because creating new groups and users can be time-consuming, especially in larger networks, the ability to pass this responsibility off to another network administrator can provide more time for you to manage other tasks.

User Accounts

User accounts, group types, and group accounts need to be discussed together for many reasons. User accounts are created so users can access objects and resources on the network and so users' access to those objects and resources can be managed effectively by administrators. In this chapter, you'll learn about the different user accounts, including the built-in accounts of Administrator and Guest, and you'll learn how to configure user accounts for the members of your organization. Before we begin, however, the relationship between users and groups should be discussed briefly.

Introduction

If you've ever taken a Microsoft class or created user accounts in Windows NT, you might have heard someone say "AGLP, AGLP, AGLP!" If you haven't, AGLP stands for Accounts, Global groups, Local groups, and Permissions. What it describes is the best way to configure user accounts and group membership. AGLP implies that when you're creating user accounts and assigning permissions, the best way to go about the task is to create user accounts first, put those user accounts into global groups, put those global groups into local groups, and then assign those local groups permissions. In Windows 2000, you can take this idea a couple of steps further by understanding how global group nesting and universal groups can be used. However, because permissions can be assigned directly to user accounts, and this section is dedicated to user accounts, I'll explain why you shouldn't configure them this way.

The Role Groups Play

Consider an administrator of a small organization that has 10 users and creates 10 user accounts. The idea of managing these 10 accounts by assigning permissions to each account seems doable. For example, User 1 may have Read permission for a certain file,

User 2 may have the ability to write to the file, and User 3 may have no access to the file but instead manages the printers on the network. What happens if this very small organization grows to 100 users? Although it might still be possible to manage user accounts this way, it would be very difficult due to the sheer number of combinations of permissions and necessary tasks. Consider now what would happen if the network grew to 1,000 users. Trying to manage a network this way would cause administrative headaches, so there are other ways to manage those accounts; the least productive way, of course, is trying to manage them all separately.

7

Consider a scenario in which those 1,000 users are all placed in one or two of five groups—say, Accounting, Marketing, Sales, Administration, and Staff. Instead of there being 1,000 accounts to manage, there are really only five. All members of a group can be managed as one unit, where changes to a group affect all members in it. This is much more productive and certainly less time-consuming.

Therefore, in considering the following information about managing user accounts, keep in mind that you will be putting those users into global groups and then possibly into local groups, and then you'll be assigning permissions to those groups. When considering assigning permissions to individual users, remember AGLP.

Built-In User Accounts

There are two built-in user accounts: Administrator and Guest. Both accounts are created automatically when Windows 2000 Server is installed, and they can be located in the Users container in the Active Directory Users And Computers console. To see these accounts for the purpose of following along visually, follow these steps:

1. Open the Active Directory Users And Computers console.

2. Double-click on the domain name, showing the available folders.

3. Open the Users container.

4. Locate the Guest and Administrator accounts.

The *Administrator account* is the account that is used to perform the administrative tasks associated with Windows 2000 Server. It is the account you use to log on to the server the first time it is booted after installation. Because it is the most powerful account on the server, it should be handled with care. Using this account, an administrator can perform any task that is required for managing the network. If a permission or right is not inherently assigned to the Administrator account, an administrator can assign it to himself.

The Administrator account cannot be deleted, but it can be renamed. Renaming the Administrator account is one of the first things you should do when Windows 2000 is installed, and renaming this account will put up one more roadblock that an intruder will have to get past to log on to the server uninvited. Renaming this account does not change the object's security identifier (SID); it changes only the logon name.

In general, Administrator accounts should be used only when necessary. You should not log on with an Administrator account and stay logged on indefinitely. Doing so could make the server vulnerable to attack through email viruses, Trojan-horse viruses, sniffers, or hackers. If you have administrator status, you should log on as a power user or other group member most of the time, and you should log on with the Administrator account only when you need to perform tasks that only administrators can complete. Some of the tasks that can be performed by an administrator are listed next. (Keep this in mind when you're assigning members to an Administrators group or allowing access to the Administrator account.)

Administrators can do the following:

- Install or upgrade the operating systems, service packs, and system drivers.
- Repair the operating system.
- Format the hard drive.
- Take ownership of files and folders.
- Back up and restore the system.
- Configure security settings such as passwords and account lockouts.
- Manage auditing logs.
- Log on locally.
- Access the computer from a network.
- Change the system time.
- Shut down the system or force a shutdown from a remote system.
- Install and uninstall device drivers.
- Add workstations to a domain.
- Create and manage user accounts and local and global groups.
- Assign user rights.
- Lock a server or unlock a locked server.
- Create program groups.
- Keep a local profile.
- Share or stop sharing printers and directories.

As you can see, and probably already know, allowing a hacker to log on to the network with an administrative account can be devastating to the security of the network. This is precisely the reason you should take the appropriate precautions by renaming the account quickly and using the account only when necessary.

The built-in *Guest account*, in contrast, is the most restrictive account by default on a Windows 2000 server. This account is disabled by default on a Windows 2000 server. This account should be enabled only on networks that are not highly concerned with security. Should the Guest account be needed, it should be used only occasionally, and the appropriate rights, permissions, and password should be configured.

The Guest account is used when a client does not have an account in the domain, or in any of the trusted domains, or if the client that needs access has an account but it is disabled. In either case, the Guest account can be used for access. The Guest account can be configured to allow access without the use of a password.

However, if you decide to enable the Guest account, you should create and configure it with care. The Guest account is an accident waiting to happen if left on its own. When a password is not set, the Guest account works this way: If a user tries to log on with a username and password, and those credentials will not allow a logon, the system will try to log on the user with the Guest account. If the Guest account is enabled, and no password is set, the user is allowed access. This type of unchecked access can cause security breaches on the network. To solve this problem, make sure you configure permissions and a password for the Guest account, if it's used.

A person using the Guest account (by default) can do two things:

- Log on to a workstation locally.

- Shut down the system.

The remaining permissions must be set manually either through group policies or by right-clicking on the Guest account and choosing Properties. By default, no boxes are checked for Allow or Deny.

To enable and properly configure the Guest account on Windows 2000 Server, you'll need to understand the options, and set permissions for the account. There are several options available for configuration, and they are performed through the Active Directory Users And Computers console, under the domain name, in the Users container. Each of the available options will be described next.

By right clicking on the Guest account in the Users container, you will see the following options:

- Copy the account and its properties

- Add members to a group

- Configure certificates through name mappings

- Disable the account

- Reset the password for the account

- Move the account

- Open the home page belonging to the account

- Send mail to the account

- Find users, contacts, or groups

- Create a new window

- Delete the account

- Rename the account

- Refresh the account

- View the properties for the account

- Get help regarding the Guest account

You can enable an account in two ways:

- Choose Enable from the list.

- Choose Properties, select the Account tab, and then uncheck Account Is Disabled, as shown in Figure 7.1.

Notice also in Figure 7.1 that you can use the Accounts tab to set logon hours, specify which computers the guest can log on to, and set account expiration.

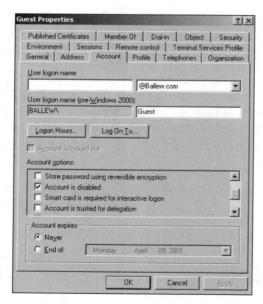

Figure 7.1
Guest properties.

Other tabs are available also.

- On the Profile tab, paths to profiles and home folders can be set.
- On the Security tab, other groups can be added, and groups or users can be deleted.
- On the Dial-In tab, restrictions can be set for remote access and callback options.
- On the Sessions tab, restrictions can be placed on session limits and reconnection configurations.

As you can see in Figure 7.1, the Guest Properties dialog box has many other tabs for managing the Guest account. These tabs will be explored in more depth for other accounts later in this chapter. For now, know that before you enable this account, make sure that all of these settings have been configured properly.

Domain User Accounts

Domain user accounts are created by administrators to allow users to access resources in the domain or anywhere on the network. User accounts can be defined in the Active Directory Users And Computers console and are created so that users can be authorized on to the network by using a logon name and password. Domain user accounts contain information that Windows 2000 uses to create an access token for the user, thus allowing the user access to the domain.

When creating a domain user account, you can specify the following information:

- Full name (must be specified)
- Password
- Password rules
- Logon name (must be specified)

After you've created the user account, you can right-click on that account and choose Properties to specify or edit any of the following settings:

- Full name, addresses, and telephone numbers
- Display name
- Description
- Office location
- Organization name, title, department, and company
- Email and Web page information
- Group membership information

- Account information and restrictions, including logon hours, computers that the user can log on to, and password settings

- Profile paths and home folders

- Dial-in rules, call-back rules, and static IP routes

- Certificate information

- Terminal Services information and configuration

Local User Accounts

Local user accounts are used only to give users access to resources on the local computer. The account is created on the computer where the resource resides, and is therefore not replicated to domain controllers on the network. The information about the account is stored in the local computer, and the user is verified by that computer's local security database. Local user accounts can be created only on Windows 2000 Professional machines or on Windows 2000 member servers running Windows 2000 Server.

On a member server, a local user account is necessary if a user needs access but the global group to which the user belongs is not in a trusted domain. No local groups are needed if proper trust relationships exist between domains. You can create a local user account by using the Local Users And Groups snap-in in a Microsoft Management Console or by using the Active Directory Users And Groups console, accessed through Administrative Tools.

When creating a local user account, you can specify the following information:

- Full name

- Password

- Password rules

- Username (must be specified)

- The account status

After you've created the user account, you can right-click on that account and choose Properties to specify or edit any of the following settings (for details, see "Properties of User Accounts" later in this chapter):

- Full name

- Description

- Password rules

- Group membership information

- Profile paths and home folders

Planning User Accounts

Before you start creating user accounts, you'll want to decide on a naming scheme to use. You'll need to think about some other issues as well—some having to do with security and some having to do with account management.

Creating Usernames

To create a user account on a Windows 2000 domain controller, you must enter at least two items: the user's first name and the user's logon name. Logon names, which can be up to 20 characters long, are used by clients to log on to the network and are used by administrators to manage user accounts. Internally, Windows 2000 uses a SID to identify users. The username that you configure isn't used by the operating system at all. The access control list uses the SID to identify the user and to determine the properties and permissions of the user's account. Because of this, you can change the username and still have the same SID, thus retaining the user's permissions and rights. This makes renaming and modifying accounts much more flexible.

Tip: *When one employee is being replaced by another employee, through promotion, demotion, or termination, it is easier to simply rename the account than to create a new one. The account keeps the same SID, and if the new employee is taking the first employee's place in the company, then groups, logon hours, dial-in properties, and so on will remain the same.*

There are many ways to decide how you will name the user accounts on your network. Described next are a few of the more common naming schemes for user accounts. Remember, the pattern you choose will most likely remain with the network for quite some time, so make these choices carefully. Keep in mind also that the network and its users will most likely develop further, so make sure there is room for growth in the naming plan.

Warning! *Although I'll suggest many options for naming schemes, each scheme has its downside. For instance, the scheme First Name, Last Initial is unwise for a large organization where there could be not only 20 Johns but also 5 John Smiths. This could pose multiple problems in a large organization when administrators try to manage usernames.*

If you have a small LAN and only a few users, you might want to consider usernames that consist of only the user's first name. I worked for a startup company in 2000, and that's exactly what we did. There were only four people in the entire office, and we all had usernames that consisted only of our first names. It was quaint, but it would have had to be changed if the company had succeeded and grown. I wouldn't suggest this plan for any organization that is expected to incur any growth in the near future. (This plan can be adapted to employ only the user's last name as well.)

A common naming scheme in small to medium-sized organizations is to use the first name and the initial for the last name. Usernames like JoliB or MaryC are usually sufficient for smaller networks, and name collisions rarely occur unless the network grows tremendously. However, there are drawbacks, and including a middle initial or full last name might be a better choice.

Another common naming scheme is to use the first initial and full last name. I see this one a lot—Jballew, Mcosmo, Jtruscott, and so on. Unless you have lots of Smiths and Joneses on the network, you'll probably be okay with this plan.

The scheme I'd suggest to most organizations is the first initial, middle initial, and last name. This will usually be sufficient for the majority of networks, and names like JABallew or MACosmo are much more individual. It isn't too hard for users to remember these names, either, and that never hurts. Most of the time, even if users have the same first and last names—for instance, Jennifer Johnson—their middle initials are different.

Note: *In an extremely large organization, you might need to create a name like JABallew1112 where the 1112 represents the last four numbers of a person's social security number. Using a scheme like this, you'll be less likely to run into duplicate usernames.*

Finally, if you need a fully secure network, you might choose to go with usernames that are created through some algorithm or code. For instance, sample usernames might be H2234R or 644TYVU4. These names are, of course, hard to remember, but combined with a complex password they can make uninvited logons much less frequent.

Tip: *A network administrator friend once stated that he keeps six locks on his front door, and each time he leaves home, he locks three of them. He says he figures that no matter how long someone stands there and picks at the locks, the person will always be bolting one lock for every lock that's picked. A clever scheme, as is creating usernames through algorithms. In an organization where security is the main concern, you can never be too protected.*

Some helpful hints in creating usernames are listed next. After deciding on the scheme you'd like to employ, incorporate the following rules and best practices:

- The characters that can't be used in a username are \ / [ ] : ; | = , + ? < >.

- If DOS clients are involved, usernames should be only 8 characters or less and not the maximum of 20.

- When you're using a home directory, the username should be only 8 characters or less, and you should make the name of the directory the same as the username.

- The username should be unique in the domain.

- Usernames should be assigned in a pattern or naming scheme. Do not randomly make up names as users join the network.

Properties of User Accounts

Besides planning usernames and logon names, you'll need to think about other issues when creating user accounts. Most of these features are related to tightening the security of the account, and some of the items are for management purposes only. This section details the remaining properties of user accounts. Later in this chapter, you'll learn how to manually create and configure a user account and its properties.

Tip: *If you want to follow along visually, open the Active Directory Users And Computers console and double-click on the Users container. Right-click on an account name and choose Properties. Figure 7.1 shows the tabs in the Properties dialog box.*

On the General tab, an administrator can set contact information, including the first name, middle initial, last name, display name, description, office location, telephone number, email address, and Web page address. The only remarkable characteristic here is the display name of the user. The display name isn't the logon name, nor is it the email address; it is any name you choose to be displayed for the user when he or she does business on the network. By default, the display name consists of the first name, middle initial, and last name as they are entered on this page. In the same vein, on the Address tab, you can set the user's address.

The Account tab allows an administrator to create a user logon name, as discussed earlier. In my network, the naming scheme is first initial, last name, as shown in Figure 7.2.

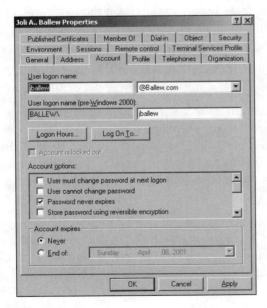

Figure 7.2
The Properties dialog box for a user account.

Notice the logon name of jballew and the additional suffix of **@Ballew.com**. With this scenario, the email and logon naming conventions can both be used. Also on the Account tab, you can set logon hours and specify which computers the user can log on to. You can also set options related to account security, such as changing the password at next logon, not having the ability to change the password, setting password expiration, and storing the password using encryption. In the section "Creating and Modifying User Accounts," I'll describe how to configure these items.

On the Profile tab, administrators can type in a profile path, a path to a logon script, or a path to a home folder. The *profile path* points to a directory associated with the user's desktop environment, including configuration of such items as the screensaver, screen colors, network connections, program groups, and the look of the Start menu or Control Panel. (Profile paths were discussed in Chapter 6, during the discussion of group policies.) The *logon script* is a batch file or command file (a program that runs when a user logs on to the network). This was also discussed in Chapter 6. Scripts can be used for many things, including saving data, cleaning up a user's disk drive, and running anti-virus programs. The *home folder* is a place where the user can store his or her data on the network server, where that user can manage folders and have full control over what is saved and deleted. The home folder can be configured by typing a local path or by connecting or mapping to another drive. Configuring a home folder will be discussed in the next section of this chapter.

On the Telephones tab, you can type in all of the user's telephone numbers, including mobile, fax, office, and home, as well as make notes. On the Organization tab, you can enter the user's title, department, company, manager, and other notes.

On the Published Certificates tab, you can list the user's issued certificates, including who they were issued by, their purpose, and their expiration. You can also add certificates either from a certificate store or from a file, and you can remove those certificates.

On the Member Of tab, you can see what groups the user is a member of. In my case, where I am both a user and an administrator, my username shows up in three groups. Those groups are Administrators (a built-in group), Domain Admins, and Domain Users (both located in the Users container). On this tab, an administrator can change a user's group memberships by adding that user to another group, deleting the user from a group, or deleting the user from all groups.

The Dial-In tab can be used to set dial-in permissions for users if those permissions haven't been currently configured in a group policy object (GPO). Dial-in properties can be configured for Remote Access Permission (dial-in or VPN) to allow or deny access, or to control access through Remote Access Policy. Callback options can be configured for No Callback (default), Set By Caller, or Always Callback To <number>. You can also apply a static IP address or static routes for dial-in options.

The Object tab describes the user as an object as it is seen in Active Directory. For example, my fully qualified domain name (FQDN) is Ballew.com/Users/JoliA.Ballew. This tab also stores such information as object class, object creation and modification dates, original Update Sequence Number (USN), and current USN. The USN is used to track changes in the objects that are stored in Active Directory. Every time information about the object is changed, the USN is incremented by one. When an object is first created, both of its USNs are the same.

The Security tab is the same as what you are familiar with from setting NTFS permissions. In the Name box, you can see which groups the user is a member of, and there may be several for each user. Users may be members of Authenticated Users, Everyone, System, Administrators, and possibly even other groups, such as Domain Administrators, Print Operators, or Backup Operators. By choosing the Advanced button, you can add, remove, view, or edit permission entries for the groups, just like you can for setting permissions in any other way.

The Environment tab is used for configuring the Terminal Services startup environment. There won't be anything configured here unless the client is using Terminal Services. If that is the case, you can configure the starting file's program name and decide how the client will connect at logon.

The Sessions tab, which also deals with Terminal Services, can be used to configure timeout and reconnection settings. You can set an active session limit, an idle session limit, and an action to take if a client is disconnected.

The Remote Control tab and the Terminal Services Profile tab are for Terminal Services configurations as well. These two tabs can be used to enable remote control and to type a path for the user's Terminal Services profile.

Once you have explored all of these options, you can decide how you'd like to configure your user accounts. The most important decision to make initially is the issue of the naming scheme for the user accounts, followed by how those accounts will be secured. As you've already learned, there are many, many ways to secure the network. You might have already made security decisions while planning group policies, designing the structure of Active Directory, and laying out the organizational structure. Configuring user accounts can now be added into the mix.

Tip: Remember AGLP. It is better to put user accounts into global groups, put global groups into local groups, and assign those local groups permissions. You can assign local groups permissions by right-clicking on a group, choosing Properties, and selecting the Security tab. This is a better way to set permissions than is assigning certain properties to users themselves.

Creating and Modifying User Accounts

In this section, you'll learn how to perform tasks such as creating local user accounts, creating domain user accounts, and modifying domain user accounts. Most of the emphasis will be placed on domain user accounts because these are the most often used, but the management of local accounts is basically the same.

The main tasks associated with modifying domain user accounts are:

- Deleting user accounts

- Renaming user accounts

- Copying user accounts

- Disabling user accounts

- Creating and using account templates

Creating the Local User Account

To create a local user account on a Windows 2000 Professional computer or on a Windows 2000 member server, follow these steps:

1. Log on to a member server or workstation as an administrator.

2. Choose Start|Run and enter "mmc" in the Open box.

3. Choose Console|Add/Remove Snap-in.

4. Choose Add, and from the resulting dialog box, choose the Local Users And Groups Snap-in.

5. If you are attempting this on a domain controller, the error message shown in Figure 7.3 will appear.

6. Select Local Computer from the dialog box, and choose Finish.

7. Select Close, then OK.

8. Expand Local Users and Groups (local).

9. Double-click on the Users container. (The Users container is also an organizational unit. I'll call it a container in this chapter.)

10. Right-click in the right pane, and choose New|User from the context menu.

11. At the very least, type a username. See Figure 7.4 for a look at the New User dialog box.

12. Choose OK.

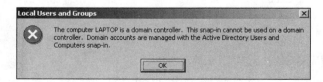

Figure 7.3
Error message.

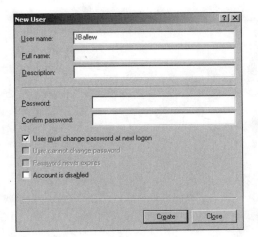

Figure 7.4
Creating a local user account.

Modifying the Local User Account

Once the local user account has been established, you can modify that account either by right-clicking on the username and choosing Properties, or by double-clicking on the username.

To edit a user account, follow these steps:

1. In the MMC that contains the Local Users And Groups snap-in, right-click on the user account you just created, and choose Properties.

2. On the General tab, you can type a description of the user or account, and you can set password restrictions. Figure 7.5 shows the options on this tab, including User Must Change Password At Next Logon, User Cannot Change Password, Password Never Expires, Account Is Disabled, and Account Is Locked Out.

3. On the Member Of tab, you can see which groups the user belongs to, and you can add or remove groups as well. To add the user to another group, choose the Add button. See Figure 7.6.

4. Select groups, such as Power Users on a Windows 2000 Professional machine, choose Add, and choose OK. You'll then see the groups listed on the Member Of tab, as shown in Figure 7.6.

5. On the Profile tab, you can type a path to a profile, a logon script, or a home folder. After typing the path, choose OK.

Other options are available by right-clicking on the username or by highlighting the username and selecting the Action menu from the console. From here you can perform the following tasks:

- Set a password for the account.

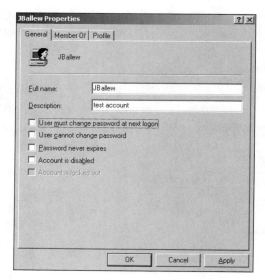

Figure 7.5
The General tab of the Properties dialog box for a local user account.

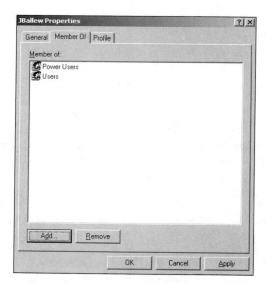

Figure 7.6
The Member Of tab of the Properties dialog box for a local user account.

- Delete the account.

- Rename the account (which will not change anything but the name; the SID will remain the same).

- Get help from Microsoft Help on creating users and groups.

In this example, I created the account JBallew and added that account to the Power Users group. The user JBallew is now a member of two groups: Users and Power Users, as shown earlier in Figure 7.6. Because this user is a member of these two groups, the user has the cumulative combination of the permissions of both.

Creating the Domain User Account

Most of the user accounts you'll be creating as an administrator will be domain user accounts. You'll set up these accounts on the domain controller, and the information will be replicated through Active Directory.

7

To create a domain user account, follow these steps:

1. Log on as an administrator.

2. Open the Active Directory Users And Computers console.

3. In the left pane, double-click on the domain name.

4. In the right pane, double-click on the Users container.

5. In the right pane, right-click in a blank area, and choose New|User. See Figure 7.7.

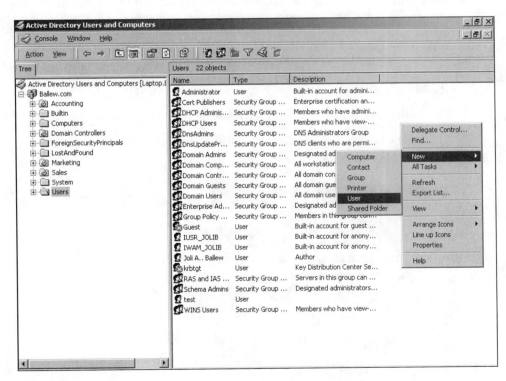

Figure 7.7
Menu choices for creating a new user account.

Tip: Notice that you can create a new computer, contact, group, printer, and shared folder as well as a new user account. Creating any of these accounts is similar to creating a new user account.

6. In the New Object – User dialog box, type in at least the first name and the user logon name. When typing the user logon name, do not put an @ after the name. If you'd like, you can type the middle initial, last name, and full name. The New Object – User dialog box is shown in Figure 7.8. Choose Next.

7. The next dialog box asks for password information. You can select from the following options:

   • User Must Change Password At Next Logon

   • User Cannot Change Password

   • Password Never Expires

   • Account Is Disabled

   Select an option, type a password, confirm the password, and choose Next.

8. The next dialog box asks you to verify the information. If the information is correct, choose Finish; otherwise, choose Back to reenter the information.

Modifying the Domain User Account

You can modify a user account by right-clicking on the account and choosing Properties.

To edit the basic settings for a domain user account, follow these steps:

1. Right-click on the user account that you want to edit, and choose Properties.

2. Choose the General tab to enter or edit the user's name, description, office location, office telephone number, email address, and Web page address.

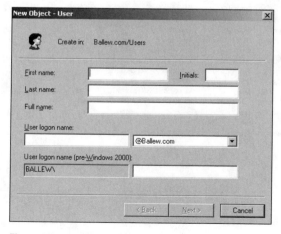

Figure 7.8
The New Object – User dialog box.

3. Choose the Address tab to enter or edit the user's street address, Post Office box, city, state or province, ZIP code, and country or region.

4. Choose the Telephones tab to enter or edit the user's home phone, pager, mobile phone, fax numbers, and IP phone, or to make notes about those numbers.

5. Choose the Organization tab to enter the user's title, department, company, and manager name, or to make notes about the user.

6. Choose the Object tab to view or edit the fully qualified domain name (FQDN) of the object (user).

7. Choose the Account tab to enter or edit the user's logon name, logon hours, computers that the user can log on to, account password options, and account expiration.

8. Choose the Profiles tab to enter or edit a user's profile path, logon script, or home folder. Creating home folders and profiles will be discussed in more depth later.

Most of the seven configuration changes listed above can be made simply by typing the requested information. Changing the logon hours, the computers that the user is allowed to log on to, and account options, such as password restrictions and account sensitivity, requires a little more work.

To change security options for a user account, follow these steps:

1. Right-click on the user account whose security options you want to change, choose Properties, and choose the Account tab.

2. To change the logon hours, click on the Logon Hours button. You will see the Logon Hours dialog box, shown in Figure 7.9.

3. By default, the user can log on any time. To change this, simply highlight the boxes representing the days and hours that you want to deny logon, and click on the Logon Denied button. This will change the denied hours' blocks from blue to white. Blue

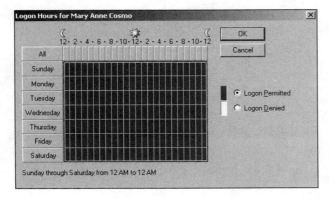

Figure 7.9
The Logon Hours dialog box.

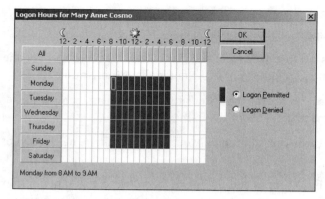

Figure 7.10
Setting user logon hours.

represents days and times the user can log on; white represents when the user cannot log on. Figure 7.10 shows logon hours for a user who is allowed to log on only during the workweek. Choose OK to return to the Properties dialog.

4. By default, the user can log on to all computers. To restrict the computers this user can log on to, choose the Log On To button on the Accounts tab.

5. To allow this user to log on to a single computer, or to specifically named computers, choose the radio button The Following Computers and type the NetBIOS names of those machines. When you're finished, choose OK.

6. In the Account Options box on the Account tab, you can configure multiple security features for the account. The following items are available:

- User Must Change Password At Next Logon
- User Cannot Change Password
- Password Never Expires
- Store Password Using Reversible Encryption
- Account Is Disabled
- Smart Card Is Required For Interactive Logon
- Account Is Trusted For Delegation
- Account Is Sensitive And Cannot Be Delegated
- Use DES Encryption Types For This Account
- Do Not Require Kerberos Preauthentication

7. On the Account tab, you can also set account expiration. Either select Never, or select End Of and then a date.

Another essential user account modification is group membership. You can see which groups the user is a member of by choosing the Member Of tab in the user account's Properties dialog. From here, you can add or delete groups as well. To modify membership information, follow these steps:

1. Right-click on the user account whose group memberships you want to change, choose Properties, and choose the Member Of tab.

2. Notice which groups the user is a member of. For a new user, there will be only one group by default: Domain Users.

3. To add that user to another group, choose Add.

4. Figure 7.11 shows the Select Groups dialog box. Select a group, choose Add, and choose OK.

5. To remove the user from a group, select that group in the Properties dialog box and choose Remove. Choose Yes to confirm this decision.

The Properties dialog box has three tabs for configuring a user account's security options, and four tabs for configuring Terminal Services options. The three tabs for general security are Published Certificates, Dial-In, and Security. To configure settings related to these items, follow these steps:

1. Right-click on the user account whose security settings you want to configure, choose Properties, and choose the Published Certificates tab.

2. If any certificates are published for this user account, you will see them listed here. To add published certificates, choose Add From Store or Add From File.

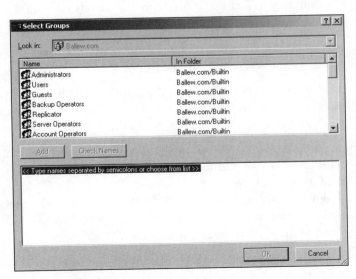

Figure 7.11
The Select Groups dialog box.

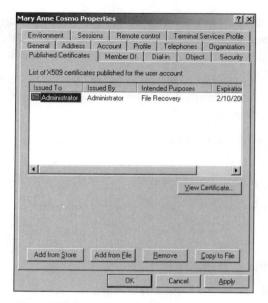

Figure 7.12
The Published Certificates tab of the Properties dialog box for a domain user account.

3. Figure 7.12 shows the Published Certificates tab, displaying the certificate, who issued it, what its purpose is, and when it expires.

4. Notice that in this dialog box you can also remove or copy the certificate.

5. To set dial-in properties, choose the Dial-In tab. By default, the dial-in and VPN permissions are set to Deny Access and No Callback. To change settings, select the appropriate radio button.

6. If you select Always Callback To, you'll need to enter a number in the appropriate box, and you'll need to configure and test that connection prior to use.

7. Finally, the Security tab offers a place to configure the security for this object, in our case, a user. Notice all of the groups associated with a single user in the example shown in Figure 7.13.

8. In this example, notice that the Account Operators group is highlighted and that this group, by default, is allowed all of the permissions available. This is, of course, because account operators have full control over accounts in a domain. If you were to scroll down and highlight another group, perhaps Authenticated Users, you'd see that that group doesn't have the same permissions. In fact, authenticated users can only read information related to the account but cannot modify the account.

9. To add, remove, or view advanced permissions, choose the appropriate tabs. Notice that you can also configure inheritable permissions for this user.

7

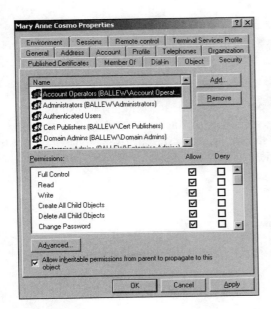

Figure 7.13
The Security tab of the Properties dialog box for a domain user account.

The four remaining tabs available for user properties configuration are Environment, Sessions, Remote Control, and Terminal Services Profile. Each of these tabs is used to configure the Terminal Services environment for a user. If you are using Terminal Services, you'll need to explore these tabs:

1. On the Environment tab, you can choose from four configuration options. These four settings allow you to start programs for the user at logon, connect client drives at logon, connect client printers at logon, and/or default to the main client printer.

2. On the Sessions tab, you can set a time limit for the Terminal Services session for never; 1, 5, 10, 15, or 30 minutes; 1, 2, or 3 hours; or 1 or 2 days. These same time limits can be set for active sessions or idle sessions as well.

3. Also on the Sessions tab, you can set rules for what happens when a session ends or a connection is broken. For instance, if the session is set to end in five minutes, at the end of that time the session can be disconnected or simply ended. Reconnection rules can be configured so that a user can reconnect from any client or from the originating client only.

4. On the Remote Control tab, you can enable or disable remote control of a Terminal Services session. By enabling remote control, you can observe the user's session and even interact with that session. This interaction can be configured such that this interaction can occur with or without the user's permission.

5. The Terminal Services Profile tab can be used to configure a user profile for the Terminal Services user. You can also configure a path to a home directory and select Allow Logon To Terminal Server.

Creating and Using Templates

When you're creating user accounts, you can save time by configuring a single user account to suit the needs of many users, copying that account, and then using it as a template. Using a template is much faster than setting specific user properties every time a new account is created. The properties that can be copied from a template user's account are:

- Description of the account

- Groups the user will be a member of

- The user's profile path (if you use %username% in the path, it can be automatically configured)

- The user's home folder path (%username% can be used in the path)

- The user's login script path (%username% can be used in the path)

- Whether or not the user can change the password

- Whether or not the password will expire

- The user's logon hours

- The account type

When you use a template to create an account, all you need to enter into the new account are the first name and user logon name. Although only two entries are needed to create an account, the following items are left blank for configuration:

- The user's logon name (required)

- The user's first name (required)

- The user's initials and last name

- The user's full name

- The password option that the user must change the password at the next logon (other password options are copied)

- The Account Is Disabled option

To create a template account and copy it for other users, follow these steps:

1. Log on as an administrator.

2. Open the Active Directory Users And Computers console.

3. Double-click on the domain name and then on the Users container.

4. In the right pane, right-click and choose New|User.

5. In the First Name box, type a name. In the Full Name box, type "Template".

6. In the Logon Name box, type a logon name. Choose Next.

Tip: *You are creating a template account, so make sure that "template" will be the display name by typing it in the Full Name box. For security, do not make the logon name "template."*

7

7. Create the password and password options. If you choose User Cannot Change Password or Password Never Expires, those settings will be kept for the user accounts created with this template account. The setting User Must Change Password At Next Logon will not.

8. After you've created the template account, right-click on it and set the security and configuration choices as you'd like them to be for the user accounts you will be creating. These settings will be applied to the new accounts. When you're finished, choose OK.

9. With the template account created, right-click on it and choose Copy.

10. You'll see the Copy Object – User dialog box, shown in Figure 7.14. Type the required information and choose Next.

11. Set the password information in the next dialog box, and choose Finish.

12. The new user account created from the template will now have the same settings as the template.

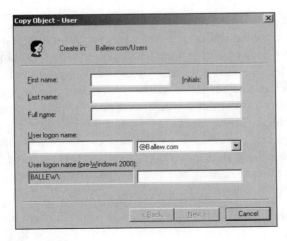

Figure 7.14
The Copy Object – User dialog box.

Miscellaneous Tasks

Several tasks can be achieved easily: deleting accounts, renaming accounts, disabling accounts, and resetting passwords, to name a few. To perform any of these tasks and more, follow the guidelines listed next.

From the Active Directory Users And Computers console, right-click on the user account for which you'd like to perform a task. From the context menu, choose the appropriate command:

- To disable the account, choose Disable Account. To enable the account again, choose Enable Account.

- To reset the password for this account, choose Reset Password.

- To rename the account, choose Rename.

- To delete the account permanently, thus losing the SID for that account, choose Delete.

- To refresh the information in the account after account information has been changed, choose Refresh.

- To move the account from this location to another, choose Move.

- To open the user's home page or send mail to this user, choose Open Home Page or Send Mail.

Profiles and Home Directories

The last items for configuration are the profiles and home directories for a user. Both of these concepts were introduced when you learned about group policies in Chapter 6, and in this section, you'll learn how they work and how to configure them.

Understanding the Local Profile

When a Windows 2000 product is initially installed, it boots with a specific configuration of desktop settings, including colors, folders, and desktop icons. When users log on to this computer with their usernames, they can change these settings to suit their individual tastes for color schemes, desktop icons, folders, network drives, shortcuts, printer settings, and more. Doing so creates a local profile for the user. The profile is saved on the computer and will be called upon the next time the user logs on. If the computer is shared with other users, those users can also create their own user profiles. Every time users log on to a computer with their logon name, they'll be given their own specific profile. On a network, the local profile is the lowest on the totem pole. It can be overridden by group policies, roaming profiles, and mandatory profiles.

It is easy to see the effects of a local profile simply by logging on as yourself, changing the desktop or the color scheme, and logging off. The next time you log on, those settings will remain. If another user logs on to the same computer and makes changes, those settings will not affect your local profile.

Understanding the Roaming Profile

Roaming user profiles are created by administrators for users who need to receive the same desktop, colors, settings, folders, and so on at every computer they visit. To create a roaming user profile, you create a user profile on a member server or domain controller, and configure the user's account to use the profile each time he or she logs on. This roaming profile is important for users who move from computer to computer to do their jobs.

Roaming profiles come in only a few varieties, the most common being standard roaming profiles, personal roaming profiles, and mandatory roaming profiles. In a *standard roaming profile*, the administrator creates a distinctive profile for all members of a specific group. For instance, an administrator for a bank may create a standard roaming profile for all bank tellers in the building. This is a good choice for this type of organization because the bank tellers will probably work at different computers during the day, will need access to just a few specific programs, and will use the same resources for logging on and connecting to printers, servers, and databases as all of the other bank tellers do. Additionally, troubleshooting problems is easier because the desktops are all the same.

Personal roaming profiles, on the other hand, can be changed by the users who employ them. In a personal roaming profile, the users receive their settings no matter which computer they log on to, and those users can change their profile at any time. Those changes are saved to a network server and will be used the next time the employee logs on. Both standard and personal roaming profiles can be stored as .dat files.

Understanding the Mandatory Profile

A roaming profile can be made *mandatory* by changing the name of the profile from the default ntuser.dat to ntuser.man. A mandatory roaming profile also follows a user to any computer, but changes made by that user are not applied to the profile. While logged on, the user can change color schemes, wallpaper, file locations, printers, and so on, but when the user logs off, those changes are not saved.

Tip: *Create the roaming profiles on a member server instead of on a domain controller. Roaming user profiles use a lot of system resources, bandwidth, and processing power. By taking the profiles off a domain controller and placing them on a member server, you can improve the performance of the domain controllers on the network.*

Creating a Roaming Profile

Creating a roaming user profile involves many steps. First, you must create a shared folder that will hold the profiles to be accessed by the users. Second, you'll need to create a user account that will serve as a model for the profile. Third, you'll create the profile for this imaginary user. Fourth, you'll copy this profile to the shared folder. Finally, you'll specify the path to the profile for users.

To create a roaming profile, follow these steps:

1. Log on to the domain controller as an administrator.

2. Use Windows Explorer to locate the root folder (system drive) C:\. Right-click and choose New|Folder.

3. Name the new folder Profiles.

4. Right-click on the Profiles folder and choose Sharing.

5. Choose Share This Folder and then OK.

6. Open the Profiles folder, and create a subfolder called Templates.

7. Close all windows; then choose Start|Programs|Administrative Tools|Active Directory Users And Computers.

8. In the Users And Computers console, create a user named TemplateProfile. Make the appropriate password choices for this user. Choose OK, then Finish.

9. Right-click on the user account, select the Member Of tab, and make this user a member of a group that has permission to log on to the domain controller. Examples include the Server Operators, Print Operators, and Account Operators groups. Choose OK.

10. Log off as administrator, and then log back on as the user TemplateProfile. You will use this account to create the new profile for the users.

Note: You create an account called TemplateProfile so a profile can be created and saved to a specific account other than the account the administrator is logged on with. The profile for the users or for specific groups might not be the profile that the administrator wants to have when she logs on, and the administrator might not want to change her own account. If you do not want to create an account for the purpose of creating a profile, you can use an existing account, or use an administrator's account other than your own.

After logging on as TemplateProfile, notice that the desktop for the domain controller looks just like it did the first time it was installed. (I love that look!) To create a profile from this account, you can begin making changes.

11. Right-click on the desktop, choose Properties, and change the display settings related to background, screensavers, appearance, Active Desktop, effects, and other settings.

12. Use Windows Explorer to define folder options, including showing hidden files, enabling offline files and folders, and viewing folders and files.

13. Create a Favorites list for Internet locations.

14. Finalize any other profile settings, such as application configuration settings, printer connection settings, network places, desktop shortcuts, and user-specific program settings.

15. Log off as user TemplateProfile and log back on as an administrator.

16. Choose Start|Settings|Control Panel and double-click on the System icon.

17. Select the User Profiles tab. Notice the profiles listed, and highlight TemplateProfile. See Figure 7.15.

18. Click on the Copy To button.

7

19. Click on the Browse button to locate the Profiles folder created earlier in the root directory, or type the name and location of the new folder like this: "C:\Profiles\ Templates". Choose OK.

Tip: *When you browse to the C:\Profiles directory, you should type a name like* templates *after it, so a new folder is created for the profile inside the Profiles folder. Otherwise, the profile contents will be directly copied into the folder without any separation from other items there.*

The profile is now copied to the Profiles folder and will be shared from here.

20. To select users or groups who will use this profile, in the Copy To box, under the words Permitted To Use, select Change.

The Select User Or Group dialog box appears, as shown in Figure 7.16.

21. Select a user who will use this profile, choose Add, then choose OK. If you see a Confirm Copy box, choose Yes and continue.

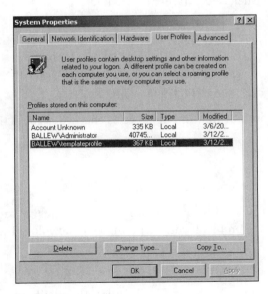

Figure 7.15
The User Profiles tab of the System Properties dialog box.

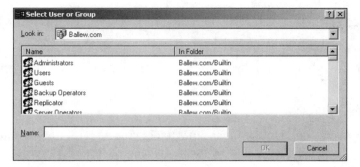

Figure 7.16
The Select User Or Group dialog box.

22. Finally, to specify the path to the profile now that it is created, open Active Directory Users And Computers, right-click on a user who will use this profile, and choose Properties.

23. Select the Profile tab. Type the path to the profile, using the form "\\computername\ sharename". In this example, the correct syntax is "\\<computername>\profiles\ templates".

Creating a Mandatory Profile

To change a roaming user profile to a mandatory user profile, follow these steps:

1. Open the Profiles folder created earlier, select the Templates folder, and open the folder.

2. Choose Tools|Folder Options.

3. Open the View menu.

4. Under Hidden Files And Folders, click Show Hidden Files And Folders.

5. If the next box, Hide File Extensions For Known File Types, is checked, remove the checkmark.

6. Choose OK.

7. Right-click on ntuser.dat and rename it ntuser.man.

You can test the roaming user profiles by logging off as administrator and logging back on as the user who has been assigned the profile. If you are prompted to download the new profile, choose Yes.

Copying a Profile

As you can probably see by now, you cannot share a profile file unless the profile is mandatory. This is because personal (roaming) profiles will be changed by the users daily and then saved back to the server throughout the day. To use the same profile for different users, you'll need to copy the profile for distribution to others. This can be done through some of the same dialog boxes shown in the previous example.

To configure a profile for multiple users, first create a profile as described earlier, and then follow the steps here:

1. With a profile created, open the Control Panel and the System icon.

2. Choose the User Profiles tab.

3. Highlight the profile you'd like to copy, and choose the Copy To button.

4. In the box Copy Profile To, type the profile path exactly as it is written on the Profile tab in the user's Properties box.

5. Select Yes to overwrite if needed; then choose OK.

6. If necessary, make adjustments to the Permitted To Use box.

Tip: You cannot use Windows Explorer to copy profiles; this must be done through the System icon in the Control Panel.

Changing the Profile Type

You can change the profile type very easily by opening the System icon from Control Panel, highlighting a profile, and choosing the Change Type button. Figure 7.17 shows the resulting dialog box. Notice that the profile can be changed from a roaming user profile to a local one or vice versa.

Deleting a Profile

You can delete a profile very easily by opening the System icon from Control Panel, highlighting a profile, and choosing the Delete button. You will be asked to verify the deletion. If you want, choose Yes to delete the profile.

Understanding Home Folders

When Windows 2000 is installed on a computer, the My Documents folder is created to hold the user's personal files on the local computer. Unless changed, this folder is where those files are stored by default. On the local computer, you can change the location of file

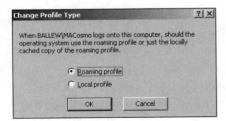

Figure 7.17
Changing the profile type.

storage by opening an application and choosing Tools|Options|File Locations. You can change the default to any folder on the hard drive.

In contrast, *home directories*, also called *home folders*, are folders that can be configured not only for the local machine but also on a network server. Creating a home folder for a user on a network server offers many advantages over allowing the user's personal documents to be stored on the local machine. Some of these advantages are as follows:

- All users on a network can have home folders on a single network server. This allows centralized administration of the folders.

- Because the user's documents are stored on a network server, the user can access the documents from any computer in the organization and from almost any computer that the user can dial in or access the network from. Computers that can access these folders can be MS-DOS, Windows 9x, Windows NT, or Windows 2000 machines.

- Backing up the data in these folders can be made the responsibility of the administrator, not the users.

- Home folders can be stored on NTFS volumes at the server level, instead of on FAT volumes possibly configured on workstations.

- Home folders aren't part of the users' roaming user profiles and thus do not slow down logons.

- The local My Documents folder can be redirected to the user's home folder on the server, thus enhancing backup and management of those documents.

Creating Home Folders

Setting up home folders on the server is quite simple. There are only two main steps involved: creating and sharing the home folder, and configuring the user account to use that folder.

To create the folders on the server, follow these steps:

1. Log on to the Windows 2000 Server as an administrator.

2. Use Windows Explorer to go to the root directory, C:\.

3. In the root directory, create a folder called "HomeDir" or something similar. (I'd always choose something eight characters or less just to be safe.)

4. Make this folder a shared folder by right-clicking on it and choosing the Sharing tab. Select Share This Folder.

5. Select the Security tab.

6. The Everyone group has Full Control of this directory by default. Choose Add.

7. Select Users and any other groups who will access the home directories, and choose Add.

8. To make the home folders work effectively, clear the checkbox for Allow Inheritable Permissions From Parent To Propagate To This Object.

9. In the security warning box, shown in Figure 7.18, choose Remove.

10. Notice that the Everyone group has been removed from the Name box. Only the users remain. The users can Read And Execute, List Folder Contents, and Read. If you need to assign the Users group more permissions or fewer, you can do so now. Most likely, these permissions are appropriate.

11. To administer these directories, you'll also need to add the Administrators group. Choose Add, choose Administrators, and choose OK.

Figure 7.19 shows the HomeDir Properties dialog box now that this process is complete. Notice that the Administrators group is highlighted in this example and that the group does not have Full Control of the folder.

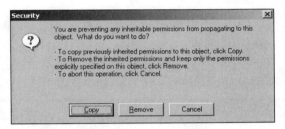

Figure 7.18
A security warning.

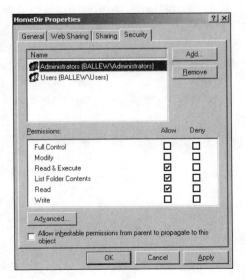

Figure 7.19
HomeDir properties.

12. Check the box for Allow Full Control so that the Administrators group has full control of the home directories. Choose OK.

To configure a user account to use a home folder, follow these steps:

1. Open the Active Directory Users And Computers console.

2. Right-click on a user account for which a home folder will be configured. Choose Properties.

3. On the Profile tab, select the Connect option.

4. Select a drive letter, perhaps the default Z, and type the path to the HomeDir folder in the To box. The path is in the form, \\computername\sharename\username, or more simply, \\computername\HomeDir\%username% in our case. See the sidebar in this section for information on the % sign.

5. Close the Active Directory Users And Computers console.

Testing the Home Folder

To test the home folder, follow these steps:

1. Use Windows Explorer to go to the root directory, C:\.

The % Placeholder

The % sign can be used as a variable when you're creating home folders for user accounts. In the previous example, you used the phrase %username% when configuring the user's home directory. The %username% placeholder was then replaced with the user's logon name. The ability to use this type of placeholder makes configuring home folders much easier, and the creation of home folders can be somewhat automated when you're using a user account template.

The %itemname% placeholder can be used to configure other items, too, including but not limited to the items listed next. (Most of these are not included for configuration in the user account properties. Many of these items are used in logon scripts and batch files.) The %itemname% placeholder can be used for:

- %homedrive%
- %homepath%
- %homeshare%
- %computername%
- %servername%
- %userdomain%
- %userprofile%
- %os%

2. Locate the HomeDir folder created earlier and open it. Inside the HomeDir folder, notice the folder for the user whose home folder was just created.

3. Right-click on that folder, choose Properties, and then select the Security tab.

   This folder can be accessed by the user and by the Administrators group. From here, you can also see that both the administrators and the user have full control.

4. Choose OK. Log off the computer and log back on as the user.

5. Double-click on the My Computer icon on the desktop, and note the new network drive leading to the home folder on the server.

Types of Groups

As you know, a group is a collection of user accounts. You learned earlier that even though permissions can be assigned to user accounts, it's more efficient to assign those users to groups and then assign the permissions to the group accounts. It's easier to manage many accounts at the same time through a single group, instead of managing each user account separately. You also know that a single user can be a member of many groups, and the effective permissions for that user are determined by the permissions of the groups he or she belongs to. In this section, you'll learn about different group scopes (local, domain local, global, and universal) and group types (security groups and distribution groups). You'll also learn how to perform the most common tasks associated with users and groups.

Local Groups

Local groups are similar to local user accounts in that they exist on a single computer for managing the user's access to resources on that computer. Local groups differ from domain local groups in that local groups are stored in the local computer's security database and not in the network server's Active Directory database. A computer's local group isn't replicated among domain controllers, and the permissions set for the local groups on the local computer are not effective on the network. Local groups are described here for the sole purpose of distinguishing them from domain local groups, which are stored in Active Directory and which apply throughout the network. Occasionally, you'll read about local groups in a domain context in other books or papers. It is important to be able to recognize the difference between the local computer group and the domain local group.

On a standalone computer that is not part of a domain, local groups can only contain local user accounts from the computer for which the local group was created. If the computer name is Workstation_02, then only users who have an account on Workstation_02 can be placed in the group. Because local groups are recognized only on the computer on which they were created, you cannot add these local groups to any other type of group, such as domain local groups, global groups, or universal groups.

On a Windows 2000 Professional machine or a Windows 2000 member server, where the computer *is* part of a domain, the local group can contain other users besides the users on the local machine. In this scenario, a local group can contain domain user accounts and global groups from the domain where the computer resides or from a domain that is trusted. However, the local group still cannot be added to other groups on the network.

It makes sense, if you think about it, that local groups cannot be configured on a Windows 2000 server, because Windows 2000 Server does not allow any other type of security database other than Active Directory. Because of this restriction and the lack of a local Security Accounts Manager database, you can't have a local group on a server.

Creating a Local Group

Configuring a local computer group is similar to creating a local user account, described earlier. To create a local group, follow these steps:

1. Open the Computer Management console. This can be done in many ways, three of which are:

   - Choose Start|Programs|Administrative Tools|Computer Management.

   - Choose Start|Run and enter "mmc". Choose Console|Add/Remove Snap-In|Add| Computer Management.

   - From the Control Panel, choose Users And Passwords; choose the Advanced tab and then the Advanced button.

2. Expand the Local Users And Groups tree.

3. Double-click on the Groups folder.

   Notice the built-in local groups Administrator, Backup Operators, Guests, Power Users, Replicator, and Users, as shown in Figure 7.20.

4. To create a new local group, right-click in the right pane and choose New|Group.

5. Type the following information:

   - *Group name*—Name the group something representative such as shift1, shift2, shift3, temp, and so on. Make sure you follow group naming guidelines such as choosing a unique name, using a name that is less than 256 characters, and not using the \ character. The group name is a required field.

   - *Description*—Although this is not a required field, type a description of the group for future reference.

   - *Members*—You can add members to the group by using the Add button. You do not need to add members at this time; the group can be created with no members initially.

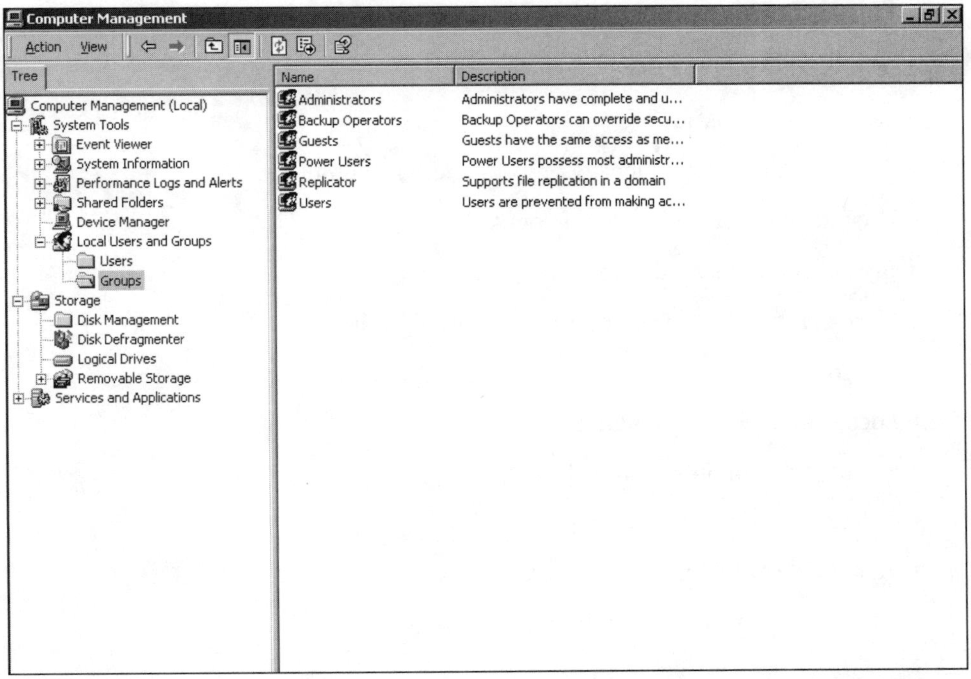

Figure 7.20
The Computer Management console.

6. To add members to the group, choose Add. Select the user or group to add; then choose OK twice.

Notice the new group located in the right pane of the Computer Management console.

Built-in Local Groups

Windows 2000 comes with six built-in local groups: Administrators, Backup Operators, Guests, Power Users, Replicator, and Users. Each of these built-in local groups has certain rights and capabilities by default, and if you assign users to these groups, those users will have the rights associated with those groups. To make good decisions about group memberships, you should understand what members of each group can accomplish.

The Administrators local group is similar to any other Administrators group in that members have full control of the system. The only default member of this group is the local administrator. Administrators have the following rights and capabilities:

- Log on locally.
- Access the computer from the network.

- Take ownership of files.

- Manage the auditing and security logs and auditing of system events.

- Change the system time.

- Shut down the system locally or from a remote computer.

- Back up and restore files and folders.

- Install and uninstall device drivers.

- Create and manage user accounts and local groups.

- Assign rights to users.

- Lock or unlock the computer.

- Format the computer's hard drive.

- Create common program groups.

- Share and stop sharing directories.

- Share and stop sharing printers.

- Create a pagefile.

- Debug programs.

The Backup Operators local group has no members by default. Backup operators have the following rights and capabilities:

- Log on locally.

- Shut down the system.

- Back up and restore files and folders.

The Guests local group is similar to any other Guests group in a domain. This group has only one default member: the Guest user account. Guests have only one right by default:

- Log on locally.

The Power Users local group is available only on Windows Professional machines and member servers. The Power Users group has no members by default. Power users have the following rights and capabilities:

- Log on locally.

- Access the computer from the network.

- Change the system time.

- Shut down the system.

- Create and manage user accounts and local groups.

The Users local group by default contains only members whose user accounts were created during the installation of the Windows 2000 Professional machine or member server. Power users and administrators can modify the properties of the Users local group. Users have the following rights and capabilities:

- Log on locally.

- Shut down the local system.

- Create and manage local groups.

- Run applications.

- Use local printers.

The Replicator group is included in all Windows 2000 products that are used with the directory replication service. This group has no members by default.

Domain Local Groups

The local groups discussed in the previous section were applicable only at the local computer level and were assigned at the local computer. The local groups discussed here are applicable at the domain level and are assigned at the domain controller. *Domain local groups* are most often used to provide the member user accounts with appropriate access to resources in the local domain. Domain local groups in a mixed-mode environment can contain user accounts, computers, and global groups. The domain local groups in a native-mode environment can consist of those objects plus other domain local groups from the same domain.

Domain local groups can consist of members from the local domain or from any trusted domain. Domain local groups can also contain accounts other than user accounts from other domains in the forest. The groups can be converted to universal groups (described later in this section) if the network is running in native mode and if the groups do not contain any other domain local groups. The groups in native mode can contain user accounts, universal groups from any domain, global groups from any domain, and other domain local groups from the same domain.

Tip: Moving from mixed mode to native mode offers many security enhancements, as previous chapters have mentioned, but the ability to apply group nesting is another perk of moving to native mode. Having the ability to add groups to groups can lessen network traffic between domains as well as simplify management of those groups.

Creating a Domain Local Group

To create a domain local group, follow these steps:

1. Log on to the Windows 2000 Server domain controller as an administrator.

2. Open the Active Directory Users And Computers console.

3. Double-click on the Users container.

4. In the right pane, right-click and choose New|Group. The New Object – Group dialog box will appear, as shown in Figure 7.21.

5. Type a group name (required) and choose the Domain Local option.

6. Choose OK, and notice the new group in the Users container.

7. To modify the properties of the new group, right-click on the new group and choose Properties.

8. The group name appears on the General tab. Here you can enter the description of the group, a group email address, and notes about the group. Make the necessary changes.

9. Select the Members tab. To add members to this group, choose the Add button.

10. Select the appropriate members or groups that will belong to the new group, and choose OK. Notice the new members in the Members Name box.

11. Select the Member Of tab to see which groups are included from the local domain or to add groups from the local domain. Adding members here is similar to Step 10.

12. Select the Managed By tab. From here, you can enter the group manager's name, office, street, city, state, country, telephone number, and fax number.

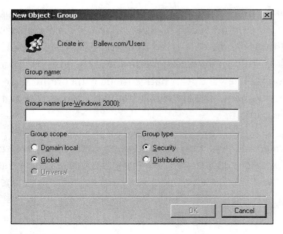

Figure 7.21
The New Object – Group dialog box.

13. Select the Object tab. Here is the object's fully qualified domain name, object class, creation and modification dates, and original and current USN.

14. Select the Security tab. Here, you can add or remove groups and set permissions for those groups. The Advanced tab offers more choices, including more permissions, auditing, and owner information.

15. Choose OK to accept the changes you've made.

Built-in Domain Local Groups

Several built-in domain local groups are available in Windows 2000 Server. They are Administrators, Backup Operators, Account Operators, Guests, Print Operators, Replicator, Server Operators, and Users. They can be located in the Active Directory Users And Computers console under the Builtin folder.

The Administrators domain local group is similar to any other Administrators group in that members have full control of both the domain controller and the domain. By default, the group's members include the Administrator account, the Domain Admins global group, and the Enterprise Admins global group. Members of the Administrators domain local group have the following rights and capabilities:

- Log on locally.
- Access the computer from the network.
- Take ownership of files.
- Manage the auditing and security logs and auditing of system events.
- Change the system time.
- Shut down the system locally or from a remote computer.
- Back up and restore files and folders.
- Install and uninstall device drivers.
- Create and manage user accounts and global groups.
- Assign rights to users.
- Lock or unlock the computer.
- Format the computer's hard drive.
- Create common program groups.
- Share and stop sharing directories.
- Share and stop sharing printers.
- Add workstations to the domain.

The Backup Operators domain local group has no members by default. Backup operators have the following rights and capabilities:

- Log on locally.

- Shut down the system.

- Back up and restore files and folders.

Note: *For security reasons, it would be a bad idea to allow the same person to back up files and folders and to restore them. That user could theoretically back up the data, modify it, and then restore it to a user's system.*

The Account Operators domain local group has no members by default. Although account operators can modify user accounts, they cannot modify the accounts in the Administrators group or any other Operators groups. Account operators have the following rights and capabilities:

- Log on locally.

- Shut down the system.

- Create, delete, and manage user accounts and global group accounts.

- Create and manage local groups.

The Guests domain local group is similar to any other Guests group in a domain. The Guests domain local group has only one default member, Guest, and one default group, the Domain Guests global group. Guests have very limited rights:

- Guests can perform only those tasks for which rights have been specifically assigned.

- Guests can access only those resources for which permissions have been specifically assigned.

- Guests cannot make permanent changes to the desktop.

- Guests can shut down the local system.

- Guests can log on to the server from the network to perform job duties.

The Print Operators domain local group is found only on Windows 2000 servers that are domain controllers. This group is used to group print operators for the specific purpose of managing network printers. Print operators have the following rights and capabilities:

- Log on locally.

- Share and stop sharing printers.

- Manage network printers on domain controllers.

- Print documents.

- Control job settings on network printers.

- Change printer properties.

- Delete printers.

- Change printer permissions.

The Server Operators domain local group is another powerful group. Server operators can perform many tasks, most of which are provided so members can back up and restore files, manage the server, and share disk resources. Server operators have the following rights and capabilities:

- Log on to the server locally.

- Change the system time.

- Shut down the system locally or from a remote computer.

- Back up and restore files and folders.

- Lock and unlock the server.

- Share and stop sharing printers.

- Share hard disk resources.

The Users domain local group is similar to the Guests domain local group because the members of this group must be granted rights and assigned permissions to perform tasks and access resources. The Users group includes, by default, the Authenticated Users special group, the Domain Users group, and the Interactive special group. The Users group should be used to house the accounts for all of the users on the network. Users have the following rights and capabilities:

- Log on locally.

- Shut down and lock the local system.

- Create and manage local groups.

- Run applications.

- Use local and network printers.

The Replicator group is included in all Windows 2000 products that are used with the directory replication service. This group has no members by default.

Global Groups

Global groups are used differently than domain local groups are, and they have different characteristics. Global groups are used mainly to group users together who access the *network* similarly, whereas domain local groups are used primarily to group users who access *resources* similarly. Global groups differ from domain local groups in two other ways. First, global groups can contain members only from the local domain, whereas a domain local group can contain members from any domain. In a global group, allowing members from only the local domain is necessary so those users can be configured with the same network resource options. Second, global group members can access resources in any domain, whereas domain local group members can access resources only in their local domain. Again, access to resources in a global group is a network-wide configuration. Because global groups can be used to assign permission to resources as well, those resources can be anywhere in the local domain, domain tree, or forest.

Creating a Global Group

To create a global group, follow these steps:

1. Log on to the Windows 2000 Server domain controller as an administrator.

2. Open the Active Directory Users And Computers console.

3. Double-click on the Users container.

4. In the right pane, right-click and choose New|Group. The New Object – Group dialog box will appear, as shown earlier in Figure 7.21.

5. Type a group name (required), and choose the Global option.

6. Choose OK, and notice the new group in the Users container.

7. To modify the properties of the new group, right-click on the new group and choose Properties.

8. The group name appears on the General tab. Here you can type the description of the group, a group email address, and notes about the group. Make the necessary changes.

9. Select the Members tab. To add members to this group, choose the Add button.

10. Select the appropriate members or groups that will belong to the new group, and choose OK. Notice the new members in the Members Name box.

11. Select the Member Of tab to add members to this global group. Adding members here is similar to Step 10.

12. Select the Managed By tab. Here you can type the group manager's name, office, street, city, state, country, telephone number, and fax number.

13. Select the Object tab. Here is the object's fully qualified domain name of the object, object class, creation and modification dates, and original and current USN.

14. Select the Security tab. Here you can add or remove groups and set permissions for those groups. The Advanced tab offers more choices, including more permissions, auditing, and owner information.

15. Choose OK to accept the changes you've made.

Built-in Domain Global Groups

You can select members to be a part of the built-in global groups, or you can create a new global group to suit your own specific needs. Windows 2000 Server comes with several built-in domain global groups: Domain Admins, Domain Guests, Domain Users, Enterprise Admins, Group Policy Creator Owners, Cert Publishers, DnsUpdateProxy, SchemaAdmins, Domain Computer, and Domain Controllers.

The Domain Admins global group is similar to any other Administrators group in that members have extensive control of the domain. There are no members in this group by default, and the members that are generally added need comprehensive administrative rights throughout the domain. There probably won't be too many users in this group because authority over organizational units and locations can be delegated. In a domain, this group is a member of the Administrators group by default. The domain administrator is also a member of this group. Domain administrators have rights and capabilities similar to any other Administrator account, only at the domain level.

The Domain Guests global group is disabled by default, as is the Guest user account. This Guest user account is the only member in the group when Windows 2000 is installed. As you would imagine, the members in the Domain Guests global group have very limited network access and can access only those resources and objects specifically assigned to their group or account. The Domain Guests global group is automatically added to the Guest domain local group.

The Domain Users global group holds users and accounts for all domain users, and as user accounts are created, they are automatically placed in this group. When the operating system is originally installed, the Administrator account is a member, along with the following accounts: Guest IUSR_computername, IWAM_computername, Krbtgt, and TsInternetUser.

The Enterprise Admins global group, only located in the domain root, is for network users who need even more freedom than domain administrators do. The members of the Enterprise Admins group have administrative control over the entire enterprise (network). This group has a couple of default members: the built-in local Administrators group and the Administrator account for the local domain. Enterprise Admin status should not be given lightly, and this group should contain only the most trusted network administrators.

The Group Policy Creator Owners global group is used when there are employees who need the ability to create group policies, but the administrator does not want to place these people in the Domain Admins or Enterprise Admins groups. By default, the only objects or users that can create group policies are these administrators, the operating system, and those users who are members of the Group Policy Creator Owners global group. When users (who are not administrators) are placed in this group, they have the ability to create their own group policies, own those policies, and edit those policies. However, non-administrators who are members of this group cannot edit any GPOs they did not create.

The Cert Publishers global group contains all of the computers that are running an Enterprise Certificate Authority. If a server on your network will be used to publish certificates in the domain, that server must be a member of the Cert Publishers group. Members of the Cert Publishers group can publish certificates for user objects in Active Directory. The Cert Publishers global group has no members by default.

The DnsUpdateProxy global group is used on networks where DHCP servers are used to dynamically update the A and PTR records for down-level clients. Although the topic is beyond the scope of this book, this global group can be employed to deal with the problems that arise when dynamic DNS updates and DHCP servers are combined with down-level clients and name resolution. The DnsUpdatePoxy global group can be used to house specific DHCP servers so that the problems that occur with these DNS records can be resolved.

The SchemaAdmins global group is available as a global group when the domain is in mixed mode, and as a universal group when the domain is in native mode. As you can probably guess, members of the SchemaAdmins group can change the schema in Active Directory. The only account included by default is the Administrator account in the root domain of the forest. Additionally, this group exists only in the root domain of a forest, and not in child domains or any other units. (If you recall, only one schema partition can exist per forest.)

The Domain Computer global group contains all of the computers that have been added to the domain, and are placed in the group by default when those computers are added. This global group contains only computers that are not domain controllers. You can see the members of this group on the Members tab of the Properties page.

The Domain Controllers global group contains all of the domain controllers that have been added to the domain, and are placed in the group by default when those computers are added. This global group only contains computers that are domain controllers. You can see the members of this group on the Members tab of the Properties page.

Universal Groups

Universal security groups are available only when the domain is operating in native mode. These groups are used to give members on the network access to resources that are located throughout the forest. Universal groups differ from both domain local and global groups for this reason and many others. Universal groups can contain users from any domain in the forest, and they can contain other universal groups or global groups from those domains as well. You may want to create a universal group if you have users who need access to certain resources in other domains—for instance, network printers, databases, or other resources in other cities or branch offices.

Note: Although the first paragraph stated that universal security groups are available only in native mode, universal distribution groups can be used while the domain is running in mixed mode. Security and distribution groups will be discussed in later sections.

When using universal groups, you should also consider the amount of replication traffic that will occur when changes to group membership occur. Because the members of the group have universal scope, it would be unwise to create a universal group for an organization whose information changes often.

Creating a Universal Group

To create a universal group, follow these steps:

1. Log on to the Windows 2000 Server domain controller as an administrator in a domain running in native mode.

2. Open the Active Directory Users And Computers console.

3. Double-click on the Users container.

4. In the right pane, right-click and choose New|Group. The New Object – Group dialog box will appear, as shown earlier in Figure 7.21.

5. Type a group name (required), and choose the Universal option (see Figure 7.22). This option will be grayed out if the domain is running in mixed mode and not native mode.

6. Choose OK, and notice the new group in the Users container.

7. To modify the properties of this group, see the previous examples in this section.

8. The group name appears on the General tab. Here you can type the description of the group, a group email address, and notes about the group. Make the necessary changes.

9. Select the Members tab. To add members to this group, choose the Add button.

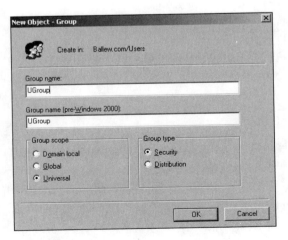

Figure 7.22
Creating a universal group.

10. Select the appropriate members or groups that will belong to the new group, and choose OK. Notice the new members in the Members Name box.

11. Select the Member Of tab to add members to this global group. Adding members here is similar to Step 10.

12. Select the Managed By tab. Here you can type the group manager's name, office, street, city, state, country, telephone number, and fax number.

13. Select the Object tab. Here is the object's fully qualified domain name of the object, object class, creation and modification dates, and original and current USN.

14. Select the Security tab. Here you can add or remove groups and set permissions for those groups. The Advanced tab offers more choices, including more permissions, auditing, and owner information.

15. Choose OK to accept the changes you've made.

Note: When the domain is switched from mixed mode to native mode, no additional built-in domain universal groups are created.

Changing Group Scope

Once a domain has been changed from mixed mode to native mode, the scope of the group can change. Group scope describes the "reach" of the group. Scope is defined in mathematics as the difference between the smallest number and the largest in a group of numbers, and it is used to describe the reach of the entire set. In Windows 2000, a universal group has universal scope, meaning that its users have access to resources in any domain. If a global group exists and you would like to change the group scope to universal, it is very easy to do. However, remember that doing so will cause lots of replication traffic when changes are made to those groups.

To change the scope of a group, follow these steps:

1. Log on to the Windows 2000 Server domain controller as an administrator in a domain running in native mode.

2. Open the Active Directory Users And Computers console.

3. Double-click on the Users container.

4. Right-click on either a global group or a domain local group that needs its scope changed, and choose Properties.

5. On the General tab, select the new group scope. There are restrictions to how the scopes of different groups can be changed. Decision Tree 7.1 shows the options.

6. Choose OK.

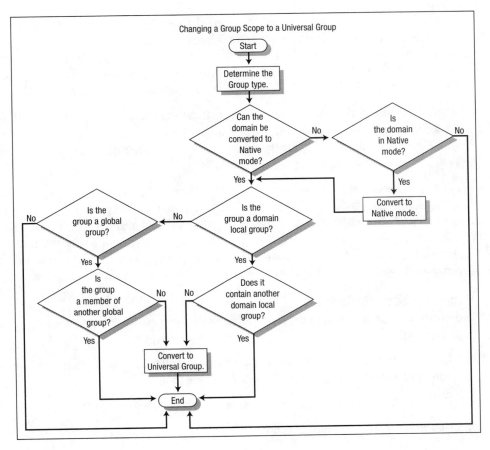

Decision Tree 7.1
Changing the scope of a group.

In a nutshell, global groups can be changed to universal groups if those global groups are not members of any other global groups. Domain local groups can be changed to universal groups if they don't contain any other domain local groups. Universal groups can't be changed to any other group because domain local and global groups are more restrictive than universal groups. Paring down the permissions of the users in a universal group would be impossible.

Security Groups

All of the groups you've created and learned about up to this point have been security groups. Domain local, global, and universal groups can be configured as security groups. The security group is used to assign permissions to resources for users in domains and forests, and it is the default type when a new group is created.

The security group works with the Windows 2000 access token that is assigned to a user when he or she logs on to the network. This token has information about the user, which security groups the user belongs to, and which rights and privileges the user has been given through those groups. This way, when a user requests access to a resource, the information about that user and his or her security groups is included in the token.

The main purpose of the security group is to gather users, computers, and other groups together to simplify the management of resource access, but security groups can be used in other ways as well. This chapter has focused so far on gathering users, but the other uses of security groups have not been explored.

Security groups can also be used with Active Directory and email programs for sending email to all members of a group. Making this feature even more appealing is the ability of an administrator to add contacts to a security group for this purpose. When the members of a group are sent an email message, so are the contacts, even though those contacts are really *members* of the group. This can be quite useful in larger organizations or in organizations where many users need to receive information about other groups.

Creating a Security Group

You create a security group in the same manner that you create any domain local, global, or universal group:

1. Log on to the Windows 2000 Server domain controller as an administrator in a domain running in either mixed mode or native mode.

2. Open the Active Directory Users And Computers console.

3. Double-click on the Users folder.

4. Right-click in the right pane and choose New|Group.

5. On the General tab, select the desired group scope and the desired group type. Security is selected by default. Name the group.

6. Choose OK.

Creating a Contact and Adding the Contact to a Group

As I just mentioned, adding contacts to a security group can be quite useful for creating email lists and keeping users informed of group activities. To create a contact and add that contact to a group, follow these steps:

1. Log on to the Windows 2000 Server domain controller as an administrator in a domain running in either mixed mode or native mode.

2. Open the Active Directory Users And Computers console.

3. Double-click on the Users container.

4. Right-click in the right pane and choose New|Contact.

5. Type the first name, initials, last name, and display name. (Only the first name is required.)

6. Right-click on the new contact and choose Properties. In the Properties dialog box, you'll see the seven tabs shown in Figure 7.23.

7

- The General tab can be used to enter the contact's full name, display name, description, office location, telephone number, email address, and Web page address. You'll need to type at least an email address here for the email properties to work in the security group.

- The Address, Telephones, and Organization tabs can be used to enter the contact's personal information.

- The Member Of tab can be used to make the contact a member of a specific group.

- The Object tab gives the object's FQDN, class, creation and modification dates, and original and current USN.

- The Security tab can be used to view who can access this contact and which permissions they have for the object.

7. Type the required information on each of these tabs, and choose OK.

8. With the contact created and configured, you can now add that contact to a security group in Active Directory. There are multiple ways to add this contact to an existing group. The fastest way is to begin by right-clicking on the new contact and choosing Add Members To A Group.

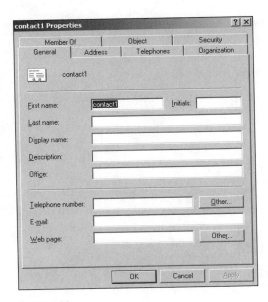

Figure 7.23
Contact properties.

9. In the resulting dialog box, choose the group to which the user should belong. Choose OK.

Note: You can also add this contact to a group by choosing Properties from the drop-down menu, selecting the Member Of tab, and choosing Add. You cannot drag and drop a user into a group, nor can you use the Move command to place a contact in a group.

The contact should now be in the appropriate group.

Testing the Addition of the Contact

To make sure that the user is in the new group, and to see what permissions the user has in that group, perform the following steps:

1. Open the Active Directory Users And Computers console, and locate the Users container.

2. Right-click on the contact that was previously placed in a group, and choose Properties.

3. On the Member Of tab, notice that the user is now part of the newly assigned group. Choose OK.

4. Right-click on the group to which the contact was added, and choose Properties.

5. Look on the Members tab to see who is a member of the group. Figure 7.24 shows a universal group and its members.

6. Choose OK to close this dialog box.

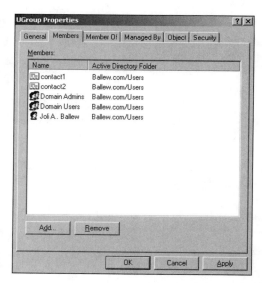

Figure 7.24
Group members.

Distribution Groups

Distribution groups are another type of group that can be configured for domain local, global, and universal groups. Distribution groups are not used for assigning permissions to resources or for managing users as security groups do. Distribution groups are used solely for email distribution among users on a network.

Creating a Distribution Group

Creating a distribution group is exactly like creating the security group described earlier, except that you select the Distribution option instead of the Security option. After the distribution group has been created, email accounts will need to be configured for the group and entered on the General tab of the Properties page for that group. Using these groups for distribution of email throughout a network will work only with programs that recognize Active Directory and can communicate with it. One application that can be used to create distribution lists or use distribution groups is Exchange 2000.

To set up a distribution group, follow these steps:

1. Log on to the Windows 2000 Server domain controller as an administrator in a domain running in either mixed mode or native mode.

2. Open the Active Directory Users And Computers console.

3. Double-click on the Users container.

4. Right-click in the right pane and choose New|Group.

5. On the General tab, select the desired group scope and the desired group type. Select the Distribution option. Name the group.

6. Choose OK.

7. Configure Exchange or other applications to use this group for distribution of emails.

That sums up the different types and scopes of groups that are available. In the next section, you'll learn more about planning the group accounts, nesting groups, using special groups, and creating your own groups.

Group Accounts

This section discusses miscellaneous tasks and characteristics related to user accounts, groups, and group accounts, and how all three of these objects and concepts work together to secure user access to network resources. I'll also provide design strategies to make your groups more effective.

I'll also discuss the Windows 2000 special-identity groups. These groups are created by the system to classify which users are on the network and who is using which resources at any given time. Although an administrator cannot modify membership in these groups, understanding what they are and their purpose will prove useful later.

Default user rights will be discussed, but this time in more detail than before. Each right will be outlined so decisions can be made regarding enabling or disabling these rights for users. Because the built-in groups have certain rights assigned by default, you will usually not want to change these rights, but there will certainly be instances when it is necessary. You'll learn why you might decide to modify or not modify these default user rights.

Finally, you'll learn how to delegate the responsibility of creating these user accounts and groups to other team members or administrators. Delegating these task responsibilities is a good way to make more time for other tasks.

Design Considerations

Group accounts play a large role in securing your network. When planning how your group accounts would be created, you probably made many decisions regarding the naming schemes of the users, the accounts, and even the email schemes. Additionally, you probably already made decisions about passwords, account lockouts, and other user conventions. Many of these decisions were made when you created your group policies as well. I won't focus on any of those items in this section; instead, I'll discuss how groups can be designed so they are the most effective they can be for a generic network.

Warning! *Microsoft has stated that a group should have no more than 5,000 members. To get around such limitations, you should use available group nesting configurations detailed in this section.*

Strategies for Local Groups

Local groups are configured most effectively when they are used to group members in the local domain or on a single computer and when those users are grouped by task or network access requirements. If a group of users on a local computer only needs access to a single application on a standalone computer, a local group and a group policy can be used to create such a configuration. In a domain, users can be grouped by their need to access the network and resources on it. As you know, the local users for a domain scope are called domain local users (groups).

You may want to create domain local groups named Accounting, Marketing, Managers, Hardware Technicians, and so on. Using this type of group strategy allows you to manage users and their groups by job function. In the Accounting group, you could add several global groups: Temporary, Junior, and Senior. Each of these global groups could contain users in those departments. You might also create a domain local group called Printers, in which you placed all of the printers on your domain, or create a domain local group called Laptops, which could be used to manage all of the laptop computers and the users who primarily use a laptop for performing their job duties.

If you decide to give the domain local users permissions and rights in a single domain, you should first place those users in a global group, and then place the global group into the local group. This is another example of the AGLP rule mentioned earlier in this chapter. To put a spin on this concept, you could just as easily place users directly in the local group, especially if the network is small. However, to accommodate network growth and minimize the chance of having to redraw those groups, I'd suggest staying with the first suggestion of including global groups in the mix. Adding users directly to local groups will not only make it impossible to assign permissions outside the domain, but it can also complicate administration of these accounts if other domains are added later. The AGLP rule's main advantage is, however, the reduction in assigning permissions for users in a domain.

If you want to include users from domains other than your local domain, but you do not want those users to have global or universal scope, you can add those users to a global group and then to the domain local group. This group will work only in the local domain, although you can add users and global groups to it. If you decide later that you'd like this local group to have access to resources in other domains, you'll need to manually create this group in the other domains. In mixed mode, you cannot add a domain local group to another domain local group, but in native mode you can.

7

Tip: Always create groups in an organizational unit such as the Users container.

One last thought about domain local groups: If you need to make a user an administrator of a domain, you should put that user in the Domain Admins global group first, and then place this global group into the local group. This strategy allows all administrators in the Domain Admins group to administer the domain. This strategy also reduces permissions assignment by allowing the domain local group to be in charge.

Strategies for Global Groups

Global groups are used most effectively when they are configured to house user accounts and computer accounts from their own domain, and these global groups are then placed in local groups in a mixed-mode domain or in local, global, or universal groups in native-mode domains. Permissions should then be assigned to the local groups. Every domain user account that is created is automatically placed in the Domain Users global group, described earlier in this chapter. By default, this group is a member of the domain local users group for the domain. This predetermined group membership again minimizes hassles associated with group permissions.

If you have several global groups that all need access to the same domain local resources, you can make those global groups members of the appropriate domain local groups. For instance, if there are three global groups called Architects, Design Engineers, and Graphic Designers, all of which need the use of the most expensive plotters in the domain, you can create two printer domain local groups: one called Printers-General and one called Printers-Plotters. The three global groups could then be placed in both groups, but the printers could be managed separately for other users.

Global groups, like domain local groups, can be named based on their users' job functions, and resources can be configured the same way. Because global groups can contain both user accounts and computer accounts, potential group names could be Managers, Sales, and Accounting, as well as Workstations, Laptops, and Legacy Machines.

Strategies for Universal Groups

Universal groups are new to Windows 2000, and they can be used only when the domain is in native mode. Universal groups are used to assign permissions for users to access resources forest-wide. Because the scope of universal groups spans multiple domains, there's no need to use universal groups in a single-domain model. Even when multiple domains exist, though, there are several problems with using universal groups, and the decision to employ them should not be made lightly.

One of the main advantages of using universal groups is that they allow incredible flexibility for group members. Members of universal groups can access resources throughout the entire forest, and with the correct permissions, members can also manage or administer those resources. In a network where all connections between the domains are fast and reliable, universal groups can be used with relative ease. As you are aware, though, this is not usually the case, and because changes to universal groups cause an inordinate amount of replication traffic, these groups might not always be useful.

You can assign permissions to universal groups in the same manner that you assign permissions to domain local groups. When using universal groups, follow similar guidelines by placing users in global groups and placing global groups in universal groups. Permissions assigned to universal groups can be configured for resources in the local domain or in any other domain in the forest.

Because of the nature of universal groups, use them only if the domain membership and permissions for resources rarely change. Consider a multiple-domain environment that contains 3 domains and 15 domain controllers. If one member of a single universal group has a change in membership, then that information must be replicated across all 3 domains and to all 15 domain controllers. Imagine what would happen if there were often multiple changes to a group or to members. This type of replication would certainly put a load on the servers and the data lines.

Note: As long as the domain is running in native mode, both domain local groups and global groups can be converted to universal groups.

Final Design Tips

There are several design tips I'd like to add that haven't previously been mentioned. When you're designing groups, consider the following:

- Do not delete the Krbtgt account in a Windows 2000 domain. It is used by Kerberos to authenticate users. Deleting this account will cause multiple problems.

- The Enterprise Admins group should contain a minimal number of members. The scope of this group is so large that problems created here could cause massive problems for the network.

- Users cannot be members of more than 1,024 groups, and although a group can have a maximum of 5,000 members, 3,000 or fewer should be assigned for stability and performance.

- Because mixed-mode domains do not use universal groups, if a forest exists where mixed-mode domains and native-mode domains trust each other, problems can arise when users of native-mode domains are migrated to mixed-mode domains. The SIDs for these users can be lost in the transfer.

- When you're considering changing a user's rights, change them by the group and not by the individual. Keeping up with individual changes to rights would be incredibly difficult.

- If you plan to incorporate groups from a NetWare server, make sure the group names are 20 characters or fewer. Otherwise, an error message will appear stating that the group cannot be accessed.

- Add computers to security groups, and then use the appropriate group policy Properties page to access the Security tab and to then access the ACL editor. Group policy filtering can then be configured.

- You can assign different printer priorities to different groups through the printers folder and through group permissions.

- Before creating groups in remote domains, make sure that you have the required permissions. Members of the Administrators group and the Account Operators group have those permissions by default. Additionally, special permissions can be granted for this purpose.

- If there are multiple domains that contain similar groups—for instance, a Sales group—make the names of those groups similar as well. Group names like Sales Chicago, Sales Dallas, and Sales Syracuse would work well.

- If you decide to change a security group to a distribution group, do so carefully. Because distribution groups do not have security features, the group members will have altered access permissions. This may cause undesired network effects. You will see the warning box shown in Figure 7.25.

- As you'll see in the next section, when you're configuring nested groups, try to keep levels of groups to a minimum. Configuring multiple groups within groups eventually causes more problems for the administrator than not employing nesting at all.

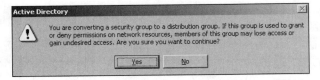

Figure 7.25
Active Directory warning.

Group Nesting

The ability to nest *security groups* in Windows 2000 is a new feature that can be used only when the network is running in native mode. Briefly, *group nesting* allows groups to be placed in other groups. Although there is no limit stating how many groups can be nested, it is best to keep nested groups to a minimum. When one group is nested into another, it is treated like a child group of its parent group. The permissions and rights associated with the parent group are inherited by the child group.

The ability to nest *distribution groups* in Windows 2000 is a new feature that can be used if the network is running in either mixed mode or native mode. Briefly, group nesting allows distribution groups to be placed in other groups with the same parent-child relationship described in the previous paragraph.

The most effective way to use group nesting is generally to add only one group to one other. When you use nesting, you need to assign permissions to objects only once for all of the groups involved, and this configuration allows easy tracking of those users and their effective permissions. If two or more levels of nesting are used, tracking these permissions becomes more complex, due to the nature of parent/child relationships. If a parent group has a child group, and that child group has a child group, and that child group has child group, well, keeping straight who has what permissions becomes quite intricate. Table 7.1 shows how groups can be nested in mixed mode.

Table 7.2 shows how groups can be nested in native mode.

There are many advantages to using nesting in universal groups. Because a universal group uses the global catalog to publish the names and properties of its users, nested universal groups can reduce the amount of replication that takes place across network lines.

Consider the following example. In an organization with branches in three cities— Chicago, Dallas, and Sacramento—three groups could be created and named for their locations. Because each branch has several supervisors, you could then place all of the branch supervisors in their own group, as a child group (nesting) in each branch group.

Table 7.1   Nesting groups in mixed mode.

Group Type	Potential Group Members
Security domain local	Global groups and accounts
Distribution domain local	Accounts, global groups, and universal groups from any domain, as well as domain local groups from within the same domain
Security global	Accounts
Distribution global	Accounts and global groups from the same domain
Security universal	n/a
Distribution universal	Accounts, universal groups, and global groups from any domain

Table 7.2   Nesting groups in native mode.

Group Type	Potential Group Members
Security domain local	Accounts, global groups, and universal groups from any domain, as well as domain local groups from within the same domain
Distribution domain local	Accounts, global groups, and universal groups from any domain, as well as domain local groups from within the same domain
Security global	Accounts and global groups from the same domain
Distribution global	Accounts and global groups from the same domain
Security universal	Accounts, universal groups, and global groups from any domain
Distribution universal	Accounts, universal groups, and global groups from any domain

I'll call the group Supervisors. You could then add the Chicago, Dallas, and Sacramento groups to a group called Enterprise Supervisors, which would be managed by an enterprise administrator. The result is that the enterprise administrator can then assign permissions to the Enterprise Supervisors group, thus securing and managing resources for the supervisors, while the branches could manage the group membership of their own supervisors group. Figure 7.26 shows this example.

Group nesting can go awry as easily as it can work; therefore, all group nesting should be properly documented and tested before being applied to the network. Consider the following example. In a large organization, one local administrator has configured a

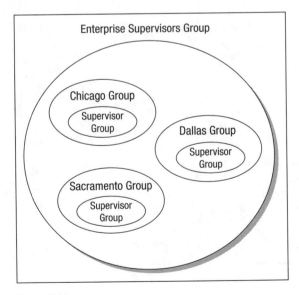

Figure 7.26
Group nesting scenario #1.

group for full-time workers who are designing a clean room and testing equipment for a new lab; these workers are members of a group called CleanRoomProject. In another part of the company, another administrator is hiring temporary employees to physically build the room, and these employees will be part of a group called CleanRoomWorkers. Because the two administrators are not in close contact, the second administrator places the CleanRoomWorkers group in the CleanRoomProject group. Later down the road, the CleanRoomProject group is given access to sensitive company information through permissions assigned via their group. Unfortunately, the CleanRoomWorkers now have access to this information as well because this group in nested in the other. Figure 7.27 shows this scenario.

The moral of the story, of course, is to fully understand which groups can be nested and why, as well as what happens to permissions and access to resources when groups are nested. There is also the underlying lesson concerning communication and keeping the lines open between all administrators on the network.

Understanding Special-Identity Groups

Other groups created by default in Windows 2000 haven't been discussed yet. These groups are created by the system to classify which users are on the network and who is using which resources at any given time. Although an administrator cannot modify membership in these groups, understanding them will prove useful later.

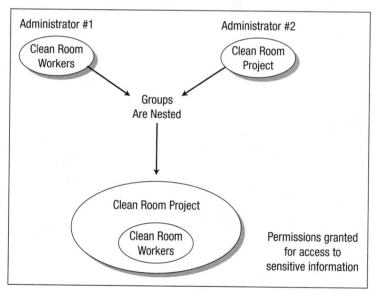

Figure 7.27
Group nesting scenario #2.

There are several special-identity groups: Anonymous Logon, Authenticated Users, Creator Owner, Dialup, Everyone, Interactive, and Network. These groups do not name specific users, but instead classify users according to their access to the computer or resource. Here's what you need to know about these groups:

- *Anonymous Logon*—There can be users on a Windows 2000 network who have not been authenticated by the operating system. These users are referred to as anonymous logons, and the group includes all users that Windows 2000 did not authenticate.

- *Authenticated Users*—If a user has a valid user account, either on the local computer or in Active Directory, then when the user logs on, he or she will become a member of the Authenticated Users group. More secure than the Everyone group, the Authenticated Users group can be used when you're configuring permissions to resources in place of the default Everyone group.

- *Creator Owner*—Every resource—including files, folders, and printers—has an owner. The creator owner is the user or group that either created the resource or took owner-ship of it. If a member of the Administrators group creates a resource, the entire group is the owner of the resource.

- *Dialup*—Many users will access the network by using dial-up resources. The Dialup group contains any user who is currently connected by a dial-up link.

- *Everyone*—All users are represented by the Everyone group. When resources are created and shared, the default group that has permissions is the Everyone group. This group has full control of the resource as well. When resources are created, this group should be removed, and other groups should be added in its place. The groups chosen might be Authenticated Users, Domain Users, or any other group that you would like to have access to the resource. Additionally, you can change the default permissions for the Everyone group from Full Control to Change or Read.

- *Interactive*—This group includes user accounts for those who are logged on at the computer. It is called the Interactive group because its members are sitting at the computer locally and interacting with resources on that computer.

- *Network*—This group includes user accounts for which a current connection is being made from a computer to a resource on the network. This is in contrast to the Interactive group, whose members are logged on locally.

Understanding User Rights

Default user rights will be discussed in this section, but this time in more detail than before. Each privilege and right will be outlined so decisions can be made regarding enabling or disabling these rights for users. Because the built-in groups and group accounts have certain rights assigned by default, and were created along with the operating system for maximum efficiency and security for your network, you will usually *not* want to change the default rights belonging to these groups. However, there will certainly be instances when it will be necessary to either modify these rights or assign them, and having a thorough understanding of the rights and privileges will prove useful.

Privileges

There are two types of rights: privileges and logon rights. Privileges were studied earlier, and the list included the familiar backing up and restoring files and directories, shutting down the system, and taking ownership. There are many other privileges to be discussed, though, some of which are familiar and some that are not. The privileges that can be configured and that will be described next are:

- Act as part of the operating system.
- Add workstations to a domain.
- Back up files and directories.
- Bypass traverse checking.
- Change the system time.
- Create a token object.
- Create permanent shared objects.
- Create a pagefile.
- Debug programs.
- Enable Trusted For Delegation on user and computer accounts.
- Force a shutdown from a remote system.
- Generate security audits.
- Increase quotas.
- Increase scheduling priority.
- Load and unload device drivers.
- Lock pages in memory.
- Manage the auditing and security logs.
- Modify firmware environment values.
- Profile a single process.
- Profile system performance.
- Replace a process-level token.
- Restore files and directories.
- Shut down the system.

- Take ownership of files or other objects.

- Undock a laptop.

You can see these rights listed by choosing Start|Programs|Administrative Tools|Local Security Policy, as shown in Figure 7.28.

Act as Part of the Operating System—A *process* is a program or a part of a program. This particular privilege allows a process to be authenticated on the network or computer, just as any user is. This allows the process to gain access to the same resources a user is allowed access to. However, this access isn't restricted to *only* what a regular user can access; some processes can also demand that additional access privileges be put in their access tokens. Allowing additional access privileges into the access token without permission can be a security risk. Additionally, some processes can create an anonymous token that can provide access to practically anything at all. Some processes can't even be tracked in audit logs because the token does not provide any primary identity information. Therefore, only low-level authentication services should require or be given this privilege.

To secure the process and its effective access, this privilege is already included in the LocalSystem account. Processes that use this privilege should use this account, rather than being specifically assigned the privilege.

Add Workstations to a Domain—Users who need to be able to add computers to a specific domain should be given this privilege or, preferably be added to a group that has this privilege by default. This allows a user to access Active Directory Users And

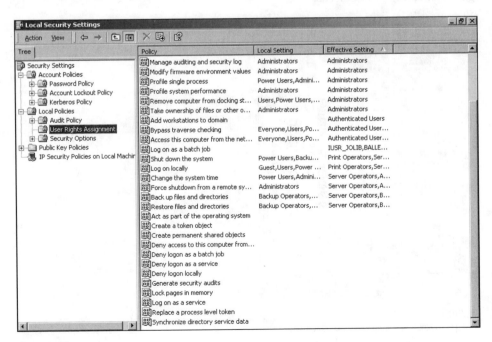

Figure 7.28
User rights assignment.

Computers and create a computer object in the Computer container housed there. You can provide this privilege through the Computer OU as well; right-click and choose Properties, select the Security tab, choose Advanced, and edit the appropriate user or group information. Figure 7.29 shows the Permission Entry For Computers dialog box and the settings for the Domain Admins group. Notice that the members of this group can create computer objects by default. You can select the Change button to permissions for other groups. (Before doing anything like this, read the section entitled "Should Modifications be Made?".)

Back Up Files and Directories—This privilege allows a user to back up files and directories on the system without having explicit permissions to access those files or folders. This privilege overrides other file and directory permissions. For instance, a user who has the right to back up files and directories on a domain controller will be able to do so even if they don't have the explicit permission to read those folders. The Back Up Files And Directories right is similar to granting the following combination of permissions: Traverse Folder/Execute File, List Folder/Read Data, Read Attributes, Read Extended Attributes, and Read.

Bypass Traverse Checking—Sometimes, a user will need access to a folder that is in a directory that he or she does not have permission to access. In order to get to Folder C, the user needs to pass through Folders A and B. Even if the user doesn't have access to the A and B folders, he can still access Folder C if given this right. The user can't list the contents of the directory or read files in the directory, but he can traverse those folders to get to the directory he needs.

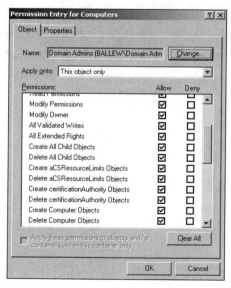

Figure 7.29
ACL permission entries for the Computer OU.

Change System Time—This user right allows the user to change the system time on a computer. The system time affects the internal clock. Members of the Server Operators, Administrators, and Power Users groups can change the system time by default.

Create a Token Object—Again, a privilege that concerns a process, this privilege allows a security access token to be created by a process that uses NTCreateToken() or another token-creation API so that the process can obtain access to a local resource. Like the privilege mentioned earlier, Act As Part Of The Operating System, processes that need this privilege should use the LocalSystem account rather than be assigned this privilege specifically.

7

Create Permanent Shared Objects—When a process needs to create a directory object by using the Windows 2000 Object Manager, it is this privilege that allows it. Kernel-mode components (detailed in Chapter 2) that need to expand the Windows 2000 object name space need this ability. Kernel-mode components have this privilege by default, so specifically assigning it isn't necessary.

Create a Pagefile—A *pagefile* is an area on the hard disk of a Windows 2000 server that is used to hold information previously stored in RAM. RAM (random access memory) can hold only so much information. When RAM is full and new information needs to be placed in RAM, some of the information can be moved to the hard disk for temporary storage. The pagefile area of the hard disk stores this information so that it can be accessed quickly when needed again. The privilege Create A Pagefile is necessary when users need either to create this file or to change the size of it. To set the pagefile's size, open the System icon in the Control Panel, select the Advanced tab, and choose Performance Options. Figure 7.30 shows the Performance Options dialog box.

Debug Programs—This privilege allows a user to attach a debugger to any process. This privilege is offered for system programmers mostly, and it is used for debugging critical system components.

Enable Trusted for Delegation on User and Computer Accounts—This privilege allows a user or object to set the Trusted For Delegation setting on another computer or user

Figure 7.30
Performance options and the paging file.

object. To set the Trusted For Delegation setting, the user must also have Write access to the account control flags on the object and must be able to write to the object's ACL. A server process that is being run either on a computer or by a user with this privilege can access resources on another computer. The process will be able to use a user's credentials as long as the user's credentials do not specifically deny it with the Account Cannot Be Delegated flag set.

When this privilege is misused or not set appropriately, a process can use delegated credentials to attack a network and thus impersonate incoming clients. Consequently, this allows viruses and other harmful entities to enter the network unchecked.

Force Shutdown from a Remote System—This privilege is straightforward; it allows a user to shut down a computer from a remote location on the network.

Generate Security Audits—The security log is used to track and trace unauthorized system access. You can view the security log through the Event Viewer (available through Administrative Tools). When this privilege is assigned, it allows processes to make entries in this log for auditing object access and generating security audits. Many events can be audited in the security log, including system restarts, shutdowns, logon processes, expired accounts, and process creation. Security logs will be discussed in depth in Chapter 8.

Increase Quotas—This privilege can be used by a process that also has Write property access to another process. This privilege is used to allow the first process to increase the processor quota assigned to the second process. *Processors* are CPUs, and *quota* is defined by Webster's Dictionary as "the share or proportion assigned to each in a division or to each member of a body." The ability to increase a processor's quota, then, can be used for both good and bad. Used properly, it can tune the system and manage processes; used improperly, it can be abused as in denial-of-service attacks.

Increase Scheduling Priority—This privilege can be used by a process or user that also has Write Property access to another process. This privilege is used to allow the user or process to increase the execution priority of another process. For a user, the scheduling priority can be increased through the Task Manager; for a process, it is done through the system. Figure 7.31 shows the processing priority as seen in Task Manager. Available priorities are real time, high, above normal, normal, below normal, and low.

Load And Unload Device Drivers—This privilege allows a user to install and uninstall plug-and-play (PnP) device drivers. *Device drivers* are programs that are installed with devices; drivers allow the user to input data and allow the operating system to send instructions to the device in a way that the device can understand. The device driver changes the instructions to a message that is sent to the device, and the device then responds to the request. This privilege affects only PnP device drivers and no others. Drivers that are not PnP can be installed only by administrators by default. Device drivers are highly trusted programs and run as trusted applications by the operating system. Therefore, this privilege can be used destructively to install hostile programs and then allow these programs access to resources, which can therefore be attacked.

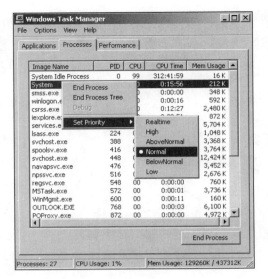

Figure 7.31
Scheduling priority.

Lock Pages in Memory—As I mentioned previously, a pagefile is an area on the hard disk of a Windows 2000 server that is used to hold information previously stored in RAM. When RAM is full and information needs to be placed in RAM, some of the information is moved to the hard disk for temporary storage. The area of the hard disk that stores this information is called a *pagefile*. The privilege Lock Pages In Memory can be assigned to processes to allow them to keep their data in RAM and not allow it to be moved to the pagefile. If a process has this privilege, the process can run very fast; however, other programs that need RAM space will suffer because of this configuration. Use it with caution.

Manage Auditing and Security Log—This privilege can be given to a user who needs to view and clear the security log in Event Viewer and who needs to specify object access auditing for resources in Active Directory, Registry keys, or files or folders. A user cannot perform object access auditing unless it has been enabled in the computer-wide audit policy settings in group policies or in group policies defined in Active Directory. This privilege does not give access to the computer-wide audit policy. Figure 7.32 shows where you can configure audit object access.

Modify Firmware Environment Values—This privilege allows a user or a process to modify system environment variables. The user can modify these variables through the System Properties dialog box. Some of these variables are the OS and its path, the location of cmd.exe, path extension names, the processor type, and the location of other files such as Temp and windir. Figure 7.33 shows the Environment Variables dialog box, which can be opened by accessing the Control Panel and right-clicking on the System icon.

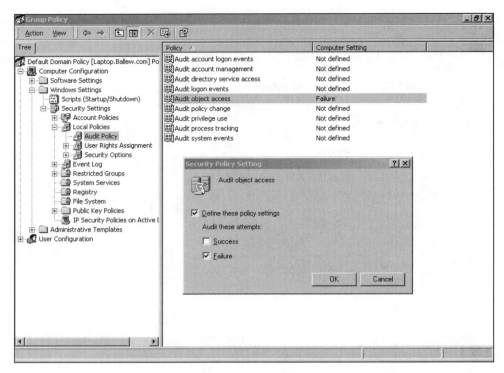

Figure 7.32
Audit object access.

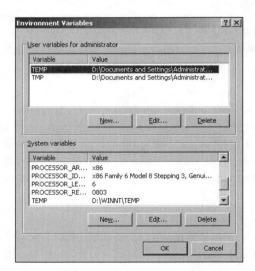

Figure 7.33
Setting environment variables.

Profile a Single Process—This privilege allows a user to monitor the performance of non-system processes with either Windows NT or Windows 2000 performance monitoring tools.

Profile System Performance—This privilege allows a user to monitor the performance of system processes with either Windows NT or Windows 2000 performance monitoring tools such as Network Monitor.

Replace a Process Level Token—Used by a process, this privilege allows the process to change the default token related to a launched sub-process. The token is used to identify a process to the OS, and it could be misused in the wrong hands.

Restore Files and Directories—This privilege allows a user to restore files and directories on the system without having explicit permissions to access those files or folders. This privilege overrides other file and directory permissions. For instance, a user who has the right to restore files and directories on a domain controller will be able to do so even if the user doesn't have the explicit permission to read those folders.

Shut Down the System—Similar to the privilege described earlier, Force Shutdown From A Remote System, this privilege allows a user to shut down the local computer. Everyone, even guests, can shut down the system if they are logged on locally to a workstation. You can disallow this by using group policies or modifying user rights.

Take Ownership of Files or Other Objects—This privilege allows a user to take ownership of objects on the network. By default, only administrators can take ownership of objects; otherwise, ownership can only be given from one user to another. Ownership can be taken from objects in Active Directory, files and folders, printers and other peripherals, Registry keys, processes, and threads.

Undock a Laptop—This privilege allows a user to undock a laptop through the Windows interface. Undocking a laptop is as simple as choosing Start|Eject PC. If this option isn't available on the Start menu, it can be added by choosing Add/Remove Programs from Control Panel. If the option still isn't available, then the user does not have the correct user right to undock the computer.

Logon Rights

There are not nearly as many logon rights available for configuration as there are privileges. Logon rights simply state how a particular user or group of users can log on to the network or how a security principal can log on as a service. The logon rights that can be configured and will be described next are:

- *Access this computer from a network*—This logon right allows a user to connect to the computer over a network. This user right is given to the Administrators, Power Users, and Everyone groups by default. You might consider removing the Everyone group and adding Authenticated Users instead.

- *Log on locally*—This logon right allows a user to log on at the local computer through an attached keyboard or other input device. The ability of a user to log on locally to a domain controller can be a security risk. Members of the Administrators, Account Operators, Backup Operators, Print Operators, and Server Operators groups can log on locally by default. Notice that groups such as Everyone and Authenticated Users do not have this right by default.

- *Log on as a batch job*—This logon right allows the user to log on using a batch-queuing program. There are several commercial batch queuing systems, usually based on Generic NQS software. These systems use a shell script to submit a batch job to a queue, and make sure that the job is run only when enough resources are available. This logon right is given to Administrators by default but to no other groups or users.

- *Log on as a service*—This logon right is used for security principals only, and it allows those principals to log on as a service. This right is not granted to any particular user or group by default. The LocalSystem account is granted this right, though, and can log on as a service as needed. If another service running under a separate account needs this right, it must be granted individually.

Should Modifications be Made?

Many user rights are available for change, as you have seen in the previous section, but when should you change these rights and when should you not? Figure 7.29, shown earlier, shows how you can change permissions for objects, groups, and OUs by changing the ACL entries for those objects. However, if you change the permissions for groups or users here, the default Windows setup will change, and the operating system will perform differently than it would by default. This could make troubleshooting seemingly simple problems much more difficult. To avoid this, see if you can place the user who needs a particular user right or permission into a group that already has the right or permission to perform the task or into a group that can do so by default. It is easier to keep track of permissions, privileges, and rights when it is done this way, and this keeps the operating system running in a more effective, default state.

In some instances, though (one in particular I'll introduce next), changing the default rights and privileges can be very useful. Consider the Guest account. This account is disabled by default, but if it is needed and enabled, changing some of the rights associated with it will make the account a little more secure.

When the Guest account is enabled and is not assigned a password, it can be used to allow users from untrusted domains and some legacy computers to access the network server on the local domain. The process involved was described earlier. The user who logs on as a guest in this manner is given rights, permissions, and group memberships belonging to the Guest account.

To enable the domain guest logon, open Active Directory Users And Computers and locate the Guest account. Right-click on the account and choose Enable from the context menu. To change permission entries—to allow the user to only view certain items or read certain information, for example—use the Security tab. You can also change the rights associated with the Guest account and allow or deny any of the rights listed earlier. For instance, you may not want the Guest account to have the user right Log On Locally, and you may want the Guest account to have the right to access a computer from the network, depending on the circumstance.

Delegating Administration

After user accounts and group accounts have been planned and named appropriately, and an overall scheme has been created, the process of creating the groups and user accounts is really quite simple. In fact, once a plan has been established, the task can be delegated to another network administrator or to administrators of OUs or other domains. Delegating authority not only reduces the number of tasks that you as an administrator must complete daily, but also minimizes the number of people who need access to the entire enterprise or need to be members of universal groups. You can also minimize the amount of time that you or another trusted administrator are logged on to the network with an Administrator account, thus improving security for the network.

The Delegation Of Control Wizard is a great utility for delegating control. This wizard allows you to grant users or groups the right to control different units and allows you to configure the rights and permissions that these users or groups have within their administrative realm. The Delegation Of Control Wizard can be used to:

- Select users or groups to whom you want to delegate control.
- Delegate responsibility for creating, deleting, and managing user accounts.
- Delegate responsibility for resetting passwords on user accounts.
- Delegate responsibility for creating, deleting, and managing groups.
- Delegate responsibility for modifying the membership of a group.
- Delegate responsibility for managing group policy links.
- Delegate responsibility for the following objects in Active Directory:
  - Computer objects
  - Connection objects
  - Contact objects
  - Group objects
  - Printer objects
  - Shared folder objects
  - Site and site link objects
  - Site link bridge objects
  - Site settings objects
  - Sites container objects

- Subnet objects and subnet container objects

- Trusted domain objects

- User objects

- Organizational unit objects

- Group Policy container objects

- IntelliMirror group and SCP objects

- MSMQ (Microsoft Message Queue) configuration objects

- If Active Directory objects are chosen, permissions on those objects can be configured for the following:

  - Read

  - Write

  - Create And/Or Delete Child Objects

  - Full Control

In the following example, I'll detail how to use the Delegation Of Control Wizard, and discuss its features and characteristics throughout:

1. Open the Active Directory Users And Computers console.

2. Choose an OU or a domain for which you would like to delegate control.

3. Right-click on the container or domain and choose Delegate Control.

4. The Welcome page of the Delegation Of Control Wizard appears. Read the description of the wizard and choose Next.

5. On the Users Or Groups page, choose Add. (See Figure 7.34.)

6. The Select Users, Computers, Or Groups dialog box appears. Scroll through the groups and user accounts, and choose a group or user who will be entrusted to preside over the OU or domain chosen in Step 2. You can choose as many as you'd like, but I'd suggest not choosing too many groups or users here.

7. After choosing the appropriate parties, choose OK to return to the Users Or Groups page shown in Figure 7.34. Choose Next.

8. The next page, Tasks To Delegate, can be used either to delegate the most common tasks or to create a custom task to delegate. Figure 7.35 shows this page and the most common tasks.

9. If you choose one or more of these common tasks, and choose not to create a custom task, then choose Next. You'll be taken to the final page of the

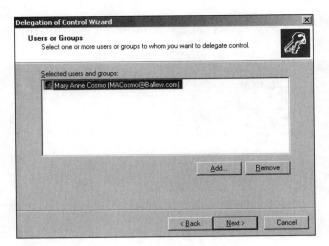

Figure 7.34
The Users Or Groups page of the Delegation Of Control Wizard.

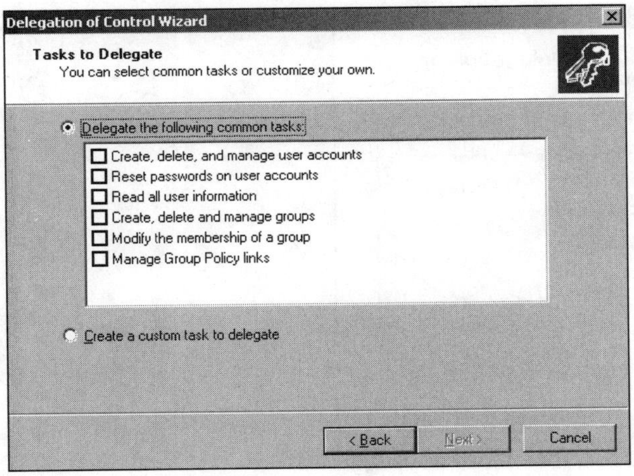

Figure 7.35
The Tasks To Delegate page.

Delegation of Control Wizard, shown in Figure 7.37. If you do select the option Create A Custom Task To Delegate, you will be shown two additional pages, the first of which is shown in Figure 7.36.

10. (Optional) Using the Active Directory Object Type page, you can select the objects in Active Directory that you'd like to delegate control of. The items were listed earlier in this section. Make your selections and choose Next.

11. The Permission page is where you can configure permissions for the objects chosen. Configure the appropriate permissions, and choose Next.

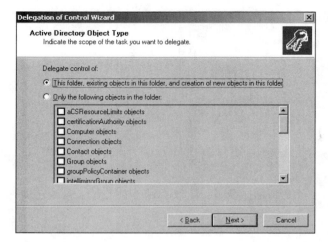

Figure 7.36
The Active Directory Object Type page.

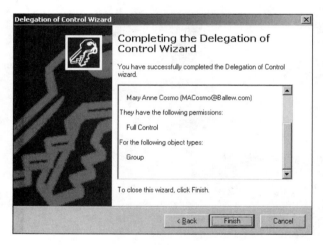

Figure 7.37
Completing the Delegation Of Control Wizard.

To see how the permissions regarding the delegation of control have affected the OU or domain for which they were configured, perform the following steps:

1. In Active Directory Users And Computers, right-click on the OU or domain that was delegated for control, and choose Properties.

2. Select the Security tab.

3. Select the Advanced tab.

4. Select the Permissions tab.

5. In the Name box, locate the user or group that was given control, and highlight it.

6. Choose the View/Edit button.

7. On the Object tab, notice the permissions, as shown in Figure 7.38.

8. On the Properties tab, notice the permissions, as shown in Figure 7.39

9. Close all of the dialog boxes.

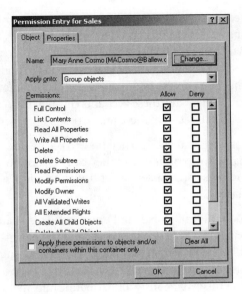

Figure 7.38
Object permissions.

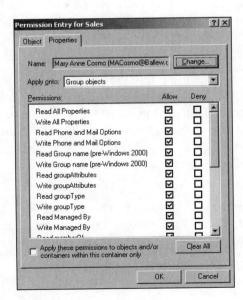

Figure 7.39
Properties permissions.

Summary

In this chapter, you learned about the different user accounts, including the available built-in user accounts. User accounts are created so users can access objects and resources on the network and so a user's access to those objects and resources can be managed effectively by administrators.

Planning for user accounts was also discussed. Some issues involved with the planning of accounts include creating an effective naming scheme for the accounts and deciding which properties and permissions those accounts will have. Each User Properties dialog box contains 15 tabs with configuration options. By accessing these tabs, you can configure logon hours, enter user information, enter profile paths and home folder information, edit dial-in information, and more. You also learned how to create and modify these accounts through the Active Directory Users And Computers console and how to set all of these properties.

Profiles and home folders were discussed as well, and you learned how to create and manage these items. Profiles can be mandatory or roaming, and they can be configured to meet the needs of almost any user. Home folders can be used to centralize the user's data and storage and to back up that data regularly.

You also learned about group scopes, including local, global, and universal. This chapter also discussed built-in groups, for both local and global group scopes, and the permissions and rights associated with each. You learned how to change a group's scope and how groups can be nested to simplify the permissions process. Security and distribution groups were discussed, too, along with some miscellaneous group account information, including group strategies, design tips, and information on special-identity groups.

User rights were introduced, and rights associated with accounts were detailed. Two types of user rights were discussed: privileges and logon rights. Built-in groups have certain rights inherently, though, and modifying the rights associated with the built-in groups was discouraged.

Finally, this chapter discussed delegating the responsibility of group and user account creation. The Delegation Of Control Wizard is used for this purpose. This wizard allows you to grant users or groups the right to control different units, and it allows you to configure the rights and permissions that these users or groups have within their administrative realm.

Moving Forward

In the next chapter, I'll move away from describing the tasks associated with installing and configuring Windows 2000 Server and will move toward optimizing the server and the network. In the next chapter, I'll discuss how to enhance the network for both performance and security.

Performance issues will include how to monitor and optimize the server's hard disks, how to use compression and encryption, how to use the Performance console, how to back up and restore utilities, and what can be achieved using System Monitor and Event Viewer.

Security issues will be discussed, including how to audit events and how to read and understand the logs associated with Security, Application, System, Directory Service, DNS Server, and File Replication Service. I'll also discuss security templates and how to use them.

7

Chapter 8

Optimizing Windows 2000 Server Performance

In this chapter, you'll be introduced to the multitude of utilities available in Windows 2000 Server that can assist you in tuning your server and network so they will perform to their optimum ability. Because a network is made up of both software and hardware, all facets of the network will need to be examined when you're attempting either to enhance performance or to monitor the system or network. Using the right disk configuration options, for instance, can not only make the network run faster but also provide fault tolerance.

In the first section, I'll be discussing many areas of disk optimization, including the Chkdsk, Disk Defragmenter and Disk Cleanup utilities, disk quotas, and pagefiles. Because disk arrays can also be used to improve performance, they will also be discussed, along with the Redundant Array of Independent Disks (RAID). Compressing files will also be discussed, because compressing files can optimize network performance in a variety of ways. Other optimization techniques include using Task Manager and Event Viewer, Quality of Service (QoS) Admission Control, the Backup and Restore utilities, and Simple Network Management Protocol (SNMP) service. Each of these available utilities and applications will be discussed.

This chapter will conclude with a detailed look at the Performance Console, System Monitor, and Network Monitor. These utilities are available in Windows 2000 to enhance and monitor the performance of the computer and the network, including both hardware and software. System Monitor can be used to collect and view real-time performance data on either a local computer or a remote one and to present that data in different forms. System Monitor offers an easily understandable graphical user interface (GUI) for doing so. Network Monitor isn't used to monitor hardware and software as System Monitor is; instead, it is used to monitor network activity. Network Monitor can be used to monitor local network traffic only, or, if you need to monitor network traffic on remote systems, you can use the Network Monitor that is included with SMS (Systems Management Server) 1.2 or 2.

Optimizing Performance

In this section, you'll learn how to use Chkdsk (I'll refer to it as Check Disk in this chapter), Disk Defragmenter and Disk Cleanup utilities, disk quotas, and pagefiles. You'll also learn how disk arrays can be used to improve network performance including a discussion on RAID.

Compressing files can also help to optimize areas of network performance. Compression can be used to save hard disk space for users or administrators, and it is available on all NTFS volumes.

The Task Manager, mentioned briefly in previous chapters, can be used to manage processes, stop and start processes, and view the performance of the computer's resources. This section will discuss the Task Manager in more detail and explain what process priorities are, what levels are available, and how threads are defined. Task Manager can be used to see which programs are running, which processes are running, and how the computer is performing.

The Event Viewer will be detailed, and the application log and the system log will be introduced. (The security log will be detailed in the next chapter, along with other security issues.) Event types will also be discussed, including the meaning of the error, warning, information, success, and failure icons. This chapter will also discuss how to archive an event log, set logging options, and use event headers.

Additional performance topics include Quality of Service (QoS) Admission Control and the Backup and Restore utilities. QoS Admission Control, which is also used to monitor the network, will install specific performance objects for this purpose. QoS Admission Control needs to be enabled and does not run by default. The Backup and Restore utility is a built-in tool located in the Accessories folder; this utility provides a wizard for backing up and restoring data and creating emergency repair disks.

The SNMP service will also be introduced. This can be used to monitor and communicate status information between a multitude of hosts, such as computers, routers, hubs, and servers. For performance purposes, SNMP can be used to monitor network performance and detect security breaches, as well as to configure remote devices on remote hosts.

Disk Monitoring and Optimization

When buying, leasing, or building the computers that would act as servers or domain controllers for your network, you probably decided that obtaining the best computer possible was the most intelligent choice. That is certainly true because, as you know, a network is only as good, fast, or reliable as its weakest link. If the domain controllers are running on the minimum requirements for hard disk space, RAM, CPU speed, and so on, the server may actually *be* the weakest link. One of the main areas where a server can be enhanced is in its hard disk. Capacity, speed, read/write performance, and fault tolerance are four very important issues related to the disk. When users need to access information on the server, they are accessing information on the disk. If the disk is slow, the users perceive the network as being slow.

To enhance the performance of your server's hard disk, you can make physical improvements as well as configuration and performance improvements. To assist you with these configuration and performance improvements, Windows 2000 provides utilities, including Check Disk, Disk Defragmenter, and Disk Cleanup. Windows 2000 also allows you to optimize pagefiles and use RAID. Physically, you can add disk arrays, larger disks, or faster disks, or you can create mirrored or striped volumes of anywhere from 2 to 32 separate physical disks. In this section, you'll learn about all of these options.

Check Disk

The Check Disk utility, which is available in all Windows 2000 operating system products, can be used to check a hard disk for file system errors and bad sectors. In order for Check Disk, also referred to as the *Error Checking tool*, to work properly, all applications must be closed before you run the utility. With Check Disk, you can let the operating system automatically fix file system errors as they are found, or have it scan the hard drive and attempt to recover bad sectors. The process is completed in phases, and the amount of time this process takes depends on the size of the hard disk. On my server, this process took only about five minutes.

When you're running Check Disk, if any applications or folders are open, a warning message will ask if you'd prefer to reschedule this operation for the next time your computer is started. This dialog box is shown in Figure 8.1 Additionally, for computers that use an NTFS file system, the information obtained by running Check Disk (such as file transactions, bad clusters, and key information) is logged.

To use Check Disk, perform the following steps:

1. Open My Computer.

2. Right-click on the volume you'd like to check, and choose Properties.

3. Select the Tools tab.

4. Under Error-Checking, choose Check Now. See Figure 8.2.

5. Choose how you'd like the disk to be repaired if errors are found, as shown in Figure 8.3.

   The disk will be checked and the application will close on its own.

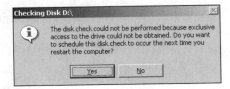

Figure 8.1
Exclusive access is necessary to run Check Disk.

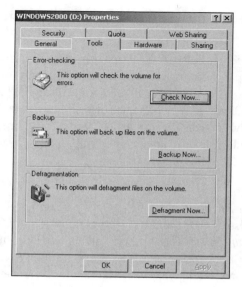

Figure 8.2
Launching Check Disk.

Figure 8.3
Check Disk options.

Disk Defragmenter

A computer writes information to a hard disk drive by starting with the first available space, or sector, and continuing to other available sectors on the drive. On a new drive, the computer saves files, folders, applications, and other information in a sequential manner. However, as files are written to the drive and subsequently erased, areas of blank space become available in various portions of the drive. At some point, another file will be saved to the hard drive, and again, the computer will try to write to the first available space on the drive. If the file requires 10MB of space, and the first sector available can house only 5MB of the file, then the rest of the file must be saved elsewhere. Because the file isn't saved in a contiguous space, the file is considered fragmented. When a hard disk is continually written to, rewritten to, erased, and written to again, the entire disk eventually becomes fragmented.

When the disk becomes fragmented, its performance suffers. If a disk read head has to move to three physical places on the disk instead of only one, it will take longer to bring up the data. If a folder needs to be created, and the only space large enough to handle the folder is in various non-contiguous places on the drive, then performance will suffer again.

To solve the problem of fragmented disks, Windows 2000 offers the Disk Defragmenter snap-in. This utility locates fragmented files and folders on a hard drive, and defragments them by moving the pieces of each file and folder to a contiguous space where they can be stored together. Disk Defragmenter also places all of the available free space at the end of the drive, and places the files and folders that are saved to the disk at the beginning. This arrangement makes accessing previously saved information faster and makes finding free space more efficient. You can use Disk Defragmenter on FAT16, FAT32, and NTFS drives.

8

Note: There was no such utility in Windows NT, and defragmenting disks was dealt with in other ways and with third-party utilities.

Warning! *Always back up a disk's data before running Disk Defragmenter. If the results are not what you expected, you can restore the data.*

There are two ways to use Disk Defragmenter. The first is to access it through the disk's Properties sheet, and the second is to add it as a snap-in to a console.

To run Disk Defragmenter from the disk's Properties sheet, follow these steps:

1. Open My Computer.
2. Right-click on the volume you'd like to defragment, and choose Properties.
3. Select the Tools tab. This screen was shown in Figure 8.2.
4. Under Defragmentation, choose Defragment Now.
5. Select the volume to be defragmented, and choose Defragment. See Figure 8.4.
6. The Analysis display area of the screen will show how the disk looks to the operating system and will include a variety of colors. This screen is shown in Figure 8.5.

Tip: *If you aren't sure if you need to defragment the disk, you can choose Analyze instead of Defragment. By looking at the analysis display, you can then make an informed decision about whether to defragment at this time or to wait.*

The analysis display shows how the disk defragmentation process is proceeding. This screen is shown in Figure 8.5.

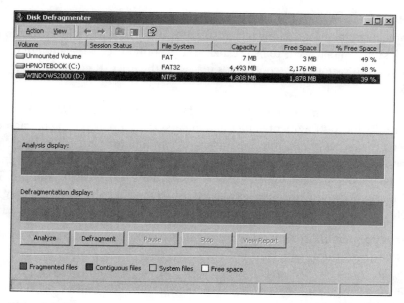

Figure 8.4
Disk Defragmenter.

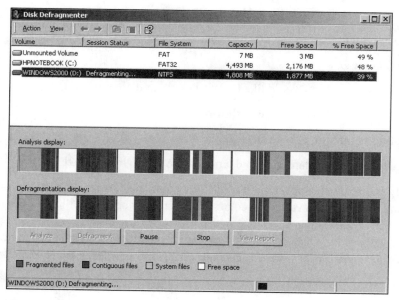

Figure 8.5
Disk Defragmenter's analysis display.

Disk Defragmenter uses different colors to represent different information (see Figure 8.5):

- Red indicates that the files are fragmented.
- Blue indicates that the files are contiguous (they are not fragmented).
- Green indicates that the files are system files.
- White indicates free space.

7. When Disk Defragmenter is finished running, close all of the dialog boxes. Figure 8.6 shows what the Disk Defragmenter screen looks like toward the end of the defragmenting process.

To use Disk Defragmenter as a snap-in, perform the following steps:

1. Choose Start|Run and enter "mmc" at the prompt.

2. Maximize both windows, and choose Console|Add/Remove Snap-in.

3. Choose Add, then Disk Defragmenter, then Close, and then OK.

4. Double-click on Disk Defragmenter.

5. Notice that Disk Defragmenter opens in the console, as shown in Figure 8.7. Choose Defragment to begin the process.

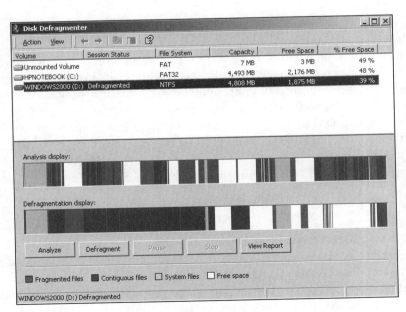

Figure 8.6
Done with defragmenting.

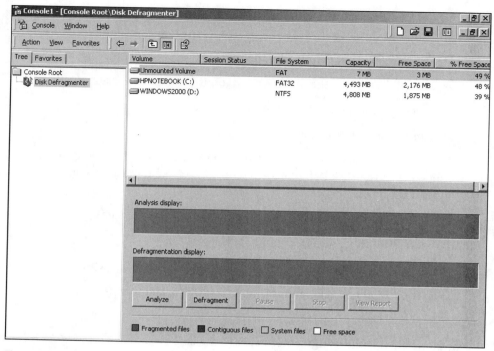

Figure 8.7
The Disk Defragmenter snap-in.

You should run Disk Defragmenter when the computer isn't in use. Disk Defragmenter is CPU-intensive, and running it will slow down any other processes currently in progress. In addition, because data is being moved to other areas of the disk, it is best left alone until Disk Defragmenter is finished running. Another way to maximize the defragmenting process is to obtain a third-party utility that can be used to schedule defragmentation monthly for the servers on the network. Scheduled Tasks and Task Manager do not offer this as an option. You should also inform users about the importance of defragmenting their own drives on workstations as well. Finally, after any large program or group of files or folders has been deleted from a computer, analyze the disks and consider defragmenting at that time.

Disk Cleanup

Disk Cleanup is a utility, accessed through Start/Programs/Accessories/System Tools, which can be used to free up space on your hard drive. You can run Disk Cleanup for any drive on the system. Disk Cleanup searches the hard drive for files that can be safely deleted, and then it prompts you for which files, if any, you want to delete. In addition, you can instruct Disk Cleanup to remove Windows components that you never use, as well as installed programs that you never access.

Some of the files that can be deleted by Disk Cleanup include the following:

- Downloaded program files
- Offline Web pages
- Old Check Disk files
- Recycle Bin files
- Temporary files, including temporary Internet files and temporary offline files
- Catalog files for the Content Indexer
- Any installed Windows components
- Any installed applications

To use the Disk Cleanup utility, follow these steps:

1. Choose Start|Programs|Accessories|System Tools|Disk Cleanup.

2. Select the drive to clean up, and choose OK.

3. Disk Cleanup will calculate how much space can be saved by cleaning up the disk and removing unused or temporary files. Select any additional files, and choose OK.

4. A confirmation box will be shown for verifying that you want to delete these files. Choose OK. The screen will show the progress of cleaning these files. On my computer, it took less than one minute and freed up around 0.5GB of hard disk space.

Note: *Disk Cleanup can also be accessed through My Computer and the local disk icon. Simply right-click on the local disk, choose Properties, and select the General tab.*

Disk Quotas

Disk quotas allow administrators to manage how much data users store on network servers. Storage numbers are calculated by determining which files or folders the user owns on the server (owning a file or folder implies that the user created the object or at least has taken ownership of it). Most organizations should limit a user's disk space. By limiting the space through quotas, you not only manage how much disk space you must have, but you also force users to consider how much data they keep and to delete unnecessary files and folders. Using disk quota utilities, you can also set quota thresholds and monitor how much space users have left before they reach their quotas.

Disk quotas can be set only on NTFS volumes, but quotas can be set for all users or for individual users on the network. When configuring disk quotas, you can set two variables: disk quota limit and disk quota warning level. If you configure a warning level, users will be informed when they are close to reaching their limits. Additionally, you can configure what will happen when a user meets or exceeds the predefined limit.

The steps listed next will describe the process of setting quotas for a specific volume. Note that when you enable disk quotas for a volume, usage is tracked for users who are new to the network after this point; to apply disk quotas to existing users on the network, you must add new quota entries as shown in this example:

1. Using administrator privileges, log on to a computer formatted with NTFS.

2. Open My Computer, right-click on the local disk, and choose Properties.

3. Select the Quota tab.

Note: *The Quota tab will not be available if the file system is FAT.*

4. Place a checkmark in the Enable Quota Management checkbox.

Note: *If the Status of the Disk Quota System is inactive, a stoplight will be displayed and quotas will not be able to be configured. Choose Enable Quota Management and then Apply, and wait for quota management to be enabled. If at any time during this configuration a Disk Quota dialog box appears, warning that the volume will be rescanned to update the new configuration, choose OK.*

5. To limit how much space users can utilize, select the Check The Limit Disk Space To option, and type a number in the text box. You'll need to make this decision based on your users' needs. Notice that the default unit size is in KB; you may need to change that to MB.

6. To set a warning level so that Windows 2000 will log an event stating that the user is approaching his or her quota limit, configure it in the Set Warning Level To box.

7. To set disk quotas so that when users exceed their hard disk space allotment, they receive an "out of disk space" message and cannot write anything further to the volume, choose Deny Disk Space To Users Exceeding Quota Limit.

8. If you do not want to limit disk usage for new users on the volume, but simply want to monitor disk usage through quotas, choose the Do Not Limit Disk Usage button.

9. To configure a quota setting for an existing member of the network, choose the Quota Entries button. The Quota Entries window is shown; see Figure 8.8.

10. Double-click on a username for whom you want to configure the disk quotas, and make the appropriate changes as necessary. Figure 8.9 shows the Quota Settings dialog box and sample configured settings. Choose OK.

11. Close the Quota Entries window, and choose OK in the disk's Properties sheet.

Listed next are some additional characteristics of disk quotas, including tips for using disk quotas and ways to enforce these quotas:

- When a user's disk space is calculated, compressed file size is ignored, and the uncompressed size of the file is used.

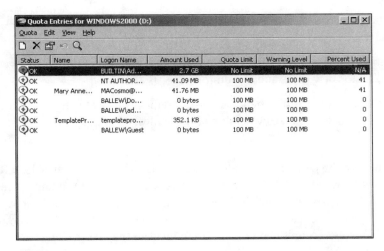

Figure 8.8
The Quota Entries window.

Figure 8.9
Configuring disk quotas.

- If a user has only 10MB of free space left in the quota for writing to the disk, applications on the server know this, even though there may be 40GB of free space on the server itself.

- Although administrators are the only members on the network who can view and change quota settings, you can allow users to view how much space they have left on the disk.

- Even if no quota limits are assigned, disk quotas can be used just to monitor the disk usage for members.

- By default, members of the Administrators group are not assigned quota limits, even when limits are set for new users and an administrator is added.

- If you need to delete a quota entry, then you need to remove all related files from the disk, or another user needs to take ownership of those files. See Figure 8.10.

Pagefiles

Another way to improve the performance of the hard disk is to better configure how RAM works with the pagefile. Windows 2000 Server can address up to 4GB of random access memory (RAM). RAM is where the operating system stores information it needs now, such as program code or drivers, or data that hasn't been saved to the hard disk. Most computers, even domain controllers, don't have 4GB of RAM; instead, they most likely have 256MB, 512MB, or 1,028MB.

As you can see, RAM is a limited commodity and it sometimes gets full. If information needs to be stored in RAM, but RAM is full, some of the information stored there must be transferred to another physical entity: the hard disk. When the information that has been transferred to the hard disk is needed again by RAM, it is brought back into memory, and when this happens, a page fault is generated. This process of transferring information between RAM and the hard disk is called *swapping*, and the problem of having excessive swapping and page faults is called *thrashing*.

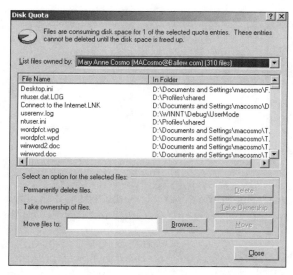

Figure 8.10
Disk Quota dialog.

The area of the hard disk that holds this transferred data is called the *pagefile* or Pagefile.sys. To see how the pagefile is configured for your server, or to configure the size or location of this file, perform the following steps:

1. Log on with administrator's rights.

2. Open Control Panel and then the System icon.

3. Select the Advanced tab.

4. Choose Performance Options.

5. Notice that the Application Response section has two options: Applications and Background Services. For a server whose primary purpose is to optimize applications, select the Applications option. For a server whose primary purpose is to perform background services, select this option.

6. Choose the Change button. Figure 8.11 shows the Virtual Memory dialog box.

7. To change the setting of the pagefile, first highlight the applicable drive, and then, in the Initial Size box, type a new number that is within the range specified. Choose Set.

Note: *Next to the Drive Volume label in Figure 8.11 is the paging file size. In this example, the paging file size is 192 – 384. The number 384 is calculated by adding the amount of physical memory and the maximum pagefile size. In this instance, 128MB of physical RAM + 256MB (the maximum Pagefile.sys size) = 384MB.*

8. Choose OK three times.

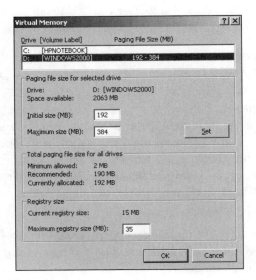

Figure 8.11
The Virtual Memory dialog box.

Listed next are some additional characteristics of pagefiles, and tips for configuring them effectively:

- The initial size of a pagefile should be at least as large as the recommended size shown in the Total Paging File Size For All Drives box in the Virtual Memory dialog box.

- If your server has more than one physical disk drive, move the pagefile off of the disk that holds the system files.

- If you're using RAID 5 on the server, you can dramatically increase the speed of access to data in the pagefile. (RAID systems will be discussed shortly.)

Physically Better Disks

Of course, you can always purchase a bigger, better, faster, or more reliable hard disk for your server or domain controller. When disk drives were first introduced, they held a mere 5MB of data that was stored on 50 24-inch platters. Now, you can buy hard drives that can hold 80 to 100GB of data on only a few platters. Recently, a hard drive was introduced that holds 30GB of data per platter and spins at 5,400 rotations per minute. Also improved is the ability of the disk to read and write data to and from the disk quickly. The read/write speed of a disk is based on many things, including the disk rotation speed, the time it takes the hard drive's read/write head to get to the data (this time is called *latency*), and the disk's transfer rates for the data it reads and writes.

Because the hard drive can be the reason a computer might perform poorly, it is well worth the money to upgrade the hard drive, add more hard drive space, or set up some sort of hard-drive RAID configuration. Additionally, an inefficient hard drive can offset any improvements made to the server via the CPU and can cause the CPU to fail to work at its full potential.

Redundant Array of Independent Disks

RAID is commonly known as Redundant Array of Independent Disks but sometimes as Redundant Array of Inexpensive Disks. RAID defines how data can be stored across multiple disks and how those disks can provide not only improved disk performance but also fault tolerance. *Fault tolerance* is the ability of a computer to recover from an event such as a power outage or hardware failure without losing any saved data or any work in progress. RAID can provide fault tolerance by writing data twice or by writing data across multiple disks in such a way that the data can be recovered if a single disk fails. There are many levels, or implementations, of RAID systems, but only three are supported in Windows 2000 systems: RAID 0, RAID 1, and RAID 5.

Note: Only RAID 1 and RAID 5 provide fault tolerance; Raid 0 only provides improvements to disks' read/write performance. Additionally, RAID 1 and RAID 5 are not supported on Windows 2000 Professional workstations.

RAID 0 is used when multiple disks are installed and data is to be striped across the disks. *Striping data* is the process of breaking up the information that needs to be written to the disks into equal pieces and then writing that data to the disks accordingly. For instance, if a disk array contains five disks, then a 20MB file would (theoretically) be broken up into five pieces, and each piece would then be written to each of those disks in order. When this happens, disk read and write time is improved because the data can be written across multiple disks faster than to a single disk. Of course, there's a lot more to it than just installing a few disks and configuring RAID 0; for instance, you have to tune the size of the stripe so that data is written to the disks somewhat evenly, and configure them so they are neither too large nor too small to work efficiently. RAID 0 is used solely for increasing disk performance and provides no fault tolerance. In this scenario, if one disk fails, all of the data is lost. Figure 8.12 shows this.

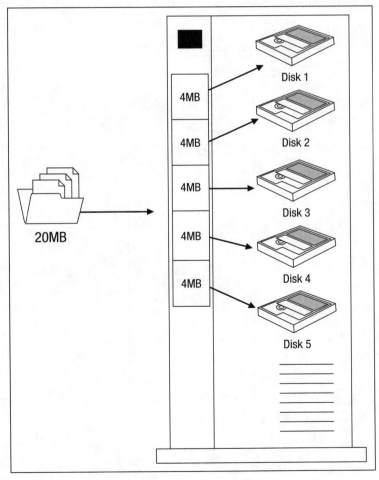

Figure 8.12
Disk striping.

Note: You can create a RAID 0 volume through Computer Management by right-clicking on an unallocated dynamic disk and choosing Create Volume. The Create Volume Wizard will guide you through this part of the procedure. Select Striped Volume when prompted. Because RAID 0 offers no fault tolerance and cannot be expanded once created, I won't go into any more detail here. Consider all of your options carefully before choosing to implement RAID 0.

RAID 1 is usually referred to as a *mirrored volume*. This scheme provides fault tolerance by writing all of the data to two physical disks instead of one. If one of the disks fails, it can be replaced and the data from the other mirror can be copied back to it. While this is taking place, the network performs as usual, with no service disruptions for its users. This implementation increases the read performance of the disk because the data is stored in two locations and the data can be read from either disk. However, this implementation decreases the write performance of the disk because all data has to be written two times, once to each disk. Figure 8.13 shows how disk mirroring works.

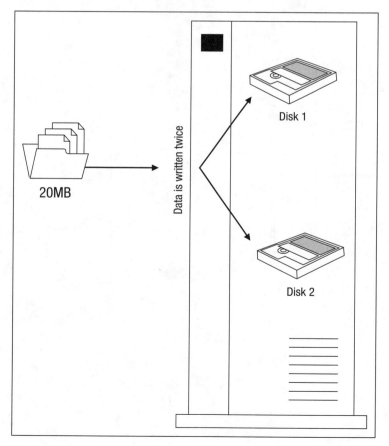

Figure 8.13
Disk mirroring.

Other conventions or characteristics associated with RAID 1 are listed next:

- RAID 1 supports both FAT and NTFS.

- System and boot partitions can be mirrored.

- Costs are higher for RAID 1 than for other implementations because an entire disk is used for mirroring and cannot be used for additional data.

RAID 5 is usually referred to as *disk striping with parity*. RAID 5 is similar to RAID 0 in that multiple disks are used, and data is broken up into pieces that are written to those disks in a specific order. Although there are major differences between these two RAID types, the main difference is that RAID 5 contains an additional disk to hold parity information. Parity is generally used in error checking to make sure that data was transferred correctly from one place to another, but when it is used in RAID systems, it creates an additional binary digit so data can be reconstructed if a single disk in the array fails. This parity information (binary digit) is stored on its own volume and provides fault tolerance. If one of the disks fails, the missing data is re-created using this parity information.

RAID 5 can be set up with a minimum of three disks—two disks for the data and one for the parity bit—but usually five or more disks are used. Up to 32 disks can be configured using RAID 5. Because a parity bit has to be calculated by the operating system and written to a separate disk, RAID 5 is best used on systems that do not require a high level of performance or on servers that require less than average write operations.

Because an entire disk or volume is reserved for parity information, determining the effective disk space requires some calculation. If a system has five disk drives, and each drive is 10GB, then it seems as though there should be 50GB available for data storage. However, one of those five drives will be used only for parity information, leaving only four drives available for data storage. Therefore, instead of calculating 5 drives × 10GB = 50GB, you need to multiply 4 drives × 10GB = 40GB to calculate available space. Mathematically this is represented as "(n-1) x the volume size of the disks" where n is the number of physical drives.

Other conventions or characteristics associated with RAID 5 are listed next:

- RAID volumes must be equal in size. If five disks exist for configuration, the first disk is 5GB, and the others are 10GB, the RAID set will consist of the lowest of those, and each will be 5GB.

- The system and boot partitions cannot be part of the striped set.

- Volumes cannot be mirrored or extended.

- Write operations are slower than on mirrored volumes, but read time is faster.

- If data has to be recovered, performance suffers.

- The more disks included in the stripe set, the less the cost of the disk used for the data stripe.

- RAID 5 supports both FAT and NTFS.

- RAID 5 requires at least three disks.

To configure new RAID 1 volumes, perform the following steps:

1. As an administrator, log on to a Windows 2000 server that contains two physical disks. These disks must contain two dynamic volumes equal in size.

2. Choose Start|Programs|Administrative Tools|Computer Management.

3. Expand the trees as necessary, and double-click on the Disk Management folder. The Disk Management screen will appear in the right pane.

4. On the first disk, select the partition that you want to mirror.

5. Right-click on the volume and choose Add Mirror.

6. Follow the on-screen instructions for completing the mirror.

To recover from a failure of a RAID 1 volume, perform the following steps:

1. Log on to Windows 2000 Server as an administrator.

2. Choose Start|Programs|Administrative Tools|Computer Management.

3. Expand the trees as necessary, and double-click on the Disk Management folder. The Disk Management screen will appear in the right pane.

4. Right-click on the volume that is not healthy, and choose Break Mirror. Confirm this selection by choosing Yes from the confirmation box.

5. There are now two independent volumes. Turn off the computer and replace the failed disk drive.

6. Reboot the system, and complete the steps for creating a new mirrored volume, as described earlier.

Tip: *If you're lucky, the disk that failed was the secondary disk and not the primary one. If the primary disk fails, use a boot disk to start the computer. This boot disk will most likely contain a boot.ini file that points to the boot partition, and if it does, the ARC path that points to the mirrored partition will need to be changed. A good administrator will have two sets of boot disks: one set whose boot.ini file points to the first mirrored volume, and one set whose boot.ini file points to the second.*

To configure RAID 5 volumes, perform the following steps:

1. Log on to Windows 2000 Server as an administrator.

2. Choose Start|Programs|Administrative Tools|Computer Management.

3. Expand the trees as necessary, and double-click on the Disk Management folder. The Disk Management screen will appear in the right pane.

4. Right-click in an area that is unallocated on a dynamic disk, and choose Create Volume. From the Create Volume Wizard, select RAID 5 as the volume type.

5. When working through the wizard, make sure to select at least three separate dynamic drives to perform as the RAID volumes.

As with other RAID implementations, you'll know if a RAID configuration has failed when the status of the drive changes from Healthy to Failed Redundancy. When this happens, the status of the individual volume that is not working is shown as Missing, Offline, or Online With Errors. There are many ways to begin recovery.

To recover from a failure of a RAID 5 volume, perform the following steps:

1. Log on to a Windows 2000 server that is configured with RAID 5.

2. Choose Start|Programs|Administrative Tools|Computer Management.

3. Expand the trees as necessary, and double-click on the Disk Management folder. The Disk Management screen will appear in the right pane.

4. Get all drives of the RAID 5 set online.

5. Back up whatever data you can.

6. If the status of the volume is Online (Errors), right-click on the volume and choose Reactivate Disk. If the drive does not change to Healthy, right-click on the volume and choose Regenerate Parity.

7. If the status of the volume is Missing or Offline, check such hardware issues as the data cable to the volume or the power to the volume. (You'll have to shut down the computer to do this, of course, and then reboot.) If the drive does not change to Healthy, right-click on the volume and choose Regenerate Parity.

8. If the status of the volume is shown as Unreadable, choose Action|Rescan Disks. If nothing happens, reboot the computer.

9. If the drive still isn't repaired, you'll have to repair the failed set. Right-click on the failed volume, choose Remove Volume, and then select a new area of unallocated space on a separate dynamic disk. This disk must be large enough to hold the data and must be a physically separate disk drive.

Decision Tree 8.1 will help you decide the appropriate course of action.

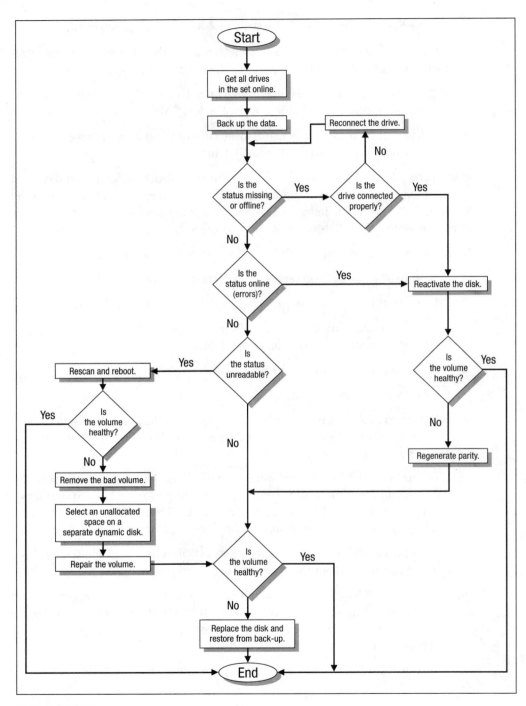

Decision Tree 8.1
RAID 5 repair.

File Compression

Compression is used to save hard disk space for users or administrators, and it is available on all NTFS volumes. Because compressed data takes up less space than does uncompressed data, more information can be stored on local hard drives. Because NTFS and Windows 2000 work together to manage compressed data, any Windows-based or MS-DOS-based application can open compressed files without needing those files to be uncompressed first by another application or utility. For instance, if Microsoft Excel is used to open a large, compressed spreadsheet, NTFS will automatically uncompress the file before it is turned over to Excel. When the file is closed again, NTFS recompresses the data before storing it.

As I mentioned earlier, when used with disk quotas, compressed files count against a user's quota as determined by the file's uncompressed size. The same is true of the operating system and its calculation of compressed files and available disk space. When a file is to be saved as a compressed file (say the file is 50MB compressed, and 75MB uncompressed), the file save operation will occur only if there is 75MB of free space on the disk. The operating system allocates space for the file based on its uncompressed size. If there isn't 75MB of free space, the user will see an error message stating that there is not enough disk space available for the file.

Tip: Bitmaps, JPEGs, GIFs, and other graphics files compress well, usually to about a quarter of their original size, whereas documents and spreadsheets compress to only around 75 to 80 percent of their original size. When compressing files, consider these files first.

To compress files and folders, follow these steps:

1. To compress a file or folder, use Windows Explorer to locate the folder.

2. Right-click on the file or folder, and choose Properties.

3. Select the General tab and choose Advanced.

4. Place a checkmark in the Compress Contents To Save Disk Space checkbox, as shown in Figure 8.14. Choose OK twice. (You must at least have Write permission for the file to do this.)

5. The Confirm Attributes Changes dialog box appears next. There are two choices:

   - *Apply Changes To This Folder Only*—The default choice, used to compress only the files in the folder that you have specifically selected.

   - *Apply Changes To This Folder, Subfolders, And Files*—Used to compress not only files contained in this folder now but also any files added to the folder later. All subfolders will be compressed as well.

Make the appropriate choice and choose OK.

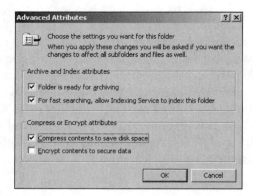

Figure 8.14
Setting compression attributes.

To show the compressed files in a different color, follow these steps:

1. Open Windows Explorer and choose Tools|Folder Options. Select the View tab.

2. The first option on the View tab is Display Compressed Files And Folders With Alternate Color. Place a checkmark in the checkbox and choose OK. All compressed files are now shown in blue.

To compress an entire drive, follow these steps:

1. Use Windows Explorer to locate the drive.

2. Right-click on the drive, and choose Properties. On the General tab, place a checkmark in the Compress Drive To Save Space checkbox.

You can also compress files and folders from a command prompt by using the **COMPACT** command. Table 8.1 lists the switches available with this command. The syntax of the command is:

```
COMPACT [/C | /U] [/S[:dir]] [/A] [/I] [/F] [/Q] [filename [...]]
```

You can also use the **COMPACT** command without parameters or with multiple file names and wildcards. The **COMPACT** command displays the compression state of the current directory and any files it contains.

Task Manager

The Task Manager, mentioned briefly in previous chapters, can be used to manage processes and applications, stop and start processes or applications, and view the performance of the computer's resources. Task Manager can be used to see which programs and processes are running and how the computer is performing.

Table 8.1   Switches for the COMPACT command.

Switch	Description
/C	Compresses the specified files. Directories will be marked so that files added afterward will be compressed.
/U	Uncompresses the specified files. Directories will be marked so that files added afterward will not be compressed.
/S	Performs the specified operation on files in the given directory and all subdirectories. Default "dir" is the current directory.
/A	Displays files with the hidden or system attributes. These files are omitted by default.
/I	Continues performing the specified operation even after errors have occurred. By default, COMPACT stops when an error is encountered.
/F	Forces the compress operation to act on all specified files, even those that are already compressed. Already compressed files are skipped by default.
/Q	Reports only the most essential information.

Every time a user starts an application, from either another application or a command line, Windows 2000 starts processes that the operating system uses to manage the program. This application has control and is said to be running in the foreground. If that program (or process) is minimized, and another is opened and used, then the second program takes over the foreground, and the first application runs in the background. A program that runs in the foreground receives a higher priority number from the operating system. This process is then given attention from the CPU and related components faster than programs with lower priorities. In addition to user-related processes, many other processes run in the background that the user never even knows about. One of Task Manager's duties is to allow the administrator or user an opportunity to manage these processes.

Processes contain threads. Threads inherit the process's base priority level. Threads are used by the CPU in "slices," and process threads are used to manage those processes by the CPU. Higher-priority threads are run before lower-priority threads.

Task Manager contains three tabs: Applications, Processes, and Performance. You can display the Task Manager either by pressing Ctrl+Alt+Del and choosing Task Manager or by right-clicking on an empty area of the taskbar and choosing Task Manager.

The Applications Tab

Figure 8.15 shows the Applications tab of Task Manager. From here, a user or administrator can stop an application, switch to another application, and start a new application.

To stop an application, select it and choose the End Task button. This is useful when a program's status is Not Responding or if you are ending multiple applications simultaneously. To switch between running applications, click on the application you want to use, and select the Switch To button. To launch a new application, choose the New Task

Figure 8.15
Task Manager's Applications tab.

button. The Create New Task dialog box will appear; it looks exactly like the Start/Run box, where you can type in a command-line task.

More information can be obtained from this tab by right-clicking on an application and choosing Go To Process. This is extremely helpful when you suspect that a particular application is causing a problem and you need to look at the processes related to that application. For instance, right-clicking on Outlook Express and choosing Go To Process opens the Processes tab, and the process msimn.exe is highlighted. This isolates the process related to this application. From the Processes tab, you can stop the process related to this application.

The Processes Tab

Figure 8.16 shows the Processes tab of Task Manager. Using this tab, you can view any parameter having to do with an application's processes. In Figure 8.16, notice the five default column headings: Image Name, process identifier (PID), CPU, CPU Time, and Mem Usage. This information can be used to troubleshoot processor bottlenecks, applications gone awry, or problems with the processes related to a specific program or application.

You can change the headings shown in Figure 8.16 to suit your personal needs by adding any of the headings listed here. Figure 8.17 shows Task Manager configured with some of these additional columns added. In order to troubleshoot processes and their process trees, you might need to see information regarding some of these parameters:

• Memory Usage Delta

• Peak Memory Usage

8

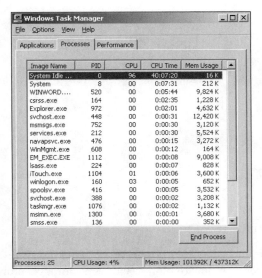

Figure 8.16
Task Manager's Processes tab, with the default column headings.

Image Name	PID	CPU	CPU Time	Mem Usage	Peak Mem Usage	Page Faults	PF Delta	Base Pri	Threads	I/O Re...
taskmgr.exe	1076	01	0:00:12	1,112 K	2,368 K	7,358	0	High	5	2
csrss.exe	164	00	0:02:40	1,156 K	3,136 K	14,179	0	High	10	619,571
winlogon.exe	160	00	0:00:06	1,996 K	8,512 K	7,295	0	High	17	1,792
msimn.exe	1292	00	0:00:01	572 K	8,540 K	2,648	0	Normal	7	77
EM_EXEC.EXE	1112	00	0:00:08	9,012 K	9,012 K	2,266	0	Normal	3	1,045
iTouch.exe	1104	00	0:00:07	3,600 K	3,612 K	1,011	0	Normal	4	764
POProxy.exe	1052	00	0:00:00	4,864 K	4,924 K	1,255	0	Normal	3	2,245
Explorer.exe	972	01	0:02:09	4,132 K	11,340 K	236,076	1	Normal	20	18,570
msmsgs.exe	752	00	0:00:31	3,120 K	6,000 K	42,552	0	Normal	10	13,170
alertsvc.exe	740	00	0:00:00	4,516 K	4,548 K	1,148	0	Normal	16	63
WinMgmt.exe	608	00	0:00:12	164 K	4,480 K	5,709	0	Normal	3	977
MSTask.exe	584	00	0:00:00	3,704 K	3,728 K	1,018	0	Normal	7	273
regsvc.exe	560	00	0:00:00	756 K	764 K	192	0	Normal	2	3
npssvc.exe	532	00	0:00:00	1,520 K	1,520 K	379	0	Normal	5	35
WINWORD....	520	00	0:06:27	7,204 K	15,896 K	17,571	0	Normal	5	129,799
navapsvc.exe	476	00	0:00:15	3,280 K	5,476 K	37,454	0	Normal	8	1,892,...
PHOTOED.EXE	452	00	0:00:03	1,008 K	8,420 K	8,005	0	Normal	4	460
svchost.exe	448	00	0:00:32	12,448 K	13,708 K	7,306	0	Normal	34	1,310,...
spoolsv.exe	416	00	0:00:05	3,544 K	4,928 K	4,458	0	Normal	12	1,008
svchost.exe	388	00	0:00:02	3,260 K	3,268 K	1,481	0	Normal	10	1,042
lsass.exe	224	00	0:00:07	584 K	4,440 K	16,879	0	Normal	14	16,133
services.exe	212	00	0:00:30	5,524 K	5,648 K	15,172	0	Normal	30	122,498
smss.exe	136	00	0:00:00	352 K	2,012 K	620	0	Normal	6	204
System	8	00	0:07:32	212 K	692 K	7,675	0	Normal	33	0
navapw32.exe	300	00	0:00:00	1,912 K	2,000 K	3,830	0	Low	1	75
System Idle ...	0	98	40:26:02	16 K	16 K	1	0	N/A	1	0

Figure 8.17
Task Manager's Processes tab, with additional column headings.

- Page Faults and Page Faults Delta

- User Objects

- I/O Reads and Read Bytes

- Virtual Memory Size

- Paged Pool and Non Paged Pool

- Base Priority

- Handle Count and Thread Count

- GDI Objects

- I/O Writes, Write Bytes, Other, and Other Bytes

In addition to adding columns, you can move the columns around by clicking and dragging, and you can sort the processes from low to high or vice versa for any column head. Figure 8.17, shown earlier, is sorted by base priority. Notice that Task Manager is running at a high priority. Any process shown on this tab can be stopped by right-clicking on it and choosing End Process. Additionally, entire process trees (the process and all of its subprocesses) can be stopped.

Note: If your server has multiple processors, another option will be available after you right-click on the process. The Set Affinity option allows you to assign a process to a particular processor. Affinity is used when you want to configure a particular process or program to use a specific single processor to improve the process's performance. This improvement will be at the expense of other processes.

If you right-click on a process, you'll see six priority levels: Realtime, High, Above Normal, Normal, Below Normal, and Low. Table 8.2 lists these priority levels and, on a scale of 1 to 31, shows where their priorities generally run. Realtime priority is generally used for kernel-mode processes and is not recommended for user applications.

Table 8.2 Process priority levels.

Priority Name	Priority Level (1–31)
Realtime	16–31
High	11–15
Above Normal	8–10
Normal	Around 8
Below Normal	6–10
Low	1–5

You might need to change the priority of a process or thread if the process that needs to run doesn't get much processor time due to other programs or threads. Although it isn't a long-term cure for a processor bottleneck, a priority change can be used as a quick fix for a single application. When changing priorities for a process, you'll receive the warning shown in Figure 8.18.

The Performance Tab

Figure 8.19 shows the Performance tab of Task Manager. The Performance tab offers a quick view of how the computer is functioning. On this tab, you can see graphs for CPU and memory usage, as well as written information concerning totals for the number of handles, threads, and processes currently running on the computer, and totals for physical, kernel, and commit memory.

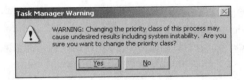

Figure 8.18
Priority change warning.

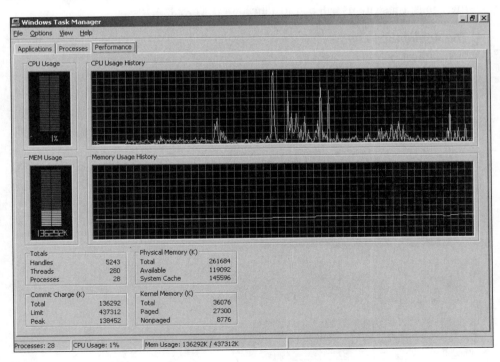

Figure 8.19
Task Manager's Performance tab.

Notice in Figure 8.19 that there are two lines in the CPU graph. The green line represents the general CPU usage, and the red line represents the number of CPU resources that are being used by the kernel operations. The kernel operations are shown as the lower of the two lines because they do not represent all of the CPU's usage. You can view the kernel CPU usage by choosing View|Show Kernel Times. You can also change the time that the data is updated or refreshed; choose View|Update Speed option and select High, Normal, Low, or Paused.

Figure 8.20 shows a computer at 100% CPU usage. If this is happening often, you should consider upgrading the CPU.

Event Viewer

The Event Viewer is used to perform a variety of tasks, most of which have to do with viewing logs that have been created by the system or defined by an administrator. By default, three logs are installed in Event Viewer: the application log, the security log, and the system log. When DNS, the File Replication Service, or other services are installed, additional logs are generated to log these activities. In this section, I'll introduce two of the three logs: the application log and the system log. I'll save the security log for the discussion on security later. In order to read and understand these logs, you'll need to understand what types of events are logged and what options are available for viewing these logs; those items will be introduced here as well.

The Application Log

The application log in Event Viewer keeps track of errors and events that occur through programs and applications. These applications can be email, anti-virus, office, data-base,

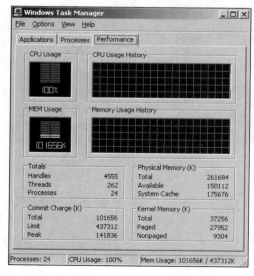

Figure 8.20
CPU usage at 100%.

and other applications, and the log contains errors, warnings, and information concerning these programs. The events that are recorded in Event Viewer through applications depend on which events the programmers of those applications decided should be recorded. In Figure 8.21, notice that application events are recorded from Dr. Watson, Norton Anti-Virus (NAV), MsiInstaller (in this case, generated from a Microsoft Office application installation), and others.

You can see more information about an event recorded in any log by double-clicking on the event in the log. For instance, to see more information on the first log entry that contains an error, double-click on the entry to see a description of the event and the action taken. Figure 8.22 shows the error generated by Winlogon. The result of the error is that access is denied to the needed resource.

Tip: You can also see the Event Properties page by right-clicking on the event and choosing Properties.

The System Log
The system log in Event Viewer keeps track of errors and events that occur in the system itself. The system log contains information, errors, and warnings that are generated not by applications but by the Windows 2000 operating system. The events that are recorded in Event Viewer through the system are preconfigured by the operating system. The

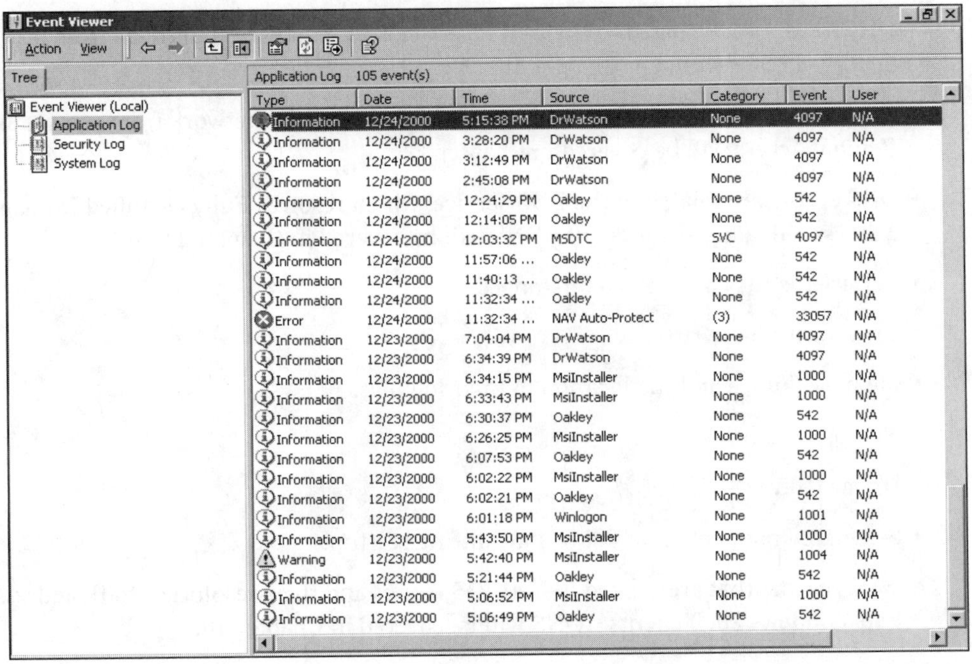

Figure 8.21
The application log.

Figure 8.22
Event Properties.

system log looks similar to the log shown in Figure 8.21. Events that are recorded in the system log include the following:

- DHCP events are related to the DHCP service and automatic TCP/IP address leasing. DHCP will be covered in Chapter 10.

- Remote Access events are related to clients accessing the network from remote sites. Remote Access will be covered in Chapter 12.

- DNS events are related to the DNS service, which resolves Fully Qualified Domain Names to IP address for clients. DNS will be covered in Chapter 11.

- Services as they are started or stopped.

- Errors with hardware.

- Memory dumps and the location of their log files.

- NetLogon failures.

- Driver failures.

- System components that fail to start during startup.

- WINS events that are related to NetBIOS names and their resolution to IP addresses for non-Windows 2000 clients. WINS will be covered in Chapter 10.

You can view events in the system log the same way as in the application log.

Action and View Menus

The Event Viewer's Action menu contains several options. They include opening a saved log file, saving a log file, creating a new log view, clearing all of the events, renaming a log file, refreshing a view, and exporting a log file. Because all of these options are self-explanatory, I'll focus on the last option, Properties.

Choosing Properties from the Action menu allows you to change how the log file is configured. Tables 8.3 and 8.4 describe the options available through the Properties page.

Table 8.3   The General tab of a log's Properties sheet.

Option	Description
Display Name	The display name of the log can be changed from "Application Log" or "System Log" to anything you'd like.
Log Name	This is the location and name of the log file, usually C:\Winnt\system32\config\<log>.Evt. The location and the name can be changed.
Size, Created, Modified, Accessed	This option shows information about the current size of the log file, when the file was created and last modified, and when it was last accessed. This information cannot be changed.
Maximum Log Size	The maximum size of the log can be set. When the file reaches this size, it will be either overwritten or cleared manually by an administrator.
Overwrite Events As Needed	Events in the log will be overwritten when the file has reached its maximum size.
Overwrite Events Older Than ___ Days	Events can be overwritten after a certain period of time. This is the default setting and is configured for seven days.
Do Not Overwrite Events (Clear Log Manually)	Full event logs must be manually cleared. You should choose this setting if you need to save and archive the logs. This setting can be configured for a single log, and the other logs can be set to clear themselves automatically.
Restore Defaults	This returns the log settings to the original configurations.
Using A Low-Speed Connection	Check this box if the connection is a slow one.
Clear Log	Check this box to clear all events from the log.

Table 8.4   The Filter tab of a log's Properties sheet.

Option	Description
Event Types	All event types are checked by default: Information, Warning, Error, Success Audit, and Failure Audit. There will be no audit entries if auditing isn't configured. (Event types are discussed next.)
Event Source	All sources are logged by default, but separate logs can be configured to log only one source, such as the Alerter Service, Workstation service, Application popup, browser, CD-ROM, DHCP, disk, IPSec, Kerberos, Modem, NetBIOS, NetLogon, Print, Remote Access, Save Dump, and more.

(continued)

Table 8.4 **The Filter tab of a log's Properties sheet** *(continued).*

Option	Description
Category	All categories are logged by default. However, if the Event Source is changed, then the categories of that event can be changed as well. For instance, if the Event Source is changed to log only the Workstation service, then the categories can be selected as well. Categories include Devices, Disk, Network, Printers, Services, Shell, and System Events.
Event ID, User, Computer	Events can be filtered by an Event ID, by a user, or by a computer; type the required information here.
From and To	Events can be filtered by date.
Restore Defaults	This returns the log settings to their defaults.

Figure 8.23 shows an application log filtered to show only errors or warnings. This log can be saved before it is cleared so that the information can be accessed later if necessary.

The Event Viewer's View menu contains several options. The options are used to change how Event Viewer looks to the user or administrator. Table 8.5 describes each of these options.

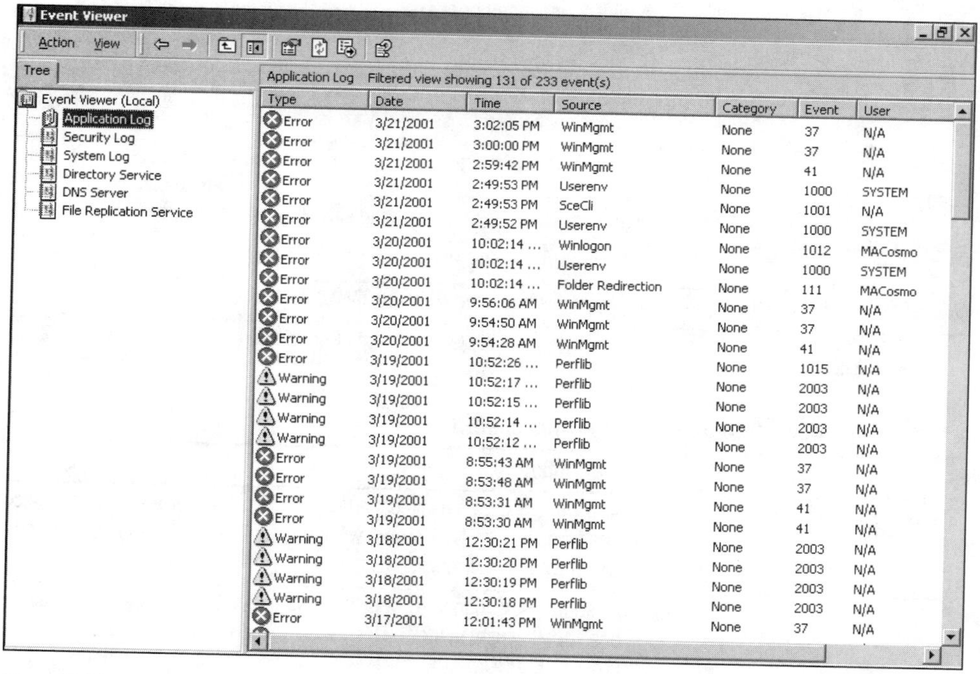

Figure 8.23
A filtered application log.

Table 8.5   Event Viewer's View menu.

Option	Description
Choose Columns	Choose this command to hide columns in Event Viewer. To troubleshoot application or system problems for specific users, an administrator might want to configure a log that contains only the user, the date and time, and the event.
All Records	Choose this command to see all of the records stored in Event Viewer for an event log.
Filter	Choose this command to filter events by using the Log Properties sheet.
Newest First and Oldest First	Choose this command to sort events by date and time.
Find	Choose this command to display the Find In Local Log page. From here, you can find information in the log based on the source, event ID, user, computer, description, or event type.
Customize	Choose this command to select which options to show or hide in the console. These items include the console tree, standard menus, standard toolbars, status bar, description bar, taskpad navigation tabs, and menus and toolbars for snap-ins.

Event Types

From the previous screenshots, you have seen errors, warnings, and information icons and information related to each. Here's a little more detail about these icons:

- Errors represent a substantial problem with either the application or the system log. Errors represent loss of data or loss of functionality of a service. Errors regarding services that fail to start at system boot are also shown in error-message boxes when the system is started. Usually, the message says that a particular service failed to start, and it refers you to the event log. The icon representing an error is a red circle with a white X through it.

- Warnings represent possible future problems with the application or system. The event itself might not be significant or cause a specific problem, but it may foreshadow an error that will occur soon because of it. For instance, a warning may be logged if detection of a particular device fails, if disk space is low, or if the domain controller cannot find a replication partner. A warning is denoted with a yellow triangle with an black exclamation point in it.

- Information is logged by applications or the system to show that certain operations have been completed successfully. For instance, information may be logged when a driver, application, or service has loaded or started successfully. Information icons are white conversation bubbles with a lower case "i" in the middle of them.

Auditing will be discussed later, but the icons representing successful and unsuccessful audits are represented by a lock for a failure audit and a key for a success audit.

Event Viewer Tasks

When an event has occurred and is recorded in one of the logs in Event Viewer, you can see more information about that event by double-clicking on it, as you are already aware. However, understanding what the information means is quite another issue. The most important information given in this information box (like the one shown in Figure 8.24) is the information recorded in the Description box.

In this example, as in other event property sheets, there is a lot of information offered. The date, time, type, user, and computer sections are self-explanatory. The other sections are:

- *Event ID*—A number associated with a particular event. In Figure 8.24, the event ID is 26. This number is always associated with pop-up messages shown during system startup. Other events have different numbers. For instance, when event log service is started, an event is logged and the number for the event ID is 6005. Event IDs are used by support personnel and product representatives to troubleshoot event errors, warnings, and system problems.

- *Source*—The name of the application or system service that logged the event. This can be the name of a program, a system component, or a driver. Like the event ID, it can be used by support personnel and product representatives to troubleshoot event errors, warnings, and system problems.

- *Category*—Describes what part of the event source is related to the event itself. This information is most important to the security log and auditing. In Figure 8.24, there is no category stated.

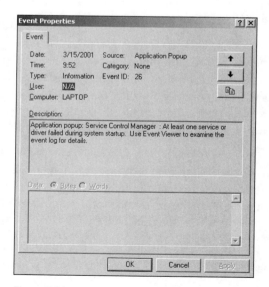

Figure 8.24
Event Properties.

In addition to using Event Viewer for troubleshooting system and application problems, there is one other task I'd like to introduce. Archiving an event log can be quite useful if it needs to be accessed later. By archiving logs once a week or whenever necessary, you can refrain from having to increase disk space for the logs or clearing them when they are full. Archiving an event log is as simple as choosing Action|Save Log File As in Event Viewer.

Log files can be saved in many formats, including event logs (*.evt), text or tab-delimited (*.txt), or, comma-separated values or comma-delimited (*.csv). When logs are saved as event logs, information about the binary data for each event is recorded. These logs can be viewed in Event Viewer but cannot be viewed in other applications such as Word or Excel. When logs are saved as text, tab-delimited, or comma-separated values, the logs can be reopened using a variety of applications, including database and word processing applications, but the binary data is not retained when you're using these files.

Event Viewer can be configured through the Security Configuration And Analysis snap-in. To configure Event Viewer through this snap-in, perform the following steps:

1. Log on to the computer as an administrator and type "mmc" at the **Run** command line.

2. Choose Add/Remove Snap-in, and choose Security Analysis And Configuration.

3. Right-click on Security Configuration And Analysis, and choose Open Database.

4. In the File Name box, type a name for the new database. Choose OK.

5. In the Import Template dialog box, select a template to use as a base for your new database. For the purpose of example only, choose basicdc.inf. (You'll learn more about these templates later.)

6. If you receive an error stating that this configuration is invalid, right-click on Security Configuration And Analysis again, but this time choose Configure Computer Now. Accept the defaults. If you do not receive an error, proceed to Step 9.

7. If you had to perform Step 6, perform this step as well. Right-click on Security Configuration And Analysis and choose Analyze Computer now. Accept the defaults.

8. If you had to perform Steps 6 and 7, right-click on Security And Configuration Analysis and choose Open Database. The database you named will be in the File Name box. Open the database.

9. Expand the Security Configuration And Analysis tree.

10. Expand the event log.

11. Highlight Settings for event logs. In the right pane you'll be able to see the available Event Log policy settings.

12. The following security settings for Event Viewer and event logs can be set by double-clicking on the policy and defining the policy appropriately. (None of these settings are defined by default, although there may be computer settings as previously configured in Event Viewer.) The configuration choices are:

- Maximum application log size

- Maximum security log size

- Maximum system log size

- Restrict Guest access to application log

- Restrict Guest access to security log

- Restrict Guest access to system log

- Retain application log

- Retain security log

- Retention method for application log

- Retention method for security log

- Retention method for system log

- Shut down the computer when the security log is full

QoS Admission Control

QoS, or Quality of Service, is a new feature in Windows 2000 that offers yet another opportunity to optimize your domain controllers and your network. QoS Admission Control standards are a set of standards that can offer more consistent and reliable networking, especially if the network is used to transmit real-time audio or video. QoS Admission Control can be used to improve media transmissions by giving those types of transmissions a higher priority than other transmissions on the network. In live video or audio streaming, data packets containing video and audio data cannot be resent if they are dropped. (If they were resent, then by the time they were received, they'd have missed their window of opportunity and wouldn't make sense to the conversation or presentation.) It is for this reason that these types of applications are given a higher priority than applications that are not time-sensitive.

Besides audio and video data, administrators can also mandate that users, other applications, or specific types of traffic be given higher priority. However, for QoS Admission Control to work correctly, every part of the network must meet the QoS Admission Control standards. Certain hardware requirements must be met, of course, but even network interface cards, routers, switches, and bridges have to be considered. If the data is sent over the Internet through an ISP, even the ISP has to meet the requirements.

The QoS Admission Control Service (QoS ACS) allows an administrator to configure who or what can obtain more bandwidth and to manage how it is used on the network. QoS Admission Control can be opened through Start|Programs|Administrative Tools|QoS Admission Control. You can then expand the Subnetwork Settings, choose a subnet, and open the Properties of that subnet by right-clicking and choosing Properties. Figure 8.25 shows the resulting dialog box.

Tip: *QoS Admission Control has to be installed from the Windows 2000 Server CD-ROM. If you don't see it under Administrative Tools, you'll need to install it. It is located under Networking Services in the Windows Components Wizard.*

If you have administrator rights, you can configure which servers can use QoS Admission Control (choose Add on the Servers tab). Additionally, logging can be enabled on the Logging tab, and parameters related to traffic, limits, and priority can be set on the other tabs. Installing, configuring, and using the QoS Admission Control Service is a rather large project. Many requirements must be met, and there are many Requests for Comments (RFCs) on the subject. To learn more about QoS Admission Control, open the Help files on Windows 2000 Server, or access Microsoft's web site, and read RFC 2386, 2696, and 2990 before starting.

Backup and Restore

Windows 2000 Server comes with a Backup utility that can be used to easily and quickly to back up data on your domain controllers or workstations. I'll go out on a limb here and say that in medium to large organizations, you'll probably want to use something a little

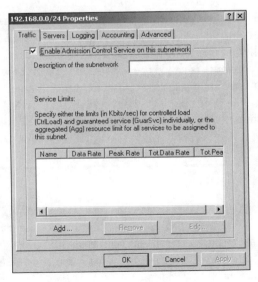

Figure 8.25
QoS Admission Control subnet properties.

more sophisticated, but for smaller networks, this might be just the right fit for you and your organization. Obviously, the purpose of backing up data is to recover from a disaster like a hard drive failure, power outage, or virus, or even from an unforeseen event like a fire or earthquake. Therefore, when you're considering how and when to back up data, keep in mind just how important the data is to the company or organization.

In this section, the Windows Backup utility will be discussed, and a walkthrough will be detailed. Options and backup types will also be discussed, as well as scheduling backup jobs using Task Scheduler. Finally, restoring data will be detailed, just in case it's ever necessary.

Tip: *Perform a complete backup at least weekly, and take the backup tapes home with you or to another location. In the case of a fire, flood, or other disaster within a building, backups kept in that building are not safe.*

Types of Backups

There are several types of backups, each used for different reasons and at different times. Before you can decide which type of backup you need, you must decide how often data is changed in your organization. In a very small network, backing up data may consist of running the Backup utility twice a month, and it may even be a scheduled event. In large networks where data changes daily, the backups will occur more frequently. In addition to deciding how often data needs to be backed up, you'll need to decide which data should be backed up. It might be necessary to back up the entire system only once a week, but make daily backups of financial data, sales records, tax information, or inventory.

The Windows 2000 Backup utility provides five distinct backup types. Some of these back up all data, some back up only data that has changed since the last backup, and some back up only the files that have changed during the day. Therefore, attributes have to exist to tell the operating system whether a certain file has recently been backed up and whether the file has changed. This attribute is called the *archive bit*, the *archive attribute*, or the *backup marker*. When a file changes, the archive attribute changes, and when the file is backed up, the attribute is either cleared or reset. While reading about the following five backup types, notice what happens to the archive bit and how it is used differently in each type.

Personal Experience

I once carpooled with a woman who worked for a large, federally insured, national bank. The bank's policy stated that each day, certain backups had to be made, and those backups had to be taken off the premises and to another location within 30 minutes of the backups being completed. This type of security is necessary with banks, of course, because the data is sensitive and highly secure; however, this type of security might well be necessary for your organization, too.

A *normal backup* is sometimes called a *full backup;* all selected files and folders are backed up. When a normal (or full) backup is performed, the archive bit is not a factor. Windows performs a full backup of the data and isn't concerned if the file has been changed since the last backup. However, during a full backup, the archive bit is reset, and it will remain in this state until data in the file is changed. Because this is a full backup, it can be used to restore a system much faster than any other type. On the other hand, it takes longer to complete and uses more physical media than any other backup type. This is a disadvantage, of course, especially if you have to wait for the backup to be completed every Friday afternoon before you can go home or if the price of the backup media is high.

8

The *copy backup* is similar to a normal backup in that all selected files and folders are backed up. It also doesn't look at archive attributes. However, unlike the normal backup, the copy backup doesn't reset them. The copy backup is good for intermediate backups of files or folders in between more complete backups, such as normal or incremental backups. Because it doesn't change the archive bit, the copy backup doesn't affect any other future backup.

In the *differential backup*, only files or folders that have the archive attribute are backed up. Having this attribute means that the file has changed since it was last backed up with a normal or incremental backup. The differential backup does not clear the archive attribute, and it is one of the faster ways to perform a backup. If you use a combination of normal and differential backups, you can restore a system with the last normal backup followed by the last differential backup.

In the *incremental backup*, the files and folders that have the archive attribute are backed up, just as in the differential backup. The difference between the two is that the incremental backup clears the archive bit. This backup type is also very fast, but restoring from an incremental backup takes longer than restoring from other types. To restore from incremental backups, you must use the last normal backup and then all incremental backups made since that time.

In a *daily backup*, all selected files and folders that have changed that day are backed up. This type of backup doesn't look at or clear archive bits. It simply looks for which files or folders have been changed on a particular date and backs up those files.

Many organizations do not rely on one type of backup, but instead use a combination of two or more types. You can combine normal and differential backups by performing a normal backup once a week, followed by differential backups on the other days. This takes a little more time while backing up but less time for restoring. Normal and incremental backups can be used the same way. Do a normal backup once a week and incremental backups on the other days. In contrast to the first scenario, this type of schedule takes less time to back up and more time to restore.

Finally, a combination of normal, differential, and copy backups works well for some organizations. It's done the same way as the previous two setups, but during the week, a copy is performed instead of another differential or incremental backup. The copy backup is added when an organization needs a snapshot of the data but doesn't want to change any attributes when doing so.

Warning! Windows 2000 Backup doesn't back up open files. Make sure all users have closed their files before you back up data.

Types of Backup Media

The backup media most commonly used in medium to large organizations consist of tape devices because those devices are convenient and have a high capacity for holding data. These devices aren't too expensive, either, and the tapes can be reused. Data can also be stored on backups on Zip drives, although the disks are fairly expensive and don't hold a lot of data. Similarly, rewritable CD-ROMs have become quite popular, as have optical drives. Backups can also be directed to another computer, a file server, a member server, or the like, and data can be stored relatively safely there. Backing up data to a file server that is in the same room as the original data doesn't provide much security in case of a disaster like a flood or fire, but backing up data to another server in another building does.

Setting Default Backup Options

You can set some default options for the Backup utility by opening it through Start| Programs|Accessories|System Tools|Backup and choosing Tools|Options from the menu bar. Listed next are some of the items available for configuration:

- Verify data after the backup is complete.

- Set restore options, including whether files should be replaced and, if so, how it should be done.

- Specify the backup type as described previously.

- Set backup log options, including detailed, summary, or none. (Detailed is the most complete, summary is the default.)

- Specify which files will be excluded from the backup.

- Specify whether mounted drives will be backed up.

- Specify whether alert messages should be shown and under what circumstances.

Figure 8.26 shows the Options screen and the choices for Default Backup Type.

Performing a Backup

To perform a backup using Windows 2000 Server's Backup utility, perform the following steps:

1. Log on to the server as an administrator, backup operator, or server operator, or as a user on a local workstation.

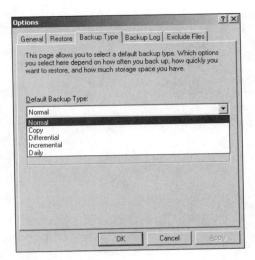

Figure 8.26
Backup options.

2. Choose Start|Programs|Accessories|System Tools|Backup to start the Backup utility. (You can also type "ntbackup" from a command line.)

3. Choose Backup Wizard, and when it appears, choose Next.

4. The Backup Wizard begins with a page offering choices for which files and folders to back up. The choices range from backing up everything, to backing up only selected files, drives, or network data, to backing up only the System State data. Make the appropriate choices and continue.

5. If you've chosen to back up everything on the computer or only the system state, the next page asks you where the data should be stored and on what type of media. If you've chosen to back up selected files, drives, or network data, an additional dialog box is offered, asking you to select which files, drives, or data should be backed up. In the second case, place a checkmark in the appropriate boxes, as shown in Figure 8.27.

6. On the Where To Store The Backup page, you can choose the location and type of media that the data should be stored to. To save to a particular location, choose the Browse button and explore to that location.

7. The Completing The Backup Wizard page appears, summarizing what you have configured for the backup. To specify additional backup options, choose the Advanced button.

8. The first page shown in the advanced section is the Type Of Backup page. From here, you can choose normal, copy, incremental, differential, or daily. You can also select the Backup Migrated Remote Storage Data option to back up the contents of files that have been migrated to Remote Storage. Make the appropriate selections and continue.

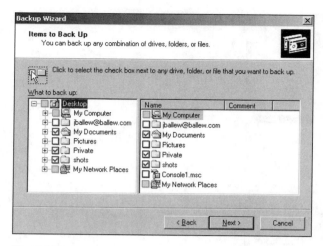

Figure 8.27
Specifying items to back up.

9. The next page, How To Back Up, offers two additional options: Verify Data After Backup, and Use Hardware Compression If Available. Place checkmarks in the boxes as appropriate, and continue.

10. The Media Options page asks you to choose how new data will be appended. Will you append this backup to the media, or replace the data on the media with this backup? If you choose to replace the data with the data in this backup, then you also have the option of allowing only the owner and the administrator to access the backed-up data. Make the appropriate choice and continue.

11. On the next page, name the backup by accepting the suggested label or typing one of your own.

12. On the next page, you can choose to back up the data either now or later. If you choose Later, you'll be asked to input a job name and a start date, and schedule the job. (Scheduling a job will be covered in the next example.) To perform the backup now, choose Now.

13. The wizard's final page summarizes the choices you have made throughout. You can choose Finish, Back, or Cancel. If you choose Finish, the backup will begin.

Note: *The time it takes to complete a backup depends on what is being backed up, how fast the data can be written to the media, and where the media is located. The simplest backup, backing up the system state to a Zip disk, took me about 8 minutes.*

14. The Backup Wizard also creates a report so the backup can be verified as successful. To see the report, simply choose the Report button. This is extremely useful when

you have the ability to start a backup and then leave it to finish on its own. Listing 8.1 provides an example of a report concerning a system state backup.

Listing 8.1   A sample backup report.

```
Backup Status
Operation: Backup
Active backup destination: File
Media name: "Media created 3/23/2001 at 9:15 AM"

Backup of "System State"
Backup set #1 on media #1
Backup description: "Set created 3/23/2001 at 9:15 AM"
Backup Type: Copy

Backup started on 3/23/2001 at 9:15 AM.
Backup completed on 3/23/2001 at 9:22 AM.
Directories: 172
Files: 2006
Bytes: 283,506,970
Time:  7 minutes and  30 seconds
```

Tip: You can manually perform a backup from the Backup tab of the Backup utility if you are not fond of using wizards.

Scheduling a Backup

Backups can be scheduled in three ways: through Control Panel|Scheduled Tasks, through the Schedule Jobs tab of the Backup utility, and by choosing Later while running the Backup Wizard. You should already know how to schedule a task from Control Panel, and the Backup Wizard makes setting a date and time intuitive.

To schedule a backup from the Scheduled Jobs tab, follow these steps:

1. Log on to the server as an administrator, backup operator, or server operator, or as a user on a local workstation.

2. Choose Start|Programs|Accessories|System Tools|Backup to start the backup utility. (You can also type "ntbackup" in the Start|Run dialog box.)

3. Select the Schedule Jobs tab.

4. This tab provides a calendar. Use the arrows to select a date for the backup, and then click on the Add Job button.

5. The Backup Wizard walks you through the same steps listed in the previous example, but on the When To Back Up page, you'll need to type a job name. The wizard is completed similarly to the previous example.

Restoring from Backup

To see the options for restoring from a backup, select the Restore tab in the Backup utility. If you choose to Start Restore from this screen, and you are trying to restore the system state, you'll see an error message that states, "The system state cannot be restored while the Active Directory service is running." The message directs you to reboot and select the advanced startup option Directory Services Restore Mode. This makes sense because the system state represents the condition of the system and includes boot files and other sensitive data.

On the other hand, backed-up files and folders that are not related to the system state can be restored at any time. To restore these types of files or folders, follow these steps:

1. Log on to the server as an administrator, backup operator, or server operator, or as a user on a local workstation.

2. Choose Start|Programs|Accessories|System Tools|Backup to start the Backup utility. (You can also type "ntbackup" in the Start|Run dialog box.)

3. Select the Restore tab.

4. This tab lists all of the backups available. Select the files or folders you need to restore to your system, and choose Start Restore.

5. Confirm the restoration to continue, or choose Advanced to see more options for restoring the data. For this exercise, choose Advanced.

6. Using the advanced options, you can do the following: restore security; restore the removable storage database; restore junction points and restore file and folder data under junction points to the original location; mark the restored data as the primary data for all replicas when you're restoring replicated data sets; and preserve existing volume mount points. Make the appropriate selections and continue.

7. Confirm the restoration again if necessary.

8. To enter the path and the file name of the backup file you want to restore, either browse to the backup or accept the default shown on the screen.

9. The restoration is completed. To see a report of the restore process, click on Report.

Tip: You'll see the same screens if you choose to restore using the Restore Wizard from the Welcome tab.

SNMP

The Simple Network Management Protocol (SNMP) service can be used to monitor and communicate status information between a multitude of hosts, such as computers, routers, hubs, and servers. For performance purposes, SNMP can be used to monitor network performance and detect security breaches as well as to configure remote devices on remote hosts. Put simply, SNMP is a way to manage remote devices on a network.

To understand how to use SNMP and what SNMP can do, you'll need to understand a few terms first:

- *Node*—A server, workstation, router, bridge, or hub that is located on a network.

- *Agent*—A node that is managed by SNMP and that responds to messages from managers and management stations. Agents can generate messages when specific events occur, such as a reboot of the system or inappropriate access.

- *SNMP manager*—A computer that is running network management software (NMS) that is used to manage agents (nodes). The manager polls the agents for information about their hardware, software, and devices.

- *Network management station (also referred to as NMS)*—A computer that runs network management software and manages updates from agents. To use the information that the SNMP service provides, you must have at least one NMS. However, the SNMP service provides only the service and the agents, not this software. To make SNMP work properly, you must configure this station with a third-party management system.

- *Management information base (MIB)*—A database that acts as a go-between for the agent and the SNMP manager. The MIB details what should be monitored on the agents, and it moves information from the agent to the NMS and back.

- *SNMP community*—A group that contains multiple hosts, used for easing administration and enhancing security.

- *Trap message*—A message sent by an agent to the MIB and then to the NMS when an event such as a system reboot, router failure, or inappropriate access has occurred.

SNMP can be used to perform the following tasks:

- Monitor network usage either by user access or group access, or by their related services.

- Monitor network performance, including processing speed, throughput, and data success and failure rates.

- Trigger alarms when lapses or security breaches—such as inappropriate access, shutdown or restarting of a node, and router failure—are detected.

- When used with NMS, obtain information from remote hosts, including device information, hardware and software information, and application usage statistics.

Installing SNMP

You may already have SNMP installed on your computer, depending on the circumstances surrounding the original installation. To see if SNMP is installed on your server and to install it if necessary, perform the following steps:

1. Log on as an administrator and open Control Panel.

2. Choose Add/Remove Programs.

3. Choose Add/Remove Windows Components.

4. Highlight Management And Monitoring Tools and choose Details. There are three options: Connection Manager Components, Network Monitor Tools, and Simple Network Management Protocol. Make sure SNMP is checked, and choose Next.

5. When prompted, choose Finish.

Exploring SNMP and Configuring an SNMP Agent

SNMP is a service, and it is configured through the Computer Management console. Once installed, the service is started by default. To locate the SNMP service, see its configuration options, and configure an SNMP agent, perform the following steps:

1. Log on to a Windows 2000 server as an administrator.

2. Open Computer Management through Start|Programs|Administrative Tools| Computer Management.

3. Expand the Services And Applications tree.

4. Open Services.

5. Right-click on SNMP Service in the right pane, and then choose Properties.

6. Select the General tab. From here, you can start and stop the SNMP service and define the startup type (automatic, manual, disabled).

7. Select the Log On tab. From here, you can configure how the system authenticates the service, and you can enable or disable hardware profiles.

8. Select the Recovery tab. From here, you can control how the computer will respond if the SNMP service fails. You can choose to take no action, restart the service, run a file, or reboot the computer, and these choices can be set differently for the first failure, the second failure, and subsequent failures.

9. Select the Dependencies tab. From here, you can see which services the SNMP servers depend on to function, and which services depend on SNMP.

10. Select the Agent tab. From here, you can enter information about the person in charge of this object (computer, router, repeater, bridge, server, etc.), the

location of the object, and the services offered by the object. The services consist of the following:

- *Physical*—Indicates that the device works at the Physical layer of the OSI model for the network. These objects can be repeaters, amplifiers, and hard disk partitions.

- *Application*—Indicates that the object runs TCP/IP applications at the Application layer of the OSI model. All Windows 2000 computers should have this box checked.

- *Datalink*—Indicates that the device works at the Data Link layer of the OSI model, like a bridge.

- *Internet*—Indicates that the device (router, gateway, or domain controller) works at the Internet layer of the OSI model.

- *End-to-End*—Indicates that the device acts as a host at the end of the OSI model. . All Windows 2000 computers should have this box checked.

11. Select the Traps tab. From here, you can type in a community name. All hosts usually are configured so they belong to the community called *public*.

12. After a community name has been added to the list, you can add a trap by choosing Add from the Traps tab. Type in a host name, IP address, or IPX address.

13. Select the Security tab. From here, you can choose to send authentication traps by placing a checkmark in the appropriate box. Additionally, you can add communities or edit community rights by choosing the Add or Edit buttons. Finally, you can configure from where SNMP packets will be accepted.

14. Close all of the boxes.

The Open Systems Interconnection Model

The Open Systems Interconnection (OSI) model is a seven-layer model that standardizes how data is moved from object to object on the network. This model standardizes how data moves from an end user's application (like an email written in Outlook Express), through the computer, network interface card, router, hub, and repeater, across the physical wire, into another user's computer, and then to that user's end application on another system. The layers, as mentioned in the Agent tab of SNMP Service Properties, start at a user's application in the Application layer, and then go down the stack through the Presentation layer, the Session layer, the Transport layer, the Network layer, the Data Link layer, and finally to the Physical layer. When the data is at the Physical layer, it is sent across the physical cable to another user's computer. At that computer, the data moves from the Physical layer up the stack, and is eventually available to the user through an application. Repeaters work at the Physical layer, bridges at the Data Link layer, and routers at the Network layer. Computers should have at least the Application, Internet, and End-to-End boxes checked in the Agent dialog box.

SNMP Tools

If you have already installed the Windows 2000 Resource Kit as described earlier in this book, then starting the additional SNMP tools will be quite easy. To start the SNMP Query utility, choose Start|Programs|Windows 2000 Support Tools|Tools|SNMP Query Utility. (If you don't see the Windows 2000 Support Tools option under Programs, you'll need to go back and install the Resource Kit before continuing.)

Using the SNMP Query utility, you can enter a node address that has an SNMP agent running on it, and query that node. You can also specify which function to execute during the query. There are several query options, located in the SNMP Function To Execute box in this utility. To perform a query, select the appropriate command from this box and choose Execute Command. The resulting information can be saved as an *.snp file for later reference. For more information on these tools, see the associated help files, especially the file snmpconcepts.chm from Windows Help.

Note: *The Windows SNMP service provides only the SNMP service and the agent; it doesn't contain the SNMP management software that is used on the NMS. Many third-party management software applications can be installed on this host to perform the duties of a management system. The NMS does not have to run on the same computer as the agents.*

Using the Performance Console

The Performance console provides two snap-ins to help you monitor and optimize your Windows 2000 server: the System Monitor snap-in and the Performance Logs And Alerts snap-in. Both of these snap-ins are available in a single preconfigured console, which you can access by choosing Start|Programs|Administrative Tools|Performance.

System Monitor is used to monitor, collect, and view real-time data about memory, disk, CPU, and network activity, and the data can be viewed in graphs, histograms, or reports. Performance Logs And Alerts can be used to create logs that record performance data automatically and to notify administrators if any problems or thresholds are encountered. By combining both of these utilities, almost any organization can get an appropriate monitoring configuration. Monitoring effectively will give administrators a heads-up on potential problems through observing and recording trends related to growth, network activity, resource usage, and workload, and this information can be extremely useful to support personnel when problems do occur.

System Monitor

The System Monitor in Windows 2000 replaces the Performance Monitor in Windows NT 4. System Monitor can be configured to perform many useful tasks, including the following:

- View and collect data regarding current activity on the local computer or a remote one.

- View collected data in a log file, chart, graph, or histogram.

- Add, delete, or highlight counters for monitoring and viewing, or freeze the display.

- Create monitoring configurations that can be saved and reused by other computers in an MMC.

- Monitor applications such as Microsoft Office by using automation.

- Update data automatically or on demand.

- Monitor and record counters for all seven layers of the OSI model.

- Establish a baseline for comparing subsequent monitoring data.

- Diagnose problems related to CPU, disks, memory, pagefiles, processes, cache, and more.

- Monitor network throughput.

How Should Monitoring Be Configured?

Because System Monitor is used for monitoring and optimizing the network, and literally thousands of monitoring configurations can be constructed, how do you decide what should be monitored? This section discusses how to determine what needs to be monitored and how often, why certain things should be monitored, and what records need to be kept.

Determining what needs to be monitored and how often is a tricky task. If too much data is monitored, the logs quickly fill up and the data is hard to decipher from those logs and graphs. If not enough data is monitored, there can be gaps in the information, and sound judgments about system performance cannot be made. If the interval for collecting data is too large or small, similar problems can occur.

If you are interested in viewing the local system or a remote computer for only a short period of time, then use the graph view, and add local computer-specific counters that represent the information you are interested in. For instance, on a local computer, you would most likely be interested in the processor time, cache, memory, paging file, and physical disk. You can add these counters and accept their defaults for interval updates. However, you can change how often a particular counter is updated if you think it is necessary. For instance, if you plan to monitor the system for only a few hours and create a log, you can configure the updates to occur every 15 seconds or so. If you plan to monitor the system for eight or more hours, you should change that figure to somewhere around five minutes. You might change the intervals because you do not want to fill up a log too quickly, cause unnecessary strain on the system, or consume an inordinate amount of disk space for holding the log files. Figure 8.28 shows each of the default counters for the five objects mentioned here.

If you are interested in monitoring the network, you should not only monitor the items listed for local systems, but also add some counters for the network as well. Remember, there are seven layers in the OSI model, so the counters you choose to monitor should

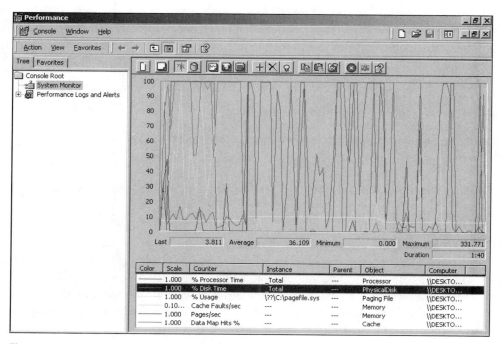

Figure 8.28
System Monitor.

reflect somewhat on each of those layers. Listed next are a few counters that relate to specific layers of the OSI model. There will be more information about these counters later, but for now, know that it is important to have a representative mix so a complete picture can be achieved. Table 8.6 shows how certain counters relate to specific layers.

If certain problems are occurring on the network, or you suspect specific problems, you can monitor these areas only. For instance, if you think that recent bottlenecks are caused by problems with RAM, you can monitor the memory, cache, and pagefile counters. If you think problems are occurring due to network throughput, you can monitor protocol and network interface counters. Again, determining how often to update the information is subjective. Updating too often or including too many counters causes the overhead to be high in terms of system resources. If you don't

Table 8.6   Counters and the OSI model's layers.

OSI Layer	Counters
Application and Presentation	Browser, Server, Redirector
Transport	TCP, UDP, NetBEUI, AppleTalk
Network	IP, NWLink, IPX/SPX
Data Link and Physical	Network Interface

update enough, you won't get the information needed to make sound judgments. With practice, you'll figure out what works best for your organization. The next subsection describes many of the most-used counters.

Keeping records of past log files can be useful to track trends and determine growth strategies. You can save log files by right-clicking in the graph and choosing Save As. These files can be saved as Web pages (*.htm) or as reports (*.tsv). They can then be reopened at any time to compare to other logs. In addition, these logs can be saved to databases, where you can use third-party database query software to analyze and draw conclusions based on that data.

Counters

There are around 50 performance objects available for configuration in System Monitor, and each of those objects has anywhere from only a few counters to more than 60 that can be chosen for monitoring. Obviously, you can't monitor everything at the same time, and you might never use any of the more obscure counters, but it is still important to know that there are hundreds available. In Table 8.7, I will introduce the counters I use most often, and describe why those counters might be used. I'll also add, wherever appropriate, the suggested threshold for those counters. (The table entry "n/a" can also mean that the threshold is subjective. For instance, when you're using the Disk Reads/Sec counter for the Physical Disk object, the threshold must be determined from the manufacturer's specifications.) Figure 8.29 shows the Add Counters dialog box.

A combination of certain counters can be used to determine bottlenecks, hardware problems, or network problems. Getting the right combination is a skill learned through lots of time and practice with monitoring networks and systems. However, there is a simple way to monitor a specific object that you believe is the cause of a bottleneck or is the root of a larger problem. When selecting a performance object, such as the processor, you can choose the All Counters option to monitor every counter under that object.

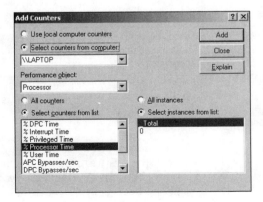

Figure 8.29
The Add Counters dialog box.

Table 8.7   Performance objects, counters, thresholds, and uses.

Performance Object	Counter	Suggested Threshold	Comments
Processor	%Processor Time	85%	Used to determine if the processor is overworked or needs to be upgraded.
Processor	Interrupts/Sec	n/a	Can be high due to a NIC or other hardware problem if system activity isn't also comparatively high. Can be used to locate CPU bottlenecks.
Processor	(_Total)\%Processor Time	n/a	Measures the activity of all of the processors in a system.
Physical disk	%Disk Time	90%	Describes the percentage of time that a disk is busy reading or writing requests.
Physical disk	Disk Reads/Sec and Disk Writes/Sec	n/a	Describes how fast data can be transferred to and from disks. The number here will need to be compared to the drive's specifications obtained from the manufacturer.
Physical disk	Current Disk Queue Length	Determined from the number of available spindles	Represents the number of requests that are waiting for attention from the disk at any given time. If this number remains high, there may be a sustained load on the drive.
Physical disk	Avg. Disk Queue Length	n/a	Represents the average of reads and writes for the disk during the sample period.
Memory	Available Bytes	Less than 4MB	If this number is greater than 4, you might need to add more RAM to the system.
Memory	Pages/Sec	20	Used to determine if page faults are a problem on the system. A number higher than 20 can mean system-wide slowdowns.
Memory	Cache Bytes	n/a	Used with Memory/Available Bytes to determine if there are memory bottlenecks or leaks. Cache Bytes is the sum of many other byte counters.
Paging file	% Usage	99%	Used to determine if the paging file is overworked or too small, and for understanding how much paging activity is happening on the system.
Server	Bytes Total/Sec	n/a	Used to determine how busy the server really is. This number represents the number of bytes that the server has sent to or received from the network.
Server	Work Item Shortages	3	A high number here can mean that services requesting attention are not being dealt with efficiently. This number is derived from how many times the STATUS_DATA_NOT_ACCEPTED result was returned.

(continued)

Table 8.7   Performance objects, counters, thresholds, and uses *(continued).*

Performance Object	Counter	Suggested Threshold	Comments
Server	Sessions Errored Out	n/a	Represents the number of sessions that were ended due to errors or to autodisconnect.
Server	Files Open	n/a	Used to determine how many files are currently open on the server, and can be used to determine the current level of server activity.
Server	Errors Logon	Shouldn't be high	Used to determine if inordinate numbers of bad logon attempts are being made.
Server	Blocking Requests Rejected	n/a	A high number here can represent an overworked server. The MaxWorkItem key in the Registry might need to be adjusted.
Network interface	Bytes Total/Sec	n/a	The rate bytes are sent and received on the network interface.
Network interface	Current Bandwidth	n/a	Used to describe the current bandwidth on the network interface.
Network segment	%Net Utilizations	40% (but it varies)	Used to describe how much of the network is being utilized during a sample period.
Network segment	Total Frames Received/Sec	n/a	Can be used to determine if bridges or routers are causing network communication problems.

By monitoring this way, you can get a great deal of information. Figure 8.30 shows the Performance console and System Monitor with all processor object counters configured.

The Diskperf Utility

In Table 8.7, you were introduced to many of the most commonly used performance objects and their counters. One of those performance objects was Physical Disk, and the Physical Disk counters were available by default. One performance object, Logical Disk, is not enabled by default. This object and its related counters must be enabled manually through the Diskperf utility. To enable Logical Disk, type **diskperf –yv** at a command prompt and reboot the computer.

The most-used counters available with Logical Disk are similar to other counters. They include % Disk Read Time, % Disk Time, % Disk Write Time, % Disk Free Space, % Idle Time, Avg. Disk Bytes (multiple counter options), Disk Bytes/Sec, and Free Megabytes.

Basic Monitoring

In the following examples, you'll learn how to use System Monitor to perform basic monitoring tasks, such as adding counters, deleting counters, getting details about counters, changing to different views, changing counter properties, highlighting counter data, and creating a custom console.

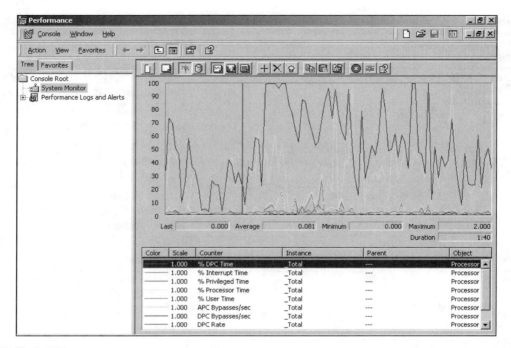

Figure 8.30
The Performance console and System Monitor with all processor object counters configured.

To open System Monitor and add or remove counters, perform the following steps:

1. Open the Performance console by choosing Start|Programs|Administrative Tools|
Performance.

2. To add a counter and begin monitoring the local computer, double-click on System
Monitor in the left pane.

3. Right-click anywhere in the right pane and choose Add Counters, or click on the Add
button (the + sign) in the toolbar at the top of the page.

4. The default performance object is Processor, and the selected counter is %Processor
Time. To add this counter, choose Add and then Close. (You can select additional
counters before closing the window if you'd like.)

5. Click on the arrow in the Performance Object box and select Memory. Notice that
Pages/Sec is highlighted by default. Add this counter; then choose Page Faults/Sec
and add it, too. Choose Close.

6. Choose Start|Programs|Accessories|System Tools|System Information. Notice how the
memory and processor counters in the graph respond to this action.

7. To delete a counter from the graph, highlight the counter that will be deleted (at the bottom of the page), and click on the Delete button (the X) in the toolbar. Delete the rest of the counters.

Getting details about counters and what they represent can also prove quite useful. To see what the available counters do, what their thresholds are (if applicable), and how the numbers are calculated, follow these steps:

1. Open the Performance console by choosing Start|Programs|Administrative Tools| Performance.

2. Right-click anywhere in the right pane and choose Add Counters, or click on the Add toolbar button.

3. In the Add Counters dialog box, select the counter that you would like more information on, and choose Explain. For instance, by choosing the performance object Physical Disk and then % Disk Time (and then Explain), you'll learn that the number calculated is the percentage of elapsed time that the drive is performing either read or write requests. From Table 8.7, you know that a number consistently over 90 percent means that the disk is overworked and may need to be upgraded.

Changing to different views when using System Monitor can be useful when the default graph isn't exactly what you need. While viewing the graph, you are viewing the current activity of the system in Chart view. To see other views, follow these steps:

1. Open the Performance console by choosing Start|Programs|Administrative Tools| Performance.

2. Right-click anywhere in the right pane and choose Add Counters, or click on the Add toolbar button. Add three to five counters.

3. Included on the toolbar are the View Chart button (graph), the View Histogram button, and the View Report button. These icons are left of the Add button (+). Select View Histogram, then View Report.

When you're using a graph, highlighting counter data can be helpful to isolate a particular object or counter. Highlighting is as simple as changing views:

1. Open the Performance console by choosing Start|Programs|Administrative Tools| Performance.

2. Right-click anywhere in the right pane and choose Add Counters, or click on the Add toolbar button. Add three to five counters.

3. Included on the toolbar are the View Chart button (graph), the View Histogram button, and the View Report button. These icons are left of the Add button (+). Make sure that Chart View is selected.

4. At the bottom of the screen, select a counter to highlight—perhaps % Processor Time for the processor object.

5. In the toolbar, select the Highlight button. (It looks like a lightbulb.)

6. Because only one counter can be highlighted at a time, to highlight another counter, simply select a different one from the list at the bottom of the screen. Figure 8.31 shows a custom console with data highlighted.

Creating a custom console might be useful when you need System Monitor to be located in the same console as Computer Management, Event Viewer, or another tool. To create a custom console, follow these steps:

1. Log on as an administrator and type "mmc" in the Start|Run box.

2. From the Console menu, choose Add/Remove Snap-In; then choose Add.

3. Highlight ActiveX Control and choose Add.

4. In the Insert ActiveX Control box, choose Next.

5. In the Control category, select All Categories.

6. In the Control Type box, select System Monitor Controls.

7. Choose Next, type an appropriate name, and choose Finish.

8. In the new console, double-click on the new entry.

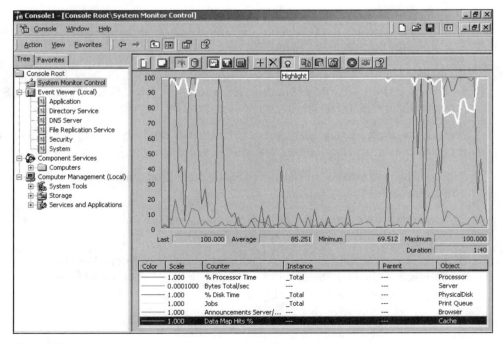

Figure 8.31
A custom Performance console.

Figure 8.31 shows a console that includes several snap-ins: System Monitor Control, Event Viewer, Component Services, and Computer Management. Understand that you can use System Monitor while also accessing these other tools simply by selecting another item in the MMC. Upon returning to the System Monitor tool, you can see that data is still being returned. Also notice that the Data Map Hits % counter for the cache object is highlighted. Data-map hits represent the percentage of time that the requested page was already in the memory at the time of the request.

Advanced Monitoring

In the following examples, you'll learn how to use System Monitor to perform advanced monitoring tasks, such as changing sampling options, changing default settings, monitoring different computers, and copying and printing data by using other applications such as Microsoft Word.

To change sampling options and default settings, you use the System Monitor's Properties sheet. To change the defaults for System Monitor, including appearance and update times, follow these steps:

1. Open the Performance console by choosing Start|Programs|Administrative Tools| Performance.

2. Right-click anywhere in the right pane and choose Properties.

3. On the General tab, set the default options for the following System Monitor properties:

   - *View*—Choose from graph, histogram, or report. Graph is the default.

   - *Display elements*—Choose to display or not to display the legend, value bar, or toolbar. All are selected by default.

   - *Report and histogram data*—Choose between default, current, average, minimum, and maximum.

   - *Appearance and border*—Choose between 3D or flat for the appearance, and choose none or fixed-single for the border.

   - *Updates*—Choose to update automatically every few seconds (you specify how many), or choose not to update automatically. A range of 5 to 15 seconds is good for short- to medium-length monitoring, but a range of 300 to 500 should be used for day-long monitoring.

   - *Duplicate counters*—Choose to allow or not allow duplicate counter instances.

4. On the Source tab, select default behaviors regarding how data should be obtained. Specify that the data should be obtained from current activity on the server or that data should be obtained from a log file. By dragging a bar across the Time Range field, you can modify how much of a specific log file you'd like to see.

5. On the Data tab, you can add counters and modify the colors used for charting them. For instance, the default color for Processor_Total, %Processor Time is red. You can change that color to any other color offered, or change the width or style. Finally, you can change the scale of the graph from default to anywhere between 0.0000001 to 100000000.0.

6. On the Graph tab, you can type a title for the graph and a name for the vertical axis. You can also show a vertical grid, a horizontal grid, and vertical grid numbers, and you can set the maximum and minimum vertical scale.

7. On the Colors tab, you can change the background color from gray to another color, as well as change the colors of borders, title bars, and more.

8. On the Fonts tab, you can change the default font and font size, and configure font effects such as strikeout and underline.

Figure 8.32 shows a specialized System Monitor configuration that includes all of these option changes.

Warning! *If you change the appearance of System Monitor, and you want to see those changes when you open System Monitor next time, you'll have to save the changes. When saving, do not accept the default name, or you will save those changes to the default System Monitor console.*

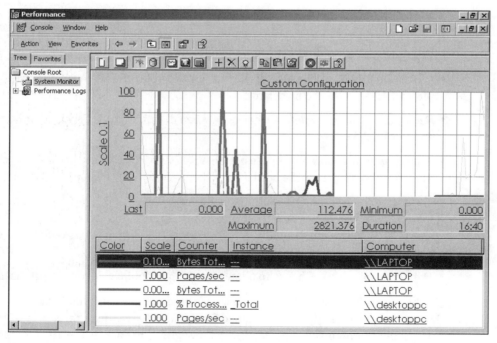

Figure 8.32
System Monitor with a custom configuration.

Monitoring another computer on the network is as simple as choosing the computer to monitor from the Add Counters dialog box. To monitor another computer, follow these steps:

1. Open the Performance console by choosing Start|Programs|Administrative Tools| Performance.

2. Right-click anywhere in the right pane and choose Add Counters.

3. Choose Select Counters From Computer, highlight the computer name that is currently listed, and type the name of a computer you want to monitor.

4. Select the appropriate counters for this computer on the local area network. Figure 8.32 shows two computers being monitored: Laptop and desktoppc.

Warning! *Although there is a down arrow next to the Select Counters From Computer box, you will not see the name of the computer in that box until you've typed it in and System Monitor has made a connection with it. Once that connection has been made, the name will appear in this box the next time you access it.*

You can incorporate Microsoft Office programs and System Monitor in many ways, including copying and printing data by using the clipboard. To incorporate System Monitor and a Microsoft Office application, follow these steps:

1. Open a Microsoft Office application such as Word.

2. Choose View|Toolbars|Control Toolbox.

3. Select the More Controls button (it's the one with a hammer and a wrench) from the toolbox.

4. From the list of controls, choose System Monitor Control.

5. Right-click on the graph and choose Properties. You can change the appearance of the graph by double-clicking on any category and accessing the options through the resulting down arrow. Make changes as necessary.

6. The control is now in design mode, and you can work with the Visual Basic script by right-clicking and choosing View|Code. When the VB GUI is launched, you can right-click on the code to access more options. You can also add counters by choosing the Exit Design Mode button from the toolbar. You can then print or save the data appropriately.

You can also save a graph and open it in another application. Right-click on the graph and choose Save As. Once saved, the graph can be opened in various applications and then printed. In addition, you can press Alt+PrintScreen to take a snapshot of what is shown on the desktop. This picture can then be printed or emailed to another user.

Finding Bottlenecks

To sum up, Table 8.8 lists which tools can be used to detect bottlenecks in the system. If you suspect that the gridlock in your system is due to memory, for instance, you can monitor the counters listed under memory. If you are not sure why the bottleneck is occurring, try these combinations of data one at a time.

As I mentioned earlier, using System Monitor to diagnose and solve bottleneck problems is a skilled art. After some experience with the monitor, you'll become more familiar with the counters and performance objects. Once familiar with these objects, you'll be better able to mix and match counters to solve problems on the network.

Performance Logs And Alerts

The Performance Logs And Alerts snap-in can be accessed through the Performance console the same way that System Monitor is. Performance Logs And Alerts and System Monitor have many other things in common as well. In Performance Logs And Alerts, you can collect performance data from local and remote computers by using counters and performance objects, as with System Monitor. Additionally, you can view this data as it is being collected or save it to a log file. However, because Performance Logs And Alerts runs as a service, data can be collected from local and remote computers even if no user is logged on to the system.

Performance Logs And Alerts has these additional characteristics:

- Logs are created in comma-separated or tab-delimited format, and they can be exported easily to database or spreadsheet programs for further analysis.

- Automatic logs can be configured, and parameters can be set for start and stop times, file names and sizes, and so on.

- Alerts can be configured to send messages when predefined thresholds are met.

- Multiple logs and alerts can run simultaneously.

- Counter logs and trace logs have some preset log settings that can be used when a custom log isn't necessary.

Table 8.8   Bottlenecks

Possible Bottleneck	Objects and Counters to Monitor
Memory	Memory object: Available Bytes and Pages/Sec counters.
Hard Disk	Physical Disk object: %Disk Time, %Idle Time, Disk Read/Sec, and Disk Writes/Sec counters. Logical Disk object: %Free Space counters. Paging File object: all counters.
CPU	Processor object: Interrupts/Sec and %Processor Time counters. Process object: %Processor Time counter.
Network	Network Segment object: %Network Utilization counter. Network Interface object: all Bytes/Sec counters. TCP object: Segments/Sec, Segments Received/Sec, Segments Sent\Sec, Frames Sent/Sec, and Frames Received/Sec counters. Server object: Bytes Total/Sec counter.

Counter Logs

Counter logs are used for the same reasons that System Monitor is: to collect data based on certain counters, such as disk, memory, paging file, processor, and server. Counter logs can be viewed in System Monitor or other applications, depending on how the logs are saved and in what form.

Note: *When you're looking at existing counter and trace logs or configured alerts, a red disk symbol means that the log is stopped, and a green symbol means that the log is started.*

To create a counter log, add counters, and set parameters for the log, follow these steps:

1. Open the Performance console by choosing Start|Programs|Administrative Tools| Performance.

2. Highlight Counter Logs.

3. Right-click in the right pane and choose New Log Settings.

4. Type a name and choose OK.

5. In the resulting dialog box, choose Add.

6. Select the counters you want to add. (For more information on adding counters or what they are used for, refer to the previous section on System Monitor.)

7. On the Log Files tab, change parameters as necessary:

   - Location

   - File name

   - End file names with _____ (sequential numbers or specific date formats), and start numbering at____

   - Log file type (binary, .csv, .tsv, binary circular)

   - Log file size (maximum or limited)

8. On the Schedule tab, you can set when the log should start and stop, and specify whether any commands need to be run when the log file closes. (You might be prompted to create this folder if it is the first time you've used the Counter log; if this happens, choose OK.)

9. To stop the log, save settings, delete the log, refresh the log, or see the log's properties, right-click on the log and make the appropriate choice.

Note: *System Monitor and Performance Logs And Alerts work together. After a log has been created and saved in Logs And Alerts, you can view the log in System Monitor by choosing View Log File Data and browsing to the log you'd like to see.*

Enabling Network Counters

Network counters aren't enabled by default on Windows 2000 Server. Network counters are used to monitor packets that are received through the network adapter. Analyzing these packets, also called *frames*, can help you solve problems with data transfer on local area networks. To enable these counters, you must install the Network Monitor Driver. To install this driver, follow these steps:

1. Log on as an administrator to the Windows 2000 server.

2. In Control Panel, open Network And Dial-Up Connections.

3. Right-click on Local Area Connection, and choose Properties. If Network Monitor Driver is already checked, it is already installed. If not, choose Install.

4. In Select Network Component Type, choose Protocol, then Add.

5. In Select Network Protocol, choose Network Monitor Driver, then OK.

6. If so prompted, insert the Windows 2000 CD-ROM and copy the needed files.

7. Complete the installation by choosing OK and Finish as necessary.

Trace Logs

Trace logs are used for logging computer activity related to system processes, and these logs can be read by third-party applications. To create a trace log, perform the following steps:

1. Open the Performance console by choosing Start|Programs|Administrative Tools| Performance.

2. Highlight Trace Logs.

3. Right-click in the right pane and choose New Log Settings.

4. Type a name and choose OK.

5. In the resulting dialog box, select the General tab and select Events Logged By System Provider. Choices here include Process Creations/Deletions, Thread Creations/Deletions, Disk Input/Output, Network TCP/IP, Page Faults, and File Details. Accept the defaults or configure as needed.

6. The Log Files and Schedule tabs are the same as in the Counter Logs dialog box. Make the appropriate choices, and then select the Advanced tab.

7. On the Advanced tab, you can change the size of the buffer (where trace data is stored temporarily until it is moved to the log file) and the number of buffers.

Note: System Monitor and Performance Logs And Alerts work together. After a log has been created and saved in Logs And Alerts, you can view the log in System Monitor by choosing View Log File Data and browsing to the log you'd like to see.

Alerts

Alerts can be set to send messages to administrators when certain thresholds have been met or exceeded. To configure alerts by using the Performance console, follow these steps:

1. Open the Performance console by choosing Start|Programs|Administrative Tools| Performance.

2. Right-click on Alerts.

3. The context menu includes two options for creating a new log: New Alert Settings and New Alert Settings From. If you have previously created a log and would like to configure alert settings from it, choose the second option; to create a new log entirely, choose the first option. If you choose New Alert Settings From, you'll be asked to browse to the location of the saved log.

4. In either circumstance, you'll see a dialog box similar to the one shown in Figure 8.33. If you have chosen to create a new alert, the boxes shown here will be empty, and you'll need to add counters before continuing. Add the counters you'd like to set alerts for by choosing the Add button.

5. After selecting the counters, set the alert values. In the example in Figure 8.33, the % Disk Time counter for the Physical Disk object is configured so that an alert will occur if the value is over 95 percent. Notice that samples are taken every second by default; you can change this number as well.

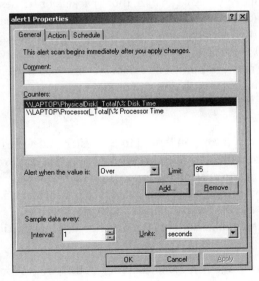

Figure 8.33
Setting an alert.

6. On the Action tab, you can configure what will happen when an alert is triggered. You can have the system do any of the following:

- Log an entry in the application event log (default)

- Send a network message to the person you specify

- Start the Performance data log

- Run a specified program

7. On the Schedule tab, you can specify when to start scanning for the data and when to stop, and what to do when an alert scan finishes. Create a schedule if necessary. Choose OK.

Warning! *Performance logs such as Trace Logs use a lot of disk space. Be careful that you don't forget that a log is being collected, and don't collect data for hours at a time, or you might be surprised when you get an "out of disk space" error.*

Using Network Monitor

Network Monitor isn't used to monitor hardware and software the same way that Systems Monitor is; instead, it is used specifically to monitor network activity. Even though counters having to do with network activity—such as how many packets have been received or discarded or the number of frame errors that occurred—can be configured in the Performance console, it offers no discrete way to analyze those packets or frames or to draw detailed conclusions about the data. Network Monitor not only allows you to capture these network frames, but also offers a GUI for analyzing them. The version of Network Monitor that ships with Windows 2000 Server can be used to monitor only local network traffic, though; if you need to monitor network traffic on remote systems, you'll need to purchase the Network Monitor that is included with SMS 1.2 or 2.

Terms and Concepts

In order to get the most out of Network Monitor, you'll need to understand a few terms and concepts first. When data is sent from one computer to another, it is sent *across the wire*, or across a physical cable or other transmission medium. The data that is sent physically from one computer to another through data lines is sent in binary form, and the data on the wire is called the *data stream*. The data stream consists of frames, sometimes referred to as *packets*, which contain not only the data but also information about the data that is being sent.

For instance, if you sent an email to a colleague on the local network, the physical or logical media along the way (repeater, hub, etc.) need to be able to easily obtain information about the data. The frames tell where the email is going, who it is from, and whether the data has arrived from its last destination safely or needs to be resent, among a host of other things. One email will be broken up into multiple frames, sent out on the wire to the destination address, and reassembled for the end recipient. To get these frames to their destination properly, each frame must contain a store of information. Every frame contains the following information:

- The source address (the originating computer)

- The destination address

- Protocol headers (describing the protocol used to send the frame)

- The data

- A trailer that verifies the data's integrity

When problems occur due to a lack of communication between two computers, and software and hardware have been ruled out as the causes, there might be a problem with these frames. Network Monitor can be used to capture these frames, view them, and analyze them.

Other terms to be familiar with before starting include the following:

- *Broadcast*—Any transmission sent to all members on a network.

- *Capture*—The process of recording frame activity on the physical wire.

- *Parser*—An application that divides protocol information into smaller chunks so Network Monitor can use the information.

- *Trigger*—A specified condition that, when achieved, causes Network Monitor to stop capturing data or execute a specific command.

Installation

Network Monitor isn't installed by default when Windows 2000 Server is installed, but the utility is on the Windows 2000 Server CD-ROM. When you install Network Monitor, the following tools are copied to your machine:

- *Network Monitor Tools*—This utility allows you to capture and analyze frames from the local network.

- *Network Monitor Agent*—This utility allows you to monitor a remote Windows 2000 machine and have the data sent to the Windows 2000 server running Network Monitor. The agent acts as a proxy application for collecting and sending the data.

To install Network Monitor, follow these steps:

1. Log on to the server with applicable permissions to install programs.

2. In the Control Panel, double-click on the Add/Remove Programs icon.

3. Click on Add/Remove Windows Components.

4. Highlight Management And Monitoring Tools and select Details.

5. Make sure that Network Monitor Tools is selected; choose OK, then Next.

6. Work through the Windows Components Wizard.

   Double-click on the Administrative Tools icon in the Control Panel, and notice the new icon for Network Monitor in the Administrative Tools window.

7. Return to the Control Panel and double-click on the Network And Dial-up Connections icon.

8. Right click on the local area connection and choose Properties. The Network Monitor Driver is now available in the components box.

Understanding the Network Monitor GUI

The Network Monitor interface contains many features. Before using Network Monitor, you should be familiar with navigating the utility. Figure 8.34 shows the interface.

The top-left frame is where captured data is shown in bar graph form. Data shown includes % Network Utilization, Frames Per Second, Bytes Per Second, Broadcasts Per Second, and Multicasts Per Second. These graphs represent the highest value found during the capture. The frame directly beneath that shows information related to captured

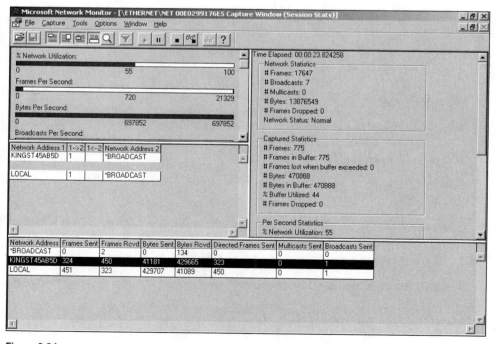

Figure 8.34
Network Monitor.

frames between two network addresses. The bottom of the screen displays additional information about the capture frames. The right frame displays statistics concerning the network and captured frames.

All tasks are done through the menus at the top of the window:

- *File*—This menu contains the usual Open, Save As, and Exit commands.

- *Capture*—This menu is probably new to you because no other Windows applications have a Capture menu option. This menu has several choices, the most used being Start And Stop, Stop And View, Pause, Continue, Display Captured Data, Clear Statistics, Addresses, Networks, and Trigger. This is the menu you'll first become familiar with when learning how to use Network Monitor.

- *Tools*—This menu can be used to identify network monitor users, find routers, resolve address, or access the Performance console.

- *Options* and *Window*—These menus are used to alter the appearance and behavior of Network Monitor.

Capturing Data

Capturing data is the heart of Network Monitor and is the reason for its existence. To begin capturing data, perform the following steps:

1. Open Network Monitor by choosing Start|Programs|Administrative Tools|Network Monitor.

2. Choose Capture|Start.

3. Once started, the capture can be stopped or paused from the Capture menu. After a minute or two, stop the capture.

4. Choose Capture|Display Captured Data.

Figure 8.35 shows captured data as accessed from the Capture menu. Notice that data has been captured between two computers (one with a name and one with a TCP/IP address), different protocols were used in the transfer, and a description of the transfer is included.

Capture Filters

You can see in Figure 8.35 that many different types of data are being captured. What if you wanted to capture only frames related to TCP, frames from a certain address pair, or frames that show a specific data pattern? That is where capture filters come in. You can filter captures by protocol (Service Access Point and EtherType), address, or data pattern.

To enable protocol capture filters, follow these steps:

1. Open Network Monitor by choosing Start|Programs|Administrative Tools|Network Monitor.

2. Choose Capture|Filter (or press F8).

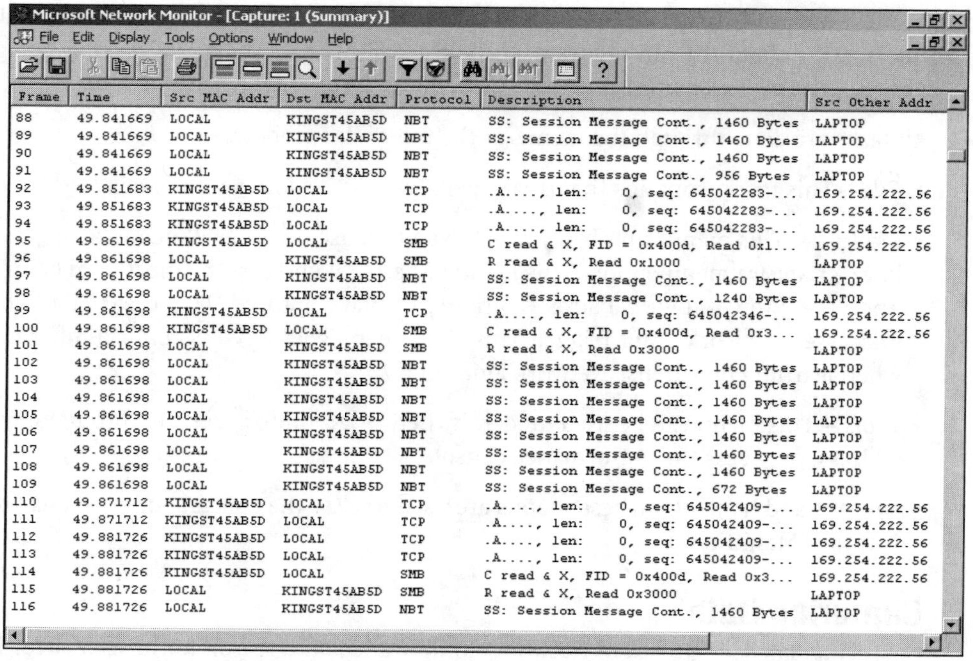

Figure 8.35
Captured data.

3. In the Capture Filter dialog box, double-click on SAP/ETYPE = Any SAP or AnyETYPE.

4. From the Capture Filter SAPs And EYPEs box, select Disable All.

5. Scroll through the choices and select the protocols you'd like to capture. Then choose Enable. Figure 8.36 shows a capture filter for TCP only. Only the choices shown in the Enabled Protocols section will be enabled. Choose OK twice.

6. Follow the procedure under "Capturing Data" again, and notice the difference in the data collected. Only data having to do with TCP will be collected.

To enable address capture filters, follow these steps:

1. Open Network Monitor by choosing Start|Programs|Administrative Tools|Network Monitor.

2. Choose Capture|Filter (or press F8).

3. Double-click on address pairs. (If you've created a SAP/ETYPE filter in the previous example, set it to Enable All before configuring address pairs to get a good picture of what happens when only address pairs are filtered.)

4. To filter data captures between two specific computers, in the left pane, select the computer at the first station, and in the right pane, select the computer at the

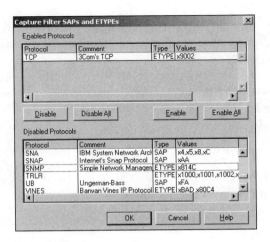

Figure 8.36
Filtering captures by protocol.

second station. Choose an arrow from the following list to specify which data will be captured:

- <—>—Captures data moving from station 1 to station 2 as well as from station 2 to station 1.

- —>—Captures data moving from station 1 to station 2 only.

- <——Captures data moving from station 2 to station 1 only.

5. If you are configuring which computers will be included in the frame capture, make sure the Include option is chosen. If you want to capture all frames *except* the data moving between these computers, make sure the Exclude option is chosen. Select OK.

6. Follow the procedure under "Capturing Data" again, and notice the difference in the data collected. Only data moving between these two computers will be captured (assuming that you chose Include).

To enable data-pattern capture filters, follow these steps:

1. Open Network Monitor by choosing Start|Programs|Administrative Tools|Network Monitor.

2. Choose Capture|Filter (or press F8).

3. Double-click on Pattern Matches.

4. In the dialog box, type the pattern of data you are looking for in either Hex or ASCII code. Specify where in the frame the data should be in the other data boxes. Choose OK.

Capture Triggers

Capture triggers can be set to capture an action that takes place when a set of conditions is met. You can set a trigger so that a network capture stops if a certain condition is met. This allows Network Monitor to respond to an event on the network when it happens. You can configure the operating system to start a batch file or executable file when Network Monitor detects a particular set of conditions on the network. When you're configuring capture triggers, you have the following options:

- *Nothing*—The default setting; no triggers.

- *Pattern Match*—Similar to filtering by data pattern; allows triggers to be configured when a particular pattern has been found in a captured frame.

- *Buffer Space*—Can be configured so that when the buffer space becomes 25, 50, 75, or 100 percent full, an executable file can be run.

- *Pattern Match Then Buffer Space*—Configured for when a pattern-match and buffer-space configuration match is met, in that order.

- *Buffer Space Then Pattern Match*—Configured for when a buffer-space and pattern-match configuration is met, in that order.

When any of these trigger matches have been met, one of three things can be configured: stop the capture, create an audible signal, or execute a command or application.

Note: When data is captured, it is stored in the server's memory buffer. The default setting for the memory buffer is the total amount of memory on the server minus 8MB. You can change the size of this buffer through the Capture menu. The data isn't saved to the hard disk until you choose File|Save As. Besides configuring the memory buffer size, you can also change the frame size. It might become important to change the frame size if there is a lot of network traffic and the memory buffer fills up quickly. For instance, you might want to filter only by source address if you're not interested in the header or data.

Analyzing Captured Data

Capturing the data was the easy part, but what does all of this information mean? You'll probably have someone in your organization far more experienced in reading this data than you are, or for problems like these, you might even hire a consultant or save the data and send it out to hardware or software support personnel. However, an introduction to what the captured data represents is certainly in line here.

There are two ways to view captured data frames, as you are aware. Figures 8.34 and 8.35 showed these two types of data representation. In Figure 8.34, the data shown was captured by choosing Capture|Stop And View; in Figure 8.35, the data shown was captured by choosing Capture|Display Captured Data. In this latter display mode, you can see more information concerning a specific frame by double-clicking on that frame. Figure 8.37 shows the resulting screen.

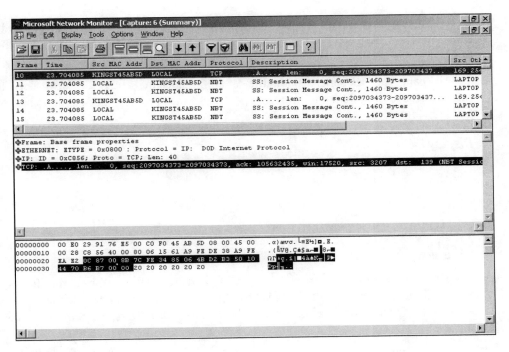

Figure 8.37
Analyzing captured data.

When you're looking at this data, notice that there are three panes containing data related to the frame you chose. The top pane is the Summary pane; this contains a single line for each frame captured in the buffer. This single line contains the following entries:

- *Frame*—Each captured frame is numbered from 1 to *n*. You can change the start number of the capture when initially configuring Network Monitor.

- *Time*—This entry tells you when the frame was captured.

- *Src MAC Addr*—This entry tells you where the data originated. This can be a NetBIOS name or a hexadecimal address.

- *Dst MAC Addr*—This entry tells you where the data is going. This can be a NetBIOS name or a hexadecimal address.

- *Protocol*—This entry specifies which protocol is associated with the frame.

- *Description*—This entry contains details about the frame and the protocol.

The middle pane is the Details pane, where the contents of the frame are arranged by the protocol layer they belong to. In Figure 8.37, notice that there are notes about the ETYPE being Ethernet, the Protocol IP, TCP, and information concerning acknowledgment number, sequence number, source and destination information, and NBT. You can obtain more information about all of these by double-clicking on them in the Details pane. Each time a different item is highlighted in this pane, the hex values related to this item are highlighted as well.

The last pane, the Hex pane, displays the data in hexadecimal and ASCII form. This data can be decoded by system engineers, support personnel, programmers, and other quali-fied individuals.

Display Filters

You can set display filters similar to the capture filters set earlier. Three display filters are available:

- Protocol

- Address

- Property

Protocol and Address filters are self-explanatory and are similar to the capture filters described earlier. Property filters are set to filter by property instances such as DNS, Comment, Ethernet, IP, Java, and NBT. To set these display filters, perform the following steps:

1. Open Network Monitor by choosing Start|Programs|Administrative Tools|Network Monitor.

2. Capture some data as described earlier.

3. Choose Capture|Display Captured Data.

4. From this display, choose Display|Filter.

5. Double-click on ANY <—-> ANY. This takes you to the Expression dialog box.

6. To configure a filter by address, select the Address tab, and under Station 1, select a computer.

7. To complete the configuration, select another computer from Station 2. In the Direction box, select either <—-> or —-> to specify the direction of displayed data between the two computers. Choose OK.

8. To configure filtering by protocol, double-click on Protocol = = Any from the Display Filter dialog box. (Or, if you are still in the Expression dialog box, select the Protocol tab.)

9. Select Disable All; then scroll through the list and enable the protocol(s) you want to filter by.

10. In the Expression dialog box, select the Property tab. This is similar to the data pattern filter in Capture configurations. Select the protocol in question, select specific items for that protocol, and select the appropriate relationship. For instance, choosing IP as the protocol offers item choices of Checksum, Flags, Header Length, Security Level, and more. Choose OK twice.

Summary

In this chapter you learned about the many ways you can optimize the performance of your Windows 2000 server. These performance enhancements can increase both performance and security. Although some of the ways mentioned involve upgrading the server's memory, hard drive, or CPU, there are other, less expensive ways as well.

You learned about disk optimization utilities available through Administrative Tools, including Check Disk, Disk Defragmenter, and Disk Cleanup, as well as system utilities and tools for configuring disk quotas and pagefiles. You also learned how Redundant Array of Independent Disks (RAID) can improve read/write performance and provide fault tolerance for the network and its users.

The Task Manager can be used to manage processes, stop and start processes, and view the performance of the computer's resources. You also learned about process priorities, process levels, and threads. Task Manager can also be used for to see which programs are running, which processes are running, and how the computer is performing.

The Event Viewer was detailed, and the application log and the system log were introduced. You learned about event types, including the meaning of the errors warning, information, success, and failure icons. This chapter also discussed how to archive an event log, set logging options, and use event headers.

Additional performance topics included QoS Admission Control, the Backup utility, and the Backup And Restore Wizard. The Simple Network Management Protocol (SNMP) service was also introduced for monitoring remote computer systems.

Finally, you learned just about all there is to know about the Performance console and System Monitor. System Monitor is used to collect and view real-time performance data on either a local computer or a remote one and to present that data in many different forms. You also learned about Network Monitor, which is used to monitor network activity. Successfully integrating all of these tools and this knowledge can greatly enhance your server's performance.

Moving Forward

In the next chapter, you'll learn about optimizing security; you'll learn how to configure auditing, how to use security templates, and what can be accomplished using Event Viewer's security logs. You'll also learn about Windows 2000 Server's licensing terms, and what you're really saying when you accept the licensing agreement during installation. Also in the next chapter, you'll learn how the Computer Management console can be used to tie together all of the utilities and tools you've learned about in this chapter and the next. Computer Management offers a place to manage and configure many aspects of server management, including sections for System Tools, Storage, and Services and Applications.

Chapter 9

Optimizing Security and Managing the Computer

Optimizing the security of your servers and managing them effectively are just as important as optimizing the performance. Just as with optimizing performance, there are multiple ways to optimize security. In this chapter, you'll learn about configuring auditing, using security templates, and encrypting data. You'll also learn how to enable and use Event Viewer's security logs. Kerberos and IPSec can be configured as well and will also be discussed. Finally, for the sake of maintaining compliance with Microsoft's licensing agreement, and to keep the network secure against auditors, licensing modes and the licensing agreement will be discussed.

Following this, you will learn how the Computer Management console can be used to tie together everything you've been introduced to in this chapter and in previous chapters. In Computer Management, you can access system tools such as Event Viewer, Performance Logs And Alerts, and Device Manager, all for enhancing performance, in one central location. You can also access Shared Folders, Disk Management, Local Users And Groups, and Services And Applications, used for enhancing security, all in that same central location. From the Computer Management console, you can even change the IPSec Agent Policies and Kerberos Key Distribution Center properties.

Optimizing Security

To optimize the security of your network, you can configure auditing for the domain controllers and the member servers. These audit logs can be saved and viewed later for comparison and maintenance. Another optimization feature is Event Viewer. In this section you'll learn how both can be used to optimize the network.

Understanding and Configuring Auditing

If you looked at the Event Viewer's security log when you were looking at the system and applications logs in the last chapter, you might have noticed it was empty. This is because the Event Viewer's security log holds information that is collected by auditing events in domains (logged-on domain controllers) or events that are local to a machine (logged-on member servers). Because auditing is not enabled by default, the log is initially empty.

Before going any further, follow these steps to enable some simple security logging for a domain controller:

1. Log on as an administrator.

2. Choose Start|Programs|Administrative Tools|Active Directory Users And Computers.

3. Expand the domain name tree, and select the Domain Controllers folder.

4. Right-click on the Domain Controllers folder, and choose Properties.

5. Select the Group Policy tab, highlight a group policy, and choose Edit.

6. Locate the Audit Policy in the console tree by expanding Computer Configuration/ Windows Settings/Security Settings/Local Policies/Audit Policy.

Note: *The policy can also be set under Domain Security Policy in Administrative Tools.*

7. Notice that there are nine items that can be audited. These items are described in Table 9.1. Choose at least one event you'd like to audit, and double-click on it. For instance, you might select Audit Account Logon Events to audit which user accounts are requesting logon validation.

8. In the resulting dialog box, shown in Figure 9.1, you can choose to audit successful logon validations, unsuccessful logon validations, or both. Because a large number of unsuccessful logon attempts could signify a security risk, such as attempts by hackers or others to gain unwanted access to the network, this is a good place to start auditing. Check Failure, Success, or both.

9. Notice that the Computer Setting has now changed from Not Defined or No Auditing to Failure (or Success, depending on the choice). Make other auditing choices as needed.

10. To view new entries in the security log, return to Event Viewer and select the security log. (You might need to right-click on the security log and choose Refresh, or perhaps even wait for an event to be written.)

So how do you decide which items to audit? If you audit too many items, the logs will fill up quickly and take up valuable disk space. Excessive auditing will also take its toll on

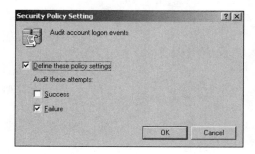

Figure 9.1
Auditing unsuccessful logon validations.

network performance. Table 9.1 describes the items available for audit and is followed by reasons you should audit certain items. This information can help you create an audit policy that is effective in your specific environment.

As you can see from Table 9.1, you can monitor several items. Before you begin monitoring indiscriminately, though, you should know a little more about auditing and the effect it can have on your system.

Auditing

Audit entries take up a lot of disk space. Each entry in the security log in Event Viewer contains information about the type of event that was recorded, the date, the time, the source, the category (if applicable), the event number, the user, and the computer that generated the event. Of course, the event is also recorded as a success or failure. Auditing successes can quickly fill up an event log, so you should be aware of some techniques for auditing that will enhance your auditing configuration. Microsoft calls these "Best Practices," and because they are so useful, I believe that summarizing them here is important:

- Audit successes and failures for logon and logoff because a high number of these events can suggest that a hacker is trying to access the network or that a random password generator is in use.

- Audit successes for logon and logoff because a stolen password can be used to break into the network. Knowing which user or computer that logon came from, what time it was generated, and so on can be very helpful when problems arise.

Table 9.1   Items available for auditing.

Item	Description of Event
Account logon event	Occurs when the domain controller is sent a request to authenticate or validate a user account.
Account management	Occurs when a user account is renamed, disabled, or enabled, or if the password is changed or set, or when an administrator creates, changes, or deletes a user account or a group.
Directory service access	Occurs when a user accesses an object stored in Active Directory. To configure this, you must select objects individually and configure them separately. You can use Active Directory Users And Computers for this task.
Logon event	Occurs when a user logs on or off, or when a network connection is made or lost.
Object access	Occurs when a user accesses a file, folder, or printer. As with Directory Service Access, due to the number of objects available, these must be configured separately.
Policy change	Occurs when a change is made to a user's rights, audit policies, or security options, or any other policy change occurs.
Privilege use	Occurs when a user has exercised a right that does not include logging on or off.
Process tracking	Occurs when an application performs an illegal action, such as requesting an invalid memory address or altering a restricted file. This information can be useful to engineers, programmers, and application designers.
System event	Occurs when a user restarts or shuts down a computer, and includes any other event that affects the system.

- Audit successes for changes to user rights, user and group management, security change policies, restarts, shutdowns, and other system events. A high success rate here may indicate that privileges are being misused or that certain users have the ability to change their rights, group membership, or security settings.

- Audit successes and failures for objects such as printers and object-access events. You can use these figures to determine if certain users are improperly accessing printers.

- Audit successes and failures for file and object access if you believe that certain users are accessing sensitive data.

- Audit successes and failures for writing to program files and process tracking. Unexpected attempts to modify applications or to create processes might indicate a virus outbreak or attack.

For auditing to be set up on a computer, the computer must be configured with NTFS, not FAT, and the user must either be logged on as an administrator or have the Manage Auditing And Security Log permission for the computer. Decision Tree 9.1 can be used to help you decide what to configure for auditing.

Auditing for Member Servers

Turning on security logging for a member server running Windows 2000 is similar to the steps for configuring security logging for domain controllers. To configure security logging for member servers, follow the steps listed next:

Note: *This is the same process for enabling security logging on a Windows 2000 Professional machine.*

1. Log on as an administrator on either a Windows 2000 member server or a Windows 2000 Professional machine.

2. Open a preconfigured console that has the Group Policy snap-in added, or configure one by choosing Start|Run, entering "mmc /a" in the Open box, and adding the snap-in to the console.

3. Expand the tree to find the Audit Policy. You'll find it in this path: Local Computer Policy/Computer Configuration/Windows Settings/Security Settings/Local Policies/ Audit Policy.

4. Click on the event you'd like to audit, and then choose Action|Security. You can also simply double-click on the event.

5. Configure success or failure as needed for the events chosen.

Advanced Auditing Tasks

To enable auditing on specific objects, files, or folders, or to enable auditing of directory service access or object access on a Windows 2000 domain controller, perform the following steps:

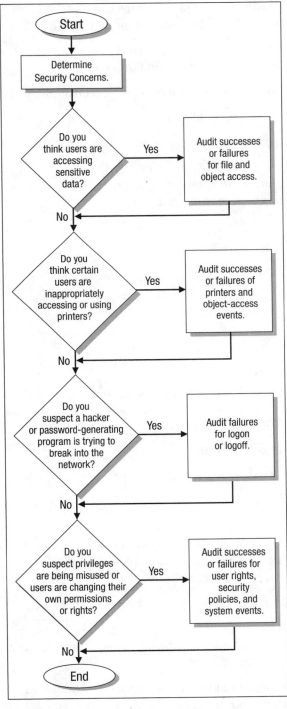

Decision Tree 9.1
Auditing.

1. Log on as an administrator or with permission to manage auditing and security. To set auditing on files and folders, make sure the drive is formatted with NTFS.

2. Use Windows Explorer to locate the file or folder you want to audit, or open the Active Directory Users And Computers console to find the object.

3. Right-click on the object, choose Properties, and select the Security tab.

4. Click on Advanced, and then select the Auditing tab.

5. Choose Add to add a user or a group for auditing. Double-click on the user or group to add it.

6. In the Auditing Entry For <filename, folder name, object name> box, select where to apply the auditing. This can be any of the following:

   • This folder only

   • This folder, subfolders, and files (default)

   • This folder and subfolders

   • This folder and files

   • Subfolders and files only

   • Subfolders only

   • Files only

7. Place a checkmark in the boxes to represent how you want to configure auditing for this folder. Be very careful that you don't go overboard; too much auditing takes up too much disk space. Choose OK three times.

To view and save the audit logs, follow these steps:

1. Log on as an administrator and choose Start|Programs|Administrative Tools| Event Viewer.

2. Click on Security Log.

3. Notice the log types of entries: A yellow key represents a successful audit, and a lock represents a failure audit. To view a particular event, double-click on it. Figure 9.2 shows an event failure related to a failed logon request.

4. To save this log file, choose Action|Save Log File As and enter a name for the file. The file is saved as a *.evt file.

Note: *From the Action menu, you can also open an existing log file, clear all events in the log file, rename or refresh the log file, or see the file's properties.*

In highly secure environments, you may need to halt the computer if the security log gets full. For instance, if you suspect a virus, password generating, or hacker attack, you can configure the computer to stop responding when the security log auditing these events

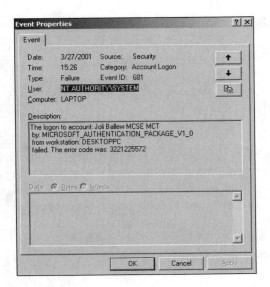

Figure 9.2
Event failure.

gets full. To configure the computer to stop when the security log is full, perform the following steps:

1. Log on as an administrator.

2. Choose Start|Programs|Administrative Tools|Event Viewer.

3. Right-click on the security log and choose Properties.

4. On the General tab, choose Overwrite Events Older Than *n* Days, or Do Not Overwrite Events (Clear Log Manually).

5. Use the Registry Editor to create or assign the following Registry-key value:

    Under HKEY_LOCAL_MACHINE\SYSTEM, expand the CurrentControlSet\ Control\Lsa tree, choose CrashOnAuditFail, and change the value to 1.

Warning! *Edit the Registry with extreme caution, and always back up the system first. Incorrect changes to the Registry can cause the system to fail to boot or to require reinstallation.*

6. Restart the computer.

If the server is configured in this way, the security log will need to be manually cleared before the server will be functional. To do this, you'll need to perform the following steps:

1. Restart the computer.

2. Log on as an administrator.

3. Open Event Viewer, and either save or clear the event log.

4. Open the Registry Editor, delete the value of 1 (in the key specified previously), and type it again.

5. Restart the computer.

Note: *If you aren't fond of editing the Registry, you can set the Local Security policy to shut down the system if it is unable to log security audits.*

Configuring Event Viewer

Event Viewer and auditing are used together to create logs for enhancing security. Event Viewer is originally set up with default settings for a maximum log size of 512KB, and logs older than seven days will be overwritten. If you are collecting these security logs to calculate growth, view trends, or collect security events for later use, you will need to change these defaults so the logs can be saved instead of overwritten. To change the defaults associated with Event Viewer, simply open Event Viewer, right-click on the security log, and choose Properties. From there, you can make the following changes on the General tab:

• *Display Name*—The name *Security Log* can be changed.

• *Maximum Log Size*—This number can be increased so that more space is available or less space is used, depending on the need.

• *Overwrite Events As Needed*—When the log is full, events will be overwritten.

• *Overwrite Events Older Than ___ Days*—Seven days is the default, but this number can be changed. You can configure it for 365 days if you want.

• *Do Not Overwrite Events (Clear Log Manually)*—Choose this if the logs should be cleared manually, in cases where each log needs to be saved.

From the Filter tab, you can filter events by event type (Information, Warning, Error, Success Audit, or Failure Audit), by event source, by category, by event ID, by user, by computer, or by date. These filters can be useful if you are looking for improper access by a specific user or computer.

Understanding the Security Configuration And Analysis Snap-In and the Security Templates Snap-In

Three main snap-ins are used to secure the network: the Group Policy snap-in, the Security Configuration And Analysis snap-in, and the Security Templates snap-in. These three utilities can be used together to form a shield of protection for the network. The Security Configuration And Analysis snap-in is used for configuring and analyzing the local computer. The Security Templates snap-in is used to create and assign security templates to one or more computers (using low, medium, or high security). The Group Policy snap-in can be combined with these snap-ins so that administrators can apply the security levels offered by the templates to the entire enterprise.

The Security Configuration And Analysis Snap-In

The Security Configuration And Analysis snap-in can be used to analyze and configure local system security. This configuration can be configured manually or by using one of the many available templates available with the Security Templates snap-in (discussed later). When these templates are applied to a local computer group policy object (GPO), the local computer can be protected from harm easily, immediately, and with an optimal level of defense.

Besides incorporating templates for security of the local machine, the Security Configuration And Analysis snap-in can be used to analyze the current state of security on the computer. Analyzing the computer for security flaws on a regular basis can prove most useful in catching defects before they become full-blown problems. The concern with changes in a computer's security configuration comes from the fact that often, when a program is installed, a certain administrative task is performed, or a group policy is changed, the result is that the computer no longer meets mandatory security requirements.

The Security Configuration And Analysis snap-in is a complicated utility. Using this snap-in, you can perform the following tasks:

- Resolve discrepancies between current security and network security requirements.

- Pay attention to or ignore suggestions by the utility regarding current security configuration, flaws, or lapses in security.

- Apply security to existing databases.

- Configure system security.

- Import and export security templates.

- Analyze system security.

- Edit an existing security configuration.

The Security Templates Snap-In

The Security Templates snap-in can be used with the Security Configuration And Analysis snap-in to set security for one or more computers on the network. The Security Templates snap-in offers many templates, and because these templates vary in level from low to highly secure, a template most likely exists that will fit your organization. These templates are simply files that contain security settings that can be applied to the local computer or to a GPO for the purpose of securing it. Security templates apply account-policy settings, including passwords, account lockouts, and Kerberos; and local-policy settings such as user rights and security event logging. Templates also have predefined policies for local group membership administration, the Registry, the local file system, and system services.

Several types of security templates are available through the snap-in. The levels include Basic, Compatible, Secure, Highly Secure, and Dedicated Domain Controller. In most instances, there is a security template of each level for both a workstation and a server. Because each template maintains a different level of security, a template such as basicdc is much less restrictive than a template such as hisecdc (think *basic security* for a *domain controller* and *high security* for a *domain controller* when you read these names). The five template levels and their templates are described in the following list.

Note: Security templates can be used only on Windows 2000 NTFS file systems, not FAT, and they are stored by default in the C:\Winnt\Security\Templates folder.

- *Basic (basicdc, basicsv, basicwk)*—Basic security configuration is available for domain controllers, servers, and workstations. This configuration is used to reverse other security configurations and return the level of security to the Windows default. These settings are applied to every aspect of security except for user rights.

- *Compatible (compatws)*—Compatible security configuration is available for workstations. This security configuration gives the local Users group strict security settings, while members of the Power Users group have a less strict environment. If Power Users need to run non-Windows-compatible applications, they can do so with these default settings; local users can run only certified applications.

- *Secure (securedc, securews)*—Secure configurations are available for domain controllers and workstations. These templates operate under suggested security settings for all security areas except files, folders, and Registry keys. File and registry permissions are configured tightly by default.

- *Highly Secure (hisecdc, hisecws)*—Highly secure configurations are available for domain controllers and workstations. These templates are used to tighten network communications. Computers using this template can communicate only with other computers using the same settings. Because these templates apply only to Windows 2000 machines on NTFS volumes, communication cannot be achieved between computers running on other operating systems, such as Windows NT or 9x.

- *Dedicated Domain Controller (dedicadc)*—This configuration is used for local user security on domain controllers.

Using the Security Configuration And Analysis and Security Templates Snap-Ins

You might have installed the Security Configuration And Analysis snap-in in the last chapter to configure Event Viewer properties, so you might be somewhat familiar with this process. However, because you'll also need to install the Security Templates snap-in, set a working database, edit the template, create a database, import and export templates, and analyze current security settings, I'll review the procedure for installing the required snap-ins first.

Installing the Security Configuration And Analysis and Security Templates Snap-Ins

To install the Security Configuration And Analysis and Security Templates snap-ins, follow these steps:

1. Log on as an administrator and type "mmc" at the Run command line.

2. From the Console menu, choose Add/Remove Snap-in and then choose Security Configuration And Analysis and Security Templates. Choose the Add button and then Close.

3. Save the console as Security.msc.

Note: *In the following examples, I'll assume you are logged on appropriately and are using this Security console with these two templates added as snap-ins.*

Creating a New Database for Applying Security and Importing a Template

To create a new database for applying security and importing a template, follow these steps:

1. Open the Security console created earlier.

2. Highlight Security Configuration And Analysis, and read the information in the right pane. This is shown in Figure 9.3.

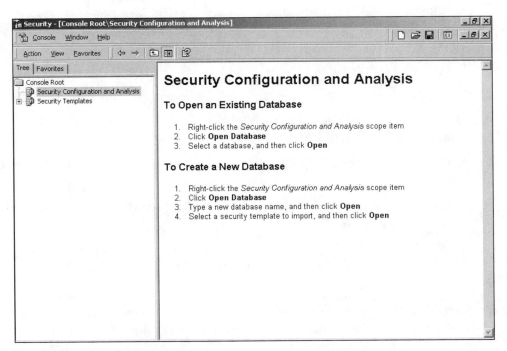

Figure 9.3
Security Configuration And Analysis in the Security console.

3. Right-click on Security Configuration And Analysis, and choose Open Database.

4. In the File Name box, type a name for the new database. I'll call mine "Database1". Choose OK.

5. In the Import Template dialog box, select a template to use as a base for your new database. Choose a security template that suits your needs. I'll choose basicdc.inf.

6. If you do not receive an error, proceed to Step 9. If you do receive an error stating that this configuration is invalid, right-click on Security Configuration And Analysis again, but this time choose Configure Computer Now. Accept the defaults.

7. If you had to perform Step 6, perform this step as well. Right-click on Security Configuration And Analysis, and choose Analyze Computer Now. Accept the defaults.

8. If you had to perform Steps 6 and 7, right-click on Security And Configuration Analysis, and choose Open Database. The database you named will be in the File Name box. Open the database.

9. Expand the Security Configuration And Analysis tree.

10. From the Console menu, choose Save.

Configuring System Security

To configure system security, simply set a working database, right-click on Security Configuration And Analysis, and choose Configure System Now. If you have previously assigned a template such as basicdc.inf and now would like to switch to a different template with higher security, perform the following steps:

1. Open the Security console created earlier.

2. Right-click on Security Configuration And Analysis, and choose Import Template.

3. In the Import Template dialog box, choose another template. I'll choose hisecdc.inf. Check the box Clear This Database Before Importing.

4. Right-click on Security Configuration And Analysis, and choose Configure Computer Now. Accept the defaults.

5. Right-click on Security Configuration And Analysis, and choose Analyze Computer Now. Accept the defaults.

6. To see the default settings for the database and computer, expand Account Policies| AccountLockoutPolicy and view the settings in the right pane.

Editing a Security Template

If you decide to apply a security template for managing a system, you can modify the existing template to suit your own needs. In the security template hisecdc.inf, the default lockout is five invalid attempts. You can change this setting (and others) if you want. To edit the security template, follow these steps:

1. Open the Security console created earlier.

2. Expand the trees under Account Policies, Local Policies, and Event Log. Select Password Policy under Account Policies.

3. Double-click on Enforce Password History. In the hisecdc.inf template, the default setting is that the password history is enforced and the password history remembers the last 24 passwords. To change this number, simply change it in the dialog box and choose OK.

4. Perform Step 3 again to change another policy setting.

5. When finished, save the console.

There are several templates and many settings available for configuration. The settings for the hisecdc.inf template are detailed in Table 9.2. Knowing how this template is configured will assist you in making decisions regarding changes to the template, or perhaps you will decide on a more or less secure template for your network.

Note: *There are many user rights and security options. Check the individual templates for configuration information.*

Analyzing the Current System Settings and Reviewing the Results

If you've changed the basic template settings, if security changes have been made to solve a network or communication problem, or if any other event has compromised system security, then the analysis part of the Security Configuration And Analysis snap-in will come in handy. Because many events can cause these security changes, you should analyze the current security of your systems often.

To analyze and review current system settings, follow these steps:

1. Open the Security console created earlier.

2. Right-click on Security Configuration And Analysis, and choose Analyze Computer Now. Accept the defaults.

3. When the analysis is complete, expand Account Policies and Local Policies, and look at the policies underneath each. Figure 9.4 shows the Account Policies/Password Policy settings.

In Figure 9.4, notice that there are white circles with checkmarks in them and red circles with white x's in them. The white circle indicates that the policy setting currently meets the proposed level of security. The red circle indicates that the current setting does not meet the proposed level of security. In this example, the maximum password age is set at 30 days in the database, but the template suggests that the setting be 42 days. To change the password age, simply double-click on the policy and make the appropriate changes.

You can also view the log file by clicking on Security Configuration And Analysis after analyzing the security settings of the machine. Figure 9.5 shows a part of this log file and the information regarding the password age discrepancy and other mismatches.

Table 9.2   Default security settings for the hisecdc.inf template.

Policy Type	Policy Component	Policy	Hisecdc.inf Setting
Account Policies	Password Policy	Enforce password history	24 remembered
Account Policies	Password Policy	Maximum password age	42 days
Account Policies	Password Policy	Minimum password age	2 days
Account Policies	Password Policy	Minimum password length	8 characters
Account Policies	Password Policy	Passwords must meet complexity requirements	Enabled
Account Policies	Password Policy	Store passwords using reversible encryption	Disabled
Account Policies	Account Lockout Policy	Account lockout duration	0
Account Policies	Account Lockout Policy	Account lockout threshold	5
Account Policies	Account Lockout Policy	Reset account lock counter after	30 minutes
Account Policies	Kerberos Policy	Enforce user logon restrictions	Enabled
Account Policies	Kerberos Policy	Maximum lifetime for service ticket	600 minutes
Account Policies	Kerberos Policy	Maximum lifetime for user ticket	10 hours
Account Policies	Kerberos Policy	Maximum lifetime for user ticket renewal	7 days
Account Policies	Kerberos Policy	Maximum tolerance for computer clock synchronization	5 minutes
Local Policies	Audit Policy	Audit account logon events	Success, Failure
Local Policies	Audit Policy	Audit account management	Success, Failure
Local Policies	Audit Policy	Audit Directory Service Access	Success, Failure
Local Policies	Audit Policy	Audit logon events	Success, Failure
Local Policies	Audit Policy	Audit object access	Success, Failure
Local Policies	Audit Policy	Audit policy change	Success, Failure
Local Policies	Audit Policy	Audit privilege use	Success, Failure
Local Policies	Audit Policy	Audit process tracking	No auditing
Local Policies	Audit Policy	Audit system events	Success, Failure
Local Policies	User Rights Assignment	No user rights are set for basic.inf	
Local Policies	Security Options	Amount of idle time before disconnecting session	15 minutes
Local Policies	Security Options	Automatically log off users when logon time expires	Enabled
Local Policies	Security Options	Number of previous logons to cache	10 logons
Local Policies	Security Options	Prompt user to change password	14 days
Local Policies	Security Options	Unsigned driver installation behavior	Do not allow installation

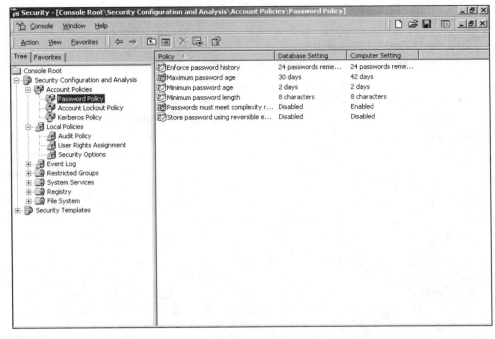

Figure 9.4
Security analysis: password policy settings.

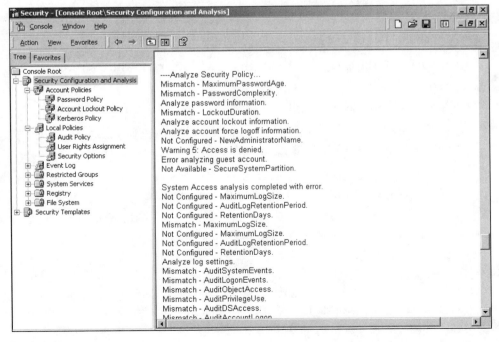

Figure 9.5
A log file with analyzed security settings.

Exporting Security Templates

Exporting the template you've created is as simple as right-clicking on Security Configuration And Analysis and choosing Export Template. When you export the template, it can be saved to the templates folder and used on other computers or by other users.

Encryption

Another way to optimize the security of the domain controller and the network is to use encryption techniques. Encrypting File System (EFS), introduced earlier, can be used to further secure sensitive data. An encrypted file is used exactly like any other file and is opened in exactly the same way. The encrypted file does not have to be manually decrypted before use, so the encryption is transparent to the user. However, if someone other than the user who encrypted the file tries to open it, he or she will receive an Access Denied message. This works similarly to a cookie on a computer's hard drive, remembering a specific user and logging him on or remembering his password automatically.

Encrypting a file consists of randomly generating a file key that is then encrypted with the user's public key. A public key identifies the user as the one person who can decrypt the file and read its contents. If the holder of the public key isn't available, a special recovery key is available to administrators, who can then gain access to the encrypted files.

Before using encryption, you should make sure you understand its characteristics:

- Encryption works only on NTFS volumes, not FAT, and if an encrypted file is moved or copied to a FAT volume, the file will lose its encryption.

- Files and folders cannot be both encrypted and compressed.

- Only the user who encrypted the file and an administrator with a recovery key can open an encrypted file.

- System files can't be encrypted.

- Just because a file is encrypted doesn't mean the file can't be moved to a non-NTFS partition or deleted entirely. Encryption isn't a cure-all for security.

- When an encrypted file is being edited by a user, it isn't encrypted. You can solve this problem by encrypting the Temp folder on your hard drive.

- You can encrypt folders that you use a lot, such as the My Documents folder. This way, when files are saved into that folder, they can be automatically encrypted.

Encrypting data when it is saved to the hard drive or during editing is one thing, but what happens to encryption when the file or folder is sent to someone through data lines? Protocols such as IPSec and Secure Sockets Layer (SSL) encrypt data while it is on the wire. Encryption across data lines works by randomly generating a file key for the encrypted data according to an algorithm created by DES (data encryption standard). DES is so advanced that it is all but impossible to break its code. DES can create a key from 72 quadrillion choices for keys—that's 72,000,000,000,000,000 choices. This key is called a *private key*, and when encrypted data is sent from one user to another, both users must hold the same private key for transmission to succeed. There's more on IPSec next.

Understanding and Configuring IPSec

When computers transfer information, if the data that is sent across the wire isn't encrypted or otherwise protected, it is susceptible to eavesdropping. Windows 2000 offers a way to protect this data while it is being transferred, provided that the computers that are communicating are using Internet Protocol (IP) on IP networks and that those computers are both running Windows 2000. IP Security (IPSec) can be used to set up tunnels for data on IP networks and to encrypt the data before transmission. Routers or switches encountered along the route simply forward this encrypted data.

Very simply, when two computers using IPSec need to communicate, they first agree on a level of security; this is determined by the highest common security policy of both computers. When this level of security is agreed upon by both parties, each computer encrypts the data before sending it and decrypts it upon receipt. This ensures that the data is safe during transmission. Windows 2000 IPSec is configured through group policies and is configured for sites, domains, organizational units, and local computers.

Although there are many books and a sea of information about the actual process of these transmissions, the components of IPSec, and the way these security associations are made, understanding these procedures is not the focus of this book. In this discussion, I simply want to help you configure IPSec for your enterprise. You'll learn how to use IPSec Monitor, create a new IPSec policy, assign IPSec to a group policy, and add a filter rule to an IPSec policy.

Using IPSec Monitor

If you are not sure if IPSec is enabled on your computer or if your IPSec communications are successful, you can use the IP Security Monitor (IPSec Monitor) to find out. Using IPSec Monitor is as simple as typing **ipsecmon [computername]** at a command prompt. Figure 9.6 shows the screen.

If the service is not enabled, you'll need to enable it through the IPSec Policy Agent Properties dialog box. The IPSec Policy Agent is responsible for implementing IPSec in Windows 2000. To start the service, follow these steps:

1. Log on as an administrator.

2. Choose Start|Programs|Administrative Tools|Services.

3. Right-click on the IPSec Policy Agent, and choose Start. (Or right-click on the agent and choose Properties.)

4. If you choose to view the Properties of the service, change the Service status to Start, and change the Startup type to Automatic.

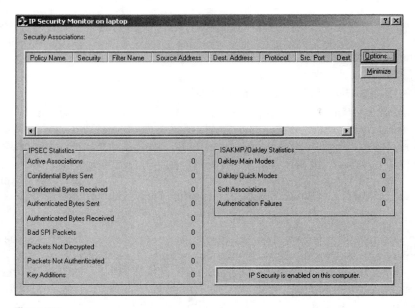

Figure 9.6
IP Security Monitor.

You can also make other changes in the default behavior of the IPSec Policy Agent by using the property sheet's other tabs: General, Log On, Recovery, Dependencies:

- *General*—Change the display name, description, and startup type, and stop or pause the service.

- *Log On*—Change the logon from the local system account to another account, and allow the service to interact with the desktop. Additionally, you can enable or disable the service for specific hardware profiles.

- *Recovery*—Change how the computer reacts to service failures. These settings can be configured for the first failure, the second failure, and subsequent failures. The settings are: Take No Action, Restart The Service, Run A File, and Reboot The Computer.

- *Dependencies*—See which services depend of the IPSec Policy Agent and which services depend on IPSec.

Adding the IP Security Policies On Active Directory Snap-In to an MMC
In order to create new IPSec policies, you must have the IP Security Policies On Active Directory snap-in configured. Follow these steps:

1. Log on as an administrator.

2. Choose Start|Run, and type "mmc" in the Open box.

3. Choose Console|Add/Remove Snap-In, and add the IP Security Policy Management snap-in.

4. Choose to manage the local computer, to manage the domain policy for this computer's domain, to manage domain policy for another domain, or to manage another computer. Choose the Finish button, Close, and OK.

5. Choose Console|Save As and save the console as IPSecPolicy.

Creating a New IPSec Policy

You can create your own IPSec policy if you do not want to depend on Windows default policies for security. To create your own IPSec policy, follow the guidelines listed here:

1. Open the IPSecPolicy console created earlier, and log on as an administrator.

2. Double-click on IP Security Policies On Active Directory; then right-click and choose Create IP Security Policy.

3. The IP Security Policy Wizard appears. Choose Next and name the new IP security policy. (For future reference, I've named my policy *New IP Security Policy 1*.)

4. On the Requests For Secure Communication page, you can enable the option to Activate The Default Response Rule. This rule states that the computer will respond to a remote computer that requests secure communications when no other rule applies. This is necessary for secure communications between computers.

5. If you left the box checked in Step 4, the Default Response Rule Authentication Method page is shown next. This page allows you to set the authentication method for this rule. Notice that Windows 2000 Kerberos is the default. You should use this option in most circumstances. Choose the second option if you need access to networks that do not use Kerberos. The third option can be used when the two communicating computers have agreed previously on a shared key. This option should be used only if Kerberos or certificates can't be employed. The choices are shown in Figure 9.7.

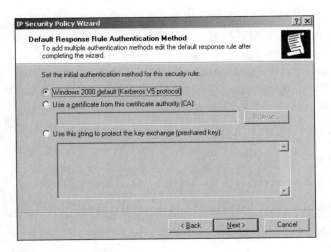

Figure 9.7
The Default Response Rule Authentication Method page of the IP Security Policy Wizard.

6. If you chose Kerberos, the next page completes the wizard and opens the new policy Properties box.

   If you chose to use a certificate authority, you'll need to choose a certificate by browsing to it. If the computer doesn't have a shared certificate store, you can select a Certificate Authority from the local machine store by answering Yes in the warning box. You won't see this warning box if you successfully locate a certificate. On the Select Certificate page, you'll need to choose a certificate as necessary.

   If you choose to use a preshared key, you'll be prompted to specify that key before continuing.

7. Either choice, once configured, opens the new policy Properties box. Here you can edit the policy's properties, such as the order of the security preference, authentication methods, the connection type, and the interval for checking for policy changes (the default is 180 minutes). The Advanced button opens a dialog box that allows you to change the key exchange settings and methods used for security.

Assigning IPSec to a Group Policy

You can assign an IPSec policy to a group policy through Active Directory Users And Computers or Active Directory Sites And Services. Adding a policy to a domain or an OU is performed through Active Directory Users and Computers, while adding a policy to a site requires using Active Directory Sites and Services.

To add an IPSec policy to a domain or organizational unit, follow these steps.

1. Log on as an administrator and open Active Directory Users And Computers.

2. Expand the domain tree, and select either an OU or the domain itself. Right-click and choose Properties.

3. On the Group Policy tab, select a group policy to which you want to assign an IPSec policy, and choose Edit. (If there isn't a policy to edit, you'll need to create one.)

4. In the console, expand Computer Configuration/Windows Settings/Security Settings/Public Key Policies/IP Security Policies On Active Directory. See Figure 9.8, and notice that there are four entries. The highlighted entry, New IP Security Policy 1, is the policy I created in the earlier example ("Creating a New IPSec Policy"); the other three are there by default.

5. To enable an existing policy, right-click on the policy and choose Assign.

To add an IPSec policy to a site, follow these steps:

1. Log on as an administrator and open Active Directory Sites And Services.

2. Expand the domain tree, and select the site. Right-click and choose Properties.

3. On the Group Policy tab, select a group policy to which you want to assign an IPSec policy, and choose Edit. (If there isn't a policy to edit, you'll need to create one.)

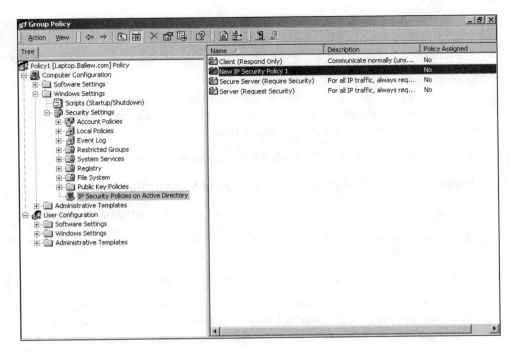

Figure 9.8
A group policy's IP Security policies.

4. In the console, expand Computer Configuration/Windows Settings/Security Settings/ Public Key Policies/IP Security Policies On Active Directory. See Figure 9.8, and notice that there are four entries. The highlighted entry, New IP Security Policy 1, is the policy I created in the earlier example ("Creating a New IPSec Policy"); the other three are there by default.

5. To enable an existing policy, right-click on the policy and choose Assign.

Warning! *IPSec policies remain active even if the GPO to which it was assigned is deleted. Make sure you unassign the policy before deleting any objects.*

Editing a Default Policy Manually
If you choose to use one of the default IPSec policies shown in Figure 9.8, but the rules for the policy don't fit your organizational needs exactly, you can change those rules.

To change default policy rules, follow these steps:

1. Log on as an administrator and open Active Directory Users And Computers.

2. Expand the domain tree, and select either an OU or the domain itself. Right-click and choose Properties.

3. On the Group Policy tab, select a group policy that you want to edit, and choose Edit.

4. In the console, expand Computer Configuration/Windows Settings/Security Settings/ Public Key Policies/IP Security Policies On Active Directory. Right-click on either Client (Respond Only), Secure Server (Require Security), or Server (Request Security), and choose Properties.

5. On the Rules tab, highlight the security rule that you want to edit, and choose Edit. The screens will differ depending on the policy that was chosen. Figures 9.9 and 9.10 show two of the screens for the Server (Request Security) policy.

6. Work through the appropriate dialog boxes and make the necessary changes.

Adding a Rule to an IPSec Policy by Using the Security Rule Wizard

1. Log on as an administrator and open Active Directory Users And Computers.

2. Expand the domain tree, and select either an OU or the domain itself. Right-click and choose Properties.

3. On the Group Policy tab, select a group policy that you want to edit, and choose Edit.

4. In the console, expand Computer Configuration/Windows Settings/Security Settings/ Public Key Policies/IP Security Policies On Active Directory. Right-click on an IP Security policy that you have previously created or on one of the default policies. Choose Properties.

5. On the Rules tab, choose Add. This starts the Security Rule Wizard.

6. On the first page, you can specify a tunnel endpoint by IP address, thus creating a direct, private connection between two computers. Make changes as necessary.

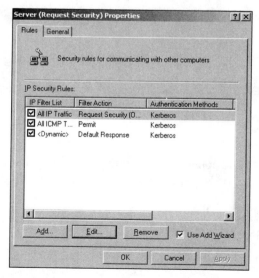

Figure 9.9
Server (Request Security) Properties.

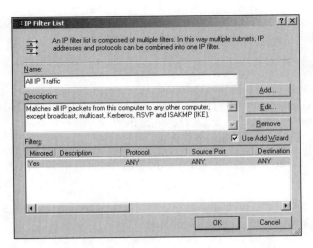

Figure 9.10
An IP filter list.

7. On the next page, you can specify that the rule be applied to all network connections, to a local area network, or to remote access. Make changes as necessary.

8. On the next page, you can change the authentication method from Kerberos to Certificate Services or Key Exchange. Make changes as necessary.

9. On the next page, you can define an IP filter list, thus selecting the type of traffic to which the rule will apply. The choices are All ICMP Traffic or All IP Traffic. Make changes as necessary.

10. The Filter Action page is next, where you can specify what action the computer should take when filtering. Choices include Permit, Request Security, or Require Security, or you can choose Add to have the Filter Action Wizard assist you in creating a new filter action.

11. The wizard finishes and offers an opportunity to edit the policy properties again.

Understanding Kerberos

The Kerberos protocol is the default protocol on Windows 2000 networks. Kerberos allows a user to log on to the domain controller one time and receive admittance to all other resources (for which the user has permission), without the user having to type a password each time. In contrast, users who log on to a workgroup must supply a password for each resource they need to access, and they have to continually identify themselves to other resources.

Kerberos, though, does more than offer the convenience of a single user logon to access resources. Before Kerberos, if a user typed a user name and the correct password, that user was authenticated on the network. With Kerberos, a third party becomes involved in this authentication. The Kerberos authentication process is as follows:

1. A client sends a request to the Kerberos service and asks for authentication.

2. The Kerberos service replies to the client with two things: a session key, and a ticket-granting ticket (TGT) to be used with the ticket-granting service (TGS). The TGS is part of the Kerberos authentication system on the domain controller, which is occasionally referred to as the ticket-granting server.

3. The client then sends a TGS request along with the TGT to the TGS or Key Distribution Center (KDC).

4. The TGS sends a reply to the client, and this reply contains a ticket for the user's target server, the session key, and the server's secret key.

5. The client then uses the session key to send a request to the target server.

6. The target server decrypts the ticket by using its secret key and obtains the session key. The session key is used to decrypt the authenticator and validate the client on the target server.

After all of this is completed, the client has a service ticket from the TGS and can use this ticket to access network services. The ticket validates the user's identity to the service and validates the service's identity to the user.

Throughout these exchanges, the TGT contains the user's SID and is encrypted. The session key is also encrypted and contains the client's secret key. All of this encryption and the inclusion of a third party (the Kerberos service) makes it very difficult for an unauthorized user to access the network or steal a private or session key. Tickets are used by the client to authenticate themselves to the target server. The ticket is encrypted, and only the target service can decrypt and read it. Tickets are usually good for about eight hours.

Again, there are many books and white papers about Kerberos, but the purpose of this chapter remains optimizing security. To optimize the security of your network, you should choose Kerberos as the policy in IPSec Policy configurations, and when necessary, change default Kerberos policies at the domain level through Active Directory Users And Computers and group policies. Even though Kerberos is installed and implemented by default on Windows 2000 systems that run Active Directory and are domain controllers, you should be aware of which options are available for configuration and how they can be changed. The following items can be configured for a Kerberos policy:

- *Enforce User Login Restrictions*—Enabling this setting allows the KDC to certify every request for a session ticket by confirming whether the user has the right to log on locally or access the computer from the network. This setting is enabled by default.

- *Maximum Lifetime For A Service Ticket*—This setting refers to the Kerberos session ticket mentioned earlier. The maximum is 99,999 minutes.

- *Maximum Lifetime Of User Ticket*—This setting refers to the TGT that is presented to the TGS. The maximum is 99,999 hours.

- *Maximum Lifetime For User Ticket Renewal*—This setting refers to the TGT and when it must be renewed. The maximum is 99,999 days.

- *Maximum Tolerance For Computer Clock Synchronization*—Authentication of clients will fail if the time settings have not been synchronized within the allotted amount of time.

To change these policies, perform the following steps:

1. Log on as an administrator and open Active Directory Users And Computers.

2. Expand the domain tree, and select either an OU or the domain itself. Right-click and choose Properties.

3. On the Group Policy tab, select a group policy that you want to edit, and choose Edit.

4. In the console, expand Computer Configuration/Windows Settings/Security Settings/ Account Lockout Policy/Kerberos Policy.

5. To change any of the policies, double-click on the policy in the right pane and make the appropriate changes.

Licensing

There are two licensing modes for Windows 2000 Server: Per Seat and Per Server. In Per Seat mode, every computer that accesses the server has to have a Client Access License (CAL). In Per Server mode, CALs are assigned to the server based on the number of connections to the server at any given time.

Per Seat Licensing

In Per Seat licensing, every client computer that will be used to access a Windows 2000 server will need its own CAL before doing so. Once it has this CAL, however, the computer can be used to access any network server running Windows 2000 Server. This is the best choice for large organizations with multiple servers and domain controllers because it is more economical than purchasing Per Server licensing. CALs must be purchased for all clients accessing the servers, including Windows 9x machines, Windows NT Workstation machines, and Windows 2000 Professional machines. A user who has a Per Seat license can always access a server with Per Seat licensing, but that user cannot be guaranteed access to a Per-Server-configured server or domain controller. Access is granted only if there is an open license available on the server, and even though the client has a Per Seat CAL, the Per Server server is still docked one CAL when network connectivity is initiated.

Per Server Licensing

Per Server licensing is configured on servers in smaller companies, where it is known exactly how many clients will need access to the server, and there is usually only one server to access. With a Per Server license, the company purchases a certain number of CALs. If the company buys 10 CALs, then only 10 people can access the server at any given time. Once this limit is reached, the eleventh client cannot log on until one of the others logs off. Per Server mode is also good for special types of servers that aren't accessed very often, such as servers used for dial-up, Internet, or remote access services.

Warning! *Although you can change once from Per Server to Per Seat at no additional cost, you can never change from Per Seat to Per Server legally. If in doubt, choose Per Server during the initial installation.*

The Licensing Agreement

If you have never actually read the agreement when installing Windows 2000 products, you probably don't know exactly what you've been agreeing to every time you've installed it. The End User License Agreement (EULA) can be found by searching the hard drive for eula.txt. After a search on my computer, I found it in two places: in the C:\Winnt\System32 directory, and in the C:\Distribution directory configured automatically during the remote installation section in Chapter 4.

You should make sure you are complying with the licensing mode you have chosen, and there is certainly information regarding the technicalities of that in the EULA. I suggest that you read the EULA agreement if you've never done so. Other things to be careful of include the following:

- You can't rent or lease the software, or *burn* copies of it for others. If you want to transfer or sell the software to another party, you can do so as long as you remove all instances of it from all of your computers.

- When you're purchasing a new computer with the operating system preinstalled, make sure you get the required books, certificates, product IDs, and the like so you can be sure the software is valid.

- If you have Windows 2000 Server installed on a domain controller, you can't also use that disk to install it on your laptop.

- If you've upgraded from Windows NT 4 to Windows 2000 Server, you still need to keep your copy of NT because all copies are treated as a single product when you're dealing with upgrades.

Managing Licenses

To view information about the licensing mode you use, open Licensing in Control Panel. Doing so will open the Choose Licensing Mode dialog box, shown in Figure 9.11.

From this screen, you can add and remove licenses, set a replication frequency, or change from Per Server to Per Seat. To perform more detailed licensing tasks, including managing licensing for the domain or enterprise, open Licensing by choosing Start|Programs|Administrative Tools|Licensing. Figure 9.12 shows this screen and the four available tabs. The Products View lists the products and the number of licenses purchased and used.

Working through the tabs is somewhat self-explanatory; there are Purchase History, Products View, Clients Per Seat, and Server Browser tabs. In the Server Browser window, you can right-click on any server in the domain or enterprise and choose Properties to get more information on that machine, to add or remove licenses, or to change from Per Server to Per Seat licensing.

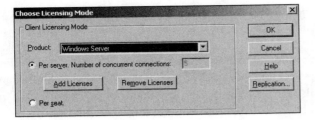

Figure 9.11
The Choose Licensing Mode dialog box.

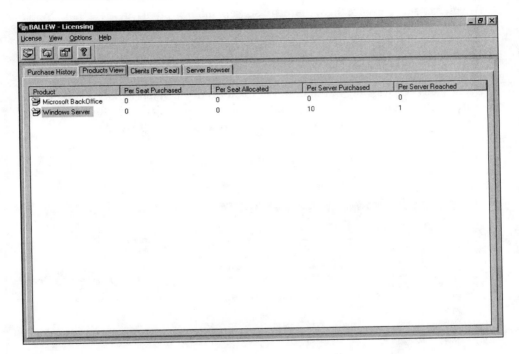

Figure 9.12
Licensing in Administrative Tools.

Note: When you remove licenses, you free up those licenses so they can be reinstalled on other machines.

Introducing the Computer Management Console

The Computer Management console, located in Administrative Tools, helps you manage your computer and remote ones by combining many of the most-used tools into one easy-to-use console. It's like having a perfect MMC that has everything you need already configured. In this section, I'll detail the three divisions of the Computer Management console: System Tools, Storage, and Services And Applications.

In this section, you'll have an opportunity to review the concepts, tools, and utilities involved in managing your computer, and you'll learn how all of these components work together. You'll also learn some new concepts, such as how to configure dynamic disks; what simple, spanned, and basic volumes are; and how services can be managed. Before starting, take a look at the console; choose Start|Programs|Administrative Tools|Computer Management. This console is also shown in Figure 9.13. System Tools is highlighted in the left pane, and the tools available are listed in the right pane.

System Tools

As you can see in Figure 9.13, there are six very different tools and folders in System Tools. You should be familiar with just about all of them by now. In this section, I'll briefly review these tools and utilities, and introduce you to a few new ones.

Event Viewer

Event Viewer is available in the Computer Management/System Tools section of the console. Event Viewer is used to monitor hardware and software performance and activities occurring on the system. Event Viewer contains logs for the following:

- Application

- Directory Service

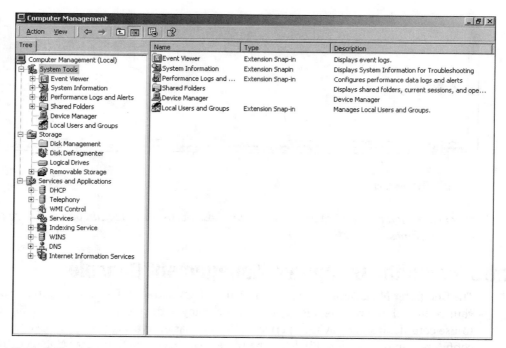

Figure 9.13
The Computer Management console.

- DNS Server

- File Replication Service

- Security

- System

For more information about these logs, how to configure them, or how to interpret them, refer to Chapter 8.

System Information

System Information offers information about your local computer system; see Figure 9.14. The summary includes items such as OS name, version, processor, BIOS, total physical and virtual memory, and more. You might consider printing this information for all of the systems in your organization. Notice that besides the System Summary, other folders are available.

Other folders in the System Summary are listed next:

- *Hardware Resources*—Contains folders and system summaries for Conflicts/Sharing, Direct Memory Access (DMA), Forced Hardware, input/output (I/O), interrupt request numbers (IRQs), and Memory.

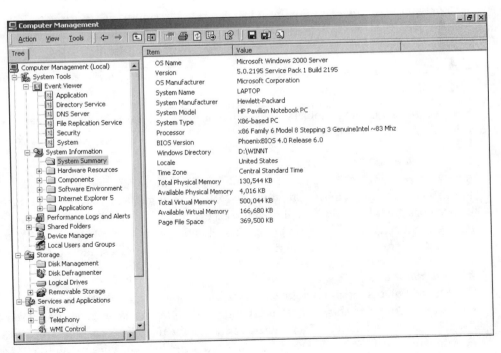

Figure 9.14
System Summary.

Personal Experience

I worked for a while as a PC technician, replacing CPU fans, memory, hard drives, and NICs, preparing them for Y2K, and so on for a rather large company. This company maintained most of the local schools' computers, so there were literally thousands to keep track of. In the schools, these computers were always being moved and jostled around, so there was never a lack of things to repair, and one was never surprised to find a lab computer acting as a teacher workstation or vice versa. One thing that was very helpful to everyone involved in this maintenance was that inside many of the cases were printouts similar to what you see in Figure 9.14. It was always nice to open up a system (especially one that wouldn't boot) and know immediately what the BIOS version was, what IRQs were being used, how much memory was installed, and anything else of importance. Occasionally, there were even notes written on the page from the last technician. I mention this here because you might be able to employ this idea in your organization.

- *Components*—Contains folders and system summaries for Multimedia, Display, Infrared, Input, Modem, Network, Ports, Storage, Printing, Problem Devices, and USB. Each folder contains invaluable information. For instance, in the Network/Adapter folder, there is information on the adapter type, service name, IP address, IP subnet, default gateway, DHCP status (enabled or not), and the adapter's MAC address.

- *Software Environment*—Contains folders and system summaries for Drivers, Environment Variables, Jobs (print), Network Connections, Running Tasks, Loaded Modules, Services, Program Groups, Startup Programs, and OLE Registration.

- *Internet Explorer 5*—Contains folders and system summaries for File Versions, Connectivity, Cache, Content, and Security.

- *Applications*—Contains folders and summaries for all of the Microsoft applications installed on the computer.

Performance Logs And Alerts

Another area of System Tools you are already familiar with is Performance Logs And Alerts. In Chapter 8, you might have configured an MMC with both Event Viewer and Performance Logs And Alerts. However, I prefer to access both of these utilities in the Computer Management console, where I can also access all of the other components described in this section. Performance Logs And Alerts offers counter logs, trace logs, and alerts.

Shared Folders

The Shared Folders section is a great place to view and manage the shares on your computer. Figure 9.15 shows the shares configured on my Windows 2000 server. You can double-click on any shared folder to view or change the user limit, caching properties, permissions, and security. You can also add a new share by right-clicking on the Shared Folders folder and choosing New File Share.

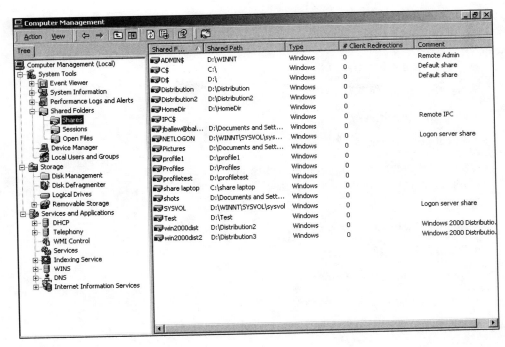

Figure 9.15
Shared folders.

Also in the Shared Folders section are Sessions and Open Files folders. The Sessions folder details all users connected, the IP address of their computers, their computer type (Windows, non-Windows, etc.), how many files they have open, how long they've been connected, any idle time, and if they are a guest or not. The Open Files folder shows which files are open, who is accessing them, and more. Through these folders, you can disconnect all sessions, all open files, or both.

Device Manager

When you opt to access Device Manager through the Computer Management console, the utility is displayed in the right pane of the console. From here, you can view the devices on your system by type or connection, or view resources by type or connection. You can also print a copy of the devices or resources, and locate problems due to hardware and resources.

Note: *When accessing Device Manager through the Computer Management console, it is shown in the right pane of the console. When accessing Device Manager from the System icon in Control Panel, it stands alone.*

For instance, to view information about the network adapter, choose View|Devices By Type, and then double-click on Network Adapters. Underneath you'll see all of the adapters installed on the system. By double-clicking on the specific adapter, you can access the NIC's properties box where you can perform all of the following tasks:

- Troubleshoot the device.

- Enable or disable the device.

- Change the properties of the device.

- See the driver details.

- Uninstall the driver.

- Update the driver.

Other devices may have different options. For instance, for the computer's modem, you can perform all of the tasks listed previously plus the following tasks (depending on the modem):

- Change the modem's speaker volume.

- Change the maximum port speed.

- Query the modem and record it in a log.

- Change default call preferences.

- See which resources the modem is using.

The point is that Device Manager is a very useful tool. You can use Device Manager to troubleshoot any device on the system, change the driver, or otherwise manage the component. In addition to viewing information by device, though, you can also view devices by connection.

Resources are components such as DMA, I/O addresses, IRQs, and memory. To see which resources are connected by type, choose this option from the View menu. Figure 9.16 shows the resources being viewed by connection. Notice how the DMA numbers are configured, what IRQs are configured, and how memory is allotted. You might want to print your computer's corresponding information for future reference.

Local Users And Groups

You may have noticed that Local Users And Groups had an X in it in Figure 9.13. This occurs because there are no local users and groups available on a domain controller. Users and groups are configured and managed in the domain under Active Directory Users And Computers. The Local Users And Groups snap-in will be available on member servers and Windows 2000 Professional workstations, however, and can be used exactly like Active Directory Users And Computers to add, remove, and manage users and groups for the local computer.

Storage

In the Storage section of the Computer Management console, you can view and configure the physical and logical disks and drives on the system, manage removable storage, defragment the disks, and configure basic and dynamic disk types as well as simple,

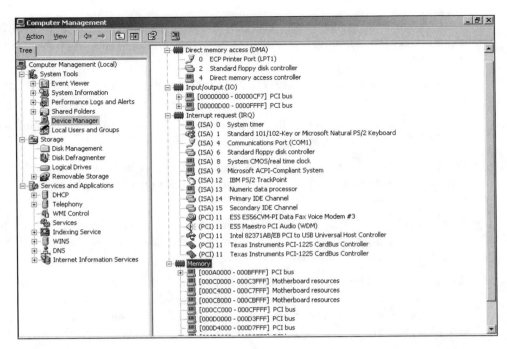

Figure 9.16
Device Manager: resources by connection.

spanned, and striped volumes. Disk Management is the big utility here, as well as the most used, so it will be discussed in detail.

Disk Management

The Disk Management utility offers many opportunities for managing the physical and logical disks on your computer and managing your network storage space. Using this utility, you can create and delete partitions and volumes, and manage disks on remote computers. You can also remove hard disks, upgrade basic disks to dynamic disks on NTFS volumes, and create simple, spanned, and striped volumes. You can perform many tasks while users are logged on without having to restart the computer. To understand what Disk Management has to offer, you need to understand these terms first:

- *Active partition*—This is the partition the computer boots from. It must be a primary partition if you're using a basic disk.

- *Basic disk*—A basic disk can contain primary partitions, extended partitions, and logical drives. It is created by default and is commonly used because it is backward-compatible with Windows NT volume sets, striped sets, mirrored volumes, and disk striping with parity. All versions of Windows, including 9x and NT, can use basic storage because it is the industry standard. Basic disks can be converted to dynamic disks without data loss.

- *Dynamic disks*—These disks can contain only dynamic volumes and cannot contain logical drives. They cannot be accessed by MS-DOS and cannot be converted to basic disks without data loss. Dynamic disks can be configured only for NTFS partitions, and cannot be configured on laptops or dual-boot systems where access is needed to other partitions.

- *Partition*—This is a portion of a disk that acts like it is its own physical disk. Partitions can be created on basic disks.

- *Volumes*—This is a portion of a disk that acts like it is its own physical disk. Volumes look like *C*: and *D*: in Disk Management and My Computer.

- *Primary partition*—On a basic disk, this is a volume from which the computer boots. You can have one, two, three, or four primary partitions on a basic disk, or three primary partitions and one extended partition.

- *Extended partition*—This is the part of a basic disk that can contain logical drives. If you want to configure more than four volumes on the basic disk, you can make one an extended partition with logical drives.

- *Simple volume*—This contains disk space from a single dynamic disk. When a basic disk is converted to a dynamic disk, it is first configured as a simple volume. You can extend this volume with space from the same disk or from other physical disks. If it is extended to other physical disks, it becomes a *spanned* volume. Simple volumes can be mirrored, but spanned volumes cannot.

- *Spanned volume*—A simple volume that has been extended to multiple physical dynamic disks is called a spanned volume. These volumes cannot be mirrored. Spanned volumes do not have to be the same size because when data is written to the volumes, it is written until the disk is full and then continued on the next disk.

- *Striped volume*—This is a volume that stores data on more than one physical dynamic disk. The data that is written to the disks is divided into data blocks that is evenly distributed to the disks; this is called *striping*. These volumes cannot be mirrored or extended. Striped volumes offer good read/write performance because the data is written to multiple disks simultaneously. RAID 5 is a type of striped volume (see Chapter 8).

Keeping all of those terms in mind, consider now what tasks can be achieved using Disk Management. Look at Figure 9.17.

In the configuration shown in Figure 9.17, there is one basic disk. This disk contains two primary partitions and one logical drive. The disk contains a DVD player and a CD-ROM drive. Partition C: is the system partition and is the active partition. Partition D: is a logical drive and is the boot partition. The boot volume and the system volume can be on the same disk, but they do not have to be. In this system, there are no options to convert to dynamic disks. This is true for two reasons: one, because the system is a portable computer; and two, because the dual boot is set up so that the logical partition can access files on the active partition. Finally, there is no option to upgrade to a dynamic disk on logical drive D: because it is not a disk, but is instead a logical drive and volume.

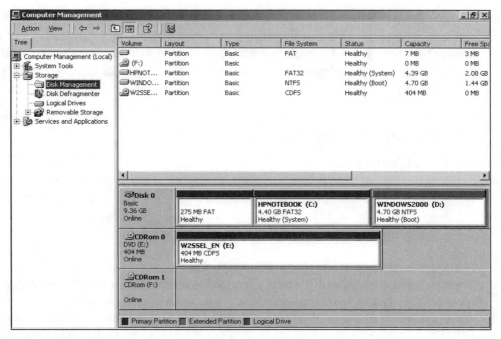

Figure 9.17
The Disk Management utility in the Computer Management console.

If your computer meets the requirements, however, upgrading a basic disk to a dynamic disk is as simple as right-clicking on the disk and choosing Upgrade To Dynamic Disk. A wizard walks you through the process. After dynamic disks have been configured, other wizards will assist you in creating spanned or striped volumes. A wizard will also help you configure RAID volumes, as detailed in Chapter 8. Finally, you can change the drive letter and path to the disk or partitions configured in Disk Management, delete and format disks that are not system or boot disks, and change which partition will act as the active partition.

In addition to creating dynamic disks and simple, spanned, and striped volumes, you can view the properties of the disk simply by right-clicking on it. From here, familiar tools are available, such as Disk Cleanup, Error-Checking, Backup, Disk Defragmenter, and Sharing.

Disk Defragmenter

You can defragment the disks from inside the Computer Management console by choosing Disk Defragmenter and then Analyze. The defragmenting utility can also be run from Disk Management, as mentioned earlier. You should defragment the drives whenever applications have been uninstalled or a large number of files have been saved or deleted. Remember to back up the drive before defragmenting it.

Logical Drives

In this section of the console, you can view the logical drives on your computer, and change the drives and their properties. To make changes, right-click on the drive and choose Properties, and select either the General tab or the Security tab. You can do the following:

- View drive properties.

- Change a drive label (name).

- Set ownership on drives.

- Set access permissions on drives.

- Set auditing of objects on drives.

- Set special permissions on drives.

Removable Storage

The Removable Storage folder, which is available under Storage in the Computer Management console, is used to manage and track the removable storage media that are currently connected. These removable storage devices don't simply consist of Zip drives and tape drives; they can also include hardware libraries and can be configured using media pools. Removable Storage can help you keep track of your devices; you can configure and control them (including ejecting or cleaning them) by adding them to pools, or you can configure them to work with the Backup utility and other applications.

The Removable Storage utility offers both system and application media pools. Media pools should be configured when many devices have the same configuration needs and contain the same types of media. There are three system media pools: Unrecognized, Import, and Free. Application media pools are created when you or a data management application need to determine what type of media can be accessed, when it can be accessed, and by whom.

Unrecognized media pools contain either media that the Removable Storage utility doesn't recognize or new media that are blank. When a device is listed here, it should be moved to a free media pool so it can be used by applications and users. Figure 9.18 shows where the Unrecognized pool is located in the Remote Storage area, plus two available media items.

Import media pools contain media that Removable Storage recognizes as being in the database, but those media haven't been used before by Removable Storage. Free media pools contain media that are not being used by any application and do not contain data that Removable Storage determines to be useful. If there are items in the Free media pool, then they are ready for use.

Application media pools are different from the three previously mentioned system media pools because application media pools are configured and created by applications or users.

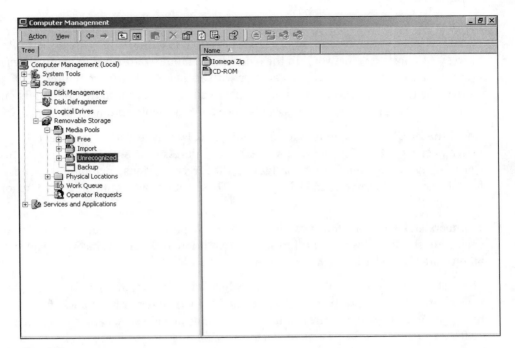

Figure 9.18
Unrecognized media pools.

You might configure the Windows Backup utility to use a particular media pool for backing up data on Mondays, and use a different pool for backing up data on Fridays.

In addition to creating and using the media pools to manage the removable media in your network, you can also use Removable Storage to perform the following tasks:

- Manage tapes and disks.
- Manage operator requests and queued work.
- Manage security for removable storage.
- View and set storage properties.
- Manage libraries.

Services And Applications

In the third section of Computer Management is Services And Applications. Here you can manage the properties of any server service or application installed on the computer. These services include WINS, DNS, and DHCP. In this section, you'll learn a little about each of these, although DNS and DHCP will be discussed at length later in the book.

DHCP

Dynamic Host Configuration Protocol (DHCP) is used to automatically assign TCP/IP addresses to hosts on a network. In the olden days, administrators had to manually visit every machine in the organization, come up with an address for that computer, keep meticulous records of those addresses, and physically type them into the computers one by one. With DHCP, these addresses can be doled out to clients automatically.

Under the DHCP tree are options for managing DHCP in the organization. The first folder, Scope, contains four folders: Address Pool, Address Leases, Reservations, and Scope Options. The second folder is for configuring the server's options, including IP addresses for gateways, WINS servers, and DNS servers. These options are configured from Action| Configure Server.

To understand what each folder can be used to accomplish, you must at least understand what address pools, leases, and reservations are. Although DHCP has its own chapter later, an introduction to basic DHCP terms is in order here.

The first folder, Address Pool, is used to see which addresses are available for clients who need them. Addresses are TCP/IP addresses, and the DHCP server has a pool of them to hand out. Addresses are usually configured as a range of addresses, perhaps ranging from 10.0.0.3 to 10.0.0.254. In this range of addresses, 50 might be assigned to clients. In this same range, you may need to exclude certain addresses for other servers, special clients, a specific peripheral, or a DNS server. You can exclude a range of addresses by right-clicking on this folder and specifying which addresses to exclude.

When a client has received an IP address from a DHCP server, that client has been given a lease for that address. The client can use this address for a certain amount of time before having to renew the lease or obtain a new address.

In the second folder, Address Leases, you can view which clients have which addresses, the lease expiration, the type of lease, a unique ID, and a description. You can manage leases from here as well, and can delete address leases as necessary.

The third folder, Reservations, is used to view which resources or clients always use the same address, like a certain network printer or specialized server. You can add a reservation by choosing Action|New Reservation. Reservations can be used with address pools and exclusions.

Finally, scope options can be configured for all kinds of hardware, including (but not limited to) routers, name servers, DNS servers, log servers, and SMTP servers. Scope options can also be set for default IP Time-to-live, broadcast address, and boot file size.

Besides the Scope folder, there are other folders available from the DHCP console. One of those folders is the Server Options folder. From here, you can configure parameters for the DHCP server clients. Besides the client needing an IP address, the client will also need a gateway address, a DNS Server address, and more. You'll also need a place to configure the scope name, lease duration, DHCP updates, and so on. These items and more can be configured through either the Server Options folder or by right-clicking on the DHCP server itself.

Telephony

Telephony Application Programming Interface (TAPI) combines available telecommunications technology with the computer to enable users to employ utilities such as HyperTerminal, Phone Dialer, Fax, Caller ID, call routing, voice mail, video conferencing, and more. To manage providers of these services, you can double-click on the Telephony folder under Services And Applications.

There are five folders in the expanded Telephony folders. The first is Unimodem 5 Service Provider, which allows you to use and install almost any modem on the market today. If you right-click on this folder, you'll be able to configure the modems on your server; you can set dialing rules, configure ports, and manage advanced settings.

The second and third folders, TAPI Kernel-Mode Service Provider and NDIS Proxy TAPI Service Provider, use an NDIS (Network Driver Interface Specification) driver that makes the connection protocol-independent, meaning that the user can connect with token ring, Ethernet, ISDN, ATM, and other protocols. Remote Access uses these services for WAN connections. You can view line names, users, and the status of the provider in these folders.

The fourth folder is called Microsoft Multicast Conference TAPI Service Provider. This service provider is included by default with Windows 2000 and is used to provide multicast video conferencing to clients on the network. Instead of sending all data and copying all data to every client who needs it, this service sends data to a single IP address for better efficiency. This not only saves on bandwidth and network resources, but also, through Computer Management, gives you a place to manage lines, users, and the status of this service and others.

Finally, Microsoft H.323 TAPI Service Provider is available to allow users to communicate using multimedia calling over IP lines and the LAN. This service allows users to communicate through modems and telephone lines with other computers using the same type of H.323 terminals on the same network or over the Internet.

WMI Control

Windows Management Instrumentation (WMI) allows you to configure this service on remote computers or local ones. WMI is used to manage an enterprise across the Internet and to configure a consistent view and universal access for all users. By right-clicking on the WMI folder and choosing Properties, you can connect to the WMI service, enable logging, backup and restore the WMI repository to a predefined file, set security, and change the default namespace for scripting. More information on WMI control can be found in the WMI Software Development Kit from the Microsoft Developer Network.

Services

The Services folder offers the same management of services that you can access by choosing Start|Programs|Administrative Tools|Services. From here, you can start and stop services, pause or restart services, or view the properties of services. At any given time, there may be 50+ services running on your computer. Some of those services include the obvious Alerter, DHCP, DNS, IPSec Policy Agent, Messenger, and Event Log, or more obscure services such as Clipbook, Smart Card Helper, or Windows Installer.

Indexing Service

The Indexing Service allows clients to use keywords or properties to search for files, folders, and documents stored on the hard disk. The Indexing Service can use up network resources quickly and should be installed only on computers and networks capable of supporting it. From this folder, you can manage the Indexing Service for both the System and Web, and specify which partitions or directories should be included in the index. Both System and Web folders contain a place to manage directories and properties and offer a place to query the catalog. Figure 9.19 shows the query utility.

WINS

Windows Internet Naming Service (WINS) dynamically maps IP addresses to NetBIOS computer names, thus allowing users to access resources by name instead of by IP address. The WINS folder contains two folders: Active Registrations and Replication Partners. The Active Registrations folder displays the list of computers and groups in the WINS database and allows you to search for certain WINS records. These searches can be performed using either the name or the owner of the record. Replication partners are

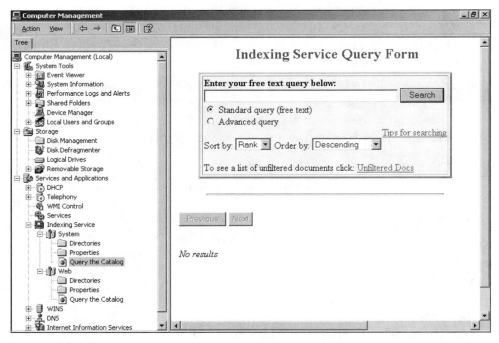

Figure 9.19
Querying the catalog.

other WINS servers that can share in the task of mapping names and addresses for clients. In this folder, you can add replication partners to increase the performance and reliability for your WINS clients and to configure settings for them.

Note: Chapters 10 and 11 cover the topic of WINS in depth.

DNS

Domain Name System (DNS) maps Internet domain names to IP addresses. It would be impractical to try to remember the IP addresses of everyone on the network or of every Web site you ever needed to visit. DNS was created to allow users to type the name of the site or user and have the translation to the IP address be transparent to the user. In a local area network, an administrator must configure the DNS server with information regarding the IP addresses of clients on the network or must set up dynamic DNS updates to do this automatically.

In the DNS folder are two other folders: Forward Lookup Zones and Reverse Lookup Zones. Forward lookup zones are configured so that a user can type a fully qualified domain name (FQDN) and receive the IP address of the resource. Reverse lookup zones do exactly the opposite, taking an IP address and returning a FQDN. You can manage or change how the zones work by using these folders. You can also add a new zone by using the New Zone Wizard. *Zones* are databases that link DNS names to their respective IP addresses or services. Zones can be primary or secondary and can be Active Directory integrated. (Chapter 11 will explain these zones, how DNS queries work, and how to create and configure zones.)

Internet Information Services

Internet Information Services, available from the Computer Management console, can be used to configure and manage services and utilities related to it. The folders include Default FTP Site, Default Web Site, Administration Web Site, Default SMTP Virtual Server, and Default NNTP Virtual Server. IIS is beyond the scope of this book; just know that IIS can be managed from the Computer Management console.

Managing Another Computer

Throughout this section on the Computer Management console, I've focused on the management of the local computer, in this case, a Windows 2000 server. You can just as easily manage a remote computer by highlighting Computer Management (Local) at the top of the console and choosing Action|Connect To Another Computer. When you're managing another computer, some things are different; for instance, under System Tools, the Local Users And Groups snap-in is enabled if the computer you are managing isn't another Windows 2000 server. On the remote computer, you may or may not see folders for IIS. You can also see open sessions for the remote computer, shared files, and even Event Viewer. Remotely managing a computer by using Computer Management is extremely efficient.

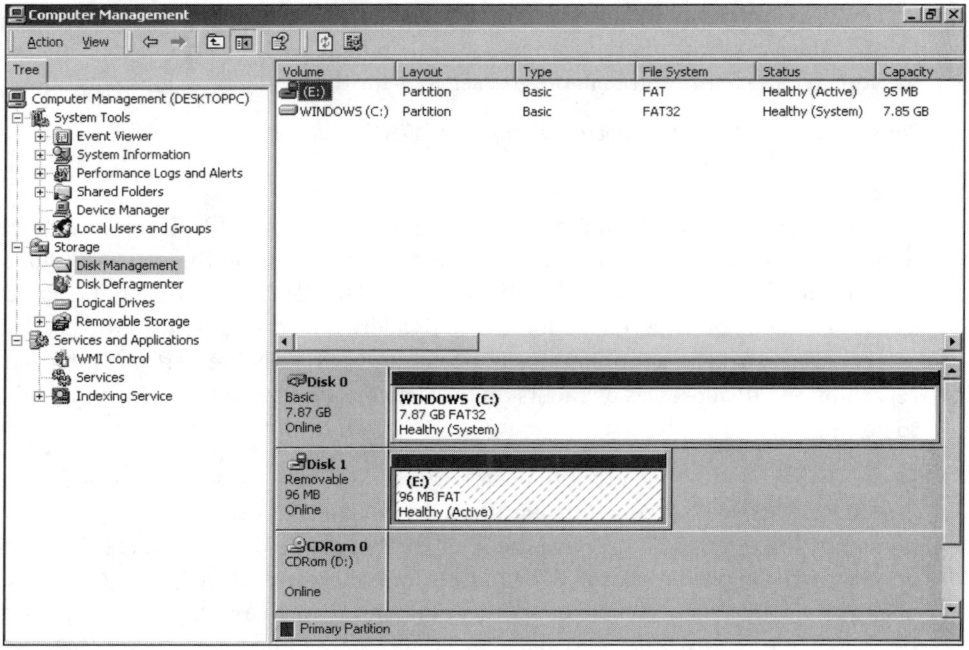

Figure 9.20
Remote administration.

Figure 9.20 shows the Computer Management console with a connection from the local computer to a computer called DesktopPC. Notice that Local Users And Groups isn't X'ed out, that Disk Management is chosen, and that there aren't any folders for WINS, DNS, or IIS because they aren't being hosted on this computer. You can also view application logs, security logs, and system logs for the remote computer, see system information, and configure Performance Logs And Alerts.

Summary

In this chapter, you learned how to improve network security and how to use the Computer Management console. In the first section, "Optimizing Security," you learned how to configure auditing and create security logs through Event Viewer. You also learned what items were auditable and what your auditing should primarily focus on, including failed logon attempts and successful changes to user rights.

Following that, you learned about the three main snap-ins that are used to secure the network: the Group Policy snap-in, the Security Configuration And Analysis snap-in, and the Security Templates snap-in. The Security Configuration And Analysis snap-in is used for configuring and analyzing the local computer. The Security Templates snap-in is used to create and assign security templates to one or more computers. The Group Policy snap-in can be combined with the other two so you can apply the security levels offered by the templates to the entire enterprise. Also in this section, you learned how to configure an existing security template.

Encryption, IPSec, and Kerberos were discussed, and creating IPSec policies was introduced. Editing these policies and utilities can play a big role in securing the network. This section also discussed licensing, including licensing modes, which one you should choose, and how to manage licenses.

Computer Management is a console that brings together many previously discussed utilities and a few new ones. The Computer Management console is a good place to manage both local and remote computers. This console includes such utilities as Event Viewer, Disk Defragmenter, Performance Logs And Alerts, and Shared Folders, and provides information about the services and applications running on the computer.

9

Moving Forward

The rest of the book will shift from installing and configuring the Windows 2000 domain controller to understanding what other servers your machine can become. For instance, you may need one particular server to be a DNS server, or need another to act as a DHCP server. In the next chapter, you'll learn about TCP/IP and DHCP, including how to configure a DHCP server, what TCP/IP is and how it works, and how to manage both TCP/IP and DHCP together.

Part IV

Using Windows 2000 Server

Configuration
Deployment
Planning
Troubleshooting

Chapter 10

Using TCP/IP and DHCP

Now that you've installed and configured a Windows 2000 server for your network, you are ready to explore the possibilities of turning that server into something even more productive and useful. In all networks, there must be some way for the computers to communicate, to locate one another, and to transfer data, files, and email. In most organizations, these clients also need access to the Internet. To achieve this, clients, servers, and network printers (among other things) need to be configured with TCP/IP addresses. In this chapter, I'll introduce TCP/IP, including an overview of how it works, what subnets and gateways are, how routing is involved, and what command-line tools can be used to troubleshoot TCP/IP communications. You'll need to know how to install and configure TCP/IP on both clients and servers. You'll also need to understand a new offering from Windows 2000 called Automatic Private IP Addressing (APIPA), used for handling TCP/IP addressing needs in smaller organizations or special circumstances.

After TCP/IP has been introduced, you'll begin to see how time-consuming it can be to manually apply and configure the addresses for all of the clients on your network. Because of this, DHCP will be introduced as a solution. DHCP servers can be used to automatically assign TCP/IP addresses to clients on the network, with little intervention from administrators once it has been set up. You'll learn how the DHCP lease process works, what scopes are and how to configure them, and how to configure DHCP options and classes.

Overview of TCP/IP

TCP/IP, or Transmission Control Protocol/Internet Protocol, is an industry-wide and uniformly accepted suite of protocols for providing communication across networks. TCP/IP provides a set of rules for communication and data transmission between networks and computers.

TCP/IP gained acceptance because it was an open architecture, meaning that companies and developers could contribute to its development. Additionally, TCP/IP became popular because computers and hardware of different makes and models could communicate effectively. This meant that Windows machines, Apple Macintoshes, Unix machines, OS/2 machines, printers, scanners, and routers could all correspond. Finally, TCP/IP gained acceptance because it became the de facto protocol of the Internet.

The TCP/IP Suite

TCP/IP is referred to as a suite of protocols because it offers support at all levels of a four-layer model that is similar to the seven-layer OSI model, and because it supports multiple protocols. The four layers of the Microsoft TCP/IP model are Application, Transport, Internet, and Network Interface, and some of the protocols, other than TCP and IP, include HTTP, FTP, Telnet, and SMTP.

Each layer of this model can be compared to the layers of the OSI model, discussed earlier, because the object of any protocol model is to create rules for sending data from an application on one computer, down through the wire, and to an application on another computer. To achieve this, there must be rules and protocols for each layer.

When an application or a user needs access to the network to send or receive data or to obtain access to a resource, TCP/IP offers two interfaces for doing so: Winsock and NetBT. In the Application layer, either Winsock (used for Microsoft Windows applications) or NetBT (used for NetBIOS applications) is chosen as the interface between the Application layer and the next layer, the Transport layer. Application-layer utilities include FTP, Telnet, Simple Network Management Protocol (SNMP), Domain Name System (DNS), POP3, and so on. The Application layer's interfaces allow users to transparently communicate with the lower layers of the model and to make successful data transfers with other computers or networks.

The next layer down, the Transport layer (responsible for transporting the data), contains two protocols: TCP and UDP. Transmission Control Protocol provides connection-oriented, reliable communication between computers, and it offers guaranteed delivery of data packets and error checking. TCP is usually used for large data transfers by applications, and it is used much differently than UDP is. User Datagram Protocol (UDP) is connectionless and does not guarantee delivery of data packets. UDP isn't used to transfer large chunks of data to specific computers; instead, it is used to transfer small packets by broadcasting them to everyone. There is no error checking because this part of the transfer is the responsibility of the applications involved.

Note: *One way to think about the differences between TCP and UDP is this: TCP is used for reliable data transfer and can be compared to calling a neighbor on the phone and speaking to him directly. UDP can be compared to using a bullhorn and sending your message to everyone on the street, hoping the neighbor you wanted to talk with hears it.*

The next layer, the Internet layer, is responsible for the routing of data packets. There are four Internet-layer protocols: Internet Protocol (IP), Address Resolution Protocol (ARP), Internet Control Message Protocol (ICMP), and Internet Group Management Protocol (IGMP). Each of these protocols routes data packets differently.

IP is a connectionless protocol that provides packet delivery for all of the protocols in the suite but does not guarantee the data packet delivery or sequence. TCP is responsible for those tasks. IP is responsible for getting the data packets from one host to another via this protocol, using routers and gateways. ARP assists in the transfer by finding out the Media Access Control (MAC) address of the machine to which the datagrams are going; this address is determined by the machine's IP address and other information. IP addresses are 32 bits long, and MAC addresses are 48 bits. All machines have MAC addresses, and each machine's is different. Conversions can be made in both directions by using an ARP cache that contains IP-address-to-MAC-address mappings. ICMP provides communication between computers that allows them to share error information. When transmission problems occur, other protocols in the stack use this information to recover. PING, discussed later, is an ICMP utility. When a PING command fails, this utility sends messages to the user. Finally, IGMP is used for multicasting transmissions, which is like broadcasting, to manage the groups that will receive the multicast. NetShow uses multicasting and IGMP for packet delivery.

10

After the data packets have worked their way through the Application, Transport, and IP layers, they are ready to go out on the wire. The Network Interface layer handles this part of the transfer. The Network Interface layer supports technologies such as Ethernet, Token Ring, Fiber Distributed Data Interface (FDDI), Frame Relay, ATM, and more. This layer provides rules for sending and receiving the data; these rules include guidelines for NICs, cables, media access units, device drivers, and so forth. When the data is on the wire, and when it is received at the target computer, the packets work their way back through the layers and are reconstructed to form an email, a file, a Web page, and so on to be read by the next user.

The IP Address

Although it is changing, the IP address is currently a 32-bit number that is assigned to every device that needs network connectivity on a Windows network. These devices include computers, network printers, network scanners, and routers. Computers or devices that have more than one NIC will need more than one IP address. Proxy servers have two NICs: one for connectivity within the network, and one for access outside the network (the Internet). For any device that connects outside a LAN or WAN that is accessed *by* the Internet, that device must have an IP address that is unique *on* the Internet. For instance, a company's external Web site, which is accessed by Internet users to place orders or view company information, must have a unique IP address on the Internet. Inside a LAN, addresses need only be unique to the LAN itself. Obtaining an address unique to the Internet is done through organizations such as the InterNIC or Network Solutions.

The 32-bit IP address is made up of four decimal octets separated by periods—for instance, 192.128.0.5 or 128.0.0.10. Like fully qualified domain names (FQDNs), though, this address is just an interface that has been created to help users cope with the 32-bit binary number that the IP address is based on. However, the number 192.128.0.5 is also an interface for users and is seen as 11000000 10000000 00000000 00000101 by the computer. As you can see, each part of the four-part 32-bit number is made up of four binary sets of digits. Because each of these four sets of digits has eight binary digits, it is referred to as four decimal octets. Depending on the first number in the octet, each IP address is separated into two parts: a network ID and a host ID. In the case of 192.128.0.5, the first part, 192.128.0.0, is the network address, and the second part, 5, is the host ID. The network ID identifies which network the host is on, and obviously thousands of networks can exist. The host ID identifies which computer is being addressed on the network, and there can be hundreds or thousands of hosts, depending on the network.

There is a lot to understand about TCP/IP and IP addressing, and the logical place to start is with the different types of addresses available. There are five, as outlined in Table 10.1. Each address class falls within a certain range of numbers and offers a certain number of network IDs and a certain number of host IDs.

Converting Binary Numbers to Base 10 and Back Again

Binary numbers in TCP/IP addresses are shown in sets of eight, as in 10111111 or 01010101. Converting these numbers to base 10 can be done with a scientific calculator or by hand. To change a binary number to base 10, you'll need to calculate each digit based on what its value is in binary, and then add up all of the digits. Look at the following example.

In a base 2 (binary) number, the digits are either ones or zeros. If the number is a one, you'll add up the number for that particular placeholder. The placeholders are worth the following in the decimal number system: <u>128 64 32 16 8 4 2 1</u>. Each of the placeholders is derived mathematically from $\underline{2^7\ 2^6\ 2^5\ 2^4\ 2^3\ 2^2\ 2^1\ 2^0}$. So, for a binary number such as 10111111, you'll have 128 + 0 + 32 + 16 + 8 + 4 + 2 + 1 = 191, and the number 01010101 is 0 + 64 + 0 + 16 + 0 + 4 + 0 + 1 = 85. You'll add up only the placeholders that contain ones, never the placeholders that contain zeros.

To change a base 10 number to binary, start with the number itself and try to subtract the largest number, 128. If you can perform this subtraction, place a 1 in the 128 placeholder, like so: <u>1 0 0 0 0 0 0 0</u>. With the remainder, see if you can subtract 64. If you can, place a 1 in the placeholder for 64, like so: <u>1 1 0 0 0 0 0 0</u>. Continue subtracting and placing ones where necessary until there are no remainders after subtracting. This number is 192.

I'll show one more example for good measure. I'll convert the number 155 to binary. Start by subtracting 128 from 155 to get 27. This means there will be a one in the 128 placeholder. Next, I'll try to subtract 64. Because I can't subtract 64 from 27, I'll put a zero in the 64 placeholder spot. Next, I'll try to subtract 32—no luck, so I'll put a zero in the 32 placeholder spot. Now I'll subtract 16 from 27 to get 11. Because I can do this, I'll place a one in the 16 placeholder spot. With 11 left, I can subtract 8 and put a placeholder of one in that spot and have three left over. That leaves a zero in the four spot, and a one in the 2 and 1 placeholders. The number in binary is 1 0 0 1 1 0 1 1.

Table 10.1   Internet IP classes and characteristics.

Class	Beginning IP Address	Ending IP Address	# of Network IDs	# of Host IDs
A	1.0.0.1	126.255.255.254	126	16,777,214
B	128.0.0.1	191.255.255.254	16,384	65,534
C	192.0.0.1	223.255.255.254	2,097,152	254
D	224.0.0.1	239.255.255.254	-	254
E	240.0.0.1	247.255.255.254	-	-

Note: IP addresses are configured in a range or scope of addresses. For instance, a LAN may have its IP addressing start for its clients at 192.128.4.25 and continue through 192.128.4.120. Additionally, addresses may be reserved for routers, gateways, network printers, and so on, in the form of a range of numbers such as 192.128.4.15 through 192.128.4.24. When your organization is assigned a group of addresses by an ISP or other entity, you will be given a range of this type. If you're configuring the IP addressing scheme to work in-house only, you should also create such a contiguous scheme.

Notice that there is no address class that contains the IP address 127.x.y.z. This address is reserved for testing on the local computer and is not a valid network address. To test the local TCP/IP stack to see if it is installed and configured correctly, you can enter **PING 127.0.0.1** (the most commonly used number, although anything up to 127.255.255.254 will work) at a command prompt. The example in Listing 10.1 shows a successful PING, indicating that TCP/IP is set up properly and working on the local machine.

Listing 10.1   A successful PING.

```
C:\>Ping 127.0.0.1
Pinging 127.0.0.1 with 32 bytes of data:
Reply from 127.0.0.1: bytes=32 time<10ms TTL=128
Reply from 127.0.0.1: bytes=32 time<10ms TTL=128
Reply from 127.0.0.1: bytes=32 time<10ms TTL=128
Reply from 127.0.0.1: bytes=32 time<10ms TTL=128
Ping statistics for 127.0.0.1:
Packets: Sent = 4, Received = 4, Lost = 0 (0% loss),
Approximate round trip times in milli-seconds:
Minimum = 0ms, Maximum =  0ms, Average =  0ms
```

So, what is the significance of the numbers 192 and 128, and the numbers 255 and 254? To understand that, you'll need to understand a little more about binary numbers and IP address configuration.

The first three numbers of the first octet determine the classes of IP addresses. In a Class A address, the first binary octet must start with a zero. In a Class B address, the first two binary numbers must be 10, and in a Class C address, the first three binary numbers must be 110. This limits how large each octet can be. In a Class A address, which begins with a zero, the smallest number is 000000001, and the largest number is 01111111. These numbers are written in binary, of course, but in base 10 (the decimal system), the numbers range from 1 to 126. In a Class B address, whose first octet has to start with 10, the smallest number is 10000001, and the largest number is 10111111, offering 128 to 192 for the first octet. In Class C, the first binary octet must start with 110, making 11000001 and 11011111 the smallest and largest numbers, respectively, offering the decimal numbers 192 to 223. Because Class D and E are not used publicly at this time, I won't detail those here.

The numbers 254 and 255 come from the octets being all ones for the middle octets and 11111110 for the last octet. The octet 192.255.255.254 is written in binary as 10111111.11111111.11111111.11111110. You may have noticed that the numbers are never all ones or all zeros. The address just shown is about as close to all ones as you can get. The address 11111111.11111111.11111111.11111111, or 255.255.255.255, is a broadcast address and is reserved. This number is used when every host needs to be sent a message. To send hosts on a single network a broadcast message, you use the following addresses:

- Class A—0.255.255.255

- Class B—0.0.255.255

- Class C—0.0.0.255

All zeros are used in RIP routing as the default route. RIP (Routing Information Protocol) is used to manage routing information in LANs. RIP transmits its routing table to other routers every 30 seconds, thus allowing all tables to contain updated information.

Subnetting and Default Subnet Masks

Besides assigning TCP/IP addresses to clients, servers, printers, and other resources, you'll need to set up other configurations. Consider what chaos would ensue if an organization using a Class A address configured one network with 500,000 hosts. Although having this many hosts is not uncommon, and organizations can have literally hundreds of thousands of clients to support, configuring them as one extremely large contiguous network isn't normally done. Obviously, maintaining a single network with 500,000 computers isn't feasible, and the network must be broken up into smaller units.

Subnetting is the process of splitting up a large network into physically separate subnetworks, or subnets, that are easier to manage. Subnetting not only makes managing a larger network possible by separating it into smaller ones, but also reduces network traffic, improves network performance, and distributes network responsibilities. To compare it to something more concrete might be to say that it's like remodeling a home when a relative moves in. You might break up the house into two or three parts instead of one, thus creating more independent living areas, reducing traffic in the kitchen or baths, or even distributing responsibilities.

Classes A, B, and C always begin with a specific set of numbers, as I mentioned earlier. Different classes also have different octet combinations of available networks and hosts. In a Class A address, the network ID is the first octet and the host ID uses the last three octets. The last three octets denote one host ID. In a Class B address, the first two octets are network IDs and the last two are host IDs. The first two octets denote one network ID, while the last two octets denote one host ID. Finally, in a Class C address, the first three octets represent the network ID and the last octet represents the host ID. If you look back at Table 10.1, you'll see that Class C addresses offered 254 hosts, and as you can see here, the last octet determines that number. If the last octet is 00000001 or 11111110, you can see that the host number is either 1 or 254.

What that basically means is this: In a Class C address that begins 192.128.0 for a network address, anywhere from 1 through 254 hosts can be configured. The clients' addresses can range from 192.168.0.1 to 192.168.0.254. And when a TCP/IP address is used, so is a subnet mask. Although you can break up this Class C network and create your own subnet masks, the default subnet masks for Classes A, B, and C are as follows:

- Class A networks use the subnet mask 255.0.0.0.

- Class B networks use the subnet mask 255.255.0.0.

- Class C networks use the subnet mask 255.255.255.0.

A *subnet mask* is really just a filter that routers can use to look at destination addresses of data packets and to send those packets on to the correct path. Subnet masks allow data transfers to determine whether or not the host they are looking for is on the local subnet. Using the same numbers mentioned earlier, if you send data from 192.128.0.1 to 192.128.0.5, then by looking at the subnet mask, the network ID, and the host ID, the hardware will know that the host is local. There won't be any need to send it out on the wire to an outside network. If you are on this network and send data to 126.64.0.8, with a different network and subnet mask, or to 192.128.0.5, with something other than a default subnet mask, then the routers know where to begin sending the data and know that the data isn't local. Because of the subnet mask, each router along the path knows if the IP address you are looking for is on one of its subnets or on another router's.

Note: In many instances, especially with the lack of Class A, B, and C address availability, class addresses are broken up into smaller units through subnetting. A Class C network has 254 hosts. However, if a client needs a Class C address, but needs only 60 addresses, it would be a waste of addresses not to somehow break up that Class C address into smaller subnets. After the address is separated, a router can be placed between the new subnets to route packets accordingly. Because the calculations required for performing this type of subnetting are quite complex, I'll leave that to the ISPs or to books dedicated solely to TCP/IP. However, you should be aware that subnetting and even super-subnetting exist.

Default Gateways

A *gateway* is a device such as a computer or router that is configured on a network so that users can access the Internet or other networks other than their local one. When you're configuring a TCP/IP address and a subnet mask for a client, you'll also need to configure a gateway if the user is to reach outside the local network. In a single network where no outside connectivity is needed, no default gateway needs to be configured.

Gateways work by maintaining a database of information about the other networks to which it's connected. For instance, if the gateway for network 1 knows about networks 2 and 3, and a packet is sent through the gateway, then the router knows which computer or network the packet should be sent to. A gateway is sometimes called an *IP router*.

In addition to sending packets to their correct destinations either locally or remotely, gateways are used to translate information as needed between protocols such as Microsoft networks and Novell NetWare networks, or between IP and IPX.

Routing

A *router* is simply a hardware device that is used to transmit data efficiently from point A to point B. Routing is a process that determines how to perform this transfer with the least amount of wasted time or effort. A router keeps a table of the routes it knows and the routes that are available and working; the router also keeps this table up-to-date. A router's main responsibility is to determine the shortest, quickest path to the destination computer. As mentioned previously, routers that act as gateways must also be able to transmit data between different technologies, like Token Ring, Ethernet, FDDI, or some other network type.

Using the IP Address and Routing Information

As you know, an IP address has two parts: the network ID and the host ID. Routers use this information to decide where and how to send data packets. Basically, a router works with the network and host IDs in the following manner:

1. When a data packet reaches a router, the router searches its routing table for a match with the destination address of the packet. Sometimes, when the destination address is located on the local network or subnet, the address is found and the packet is sent directly.

2. If the router doesn't see an exact match for the destination address in its routing table, it will search the table for a match with the destination network ID only,

ignoring the host ID. If the destination network ID is found, the packet is forwarded at that time. The next router will look at the host ID and route the data to the correct destination address. If the router doesn't have an entry for the destination network ID, then the router tries the default gateway.

3. If a default gateway is found, the data is sent to the default gateway router, and the process begins again. If the default gateway isn't found, the router returns the packet to its sender with a "host unreachable" error.

For the router to access other networks, it must be outfitted with the appropriate IP addresses as well. For instance, if a router connects a Class C network to a Class A network, that router must have the appropriate configuration. Figure 10.1 shows an example of a router of this type.

10

Routing tables play an important part, of course, and every time a computer is booted, it loads its routing table into memory. Table 10.2 shows a sample routing table. (You can see your routing table by typing **route print** at a command prompt.)

Notice the network destination addresses, subnet masks, and gateways used by the routing table. When data needs to be sent, these items describe the path that the data will take to try to get to its destination.

You can also use the Tracert tool with the Route Print command to determine what these IP addresses represent. For instance, if I enter the command **tracert 208.228.170.61**, it returns with the results shown in Figure 10.2, showing that the default gateway is actually my desktop PC. These command-line tools and others will be discussed in the next section, "Command-Line Tools."

Table 10.2   A sample routing table and its active routes.

Network Destination	Netmask	Gateway	Interface	Metric
0.0.0.0	0.0.0.0	208.228.170.61	208.228.170.61	1
66.6.196.134	255.255.255.255	208.228.170.61	208.228.170.61	1
127.0.0.0	255.0.0.0	127.0.0.1	127.0.0.1	1
169.254.0.0	255.255.0.0	169.254.222.56	169.254.222.56	1
169.254.222.56	255.255.255.255	127.0.0.1	127.0.0.1	1
169.254.255.255	255.255.255.255 169.254.222.56	169.254.222.56	1	-
208.228.170.61	255.255.255.255	127.0.0.1	127.0.0.1	1
208.228.170.255	255.255.255.255	208.228.170.61	208.228.170.61	1
224.0.0.0	224.0.0.0	169.254.222.56	169.254.222.56	1
224.0.0.0	224.0.0.0	208.228.170.61	208.228.170.61	1
255.255.255.255	255.255.255.255	169.254.222.56	169.254.222.56	1
Default gateway:	208.228.170.61	-	-	-

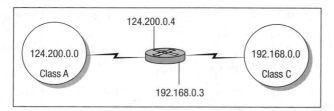

Figure 10.1
Router.

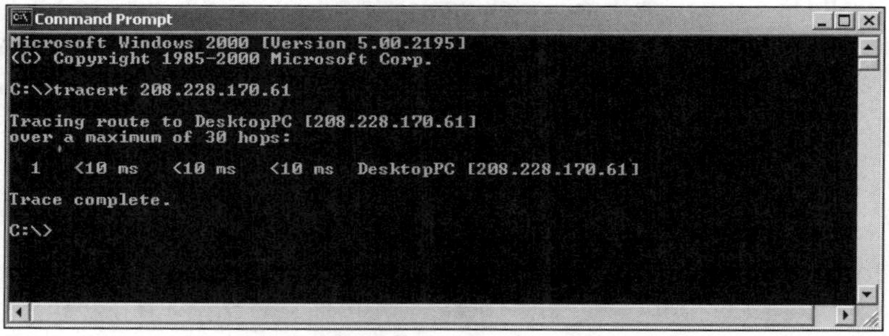

Figure 10.2
Tracert.

Addressing Tips

To create a workable TCP/IP addressing scheme, it's imperative that you understand which TCP/IP addresses will work with which subnets and gateways. Obviously, certain subnet masks are used with certain IP address classes, and gateways have to have addresses configured for accessing both networks. Listed next are some tips for creating a TCP/IP addressing scheme for your network, as well as a summary of some of the ideas mentioned earlier:

- The first octet cannot be 127; that is the loopback address.

- Neither the network ID nor the host ID can be all zeros or ones.

- The network ID on a LAN isn't unique, it is shared, but the host ID for each computer or resource must be unique.

- The source and destination addresses and the subnet masks are used by routers to determine if the transfer is for the local subnet or a remote one.

- No octet can have a value greater than 255.

- The gateway or router must be configured with a network ID so that clients on the local subnet can access it.

- A computer that acts as a proxy server will need two IP addresses: one for local traffic, and one for remote (Internet) traffic.

- The addresses in the sequence 169.254.0.0 through 169.254.255.255 are reserved and used for APIPA. You cannot use these addresses.

Command-Line Tools

No matter how much care you take in creating a TCP/IP addressing scheme, problems will arise, and you'll need to troubleshoot them. Microsoft offers some command-line tools for dealing with these problems, and the tools and their uses are outlined next.

PING

If you think that TCP/IP problems are causing the problem and you have ruled out physical problems with cables, NICs, or power to the machine, start troubleshooting with the PING utility. If you can successfully ping the loopback address, then you can rule out the possibility that TCP/IP is installed incorrectly or not bound to the NIC properly. Typing **ping 127.0.0.1** at a command prompt should be your first step. If you cannot ping the loopback address, consider reinstalling TCP/IP or at least looking over the configuration. Even if you aren't connected to any network, you'll get a successful ping because PING is an internal check.

If pinging the loopback address works fine, then the next step is to begin pinging local hosts, then gateways, and then remote hosts. PING can help you determine how deep the problem is. For instance, if you can ping a local host but not the default gateway, then you most likely have found your problem. It probably involves an incorrectly configured gateway address on the client or a gateway that isn't functioning on the network. If you can ping a local host and the default gateway, but not a remote host on the other side of that gateway, then you have some sort of routing problem.

Tracert

When a route breaks down on the way from the destination computer to its target, the Tracert route-tracing utility can tell you exactly where the packet got lost. Sometimes these problems lie in the gateway on your local network, and sometimes they lie with other routers not belonging to you or under your control. To use Tracert, simply type "*c:\tracert<IPaddress>*" and look at the route the packets took while getting to that address. If there is a breakdown along the route, you'll be able to tell at what point the packets were lost. Listing 10.2 shows a successful Tracert command for a local host, and this route includes only one hop. Listing 10.3 shows a Tracert command for a remote host, where the request has timed out (failed).

Listing 10.2   Tracert to a local host.

```
C:\>tracert 169.254.234.226

Tracing route to LAPTOP [169.254.234.226]
over a maximum of 30 hops:
1   <10 ms   <10 ms   <10 ms  LAPTOP [169.254.234.226]
Trace complete.
```

Listing 10.3   Tracert to a remote host.

```
C:\>tracert 10.0.0.4
Tracing route to 10.0.0.4 over a maximum of 30 hops
1    *        *        *       Request timed out.
2    100 ms   101 ms   100 ms  196-129.istrength.net [66.6.196.129]
3    110 ms   100 ms   131 ms  208.228.175.254
4    *        *        *       Request timed out.
5    *        *        *       Request timed out.
.
.
.
.
29   *        *        *       Request timed out.
30   *        *        *       Request timed out.
Trace complete.
```

IPConfig

The **ipconfig** command with the **/all** switch can be used to displays statistics about the local computer's IP address, host type, DNS suffix, subnet mask, and more. This information can be quite useful in troubleshooting such IP address problems as incorrectly configured gateways, subnets, and DNS server addresses.

Listing 10.4 shows an example of an **ipconfig /all** command on a local workstation.

Listing 10.4   Using the ipconfig /all command.

```
C:\>ipconfig /all
Windows 2000 IP Configuration\

Host Name . . . . . . . . . . . . : DesktopPC
Primary DNS Suffix  . . . . . . . :
Node Type . . . . . . . . . . . . : Broadcast
IP Routing Enabled. . . . . . . . : No
WINS Proxy Enabled. . . . . . . . : No
Ethernet adapter Local Area Connection:
```

```
Connection-specific DNS Suffix  . :
Description . . . . . . . . . . . : Realtek RTL8029(AS) PCI Ethernet Adapter
Physical Address. . . . . . . . . : 00-C0-F0-45-AB-5D
DHCP Enabled. . . . . . . . . . . : Yes
Autoconfiguration Enabled . . . . : Yes
Autoconfiguration IP Address. . . : 169.254.222.56
Subnet Mask . . . . . . . . . . . : 255.255.0.0
Default Gateway . . . . . . . . . :
DNS Servers . . . . . . . . . . . :

PPP adapter Internet:
Connection-specific DNS Suffix  . :
Description . . . . . . . . . . . : WAN (PPP/SLIP) Interface
Physical Address. . . . . . . . . : 00-53-45-00-00-00
DHCP Enabled. . . . . . . . . . . : No
IP Address. . . . . . . . . . . . : 208.228.170.171
Subnet Mask . . . . . . . . . . . : 255.255.255.255
Default Gateway . . . . . . . . . : 208.228.170.171
DNS Servers . . . . . . . . . . . : 207.252.204.136
                                    207.18.144.45
NetBIOS over Tcpip. . . . . . . . : Disabled
```

You can tell from this display that the computer's name is DesktopPC, that it has an Ethernet adapter with DHCP and automatic IP addressing enabled, and that the local area network connected via the Ethernet card isn't connected to an outside network because no gateway is configured. You can also tell that there is a connection called Internet, which does not have DHCP enabled and which uses DNS servers for name resolution on the Internet. From this you can conclude that there must be an ISP or other entity involved in connecting this computer to the outside world, probably through a modem or other connecting device that doesn't go through the local area network.

Other Command-Line Tools

Several additional command-line tools are available for troubleshooting TCP/IP connections. Table 10.3 describes some of these other tools.

Table 10.3 Miscellaneous command-line tools for troubleshooting TCP/IP connections.

Command	Description
Arp	Used to display locally resolved IP addresses as physical (MAC) addresses.
Nbtstat	Used to display connections using NetBIOS over TCP/IP and their statistics.
Netstat	Used to display TCP/IP connections and current protocol statistics. Listing 10.5 shows an example of an active TCP/IP session on a Windows 2000 workstation.
Route	Used to display the local routing table.
NSLookup	Used to help solve DNS hostname resolution problems.

Listing 10.5   Netstat.

```
C:\>netstat
Active Connections
Proto Local Address Foreign Address State
TCP DesktopPC:4627 LAPTOP:netbios-ssn ESTABLISHED
TCP DesktopPC:4634 205.138.3.62:http TIME_WAIT
TCP DesktopPC:4640 ns-100.waymark.net:pop3 TIME_WAIT
TCP DesktopPC:4645 ns-100.waymark.net:pop3 TIME_WAIT
TCP DesktopPC:4648 www.swynk.com:http ESTABLISHED
TCP DesktopPC:4649 www.swynk.com:http ESTABLISHED
TCP DesktopPC:4650 205.138.3.62:http TIME_WAIT
TCP DesktopPC:4651 ns-100.waymark.net:pop3 ESTABLISHED
TCP DesktopPC:4653 128.11.60.80:http ESTABLISHED
TCP DesktopPC:4655 207.68.183.62:http SYN_SENT
TCP DesktopPC:4656 63.236.18.129:http SYN_SENT
TCP DesktopPC:4657 www.law9.hotmail.com:http ESTABLISHED
```

Notice that there are several connections—some established, some in transit (sent), and some in waiting. The first connection is a NetBIOS connection from the desktop PC to the laptop, and this connection is established. The first three **TIME_WAIT** connections show an Internet POP3 mail account being accessed. The connection to **www.swynk.com** is established, as is a connection to **waymark.net**, a mail server. Finally, a connection to **hotmail.com** is established, as shown at the end of the listing.

Installing and Configuring TCP/IP

TCP/IP is most likely already installed on your computer, but if it isn't, you'll learn how to install it in this section. Also, you'll learn about the three ways to use TCP/IP addressing: dynamic addressing using DHCP; static addressing and configuring addresses manually; and automatic addressing using APIPA, a new feature of Windows 2000.

If your network supports dynamic TCP/IP addressing and uses DHCP, then you'll only need to configure the computer to obtain an IP address automatically in the IP Properties dialog box in My Network Places. This is the default setting for client computers running Windows 2000, Windows NT, or Windows 9x. However, for servers, you'll probably want to configure a static address. Static addresses are configured manually with the Use The Following IP Address option in the IP Properties dialog box.

Certain computers cannot be DHCP clients and receive their IP address automatically. For instance, computers that will act as DHCP servers cannot also be DHCP clients, and DNS servers must have a static address so users and applications can always find them when needed. Computers that act as gateways or routers must also have a static address assigned. On the client side, to enable callbacks from a remote access server, the client must be configured with a static IP address. Other resources needing static IP addresses include network printers, network scanners, or any other network resource that is accessed regularly.

If you have determined that you need a static address for a particular computer or resource, you must not only obtain an address for that resource's NIC that is unique on the network, but you must also obtain information about the subnet mask, the gateway or router, and the DNS domain name and address for a DNS server on the network. If a WINS server is used, that address is also needed.

Finally, you can configure your TCP/IP addressing scheme to use Automatic Private IP Addressing (APIPA). To use this type of addressing, you can have only a limited number of servers, the network must not be connected to the Internet, and the network must consist of only one segment. If these requirements are met, APIPA can be easily configured and managed because a default gateway, DNS server, or WINS server don't need to be configured.

10

Installation

To install TCP/IP, perform the following steps:

1. Log on as an administrator.

2. Choose Start|Settings|Control Panel and open Network And Dial-Up Connections.

3. If no local area connections exist, choose Make New Connection. If a local area connection exists, TCP/IP may already be installed. To configure TCP/IP for an existing connection, skip to Step 6.

4. If no local area connections exist, you'll need to configure one. In the Network Connection Wizard, choose the type of network connection you want to create, based on your networking needs. The choices are:

   • Dial-up to private network

   • Dial-up to the Internet

   • Connect to a private network through the Internet (for VPN tunneling)

   • Accept incoming connections

   • Connect directly to another computer

5. Depending on the choice you make in Step 4 and on the type of computer for which you are configuring the connection, you'll need to continue to work through the wizard to set up this local connection. If you've chosen to dial either a private network or the Internet through an ISP, or you've chosen to set up a VPN through the Internet, you'll be asked for phone numbers and similar information. If you've chosen to accept incoming connections, you'll need to switch over to Routing And Remote Access to continue if you're on a domain controller. And finally, if you've chosen Connect Directly To Another Computer, you'll be asked to define the role of

the computer you are connecting to, define your own computer, and, depending on the circumstance, use Routing And Remote Access to finish that as well. Either way, a local area connection must exist for you to install TCP/IP and to configure TCP/IP properties for the connection.

6. Right-click on the new local area connection or an existing one, and choose Properties.

7. In the General box, look for Internet Protocol (TCP/IP) in the Components area. If it isn't there, choose Install.

8. In the Select Network Component Type box, choose Protocol; then choose Add.

9. In the Select Network Protocol box, choose TCP/IP. (There are several others, including AppleTalk, DLC, NetBEUI, and NWLink IPX/SPX.) Choose OK.

10. TCP/IP is now installed. Choose OK to close this dialog box.

Static Addressing

With TCP/IP installed, you can now configure it with a static or dynamic address. To assign a static TCP/IP address, perform the following steps:

1. Log on as an administrator.

2. Choose Start|Settings|Control Panel and open Network And Dial-Up Connections.

3. Right-click on the connection for configuration, and choose Properties.

4. Highlight Internet Protocol and choose Properties.

5. In the Use The Following IP Address box, type the IP address, the subnet mask, and the default gateway. Next, type the preferred DNS server address. Choose Advanced.

6. In the Advanced TCP/IP Settings dialog box, on the IP Settings tab, choose Add to add more IP addresses, subnet masks, or gateways for use by this network connection.

7. On the DNS tab, choose Add to add the IP addresses of more DNS servers. Other items on the DNS tab allow you to append suffixes to unqualified names, and to register this connection's addresses in DNS.

8. On the WINS tab, choose Add to add WINS addresses, enable LMHOSTS lookup, and enable or disable NetBIOS over TCP/IP.

9. On the Options tab, you can change IP security settings or apply TCP/IP filtering. Choose OK until all boxes are closed; then restart the computer if necessary.

Tip: After installing or configuring TCP/IP, you can always test the setup by using the troubleshooting utilities mentioned earlier. Pinging the loopback address or the local host will let you know whether the installation was successful.

Automatic Private IP Addressing

One of the new features of Windows 2000 is the ability of TCP/IP to configure itself using Automatic Private IP Addressing. APIPA works like this:

1. When a computer logs on to the network, it needs an IP address. If the computer has a static address configured, it uses that address. If the computer is configured to obtain an IP address automatically, it looks first for a DHCP server to give it one. If there is a DHCP server on the network, the computer obtains an IP address from this server.

2. If no static address is configured, and no DHCP server exists (or if the DHCP server isn't online), then the client is unable to obtain an address. Before APIPA was introduced, this was the end of the network connection attempt. With Windows 2000, however, the client is given an address through APIPA.

3. APIPA steps in and generates an address for the client, giving the client access to the local network. The address is in the form 169.254.x.y, where the x and y combination identifies the client on the network and is unique. A subnet mask of 255.255.0.0 is also assigned. While this IP address generation is taking place, if duplicate addresses are assigned, the address is revoked and another one is generated.

4. When an address and a client are successfully matched, the client computer broadcasts this address to the network. The computer uses this address until a DHCP server is brought online and receives additional addressing information.

Because of this, a simple network can be set up simply by plugging a few computers into a hub and turning them all on. No DHCP or DNS servers need to be configured, and no advanced knowledge of TCP/IP is required.

If you noticed in Step 3, no default gateway was configured for the client computers. Without a gateway, clients using APIPA cannot access anything outside the local area network. Therefore, APIPA is useful only in emergencies and on small LANs that don't need outside access and that don't have more than one network segment.

In Listing 10.4, notice two sections: One shows information regarding an Ethernet adapter using an autoconfiguration address 169.254.222.56 (using APIPA), which allows access through the NIC and to the local network. The second section shows an Internet connection via a modem using an ISP and the information here:

```
IP Address. . . . . . . . . . . : 208.228.170.171
Subnet Mask . . . . . . . . . . : 255.255.255.255
Default Gateway . . . . . . . . : 208.228.170.171
DNS Servers . . . . . . . . . . : 207.252.204.136
```

Disabling APIPA

APIPA is enabled by default. Disabling it requires a change in the Registry. It is changed through the IPAutoconfiguration Enabled value in the HKEY_LOCAL_MACHINE\ SYSTEM\CurrentControlSet\Services\Tcpip\Parameters\Interfaces\Adapter_GUID subkey. The default value is 1; to disable APIPA, change this value to zero.

Warning! *Any changes to the Registry can potentially bring down a system and even require it to be reinstalled. Be very careful when making changes such as these, and always back up your data before doing so.*

Enabling APIPA for Use by a Client

To enable a computer to use APIPA, perform the following steps:

1. Log on as an administrator.

2. Choose Start|Settings|Control Panel and open Network And Dial-Up Connections.

3. Right-click on the connection for configuration, and choose Properties.

4. Highlight Internet Protocol and choose Properties.

5. Select the option Obtain An IP Address Automatically.

6. Connect the computer to a single-segment network through a simple hub.

Dynamic Addressing

In order to use dynamic addressing, you'll need to configure the clients, as shown in the previous example, by setting them up to obtain their IP addresses automatically. However, with dynamic addressing, you'll also need to set up a DHCP server from which the clients can obtain those addresses. When properly configured, DHCP can assign IP addresses, subnet masks, and gateways for all of the clients on the network. In the next section, you'll learn about DHCP servers, including how to configure them and how they complete the processes involved in assigning addresses and leases, scopes and configurations, and more.

Overview of DHCP

As you are certainly aware by now, DHCP can be used to simplify and automate how TCP/IP addressing is handled on a network. Windows 2000 Server contains a DHCP service that can be enabled and configured to handle this task. Because each computer must have its own unique name and address on the network, the administration of these items can quickly become a large task in a medium-size to large network.

DHCP not only simplifies the administration of these addresses and associated clients, but is also much more reliable than static addressing. When an administrator has to manually type in addresses on hundreds of computers and keep track of which addresses have been used and which haven't, the odds for making an error in those configurations are pretty good. Any replication of addresses will cause network problems as well, and incorrectly configured subnet masks or gateways will prevent clients from accessing both local and remote hosts. If the network is anything other than a very small and manageable network, you should seriously consider setting up at least one or two DHCP servers.

DHCP servers also enable administrators to specify global and subnet-specific parameters, such as scopes and superscopes, and centrally administer them. A *scope* is a contiguous range of IP addresses available for clients on the network. A single scope is usually used for a single physical subnet, and this scope provides the DHCP server with a pool of addresses to generate from. *Superscopes* are groups of scopes that are used to support numerous logical IP subnets on the same physical subnet.

10

Additionally, DHCP servers make it much easier to move clients from one subnet to another. When a client is moved, its old IP address is put back in the scope (or address pool), and it can be used by another client on that subnet. When the client is moved to its new subnet, it simply obtains a new address from the DHCP server serving the new network. This happens because the client is configured to obtain an address automatically and, as you will see later, simply works through the process of obtaining a new address from a new DHCP server on the new network.

DHCP is a TCP/IP standard and is an extension of the Bootstrap Protocol (BOOTP). BOOTP is an earlier protocol that allowed diskless clients to obtain their own IP addresses, obtain the address of the server, and obtain a file to be loaded into memory and executed, all without user involvement. How BOOTP works is described next, and this process is the basis of the DHCP lease process described later in this section.

Here is how BOOTP works:

1. The client has a unique ID, which is not an IP address and which is discovered when the computer boots. This unique ID is its MAC address.

2. The client sends a broadcast request for an IP address to everyone on the network; this request includes the MAC address of its machine. This request is a *bootrequest* packet.

3. The server sees the request and responds with a *bootreply* packet. The server has a database that contains MAC-address-to-IP-address mappings. The server offers an IP address.

4. The computer accepts the address and is initiated onto the network. At this time, an executable file can be run that starts an operating system or otherwise configures the client and makes it functional.

The Lease Process

When an organization uses DHCP to automatically assign TCP/IP addresses to clients on its network, those addresses aren't assigned and then left with the client computer forever. The client only borrows them from the server for a predetermined period of time.

This arrangement is called a *lease*, and when the lease of the IP address is up, the server revokes it. If the client still needs an IP address, the client then requests a new one. Of course, it's a lot more complex than that, but the point is that a leased IP address doesn't last forever.

This leasing arrangement eliminates many potential problems. For instance, suppose a network has a Class C address and has approximately 254 addresses available. A few of those addresses will be configured as static addresses for DNS and DHCP servers, a few addresses will be configured for remote access clients, and perhaps some addresses will be configured for network printers. In the Class C network in this scenario, perhaps there are 235 available addresses for clients. This will work fine, of course, as long as there are fewer than 235 clients needing IP addresses, but this is not always the case. Suppose there were 350. When DHCP releases IP addresses that aren't in use—computers that have been shut down, computers that have been inactive for a day or two, or computers that have been taken offline because they are laptops or have been moved—those IP addresses are free for another client on the network to use them.

For a client to use addresses from a Windows 2000 DHCP server, the client must be running one of the following operating systems:

- Windows 2000

- Windows NT Server 3.51 or later

- Windows NT Workstation 3.51 or later

- Windows 9x

- Windows for Workgroups 3.11 running Microsoft TCP/IP-32

- Microsoft Network Client 3 for Microsoft MS-DOS with the real-mode TCP/IP driver

- LAN Manager version 2.2c for MS-DOS (LAN Manager 2.2c for OS/2 isn't supported)

Leases are initiated when a DHCP client is booted and tries to connect to the network for the first time, when a server drops a lease, when a DHCP lease expires, or when a new lease is requested. The sections that follow explain the process by which the client obtains a lease and the server assigns one.

DHCP Discover Message

When a client is initiating a network connection, the client does not know anything about an IP address, subnet mask, or gateway. The client begins the lease acquisition process by using a limited version of TCP/IP and sending out a DHCPDISCOVER broadcast to all of the DHCP servers on the network. This message is encapsulated in a UDP packet, is sent with a local IP broadcast address of 255.255.255.255 (the destination address), and uses 0.0.0.0 for the source address. If there is a DHCP server on the local network or subnet, that DHCP server will respond with a DHCPOFFER message. If there is no such local DHCP server, the request must be forwarded to an IP router that supports the transmission of DHCPDISCOVER broadcast messages. (Routers don't generally send broadcasts.) All DHCP communications are done over two ports: UDP 67 and 68.

Because the computer is sending the source address as 0.0.0.0, the server will not be able to identify it with only that information, so the computer sends its MAC address and computer name as well.

Note: *When a DHCP client has an IP address lease and shuts the computer down, the lease is still active and can be used when the computer is booted again, provided that the lease has not expired.*

DHCP Offer Message

All of the DHCP servers on the network that receive the DHCPDISCOVER message then respond with an offer of an IP address. This offer is called DHCPOFFER and contains the following information:

- The client's MAC address

- An available IP address from that server's scope of addresses

- An appropriate subnet mask

- A lease term (how long the lease will be good for)

- The address of the server that is making the offer

This offer is also a broadcast message because the computer does not yet have an IP address.

The client picks the first IP address offered while, at the same time, all DHCP servers reserve the addresses they've offered. It is necessary that all DHCP servers reserve their offered addresses until each server is certain that its address has been chosen or it hasn't. When that information is available, a server can either mark the address as in use or put it back in the pool for another client's request.

DHCP Request Message

Once a client has accepted an offer, that client must send another broadcast message to all of the DHCP servers on the network so that each server that made an offer is told which offer the client accepted. The server that issued the winning IP address makes a note that the address is in use, while the servers that did not have their addresses accepted can put them back in the pool. This client broadcast is called a DHCPREQUEST message and includes the winning server's IP address.

DHCP Acknowledgement Messages

The final step in the lease process occurs when the client receives an acknowledgement from the DHCP server that the lease has been granted. This is called a DHCPACK message, which is another broadcast message, and it contains a valid lease and other information, including the lease duration. Once the lease is received and accepted, the client is considered a DHCP client and can access the network as appropriate. DHCPACK messages are also sent during lease renewal, when the client's lease is almost up and is requesting to continue using the lease.

Another type of acknowledgement message, the DHCPNACK message, can be sent when the lease request isn't successful. This broadcast message is sent when either of the following conditions is met:

- The client is trying to obtain a lease on a previously held address, and that address is no longer available because of changes in scope on the DHCP server.

- The client is requesting to renew a lease after moving to a new subnet, and the address is not available.

Note: *The DHCP client can perform a check in which an ARP request might suggest that the address is already in use. Although this is rare, the client would then decline the request and begin the process again. This "decline" message is sent as a DHCPDECLINE message from the client to the server.*

DHCP Lease Renewal

Because leases aren't good forever, at certain times during the lease, the client will try to renew the lease of the IP address. The first time a computer tries to renew its lease is when its lease is 50 percent up. Suppose a lease is good for 48 hours. At the 24-hour mark, the computer will try to renew its lease by sending out a DHCPREQUEST message to the server that issued the lease. Because the computer has a lease and knows from where the lease came, the message is a directed message instead of the usual broadcast. If the DHCP server is available, it usually renews the lease and sends a DHCPACK message with new lease parameters. If the DHCP server isn't available, other measures are taken.

If the lease renewal is not successful, the client does nothing else until the 87.5 percent mark—in this example, at 42 hours. At this time, the client broadcasts a DHCPREQUEST message to any DHCP server on the network. Requests are followed by either DHCPACK or DHCPNACK from available servers, and either the lease is renewed or it isn't. If it isn't renewed, the client continues to try to renew the lease at various intervals until the lease expires or until a lease is obtained. If the lease expires before the client receives an acknowledgement from a DHCP server, the client must surrender the IP address and begin the process again.

Note: *Keep the concept of APIPA in mind during discussions about unsuccessful lease renewals. If a client's lease runs out and there is no DHCP server online, the client can be given an IP address—in the form of 169.254.x.y—that will work on the local subnet.*

DHCP Release

Although command-line utilities and switches are available for renewing and releasing leases, most lease releases are simply caused by computers being taken offline, computers being moved, or leases expiring. Microsoft DHCP clients do not initiate DHCPRELEASE messages when they shut down.

Note: If a computer has more than one NIC, then the computer will go through the lease process for every NIC configured on the machine.

Tip: You can use command-line utilities and their switches for managing DHCP leases. The **ipconfig /release** and **ipconfig /renew** commands are the most commonly used. When a client will be moved to a different network and will not need its current lease, administrators can type **ipconfig /release** at a command prompt to force the client to send a DHCPRELEASE message. When a user wants to renew a lease manually, the **ipconfig /renew** command can be used to send a DHCPREQUEST message to the DHCP server. When this is done, the DHCP server sends an updated lease if it is available. If the server is not available, an error message is displayed and the client continues to use its existing lease.

10

Scopes and Reservations

When you configure a DHCP server, one of the first things you configure after installation is a scope of available IP addresses. A *scope* is a range of addresses that can be leased to clients on the network. Each subnet on the network can have only one scope of addresses, and those addresses must be contiguous. For instance, you might configure a scope such as 168.140.2.0 through 168.140.2.250. When you need to use addresses from more than one continuous range of numbers, as shown here, you can do so by creating the scope from the lowest IP address to the highest and then excluding the addresses that cannot be used. Addresses that are excluded are not offered to clients for lease.

Scopes are configured with a name, a subnet mask, a range of addresses, and a time interval that describes the lease duration. Because the DHCP server itself must have a static IP address, this address must be excluded from the scope if it is in the scope's range. Other static addresses must also be excluded for computers, network printers, or laptop clients that have those addresses configured. After all of this has been set up, the remaining addresses are ready for lease.

Tip: When you are making a list of static addresses previously assigned for exclusion, make sure you remember to include other DHCP servers, non-DHCP clients, diskless workstations, and routing and remote access clients.

The default lease duration is eight days; in the example used earlier, the lease was set to 48 hours. When configuring a scope, you have the opportunity to change the lease duration. If there aren't enough IP addresses available, or if computers on your network are moved around a lot, then you need to make sure that the IP addresses that you do have are recycled often. By shortening the lease duration, you can achieve just that. If you have plenty of IP addresses, and the clients don't change locations often, you probably won't need to make any changes here. If you have plenty of IP addresses, and the clients don't change locations often, but you need to reduce network traffic due to DHCP requests, acknowledgements, and such, you can increase the lease duration. Decision Tree 10.1 details lease duration decisions.

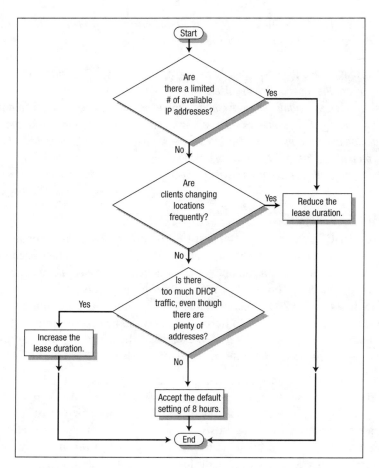

Decision Tree 10.1
Lease durations.

Although only one scope can be configured per subnet, multiple scopes can be configured on a single DHCP server for centralizing the administration of multiple subnets. In contrast, if only one DHCP server exists, it must be configured with at least one scope. In medium to large organizations, though, multiple DHCP servers usually exist for fault tolerance and load balancing. When multiple DHCP servers exist, you'll also have to make sure that none of their scopes overlap. As you know, when duplicate IP addresses occur on a network, communication problems occur. Duplicate addressing is usually caused by static addressing typos, exclusion configuration problems, or incorrectly configured (overlapping) scopes.

Reservations and exclusions are similar in that the addresses are not available for lease to DHCP clients in the way they are generally assigned to clients. Whereas *exclusions* are for addresses statically assigned to certain resources (including non-DHCP clients) and cannot be leased, *reservations* are IP addresses that are permanently leased to a particular object through the DHCP server. For instance, a print server, a fax server, a mail server, or perhaps even a specific user will always be reserved, and thus assigned, the same address to lease each time. The devices that are configured with address reservations are DHCP clients and perform a specific duty for the network.

The 80/20 Rule

In larger networks, more than one DHCP server is often configured for a single subnet. When more than one DHCP server is available, fault tolerance increases, so if one of the DHCP servers goes offline, the others can take over until the problem is resolved. The 80/20 rule states that if there are two DHCP servers for a single subnet, the first DHCP server should be configured with 80 percent of the available addresses, and the second DHCP server should be configured with 20 percent. The thought is that if the first server goes down, the second will have enough addresses to renew and will give new leases for a reasonable period of time until the first server is repaired.

10

DHCP Scope Parameters Defined

When you're configuring the scope for a DHCP server, there are several parameters, as I mentioned earlier in this section. Table 10.4 lists these parameters as you will see them when you begin installing DHCP. Make sure you know exactly what you want to specify in each of these parameters before beginning that installation. This book's CD-ROM includes a blank worksheet, which you can use to make notes concerning your specific scope configuration.

Table 10.4   Scope parameters.

Parameter	Description
Name	The name of the scope. Make sure the name is descriptive and represents the subnet in some way.
Description	A description of the scope, its subnet, or any other notes. Optional.
Start IP Address	The starting IP address from which clients can lease addresses.
End IP Address	The ending IP address from which clients can lease addresses.
Subnet Mask	The subnet mask that clients will be assigned with their IP addresses.
Start IP Address (For Excluded Range)	Used to exclude certain ranges of addresses. This parameter defines the start address. Optional.
End IP Address (For Excluded Range)	Used to exclude certain ranges of addresses. This parameter defines the ending address. Optional.
Lease Duration	Defines how long a lease can be used by a client before it must be renewed. The duration is specified in days, hours, and minutes. The default is 8 days.

DHCP Options and Classes

Once a scope has been created, DHCP options can be configured for servers and clients. There are several option types: predefined, server, scope, and client, although predefined options are simply configurations of the other three. In addition to these option types, several class options are available, representing both vendors and users.

Predefined Options

You can set predefined options for your DHCP server by opening the DHCP console (Start|Programs|Administrative Tools|DHCP) and choosing Action|Set Predefined Options. From here, you can select standard options from server options, scope options, and client options. You can add, remove, or edit these options, and thus standardize how those options will be used for the DHCP server or its clients.

Server Options

Server options are configured to represent all DHCP clients on the network and are used when every client requires the same configuration. For instance, all clients may need the same DNS server, default gateways, or WINS servers. Server options are used by default but are overridden by scope or client options. These server option settings will be the default settings for all of the clients on the network that lease an address from the DHCP server.

To set server options perform the following steps.

1. Log on as an administrator to the DHCP server.

2. Open the DHCP console from Start|Programs|Administrative Tools|DHCP.

3. Expand the tree in the left pane and highlight the folder Server Options.

4. Choose Action|Configure Options from the menu bar.

Note: *The Action|Configure Options dialog box will change depending on what folder is highlighted in the tree. Figure 10.3 shows the dialog box for this instance.*

In the Server Options dialog box, you can select an item to be configured, such as a DNS server, and then type the server name and its IP address. Some of the other common items that are configured here are listed next. These are configured on the General tab. (You can see the screen in Figure 10.3.) Server options are:

- Router

- Name Servers

- Log Servers

- Cookie Servers

- DNS Domain Name

- Broadcast Address

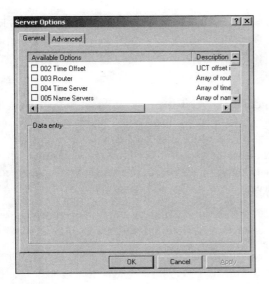

Figure 10.3
Server Options.

- ARP Cache Timeout

- TCP Default Time-To-Live

- WINS Servers

- NetBIOS Scope ID

- Simple Mail Transfer Protocol (SMTP) Servers

- Post Office Protocol (POP3) Servers

- Network News Transfer Protocol (NNTP) Servers

- World Wide Web (WWW) Servers

Configuring these options will allow all clients who lease addresses to use these settings by default. Typing the name and IP address of the server configures most of these settings, but some are configured with data entry information. On the Advanced tab, you can configure the Vendor classes and the User classes. Vendor classes include DHCP Standard Options, Microsoft Options, Windows 2000 Options, and Windows 98 Options. User classes include BOOTP classes, Routing And Remote Access classes, and Default User classes. All of these classes are described in more depth at the end of this section.

Scope Options

Scope options are configured for clients who lease their addresses from a specific scope of addresses. You could have different scopes and gateways for different subnets, and these different clients could have their settings configured here. Scope options override server options.

To set scope options, you select the Scope Options folder in the DHCP console and choose Action|Configure Options. The Scope Options dialog box is similar to the Server Options dialog box, which is shown in Figure 10.3 and used to set client options.

Client Options

Client options are configured for clients on the network that have reserved client leases. Client options override scope and server options and are configured through the Action menu in the DHCP console. If you are just setting up a DHCP server, however, you won't be able to set client options because you don't yet have any reservations configured. Client options apply to only those specific clients that have reserved IP addresses configured in the DHCP server.

After you have configured a reservation for a particular client on the network, you can select that client in the DHCP console, choose Action|Configure Options, and set the options as needed.

Classes and Class Options

There are two types of classes related to DHCP: Vendor and User. Vendor classes are configured when clients need to be identified by their vendor type while obtaining a lease from the server. That vendor type may be Windows 2000, Windows 98, or standard DHCP options. If you want to define other Vendor classes besides Microsoft classes, you'll need to define those yourself. By allowing specific vendor applications to work with DHCP, Vendor classes provide support for multiple-vendor environments.

User classes are configured to separate different types of users into groups so that their options can be configured appropriately. For instance, all remote access clients might be grouped together so that they can receive their leases from a certain scope or have a specific DNS or gateway server assigned only to them. Laptop users might be given a lease time that is shorter than that given to the rest of the users. Also, BOOTP clients can be configured with specific servers, such as log servers, resource location servers, or swap servers.

Class options, both Vendor and User, are configured from the Advanced tab in the Server Options or Scope Options dialog boxes.

Vendor classes include the following settings:

- *DHCP Standard Options*—This is the default setting for the Vendor class. These options include those seen on the General tab mentioned earlier in "Server Options." These include items such as DNS servers, routers, WINS servers, WWW servers, and POP3 servers.

- *Microsoft Options*—This setting contains three configurable options, including Microsoft Disable NetBIOS Option, Microsoft Release DHCP Lease On Shutdown, and Microsoft Default Router Metric Base.

- *Microsoft Windows 2000 Options*—This setting contains the same options as the Microsoft Options setting has. All clients configured to use this option class will receive these settings with the lease.

- *Microsoft Windows 98 Options*—This setting can be configured for Windows 98 Vendor classes.

User classes include the following settings:

- Default User Class

- Default BOOTP Class

10

- Default Routing And Remote Access Class

For the majority of options introduced in this section, any locally defined option will override the option configured here. For instance, if more than one option exists, a locally assigned DNS server address will be used instead of the DNS server address configured in the server, scope, or client options set through the DHCP console.

Beyond the local settings' overriding these DHCP options, other overrides exist in certain circumstances. Server options can be overridden by both the scope options and the client options. Scope options can be overridden by client options. However, if a scope option has been set for the Routing And Remote Access class on the Advanced tab, then only Routing And Remote Access clients will be configured with those settings. If a default user has scope options configured, that user will not receive options configured for Routing And Remote Access clients. In other words, configured Vendor and Client classes will receive their own settings, and no one else will. Scope settings are still overridden by client settings, though, so make sure your options are set appropriately. In most instances, the default settings will work just fine.

BOOTP Clients

Earlier, the Bootstrap Protocol (BOOTP) was discussed as the precursor to Windows DHCP. Because of this, there will most likely be times when you'll need to support these BOOTP clients. BOOTP was created to support diskless clients on older workstations, and you may have several of these on your network. As I mentioned earlier, it is the Bootstrap Protocol that allows these clients to boot up, access the network, and participate in a network successfully.

In the days of Windows NT, these clients had to be configured to use a static address or had to be issued a client reservation. In Windows 2000, however, these clients can now be a part of the regular DHCP lease process as long as some special configurations are set to accommodate them.

If a BOOTP client simply wants to obtain an IP address, without using a client reservation, a special BOOTP pool of addresses can be configured. You can also configure specific options for all of the BOOTP clients by making changes on the Advanced tab of the Server Options, Scope Options, and Client Options dialog boxes. If a client needs also to obtain boot file information, you'll still need to add client reservations, and you'll need to configure a BOOTP table. This table contains the name of the boot image file, the path to the file that contains the image, and the Trivial File Transfer Protocol (TFTP) file server that will be used to hold those files until needed. You can add entries to this table through the DHCP console. In the "Configuring and Implementing DHCP" section, you'll learn how to perform these tasks.

Remote Access Clients

Remote access clients gain entry into the network server by dialing into the server from a remote location. These clients are usually telecommuters, temporary guests to the network, or laptop users. The clients dial in (or otherwise connect) to a remote access server using Point-to-Point Protocol (PPP) or Serial Line Internet Protocol (SLIP), and the clients can then access the network as if they were physically in the office or building.

Remote access servers can be configured to use some of the available DHCP IP addresses for their clients. These addresses are obtained from the DHCP server before any clients log on, and these addresses are cached at the remote access server. Remote access servers act like proxy DHCP servers for these clients. *Proxy* means that something acts as a surrogate or substitute for the real thing. When a remote access server offers a remote access client an IP lease, the lease has no expiration or time configured. This is because the remote access server handles how long the client can stay connected and simply takes care of the address lease when the client logs (or is logged) off the network.

As seen in previous examples, for these users, Windows 2000 offers a default class called the Default Routing And Remote Access class. This User class identifies those clients that are making a PPP or SLIP connection through a remote access server, and this class can be configured to assign certain option settings to these users as they obtain their leases.

New Features of Windows 2000 DHCP

Windows 2000 DHCP has several new features. Each enhancement further simplifies and refines the DHCP lease process. You are already aware of one of the new features, Automatic Private IP Addressing (APIPA), and you have been introduced to some of the other new features already in this chapter. This section will summarize these new concepts as well as others not previously mentioned.

APIPA comes into play when the DHCP server on your network is taken offline or goes down unexpectedly. APIPA offers clients addresses in the form of 169.254.x.y, and APIPA IP addresses can be used to access the local subnet until the DHCP server is repaired. Besides this feature, there are several others worth mentioning.

A new type of scope called a *multicast scope* is available. This scope enables clients to lease Class D IP addresses for configuring multicast broadcasts and groups.

Dynamic support for BOOTP clients permits these clients to be configured on the network without your having to statically assign them addresses or reserve leases for them. This feature allows administrators to more easily configure and manage large BOOTP networks that contain diskless or legacy workstations requiring such support.

DHCP and DNS can now work together to provide dynamic updates for DHCP clients as long as there are DNS servers that can support these dynamic updates on the network. DNS servers keep track of which IP addresses are mapped to which hostnames. If Workstation_01 has an IP address of 192.168.0.5, then the DNS server knows that mapping and keeps track of it. The DNS server can then resolve that name for other clients on the network that need it. Clients who lease an IP address have IP addresses that change often. For DHCP and DNS to be used together, there would have to be something in place so that the DNS server could keep track of the changes. This is the purpose of Dynamic DNS (DDNS) updates.

10

Another innovative feature is the authorization of DHCP servers by Active Directory for computers that are new to the network. Discussed earlier, this authorization keeps unauthorized servers from servicing the network and thereby creating multiple communication problems for users. Superscopes are also available; they can be used to enlarge the IP address space on the network without disrupting currently active scopes. You'll learn more about these two types of scopes and how to configure them later in the chapter. User and Vendor classes are also new to Windows 2000 and have been introduced.

New performance objects for DHCP are available in Performance Monitor. You can monitor many objects related to the DHCP server's performance, and listed next are just a few of them:

- Discovers/sec—DHCPDISCOVER
- Offers/sec—DHCPOFFER
- Requests/sec—DHCPREQUEST
- Informs/sec—DHCPINFORM
- Acks/sec—DHCPACK
- Nacks/sec—DHCPNACK
- Declines/sec—DHCPDECLINE
- Releases/sec—DHCPRELEASE

Having the ability to monitor these objects and more through Performance Monitor greatly increases the chances that the server can be optimized and can perform at the best levels possible.

Optimizing the DHCP Servers

Listed next are some ways that you can optimize the configuration of the DHCP server(s) on your network. Some of these tips are offered by Microsoft, and some simply come from experience. Spending time optimizing your DHCP servers now will pay off in the long run. Keep the following tips in mind:

- Do not configure one DHCP server to maintain more than 8,000 clients. Microsoft's number is 10,000, but there's no fixed limit.

- Each DHCP server should have no more than 1,000 scopes defined for use by clients.

- Have at least two DHCP servers, if possible, for anything other than a small network of 500 or fewer clients, and configure these servers with the 80/20 rule mentioned earlier.

- If a network is connected with a slow WAN link, configure a DHCP server on both sides of the link to avoid slow transmissions.

- The DHCP server should have really fast disk drives so that the requests are handled quickly.

- For a router to forward DHCP requests, the router must be capable of passing both DHCP and BOOTP requests across it. If it isn't, you'll need to configure a computer to act as a DHCP relay agent. This relay agent can be another router capable of forwarding these requests, or it can be a Windows 2000 server configured for Routing And Remote Access. You can also place a Windows NT server in between the DHCP client and the IP router to act as a relay agent.

- Do not deactivate a scope when what you really want to do is temporarily disable it. Deactivating a scope causes the DHCP server to stop recognizing those addresses as valid and can cause multiple network problems. Deactivate a scope only when you are positive that you want to remove the scope for good. To change the scope, it is better to edit it or create exclusion addresses instead.

- When more than one DHCP server exists, make sure that you have reserved those DHCP static addresses from all of the scopes on all of the DHCP servers.

- Increase and reduce lease times as noted earlier. Use longer leases for less-mobile users, and shorter leases for laptop or more-mobile users. In a smaller network, leases can even be configured not to expire at all.

- As you'll see in Chapters 11 and 12, DHCP servers can be configured to work with DNS servers and Routing And Remote Access servers. You should take advantage of these capabilities.

- Install the first DHCP server on your network on a domain controller or a member server, not on a standalone server.

- Allow server log files to audit the DHCP Server service. Using event logs, you can see successes related to leases and requests, and see failure related to authorizations, unreachable domains, network failures, and more. Additionally, you can audit cached authorizations and see information related to rogue DHCP detections.

- Use Option classes to separate users on the network and to obtain specific information regarding their leases and logons.

- Take advantage of the new Performance Monitor counters to optimize your DHCP server(s).

Installing DHCP

10

In this section, you'll learn how to install DHCP and create a DHCP server. The server must meet certain requirements, such as having a static TCP/IP address, and those issues will be discussed. You'll also need to activate the server after the DHCP service has been installed. Once the server has been authorized by Active Directory, the DHCP server will be ready for use.

Server Requirements

The DHCP service has certain network requirements. First, the network must be running TCP/IP, and at least one computer must be a Windows 2000 server. This server can be a domain controller, a standalone server, or a member server. This server must have a static TCP/IP address because a DHCP server cannot also be a DHCP client. If this is the first DHCP server on the network, do not install it on a standalone server.

To configure your Windows 2000 server with a static TCP/IP address, perform the following steps:

1. Log on as an administrator and open the Control Panel.

2. Open Network And Dial-Up Connections.

3. Right-click on the local area connection you want to manage, and choose Properties.

4. Highlight Internet Protocol in the Components box, and choose Properties.

5. In the Internet Protocol Properties box, choose Use The Following IP Address.

6. Enter an IP address that you can use for this DHCP server, and enter an appropriate subnet mask and a gateway address. (If this network doesn't need to access any entity outside the LAN, a gateway address isn't needed.)

7. If you use a preferred DNS server, type in this address. If this computer will also serve as the DNS server, do not type in an address.

8. Choose the Advanced button if you need to configure alternate IP settings, DNS, WINS, or other options.

After the server is configured with a static IP address, other DHCP requirements include the following:

- Installing the DHCP service

- Configuring the DHCP scope

- Activating the new scope

- Authorization by the Active Directory service

In the sections that follow, you'll learn how to install the DHCP service, configure scopes, activate scopes, configure clients, and manage leases, options, and classes.

DHCP Server Installation

To install a DHCP server, follow the steps listed next. (Make sure the computer is configured with a static IP address as shown in the previous section.)

1. Log on as an administrator and open the Control Panel.

2. Choose Add/Remove Programs.

3. From the Windows Components Wizard, highlight Networking Services.

4. Choose the Details button, and check Dynamic Host Configuration Protocol (DHCP). Choose OK, then Next.

5. Choose Start|Programs|Administrative Tools|DHCP to test the installation.

6. If the installation was successful, and TCP/IP was configured and bound correctly to the NIC, you'll see the screen shown in Figure 10.4.

Authorizing a DHCP Server

Before the DHCP server can be used by clients or configured by administrators, the Active Directory service must authorize it first. This authorization prevents DHCP servers from being configured or started on the network unintentionally; an unexpected DHCP server on the network can cause multiple TCP/IP network problems.

Unintended DHCP servers cause network problems because they will offer or lease TCP/IP addresses that will most likely not be valid on the subnet. Even if those addresses are valid, they will probably conflict with others already leased. If clients on the network are given bogus addresses, these clients will be unable to reach the domain controller and will fail to log on to the network. If they are given duplicate addresses, havoc will ensue for network communications. Because of this, Active Directory is assigned the duty of ensuring that the DHCP servers that are authorized are legal.

Unauthorized servers are detected, and valid servers are authorized, by utilizing specific types of messages called *DHCP information messages*, or DHCPINFORM. A DHCPINFORM message is sent when the DHCP service starts. This message is a

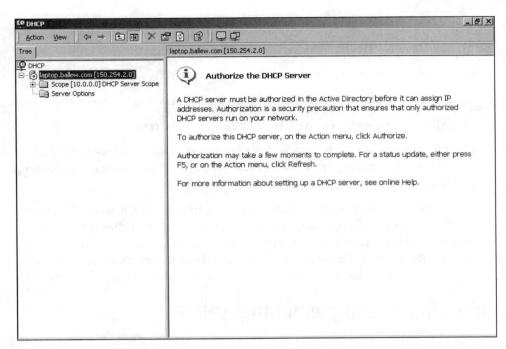

Figure 10.4
A successful DHCP installation.

broadcast message sent to the root domain of the network that contains other (or no) DHCP servers. The other DHCP servers on the network (if they exist) then reply with a DHCPACK message, which contains information about other DHCP servers on the network. The initiating DHCP server now has a list of other DHCP servers on the local network and has information regarding the root domain.

If no other DHCP servers exist on the network, and if the network is a confined network such as one used for testing, then the DHCP server is authorized. If the DHCP server is being configured as the first DHCP server on the network and is being configured on a domain controller or member server, it is also authorized. If this is not the case, the initiating computer checks for the directory service from other computers on the network. One of the existing DHCP servers will be running on a domain controller or a member server. When a directory service is found, final checks are made.

Warning! *Your first DHCP server should be installed on a domain controller or a member server, not on a standalone server. If it is installed on a standalone server, DHCP authorization will not work properly.*

If the initiating computer is to be authorized, its IP address must be on the authorized DHCP server list. For member servers, this list is in directory services for the DHCP server list; for standalone servers, this list is in directory services for the root of the enterprise.

To authorize a newly installed DHCP server, follow these steps:

1. Log on as an administrator.

2. Choose Start|Programs|Administrative Tools|DHCP.

3. Choose Action|Authorize. The authorizing process might take a few minutes.

4. When the process is complete, choose Action|Refresh.

5. The right pane will no longer have information about authorizing the server. Instead, this pane will have information about the IP address of the server scope and will show its status as Active. Close the console.

You may want to use the DHCP snap-in for managing the DHCP server. This snap-in isn't available until you install the DHCP service unless you choose to install Adminpak.msi from the Windows 2000 Server CD-ROM. Either way, using the DHCP snap-in allows you to view detailed information about scopes and reservations, create and modify scopes, view reservation options, and view address leases for clients.

Configuring and Implementing DHCP

After installing and authorizing the DHCP service, you can begin the task of configuring the new DHCP server and implementing it on the network. In this section, you'll learn how to configure scopes and reservations, configure DHCP clients, configure options and classes, manage clients and leases, and configure and manage both BOOTP clients and remote access clients.

Configuring Scopes

Several tasks are involved with configuring scopes and reservations on the new DHCP server. You can create new scopes, remove scopes, exclude addresses, activate and deactivate the scope, and change scope properties.

Creating a New Scope

To create a new scope on a DHCP server, follow these steps:

1. Log on as an administrator.

2. Choose Start|Programs|Administrative Tools|DHCP.

3. In the domain tree, open the DHCP server for which you want to configure a scope.

4. Choose Action|New Scope.

5. The Welcome page of the New Scope Wizard appears. Choose Next, and type in a name and description of the scope you are creating. Figure 10.5 shows this screen.

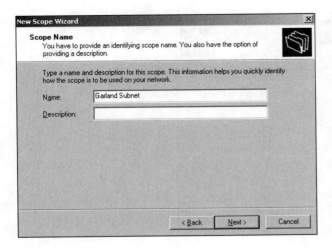

Figure 10.5
The New Scope Wizard.

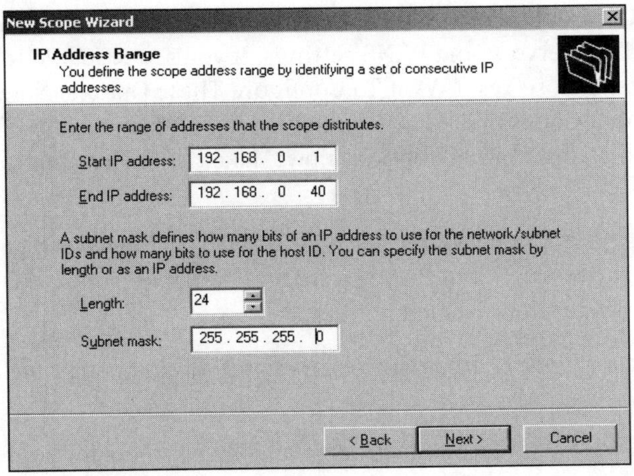

Figure 10.6
IP address range.

6. The New Scope Wizard continues with the page shown in Figure 10.6. Type in the starting and ending addresses for the new scope, and enter the subnet mask. (The default subnet mask will be written in, but it can be changed if you are subnetting the network and you choose a different length for the network ID and the host ID.)

7. The next page allows you to add exclusions for the address range input in the previous page. Type in any excluded addresses. (Excluding addresses is covered later.)

8. The next page, shown in Figure 10.7, allows you to change the duration of the offered leases. As you can see, the default lease is 8 days. Change the lease to suit your needs, based on decisions made earlier in this chapter.

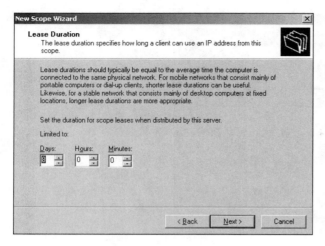

Figure 10.7
Lease duration.

9. The next page allows you to configure this server's DHCP options, including any IP addresses or routers, DNS servers, and WINS settings. If you are prepared to configure these addresses, choose Yes, I Want To Configure These Options Now; otherwise, choose No, I Will Configure These Options Later. For the purpose of instruction, I'll choose to configure these options now. Make the choice appropriate for your organization.

10. On the next page, you can configure a router's IP address. This is the default gateway that clients will be configured with when they receive an IP address from the DHCP server. Type in the appropriate gateway and continue.

Note: *A gateway is needed only if your clients need to access resources outside the local intranet.*

11. The next page allows you to specify the domain name and DNS servers for your clients. You'll need to specify a parent domain first, followed by the name of the DNS server that clients will use and its IP address. Type in the correct configuration and continue. If you don't know the IP address of the DNS server, but you know its name, you can type in the name and choose Resolve. The IP address of the DNS server will be included automatically.

12. In the next page, you'll need to type the names of any WINS servers on the network. WINS servers convert NetBIOS computer names to IP addresses. You may or may not have a WINS server.

13. When all of these items have been configured, the wizard finishes and asks you if you want to activate this scope now or later. Make the appropriate choice for your network; then choose Next and Finish.

If you've configured the scope correctly, when the wizard finishes, you'll see the new scope listed in the right and left panes of the DHCP console, as shown in Figure 10.8.

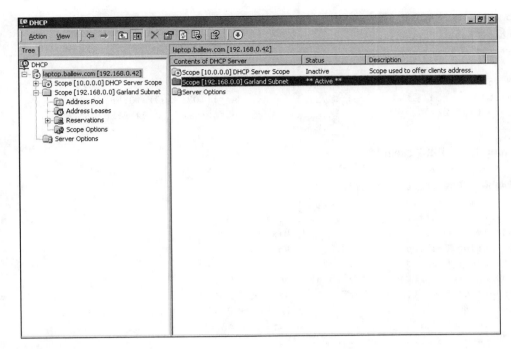

Figure 10.8
The new scope.

In this example, I created a scope for the subnet Garland. I configured the range of addresses from 192.168.0.1 through 192.168.0.40, and the DHCP server's address is 192.168.0.42. After I activated the scope, I configured two clients with the new leases by using the **ipconfig /renew** command. Listings 10.6 and 10.7 show the first two clients' addresses and lease duration. Notice that no gateway was configured for this network. The information important to take note of is highlighted, and the lease has been set to the maximum of 999 days. Client configuration will be covered in the next section.

Listing 10.6   DHCP client #1.

```
C:\>ipconfig /all
Windows 2000 IP Configuration
Host Name . . . . . . . . . . . . : DesktopPC
Primary DNS Suffix  . . . . . . . : Ballew.com
Node Type . . . . . . . . . . . . : Broadcast
IP Routing Enabled. . . . . . . . : Yes
WINS Proxy Enabled. . . . . . . . : No
DNS Suffix Search List. . . . . . : Ballew.com
Ethernet adapter Local Area Connection
Connection-specific DNS Suffix  . : Ballew
Description . . . . . . . . . . . : Realtek RTL8029(AS) PCI Ethernet Adapter
Physical Address. . . . . . . . . : 00-C0-F0-45-AB-5D
DHCP Enabled. . . . . . . . . . . : Yes
Autoconfiguration Enabled . . . . : Yes
```

```
IP Address. . . . . . . . . . . . . : 192.168.0.2
Subnet Mask . . . . . . . . . . . . : 255.255.255.0
Default Gateway . . . . . . . . . . :
DHCP Server . . . . . . . . . . . . : 192.168.0.42
DNS Servers . . . . . . . . . . . . :
Lease Obtained. . . . . . . . . . : Sunday, April 08, 2001 10:58:25 AM
Lease Expires . . . . . . . . . : Friday, January 02, 2004 9:58:25 AM
```

Listing 10.7   DHCP client #2.

```
C:\>ipconfig /all
Windows 2000 IP Configuration
Host Name . . . . . . . . . . . . : PIII
Primary DNS Suffix . . . . . . . : Ballew.com
Node Type . . . . . . . . . . . . : Mixed
IP Routing Enabled. . . . . . . . : No
WINS Proxy Enabled. . . . . . . . : No
Ethernet adapter Local Area Connection:
Connection-specific DNS Suffix  . : Ballew
Description . . . . . . . . . . . : Intel(R) PRO/100+ Management Adapter
Physical Address. . . . . . . . . : 00-D0-B7-5A-CD-10
DHCP Enabled. . . . . . . . . . . : Yes
Autoconfiguration Enabled . . . . : Yes
IP Address. . . . . . . . . . . . : 192.168.0.1
Subnet Mask . . . . . . . . . . . : 255.255.255.0
Default Gateway . . . . . . . . . :
DHCP Server . . . . . . . . . . . : 192.168.0.42
DNS Servers . . . . . . . . . . . :
Lease Obtained. . . . . . . . . . : Sunday, April 08, 2001 10:57:18 AM
Lease Expires . . . . . . . . . : Friday, January 02, 2004 9:57:18 AM
```

Removing or Deactivating a Scope

Removing or deactivating a scope is as easy as right-clicking on the scope and choosing the appropriate command. As I mentioned earlier, though, deactivating is most often the better choice when a scope needs to be decommissioned.

To remove or deactivate a scope, perform the following steps:

1. Log on as an administrator.

2. Choose Start|Programs|Administrative Tools|DHCP.

3. In the domain tree, open the DHCP server that contains the scope you need to either deactivate or delete. (Activating scopes is done using the same tools.)

4. To deactivate a scope that is active, right-click on the scope in either pane, and choose Deactivate.

5. To delete a scope completely, right-click on the scope and choose Delete.

Note: There are several ways to determine the status of a scope. Next to the scope is either a red down arrow or a green up arrow. A red down arrow means that the scope is inactive, and the green arrow means that the scope is active. Additionally, you can highlight the domain name in the left pane, and in the right pane all configured scopes will be shown. They'll be listed as either Inactive or Active under Status in this pane.

Excluding Addresses from a Scope

To exclude addresses from a scope, perform the following steps:

1. Log on as an administrator.

2. Choose Start|Programs|Administrative Tools|DHCP.

3. In the domain tree, open the DHCP server that contains the scopes that you'd like to manage.

4. Right-click on the Address Pool for this DHCP server, and choose New Exclusion Range. The pool is located at DHCP/*applicable server*/*applicable superscope* (if used)/*scope*/Address Pool.

5. In the Add Exclusion box, type the starting and ending IP addresses of the range to exclude. Choose Add, then Close. Figure 10.9 shows the resulting configuration in the DHCP console.

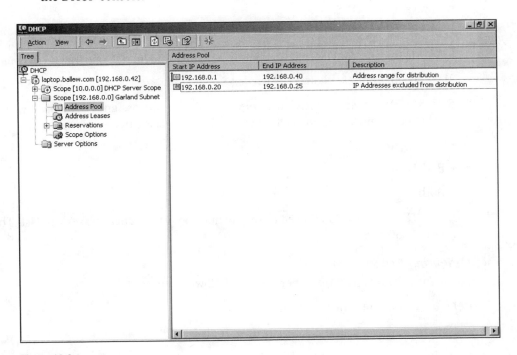

Figure 10.9
IP addresses excluded from distribution.

Changing Scope Properties

You can manage a scope's properties through the Action menu. Several DHCP scope properties can be set. To change or view a scope's properties, perform the following steps:

1. Log on as an administrator.

2. Choose Start|Programs|Administrative Tools|DHCP.

3. In the domain tree, open the DHCP server that contains the scopes that you'd like to manage.

4. With the scope highlighted, choose Action|Properties.

5. The Scope Properties dialog box appears. On the General tab, you can change the scope name, the starting and ending IP addresses, and the lease duration. The lease duration can be set as unlimited as well. Make the appropriate changes as needed.

6. Select the DNS tab. Changes made concerning DNS and DHCP server integration can be made here. You can do any of the following:

   • Automatically update DHCP client information in DNS.

   • Update DNS only if a DHCP client requests it.

   • Always update DNS.

   • Discard forward lookups when the lease expires.

   • Enable updates for DNS clients that do not support dynamic update.

   Make the appropriate changes as needed.

7. Select the Advanced tab. To change how IP addresses are assigned dynamically, and to which clients, make the choice that will suit your specific needs:

   • DHCP Only

   • BOOTP Only

   • Both

   If BOOTP is chosen, you'll need to specify how long those client leases will last. The default is 30 days.

Configuring Reservations

To configure client reservations, perform the following steps:

1. Log on as an administrator.

2. Choose Start|Programs|Administrative Tools|DHCP.

3. In the domain tree, open the DHCP server that contains the scopes that you'd like to manage.

4. Open the Reservations folder. Notice that the right pane contains information about configuring reservations. You will not see this information if reservations are already configured.

5. Right-click on the Reservations folder, and choose New Reservation; or choose Action|New Reservation.

6. In the resulting dialog box, type the name of the reservation, the IP address of the reservation, the MAC address of the computer that will use this reservation, and the description of the reservation.

7. Select the type of client that will be using this address: DHCP Only, BOOTP Only, or Both. Choose Add, then Close.

10

You can view the properties of this client reservation by right-clicking on the reservation in the left pane of the DHCP console and choosing Properties. On the General tab, you can see the Reservation name, the MAC address, the description, and the supported type of client. On the DNS tab, you can configure how DNS will work with this client and how update information will be handled between this client and the DHCP server.

Note: You cannot use excluded addresses as reserved addresses for clients. Reserved addresses must come from the DHCP scope of available addresses.

Configuring DHCP Clients

With the DHCP server, scopes, and reservations installed, you can now configure your clients to use them. Client requirements are listed in the section called "The Lease Process," earlier in this chapter. Most clients that you'll have on your network will be configurable.

To configure a Windows 2000 Professional workstation to use the new DHCP server, perform the following steps:

1. Log on as an administrator and open the Control Panel.

2. Open Network And Dial-Up Connections.

3. Right-click on the local area connection you want to manage, and choose Properties. Figure 10.10 shows this screen. Notice that this computer has two connections: one for Internet connectivity via a modem, and one connection to the local network via an Ethernet adapter.

4. Highlight Internet Protocol in the Components box, and choose Properties.

5. In the Internet Protocol Properties dialog box, choose Obtain An IP Address Automatically.

6. After it's configured, enable the local area connection. The lease process described earlier begins.

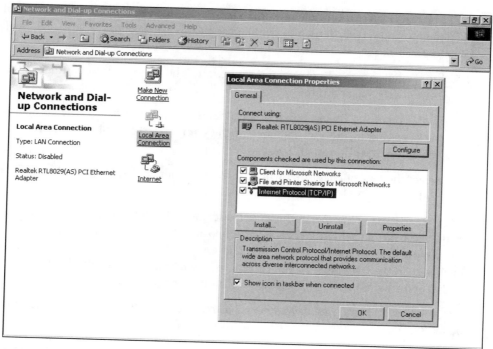

Figure 10.10
Client configuration.

You can watch the lease process in action by entering **ipconfig /renew** at a command prompt at the client's workstation. Listings 10.6 and 10.7 showed the result of the **ipconfig /renew** command on two such clients.

Configuring Server Options and Classes

For the DHCP server, you can configure server options—including default gateways, and WINS servers—through the Server Options folder in the DHCP console. Similar to scope options, server options are also used to set the IP addresses for clients who obtain leases. Unlike scope options, however, server options affect all scopes on the DHCP server. From the Server Options folder, classes can be configured as well. The process for configuring these options is similar to the configuration of scope options.

Configuring Basic Server Options

To configure server options, follow these steps:

1. Log on as an administrator.

2. Choose Start|Programs|Administrative Tools|DHCP.

3. In the domain tree, locate the folder Server Options. Double-click on this folder.

   In the right-hand pane of the DHCP console, you'll see the information screen shown in Figure 10.11.

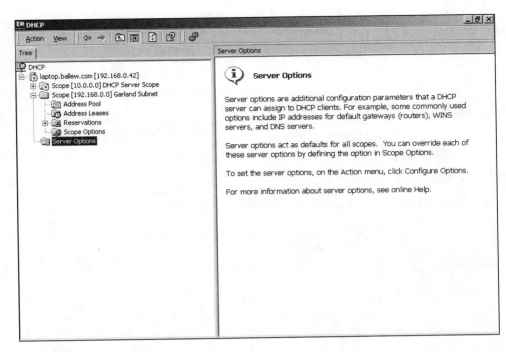

Figure 10.11
DHCP server options.

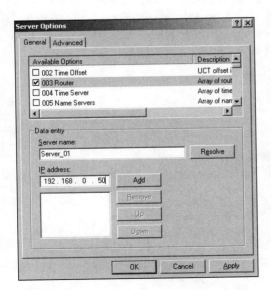

Figure 10.12
Configuring server options.

4. With the Server Options folder highlighted, either choose Action|Configure Options, or right-click and choose Configure Options. The Server Options dialog box is shown in Figure 10.12 with Router checked for configuration.

5. On the General tab, you can input IP addresses for any resources that a lease recipient might need. These are the same options that were mentioned earlier for scope configuration. Some of these entities include routers, DNS servers, cookie servers, and WINS servers, but other information can be configured as well. Choose the item(s) you want to change, and configure them appropriately in the Data Entry box. Choose OK.

Configuring Basic Server Classes

To configure Server classes, perform the following steps:

1. Log on as an administrator.

2. Choose Start|Programs|Administrative Tools|DHCP.

3. In the domain tree, locate the folder Server Options. Double-click on this folder to open the Server Options dialog box.

4. Select the Advanced tab.

5. To configure a class option, select one of the available classes from the Vendor Class or User Class drop-down lists on this screen. They are the same as scope classes and are listed in the sidebar for reference. This Advanced tab and the available User classes are shown in Figure 10.13.

Defining User and Vendor Classes, Setting Predefined Options

You can configure new User or Vendor classes as well as new options. Additionally, you can modify or remove options and create predefined options. All of this is done through the Action menu with the applicable DHCP server highlighted.

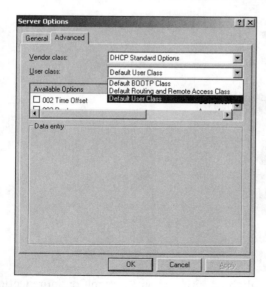

Figure 10.13
Advanced tab—Vendor and User classes.

User and Vendor classes are used to group together clients that are alike for the purpose of assigning IP addresses to them. Everyone included as a member of a specific User or Vendor class will receive addresses from a certain part of the IP address pool and will receive a configuration specific to the class. If the predefined User or Vendor classes do not meet your network needs, you can create your own. For instance, you might create a User class that is configured for all of the users in Office_01, and create another for all of the users who use a dial-up connection to the Internet. New Vendor classes might be created to group together all users of specific laptops, or all clients running a specific OS or using a specific NIC or modem.

To configure Vendor classes, you'll need to obtain the required information from the vendors themselves, and for User classes, you'll need to define the appropriate User class ID information. You can find the latest information about User classes at **ftp://ftp.isi.edu/ in-notes/rfc3004.txt**. After the new classes are configured on the server, they'll also need to be configured at the client.

Several tools from Microsoft can assist you with creating new classes, creating new options, and modifying those options. Although explaining all of the Vendor and User classes is not possible in this setting, I can introduce you to the most basic tasks associated with these concepts.

Tip: For Windows 2000 DHCP clients, only Windows 2000 computers can use this type of option class setting. Older clients do not use this option type because they do not send a class ID or recognize the data. The default User class does support these legacy clients, though, and should be used as necessary.

To create a new User or Vendor class, perform the following steps:

1. Log on as an administrator.

2. Choose Start|Programs|Administrative Tools|DHCP.

3. In the domain tree, highlight the DHCP server.

4. Choose Action|Define User Classes to define a new User class, or choose Action| Define Vendor Classes to define a new Vendor class.

5. Figure 10.14 shows the resulting dialog box if Define User Classes is chosen from the Action menu. There are two classes defined: BOOTP Class and Default Routing And Remote Access. To define a class of your own, choose Add.

6. In the New Class dialog box, type a display name, a description, and a class ID. Information on class IDs will need to be obtained from Microsoft's Web site or the Microsoft Windows help system. Choose OK.

7. When you're setting a new Vendor class, you'll use the DHCP Vendor Classes dialog box, which is similar to the screen shown in Figure 10.14. To define a new vendor class, choose Add.

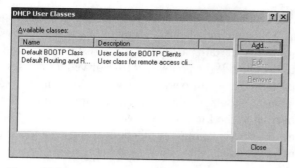

Figure 10.14
User classes.

8. In the New Class dialog box, type a display name, a description, and a class ID. Information on class IDs will need to be obtained from the vendors themselves. Choose OK.

To set or modify predefined options and values for a specific class, perform the following steps:

1. Log on as an administrator.

2. Choose Start|Programs|Administrative Tools|DHCP.

3. In the domain tree, highlight the DHCP server.

4. Choose Action|Set Predefined Options.

5. In the Option Class drop-down list, select DHCP Standard Options, Microsoft Options, Microsoft Windows 2000 Options, or Microsoft Windows 98 Options.

6. In the Option Name drop-down list, select the option to predefine for the DHCP server such as a router, DNS server, LPR server, or any of the other available option names. After choosing the option, you can edit the option name or description, or you can add more options. Make the appropriate changes and choose OK. Figure 10.15 shows the screen.

To remove options created for the DHCP server under predefined options, perform the following steps:

1. Log on as an administrator.

2. Choose Start|Programs|Administrative Tools|DHCP.

3. In the domain tree, highlight the DHCP server.

4. Choose Action|Set Predefined Options.

5. Select the option you've added previously, and choose Delete from the Predefined Options And Values dialog box, as shown in Figure 10.15.

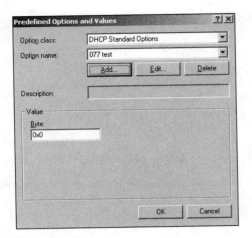

Figure 10.15
The Predefined Options And Values dialog box.

If you've created a new User or Vendor class, you'll need to configure the client to use this new class. To do this, you'll have to configure the client with the necessary DHCP class ID information. To do this, follow the steps listed here:

1. Log on to a DHCP-enabled client as an administrator.

2. Choose Start|Programs|Accessories|Command Prompt.

3. At the prompt, type **ipconfig /setclassid <Local Area Connection>** *NewClassID* (*NewClassID* can be anything you like).

If everything has been properly configured on both ends, the message "DHCP ClassID successfully modified for adapter 'Local Area Connection'" will be displayed. You can see the new class ID by typing **ipconfig /all** at a command prompt on the client machine. Listing 10.8 shows the output.

Listing 10.8   A client's new class ID.

```
Windows 2000 IP Configuration
Host Name . . . . . . . . . . . . : DesktopPC
Primary DNS Suffix  . . . . . . . : Ballew.com
Node Type . . . . . . . . . . . . : Broadcast
IP Routing Enabled. . . . . . . . : Yes
WINS Proxy Enabled. . . . . . . . : No
DNS Suffix Search List. . . . . . : Ballew.com
Ethernet adapter Local Area Connection:
Connection-specific DNS Suffix  . : Ballew
Description . . . . . . . . . . . : Realtek RTL8029(AS) PCI Ethernet Adapter
Physical Address. . . . . . . . . : 00-C0-F0-45-AB-5D
DHCP Enabled. . . . . . . . . . . : Yes
Autoconfiguration Enabled . . . . : Yes
```

```
IP Address. . . . . . . . . . . . : 192.168.0.2
Subnet Mask . . . . . . . . . . . : 255.255.255.0
Default Gateway . . . . . . . . . :
DHCP Class ID . . . . . . . . . . : NewClassID
DHCP Server . . . . . . . . . . . : 192.168.0.42
DNS Servers . . . . . . . . . . . :
Lease Obtained. . . . . . . . . . : Monday, April 09, 2001 10:56:16 AM
Lease Expires . . . . . . . . . . : Monday, January 18, 2038 9:14:07 PM
```

Configuring and Managing Clients and Leases

You can see which clients on the network currently have leases by opening the Address Leases folder under the appropriate scope. To see what leases are being used on your server, perform the following steps:

1. Log on as an administrator.

2. Choose Start|Programs|Administrative Tools|DHCP.

3. In the domain tree, expand the DHCP server tree, expand the scope in question, and then click on Address Leases. Figure 10.16 shows a sample screen.

From here, you can perform one other task associated with managing client leases: deleting the lease. To delete the lease, simply right-click on it and choose Delete. You

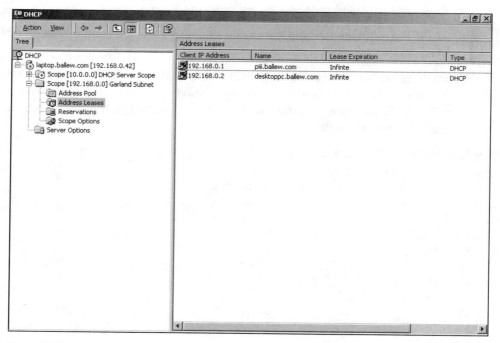

Figure 10.16
Active client leases.

can also use this interface to sort leases by client IP address, name, lease expiration, and type. Each lease also has a unique ID that you can view by scrolling right in the right pane.

Note: Deleting a client reservation is not the same as deleting the lease. To delete a client reservation, click on Reservations in the console tree, and find the reservation to remove. Right-click on the reservation and choose Delete.

Advanced Features of DHCP

In this section, you'll learn how to perform more advanced tasks on the DHCP server, including configuring and managing BOOTP and remote access clients, backing up and restoring the DHCP database, reconciling scopes, and using multiscopes. You'll also learn how Internet Connection Sharing (ICS) affects the DHCP process and configured scopes and how such a configuration disrupts a network.

Configuring and Managing BOOTP and Remote Access Clients

You already know what BOOTP is and how it works. You also know how to configure specific leases and groups that affect only BOOTP clients. However, managing BOOTP clients can be a little more complicated than simply configuring a few User classes and setting a few default DNS servers for them to use. In this section, you'll learn about the BOOTP table, how to manage it, and how to change the lease time for remote access clients.

The BOOTP Table

If you are supporting, or plan to support, BOOTP clients, you'll need to take a look at the BOOTP table. To do this, perform the following steps:

1. Log on as an administrator.

2. Choose Start|Programs|Administrative Tools|DHCP.

3. Highlight the DHCP server, and choose Action|Properties.

4. Select the option Show The BOOTP Table Folder. Choose OK.

To create a new boot image, perform the following steps:

1. Right-click on the BOOTP table folder, and choose New Boot Image.

2. In the Add BOOTP Entry dialog box, you can enter a boot image file name, a path to the boot image, and a TFTP file server that contains the image.

3. To add an entry to the BOOTP table, fill in the required information and choose Add.

Configuring Reservations for BOOTP Clients

You may also need to configure reservations for BOOTP clients under the specific circumstances mentioned earlier. To configure a reservation for a BOOTP client, perform the following steps:

1. Log on as an administrator.

2. Choose Start|Programs|Administrative Tools|DHCP.

3. In the domain tree, open the DHCP server that contains the scopes that you'd like to manage.

4. Open the Reservations folder. Notice that the right pane contains information about configuring reservations. You will not see this information if reservations are already configured.

5. Choose Action|New Reservation, or right-click on the Reservations folder and choose New Reservation.

6. In the resulting dialog box, type the name of the reservation, the IP address of the reservation, the MAC address of the computer that will use this reservation, and a description of the reservation.

7. Select BOOTP Only from the Supported Types folder. You'll see the reservation in the right-hand pane, as shown in Figure 10.17.

Note: You cannot use excluded addresses as reserved addresses for clients. Reserved addresses must come from the DHCP scope of available addresses.

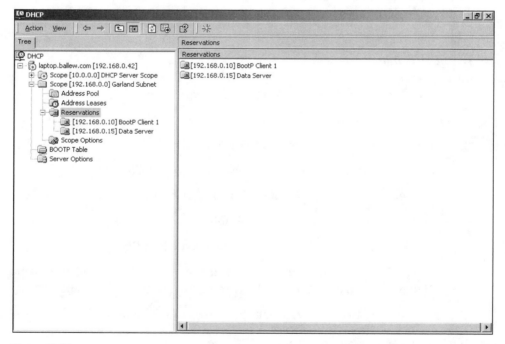

Figure 10.17
BOOTP client reservation.

Changing the Lease Time for Remote Access Clients

Another task that may need to be done is to change the default lease time for remote access clients. To change this default lease time, perform the following steps:

1. Log on as an administrator.

2. Choose Start|Programs|Administrative Tools|DHCP.

3. In the domain tree, open the DHCP server that contains the scopes that you'd like to manage.

4. Right-click on the Scope Options folder, and choose Configure Options. If you have a reserved scope configured, you'll see it in the right pane. If this is the case and you want to configure this client, you can right-click and choose Properties.

5. Select the Advanced tab. (Both choices in Step 4 open the Scope Options dialog box.)

6. In the User Class drop-down list, select Default Routing And Remote Access Client.

7. In the Available Options box, select 051 Lease.

8. In the Data Entry box, Long is set to 0×0. To change this default entry to one hour, change it to 0×3600; for two hours, use 0×7200, and so on.

Almost any other option for a BOOTP client or a Routing And Remote Access client can be configured in one of the ways described in this chapter. For instance, to add a dynamic BOOTP client to a scope, you can select the applicable scope in the DHCP console, choose Action|Properties, and choose the option Both or BOOTP Only. This information can usually be changed in the same way that DHCP clients are managed.

Backing Up and Restoring the DHCP Database

Windows 2000 Server automatically backs up the DHCP database every 60 minutes by default. This backup is stored in the %systemroot%\System32\DHCP\Backup\Jet\New folder. Windows 2000 Server also automatically restores a corrupt database when the DHCP service is stopped and restarted.

Stopping and Starting the DHCP Service

There are several ways to start, stop, resume, or pause the DHCP service. Three will be mentioned in this section. For all of these tasks, log on to the DHCP server that needs to be managed.

My personal favorite is to manage services such as these by choosing Start|Programs| Administrative Tools|Services|DHCP Server. Figure 10.18 shows the DHCP Server Properties dialog box. By using the Services utility, you can perform multiple configuration tasks in a single dialog box. You can perform the following tasks:

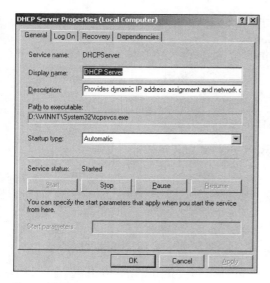

Figure 10.18
The DHCP Server Properties dialog box.

- *General tab*—You can see the display name, the description, and the service status. You can stop, pause, start, or resume the DHCP Server service. (When you're performing these operations in the DHCP console, no such interface exists.)

- *Log On tab*—You can choose to log on with a local system account, or specify an account. You can also enable or disable the DHCP service with certain hardware profiles.

- *Recovery tab*—You can configure how the server will respond to failures for the first, second, and subsequent failures, and specify if and when the service will be restarted.

- *Dependencies*—You can see what the DHCP server depends on to work properly, and see which services depend on DHCP.

Another way to start, stop, resume, or pause the service is through the DHCP console you've become familiar with in this chapter. You can manage the DHCP server by following these steps:

1. In the DHCP console, highlight the DHCP server to be managed.

2. Right-click on the server name in the right pane, and choose All Tasks.

3. Choose Start, Stop, Pause, Resume, or Restart.

Finally, you can perform these tasks at a command prompt, using the following commands:

- **net start dhcpserver**

- **net stop dhcpserver**

- **net pause dhcp server**

- **net continue dhcpserver**

Changing the Default Backup Interval

As I mentioned earlier, Windows 2000 backs up its own DHCP database to the hard drive every 60 minutes. You can change this default interval if you want, but the change is made in the Registry. As you are aware, changing the Registry is a dangerous and potentially damaging act. If you must, you can change it by following these steps:

1. Log on as an administrator. Back up the Registry and all of the data on the system.

2. Choose Start|Run, and enter "RegEdit32" in the Open box.

3. Expand the trees in the Registry, and locate the following entry:

   HKEY_LOCAL_MACHINE\SYSTEM\CurrentControlSet\Services\DHCPServer\Parameters

4. Locate the BackupInterval entry. The default is Reg_DWORD 0x0000003c(60). The 60 represents 60 minutes. Make the appropriate change and close the Registry.

Manually Compacting the DHCP Database

This section won't be of much use to you if you are running your DHCP server on a Windows 2000 machine (which I hope you are). When a DHCP server is run on a Windows 2000 Server platform, compacting the database is done automatically when the database grows to over 30MB in size. However, if you are running only a few Windows 2000 servers on your network, and your DHCP servers are running older operating systems, you'll need to compact the database manually. You can manually compact and repair the DHCP database with the command-prompt utility Jetpack.exe.

The syntax for the Jetpack utility is as follows:

```
jetpack database_name temporary_database_name
```

For example, in the command

```
jetpack dhcp.mdb tmp.mdb
```

dhcp.mdb is the DHCP database file, and **tmp.mdb** is the temporary database file. These files are found in the %systemroot%\System32\DHCP directory. You should not rename or delete these files.

To use this utility, you'll need to stop DHCP first, run this command, and then start the DHCP service again.

Manually Backing Up the DHCP Database

You can manually back up the DHCP database in many ways, including by using the Windows 2000 Backup utility, by using a multitude of third-party tools, and even by simply copying the dhcp.mbd file. Figure 10.19 shows the DHCP folder and this file checked using the Backup utility under Accessories.

Manually Restoring the DHCP Database

Just as there are multiple ways of backing up a DHCP database, there are multiple ways of restoring it. You can use the Backup utility shown in Figure 10.19, you can restore from tape, and you can restore by copying the dhcp.mdb file back to the server. However, because the DHCP database is restored automatically each time the DHCP server is stopped and restarted, it makes sense to use that approach first when you're considering recovery options.

If you are a Registry fanatic, you can manually restore the DHCP database there. To manually restore the DHCP database by using the Registry, perform the following steps:

1. Log on as an administrator. Back up the Registry and all of the data on the system.

2. Choose Start|Run, and enter "RegEdit32" in the Open box.

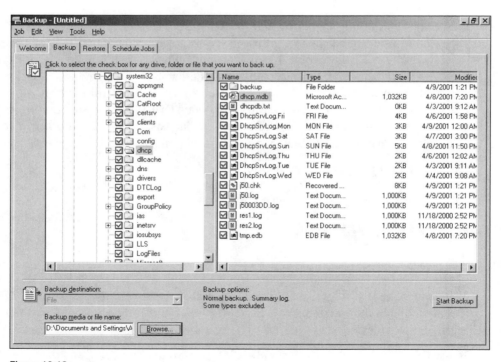

Figure 10.19
Using the Backup utility to back up the DHCP database.

3. Expand the trees in the Registry, and locate the following entry:

    HKEY_LOCAL_MACHINE\SYSTEM\CurrentControlSet\Services\DHCPServer\ Parameters

4. Locate the RestoreFlag entry. The default is Reg_DWORD 0x00000000(0). To restore the registry, change the 0 in the parentheses to a 1.

5. Close the Registry window, and then restart the DHCP service. The flag will be set back to 0 when the database is restored.

One last way to restore the DHCP database is to copy the contents of the %systemroot%\ System32\Dhcp\Backup\Jet folder to the %systemroot%\System32\Dhcp folder and restart the DHCP service.

Moving the DHCP Database to Another Server

There will be times when a computer can no longer handle the duties of being a DHCP server or when the DHCP database is being moved to another server to prevent this from happening. In any event, sometimes DHCP databases must be moved to keep up with changing times and a growing network.

To move a DHCP database to another server, follow the guidelines listed here:

1. Log on to the source server as an administrator.

2. Stop the DHCP Server service, as described earlier.

3. Choose Start|Programs|Administrative Tools|Services, and open DHCP Server.

4. On the Log On tab, select Disable. (This is necessary so the service doesn't start automatically.)

5. Locate the %systemroot%\System32\DHCP folder on the source computer, and copy it to a temporary folder on the target computer. I'll refer to this folder as Temp.

6. Save the following Registry key as a text file:

    HKEY_LOCAL_MACHINE\SYSTEM\CurrentControlSet\Services\DHCPServer

    You can save a key by selecting it, choosing Registry|Save Key, entering a name in the Name box, and saving the file. Make sure you choose Save Key and not Save Subkey, or the operation will fail.

7. Locate the %systemroot%\System32\DHCP folder on the source computer again, and delete this folder from the source computer.

8. Uninstall DHCP from this server through Add/Remove Programs in Control Panel.

9. On the new (target) computer, log on as an administrator, and install DHCP.

10. After installation, the service will be running, and you must stop the DHCP Server service before continuing.

11. Rename the System.mdb file to System.src in the temporary (Temp) folder.

12. To replace the existing directory, copy the DHCP server directory tree from the Temp folder to the %systemroot%\System32\Dhcp folder.

13. On the target machine, restore the Registry key HKEY_LOCAL_MACHINE\SYSTEM\ CurrentControlSet\Services\DHCPServer folder with the saved information from the source DHCP server. (See Step 6.) You'll have to use Regedit32 again to access the registry. Make sure you are not trying to restore this key from a remote computer, or the operation will fail.

14. In Restore Key, under File Name, use "%systemroot%\System32\DHCP\backup\ Dhcpcfg", and choose Yes when prompted to make changes.

15. Close the Registry editor, and start the DHCP service.

16. Finally, reconcile the scopes, as detailed in the following section.

Reconciling Scopes

Occasionally, you'll need to reconcile the scope or scopes on your DHCP server. To reconcile means to resolve, merge, or otherwise bring together the scopes on your network. To reconcile a scope for a particular subnet, perform the following steps:

1. Log on as an administrator.

2. Choose Start|Programs|Administrative Tools|DHCP.

3. In the domain tree, open the DHCP server that contains the scopes that you'd like to manage.

4. Right-click on the scope to reconcile, and choose Reconcile.

5. Choose Verify from the resulting dialog box.

6. The scopes on the network are compared to the scope information in the database and are listed in the Reconcile box, as shown in Figure 10.20. You'll then receive a message that the database is consistent.

To reconcile all scopes when a DHCP database has been moved, as in the previous section, or to simply reconcile all scopes in the DHCP server, perform the following steps:

1. Log on as an administrator.

2. Choose Start|Programs|Administrative Tools|DHCP.

3. In the domain tree, open the DHCP server that contains the scopes that you'd like to manage.

4. Right-click on the DHCP server name, and choose Reconcile All Scopes.

5. Choose Verify from the resulting dialog box. In this instance, either you'll see a box that informs you that the database is consistent, or you will see a warning message.

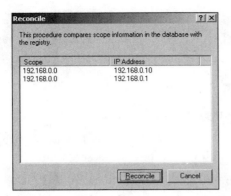

Figure 10.20
Reconciling scopes.

10

Multicast Scopes

Multicast scopes have not been discussed in depth yet; they have only been briefly intro-duced as a way to configure Class D addresses for IP multicasting. *Multicasting* is the process of delivering information from one point on the network or Internet to several (or multiple) clients by using broadcast technology. These multicast data packets can be transmitted in three ways:

- The data can be sent to specific addresses, called *unicast endpoint addresses*. The endpoint can then redistribute the data to the network as necessary.

- The data can be sent using a broadcast address. Broadcasting is similar to a tornado siren in that it can be heard by anyone in the local vicinity (intranetwork) but cannot be heard far away (internetwork). This limitation occurs because broadcasts are not forwarded across routers. This type of broadcast is disruptive to the network because everyone on the local network hears it.

- The data can be sent using a multicast address. Multicast addresses differ from broad-cast addresses in that they affect only the clients that are listening. While broadcasting is like a tornado siren, multicasting is like a radio transmission. Only those that have their radios turned on will hear the message. This is the best way to configure multicast data transmissions because computers that aren't configured for listening aren't dis-turbed and because routers can be configured to forward these packets across subnets.

Multicast addresses are Class D addresses in the range of 224.0.0.0 to 239.255.255.255. The clients that receive these multicasts are configured as groups of users and are employed in a manner similar to email communities. What that means is, users who belong to multicast groups can receive multicasts from particular sources and will be configured to listen to those sources for transmissions. Additionally, users can belong to multiple multicast groups at the same time. Like email communities, users can join or leave these groups at any time.

Configuring a Multicast Scope

To configure a new multicast scope for your DHCP server, perform the following steps:

1. Log on as an administrator.

2. Choose Start|Programs|Administrative Tools|DHCP.

3. Right-click on the DHCP server name, and choose New Multicast Scope.

4. The New Multicast Scope Wizard starts. Choose Next. On the following page, you'll need to type the name of the new multicast scope and a description.

5. The next page asks for starting and ending IP addresses for this scope and a TTL (Time-To-Live) setting. The default TTL is 32, meaning that the multicast will travel through 32 routers before being discarded. Make sure you configure an addressing scheme that offers at least 256 addresses, or you'll get an error message and you'll have to try again.

Note: *If you are configuring a scope for a private network, begin with 239.192.0.0 and subnet mask 255.252.0.0. This range allows you to configure up to 262,144 addresses for your network. If you are configuring a scope for the Internet or other public network, start with the address 233.0.0.0. The reasoning behind this is complex, but if you'd like to learn more about public IP multicast addressing, information can be obtained from* **http://www.ietf.org/.** *Additional information can also be obtained from your ISP or the Internet Assigned Numbers Authority (IANA).*

6. The next page asks for exclusion addresses. Add any necessary exclusions before continuing.

7. On the next page, you'll set the lease duration. The default is 30 days. Make the appropriate changes and continue.

8. On the next page, you'll need to choose to activate this scope now or later. Activate the scope now if it is possible on your network.

9. Choose Finish, and notice the new multicast scope in the right pane of the DHCP console.

Managing a Multicast Scope

After configuring the scope, you can manage it by right-clicking on it in the DHCP console, and choosing Properties. In the Properties dialog box, you can view or configure the same items you initially set up when you created the scope. These include the following:

- *On the General tab*—Enter the scope name, starting and ending IP addresses, TTL, lease duration (can be unlimited), and a description of the scope.

- *On the Lifetime tab*—The lifetime of the scope can be configured as Infinite or with a lifetime configured from today's date to any date in the future, or to any time in the future. For instance, the multicast scope could be configured to expire the day it was created, but later in the afternoon—after the broadcast is complete.

Superscopes

A *superscope* is a collection of member scopes that are activated together and used to support multiple logical IP subnets within the same physical subnet. A superscope, which contains multiple member scopes, is administered as one entity. Superscopes can be made of scopes on the same logical subnet or from subnets on the other side of a DHCP relay agent. You can use superscopes to solve problems related to depleted address pools by allowing the subnet to use addresses from another scope in another physical area of the network. Superscopes can also be used when two DHCP servers need to be configured for the same subnet to administer two separate IP networks in the same physical location.

10

Warning! *Although I've stated that superscopes can be administered as a single entity, and that is technically true, the member scopes must be configured independently. It is not the purpose of the superscope to allow management of all of the member scopes at the same time; the superscope is used only to group those scopes together in one place.*

Creating and Activating a Superscope

To begin using superscopes, you'll need to create and activate them. To create and activate a superscope, perform the following steps:

1. Log on as an administrator.

2. Choose Start|Programs|Administrative Tools|DHCP.

Multicasting

To actually use these scopes and to enable IP multicast conferencing, be it video, audio, or otherwise, you'll need to do a lot more configuring. This chapter covers only TCP/IP and DHCP and is concerned only with scopes and the actual numbers and processes involved, not with configuring a multicast server. If you want to enable multicasting (in particular, video and audio conferencing, or IP Telephony) and use it on your network, you'll need to begin by purchasing, installing, or configuring the following items:

- TCP/IP network

- QoS Admission Control and RSVP

- Windows 2000 with Active Directory

- Site Server Internet Locator Service

- DHCP Server

- Multicast Address Dynamic Client Allocation Protocol (MADCAP)

- Workstations with speakers, sound and video cards, and other multimedia hardware

- Appropriate ranges and scopes

More information can be obtained from Microsoft's Web site, and links to the relevant pages will be included on this book's CD-ROM.

3. Highlight the DHCP server name, and choose Action|New Superscope.

4. The New Superscope Wizard starts; choose Next to continue. Type in the name of the superscope.

5. On the next page, you must select the scopes that will be added to the superscope. Here you'll see all of the configured scopes on your network. Select the scopes that you want to have in this superscope, and choose Next.

6. The wizard completes. Read the summary box to verify the information, and choose Finish. Notice that the new superscope is listed in the right pane. To see the status of the new superscope, double-click on it in the right pane. In the left pane, it will be shown as active.

Adding a Scope to a Superscope

To add a scope to the new superscope, perform the following steps:

1. Log on as an administrator.

2. Choose Start|Programs|Administrative Tools|DHCP.

3. Highlight a scope that is *not* a member of the superscope you are configuring.

4. Choose Action|Add To Superscope. In the resulting dialog box, you'll see a list of available configured superscopes. To add this scope to the superscope, highlight it and choose OK.

Removing and Deactivating a Superscope

When a superscope is deactivated, all of the member scopes in it are deactivated as well. If the superscope is being used to lease addresses to users on the network, those users will not be able to renew their leases. Removing (or deleting) a superscope is a little different. When a scope is deleted, only the superscope itself is deleted, not the member scopes. The member scopes are returned to their original positions as independent scopes in the DHCP console. Removing or deactivating a superscope is easily achieved.

To remove or deactivate a superscope, follow these steps:

1. Log on as an administrator.

2. Choose Start|Programs|Administrative Tools|DHCP.

3. To deactivate the superscope: Highlight the superscope to be deactivated, and choose Action|Deactivate.

   To delete the superscope: Highlight the superscope to be deleted, and choose Action| Delete. You'll be asked to verify that you understand that only the superscope is being deleted, not all of the child scopes. Choose OK.

Note: Microsoft uses both member scopes and child scopes to refer to the scopes that are included in a superscope.

Internet Connection Sharing and DHCP

The last topic for DHCP, scopes, addresses, and servers must address what happens to those items when Internet Connection Sharing (ICS) is established for a network using DHCP for IP address leasing.

ICS is configured on a computer that has both a dial-up connection and a network adapter. The modem or dial-up hardware is configured to access the Internet. Through the Properties tab of this connection, a user can configure the connection to be shared by other users on the network. When you make this configuration change, the computer that is configured for ICS takes over many roles for the network. For instance, the computer now provides Network Address Translation, IP addressing, and name resolution services for all of the computers on the network. ICS works wonderfully in a small office, but doesn't work well at all in larger environments (in this context, anything over 10 or so users).

The reason for this is quite understandable. The computer that offers ICS is now the gateway for the entire network and takes over the responsibility of assigning TCP/IP addresses to the network. Because of this, the computer becomes a DHCP server. The problem is that the address it uses is 192.168.0.1, which will most likely cause problems on your already configured network. To make this work, you'll have to reconfigure the addresses of the other computers to obtain an IP address automatically, and the settings made for DHCP previously will not be of use.

Note: *Network Address Translation (NAT) can be used with Internet Connection Sharing and small home offices to allow more flexibility. NAT will be discussed in depth in Chapter 12.*

Using Internet Connection Sharing

If you run a small home-office network and have DHCP configured, you may be able to quit using (or not use) DHCP and instead assign TCP/IP addresses or use APIPA for addressing. If you decide to go in this direction, then you can configure ICS.

To configure ICS for your network, perform the following steps:

1. Log on as an administrator to the server or workstation that contains the dial-up connection you want to share.

2. Open Control Panel, and then open Network And Dial-Up Connections.

3. Right-click on the connection to share, and choose Properties.

4. Select the Sharing tab. Place a checkmark in the Enable Internet Connection Sharing For This Connection checkbox. Choose OK.

5. If the system identifies your network as having any of the items listed previously, such as DHCP servers and the like, you'll see the error message shown in Figure 10.21. If you want this configured computer to dial this connection when others on the network

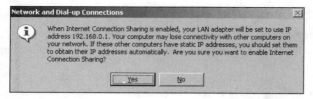

Figure 10.21
Information about ICS.

request access, place a checkmark in the Enable On-Demand Dialing checkbox as well.

6. If the system does not have any conflicts with the DHCP server, DNS servers, or any other previously listed hazard, the setting will be completed without incident.

Optimizing the DHCP Server

Implementing the monitoring options offered by Windows 2000 can help you optimize both the performance and the security of the DHCP server. The Performance console has several new counters that serve this purpose; the new counters include acknowledgements per second, informs per second, and discovers per second, to name only a few. You can configure audit logging through the DHCP console and examine audit log files. In the audit log files, event codes can be analyzed to determine what problems have occurred with the DHCP server and its clients. Some of these events include successful or failed authorizations, or indicate whether or not the servers were reached by clients. The DHCP server can be configured to detect address conflicts as well. In this section, you'll learn about all of these techniques and the utilities involved in maximizing the performance of your DHCP servers.

Address Conflict Detection

One easy way to optimize the performance of the DHCP server is to configure it to detect address conflicts. It is not set to detect these conflicts by default, and, as you are aware, conflicting addresses can become quite a difficult problem to solve when it occurs on a network.

When you enable address conflict detection, this is how it works: Each time the DHCP server prepares to lease an address, it first pings that address to see if it is in use. If the ping is successful, then the address is in use, and if not, the address is available. The only downsides of enabling this detection are a one-second delay while the ping is being performed and the bandwidth that this service uses on the network. Of course, in a smaller network, this may not be a problem; in larger networks with thousands of clients, this *optimization* tool might not optimize the network at all.

Note: *Address conflict detection isn't to be turned on and left on indefinitely. Because of* *the network traffic it generates, it should ideally be used only when you're troubleshooting network connection problems.*

Enabling Address Conflict Detection

To enable address conflict detection, perform the following steps:

1. Log on as an administrator.

2. Choose Start|Programs|Administrative Tools|DHCP.

3. Highlight the DHCP server, and choose Action|Properties.

4. On the Advanced tab, set the conflict detection attempts to a number greater than the default of zero. Choose OK.

10

Warning: *More is not always better. The number you choose in Step 4 is the number of times the DHCP server will ping the address before leasing it. Pinging the address five times (the limit) would generate unnecessary network traffic.*

The Performance Console

In Chapter 8, the Performance console was discussed at length, but using the Performance console to optimize a DHCP server was not. You can use the Performance console to watch the performance of the DHCP server and to monitor the problems occurring with it. Before continuing on this subject, perform the following steps to look at what the Performance console has to offer:

1. Log on as an administrator to the DHCP server or to a domain controller on the network.

2. Open the Performance console (choose Start|Programs|Administrative Tools| Performance).

3. Click the + button at the top of the screen. In the counters screen, connect to the computer that manages the DHCP service.

4. Select DHCP Server in the Performance Object drop-down list box.

Notice the number of counters in the counter list. In the next section, you'll learn what these counters are used for and what they represent.

The Counters

The Performance console provides 14 counters that can be used to monitor the network. Understanding what these counters can be used for is imperative to successful optimization and monitoring. Listed next are these 14 counters and their characteristics and uses:

- *Acks/Sec*—This counter monitors the rate at which the DHCP server sends acknowledgement messages to clients. Acknowledgements contain IP address leases and other information for clients. If this number is unusually high, you might consider increasing the length of the leases given to clients.

- *Active Queue Length*—When DHCP is processing requests, some clients must wait in a queue for their turn to come up. This counter shows the number of packets that are in the queue of the DHCP server, thus representing current unprocessed requests. An unusually high number here can indicate that network traffic is high and there isn't enough bandwidth for current network traffic, or that the DHCP server needs to be upgraded to a faster processor or more RAM.

- *Conflict Check Queue Length*—When address conflict detection is enabled, there will be clients waiting for ping results to be returned and address leases to be sent. This counter shows how many packets are waiting for ping results in the DHCP server queue. A high number here can indicate that network traffic is high or that conflict detection attempts is set too high in the DHCP server's advanced properties.

- *Declines/Sec*—When a client declines a DHCP address lease, it is usually because some other utility is in effect causing that client to test the address before accepting it. This counter shows how many declines are accepted by the server each second. A high number of declines at the server indicates that lots of clients are finding address conflicts on the network and refusing certain addresses. Under these circumstances, you should enable address conflict detection to begin the troubleshooting process.

- *Discovers/Sec*—When a client needs an IP address from the DHCP server, the client starts the process of obtaining one by using a discover message. This counter shows the number of discover messages the server receives every second. This number is usually high in the morning when the users on the network try to obtain network access at the same time. The number should not be high at other times. If the number is unusually high at any given time, you might suspect a virus or a malfunctioning NIC on the network.

- *Duplicates Dropped/Sec*—When a DHCP relay agent or other hardware sends packets to the server, duplicate packets can be received. This counter shows how many duplicate packets are dropped each second by the DHCP server. A high number can be indicative of many problems, but it most likely indicates that the server isn't responding fast enough to client requests.

- *Informs/Sec*—Information messages are sent by clients to the server to obtain information about the server's configuration. Clients who are already configured with an IP address are the only ones who send this message.

- *Milliseconds Per Packet (Avg.)*—When a DHCP server needs to send any kind of response, the time it takes to send that response is measured with this counter. If this number is extremely or unexpectedly high, there might be a server problem having to do with hardware or other internal components.

- *Nacks/Sec*—DHCP servers send negative acknowledgements to clients when the

DHCPREQUEST is not successful, as in the case of a client trying to lease its previous IP address or trying to lease an invalid address. This counter shows the number of negative acknowledgements the server sends out per second. High numbers here might indicate that the server's scopes are configured incorrectly or that they are deactivated. Certain users, such as laptop users moving from subnet to subnet, also can cause high negative acknowledgements.

- *Offers*/Sec—After a client has sent a discover message, all DHCP servers respond with offers. This counter monitors the number of offers per second received by the DHCP server being monitored. A high number of offers can indicate increased network traffic and will occur during network logon periods, such as when users all log on at the same time each morning.

- *Packets Expired/Sec*—When packets are in the DHCP server message queue and waiting to be processed, they can expire or time out if it takes more than 30 seconds to process the request. This counter shows the number of these packets that expire each second while in this queue. A high number here indicates that the DHCP server is overworked and can't process the requests required of it (thus the server is taking too long to process the packets). This problem could be hardware related or network related.

- *Packets Received/Sec*—This counter shows the number of packets that the DHCP server receives (total) each second. A high number here can indicate high network traffic to the server.

- *Releases/Sec*—When a client no longer wants a lease, the lease is released. This is usually done by using the **ipconfig /release** command because simply logging off does not release a lease. Leases simply expire in most instances. This number is usually low for most organizations.

- *Requests/Sec*—Clients send request messages when the DHCP server has offered a lease and the client wants to accept it. This message is sent to all DHCP servers so they'll know an offer has been accepted. Requests are also sent when clients want to renew their current leases. If this number is high, you might consider increasing scope lease durations.

Sample Performance Monitor for a DHCP Server

How you configure the Performance console to monitor a DHCP server (or servers) is entirely up to you. You'll need to take into account what you think is happening and what you think is necessary to monitor. On my network, I don't think that DHCPDECLINE messages are going to be a problem because I have a very small network and plenty of addresses. In addition, there aren't any address conflicts or similar problems that I've ever noticed. However, I do think it's necessary to monitor whether or not packets are expiring, how many packets are received per second, and perhaps even how many discover, offer, request, and acknowledgement packets there are. Figure 10.22 shows this console.

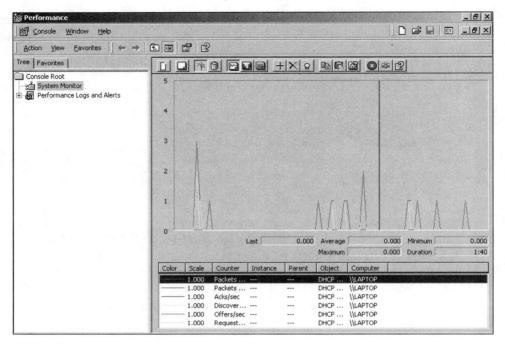

Figure 10.22
Performance console—DHCP counters.

Audit Logging

DHCP audit logging is another way to optimize the performance and security of the DHCP server and its clients. Auditing allows administrators to stay on top of what's happening on the server, watch for security breaches, and keep track of DHCP-related events such as lease offers and server access. DHCP auditing for Windows 2000 also offers disk checking to make sure that the log file is not getting too large and that the disk has enough space to store the log file successfully. These items and more will be discussed in this section.

Enabling Audit Logging

As you learned earlier, audit logging must be enabled before it can be used. The same is true of DHCP audit logging. Before getting too deep into this discussion, you should enable audit logging on your DHCP server. To enable logging, perform the following steps:

1. Log on as an administrator to the DHCP server or an appropriate domain controller or member server.

2. Choose Start|Programs|Administrative Tools|DHCP to open the DHCP console.

3. Make sure the DHCP server is highlighted, and choose Action|Properties.

4. On the General tab, place a checkmark in the Enable DHCP Audit Logging checkbox. Close the Properties dialog box.

With auditing enabled, you can now begin using log files to monitor the DHCP server.

Changing Auditing Parameters

The directory path for where auditing logs are stored can be changed in the DHCP console. To change the path, follow these steps:

1. Log on as an administrator to the DHCP server or an appropriate domain controller or member server.

2. Choose Start|Programs|Administrative Tools|DHCP to open the DHCP console.

3. Make sure the DHCP server is highlighted, and choose Action|Properties.

4. On the Advanced tab, there are two paths that can be changed: the audit log file path and the database path. Both are located in the %systemroot%\Winnt\System32\dhcp folder.

Changing the maximum size of the log file and the interval for disk checking is done through the Registry. To make these changes and others, perform the following steps:

1. Log on to the appropriate server as an administrator.

2. Choose Start|Run, and enter "Regedit32" in the Open box.

3. Browse through the trees to the HKEY_LOCAL_MACHINE\SYSTEM\ CurrentControlSet\Services\DHCPServer\Parameters folder.

4. The right pane contains several settings that can be changed, and the following list contains some of the options that are most often configured:

   - *BackupDatabasePath*—The default is %systemroot%\System32\dhcp\backup.

   - *BackupInterval*—The default is 60 minutes.

   - *DatabaseName*—The default is dhcp.mdb.

   - *DatabasePath*—The default is %systemroot%\System32\dhcp.

   - *DhcpLogDiskSpaceCheckInterval*—The default is every 50 events.

   - *DhcpLogFilePath*—The default is %systemroot%\Winnt\System32\dhcp.

   - *DhcpLogFilesMaxSize*—The default is seven stored log files, one for each day of the week, with a maximum log-file size of 1MB.

   - *DhcpMinSpaceOnDisk*—The default is 20MB.

Audit logs are named by the DHCP service depending on the day of the week they are created. Logs are called DhcpSrvLog.Mon, DhcpSrvLog.Tue, and so on (see Figure 10.23).

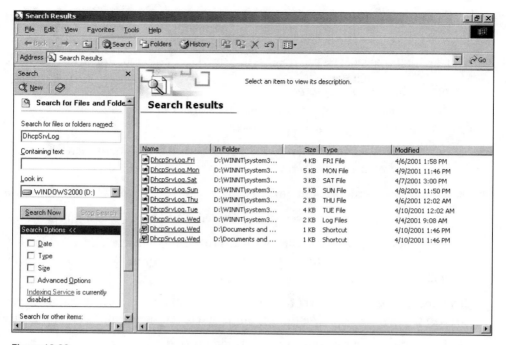

Figure 10.23
DHCP server log files.

As the seventh day rolls around, the file is either overwritten (if it has not been modified in the last 24 hours) or amended (if the file has been modified during the last 24 hours). Audit logging starts and ends daily at 12:00 A.M.

Reading Audit Log Files

Once you've enabled audit logging, you can view these logs in Notepad, Microsoft Word, or another similar program. If you've enabled audit logging and you'd like to view an audit log, perform the following steps:

1. Log on as an administrator at the server where the log is stored.

2. Choose Start|Search|For Files Or Folders, type "DhcpSrvLog", and choose Search Now.

Note: *The default location for these files is the %systemroot%\System32\DHCP folder. However, with the opportunity having been made available already to change the location of this file, it is best to locate the file this way to meet all users' needs.*

3. In the right pane under Search Results, you'll see files that look like those shown in Figure 10.23. In this example, notice that there are several log files for different days of the week. Open the latest file.

4. If prompted, choose to open the file in a text editor program such as Notepad or WordPad, or an office application like Microsoft Word for Windows.

Listing 10.9 shows part of a sample log. Notice the events being audited and their event codes. Event code numbers and the most common codes will be discussed in the next section.

Listing 10.9   DHCP server log.

```
Microsoft DHCP Service Activity Log

ID Date,Time,Description,IP Address,Host Name,MAC Address
63,04/10/01,00:52:20,Restarting rogue detection,,,
51,04/10/01,00:53:20,Authorization succeeded,,Ballew.com,
63,04/10/01,08:43:48,Restarting rogue detection,,,
51,04/10/01,08:44:48,Authorization succeeded,,Ballew.com,
11,04/10/01,09:23:25,Renew,192.168.0.15,PIII.Ballew.com,00D0B75ACD10
11,04/10/01,09:46:47,Renew,192.168.0.15,PIII.Ballew.com,00D0B75ACD10
11,04/10/01,09:49:09,Renew,192.168.0.15,PIII.Ballew.com,00D0B75ACD10
63,04/10/01,09:51:09,Restarting rogue detection,,,
51,04/10/01,09:52:09,Authorization succeeded,,Ballew.com,
15,04/10/01,10:12:35,NACK,192.168.0.15,PIII.Ballew.com,00D0B75ACD10
11,04/10/01,10:13:03,Renew,192.168.0.15,PIII.Ballew.com,00D0B75ACD10
11,04/10/01,10:13:05,Renew,192.168.0.15,PIII.Ballew.com,00D0B75ACD10
63,04/10/01,10:58:30,Restarting rogue detection,,,
51,04/10/01,10:59:31,Authorization succeeded,,Ballew.com,
63,04/10/01,12:05:51,Restarting rogue detection,,,
51,04/10/01,12:06:52,Authorization succeeded,,Ballew.com,
12,04/10/01,12:53:47,Release,192.168.0.15,PIII.Ballew.com,00D0B75ACD10
10,04/10/01,12:56:28,Assign,192.168.0.2,DesktopPC.Ballew.com,00C0F045AB5D
12,04/10/01,12:57:04,Release,192.168.0.2,DesktopPC.Ballew.com,00C0F045AB5D
10,04/10/01,12:57:10,Assign,192.168.0.2,DesktopPC.Ballew.com,00C0F045AB5D
12,04/10/01,12:57:14,Release,192.168.0.15,PIII.Ballew.com,00D0B75ACD10
11,04/10/01,12:57:19,Renew,192.168.0.15,PIII.Ballew.com,00D0B75ACD10
63,04/10/01,13:13:13,Restarting rogue detection,,,
51,04/10/01,13:14:14,Authorization succeeded,,Ballew.com,
11,04/10/01,13:17:46,Renew,192.168.0.15,PIII.Ballew.com,00D0B75ACD10
```

Seven different components are written for each entry to the log. Each of these components further defines the event. The first component is the ID of the event. IDs, also referred to as *event IDs* or *event codes*, describe the event type, such as starting or stopping a log, leasing an address, or denying a lease.

Besides the ID, the event's date and time are recorded. A description of the event is next, and in this listing you can see that most events have to do with assigning, renewing, and releasing leases and with authorizing the DHCP service. Finally, information about the clients themselves is listed (the client's IP address, hostname, and MAC address). The combination of all of this information makes it possible to pinpoint problems and to identify all DHCP service events that have taken place during the day.

10

Common Event Codes

The first entry in each log event is an ID code, which identifies the event that took place. There are several event codes ranging from 0 to 60+. The most commonly seen ID numbers are the following:

- **00**—The audit log was started.
- **01**—The audit log was stopped.
- **02**—The audit log was paused due to low disk space.
- **10**—A client received a new IP address lease.
- **11**—A client renewed an IP address lease.
- **12**—A client released an IP address lease.
- **13**—The DHCP service determined that a lease was already in use on the network.
- **14**—The address pool (scope) ran out of addresses to lease, and a lease request could not be filled.
- **15**—A client requested a lease, and the request was denied for reasons other than running out of leases.
- **20**—A client was leased a BOOTP address.
- **21**—A client was leased a dynamic BOOTP address.
- **22**—A client did not receive a BOOTP address lease because the scope was depleted.
- **23**—A BOOTP IP address was deleted after the server discovered that the lease was not in use.
- **50**—The DHCP server was unable to locate the domain.
- **51**—The DHCP service was started on the network.
- **54**—The DHCP service was not authorized on the network.
- **55**—The DHCP server was authorized to start on the network.
- **56**—The DHCP server was not authorized and thus the service was shut down.
- **59**—The DHCP server could not be authorized due to a failure in the network.
- **60**—The DHCP server could not find a domain controller to determine whether the server is authorized on the network.
- **62**—Another DHCP server was found on the network.
- **63**—The DHCP server is trying to determine whether it is authorized on the network.

DHCP and WINS

In this last section, I'll discuss the Windows Internet Naming Service (WINS) and how it is incorporated with a DHCP network. You'll learn what WINS is and what it is used for, what the requirements are for servers and clients, how to install the service, how to use the WINS snap-in, and how to manage and administer DHCP clients who use WINS. Understanding how WINS and DHCP work together is imperative if your network supports down-level clients such as Windows 98 or Windows NT 4 clients.

What Is WINS?

WINS is used in mixed environments (containing legacy clients) where NetBIOS names are used for communication. NetBIOS, which is short for Network Basic Input/ Output System, is a program that is used to enable applications and clients to communicate on a local area network. These networks can be Ethernet, Token Ring, or Windows networks. NetBIOS is not routable, requiring another protocol like TCP/IP to be configured in wide area networks or internetworks.

Computers that run Windows NT, Windows 9x, DOS, or OS/2 communicate using NetBIOS names. These are not the same as the fully qualified domain names that are used on Windows 2000 networks, so they require special attention. WINS, then, is basically a NetBIOS name server, mapping these NetBIOS names to their respective IP addresses.

A problem arises when NetBIOS clients who use a WINS server for NetBIOS-name-to-IP-address resolution have addresses that change often because those clients are DHCP clients as well as WINS clients. The WINS server must be able to keep track of those names and ever-changing addresses in some manner.

Note: Windows 2000 uses DNS, not WINS, for name resolution. However, to support down-level clients, WINS is still needed.

The WINS Name Registration Lease Process

WINS clients, like DHCP clients, must request and lease a NetBIOS name from the appropriate server. The WINS server accepts name registration requests from its clients and determines if the name can be leased temporarily to the client. If it can, the name is leased along with a TTL for the lease. The WINS server stores this name, along with the client's IP address, in its database. Like DHCP, the WINS client must renew the name at certain intervals by querying the WINS server. This process is complex, but understanding it is not crucial to installing and configuring a WINS server. However, it is important to understand what happens when a client tries to communicate with another client on the network.

Communicating with Other Clients

After a WINS client has obtained a name lease and has an IP address from a DHCP server, the client is ready to communicate with others on the network. To do this, the client will need the IP address of the client. WINS clients resolve IP addresses in this manner:

1. Because each WINS client maintains a cache of successfully resolved NetBIOS-name-to-IP-address mappings, it checks this cache first for the IP address of the client it wants to communicate with.

2. If the information isn't found, the WINS client sends the name to the WINS server. This request goes to the primary WINS server if two or more exist on the network. The primary WINS server is queried a maximum of three times. If the primary server is still unavailable, the request is sent to the secondary WINS server.

3. Either the request is resolved, or it isn't. If the request is resolved, the client is sent the IP address; otherwise, the WINS server sends the client a message saying that the name doesn't exist and then sends a broadcast to the network.

4. These broadcasts can be used to resolve the names successfully.

WINS Requirements

To configure a new WINS server on a Windows 2000 network, it must be running Windows 2000 Server, and it can be either a domain controller or a member server. The server must have WINS installed and have a static IP address, a subnet mask, and a default gateway. The server can also be configured to work with DHCP and DNS servers or to work through static mappings in the WINS server database.

WINS clients must be configured with the IP address of at least one WINS server, called a primary WINS server, or optimally with two, a primary and a secondary server. WINS clients can be running any of the following operating systems:

- Windows 2000

- Windows NT Server 3.5 or later

- Windows NT Workstations 3.5 or later

- Windows 95 or 98

- Windows for Workgroups 3.11 running Microsoft TCP/IP-32

- Microsoft Network Client 3 for Microsoft MS-DOS with the real-mode TCP/IP driver

- LAN Manager version 2.2c for MS-DOS

Installing WINS

One of the first things that needs to be done to use WINS on the network is to install a WINS server. To install a WINS server, follow these steps:

1. Log on, as an administrator, to the computer that will act as the new WINS server for the network.

2. Choose Start|Settings|Control Panel.

3. Open Add/Remove Programs.

4. Choose Add/Remove Windows Components from the left pane.

5. In the Windows Components Wizard, highlight Networking Services and choose Details.

6. Place a checkmark in the Windows Internet Naming Service (WINS) checkbox, and choose OK. Then choose Next and Finish.

Configuring DHCP to Use WINS

For DHCP and WINS to work together, the DHCP server must be configured properly. Perform the following steps to achieve this configuration:

1. Log on to the DHCP server as an administrator.

2. Choose Start|Programs|Administrative Tools|DHCP to open the DHCP console.

3. In the left pane, select Server Options.

4. Choose Action|Configure Options.

5. In the Server Options dialog box, select the 044 WINS/NBNS Servers option.

6. In the Server Name box, type the name of the WINS server; then choose Resolve.

7. Choose Add to add this information.

8. Next, select the 046 WINS/NBT Node Type option.

9. In the Byte box, type "0x8" instead of 0x0. (The notation 0x8 represents node type h-node. This node type configures clients to check with the WINS server first for name resolution.) Choose OK.

Note: *There are several node types including B-node, P-node, M-node, and H-node, referring to broadcast, peer-to-peer, mixed, and hybrid respectively. H-node first tries to resolve a name by contacting the name server directly, and if that doesn't work, it uses a broadcast to resolve the name.*

In the right pane, you'll see a new option name, 044 WINS/NBNS Servers, and an IP address for that server. Before continuing, you should configure the WINS server to point to itself in the Advanced Settings for the TCP/IP properties. To do this, perform the following steps:

1. Log on to the WINS server as an administrator.

2. Right-click on My Network Places, and choose Properties.

3. Right-click on the local area connection, and choose Properties.

4. Highlight TCP/IP in the Components box, and choose Properties.

5. Choose the Advanced button, followed by the WINS tab.

6. Choose Add, and type the IP address of the WINS server. Choose Add again and close the dialog boxes.

You can see the service in action by opening the WINS console through Start|Programs| Administrative Tools|WINS, or you can add the WINS snap-in to a new or existing console by typing "mmc" at the Start|Run command and choosing Add/Remove Snap-in. The WINS console will be discussed next.

Configuring Clients Who Use Both WINS and DHCP

For users to use the WINS server, they must be configured. The following steps outline this procedure:

1. Log on to the DHCP client as an administrator.

2. Right-click on My Network Places, and choose Properties.

3. Right-click on the local area connection, and choose Properties.

4. Highlight TCP/IP in the Components box, and choose Properties.

5. Choose the Advanced button, followed by the WINS tab.

6. Choose Add, and type the address of the WINS server configured earlier. Close all of the dialog boxes. See Figure 10.24.

With clients configured to use the WINS server, you can now open the WINS console to manage these clients and server settings.

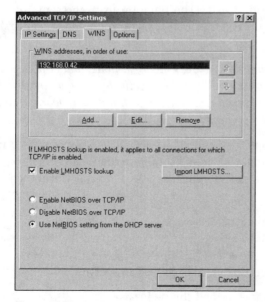

Figure 10.24
Configuring WINS clients.

Using the WINS Console

The WINS console is used to manage the WINS server and its clients. You can use this console to perform several tasks, including viewing server status, configuring how often the server will be updated, displaying server statistics, configuring replication settings, backing up the database, verifying the database, and viewing active registrations. In this section, I'll discuss most of these tools and configurations, along with registration and replication.

Note: *After the first example on configuring replication, I'll assume that you are logged on correctly and are using the WINS console. Right-clicking or double-clicking on a specific folder and choosing the correct menu item will enable you to complete the remaining steps for all of these tasks.*

10

Replication and Replication Partners

If the network has more than one WINS server, the servers should be configured to be replication partners. Replication partners offer fault tolerance and load balancing for the WINS clients. These *replication partners* can be configured as pull partners or push partners or both. A *pull partner* is configured to pull replication data from its push partner; pull partners obtain information because they've requested it. A *push partner* sends the data to the pull partner who requested it.

When a network has primary and secondary WINS servers, it is best to configure them as both push and pull partners of each other. When data is replicated or sent to a partner, only changes made to the database are sent, not the entire database. These partners can be configured to push or pull information when the WINS service starts or at specific intervals throughout the day.

To configure a replication partner, perform the following steps:

1. Log on as an administrator.

2. Choose Start|Programs|Administrative Tools|WINS to open the WINS console.

3. Right-click on Replication Partners in the left pane, and choose New Replication Partner.

4. In the New Replication Partner dialog box, type the name or browse to another WINS server. Choose OK.

5. Once the new server is configured as a replication partner, you can choose Replicate Now from the same menu and start the replication manually.

Changing the Update Status

In the WINS console is a folder named Server Status. By clicking on this folder, you can see the status of the WINS server, the last update, and the name and IP address of the server. The status information tells you whether the WINS server is responding, and the last update can be used to see if updates have been done recently. You can change the update times from the default of five minutes to another number by right-clicking on the Server Status folder and choosing Properties. This number can be set to anything between 1 minute and 59 minutes.

Viewing Server Statistics

You can view server statistics in the WINS console by right-clicking on the server name in the left pane and choosing Display Server Statistics. The WINS Server Statistics box gives information on the following statistics, all of which can be very useful in troubleshooting problems with the WINS server:

- Server start time
- Last periodic replication
- Last manual replication
- Last address change replication
- Total queries
- Records found
- Records not found
- Unique registrations
- Conflicts
- Renewals
- Group registrations
- Total registrations received
- WINS partner
- Number of replications

WINS Server Properties

You can view or change the WINS server properties by right-clicking on the WINS server in the left pane of the WINS console and choosing Properties. There are four tabs for configuring the server properties: General, Intervals, Database Verification, and Advanced.

On the General tab, you can change how often the WINS server automatically updates the server statistics you looked at earlier. By default, the setting is 10 minutes. You may want to raise this number if this information isn't used often or if you want to take pressure off the CPU or other resources, or you might want to lower this number during troubleshooting sessions. You can also create a path for the database backup, which will be discussed later. If you want to back up the database each time the server is shut down, you can check the appropriate box here.

The Intervals tab lets you configure how often records are renewed, deleted, and verified. WINS records contain information about NetBIOS computer names and their IP addresses, and these records need to be reviewed often for validity on the network. Figure 10.25 shows the defaults; you can change these to suit the needs of your organization. If you discover, through server statistics, that there's a low number of records found, and there's a high number of records not found, you might consider lowering these numbers.

The Database Verification tab allows you to verify the database consistency every few hours and to verify this database against either owner servers or randomly selected partners. Verifying the database consistency will be useful if you are having problems with database integrity or if the network is very large and database entries change often.

10

The Advanced tab allows you to log WINS activities for troubleshooting purposes and to configure the WINS server for dealing with bursts of activity. Those settings can be set to low, medium, high, or custom, and they are used to determine how many requests the server can handle at one time before clients have to retry registering or renewing. You can also change the database path for the WINS database.

Scavenging the Database

Scavenging is the term used for weeding out the invalid WINS entries in the WINS database. This database retains entries that have been released or are outdated, were registered at another WINS server, and then were replicated to this one. Thus, some of the records in the database are outdated and need to be removed. To scavenge the database and clear it of these outdated entries, right-click on the WINS server name and choose Scavenge Database. You should scavenge the database before backing it up.

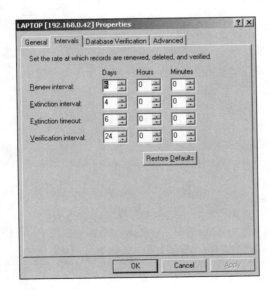

Figure 10.25
Intervals.

Backing Up the Database

When you configure the WINS database for backup, it is backed up automatically every three hours by default. You can back up the database by right-clicking on the WINS server name and choosing Back Up Database. Then you'll browse to the folder to which the database will be backed up and choose OK. Backing up the WINS database, although not configured by default, should be configured for fault tolerance.

Finding Records by Name or by Owner

To find a specific record in the WINS database, you can search the database by name or by owner. To find a record by name, right-click on the Active Registrations folder in the WINS console and choose Find By Name. Type the name or the first few letters of the name you want to find, and choose Find Now. The results will be shown in the right pane of the WINS console, as shown in Figure 10.26, along with the Find By Name dialog box.

In Figure 10.26, notice that the search returns not only the record name, but also the type, the IP address, the state, the owner, and the version. To get more information on the record, double-click on the record name to see the Properties sheet for that entry. Figure 10.27 shows this screen.

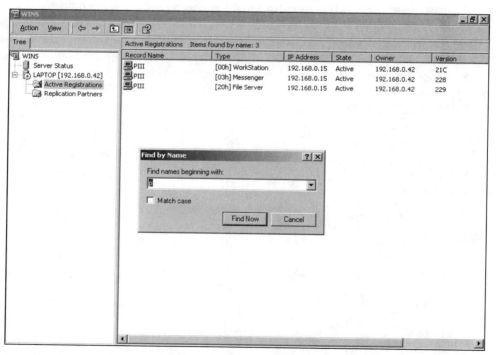

Figure 10.26
Finding a record by name.

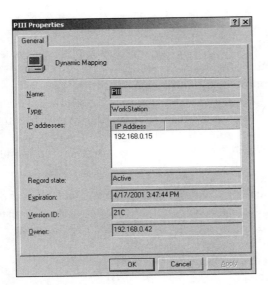

Figure 10.27
Properties for a record in the WINS database.

You can also search the database by owner; right-click on the Active Registrations folder in the WINS console and choose Find By Owner. In the resulting dialog box, you can search by a specific owner or by all owners. Again, by double-clicking on any of these entries, you can see the Properties sheet for them.

Active Registrations

If you searched earlier for a specific name or owner record, you saw entries in the right pane along with their status, type, IP address, and more. This is a list of active registrations. The Active Registrations folder can be used to find and list all clients on the network that are using the WINS server or connected to it. To see all active registrations, choose Find By Owner from the context menu and select All Owners.

If you want to filter the active registrations you see, you can choose the Record Types tab from the Find By Owner dialog box of the Active Registrations folder. Simply uncheck the boxes you want to filter out, and choose Find Now.

Creating Static Mappings

You can create a new static mapping for the WINS server by right-clicking on the Active Registrations folder and choosing New Static Mapping. In the New Static Mapping dialog box, type the computer name, the NetBIOS scope (optional), the type, and the IP address of the computer to receive the mapping. The type can be Unique, Group, Domain Name, Internet Group, or Multihomed.

Summary

In this chapter, you learned about TCP/IP and DHCP. TCP/IP is a suite of protocols used for communication on the Internet and for Windows networks. TCP/IP is configured on both servers and clients so they can communicate with one another. IP addresses are made up of four decimal octets consisting of ones and zeros, and these addresses are not usually employed by users. Instead, users generally initiate communications with other computers by using their computer names, fully qualified domain names, or NetBIOS names. Other entities are responsible for changing those names into IP addresses and allowing a connection.

IP addresses can be configured manually by typing the appropriate address, subnet, and gateway into all client workstations. This type of configuration is time-consuming and accident-prone. In a small network, APIPA can be used. This automatic IP addressing is useful when the network doesn't have a lot of clients and doesn't need access to the Internet or another network. Because APIPA doesn't offer a gateway, outside communications are not possible.

DHCP is offered as a way to automatically assign IP addresses for large or small networks. A DHCP server is configured with a scope of addresses that it can lease to clients, so clients do not have to be configured manually. This automation reduces administrative tasks, eliminates data-entry errors, and reduces the number of duplicate addresses on the network. A DHCP client can be automatically assigned an address when it needs one.

This chapter also discussed DHCP and leases, including how leases work, what scopes are and how they are configured, and how to enable logging for the DHCP servers on your network. Many other tasks associated with DHCP servers were also covered.

Finally, WINS servers and clients were introduced, including why a WINS server is needed on a mixed network. Also discussed was how WINS and DHCP work together.

Moving Forward

In the next chapter, you'll learn about DNS and name resolution on a Windows 2000 network. You'll also learn more about DHCP and how it works with DNS to dynamically update records on the DNS server. Used to map FQDNs to IP addresses on a network, DNS is necessary to allow communications between clients.

Chapter 11

DNS, DDNS, and Name Resolution

DNS is an abbreviation for Domain Name System, and DDNS refers to the Dynamic Domain Name System. Both represent a system in which users can log on to a network or the Internet, type in a fully qualified domain name (FQDN), and have that name resolved to an IP address. It is the DNS servers that resolve these names to IP addresses. In this chapter, you'll learn about DNS, DDNS, and how this name resolution works. You'll also learn how to install a DNS server, how to configure the server, and how to manage and optimize the DNS service.

There are many aspects of DNS to understand before you undertake the installation and use of a DNS server on your network. To use the DNS server effectively, you must understand what the DNS service consists of. You need to know how the DNS database is created, what zones are, what name servers do, what types of DNS records are available, and what they are used for. You'll also need to understand how the name resolution process works so that you can troubleshoot that process efficiently when errors occur.

After that, you'll be ready to install and configure the DNS server. Installation deals with both servers and clients, and there are many configuration tasks. These include configuring servers and clients, creating primary and secondary zones, creating forward and reverse lookup zones, and adding records to those zones. You'll also learn how to integrate WINS and DHCP servers with the new DNS server, as well as how those entities work together.

Monitoring and optimizing the server are detailed also, including how to use the Performance console, enable logging, and use command-line utilities for troubleshooting and monitoring. Finally, security options will be discussed.

Overview of DNS

As you learned in the last chapter, computers communicate over the Internet and in networks by using IP addresses such as 192.128.0.5 or 120.4.4.8. Most users don't like to remember these numeric IP addresses, though, and instead prefer to type in a friendly name like **www.microsoft.com**, **workstation06.Ballew.com**, or **www.yahoo.com**. With DNS, they can. DNS servers are responsible for taking a name like **www.yahoo.com** and resolving this FQDN to an IP address that computers, gateways, routers, and servers can all understand.

Windows 2000 networks use DNS to resolve their own IP addresses because new features of the operating system enable intranets to act and work more like the Internet than ever before. A name like **Graphics1.Dallas.Ballew.com** is still easier to remember than 192.168.5.10 and is very helpful to users on the local network. DNS is useful on both the Internet and an intranet because often, even when the IP addresses change due to DHCP or other factors, the FQDNs generally remain the same. I doubt that the name **www.yahoo.com** is going to change in the near future, although the IP address might. The translation and resolution of the name to the IP address is transparent to the user.

In this section, you'll learn the basic terms and characteristics associated with DNS servers and services, and you'll learn how the DNS namespace is organized on the Internet.

The DNS Database

The DNS database, referred to also as the *domain namespace*, is made up of several types of domains. They're called domains on the Internet or in a DNS namespace, but they aren't exactly like the domains you're used to. In a Windows 2000 domain, you have a specific number of computers and servers, and the domain is a unique entity that you control. The term "domain," when used in DNS lingo, represents a piece of the DNS namespace. One common DNS domain is the **.com** domain. To explain this in more depth, I'll discuss the domains available on the Internet (listed next) and in the DNS hierarchy, and compare the types of domains and their names to your unique namespace on your network.

The Root Domain

The root domain on the Internet is the third dot (**.**) in the name **www.microsoft.com** and is invisible. The root domain is managed by lots of different organizations, but Network Solutions, Inc., currently maintains domain name registration and the central DNS file server. This organization and other agencies work together to replicate the information on the central server to 12 other nationwide servers daily to keep the information up-to-date. This central server maintains a list of the top-level domains, described next.

Top-Level Domains

There are several top-level domains now, and most likely, there are more to come soon. In fact, when this book was being written, several new top-level domains were being considered. Here are a few of the most common top-level domains:

- **.com**—Used by commercial organizations such as Microsoft (**www.microsoft.com**), Yahoo! (**www.yahoo.com**), or Ask Jeeves (**www.ask.com**).

- **.gov**—Used by government organizations such as the White House (**www.whitehouse. gov**), the IRS (**www.irs.gov**), or the U.S. Department of Health and Human Services and related agencies (**www.health.gov**).

- **.edu**—Used by educational institutions such as the University of Texas at Arlington (**www.uta.edu**), the University of California at Berkeley (**www.berkeley.edu**), or the Massachusetts Institute of Technology (**www.mit.edu**).

- **.org**—Used by noncommercial or nonprofit organizations such as the Society for the Prevention of Cruelty to Animals (**www.spca.org**) or Straydog, Inc. (**www.straydog.org**).

- **.net**—Used by organizations such as ISPs or other large-scale Internet-based services; **www.waymark.net** (Waymark Communications) is an example.

*Note: Even if your network isn't connected to the Internet or available on the Internet, you can still relate to these examples. For instance, my network's name is **Ballew.com**. Second-level domains are similar to the offices **Dallas.Ballew.Com** or **FortWorth. Ballew.com**. If you use Windows 2000, you'll have already configured something similar. Even the computer names have a similar feel: **Laptop.Ballew.com** and **DesktopPC. Ballew.com**.*

Second-Level Domains

If a domain name like **www.uta.edu** is registered, the organization can also register a second-level domain name for use on the Internet. A second-level domain name can be something like **ftp.uta.edu** or **classes.uta.edu**.

Hostnames

When a DNS name is created, the part of the name written farthest to the left is called the *hostname*. Usually this is configured only for private networks, but sometimes specific entities on the Internet use such a configuration. Hostnames look like this: **DesktopPC. Garland.Ballew.com** or **Printer04.Dallas.Ballew.com**.

Your Domain Namespace

As you can tell, DNS must be used to communicate over the Internet. When you request a connection to **www.microsoft.com**, for example, the name is first sent to a DNS server that can resolve the name to an IP address; then the results are sent back, and the computer is connected. Sometimes, these addresses are cached in the local browser, sometimes the ISP or another close server knows the address, and sometimes the process is more complex. Whatever the case, the same is true on your network. When a client on your network needs to resolve a name like **Printer04.Dallas.Ballew.com**, the name must first be resolved to an IP address before the client can connect.

So, how do you know if you need to configure your own DNS server? You'll need a DNS server if you have an Internet domain name and want to create subdomains; if you want to create a domain, install a domain controller, or manage the DNS servers locally; or if you are running a firewall that prevents you from using an ISP or other outside entity for internal DNS resolution.

Note: DNS is required by the Netlogon service for locating Windows 2000 domain controllers.

Zones

A *zone* is a division of the DNS namespace. The zone stores information about that portion of the namespace and becomes the authoritative source of information for that division of the namespace. The zone is simply a database of information about a particular part of a domain. Zones are used to break up the domain namespace into manageable sections for the purpose of delegating responsibility or easing administrative tasks.

Zones are configured for reasons other than delegating responsibility, though. You can create a zone to extend the namespace and add subdomains or to reduce the traffic of a single-zone configuration on a network. When zones are created, a standard primary zone is created first, and the database is stored as a text file. This file contains the resource records for a single DNS server. This zone information can be replicated to other DNS servers for fault tolerance and network performance. Secondary zones can then be configured to provide redundancy and fault tolerance, to reduce load, to partition network traffic across WAN links, or to delegate responsibility.

Zones should ideally be created to delegate responsibility and reduce load. Before zones are created, proper planning should be done. You can study the network topology and design zones around physical locations or departments. You can also review the traffic on your network to determine where zones should be created and where additional DNS servers should be configured. When you're configuring and planning zones, take into account the traffic that zone transfers will create.

Zone Transfers

Because zones contain the information about a particular DNS server and namespace partition, it is important that there be fault tolerance for the zone database files. Usually, multiple DNS servers are configured for this purpose. When a new secondary server is introduced on the network, this server obtains a full copy of the DNS zone database files from the primary DNS server. This causes quite a bit of traffic, and transfers must be configured to update information regularly to ensure its validity.

Transfers after this initial transfer do not move the entire database. Windows 2000 supports *incremental zone transfers*, which allow the DNS servers to compare information before transmitting data. If the databases are the same, then no transfer takes place, and if the databases are different, then only the differences are replicated. (Such was not the case in Windows NT DNS zones.) Zone transfers usually occur due to preconfigured interval copy settings, but transfers can also occur when a secondary server is notified of zone changes by the primary server or its master server or if a transfer is manually initiated.

These zone database files are stored on the DNS name server. Every zone has at least one name server, and changes in the master zone's database file need to be made from this primary zone server. Multiple servers can exist for one zone and are encouraged.

Records

The DNS database contains records known generally as *resource records*. There are several types of resource records, but you'll probably be concerned with only a handful. Those records are detailed here, including their names, descriptions, and purposes.

Address Records

The address (A) record, often referred to as the *host (A) record*, is used to map a host computer name or other network device name to an IP address. The A record contains three parts: the domain name that contains the host, the hostname itself, and the host's IP address. When a hostname is combined with a domain name, it becomes a FQDN. This record is automatically generated when a resource with a FQDN is introduced on the network.

Canonical Name Records

The canonical name (CNAME) record is used to create an alias for a specific computer or resource on the network. Using CNAMEs allows administrators to hide various details about the internal company configurations from outsiders and to shorten long, unwieldy names. For instance, the name **open.web.garland.ballew.com** might be configured for users as **www.ballew.com** or **www.sales.ballew.com**. The CNAME record has three parts: the alias domain name, the alias name, and the hostname of the department or resource.

Mail Exchange Records

A mail exchange (MX) record is the record for the server that processes the email for an organization. This record can be configured for a host or a domain and contains three parts. The first two parts are the domain name where the mail is processed and the mail server's DNS name. This name is a FQDN. The third part of the record is the preference number. This number is between 0 and 65,535; it indicates the mail server's priority when compared to other mail servers on the network. The mailer first tries the server with the lowest priority and moves up the ladder until the mail is successfully transferred.

Name Server Records

Every domain has an authoritative name server, and the name server (NS) record identifies that server. This record has two parts: a domain name and the DNS name server's name (the one that holds the A records).

Pointer Records

Most of the time, a user needs to type in a FQDN and have it resolved to an IP address. Occasionally, though, a user will need to type in an IP address and have it resolved to a hostname. The pointer (PTR) record contains information about the subnet, the host's IP address, and the host's FQDN.

11

Start of Authority Records

The Start of Authority (SOA) record contains information that identifies the DNS name server that is the authority for the domain. SOA records are used to identify the primary zones and servers for a domain. The SOA record contains information about the primary server's owner, the responsible person, the serial number, the refresh interval, the retry interval, the expire interval, and the default Time-To-Live (TTL). These components of the SOA record will be discussed in detail later in the section entitled Resource Records.

Active Directory Integration

When you install Active Directory on a Windows 2000 computer, you are asked to specify a DNS name if one exists. If no DNS server exists on the network, then the DNS service is installed on the computer as Active Directory is installed. During this installation, you are asked to create a DNS name.

Active Directory and DNS are integrated, meaning that you can configure DNS components such as zones and replication of them in the Active Directory consoles. Using Active Directory for storing DNS zone database files not only provides better security, but also allows the DNS zone information to be replicated through Active Directory instead of through DNS. This system allows only the information that has changed to be replicated, and not the entire zone database. (Such is not the case in the older NT model.)

Additionally, as new domain controllers are added to the domain, the DNS zone database is replicated automatically. This allows the other domain controllers to hold their own zone information and to act as primary DNS servers for their areas. Where DNS servers were usually installed as additional resources in NT domains, now Active Directory can simply transfer the information along with other changes to the necessary domain controllers. This system allows the domain controllers to have their own read/write copy of the zone database files and to share in the tasks associated with it.

When Active Directory is installed and a DNS server is set up, you can decide what kind of zones you want to configure. Although Active Directory zones are the logical and most secure choice, you can also configure standard zone storage using a text-based file. This text file is stored in the %systemroot%\System32\DNS folder. In either case, if only one primary or standard DNS server is installed, it offers a single point of failure for the network. Ideally, secondary DNS servers should be installed, and zone transfers should be configured. This can reduce network traffic, provide fault tolerance, enhance load balancing, and streamline database replication.

Overview of DDNS

DNS zone database files contain information, including FQDNs and their associated IP addresses, for clients and resources on the network. In the olden days, this information didn't change much and was managed by manually typing in the names and IP addresses and creating the mapping files by hand. This worked fairly well because once an IP address was configured for a machine, it usually didn't change that often.

With the creation of DHCP, mobile computers, and ever-changing networks, maintaining these manually created mapping files became impossible. Consider having the task of manually typing in all of this information as it changed dynamically with DHCP, mobile, or remote access clients. Because of this need, Dynamic DNS was created. Dynamic DNS allows clients to register and update their DNS resource records with a DNS server every time a change occurs. Dynamic DNS, often referred to as *dynamic update*, can be enabled or disabled on any zone configured on a Windows 2000 server. Dynamic DNS works for Active Directory-integrated zones and standard primary zones. By default, client computers will update their A records with the DNS server when configured to use TCP/IP as the network protocol and when offered a DNS server with which to update.

Every time a client IP address is added, removed, or changed in the TCP/IP Properties sheet, any time a client's IP address lease changes or is renewed with a DHCP server, or any time a computer is turned on, a dynamic update is sent from the client to the DNS server. The DHCP client service sends this request to update the information because the change may have occurred because of DHCP, and DNS will need to synchronize its name-to-address mappings for the computer.

Note: *Microsoft has provided multiple white papers detailing how the process works. For more information, see the links to Microsoft's Web site and accompanying papers from the CD-ROM included with this book.*

More Features and Benefits of DNS and DDNS

There are several features still not mentioned concerning DNS servers and clients. Each of these features makes using Windows 2000, DNS, and DHCP even more appealing. You can obtain more information on these features from Microsoft Help or from Microsoft's Request for Comments. These are the features:

- DNS is an open protocol and is used worldwide. It is also used with TCP/IP on the Internet.

- DNS works well with other DNS services and with various Berkeley Internet Name Domain (BIND) versions.

- DNS works with WINS, DHCP, and older versions of Microsoft DNS.

- Several tools are available such as the DNS console, the Configure Your Server utility, and various command-line utilities such as NSLookup and IPConfig.

- Performance tools are available through the Performance console, auditing, and trace logging and debugging.

- DNS offers various resource record types besides the ones previously mentioned. These additional records include mail group, responsible person, route through, and service locator records, to name a few.

Name Resolution

What happens from the time you type in a name like **www.microsoft.com** or **graphics1. garland.ballew.com** to the time you are actually connected to the resource or Web site? The answer to that question is quite complex, but the answer begins with name resolution. Name resolution is the process of resolving a name to its IP address; this process is completed through DNS databases and network hardware and software.

If you need the address or phone number of a friend, you can find that information in a number of ways. If you know the information, you can say it is cached, similar to a locally cached IP address. If you need to consult a phone book, you can compare the phone book to the local DNS zone database file. If the number isn't in the phone book, and you have to call Information for the number, you can compare that to contacting a non-local DNS server outside the network or consulting your ISP. These searches are considered *forward lookups*—when you know the name and you need the number (FQDN to IP address). There are also *reverse lookups*, which are a little more complex. Reverse lookups are necessary when you know the number but need the name. In this instance, you can consult a Mapsco (**www.mapsco.com**) or the Internet, or, using a DNS server, you can use NSLookup, along with other utilities.

In order to understand how DNS works and to be successful at troubleshooting the DNS servers on your network, you'll need to have a thorough understanding of the lookup processes.

Forward Lookups

When a client sends a request to be connected to a resource by using its FQDN, a forward lookup takes place. The request is passed to the local name server first, and that server tries to resolve it. If the local name server doesn't know the IP address of the resource, the request is passed on to another name server for resolution. The entire forward lookup process is detailed next (Decision Tree 11.1 shows this process also):

1. A user types an address such as **www.yahoo.com** or **graphics01.garland.ballew.com** into a Web browser and presses Enter.

2. The client computer sends this query to the local name server.

3. The local name server checks its zone database files for the name-to-address mapping matching this query; this mapping is known as the A record. In the case of **www.yahoo.com**, the local name server does not have authority over **yahoo.com**, so the request is sent on to a DNS root server. In the case of **graphics.garland. ballew.com**, if the local name server does have authority over the **ballew.com** domain, then the request is completed and the local name server sends the IP address to the client.

4. If the address isn't local to the network, and the root name server is queried, the root server sends back a referral to the **com** name servers.

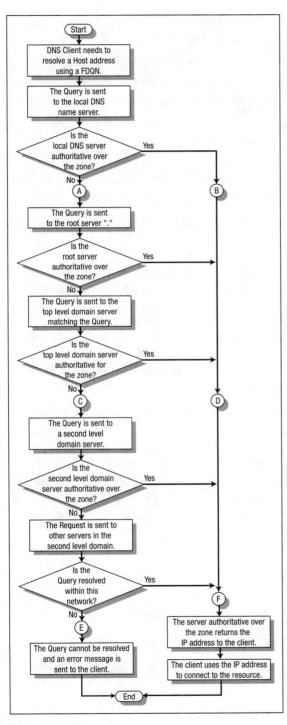

Decision Tree 11.1

The forward lookup process.

5. The client initiating the request then sends a request to the **com** name server, which responds to the client with a referral to the Yahoo! name servers.

6. The client initiating the request then sends a request to the Yahoo! name server, which does indeed have the authority to resolve the name. Yahoo! servers send the IP address of the resource or Web page **www.yahoo.com** to the client's local name server.

7. The local name server then sends this address to the client, who can now request a connection to **www.yahoo.com** by using its IP address.

*Note: Local name servers cache information they receive for an hour in case the same information is needed again. If it is, the local name server has information regarding the **com** domain, the **yahoo** domain, and more, and can resolve those addresses faster the next time. Caching will be covered in more detail later.*

Reverse Lookups

As I mentioned earlier, reverse lookups are a tad more complex than forward lookups. A reverse lookup is used when you need to resolve an IP address like 64.58.76.176 to a FQDN like **www.yahoo.com**. Because DNS was originally created for resolving FQDNs to IP addresses, this process took more time to develop and required more resources. Consider trying to look up a phone number in a phone book. Phone books weren't originally developed to be used this way. The only way to find the name that corresponds to a specific phone number is to look at every number in the book. This would be fairly time-consuming.

To allow users to type in an IP address and have it resolved to a FQDN, the **in-addr.arpa** domain was created. This domain creates a *reverse namespace* where IP addresses can be resolved easily. Basically, the **in-addr.arpa** domain is configured in reverse from a forward lookup zone. For instance, to resolve IP addresses in the 192.168.5.0 through 192.168.5.65 range, the reverse lookup zone would contain entries for 5.168.192. The subdomains are named for each of the IP octets, and the order of the IP octets is reversed. In later sections, when you learn about the troubleshooting tools and command-line tools, NSLookup will be introduced. Listing 11.1 shows how NSLookup can be used to resolve an IP address to a FQDN.

Listing 11.1   A reverse lookup.

```
C:\>nslookup 64.58.76.176
Server: ns1.istrength.net
Address: 207.252.204.136

Name: www7.dcx.yahoo.com
Address: 64.58.76.176
```

This lookup was completed faster than I could blink my eyes, and the name for the IP address 64.58.76.176 was returned as a **yahoo.com** server. This tool, used locally, can aid in troubleshooting and can be used by applications and other entities for communications on the network or Internet. Here are the steps involved in a reverse lookup:

1. A client sends a request for communication to another resource by using the resource's IP address. The IP number is typed into the user's Web browser or is initiated through the **nslookup** command.

2. The DNS server receives the request for a PTR record that maps this address to the FQDN of the resource.

3. Because the requested record is a PTR record, the resolver reverses the address and adds **.in-addr.arpa** to the end of the address. An example of this would be **176.76.58.64.in-addr.arpa**.

4. When the **in-addr.arpa** domain is contacted (and this is achieved the same way that forward lookups are processed), the PTR record information is sent to the client and the address is resolved.

Note: You can create your own reverse lookup zones on your private network. This will be explained later.

Caching

As the local name server processes forward lookup queries for clients, it stores the information it receives along the way in its local cache. For instance, in a simple query for **www.yahoo.com**, several domain namespaces are contacted, including the root domain, the **com** domain, and the **yahoo** domain. This information is saved for an hour by default in the local cache, so the next time the same information is needed, the server can immediately go to the domain namespace and obtain the required information. This information can decrease network traffic if the cache Time-To-Live interval is set high, but if up-to-date information is needed, the cache TTL should be set to something lower than 60 minutes. After the TTL expires, the name server deletes these results from its cache.

Caching-Only DNS Servers

When networks or subnets are separated by slow WAN links, you might consider installing a caching-only DNS server on those remote links. Caching-only servers are not authoritative for any zones or domains; these servers simply work to resolve and cache queries and query information for a given domain. They do not perform zone transfers, so they reduce WAN traffic even more. Initially, the cache is empty and takes some time to build, so patience is necessary with a new caching-only server, but over time and after the cache is built, network traffic will improve.

11

Installing DNS

Now that you are somewhat familiar with the terms and concepts related to DNS, you can consider the installation and configuration of it. If you have a domain controller that has Active Directory installed on it, then the DNS service is already installed and only needs to be configured. However, to set up a new DNS server or to create a secondary DNS server, you'll need to understand how DNS is installed in these circumstances.

Planning for the DNS Servers

Before installing DNS or configuring zones, make a detailed drawing of the network as you did in Chapter 3, and make some decisions regarding the servers and the zones you'll configure. In the following worksheet, answer the questions and make notes regarding each entry. By doing so, you'll be able to decide how many servers you need, how you want to configure zones, and how the DNS servers will be used.

DNS server worksheet.	
Question	**Notes**
Will the server act as a domain controller or as a member server?	
Which server will act as the primary DNS server?	
Which server will act as the secondary DNS server?	
Where might bottlenecks occur with DNS zone transfers?	
Where on the network do users have slow responses when logging on?	
How will fault tolerance for local and remote sites be handled?	
Will you have down-level machines acting as DNS servers?	
How will zones be configured? Is more than one zone needed?	
How many zones will each server host and maintain?	
How large are the zones to be configured?	
Is it possible to put a DNS server on each subnet?	
Can caching-only servers be used for remote networks?	
How will users obtain DNS information if their local DNS server goes offline? Will secondary servers be available on each subnet?	
Is it possible to use Active Directory integrated zones instead of standard primary zones?	
How will dynamic updates be used?	
What effect will zone transfers have on slower areas of the network or on those separated by WAN links? Will DNS servers be installed on those networks?	
How will you test this new zone configuration in a lab? Can you?	

One more step before the installation: Does the computer meet the requirements for a DNS server? To answer this last question, first make sure the computer meets the requirements listed earlier for a domain controller or member server, and then consider the following items:

- DNS servers need around 4MB of RAM to start with no zones configured.

- For each resource record added to the zone, the server needs about 100 bytes of additional memory. For instance, if 5,000 resource records exist, then 500KB of additional memory will be needed.

- To improve performance of a DNS server, add more RAM.

- The DNS server should be configured with a static IP address. Before installing the server, make sure this address has been properly set.

Installing the DNS Service

To install the DNS service on a member server or for adding a secondary DNS server, perform the following steps:

1. As an administrator, log on to the server to be installed as a DNS server.

2. Choose Start|Settings|Control Panel, and open Add/Remove Programs.

3. Select Add/Remove Windows Components from the left pane.

4. In the Windows Components box, highlight Networking Services and choose Details.

5. Place a checkmark in the Domain Name System (DNS) checkbox, and choose OK.

Installing a DNS Server

To create a DNS server after the DNS service is installed or on a domain controller with Active Directory installed, perform the following steps:

1. As an administrator, log on to the server to be installed as a DNS server.

2. Choose Start|Programs|Administrative Tools|DNS to open the DNS console.

3. Right-click on DNS in the left pane, and choose Connect To Computer.

4. In the Select Target Computer dialog box, select This Computer. Choose OK.

If you click on the Forward Lookup Zones folder, you'll notice that two zones are created already. The root domain is first and is shown with a dot, and the domain that the computer is a member of is shown second. Figure 11.1 shows the resulting screen.

Note: You can also create your own management console by adding the DNS snap-in to an existing console or a new one.

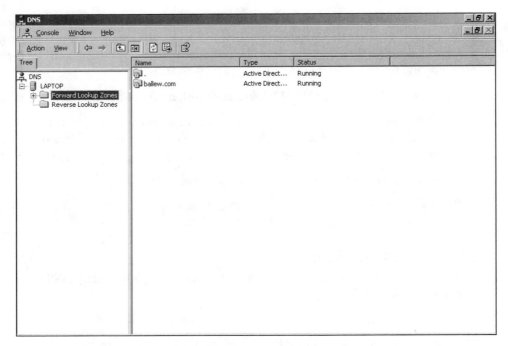

Figure 11.1
The DNS console.

Installing a Caching-Only Server

To install a caching-only server, perform the following steps:

1. As an administrator, log on to the server to be installed as a DNS server.

2. If the server isn't configured with a static TCP/IP address, configure it with one by right-clicking on the local area connection through Network And Dial-Up Connections.

3. Choose Start|Settings|Control Panel, and open Add/Remove Programs.

4. Select Add/Remove Windows Components from the left pane.

5. In the Windows Components box, highlight Networking Services and choose Details.

6. Place a checkmark in the DNS checkbox, and choose OK.

7. Choose Start|Programs|Administrative Tools|DNS to open the DNS console. Right-click on DNS, and choose Connect To Computer. Select This Computer.

8. Do not configure the DNS server with zones, but verify that the server root hints are configured properly; you can do this by right-clicking on the DNS server just installed and choosing Properties.

9. Select the Root Hints tab.

10. For this DNS server to cache information effectively, it needs to be configured with the root server for the DNS namespace. Choose Add to add root servers to this list.

Installing Clients

For the sake of continuity, I'll describe installing clients here. However, you won't be able to use DNS effectively without configuring the server first. Configuration of the DNS server includes adding zones, modifying and viewing records, and setting special configuration options. To configure a client for DNS, perform the following steps:

Note: The clients here have previously used static IP addresses.

1. As an administrator, log on to the client workstation (it must be configured with TCP/IP).

2. Right-click on My Network Places, and choose Properties.

3. Right-click on the local area connection, and choose Properties.

4. Highlight Internet Protocol (TCP/IP), and choose Properties.

5. On the General tab, choose the Advanced button.

6. On the DNS tab, choose Add.

7. In the TCP/IP DNS Server dialog box, type the IP address of the DNS server you want the client to use. Choose Add.

8. Choose OK three times to exit.

Configuring DNS

There are seemingly hundreds of items that can be configured in the DNS server, including different types of zones, interfaces, forwarders, and resource records. In this section, you'll learn about the different configuration options, including what must be done for DNS to work properly and effectively.

Zones

One of the first items to consider is the creation of zones for your DNS server. You have decided that you need to create some additional zones after going through the checklist offered previously or due to network traffic or size. If so, use the following procedures for the specific zone you'd like to create.

Creating a Standard Forward Lookup Zone

To create a standard forward lookup zone, follow these steps:

1. As an administrator, log on to the DNS server to be configured.

2. Choose Start|Programs|Administrative Tools|DNS to open the DNS console.

3. Right-click on the Forward Lookup Zones folder, and choose New Zone. Choose Next when the New Zone Wizard appears.

4. The first page in the wizard requires you to select the type of zone you want to create. There are three choices:

   - *Active Directory-integrated*—Stores the new zone in Active Directory to provide secure updates and integrated storage.

   - *Standard Primary*—Stores a master copy of the new zone as a text file, allowing the exchange of DNS data on this computer with other DNS servers using the same text-based methods. These computers might be older non-Windows-2000 machines.

   - *Standard Secondary*—Creates a copy of an existing zone to help balance the load of the primary servers and to enable fault tolerance.

   Choose Standard Primary.

5. Type the name of the new zone in the Zone Name text box.

6. The next page is the Zone File Configuration page. You can do either of two things here: Create a new file with the suggested name for the zone database file, or use an existing file. Select the option that meets your needs.

7. Verify that the information on the Summary page is correct, and choose Finish. You'll be able to see the new zone in the right pane of the DNS console.

Creating an Active Directory-integrated Zone

To create an Active Directory-integrated zone, follow these steps:

1. As an administrator, log on to the DNS server to be configured.

2. Choose Start|Programs|Administrative Tools|DNS to open the DNS console.

3. Right-click on the Forward Lookup Zones folder, and choose New Zone. Choose Next when the New Zone Wizard appears.

4. The first page in the wizard requires you to select the type of zone you want to create. Select Active Directory-integrated.

5. Type the name of the new zone in the Zone Name box.

6. Verify that the information on the Summary page is correct, and choose Finish. You'll be able to see the new zone in the right pane of the DNS console.

Creating a Standard Secondary Lookup Zone

To create a standard secondary lookup zone, follow these steps:

1. As an administrator, log on to the DNS server to be configured.

2. Choose Start|Programs|Administrative Tools|DNS to open the DNS console.

3. Right-click on the Forward Lookup Zones folder, and choose New Zone. Choose Next when the New Zone Wizard appears.

4. The first page in the wizard requires you to select the type of zone you want to create. Select Standard Secondary.

5. Type the name of the new zone in the Zone Name box.

6. The next page is the Master DNS Servers page. Type in the name of, or browse to, the DNS server from which you want to copy the zone. You can add multiple DNS servers here, and those servers will be contacted in the order in which they are shown on the list. The order of the DNS servers can be changed. See Figure 11.2 to view the Master DNS Servers page of the wizard.

7. Verify the settings on the Summary page, and choose Finish.

Creating a Reverse Lookup Zone

To create a reverse lookup zone, follow these steps:

1. As an administrator, log on to the DNS server to be configured.

2. Choose Start|Programs|Administrative Tools|DNS to open the DNS console.

3. Double-click on the Reverse Lookup Zones folder.

4. Choose Action|New Zone. When the New Zone Wizard appears, choose Next.

5. The first page in the wizard requires you to select the type of zone you want to create. There are three choices: Active Directory-integrated, Standard Primary, and Standard Secondary. Select the correct type of zone, and continue.

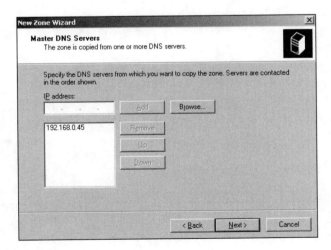

Figure 11.2
Specifying master DNS servers.

6. In the Reverse Lookup Zone box, type in the network ID. This number will be the first number in the IP address quartet for a Class A address, the first two numbers in the quartet for a Class B address, or the first three numbers in the quartet for a Class C address. Type in your network ID, and continue.

7. On the Zone File page, either accept the new file name offered or choose an existing file.

8. Verify that the settings are correct, and finish the wizard. You'll see the new reverse lookup zone in the right pane of the DNS console, as shown in Figure 11.3.

Configuring Zone Properties

With various zones configured, you will need to configure the zone properties on occasion. To configure existing zone properties, perform the steps outlined next:

1. As an administrator, log on to the DNS server to be configured.

2. Choose Start|Programs|Administrative Tools|DNS to open the DNS console.

3. Right-click on a zone to configure, and choose Properties. Figure 11.4 shows a Properties dialog box for an Active Directory-integrated zone.

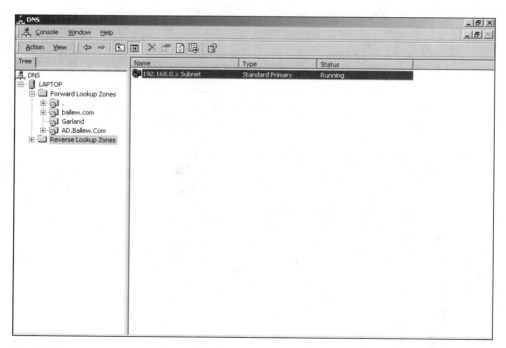

Figure 11.3
A reverse lookup zone.

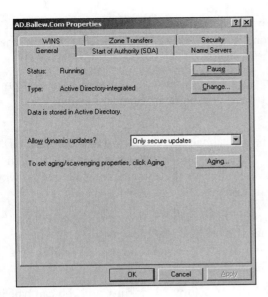

Figure 11.4
Properties dialog box for an Active Directory-integrated zone.

Note: The Properties dialog box for a primary or secondary standard zone looks similar to this screen except that the standard zone's dialog box does not contain a Security tab. Also, on the General tab of a primary or secondary zone's Properties dialog, there are no options for secure dynamic updates; there are only options for dynamic updates as a yes/ no configuration. Active Directory-integrated zone configurations are better suited to Windows 2000 networks for this reason and should be used whenever possible.

There are several tabs in this dialog box, and each tab has zone options that can be modified. To configure the DNS zones properly, you'll need to understand what each item offered for configuration is used for.

The General tab is used to allow dynamic updates for a zone or to change how dynamic updates are configured for the zone. In the Allow Dynamic Updates drop-down list shown in Figure 11.4, you can change the dynamic update configuration to Yes, No, or Only Secure Updates. The default is Only Secure Updates, and this should be used whenever possible. (As mentioned in the note earlier, there is no option for secure updates when you're using a standard zone. Only Active Directory can guarantee secure updates, thus the option is available only in Active Directory-integrated zones.)

Also on the General tab is the option to set aging and scavenging for the zone. Aging and scavenging are used to clean up the zone database files that become cluttered with resource records that are no longer valid or useful. When a computer logs on to the network, the computer's A (address) record is registered with the DNS server, and if the computer isn't logged off the network properly, its A record isn't deleted. This can cause numerous problems for the database. In the section "Monitoring and Optimizing the DNS Server," later in this chapter, you'll learn more about aging and scavenging.

Finally, using the General tab, you can pause, stop, and start the zone DNS service. Click on the Pause button while the DNS zone is running, or click on the Start button when the DNS zone has been paused.

Directly underneath the Pause button is the Change button. You can use this button to change the zone type between Active Directory-integrated, Standard Primary, and Standard Secondary.

Using the Start Of Authority (SOA) tab, you can view or change information in the DNS zone's SOA record. The SOA record is the resource record that contains information about the DNS name server that is the authority for the domain. Later I'll discuss why you'd want to change the settings for this record.

On the Name Servers tab, you can add, edit, or remove name servers to be used for this zone. This tab lists the server name and its IP address. By choosing the Edit button, you can change the name server being used to another, or you can remove certain name servers from the list of available servers for this zone.

On the WINS tab, you can configure WINS to use forward lookups, and you can type in the IP address of the WINS server. A later section explains how DNS and WINS work together and are integrated.

On the Zone Transfers tab, you can allow zone transfers to other servers on the network. These zone transfers can be configured for any server on the network, for only the servers listed on the Name Servers tab, or for only specific servers listed by IP address. You can also choose to automatically notify secondary servers when configuration of the zone changes to the servers listed on the Name Servers tab or to specific servers listed by IP address. By default, secondary servers will be automatically notified.

Finally, use the Security tab to specify which Active Directory permissions will be assigned to this zone. The usual options apply here. Some of the default permissions are:

- Enterprise Admins, DNS Admins, SYSTEM, and Domain Admins have full control.

- Administrators can read, write, and create child objects.

- Authenticated users can create child objects only.

- Everyone can read objects.

Changing the Zone Type

You might decide after some time that you'd like to change your standard primary zone to an Active Directory-integrated zone, or that you'd like to change a standard secondary zone to a primary zone. To change the zone type, perform the following steps:

1. As an administrator, log on to the DNS server to be configured.

2. Choose Start|Programs|Administrative Tools|DNS to open the DNS console.

3. Right-click on the zone that you'd like to change, and choose Properties.

4. On the General tab, choose Change.

5. Select the zone type you'd like the zone to be configured as.

Delegating Zones

Sometimes, zones are created so that other people in the network can manage the DNS namespace. This delegation can be to a specific physical location or department, or even to a group of users on a particular subnet. You can create a zone delegation by performing the following steps:

1. As an administrator, log on to the DNS server to be configured.

2. Choose Start|Programs|Administrative Tools|DNS to open the DNS console.

3. Right-click on the zone that you'd like to create a delegation for, and choose New Delegation.

4. The New Delegation Wizard appears; choose Next. On the first page, type the name of the delegated domain, and verify the FQDN of the domain name.

5. On the next page, you will need to add a name server for that domain. Choose Add.

6. Type in the server name or browse to the server. Choose the Resolve button to input the IP address of that server.

7. In the Browse box, highlight the Forward Lookup Zones folder, and choose OK.

8. On the next page, choose the zone to be delegated, and highlight an appropriate host. The Name Servers page appears again with the newly configured zone delegation, as shown in Figure 11.5.

9. On the next page, verify the new delegation before completing the wizard.

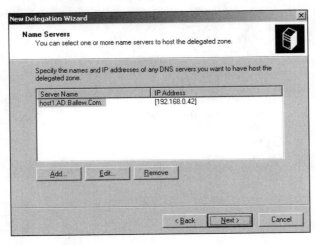

Figure 11.5
Delegating a zone.

Adding a New Domain to a Zone

To add a new domain to a zone, perform the following steps:

1. As an administrator, log on to the DNS server to be configured.

2. Choose Start|Programs|Administrative Tools|DNS to open the DNS console.

3. Highlight the appropriate zone that contains the resource record you want to modify, and notice the records in the right pane.

4. Right-click on the zone, and choose New Domain.

5. Type in the name of the new domain.

Resource Records

Zone database files consist of resource records. Resource records contain information about the resource's owner, its TTL, its class, its type, and record-specific data that describes the resource. Several types of records can be added to a zone database file, and those records can be modified as needed. In this section, you'll learn a little more about resource records, including how to add different types of records, how to modify SOA records, and how to add a domain to a zone.

Adding Host (A) Records

As you know, A records provide information about the DNS domain name and its IP address. Host (A) records can be created manually for static TCP/IP clients through the DNS console, but only computers that need to share resources on the network need an A resource record. For any client to be identified by others on the network, it needs to have its DNS domain name represented with an A record in the zone database file.

Note: *A records are also called host A records, thus the selection of New Host from the menu during configuration.*

To manually add an A record to a zone, perform the following steps:

1. As an administrator, log on to the DNS server to be configured.

2. Choose Start|Programs|Administrative Tools|DNS to open the DNS console.

3. Open the applicable forward lookup zone in the Forward Lookup Zones folder.

4. Right-click on the zone, and choose New Host.

5. In the New Host dialog box, type the name of the new A record, along with the IP address. If you want to create an associated PTR record, select that option.

Adding Pointer Records

Pointer (PTR) records are created when reverse lookups need to be completed. When creating a new host A record, you can choose to create the respective PTR record at the same time. To create a new PTR record, perform the following steps:

1. As an administrator, log on to the DNS server to be configured.

2. Choose Start|Programs|Administrative Tools|DNS to open the DNS console.

3. Open the applicable forward lookup zone in the Forward Lookup Zones folder.

4. Right-click on the folder, and choose Other New Records.

5. Scroll down to Pointer and choose Create Record. Figure 11.6 shows this screen.

6. Type in the Host IP number and the Host Name. You can browse to the host name. Choose OK, then Done. You'll notice the new record in the right pane of the zone.

Modifying SOA Records

An SOA record defines the resource record that contains information about the DNS name server that is the authority for the domain. You might want to change the default settings of the SOA record to enhance performance on your network or to change the primary server or responsible person for the zone. Listed next are the options you'll see when you modify these records, followed by the steps necessary to modify them. Here are the options:

- *Serial Number*—The serial number is used by zones and the operating system to determine whether a zone needs to be replicated to other secondary servers on the network when zone transfers are scheduled. The serial number is incremented by one each time a resource record in the zone changes. You can increment the zone by using the Increment button or by typing in a new number.

- *Primary Server*—The DNS server has an owner, or a primary server, for the zone being configured. You can change this server by choosing the Browse button and choosing another DNS server on the network.

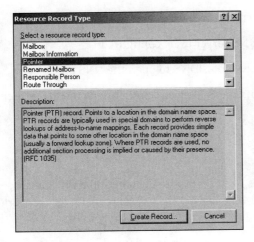

Figure 11.6
Creating a new PTR record.

- *Responsible Person*—This setting lists the person responsible for this DNS zone. To change the responsible party, choose the Browse button or type in the correct name. The name is written in the form **administrator.ballew.com** but is really an email address. The period between the name and the domain takes the place of the @ sign.

- *Refresh Interval*—The default refresh interval is 15 minutes, but this can be changed from one minute to any number of days. The refresh interval is the time that a secondary DNS server waits before renewing the zone information for its database. When the refresh interval is met, the secondary DNS server requests a copy of the primary DNS server's SOA record and checks this record's serial number with its own. If the numbers are different, indicating that changes have been made, then the secondary server requests a zone transfer. If the serial numbers are the same, no transfer of information takes place.

- *Retry Interval*—If a zone transfer fails, the retry interval denotes the amount of time that the secondary server will wait before attempting another transfer. The default is 10 minutes.

- *Expires After*—This number represents the time that will elapse after the refresh interval has failed to obtain a successful zone transfer. The secondary server will stop responding to client queries because it will deem its database unreliable and not current. The default is one day.

- *Minimum (Default) TTL*—This number is the minimum value that resource records use that aren't configured already with a TTL. This minimum default is sent with query responses to let other entities know how long the records should be cached. The default is one hour.

- *TTL For This Record*—This setting shows the TTL for this particular record.

To modify any of these properties, perform the following steps:

1. As an administrator, log on to the DNS server to be configured.

2. Choose Start|Programs|Administrative Tools|DNS to open the DNS console.

3. Right-click on the zone that contains the SOA record you want to modify, and choose Properties.

4. Select the SOA tab and make the necessary changes.

Modifying Resource Record Properties

To modify an existing record's properties for the purpose of changing its IP address, changing the permissions on the record, or updating the associated PTR record, perform the following steps:

1. As an administrator, log on to the DNS server to be configured.

2. Choose Start|Programs|Administrative Tools|DNS to open the DNS console.

3. Highlight the zone that contains the resource record you want to modify, and notice the records in the right pane.

4. Right-click on the record you want to modify, and choose Properties.

5. In the Properties dialog box, change the IP address, and/or choose to update the associated PTR record on the resource record tab. (This tab will have various names depending on the record being changed.)

6. You can change the permissions for this record on the Security tab if necessary. Make the appropriate changes and choose OK.

Note: Deleting a record is as simple as right-clicking on the record and choosing Delete.

11

WINS Integration

If your network has legacy operating systems communicating using NetBIOS names, those clients will need another way to resolve names other than with DNS servers. NetBIOS names will not be found in the DNS domain namespace. To accommodate these clients, you'll need to integrate WINS with DNS. When this is done, two special resource records are created: the WINS and the WINS-R records. The WINS record indicates who the WINS server is and its IP address, and the WINS-R record is used to enable reverse lookups for WINS clients.

WINS lookup integration is available only with Windows DNS servers. Using a combination of Windows DNS servers and other DNS servers can cause interoperability issues. These special issues will be discussed later in this section. WINS lookup is most effectively used when only Windows DNS servers are configured. Additionally, by default, WINS resolves only the names in the zone root or names that are direct descendants of that root, but not names in subdomains. You should put WINS hosts in a single zone if possible because resolution will work properly and be easier to configure and manage.

The WINS Lookup Process

When clients access the DNS server and need a NetBIOS name, and no A record exists for that name, the client's request is sent to the network. The WINS lookup process works like this:

1. The client sends a request to the preferred DNS server for the purpose of locating another resource's IP address to initiate communications.

2. The preferred DNS server looks in its zone database to see if it has a matching A record.

3. If the preferred DNS server doesn't find the record, then the normal process of resolving the FQDN ensues. This process was described earlier. When the results are found, they are sent to a Windows DNS server on the network.

4. When the DNS lookup process has located the authorized server, resolution continues because the query is for a NetBIOS name. Because the host A record does not exist, if the DNS server is WINS-enabled, the rest of the steps are performed.

5. The DNS server removes the domain name from the FQDN request that was sent and uses the hostname only for its communication with the WINS server. Remember, the hostname is the name farthest to the left. For example, in **host1.ballew.com**, the hostname is **host1**.

6. The DNS server sends a request to the WINS server using the hostname, and sends it as a NetBIOS request.

7. Either the WINS server resolves the name and returns the IP address to the DNS server, or the WINS server does not resolve the name and the resource isn't found.

8. The WINS server sends the IP address of the resource to the Windows DNS server, which in turn sends it to the preferred DNS server for the client.

9. The preferred DNS server sends the IP address to the client.

Configuring a WINS Server

Configuring a WINS server involves two distinct tasks. The first task is to enable a WINS lookup in a zone root domain, and the second task is to enable a WINS reverse lookup in an **in-addr.arpa** domain.

To enable a WINS lookup in a zone root domain, perform the following steps:

1. As an administrator, log on to the DNS server to be configured.

2. Choose Start|Programs|Administrative Tools|DNS to open the DNS console.

3. In the left pane, select the Forward Lookup Zones folder.

4. In the right pane, right-click on the zone to configure with WINS integration, and choose Properties.

5. Select the WINS tab.

6. Place a checkmark in the Use WINS Forward Lookup checkbox.

7. Type in the IP address of the WINS server. Choose Add, then OK. You'll be able to see the new zone in the right pane.

Before you can enable a WINS reverse lookup in an **in-addr.arpa** zone root domain, you'll need to have a reverse lookup zone configured first. (If you need to configure a reverse lookup zone, see the section "Creating a Reverse Lookup Zone.") To enable a WINS reverse lookup in an **in-addr.arpa** zone root domain, perform the following steps:

1. As an administrator, log on to the DNS server to be configured.

2. Choose Start|Programs|Administrative Tools|DNS to open the DNS console.

3. In the left pane, select the Reverse Lookup Zones folder.

4. In the right pane, right-click on the zone to configure with WINS integration, and choose Properties.

5. Select the WINS-R tab.

6. Place a checkmark in the Use WINS-R Lookup checkbox, and type in the domain to append to the returned name. You'll be able to see the new zone in the right pane.

Tip: If a specific zone uses WINS lookup, but only one of the zone's authoritative servers is WINS-enabled, you'll have problems with NetBIOS name resolution that will be hard to pinpoint. Make sure that all of the authoritative DNS servers for a zone are WINS-enabled if WINS clients are present.

11

WINS Advanced Properties

You can modify how DNS and WINS work together by changing a few of the advanced properties. These properties include cache time-out and lookup time-out.

Cache time-out is a value that represents how long the DNS server should cache information gained from a WINS server. The default is 15 minutes. You might consider changing this number to something higher if the WINS server's information doesn't change much or if the WINS transfers are causing a large amount of traffic. You'll need to lower this number if the information on the WINS server needs to be kept up-to-date as often as possible.

Lookup time-out is a value that represents how long the DNS server (service) will wait after a request has been made to a WINS server. The default value is 2 seconds. You might consider raising this number if the WINS server is physically distant from the DNS server, if the WINS computer is running on minimal resources, or if the link to the server is slow.

To change these time-outs, perform the following steps:

1. As an administrator, log on to the DNS server to be configured.

2. Choose Start|Programs|Administrative Tools|DNS to open the DNS console.

3. In the left pane, select the Forward Lookup Zones folder.

4. In the right pane, right-click on the zone to configure with WINS integration, and choose Properties.

5. Select the WINS tab, and choose Advanced.

6. Type in the new cache time-out or lookup time-out as needed.

Special Cases

When you are using a mix of Microsoft DNS servers and other DNS servers, you'll need to enable the option to prevent replication so zone data transfer failures can be avoided when Microsoft DNS servers try to replicate to the non-Microsoft WINS servers. To enable this restriction, perform the following steps:

1. As an administrator, log on to the DNS server to be configured.

2. Choose Start|Programs|Administrative Tools|DNS to open the DNS console.

3. In the left pane, select the Forward Lookup Zones folder or the Reverse Lookup Zones folder.

4. In the right pane, right-click on the zone to configure with WINS integration, and choose Properties.

5. Select the WINS tab or the WINS-R tab.

6. Place a checkmark in the Do Not Replicate This Record checkbox.

Special Options for DNS Servers

When you're configuring your DNS server, you might need to set several additional options in some instances. In this section, I'll introduce a few of these options and detail how they are configured. Some of these include restricting a DNS server to accept requests from only certain clients, changing how the DNS server boots, and restoring the server to its defaults.

Restricting a Multihomed DNS Server to Use a Specific NIC for Client Queries

If the DNS server has multiple NICs, and you want only one of those interfaces to respond to client queries, perform the following steps:

1. As an administrator, log on to the DNS server to be configured.

2. Choose Start|Programs|Administrative Tools|DNS to open the DNS console.

3. Right-click on the DNS server in the left pane, and choose Properties.

4. By default, the Listen On parameter is set to listen to all IP addresses on the network. Select the parameter Only The Following IP Addresses.

5. Type in the IP addresses one at a time for the NICs that the DNS server should respond with (or listen with). Click on Add each time. You'll have to configure the server to listen with at least one IP address.

6. Remove any preconfigured IP addresses that the server should not listen to; do this by highlighting them and choosing Remove. Choose OK when you're finished.

7. With the DNS server still highlighted, right-click and choose All Tasks.

8. Select Stop to stop the DNS service.

9. With the DNS server still highlighted, right-click and choose All Tasks, and Start.

Changing How the DNS Server Boots

The DNS server service starts by accessing the Windows 2000 server's Registry and looking at information stored there. The zone data is stored in the Registry along with other information. If you do not want the DNS service to start from the Registry, but you would like it to boot up either using a file or from data stored in Active Directory-integrated zones, you certainly can configure it to do that. Follow these steps:

1. As an administrator, log on to the DNS server to be configured.

2. Choose Start|Programs|Administrative Tools|DNS to open the DNS console.

3. Right-click on the DNS server in the left pane, and choose Properties.

4. Select the Advanced tab. Notice the section called Load Zone Data On Startup.

5. Select one of the three options: From Active Directory And Registry; From File; or From Registry.

Warning! *If you choose to use a file for the DNS boot configuration, you'll need to name the file boot.txt and store it in the %Systemroot%\Winnt\System32\DNS folder. Otherwise, the DNS service will not know where to find the file and will not initiate properly. Also, if there are any Active Directory-integrated zones, you will receive the error message shown in Figure 11.7.*

If you receive the error message shown in Figure 11.7 and you still want to use a file to boot the DNS service from a file, you'll have to change all of the Active Directory-integrated zones to standard zones. I wouldn't recommend this, but if you must, you can do so by right-clicking on the Active Directory-integrated zones, choosing Properties, selecting the General tab, and changing the zone types. Once this is done, the configuration will be completed successfully.

More on DNS Clients

Before I move on to managing DNS, I'll return once more to clients and their configuration settings. Two types of clients will be discussed here: clients that have static IP addresses, and DHCP clients. You already know how to configure a DHCP client manually, but the instructions offered earlier required physically attending to the specific machine and typing in the DNS server's IP address at the computer. Remember that in Chapter 10, you learned how to configure clients with scope-based options to use a specific DNS

Figure 11.7
Boot file error message.

server, eliminating the need to visit each machine and input that number for each one. There are other client options as well. In this section, I'll introduce some ways to simplify your initial configuration of the clients and their DNS and WINS needs.

Static Clients

Clients that have static IP addresses must be dealt with individually. In the case of the DNS server and its listening to clients, those IP addresses had to be input manually and must be managed manually. For clients that need static IP addresses, the same is true.

To configure a client with a static IP address, perform the following steps:

Tip: Before starting, make sure you have the required information for the DNS and WINS servers on the network (as necessary), including their hostnames, the primary and secondary servers' IP addresses, and any DNS suffixes that need to be appended for resolving names other than FQDNs.

1. Log on to the client workstation as an administrator.
2. Right-click on My Network Places, and choose Properties.
3. Right-click on the local area connection, and choose Properties.
4. Highlight Internet Protocol (TCP/IP), and choose Properties.
5. Select Use The Following IP Address. Type in an IP address that is not being used by any other client and that is not in the range of IP addresses available for lease by the DHCP server.
6. Click in the Subnet Mask window. The default subnet mask will appear for the IP address you typed in. If you are using a subnet mask other than the default subnet mask, make the necessary changes.
7. If a default gateway is used, type in the IP address.
8. On the General tab, choose the Advanced button.
9. On the DNS tab, choose Add.
10. In the TCP/IP DNS Server dialog box, type the IP address of the DNS server that you want the client to use. Choose Add.
11. Select the WINS tab if you need to add a WINS server's IP address. Choose Add, and type in the IP address of the WINS server. Choose OK three times to exit.

DHCP Clients

With DHCP clients, you can configure those clients to obtain information about their WINS and DNS servers automatically and at the same time they receive information regarding their IP addresses. You learned a little about that in the last chapter.

When Windows 2000 clients are installed, they are set to obtain an IP address automatically by default. This is done because the installation program does not know what IP address to use and wouldn't be able to configure it automatically. If no address is manually configured by an administrator during the installation, the client will try to obtain an IP address automatically and will try to obtain the DNS server address automatically as well. When this is the case, options can be configured on the server so that these clients will obtain the correct information about WINS, DNS, and IP addresses without the administrator's ever having to visit the machine.

To configure the server in this way, perform the following steps:

1. Log on as an administrator.

2. Choose Start|Programs|Administrative Tools|DHCP.

3. In the domain tree, highlight the DHCP server.

Note: *Let's stop here for a moment and decide how you want to configure the options. As you know, you can configure options for the DHCP server as predefined options, you can create options that apply to only specific scopes or only a single scope, or you can configure server options. (See Chapter 10.) For the sake of example, I'll choose two: configuring options for a specific scope, and configuring predefined options for the DHCP server. You can make whatever choice is necessary for your environment.*

To configure scope options, perform the following steps.

1. Highlight the scope you want to configure, and locate the Scope Options folder under that scope or in the right pane.

2. Right-click on the Scope Options folder, and choose Configure Options.

3. On the General tab, place a checkmark in the 006 DNS Servers checkbox.

4. Type in the server name and IP address for the DNS server. Choose Add. (The Resolve button will resolve the address for you.)

5. On the same tab, place a checkmark in the 044 WINS/NBNS Servers checkbox.

6. Type in the server name and IP address for the WINS server. Choose Add. Choose OK. (The Resolve button will resolve the address for you.)

   Notice that the right pane lists options: one for the DNS Servers, one for the DNS Domain Name, and one for the WINS server.

To configure DHCP predefined options perform the following steps.

1. Right-click on the DHCP server in the left pane, and choose Set Predefined Options.

2. This screen differs from the Scope Options screen and does not have any tabs. From the screen that is available, Predefined Options And Values, choose an appropriate option class for this configuration. I'll choose DHCP Standard Options.

3. In the Option Name box, choose 006 DNS Servers.

4. Click on Edit Array.

5. Type the server name in the Server Name box, and type the IP address of the DNS server. (The Resolve button will resolve the address for you.) Choose Add, then OK.

6. Back at the Predefined Options And Values screen, in the Option Name box, choose 044 WINS/NBNS Servers.

7. Click on Edit Array.

8. In the next screen, type in the server name and IP address of the WINS server, and choose Add. (The Resolve button will resolve the address for you.) Choose OK again.

Tip: Another useful addition here is to add the default gateway.

To test the configuration, perform the following steps:

1. Log on to the client workstation as an administrator.

2. Open Start|Programs|Accessories|Command Prompt.

3. Enter "ipconfig /release" at this prompt.

4. Enter "ipconfig /renew" at this prompt.

5. Enter "ipconfig /all" at this prompt.

In the section titled "Ethernet Adapter Local Area Connection," or whatever applies to your specific setup and hardware, notice that the client now has the specified DNS server, the specified WINS server, and a DHCP leased address.

Managing DNS

Now that you've installed and configured a DNS server and clients, you'll need to know a little about managing those servers and clients and their zones. In this section, you'll learn about enabling DNS on multihomed servers, modifying the DNS server cache, stopping and starting the DNS service, manually updating server data files, using secondary servers, and more. For clients, you'll learn how to configure multiple names for clients and how to optimize client settings. Finally, for managing zones, you'll learn how to optimize settings for zones, manage zone database resource records, and manage reverse lookup zones.

Managing Servers

As you are aware, installing and configuring a server of any type is usually the easy part of the assignment. The harder tasks involve managing those servers on a daily basis and making sure they are working properly and are effectively configured. I've talked about many different configurations that can be set on the DNS server and its clients, but some tasks are ongoing, such as starting or stopping the service or manually updating server data files. In this section, you'll learn some of the behind-the-scenes activities that administrators must consider and perform when managing DNS servers for a network.

Managing the DNS Service and Modifying or Clearing the Cache

If the DNS server isn't responding to clients, and you've ruled out a physical problem with cables or NICS, you may want to see if the DNS service is started. You can see if this service is started, pause the service, or stop the service by right-clicking on the DNS server in the DNS console and choosing All Tasks. You can stop and start the service as a kind of rebooting.

You can also manage the DNS service through Start|Programs|Administrative Tools| Services. Here, you can manage settings for both the DNS server and the DNS clients. For both, you can stop, pause, restart, resume, and start the service, as well as view the service's related properties. You can also configure the following properties for the server or the client services (this is not a complete list):

- Startup Type—This defaults to automatic.

- Hardware Profile—You can enable or disable the service for certain hardware profiles.

- Recovery—Configure how the server will respond if there is a failure and how subsequent failures will be handled. The default is to take no action, but you can set this option to have the service restart, to have a specific file run, or to reboot the computer.

The cache contains a list of root name servers for the Internet, and this cache rarely needs to be changed. The only time you'll need to modify the cache is when the root name servers change. You modify the cache through the Root Hints tab of the Server Properties dialog box. Before modifying this cache, however, you should check the InterNIC for any updates to the root name servers. If no changes have been made, then no modifications are necessary. You can modify the cache by performing the following steps:

1. Log on as an administrator.

2. Choose Start|Programs|Administrative Tools|DNS to open the DNS console.

3. In the domain tree, highlight the DNS server.

4. Right-click and choose Properties.

5. On the Root Hints tab, you'll see entries for the Server Name and IP address of other DNS servers on the network if the server you are configuring is a root server.

6. To change a record, highlight it and choose Edit. To delete a record, highlight it and choose Remove. To add a record, choose Add.

Modifying the cache and *clearing* the cache are two different things. When you modify the cache, as in the previous example, you are changing the roots and root hints that the server uses to resolve client queries. On the DNS server, you can clear the local cache of previously resolved entries by right-clicking on the DNS server name in the DNS console and choosing Clear Cache.

Securing the Cache Against Pollution

When a DNS server makes a query, the server caches information it finds during that query in its local DNS cache. Generally, DNS servers add to the cache resource records that are included with referral answers sent as a result of a query to another root server. These "extra" records may include caching **msn.com** when you're searching for **microsoft.com**, for example, and they are technically unrelated. However, including these referrals in the cache can speed up access for others who need a similar query resolved.

This storage of referrals is sometimes referred to as *pollution of the cache*. You can configure the DNS server not to cache these non-related entries. This keeps the cache clean and avoids cache pollution. To configure your server to secure the cache against this type of pollution, perform the following steps:

1. Log on as an administrator.

2. Choose Start|Programs|Administrative Tools|DNS to open the DNS console.

3. In the domain tree, highlight the DNS server.

4. Right-click and choose Properties.

5. Select the Advanced tab.

6. Place a checkmark in the Secure Cache Against Pollution checkbox.

Manually Updating Server Data Files

You may need to update server data files manually if you've changed information in the data files or if you need to troubleshoot DNS problems on the network. You might also want to update the files manually if you've recently stopped and restarted the DNS service or performed maintenance on the server. You can manually update server data files by performing the following steps:

1. Log on as an administrator.

2. Choose Start|Programs|Administrative Tools|DNS to open the DNS console.

3. In the domain tree, highlight the DNS server.

4. Right-click, and choose Update Server Data Files.

Secondary Servers

You might have already installed and configured a few secondary servers on your network for fault tolerance and load balancing. You probably took into consideration the impact that the zone transfers would have on your network, too. However, managing those servers on a day-to-day basis requires that you monitor them carefully, that you make sure they are located and configured to maximize network throughput and communications, and that they aren't putting any extra load on the network or costing too much money to maintain.

If you've placed your secondary servers in a high-traffic area of the network, you're off to a good start. You might also consider the following tips for managing these secondary servers:

- Put the secondary server in an area close to the clients who need it most.

- Restrict zone transfers from the primary DNS server to only authorized secondary servers so you can hide the details of the network from outsiders who might try to hack into the network. This can be done through the Notify button on the Zone Transfers tab in the appropriate zone.

- Place a secondary server on the other side of a router on other subnets for fault tolerance.

- Remember that secondary servers inherently increase network traffic because of the necessary zone transfers. Configure the zone transfers accordingly, and do not add unnecessary secondary servers.

- If secondary servers are causing too much network traffic and bogging down a slower WAN link, consider changing the role of the server to a primary DNS server.

Adding Network Adapters to the DNS Server

To enhance DNS server performance, you can add multiple network interface cards to the DNS server. DNS can work on all of the NICs of a DNS server when properly configured. To enhance server performance, add the network cards as appropriate, and then perform the following steps to configure the server:

1. Log on as an administrator.

2. Choose Start|Programs|Administrative Tools|DHCP.

3. In the domain tree, highlight the DHCP server.

4. Right-click and choose Properties.

5. On the Interfaces tab, select All IP Addresses.

The server is now configured to listen for client queries with all of its installed NICs. To configure it to listen with only specific NICs, see the section "Restricting a Multihomed DNS Server to Use a Specific NIC for client Queries" earlier in this chapter.

Managing Clients

Once clients are set up and using DNS, only a few items will need tweaking. You can configure a DNS domain's suffix search list to revise a client's DNS search capabilities; you can do this by adding suffixes to the client's search list to revise or manage the DNS query process for that client.

Appending DNS Suffixes through the TCP/IP Advanced Tab

If users need to resolve names that are not FQDNs, you can configure the DNS suffix search list to search for the names using preconfigured domain name suffixes. When a user types in an unqualified domain name like **Computer_01** or **Printer_04**, the DNS Client services will try to find this particular resource by first testing a set of suffixes, then contacting other DNS servers, and finally querying those servers for the resource. This is handy when users generally type in shorter names for resources that reside in one (or more than one) domain.

When no entries are configured in the suffix list in TCP/IP properties for the client computer, then the client resolves DNS queries in the usual way, as described earlier in this chapter. If entries are configured in the DNS suffix box, then the process changes when requests to resolve the non-FQDNs are made. When suffixes are listed, only the FQDNs that can be made with the shorter, unqualified resource name plus the suffix are searched for.

Tip: *If the list has several entries, the first one is tried first, the second one second, and so on. Once the query is resolved, the suffixes further down the list aren't checked. Therefore, it is best to list the suffixes in order of their expected use.*

To configure a client to use appended suffixes for short, unqualified domain names, perform the following steps:

1. Log on to the client workstation as an administrator.

2. Right-click on My Network Places, and choose Properties.

3. Right-click on the local area connection, and choose Properties.

4. Highlight Internet Protocol (TCP/IP), and choose Properties.

5. Choose the Advanced button, and then select the DNS tab.

6. To add a suffix to the search list, choose Append These DNS Suffixes (In Order).

7. Choose Add. Then type in the name of the suffix you want to append. Close all of the boxes.

Note: *The default is to append primary and connection-specific DNS suffixes and to append parent suffixes of the primary DNS suffix for the DNS client. This allows a client to resolve non-FQDNs by using all of the primary suffixes and all connection-specific suffixes, not just one specifically configured.*

Managing Zones

Managing a DNS server implies managing its zones and zone records. You already know quite a bit about configuring zones, stopping and starting zones, notifying other DNS servers with zone updates, and configuring zone transfers, but day-to-day management tasks associated with zone database records and reverse lookup zones haven't been discussed. When new resources are introduced to a zone, new zone records will have to be added to the zone, and even though you know *how* to create a new record, you may not understand *when* to create a new record. In this section, you'll learn more about why certain records are created and what additional records are available. Managing reverse lookup zones will also be discussed.

Managing Zone Database Resource Records

In this section, I'll list many of the available resource records and explain why they should be added. Some of these records are added automatically for computers running Windows 2000 and using DHCP and Dynamic DNS. However, such a pristine environment isn't always the case with networks, and many records will have to be manually added. These are the resource records:

- CNAME (alias)

  - Must be added when a computer needs an alias (or second) name, such as when a server will act as both a Web server and a Telnet server.

  - Used to provide an alias name, such as **www.ballew.com**, for client access to a computer. The real name might be something like **servergroup.home.dallas. ballew.com**.

- Host (A)

  - Must be added for any resource on the network that will share its resources.

  - Must be added for any resource on the network that needs to be accessed by its DNS name so others can resolve the name through a query.

- Integrated Services Digital Network (ISDN)

  - Used when a DNS domain name needs to be mapped with an ISDN telephone number.

- Mail exchange (MX)

  - Used so email applications can locate a mail server by using the mail server's DNS name.

  - Configured for the mail servers that process mail for the domain.

  - Each MX record must also have an A record.

- Pointer (PTR)

  - Needed only for reverse lookup zones.

- Service locator records

  - Used for locating Active Directory domain controllers on a network and are usually created automatically.

In contrast to resource records, there are authority records. Authority records include the Start of Authority (SOA) record and the name server (NS) record. These records are required and are automatically created when the Add New Zone Wizard is used.

- SOA

    - Used to indicate the name of the primary server and the origin of the zone, along with other fundamental properties of the zone such as expiration, refresh intervals, and renewal.

    - The SOA record is the first record in a zone.

- NS

    - Used to designate which name servers are authoritative for a zone.

    - If this record exists for a name server, the zone's clients consider the server authoritative for the zone.

Other types of records are available: AAAA (Ipv6 host address), AFSDB (Andrew File System Database), ATMA (asynchronous transfer mode address), HINFO (host information), MB (mailbox), MG (mail group), MINFO (mailbox mail list information), MR (mailbox renamed), RP (responsible party), RT (route through), TXT (text), WKS (well-known service), and X25. These records are used for identification of resources similar to the other records mentioned. You can learn more about these records from RFCs 1886, 1183, and 1035.

Managing Reverse Lookup Zones

Managing reverse lookup zones is another task an administrator must deal with on a regular basis. Reverse lookup zones allow clients and applications to access hosts based only on the knowledge of their IP addresses.

The first step in making reverse lookup zones easier to manage is to place a checkmark in the Update Associated PTR Record checkbox when you're adding a record to a forward lookup zone. Performing this small step will ensure that the record's associated pointer record is created when the host (A) record is, and will eliminate the need to create that file manually. See Figure 11.8.

Another way to improve the management of these zones is to use DHCP and Dynamic DNS on the network. With both enabled and configured, you can have the DHCP clients automatically update their records with the DNS server, and their associated records will be managed automatically. DHCP and Dynamic DNS can be configured to help with legacy clients as well and simplify the management of their records.

Finally, Windows 2000 Professional clients automatically register their pointer records when an IP address is obtained from a DHCP server. If at all possible, clients should be moved to Windows 2000, or at least a new standard should be put in place to ensure that all new clients on the network will be running Windows 2000.

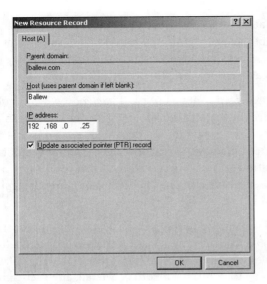

Figure 11.8
Update associated PTR record.

Monitoring and Optimizing the DNS Server

With the DNS server(s) up and running, your attention should now turn to monitoring and optimizing the server(s). In this section, you'll learn many techniques for monitoring your servers, including how to automatically or manually scavenge certain records. You'll also learn how to test and query the DNS server.

Following that, you'll learn how the Performance console is used and what counters are available for monitoring. You'll also be introduced to logging options. You can log events to assist in finding problems related to queries, updates, notifications, and more. You can view these logs using WordPad. Event Viewer can also be used with DNS monitoring, and you can use this utility to connect to the DNS server and view statistics and information.

Finally, you'll learn the main command-line tools and utilities that can be used to manage DNS. These include more IPConfig switches, NSLookup, and Dnscmd.

Aging and Scavenging Records

When computers or services use Dynamic DNS to automatically update their resource records with the DNS server, the records that are stored by the DNS server can sometimes become stale or invalid. This can cause the DNS server to offer information to clients that is not up-to-date or legitimate. Usually, these invalid records are stored in the DNS zone database because a computer was disconnected improperly from the network. When this happens, the computer does not have time to remove the A record, so it remains on the server.

Over time, these records can accumulate in the DNS server's database and can cause various intermittent problems. Some of these problems include taking up valuable disk space on the server, slowing down the server's response time, offering outdated information to clients, and causing communication problems with other DNS servers.

When you're using Active Directory-integrated zones, *aging* and *scavenging* techniques used by the DNS server can help remove these stale records and bring the DNS database back to normalcy. In particular, DNS places timestamps on the resource records that are dynamically added to the database. Determined by the refresh interval of the record, the record is deleted (scavenged) when its time is up. For manually added records, there is no automatic deletion by default, and those records must be manually configured to expire or must be manually deleted.

If there is a downside to the aging and scavenging process, it is the fact that improper configuration of it can cause more problems than would occur if the records were left alone. If the scavenging process removes valid records, or if they are accidentally deleted, then DNS client queries can fail. Not only that, but if a record is deleted, any user can create a new record for the resource and take ownership of it, even if security precautions are put in place to prevent such activities. Configuring aging and scavenging properly requires a little more knowledge on the subject.

Precautions for Aging and Scavenging

Before enabling aging and scavenging, you need to consider a few precautions and prerequisites. First, understanding some of the terms not previously mentioned is important to proper configuration. Listed next are a few of these terms:

- *No-refresh interval*—This interval represents the date and time the record was last refreshed and the date and time when the record will be refreshed again. This interval is necessary so there won't be an inordinate number of write operations to the Active Directory database. The default is 7 days and is configured zone-wide.

- *Refresh interval*—This interval represents the earliest date and time the record can be refreshed and the earliest date and time the record can be scavenged. The default is 7 days and is configured zone-wide.

- *Record refresh*—This interval represents when a DNS dynamic update will be processed for a record when the record's timestamp is revised.

- *Record update*—This interval represents when a DNS dynamic update will be processed for a record when the record's timestamp and other characteristics are revised.

- *Start scavenging time*—This is a specific time when scavenging can start. Start scavenging time = current server time + refresh interval.

- *Scavenging period*—This is the amount of time between scavenging events. The default is 7 days, but this setting can be reduced to as low as one hour.

- *Scavenging servers*—This advanced parameter can be left unconfigured, but if you enter server IP addresses here, you can choose specific servers for performing DNS scavenging. If this setting is left blank, all Windows 2000 DNS servers will attempt to scavenge records for their zones.

Additionally, scavenging and aging must be enabled at the DNS server and for the zone to be scavenged. This scavenging can be automated or manually performed. When automatic scavenging is enabled, the records are scavenged based on the number in the scavenging period setting. For manual scavenging, the scavenging is performed as the administrator sees fit.

Automatic Scavenging

To set aging and scavenging properties for a DNS server, perform the following steps:

1. Log on as an administrator.

2. Choose Start|Programs|Administrative Tools|DNS to open the DNS console.

3. In the domain tree, highlight the DNS server.

4. Right-click, and choose Set Aging/Scavenging for all zones.

5. Place a checkmark in the Scavenge Stale Resource Records checkbox.

6. For now, accept the defaults for the no-refresh interval and the refresh interval, leaving them both at 7 days. Choose OK.

Note: If changing the default of 7 days is necessary, don't increase the value to a high number. This action will weaken how well aging and scavenging work.

7. Confirm aging and scavenging in the next dialog box, and check the Apply These Settings To The Existing Active Directory-Integrated Zones checkbox.

8. Next, from the tree in the left pane, choose a specific zone that will be configured for scavenging.

9. Right-click on the zone, and choose Properties.

10. On the General tab, choose the Aging button.

11. Place a checkmark in the Scavenge Stale Resource Records checkbox.

12. For now, accept the defaults for the no-refresh interval and the refresh interval, leaving them both at 7 days. Choose OK.

13. If you've chosen a primary zone, choose Yes in the DNS box informing you that the zone file format will change.

Note: Automatic scavenging can also be configured by right-clicking on the DNS server, choosing Properties, selecting the Advanced tab, and selecting Enable Automatic Scavenging Of Stale Records.

Manual Scavenging

To begin manual scavenging of records, perform the following steps:

1. Log on as an administrator.

2. Choose Start|Programs|Administrative Tools|DNS to open the DNS console.

3. In the domain tree, highlight the DNS server.

4. Right-click on the DNS server, and choose Scavenge Stale Resource Records. Choose OK to verify the choice.

Viewing Advanced Properties

To see when a DNS server can next start scavenging stale records, or to view other advanced properties about the DNS server and its zones, perform the following steps:

1. Log on as an administrator.

2. Choose Start|Programs|Administrative Tools|DNS to open the DNS console.

3. In the domain tree, highlight a DNS zone.

4. Choose View|Advanced.

5. Choose Action|Properties.

6. On the General tab, choose Aging.

7. In the Zone Aging/Scavenging Properties dialog box, notice the date and time for the next time that records will be scavenged. See Figure 11.9.

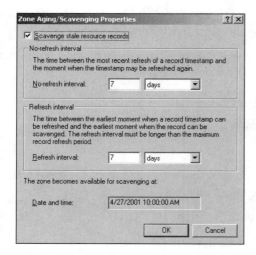

Figure 11.9
Date and time of next scavenging event.

Notice also that when View|Advanced was chosen with the zone selected in the console, other information appeared in the left pane, including more information on the reverse lookup zones and record types.

Setting Properties on a Specific Record

Aging and scavenging properties can be set for individual records if necessary. To set these properties, perform the following steps:

1. Log on as an administrator.

2. Choose Start|Programs|Administrative Tools|DNS to open the DNS console.

3. In the domain tree, highlight the DNS zone that contains the record.

4. In the right pane, right-click on the record, and choose Properties.

5. If the record was manually added, select the checkbox to allow aging and scavenging to occur for this record. If the record was dynamically added, clear the checkbox to prevent aging and scavenging for this record.

Testing and Querying the DNS Server

You can test the DNS servers on the network when performing troubleshooting as communication problems arise. To test connectivity to the servers, you can do two types of queries: simple queries, and recursive queries.

In a simple query, the DNS server queries itself. The DNS server acts as a client and queries itself (a DNS server) for DNS resolution. In a recursive query, a simple query is performed, but the client also asks the server to perform a recursive query to resolve an NS-type query for the root of the DNS domain namespace. This type of query is helpful in determining if problems on the network are occurring with server root hints or zone delegations. A recursive query will attempt to query other DNS servers to perform this task. To do these test queries, perform the following steps:

1. Log on as an administrator.

2. Choose Start|Programs|Administrative Tools|DNS to open the DNS console.

3. In the domain tree, right-click the DNS server, and choose Properties.

4. Select the Monitoring tab.

5. There are two test-type options, and you can select either or both: A Simple Query Against This DNS Server; or A Recursive Query To Other DNS Servers.

6. Choose Test Now. Figure 11.10 shows both types of queries passing this test.

Notice that this dialog box also has an option that allows you to perform automatic testing at certain intervals. The default is one minute. This performance checking should not be enabled all of the time, though, because this would generate unnecessary traffic.

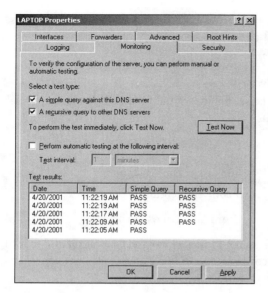

Figure 11.10
DNS test queries.

The Performance Console

Monitoring the Windows 2000 DNS servers on your network can prove useful in many ways. DNS is a critical part of a Windows 2000 network, performing the tasks necessary to provide IP addresses to clients who access resources by using their hostnames. Because DNS is such a critical service, maintaining the servers and keeping them in top form is imperative.

One of the best ways to monitor a DNS server's performance is through the Performance console, accessed from Start|Programs|Administrative Tools. Monitoring the servers allows administrators to obtain benchmarks for estimating current and future needs for the servers, to troubleshoot problems with the servers, and to determine if any bottle-necks exist or if any single piece of hardware is slowing down the server's performance.

In this section, I'll introduce some of the Performance console's most-used counters for monitoring the DNS servers. The counters vary in monitoring tasks and range from measuring overall performance to monitoring specific items, such as dynamic updates queued and TCP queries received.

Before starting, open the Performance Monitor by performing the following steps:

1. Log on as an administrator.

2. Choose Start|Programs|Administative Tools|Performance Monitor.

3. Highlight System Monitor in the left pane.

4. Click on the Plus sign, and then select the computer you want to connect to by using the Select Counter From Computer option.

5. In the Performance Object area, choose DNS.

Note: In the following examples of DNS counters, the thresholds are similar to those for other related counter types. You can find more information on these counters in the Windows 2000 Resource Kit, but generally, extremely high or low numbers indicate a problem. In the following sections, I'll introduce you to some of the most-used counters and what can be done to improve problems related to them.

Performance Counters

The Performance console has four *overall* performance counters that can be used to monitor the general performance of the DNS server. Monitoring the overall performance of the server can be a great place to start monitoring, and it can identify problems with server overload or heavy DNS traffic. If any of these counters are high on a regular basis, you might consider adding other DNS servers to lighten the load or reconfiguring the zones on the subnet. These are the counters:

- *TCP Query Received*—The total number of queries the DNS server receives from DNS clients

- *Total Query Received/Sec*—The average number of queries received from clients every second

- *Total Response Sent*—The total number of responses sent to clients from the DNS server

- *Total Responses Sent/Sec*—The average number of responses sent to clients from the DNS server every second

Zone Transfer Counters

To monitor zone transfers and to create a baseline or obtain other information about how zone transfers are being handled by the DNS server, use the four counters listed next. High numbers for the first three counters could indicate heavy zone-transfer traffic or poor links between zones. To solve problems here, consider changing the zone types or configuring better links. The last counter can be used to determine how much of the zone transfer traffic is successful. These are the counters:

- *Zone Transfer Failure*—The total number of zone transfers that have failed between the master DNS server and its secondary servers

- *Zone Transfer Request Received*—The total number of zone transfer requests that have been received by the master DNS server

- *Zone Transfer SOA Request Sent*—The total number of SOA zone transfer requests sent by the secondary DNS server to the master DNS server

- *Zone Transfer Success*—The total number of successful zone transfers done by the master DNS server

DNS Server Memory Counters

Four counters are available for monitoring the DNS server's memory use. These counters can be used to determine if the server's memory is the cause of a DNS bottleneck. If the numbers shown when monitoring these counters is generally high, you might need to install more memory in the DNS server, run memory-intensive programs on servers other than the DNS servers, or reconfigure zones or zone types. These are the DNS server memory counters:

- *Caching Memory*—The total amount of RAM that the DNS server is using for caching

- *Database Node Memory*—The total amount of RAM that the DNS server is using for database nodes

- *Nbtstat Memory*—The total amount of RAM that the DNS server is using for Nbtstat

- *Record Flow Memory*—The total amount of RAM that the DNS server is using for record flow

Dynamic Update Counters

Nine dynamic update counters can be used to monitor and troubleshoot problems with DNS and DHCP dynamic updates. The two counters detailed here are NoOperation counters. They indicate that a dynamic update was scheduled, but there was no new information to be transferred. A high number here could indicate that dynamic update intervals could be lowered. These are the two NoOperation counters:

- *Dynamic Update NoOperation*—The total number of NoOperation or empty dynamic update requests received by the master DNS server

- *Dynamic Update NoOperation/Sec*—The average number of NoOperation or empty dynamic update requests received by the master DNS server each second

The remaining seven dynamic update counters can be used to determine if dynamic updates are working efficiently for the DNS server. If these counter numbers are generally high, traffic for dynamic updates could be causing network problems. These counters are similar to counters already described and are self-explanatory:

- Dynamic Update Queued

- Dynamic Update Received

- Dynamic Update Received/Sec

- Dynamic Update Rejected

- Dynamic Update TimeOuts

- Dynamic Update Written To Database

- Dynamic Update Written To Database/Sec

Recursive Query Counters

Recursive queries are received by the DNS server from other DNS servers for help resolving hostnames to IP addresses. During this process, the DNS server gains information about the DNS domain namespace and caches the information. To monitor how well the recursive querying processes are working, the following counters are available. Again, these counters are self-explanatory, either being total counters or averages per second, as indicated by the name. If there are problems here, such as a high number of failed recursive queries, you might try modifying the root hints on the DNS server. Other counters can indicate a high level of DNS traffic, thus indicating that more DNS servers are needed or that zones need to be reconfigured. There are the recursive query counters:

- Recursive Queries

- Recursive Queries/Sec

- Recursive Query Failure

- Recursive Query Failure/Sec

- Recursive TimeOut

- Recursive TimeOut/Sec

Secure Dynamic Update Counters

Active Directory-integrated zones use secure dynamic updates. No other zones use this type of update process. Three counters are available for monitoring secure dynamic updates. A high number of failures or successes could mean that the DNS server or zone is overloaded and needs to be reconfigured or upgraded. These are the counters for secure dynamic updates:

- Secure Update Failure

- Secure Update Received

- Secure Update Received/Sec

WINS Lookup Counters

The WINS server is responsible for resolving hostnames to IP addresses for the legacy computers on the network and must also be monitored carefully. The following counters are available for WINS forward lookups and reverse lookups sent and received. High numbers here can indicate elevated WINS traffic levels and can be the source of WINS client bottlenecks. Additional WINS servers might be considered if these numbers are unusually high. These are the WINS lookup counters:

- WINS Lookup Received

- WINS Lookup Received/Sec

- WINS Response Sent

- WINS Response Sent/Sec

11

- WINS Reverse Lookup Received

- WINS Reverse Lookup Received/Sec

- WINS Reverse Response Sent

- WINS Reverse Response Sent/Sec

Other Counters

There are several other counters available for UDP and TCP queries received and responses sent, a couple of counters regarding notifications sent and received, and seven
counters for monitoring incremental zone transfers. These counters and more information on them can be found in the Performance console and can be used as necessary.

Logging

Another monitoring tool available with Windows 2000 DNS servers is logging. Logging in
DNS is used for debugging purposes when you're troubleshooting specific problems with
the DNS server. You can track DNS activity on the server and view this activity using
WordPad. Logging should not be used all the time; use it only when you're troubleshooting the server. Logging is CPU- and network-intensive and may cause performance
problems when used regularly.

Enabling Logging on the DNS Server

Because logging is disabled by default, it will need to be enabled prior to use. You can
enable the DNS server for logging by performing the following steps:

1. Log on to the DNS server as an administrator.

2. Choose Start|Programs|Administrative Tools|DNS to open the DNS console.

3. Right-click on the DNS server to configure, and choose Properties.

4. Select the Logging tab.

5. Select the events to log from the Debug Logging Options box. See Figure 11.11.
   (These events will be described next.)

*Note: These events will be logged in the %systemroot%\System32\Dns\Dns.log by
default.*

Logging Options

As you can see in Figure 11.11, there are 11 items available to log. Logging all of them at
once will put an incredible strain on the server, and the results will be harder to decipher
when you're reading the log than they will be if you choose only a few. When enabling
logging, carefully decide what needs to be logged and why. These are the logging options:

- *Query*—Clients send DNS servers queries, and this option is used to track those queries
  that are received.

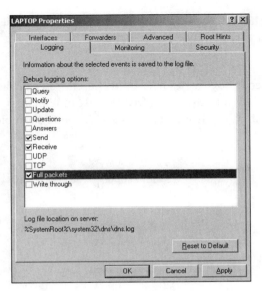

Figure 11.11
Enabling DNS logging.

- *Notify*—Other servers send DNS servers notification messages about zone transfers and changes to their databases. This log option tracks those notifications.

- *Update*—Client computers send DNS servers updates concerning their hostnames and IP addresses. This log option tracks those update notifications.

- *Questions*—When a DNS server receives a query from a client, the message contains a question section. This log option logs the contents of this question section for each message received.

- *Answers*—When a DNS server sends a query's answer to a client, the message contains an answer section. This option logs the contents of this answer section for each message sent.

- *Send*—DNS servers send query messages to other servers when they can't resolve the query themselves. This option logs those query messages.

- *Receive*—The DNS server service receives query messages from clients, and this log tracks how many of these messages are received.

- *UDP*—Some messages are sent over UDP ports instead of over TCP ports. This log tracks those requests.

- *TCP*—Some messages are sent over TCP ports instead of over UDP ports. This log tracks those requests.

- *Full Packets*—The DNS server writes and sends data to clients. This option logs how many full packets are sent and written by the DNS server.

- *Write Through*—As data is written through the DNS server service and back to the zone, these events can be logged if you select this option.

Viewing the DNS Server Log File

After logging has been enabled and specific log entries have been chosen, you can view those entries by going to %systemroot%\Winnt\System32\Dns\Dns.log in Windows Explorer and opening the file using Notepad or WordPad. Listing 11.2 shows a sample log file with all parameters chosen.

Listing 11.2   Partial dns.log file.

```
Snd     127.0.0.1      011c  R Q [8085 A DR  NOERROR] (9)desktoppc(6)Ballew(3)com(0)
UDP response info at 00481A3C
Socket = 464
Remote addr 127.0.0.1, port 1103
Time Query=81328, Queued=0, Expire=0
Buf length = 0x0200 (512)
Msg length = 0x0036 (54)
Message:
*
*
Name       "(9)desktoppc(6)Ballew(3)com(0)"
QTYPE   A (1)
QCLASS  1
ANSWER SECTION:
Offset = 0x0026, RR count = 0
Name       "[C00C](9)desktoppc(6)Ballew(3)com(0)"
TYPE    A  (1)
CLASS   1
TTL     1200
DLEN    4
DATA    192.168.0.2
```

This listing has information on the type of requests (**snd**), who the request was for (**(9)desktoppc(6)Ballew(3)com(0)**), the message sent, the type and class of message, and the answer. This is not a complete log or even a complete listing, but it does give you an idea of the complexity of information received in these logs.

Note: The beginning of the log file itself contains more information concerning these numbers and the data that is logged here.

Using Event Viewer

Another option for monitoring the DNS server, Event Viewer offers an ideal way to quickly determine if there are problems with the DNS server and, if so, what specific problems are occurring. Before going any further, view the current DNS server log on your DNS server by performing the following steps:

1. Log on as an administrator.

2. Choose Start|Programs|Administrative Tools|Event Viewer.

3. Right-click on Event Viewer in the left pane, and choose Connect To Another Computer.

4. In the Select Computer dialog box, browse to the DNS server, or choose Local Computer if the computer you are working with is the DNS server.

5. Highlight DNS Server in the left pane.

The right pane provides plenty of information about what's been happening with the DNS server. Hopefully, the majority of those entries are information balloons or warnings. Errors indicate a server problem, which is generally an event that has failed to occur properly. Each event is listed with the event type (such as information, error, or warning), the date, the time, and the source of the event, along with the event ID. Event IDs indicate what type of event it was. Many event IDs can be shown, and the most common codes are listed next:

- *2*—The DNS service has started successfully.

- *3*—The DNS server has shut down.

- *414*—The DNS server does not have a primary DNS suffix configured. DNS suffixes can be configured from the Network Identification tab of the System Properties dialog box, accessed through the System icon in Control Panel.

- *708*—The DNS server does not have any zones configured and will act as a caching-only DNS server.

- *3150*—The DNS server has written another version of the zone file.

- *4000*—The DNS server could not open Active Directory. The zone will not be loaded.

- *6527*—A DNS zone has been shut down because it could not obtain a successful zone transfer in its allotted time. The zone expired.

- *9999*—The DNS server has encountered runtime events, usually caused by the reception of bad packets or by excessive replication traffic.

Command-Line Tools

Command-line tools are available for monitoring and optimizing the DNS server, and they can also be used for troubleshooting when problems arise. There are several that may prove useful, and I've included my favorites in this section.

ipconfig /displaydns

The **ipconfig** command is not new, but the **/display** switch is, and it works only with computers running the DNS Client service on Windows 2000 computers. This command is used to view the contents of the DNS client resolver cache, which includes information about recently obtained resource records from previous queries to the DNS server. It is this information that the client accesses when first trying to resolve a DNS query. If you think this cache is corrupt, you can view it with this command and then flush and reset it to obtain a valid cache of information. Listing 11.3 shows the contents of a DNS client cache. Notice that the record information includes the record name, record type, and the IP addresses of the servers being accessed. Having the information about the servers on the network can be quite useful when you're troubleshooting DNS problems.

Listing 11.3 Partial DNS client cache.

```
C:\>ipconfig /displaydns |more
Windows 2000 IP Configuration


ns.waymark.net.
--------------------------------------------------------
Record Name . . . . . : NS.waymark.net
Record Type . . . . . : 1
Time To Live  . . . . : 4179
Data Length . . . . . : 4
Section . . . . . . . : Answer
A (Host) Record . . . :
207.18.144.2


localhost.
--------------------------------------------------------
Record Name . . . . . : localhost
Record Type . . . . . : 1
Time To Live  . . . . : 31044003
Data Length . . . . . : 4
Section . . . . . . . : Answer
A (Host) Record . . . :
127.0.0.1


dns3.jp.msft.net.
--------------------------------------------------------
Record Name . . . . . : DNS3.JP.MSFT.NET
Record Type . . . . . : 1
Time To Live  . . . . : 79705
Data Length . . . . . : 4
Section . . . . . . . : Answer
A (Host) Record . . . :
207.46.72.123


services.msn.com.
--------------------------------------------------------
Record Name . . . . . : services.msn.com
Record Type . . . . . : 5
Time To Live  . . . . : 2245
```

```
Data Length . . . . . : 4
Section . . . . . . . : Answer
CNAME Record  . . . . :
go.msn.com
Record Name . . . . . : go.msn.com
Record Type . . . . . : 1
Time To Live  . . . . : 2245
Data Length . . . . . : 4
Section . . . . . . . : Answer
A (Host) Record . . . :
207.68.183.61

-- More   --
```

ipconfig /flushdns

If, after viewing the DNS resolver cache for the computer in question, you find problems with the cache, you can empty and reset the cache to correct the problems in it. The command for flushing the DNS client resolver cache is **ipconfig /flushdns**. As with the **/displaydns** switch, this utility is available only on computers running Windows 2000 DNS Client services.

Note: *If the computer is accessing information from a local Hosts file, then problems with this cache could be caused by incorrect entries in this file. If this is the case, the Hosts file will need to be repaired.*

ipconfig /registerdns

The **/registerdns** switch is used when there are problems with failed DNS dynamic registration for a client. If dynamic update has been enabled, and there are no problems with the server or zone—such as a network failure or lack of support for dynamic updates—the solution might be to manually update the DNS name and IP address of the computer with the servers on the network. The **ipconfig /registerdns** command allows this information to be manually initiated without rebooting the client computer.

To reregister a client's DNS name and IP address with the DNS server, perform the following steps:

Note: *Remember, this switch works only with clients running Windows 2000 and DNS Client services.*

1. As an administrator, log on to the computer that needs its records automatically updated with the server.

2. Open a command prompt.

3. Enter "ipconfig /registerdns". If there are multiple adapters, specify the name of the specific network adapter that you want to reregister. The syntax is

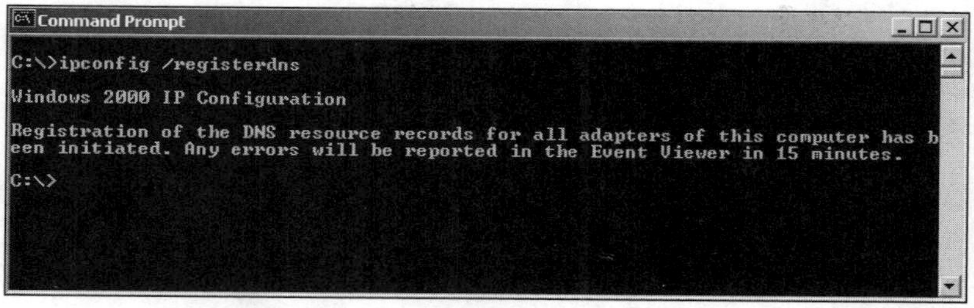

Figure 11.12
The ipconfig /registerdns command.

> **ipconfig /registerdns [*adapter*]**. The adapter name is the name the machine uses for the NIC and not an arbitrary name.

Figure 11.12 shows this command and the resulting dialog. Notice that information will be detailed in the Event Viewer regarding this change in 15 minutes.

NSLookup

The NSLookup utility was mentioned briefly earlier. NSLookup can be used for troubleshooting problems with DNS queries and related DNS servers. There are 26 **nslookup** subcommands available, and information on these commands can be found from the Microsoft Help files by searching for NSLookup.

The main reason NSLookup is used is to enable a user to interact with the DNS server. NSLookup can be used to display resource record information from the server and to troubleshoot name resolution problems. NSLookup has two modes: interactive and non-interactive. When only one piece of information is needed, non-interactive or command-line mode is used, but when more information is needed, interactive mode is best. To obtain information about the DNS server and its availability, simply type "nslookup" at a command prompt, as described later.

The syntax for the **nslookup** command is as follows:

```
nslookup [-option] [computer to find | - [server]]
```

The **–option** parameter is one of the 26 subcommands, and the **computer** and **server** parameters name particular machines to use. If the server name isn't specified, the default server will be used.

The first step in troubleshooting DNS problems with the default server is simply to type **nslookup** at a command prompt. If connectivity to the default server is working, then the server's name and IP address will be returned. Another common method is to type **nslookup** followed by the default server's IP address, followed by the loopback address, as shown in Figure 11.13.

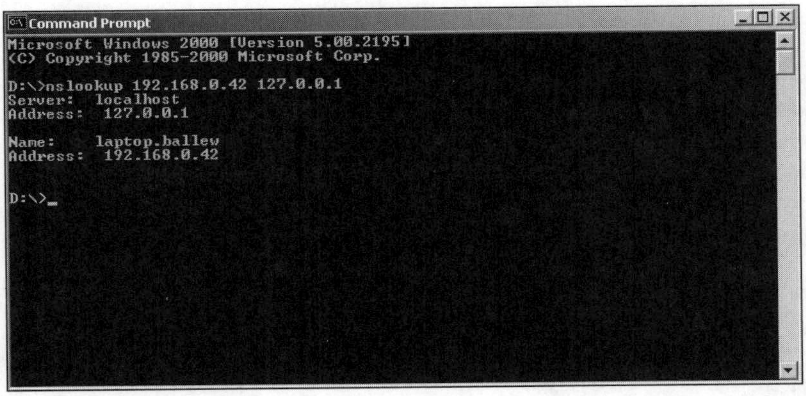

Figure 11.13
The **nslookup** command.

If the request fails, error messages will be shown. The request might time out, might get no response, or might not find any records, or the network might be unreachable. No matter; whatever error message is received is a clue to the problems on the network, and with that information, you can use **nslookup** subcommands to further define the problem and find the solution.

Dnscmd

To manage DNS servers by using batch files and scripts, to automate administration, to configure existing DNS servers, and to configure new DNS servers on the network, Windows 2000 offers the Dnscmd command-line utility. This utility is installed from the \support\enterprise\reskit folder on the Windows 2000 Server CD-ROM. After it's installed, you can get information about the utility and its switches by typing **dnscmd /?** at a command prompt.

All of the command switches available with this utility are shown in Figure 11.14, and Listing 11.4 shows information received by entering the **dns /info** command. As you can see from the figure, there are many commands that can assist in administering the DNS server from a command line, including switches such as **/ClearCache**, **/ZoneInfo**, **/StartScavenging**, and **/Statistics**.

Listing 11.4   The dnscmd /info command.

```
D:\>dnscmd /info
Query result:
Server info:
ptr = 00075960
server name = Laptop.Ballew.com
version = C2000005
DS container= c
Configuration:
DwLogLevel = 00000000
```

```
DwDebugLevel = 00000000
dwRpcProtocol = FFFFFFFF
dwNameCheckFlag = 00000002
cAddressAnswerLimit = 0
dwRecursionRetry = 3
dwRecursionTimeout = 15
dwDsPollingInterval = 300
Configuration Flags:
FBootMethod = 3
fAdminConfigured = 1
fAllowUpdate = 1
fDsAvailable = 1
fAutoReverseZones = 1
fAutoCacheUpdate = 0
fSlave = 0
fNoRecursion = 0
fRoundRobin = 1
fLocalNetPriority = 1
fStrictFileParsing = 0
fLooseWildcarding = 0
fBindSecondaries = 1
fWriteAuthorityNs = 0
Aging Configuration:
ScavengingInterval = 168
DefaultAgingState = 1
DefaultRefreshInterval = 168
DefaultNoRefreshInterval = 168
ServerAddresses:
Addr Count = 1
Addr[0] => 192.168.0.42
ListenAddresses:
NULL IP Array.
Forwarders:
NULL IP Array.
forward timeout  = 5
slave = 0
Command completed successfully.
```

In Listing 11.4, the highlighted information should look familiar. There is information on the server name and its PTR record, reverse zones, cache, aging and scavenging, listening addresses, and more. The information looks similar to the way it is shown in the Registry. In addition, there are a few items not yet covered—in particular, forwarders, round robin, and local subnet priority. These items are advanced configurations and are discussed in the next section.

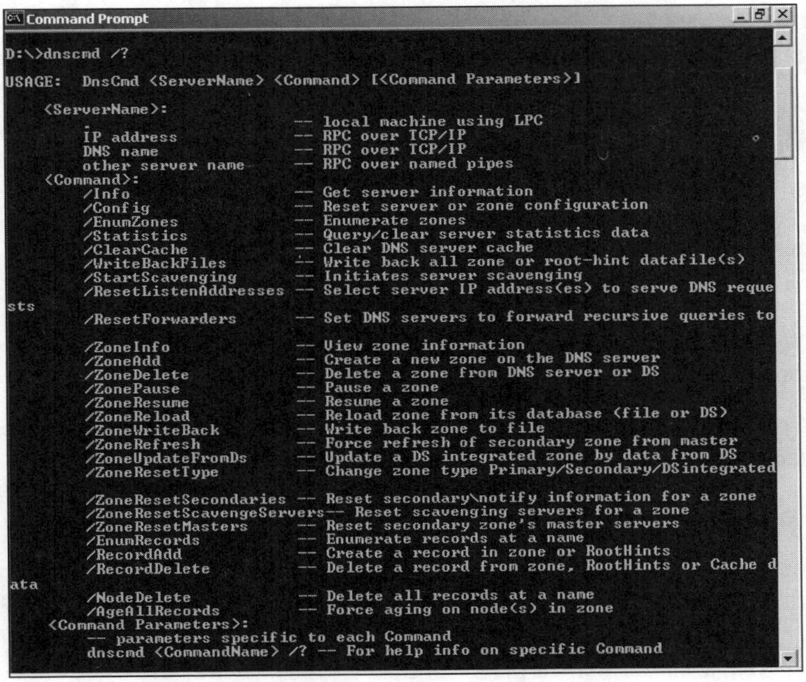

Figure 11.14
Switches for the **dnscmd** command.

Advanced DNS Server Configuration

The DNS server can be configured with even more options than those already discussed. For instance, *forwarders*, a kind of DNS server, can be configured to improve DNS query performance on the network. In addition, the DNS server can be configured to use *round-robin* to share and distribute the DNS load on the network; *local subnet priorities* can be set so that certain subnets get priority over others; and zones can be configured to perform *fast zone transfers*. All of these advanced server configurations can be set on the DNS servers to allow for maximum performance on the network. In this section, these items will be discussed, along with how to configure the DNS servers to take advantage of these features.

Why Use Forwarders?

Forwarders can be used so that DNS servers will send all of their recursive queries to a forwarder instead of trying to resolve the queries themselves. Forwarders provide a way for the DNS server to become a kind of DNS client to another server. This configuration allows a DNS forwarder to be placed on the other side of a firewall to enhance security, to provide a buffer between a fast intranet and a slower Internet, and to provide a better cache of information for the clients on the network, all in a single location.

Configuring a Forwarder

To configure a server that is not a root DNS server to use forwarders, perform the following steps:

1. Log on to the DNS server as an administrator.

2. Choose Start|Programs|Administrative Tools|DNS to open the DNS console.

3. Right-click on the DNS server in the left pane, and choose Properties.

4. On the Forwarders tab, select Enable Forwarders.

5. Type in the name of the IP address of the server that will act as the forwarding server, and choose Add.

Note: The Enable Forwarders option will be grayed out if the DNS server is a root server for your network.

What Is Round-Robin?

Round-robin, in general terms, is the process of taking turns. In a round-robin game, all teams play each other by taking turns until all teams have played. In this instance, it is the NICs that take turns servicing client requests. Round-robin is used to balance the load on computers that are multihomed (have multiple NICs configured). Round-robin works when multiple host (A) resource records exist for a queried name in a zone. When a forward lookup query is sent to the multihomed device, and that device has been configured with two or more IP addresses, each IP address has its own A record. When a client queries the DNS server for the record, the first record is accessed. The next time the same record is accessed, the records are rotated and the second client gets the second instance of the record. If there are more A records for the resource, they continue to be rotated to share the load of accessing the A resource records for this device. This rotation of resource record data returned in a query answer is called *round-robin*.

Configuring Round-Robin

To enable or disable round-robin at the DNS server, perform the following steps:

1. Log on to the DNS server as an administrator.

2. Choose Start|Programs|Administrative Tools|DNS to open the DNS console.

3. Right-click on the DNS server in the left pane, and choose Properties.

4. On the Advanced tab, either add or remove a checkmark in the appropriate checkbox to enable or disable round-robin for this server.

Local Subnet Prioritization

As a default procedure, the DNS server responds to DNS client queries by using local subnet prioritization. This is used only if a client requests (or resolves to) a resource for which more than one Host (A) record exists, as in the case of a multihomed computer. The client will try to connect to the host by using its closest and fastest connection.

Local subnet prioritization works like this: If a client's IP address is 192.168.0.5, and the query results for the resolved resource have more than one IP address, then those addresses are sorted by proximity to the client. For instance, if the multihomed computer is the query result and the computer has three IP addresses configured (192.168.5.10, 120.0.5.2, and 15.0.0.8), then the DNS server will pass those results on to the client with its closest connection at the top of the priority list. In this case, that would be 192.168.5.10 because it is a Class C address and so is the client.

Configuring Local Subnet Priorities

To disable local subnet priorities, perform the following steps:

1. As an administrator, log on to the DNS server to be configured.

2. Choose Start|Programs|Administrative Tools|DNS to open the DNS console.

3. Right-click on the DNS server in the left pane, and choose Properties.

4. On the Advanced tab, uncheck Enable Netmask Ordering.

Note: *If local subnet prioritization and round-robin are both enabled, local subnet prioritization will prevail. However, records will continue to be rotated as a secondary technique of arranging the query answer list.*

Fast Zone Transfers

By default, all DNS servers use fast zone transfers when sending zone information. This format allows the records to be compressed and allows TCP messages to contain multiple records during a transfer. If the network has some servers that do not support this faster zone transfer format, such as BIND servers prior to version 4.9.4, then this feature should be disabled.

To enable or disable fast zone transfers, perform the following steps:

1. As an administrator, log on to the DNS server to be configured.

2. Choose Start|Programs|Administrative Tools|DNS to open the DNS console.

3. Right-click on the DNS server in the left pane, and choose Properties.

4. On the Advanced tab, add or remove the checkmark in the BIND Secondaries checkbox.

Recursion

When using forwarders to complete DNS queries, a DNS server will attempt to resolve the query by requesting the information from its configured forwarder. However, if the forwarder fails to obtain the required answer, the DNS server will try to resolve the query itself by using iterative queries and standard recursion. If forwarders are to be used exclusively, and those DNS servers should not try to resolve the queries if the forwarders fail, then the Do Not Use Recursion option needs to be set for the server. This means that if the query information isn't found in the server's zone or by the forwarder, the query will fail.

Note: The Do Not Use Recursion option will be grayed out if this is a root server or if no forwarders are enabled for this DNS server.

To configure a DNS server to use forwarders exclusively, perform the following steps:

1. Log on to the DNS server as an administrator.

2. Choose Start|Programs|Administrative Tools|DNS to open the DNS console.

3. Right-click on the DNS server in the left pane, and choose Properties.

4. On the Forwarders tab, place a checkmark in the Do Not Use Recursion checkbox.

Note: Recursion can be disabled on the Advanced tab as well.

Fail On Load If Bad Zone Data

When the DNS server loads a zone, the server records any errors it finds with the data and continues to load the zone. The bad data is ignored, but the zone is still loaded. To configure the zone to fail if bad zone data is found, perform the following steps:

1. Log on to the DNS server as an administrator.

2. Choose Start|Programs|Administrative Tools|DNS to open the DNS console.

3. Right-click on the DNS server in the left pane, and choose Properties.

4. On the Advanced tab, place a checkmark in the Fail On Load If Bad Zone Data checkbox.

Summary

In this chapter, you learned about DNS, Dynamic DNS, how DNS works with WINS, and how DNS servers are installed and configured to work efficiently on the network. An overview of DNS explained why DNS is needed and what role hostnames and IP addresses play in the name resolution game.

You learned the terms associated with DNS, including domain types, zone types, and record types. You also learned how DNS and Active Directory can work together to secure the DNS records and resources. You learned that when you install Active Directory on a Windows 2000 computer, you are asked to specify a DNS name if one exists; if no DNS server exists on the network, then the DNS service is installed on the computer as Active Directory is installed. The integration, then, between DNS and Active Directory makes each feature a requirement of the other.

Dynamic DNS was introduced as a way to keep track of ever-changing hostname-to-IP-address mappings created by the addition of mobile computers and DHCP on the network. You learned that DNS and DHCP can be configured to work together to update these records automatically, reducing manual administration of these records.

The processes involved in name resolution were introduced next, and a detailed look at the DNS query process was included. In order to troubleshoot DNS query problems, you need a thorough understanding of both forward and reverse lookups.

After DNS is installed, it has to be configured. The rest of the chapter dealt with how the DNS servers and clients could be best configured to run optimally. This includes creating different types of zones, configuring their properties, and managing their records.

11

Following that, WINS was discussed, and you learned why WINS is used and how to configure a WINS server and clients. And finally, I discussed managing and optimizing the DNS servers. These tasks include managing zones, aging and scavenging records, using the Performance console, logging, and using the Event Viewer. I also discussed command-line tools and advanced server configurations, such as using round-robin and subnet prioritization.

Moving Forward

The next chapter (the last one) will introduce routing and remote access. You'll learn how to set up a remote access server and use the routing services available in Windows 2000 Server to set up your own virtual private network, allowing users to connect from home or while away on business, and you'll learn how to manage both the servers and the clients. Routing and Remote Access is no longer just for large organizations or enterprise networks. In the next chapter, you'll learn how to configure it for your network and clients, and what advantages it will bring to your organization.

Chapter 12

Routing and Remote Access

In this final chapter, I'll introduce the Routing and Remote Access Service available with Windows 2000 Server. The Routing and Remote Access Service (RRAS) provides two configurable components: a multiprotocol router and a remote access server. These components can be used to enable network users to telecommute, to access their files and folders while on the road, and to retrieve email from the network server when away from the office, to name a few of the applications. RRAS can also be used in small home offices to allow the owner or proprietor to easily configure a computer as a dial-up server for only a few people or to allow server-to-server communications using dial-on-demand configurations in larger organizations. Because these types of business solutions are being used more and more often, the role that RRAS will play in networks will increase quickly.

In this chapter, all aspects of RRAS will be discussed, including the components of a remote access server and router, the protocols used with both, and installation and configuration of the remote access server and clients. There are many ways to set up the server and clients, including using the server as a dial-up server, using a virtual private network (VPN), using the server for Internet Connection Sharing, and using the server with Network Address Translation. Each of these installations and configurations will be addressed in this chapter.

After the remote access server is set up, configured, and in use, monitoring and optimizing the remote access server become important. Toward the end of the chapter, the Performance console, Network Monitor, logging, auditing, and routing tools will be discussed in depth. Additionally, creating and managing the user accounts and their policies will be introduced.

Overview

The Routing and Remote Access Services are combined as a single service in Windows 2000 Server because together they provide point-to-point connections for clients and servers using dial-up, demand-dial, VPNs, and more. RRAS provides an administrator with a single console and utility for managing the Remote Access Service (RAS) and its clients. Using RRAS, a remote access network and/or a router can be configured for any type of network, from a small, two-computer home office to a large network containing thousands of clients and servers. RRAS is easy to install and configure, and it serves multiple purposes for networks.

This section introduces the features and components of both the remote access server and the router, as well as some of the different types of physical connections that can be used with them.

Remote Access Server

A computer can be installed as a remote access server so it can provide remote access connectivity for clients not physically sitting at the network. Remote access clients can use IP, IPX, AppleTalk, or NetBEUI, and those clients can connect to the remote access server over any of the LAN and WAN configurations and NICs that are supported in Windows 2000. Additionally, these connections can be configured on a variety of physical connections, including Frame Relay, ISDN, digital cable, and standard dial-up lines.

Components and Features

The RAS part of RRAS has many components. One of these components is demand-dial routing. Demand-dial routing can reduce the cost of WAN communications because you can configure the server and the client to connect with each other only when communication needs to take place or data needs to be sent. This way, the WAN link is used on an as-needed basis and costs are kept to a minimum. Additionally, the configuration can be further defined to disconnect when the connection has been idle for a certain period of time.

Another feature of RAS is the ability to encrypt data during transmission and *tunnel* the data when it is sent on the Internet. There are two tunneling protocols: Point-to-Point Tunneling Protocol (PPTP) and Layer 2 Tunneling Protocol (L2TP). Tunneling allows data to be encapsulated, encrypted, and authenticated. These security measures are added benefits of using RRAS and are more secure than many other VPN solutions.

RAS can also be configured to use bandwidth efficiently. The Multilink feature is a way to combine the bandwidth of multiple WAN links to create a larger channel that contains the combined bandwidth of the available links. Multilink with Bandwidth Allocation Protocol (BAP) enhances this bundling of links by adding and dropping lines based on the amount of traffic that is using the link. RAS also supports the following authentication protocols:

- Password Authentication Protocol (PAP)

- Shiva-PAP (SPAP)

- Challenge Handshake Authentication Protocol (CHAP)

- Microsoft Challenge Handshake Authentication Protocol (MS-CHAP)

- Extensible Authentication Protocol (EAP), including EAP-TLS and EAP-MD5

- Remote Authentication Dial-In User Service (RADIUS)

These authentication protocols, the routing protocols mentioned later in this section, the tunneling protocols PPTP and L2TP, and other protocols will be discussed in depth in the section "Protocols for Routing and Remote Access."

RRAS also comes with multiple wizards for configuring the components of the remote access server and for simplifying tasks for the administrator. Wizards make the configuration of components straightforward and less prone to errors during setup.

Other security features available with RRAS include the capability to use smart cards for remote access clients and the ability to set policies for these clients from the RRAS console and through remote access policies. With these policies, you can define how access is allowed, whether callback numbers are configured, how long a session can be, and more.

Finally, Internet Connection Sharing (ICS) is available for users in a small office so that one Internet connection can be shared among multiple clients or computers. This is a great way to give users occasional access to the Internet when they do not need a dedicated line or continuous access.

Multiprotocol Router

The second half of RRAS is the routing part. Windows 2000 Server can be configured to act as a fully functional multiprotocol router. The routing protocols supported by this router include the following:

- Routing Information Protocol (RIP) for IP
- Open Shortest Path First (OSPF)
- DHCP Relay Agent
- IP multicast routing
- RIP for Service Advertisement Protocol (SAP) for IPX
- AppleTalk routing
- Network Address Translation

These protocols allow the router to communicate with many types of networks and operating systems and can be used effectively with networks of all sizes. These protocols and others will be described in detail later.

Other RRAS Features

A few other features are worth mentioning at this time. Each will be described in more depth later, and each plays an important role in the configuration and effectiveness of the remote access server.

Virtual Private Networking

More and more often, users are connecting to their network's intranet via the Internet. This access is the result of more mobile computing and the creation of larger networks that span multiple physical locations. Connecting these users and offices with a dedicated physical line is too expensive for most organizations to afford. Access through the Internet is inherently not as secure as LAN communications within an intranet, however. Therefore, to allow users access to the corporate intranet through the Internet, communications must be made secure. Virtual private networks (VPNs) can be configured using the Windows 2000 tools to secure such communications.

VPNs are used to keep information private, ensure that data was received, prevent eavesdropping, and authenticate users. When Windows 2000 VPNs are configured, the data that is sent over the Internet is encapsulated and encrypted. Encrypted data is useless to hackers who capture it, and encapsulated data is placed inside another type of data frame so that it is hidden as well.

There are several types of VPNs, all having to do with some form of Internet-to-intranet communications. VPNs include dial-up clients, intranet servers, firewalls, and tunneling protocols. VPNs will be discussed in more depth later in the chapter.

Connection Manager and Connection Point Services

Connection Manager is a preconfigured dialing tool for users who access the remote access server on the corporate intranet, on a VPN, or via a commercial ISP. Connection Manager contains the settings that a user needs to connect to the required server; these settings include dial-up networking entries, VPN support, a phone book, help files, and connection actions. An administrator using the Connection Manager Administration Kit that ships with Windows 2000 Server configures these settings.

Administrators use Connection Point Services to automatically update phone-book entries for clients. These entries contain phone numbers and other information for calling into the remote access server. The clients can be configured to download files automatically when they (clients) dial into the server.

Internet Authentication Service

Internet Authentication Service (IAS) is a Windows 2000 add-on component for authenticating and authorizing dial-in and VPN clients. You don't have to use IAS to make remote access work, but it does have its benefits.

IAS offers authentication protocols for most types of clients, be they AppleTalk, Windows NT, Windows 2000, or a variety of others. These authentication protocols add an extra measure of security to the network. IAS can also be used with remote access policies for the management of remote access client permissions. The RADIUS protocol, used with IAS, can be used for logging communications between all of the network access servers and the IAS server. This log includes entries for successes, account lockouts, failures, and more.

Physical Connection Options

There are many ways to connect a remote access client and a remote access server. When you're setting up the remote access server and clients, it is important to start with a reliable and affordable telecommunications option that will work for your organization. If the network is large and in physically different areas, the options listed here can vary in availability.

Plain Old Telephone Service

Plain Old Telephone Service (POTS), also known as Public Switched Telephone Network (PSTN), is widely used in remote access configurations. Telephone lines are available from just about any hotel room or home office, and they are inexpensive. Although this type of communication has limited bandwidth potential, it is a great way to enable communication between clients and remote access servers.

12

If multiple PSTN lines are available, those lines can be configured with Multilink to provide an alternative to higher-bandwidth lines that are leased and more expensive. In larger organizations, modem banks containing hundreds of modems can be configured to use these types of lines as well.

To use POTS for remote access, the only hardware needed is a modem on each end of the connection. This simplicity makes telephone service lines a great option for small home offices and little-used remote access servers. Telephone lines transfer analog signals from a user's computer to the local telephone switching office, where the signals are then changed to digital signals and transmitted further. Converting the digital signals of the computer to the analog lines for the initial transfer to this switching station requires a modem (modulator/demodulator). The transfer of the analog signals back to digital signals at the station causes the transmission to be "noisy." When digital switches and V.90 modems are used, this noise is not created.

Digital Links and V.90

Digital links and V.90 modems can be used with PSTN to make the telephone lines send data faster than they would normally. The data can be sent faster because of the lack of signal noise. For PSTN to be used in this manner, several things must happen: the client must be using a V.90 modem; the RAS server must be using an appropriate V.90 digital switch; the connection between the two must be a digital link to the PSTN; and there cannot be any analog-to-digital conversions in the path from the client computer to the RAS server. Some digital links include ISDN and T carriers.

ISDN

Integrated Services Digital Network (ISDN) is a high-speed digital dial-up service that can be used as an alternative to PSTN. ISDN offers speeds up to 128Kbps and can send data, voice, and video over existing telephone wiring configurations. For a client to use an ISDN connection, the client and server must be configured with a special ISDN card, and the transmission link must not have any analog-to-digital conversions. The ISDN card is not the same as a modem.

There are two types of ISDN channels: B-channels and D-channels. B-channels are used to send voice, video, or data, and these channels offer bandwidth at a rate of 64Kbps. D-channels are used for call management, and they include information about how the call is set up and how it is ended. The size of the D-channel varies depending on how many B-channels are used.

Smaller organizations usually obtain Basic Rate Interface (BRI) ISDN lines, and larger organizations tend to use Primary Rate Interface (PRI) ISDN lines. BRI uses two B-channels and a 16Kbps D-channel and has a total bandwidth of 144Kbps. PRI uses 23 B-channels and one 64Kbps D-channel and has a total bandwidth of 1.536Mbps. Of course, total bandwidth and actual data transmission rates are not this high because the D-channel transmits only call data.

X.25

X.25 is a protocol used on packet-switched networks (PSNs). These networks are accessed through a Packet Assembler Disassembler (PAD) device. In order to use the X.25 protocol on a PSN, the client must be configured with one of these devices or must be able to dial into a PAD at an X.25 network. Windows 2000 supports the X.25 protocol by allowing the client computer to use an X.25 card or dial into a PAD from an analog modem via an X.25 carrier. The RAS supports direct connections to X.25 networks via an X.25 smart card.

ATM

Asynchronous Transfer Mode (ATM) and ATM adapters are used to connect to Asymmetric Digital Subscriber Lines (ADSL) or other public and private networks. ATM and ADSL are becoming more and more popular as both a home-office and company alternative to more expensive T-lines and slower and less efficient ISDN lines. ADSL equipment can be in the form of either an Ethernet cable or a dial-up interface. When an Ethernet cable is used, the ADSL connection works like a regular Ethernet connection, but when a dial-up connection is configured, the connection sends data by using ATM and the ATM adapter.

Depending on the type of cable it is running over, ATM can run at different speeds, from 1.544Mbps all the way to 2.488Gbps. ATM can also travel over a kilometer without any problem. Because of this flexibility, ATM is well suited for larger organizations and networks as well as for single connections.

ATM providers offer many choices for service, including the following:

- *Available Bit Rate (ABR)*—The ATM provider guarantees a minimum throughput, but data is sent at higher throughput levels when additional bandwidth is available.

- *Unspecified Bit Rate (UBR)*—The ATM provider does not guarantee any minimum throughput of data.

- *Variable Bit Rate (VBR)*—The ATM provider guarantees an average throughput over a specified period of time, but data isn't guaranteed always to be sent at that speed.

- *Constant Bit Rate (CBR)*—The ATM provider guarantees a constant rate for data throughput.

T Carriers

T carriers include T1 and T3 lines and fractional T1 lines. T carriers lease these digital lines in 64Kbps channels to clients for transmitting data, voice, and video. T lines often join two sites and are expensive. They offer the bandwidth needed for companies requiring more than ISDN or other choices can offer. T1 and T3 lines do transmit data at a high rate, though, and are well worth the expense if that is what the organization needs to function properly.

Here's what you need to know about the three types of T lines:

- *Fractional T1*—Sometimes called DS-0. The customer has the option of ordering only the number of 64Kbps channels needed.

- *T1*—A more expensive alternative, also referred to as DS-1, offers 1.544Mbps.

- *T3*—The most expensive T-carrier choice, also referred to as DS-3, offers bandwidth at a rate of 44.763Mbps.

Frame Relay

Frame Relay can be used in LANs as a cost-effective way to transmit data intermittently. Frame Relay is not a continuously leased line, although to users, it looks like one. With Frame Relay, data is transmitted at high speeds (56Kbps, 1.544Kbps, or 45Mbps), and cost is calculated based on usage. Frame Relay does not include error-checking, though, and any errors that occur are the responsibility of the Frame Relay endpoints. The data that contains errors is re-sent as needed; however, the number of errors on digital networks is quite small compared to the number of errors on analog networks.

Protocols for Routing and Remote Access

RRAS involves a router, a remote access server, encapsulation and encryption of data, and the incorporation of LANs, VPNs, and the Internet. Every item in this list has its own associated protocols. To configure the remote access server correctly, and to make it work efficiently for your network, you need a thorough understanding of all of these protocols. This section introduces authentication protocols, routing protocols, tunneling protocols, LAN protocols, and VPN protocols. The TCP/IP protocol suite doesn't really need to be covered here because it has already been discussed at length, but a short mention will be included for continuity.

Routing Protocols

The routing protocols include Routing Information Protocol (RIP) for IP, Open Shortest Path First (OSPF), DHCP Relay Agent, IP multicast routing, RIP for Service Advertisement Protocol (SAP) for IPX, AppleTalk routing, and Network Address Translation.

Routing Information Protocol for IP

RIP for IP is a distance-vector protocol that is widely used in small to medium-sized organizations or in organizations that are contained in a single physical entity or under one administrative body. RIP for IP is generally chosen as the protocol of choice for small intranets configured for corporations or home offices. This protocol routes data within the network.

Every 30 seconds, a RIP router sends messages (called *advertisements*) to all of the other routers it knows. When something changes in a RIP routing table, the router also advertises that change to other routers. The RIP router then uses the information in these tables to determine the distance from itself to other routers and networks. The router calculates this distance by looking at the number of hops between each router. This calculation allows the RIP routers to choose the best route based on the lowest number of hops; this route becomes the least expensive route in terms of cost and time.

Open Shortest Path First

Because RIP for IP won't work for large networks (due in large part to the fact that it sends out advertisements every 30 seconds), other options have to be available. OSPF is one of those options. OSPF is a routing protocol that uses link state advertisements (LSAs) to inform other routers in the local area of changes in its routing table. These link state updates are stored in a router's link state database (LSDB). These databases are then synchronized with routers that neighbor each other. An algorithm is then used to figure out the shortest path to a destination, based on the information in the LSDB.

DHCP Relay Agent

One of the problems with using DHCP on networks that use routers is that routers don't generally forward broadcasts. As you know, DHCP uses broadcasts to request, lease, assign, and release DHCP TCP/IP addresses. For these broadcasts to be forwarded across network segments, a DHCP relay agent must be installed.

RRAS includes such a utility. A Windows 2000 server can be turned into a router that can act as a DHCP relay agent for the network. This relay agent will listen for DHCP broadcasts and will forward those to specific DHCP servers on the network. The relay agent will also send the DHCP server's broadcasts to clients on the other side of the router. This configuration allows a DHCP server to service clients that are not on the same network as the DHCP server.

IP Multicast Routing

Multicasting is the transmission of data to multiple hosts at the same time. These hosts are members of a multicast group, and they use the Internet Group Management Protocol (IGMP) to listen for multicast broadcasts. Multicasting is like a radio broadcast; clients who want to listen can, and those who don't want to listen, don't.

Windows 2000 routing supports multicast forwarding and limited multicast routing. Multicast forwarding is used when a router sends multicast data to the network where the hosts (who are members of a multicast group) are located and listening. Multicast forwarding keeps unnecessary traffic from being sent to networks that don't have anyone listening for these broadcasts. For multicast forwarding to work, both the clients and the server must be capable of dealing with multicasts.

Multicast routing is used when one multicast router informs another multicast router of its routing table and multicast group information. Windows 2000 systems can send and receive IP multicast traffic, but they do not contain any multicast routing protocols.

RIP for Service Advertisement Protocol for IPX

Because not all networks are Windows-based or Windows-only networks, support for other network types, operating systems, and protocols is necessary. Novell NetWare networks use IPX, and the Windows 2000 router can be used when Novell NetWare is involved in a Windows-based network. The router can be configured to broadcast IPX network routes to other routers on the network; SAP enables file and print servers to advertise their addresses and services as well. Other components of IPX support include:

- *NetBIOS over IPX*—Used to support file and printer sharing on IPX internetworks.

- *RIP for IPX*—Used to configure static routes and RIP route filters on IPX internetworks.

- *IPX packet filtering*—Used to filter packets coming into and going through the router; packets can be filtered by destination IPX network, socket numbers, packet types, and nodes.

AppleTalk Routing

Windows 2000 Server can act as a router for AppleTalk Macintosh networks and can connect to them and perform routing for them. No other software is needed by the clients or the server for this router to function. Although newer Macintosh networks use TCP/IP, some older networks still use AppleTalk.

Network Address Translation

Network Address Translation (NAT) allows a home-office user, a small ISP, or other similar network user to connect his or her network to the Internet without having a public IP addressing scheme for the internal network. NAT allows these networks to use private IP addresses for the intranet and use one public IP address for the Internet. The network address translator component acts as a proxy between the intranet and the Internet, thus allowing the smaller intranet to use any internal addressing scheme while still accessing the Internet with the network.

Authentication Protocols

The authentication protocols include Bandwidth Allocation Protocol (BAP), Password Authentication Protocol (PAP), Shiva-PAP (SPAP), Challenge Handshake Authentication Protocol (CHAP), Microsoft Challenge Handshake Authentication Protocol (MS-CHAP), Extensible Authentication Protocol (EAP), including EAP-TLS and EAP-MD5, and Remote Authentication Dial-In User Service (RADIUS).

Bandwidth Allocation Protocol

BAP is used with Multilink connections to introduce another way to efficiently use the extra lines in an ISDN link or multiple dial-up lines. BAP can be configured to add available links when extra bandwidth is required and to remove them when the bandwidth is no longer needed. BAP is a PPP Link Control Protocol; it can also be used to assist dial-up customers by offering those clients other phone numbers as they become available. BAP clients do not need to be told of the new connections because the RAS server can send these numbers to them. Because BAP dynamically adds and drops lines based on need, make sure that you are careful with pay-as-you-go connections and BAP; you can get a pretty hefty bill if you aren't fully aware of what BAP is doing.

Password Authentication Protocol

PAP authenticates clients using clear text passwords. PAP is not the most secure authentication method for this reason, and it is used only when the client and the server can't negotiate any other way to authenticate. The passwords are sent in clear text form, meaning that anyone with the right tools can obtain those passwords from the wire. There are other security concerns as well, such as leaving the server open to replay attacks and other similar security flaws. PAP should be used only when no other form of authentication can be negotiated between the two communicating machines.

Shiva-PAP

More secure than PAP, but less secure than any other authentication protocols mentioned in this section, is Shiva-PAP. Shiva clients can dial into Windows 2000 servers, and Windows 2000 clients can dial into Shiva servers by using encrypted password authentication. This encryption is two-way reversible and is used by both clients and servers. Although more secure than clear text passwords, encrypted password authentication is still not the ideal way to authenticate users; it should be used only when other protocols cannot be.

Challenge Handshake Authentication Protocol

There are three types of CHAP, and this one is the least secure of the three. Although CHAP is a better authentication scheme than PAP or Shiva-PAP and is well known and widely used, the CHAP algorithm for this protocol is familiar and can be hacked more easily than for other protocols.

CHAP uses a challenge-response authentication process between the client and the server; the password is hashed (encrypted) before it is sent on the wire, and each entity must know the password. These passwords are stored on the machines in reversible-encrypted format for further security.

Microsoft Challenge Handshake Authentication Protocol

Another form of CHAP, MS-CHAP is more secure than the CHAP mentioned in the previous section. In CHAP, the password originates as a clear text password during the initial hash used for identification, and even though the passwords are stored using encryption, clear passwords are still in use. MS-CHAP doesn't require clear text passwords on the server that performs the client authentication, and MS-CHAP stores a hashed version of the password that is used in the challenge-response process. The clear text passwords are never used. MS-CHAP uses 40-bit encryption and the same key for each connection that uses the same password. Although more secure than CHAP, it is less secure than MS-CHAP v2.

Microsoft Challenge Handshake Authentication Protocol V2

MS-CHAP v2 is the most secure CHAP version available at this time. For the first time, this version of CHAP allows mutual authentication of clients and servers, whereas the other two versions offered only one-way authentication of the client and not of the server. In addition, the same key is not used for each connection using the same password; instead, a new key is generated using the password and other information sent during authentication. MS-CHAP v2 also offers a higher level of security for legacy computers than do the other versions. Although MS-CHAP v2 is a fairly secure authentication protocol, it is not as secure as EAP.

Extensible Authentication Protocol

Using Extensible Authentication Protocol (EAP) is one of the most secure ways to negotiate a remote access connection. EAP supports multiple authentication techniques, including token cards, MD5-Challenge, Transport Level Security (TLS), and smart cards. EAP, when used with smart cards, offers one of the strongest levels of security possible and can be enabled domain-wide. EAP with TLS can be used with security certificates, another highly secure method of authenticating clients. TLS offers mutual authentication with symmetric and asymmetric encryption, encryption algorithms, and private keys for encryption. The TLS authentication technique works only with domain servers and will not work with standalone servers.

LAN Protocols

The LAN protocols supported by RRAS include TCP/IP, IPX, NetBEUI, and AppleTalk.

TCP/IP

As you know, TCP/IP is the most widely used LAN protocol in the world, and it's the protocol used to communicate over the Internet. Windows 2000 RRAS supports TCP/IP as a remote access protocol. The RAS must be informed of how its clients should receive IP addresses. IP addressing for clients is configured using static addresses, using APIPA (Automatic Private IP Addressing), from a pool of addresses on the RAS, or from a DHCP server pool.

When remote access clients do not obtain their IP addresses from a DHCP server, the RAS must be configured with a pool of addresses for leasing to these clients. This pool of addresses does not have to be part of the LAN's address pool. If it isn't from the LAN's pool of addresses, make sure that routing is enabled on the server, or configure the required static routes. If it is part of the LAN's pool of addresses, make sure that no IP addresses given to remote access clients are in use anywhere else on the network.

Remote access clients can also be configured with static IP addresses on their laptops or remote machines. This can be easily done from the TCP/IP Properties sheet of the client's computer.

When clients get their addresses from a DHCP server, the remote access server must be configured to use the DHCP Remote IP Addresses option. Then, when clients of the remote access server need a connection, the RAS server retrieves an address from the DHCP server and gives it to the client. Technically, the RAS obtains these addresses in groups of 10 from the DHCP server and manages the leases it owns. When a client disconnects, the RAS puts that address back in its pool of addresses. When the RAS runs out of addresses, it obtains 10 more.

If the DHCP server isn't available, RAS uses APIPA to lease addresses. Although limitations of APIPA include not being able to configure the client with a subnet mask or default gateway, it at least gets the client logged on to the server and working. When a DHCP server comes back online, the RAS server will begin obtaining its groups of addresses and leasing them to clients.

Tip: On a RAS server, the default DHCP setting of obtaining IP addresses in groups of 10 can be changed. This change can be made only in the Registry in HKEY_LOCAL_MACHINE\System\CurrentControlSet\ Services\RemoteAccess\Parameters\Ip\InitialAddressPoolSize.

Internetwork Packet Exchange

Remote access clients using Internetwork Packet Exchange (IPX)—such as Novell NetWare clients—can access a Windows 2000 remote access server that is running the NWLink IPX/SPX/NetBIOS Compatible Protocol. The server acts as an IPX router and transmits the data to the network. RAS can also assign TCP/IP addresses to these clients in a manner similar to the process mentioned in the previous section.

NetBEUI

NetBEUI clients can be remote access clients as well. Those clients will need a NetBIOS gateway configured. This gateway adds the client's NetBIOS name to the name table on the server and transfers the NetBIOS traffic to the required resource. The gateway is responsible for managing the data that is transferred between the two entities, and it handles any protocols and protocol translations necessary for communication.

AppleTalk

Macintosh clients can be remote access clients. The remote access server must be running the AppleTalk protocol, and the clients must be Macintosh clients.

Remote Access Protocols

The remote access protocols supported by RRAS include Point-to-Point Protocol (PPP), the Serial Line Internet Protocol (SLIP) client component, and the Microsoft RAS protocol, also known as Asynchronous NetBEUI (AsyNetBEUI).

Point-to-Point Protocol

PPP is responsible for creating, maintaining, and ending a logical link between the remote access client and the remote access server. PPP is the recommended protocol for remote access clients and servers because it can negotiate connections with clients using any of the supported LAN protocols: TCP/IP, IPX, NetBEUI, or AppleTalk. Any client capable of using PPP can use the remote access servers; this includes most Windows clients, Unix clients, Linux clients, and Macintosh clients.

Many networks, organizations, and ISPs use PPP for providing remote access connectivity. PPP is used for negotiating the size of the packets and how they are framed, how a client will log on, how a client will obtain an IP address, and other services between client and server. PPP supports dial-up remote access, VPN remote access, demand-dial routing, and more.

Serial Line Internet Protocol Client Component

SLIP is older than PPP and doesn't offer as much functionality. Clients who need to use SLIP for connecting to a SLIP remote access server can do so, but a Windows 2000 server cannot be configured as a SLIP server and does not accept dial-up connections from SLIP clients. SLIP clients do not have a choice of protocols and must use TCP/IP. SLIP doesn't support the authentication protocols mentioned earlier. SLIP passwords are not encrypted, which means that clear text passwords are on the wire. SLIP should be used only in rare circumstances; otherwise, PPP should be configured.

Microsoft RAS Protocol

Even in networks where the servers are running Windows 2000, the clients might not be quite so up-to-date. On networks with legacy remote access clients—such as Windows NT 3.1, Windows for Workgroups, MS-DOS, and LAN Manager—there has to be a protocol with which they can connect to the remote access server. PPP might not work with these older clients, and SLIP certainly won't, so Microsoft created its own Remote Access Service protocol for these clients. This protocol enables these older clients to act as remote access clients on Windows 2000 networks.

VPN Tunneling Protocols

Several VPN tunneling protocols are available, including Point-to-Point Tunneling Protocol (PPTP), Layer 2 Tunneling Protocol (L2TP), IPSec, a layer-3 protocol, and IP-IP. These protocols may work together or independently.

Point-to-Point Tunneling Protocol

PPTP is an extension of PPP used to encapsulate PPP frames for secure (tunneled) transmission over the Internet or for LAN-to-LAN communications. The data that is encapsulated can also be compressed and encrypted if necessary. When you're using a Windows 2000 server, PPP encryption can be used only when combined with the EAP-TLS or MS-CHAP authentication protocols. PPTP is less complex and secure than other forms of tunneling protocols.

PPP offers authentication for both the VPN client and the server, thus further securing both from attack and preserving the identities of the clients. When EAP or MS-CHAP v2 is used, stronger encryption keys are created, using both the password and other authentication data. Also, separate keys are created for sending and receiving data. Because PPTP does not require a public key infrastructure, it is easy to set up and manage. PPTP is best used with small networks and home offices or with offices using NAT.

Note: PPTP also supports PAP, SPAP, CHAP, and MS-CHAP v1.

Layer 2 Tunneling Protocol

L2TP is similar to PPTP in several ways: a tunnel is created between the client and the server; the same authentication methods are used (PAP, MS-CHAP, CHAP, and EAP); and compression is inherited from PPP. What differs is the encryption methods. PPTP uses the encryption from PPP, whereas L2TP uses one of three other encryption methods: 40-bit DES (data encryption standard), DES, and Triple DES. Provided by IPSec, this encryption provides per-packet authentication, integrity checks, and more. Integrity checks are provided by hash message authentication codes configured with shared secret keys that prove that the data has not been changed or tampered with while in transit.

The encryption methods are agreed upon when the client and server create their connection. Here's what you need to know about the DES encryption methods:

- *Triple DES*—The strongest form of encryption, also called 3DES, uses two 56-bit keys that provide the highest level of encryption available from Windows 2000. Triple DES goes over each bit of data three times, ensuring its validity, and at the same time slows down transmissions of data. The high overhead associated with 3DES makes it useful only on networks that need this highest level of security.

- *DES*—The middle form of encryption, DES uses one 56-bit encryption key. DES is generally acceptable for most networks.

- *40-bit DES*—This is the least secure method of DES encryption, and it uses only 40-bit keys for encrypting data. It is used mainly outside North America to meet restrictions placed on the export of encryption tools.

IPSec Tunneling

IPSec tunnel modes encapsulate entire IP datagrams for transport over the Internet or an intranet. In this process, the entire datagram is encrypted with ESP (Encapsulating Security Payload), and the result of that is encapsulated, thus making hacking into such data nearly impossible. When the destination server or router receives the datagram, it is then stripped of its headers, decrypted, and processed.

IPSec tunneling is used mainly for communicating with routers and gateways that do not support L2TP/IPSec or PPTP VPN tunneling. This type of tunneling is only supported in server-to-server or router-to-router scenarios and is not supported for client-to-server remote access VPN connections. L2TP or PPTP should be used in those instances. For more information on IPSec tunneling, see the Windows 2000 Resource Kit and search for "IPSec." IPSec tunneling should not be configured for servers or gateways unless the entire process is understood completely.

IP-IP

IP-IP is another tunneling technique that is used to tunnel multicast traffic over network routers that do not support multicast routing. The IP packet is encapsulated with an IP header and sent via a virtual network to its destination. The IP data includes IP, TCP, UDP, or ICMP headers and data. There are no encryption services with IP-IP data transmission.

Installation

"Installation" isn't necessarily a good title for this section because the Routing and Remote Access console is available by default from the Administrative Tools menu when Windows 2000 Server is installed. However, as is shown in Figure 12.1, when the console is accessed for the first time, the service is not enabled. In this section, I'll cover enabling a RRAS server—in essence, installing it—as well as installing a multiprotocol router, a VPN server, and an Internet connection server.

Installing a Remote Access Server

To install (enable) a Windows 2000 remote access server, perform the following steps:

1. As an administrator, log on to a computer running Windows 2000 Server. This computer can be a domain controller, member server, or standalone server, but if the computer is a standalone server, some functionality will be lost.

2. Choose Start|Programs|Administrative Tools|Routing And Remote Access to open the Routing and Remote Access console. You'll see the screen shown in Figure 12.1.

3. Highlight the server, and choose Action|Configure And Enable Routing And Remote Access.

4. The Routing And Remote Access Server Setup Wizard appears; choose Next.

5. The Common Configurations page offers five choices for the new remote access server. From the list, choose Remote Access Server.

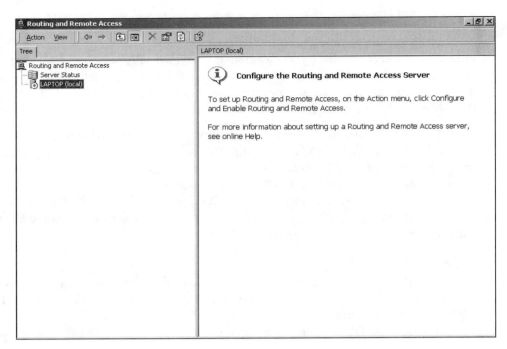

Figure 12.1
The Routing and Remote Access console.

Note: The options in this list are shown in the sidebar. Before continuing, make sure you know what kind of server you want to install, choose the appropriate option, and then choose the appropriate section for installing that server type. This section covers the Remote Access Server option.

6. The next page prompts you to select the protocols that remote clients will use. If the protocols you need aren't in this list, choose No, I Need To Add Protocols, and select the protocols you need. If the protocols you need are in this list, choose Yes, All Of The Required Protocols Are On This List. Choose Next.

7. The next page requires you to select how clients will obtain their IP addresses. If you use a DHCP server, select Automatically. If you need to specify a range of addresses, select the From A Specified Range Of Addresses option. If you choose to configure a range of addresses, simply type the range in the next wizard page.

8. You now need to decide if you want to set up this server to use RADIUS. For this example, I'll stick with a fairly straightforward installation and choose No. The wizard's summary screen appears next, and the process is complete.

Note: RADIUS servers will be discussed in the section "Internet Authentication Service."

Common Configurations through the Routing and Remote Access Setup Wizard

The Common Configurations page in the Routing And Remote Access Server Setup Wizard offers the following options:

- *Internet Connection Server*—Used in small home offices with fewer than 10 workstations. Enables all of the computers on the local network to connect to the Internet through one connection configured through this server.

- *Remote Access Server*—Used in any size organization or network to enable remote computers to dial into this computer or the local network.

- *Virtual Private Network Server*—Used in any size organization or network to enable remote computers to connect to this network through the Internet.

- *Network Router*—Used in any size organization or network to enable this computer to act as a router to manage communications with other networks.

- *Manually Configured Server*—Used to start the routing and remote access server with the default settings. (This option won't be covered in this section.)

12

Installing a Virtual Private Network Server

To install a VPN server, perform the following steps:

1. As an administrator, log on to a computer running Windows 2000 Server. This computer can be a domain controller, member server, or standalone server, but if the computer is a standalone server, some functionality will be lost.

2. Choose Start|Programs|Administrative Tools|Routing And Remote Access to open the Routing and Remote Access console. You'll see the screen shown in Figure 12.1.

3. Highlight the server, and choose Action|Configure And Enable Routing And Remote Access.

4. The Routing And Remote Access Server Setup Wizard appears; choose Next.

5. The Common Configurations page offers five choices for the new remote access server. From the list, choose Virtual Private Network (VPN) Server.

6. The next page prompts you to select the protocols that remote clients will use. If the protocols you need aren't in this list, choose No, I Need To Add Protocols, and select the protocols you need. If the protocols you need are in this list, choose Yes, All Of The Required Protocols Are On This List. Choose Next.

7. On the Internet Connection page, select the Internet connection that this server will use. This can be a LAN connection or an existing Internet connection.

8. The next page requires you to select how clients will obtain their IP addresses. If you use a DHCP server, select Automatically. If you need to specify a range of addresses, select the From A Specified Range Of Addresses option. If you choose to configure a range of addresses, simply type the range in the next wizard page.

9. You now need to decide if you want to set up this server to use RADIUS. For this example, I'll stick with a fairly straightforward installation and choose No. The wizard's summary screen appears next, and the process is complete.

Installing an Internet Connection Server

To install an Internet connection server, perform the following steps:

1. As an administrator, log on to a computer running Windows 2000 Server. This computer can be a domain controller, member server, or standalone server, but if the computer is a standalone server, some functionality will be lost.

2. Choose Start|Programs|Administrative Tools|Routing And Remote Access to open the Routing and Remote Access console. You'll see the screen shown in Figure 12.1.

3. Highlight the server, and choose Action|Configure And Enable Routing And Remote Access.

4. The Routing And Remote Access Server Setup Wizard appears; choose Next.

5. The Common Configurations page offers five choices for the new remote access server. From the list, choose Internet Connection Server.

6. On the Internet Connection Server Setup page, choose Set Up A Router With The Network Address Translation Routing Protocol.

Note: *If you choose Set Up Internet Connection Sharing, an information box will appear. It states that you'll need to set up Internet connection sharing from the Network And Dial-Up connections folder. You can choose to view the help files on this subject or choose Cancel to return to the wizard.*

7. The Internet Connection page asks you to select an Internet connection that already exists or create a new demand-dial Internet connection. Demand-dial connections are dialed when a client needs to send data; they are used on an as-needed basis. If you choose a local area connection, work your way through the final pages and finish the wizard. If you choose to create a new demand-dial Internet connection, the Demand Dial Interface Wizard begins.

8. The Routing and Remote Access Service is started, the new wizard begins, and the first page that needs information asks for the name of the interface for the new connection. I'll accept the default of Remote Router.

9. In the Connection Type box, choose to connect by using a modem, ISDN adapter, or other physical device, or choose to connect by using virtual private networking. If you've chosen to connect by using a modem, ISDN adapter, or other physical device, perform Steps 10 through 12. Otherwise, skip to Step 13.

10. Type in the phone number or IP address of the remote server you are dialing, and configure any alternate numbers through the Alternates button.

11. On the next page, choose how protocols and security options will be configured. See Figure 12.2.

12. On the next page, type the dial-out credentials, including the user name, the domain name, and the password, and complete the wizard.

13. For configuring a connection using a virtual private network (continued from Step 10), select a type of VPN interface to create. There are three types: Automatic Selection, PPTP, and L2TP. Make the choice that fits your network and business needs, and continue.

14. On the Destination Address page, enter the hostname or IP address of the router to which you are connecting.

15. On the next page, choose how protocols and security options will be configured. See Figure 12.2. (The last two options might be grayed out.)

16. On the next page, type the dial-out credentials, including the user name, the domain name, and the password, and complete the wizard.

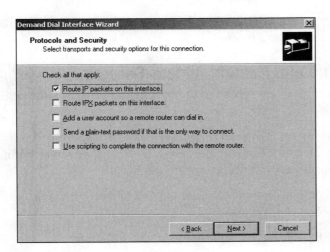

Figure 12.2
Choosing protocols and security options.

Installing a Multiprotocol Router

To install a multiprotocol router, perform the following steps:

1. As an administrator, log on to a computer running Windows 2000 Server. This computer can be a domain controller, member server, or standalone server, but if the computer is a standalone server, some functionality will be lost.

2. Choose Start|Programs|Administrative Tools|Routing And Remote Access to open the Routing and Remote Access console. You'll see the screen shown in Figure 12.1.

3. Highlight the server, and choose Action|Configure And Enable Routing And Remote Access.

4. The Routing And Remote Access Server Setup Wizard appears; choose Next.

5. The Common Configurations page offers five choices for the new remote access server. From the list, choose Network Router.

6. The next page prompts you to select the protocols that remote clients will use. If the protocols you need aren't in this list, choose No, I Need To Add Protocols, and select the protocols you need. If the protocols you need are in this list, select Yes, All Of The Required Protocols Are On This List. Choose Next.

7. On the Demand-Dial Connections page, choose Yes or No to specify how you want to configure demand-dial at this time. Demand-dial can also be configured after this wizard finishes and will be discussed in depth in the "Configuring the Server" section, so I'll choose No for this example.

Choosing No here causes the wizard to finish. The Routing and Remote Access Service is started, and the computer is set up as a router.

Adding Other Routing and Remote Access Servers

To add more routing and remote access servers to the console, perform the following steps:

1. As an administrator, log on to a computer running Windows 2000 Server. This computer can be a domain controller, member server, or standalone server, but if the computer is a standalone server, some functionality will be lost.

2. Choose Start|Programs|Administrative Tools|Routing And Remote Access to open the Routing and Remote Access console.

3. Highlight Routing And Remote Access, and choose Action|Add Server.

4. Choose how you want to add the server, as shown in Figure 12.3.

Once the domain name or computer name has been typed in, or a RRAS server has been chosen from Active Directory, the server will be added to the console and will be available for management.

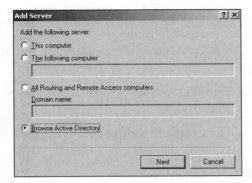

Figure 12.3
The Add Server dialog box.

Configuring the Server

Now that the remote access server has been enabled, it needs to be configured to work effectively for clients and the network. This section explains some of these configuration tasks, including creating a static IP address pool for the remote access server and its clients, integrating DHCP, enabling Multilink, using smart cards, and configuring protocols.

Also covered are topics concerning dial-up connections and demand-dial as well as how routers can be managed. For connections, the server and client configurations will both be addressed, and for the routers, protocols, devices, and how to connect the internal network to the Internet.

Configuring a Remote Access Server

The remote access server, though enabled and installed, isn't of much use until it's been configured properly. Depending on how the server was enabled and what choices were made through the wizards, the topics presented here may or may not apply to your particular circumstance. The best way to use this part of the chapter is to skim the topic titles and perform the tasks that apply to your network. For example, the first section, "Creating a Static IP Address Pool," will apply to only those network administrators who do not use DHCP or static addresses preconfigured on their clients. The second section, "Integrating with DHCP," obviously won't apply to those administrators who have created a static IP address pool. Throughout this section, simply configure what applies to you, and skip the rest.

Creating a Static IP Address Pool

To configure a static IP address pool for remote access clients on a network where DHCP is not used at all or is not used to administer remote access clients, perform the following steps:

1. As an administrator, log on to a computer running Windows 2000 Server and acting as a remote access server. This computer can be a domain controller, member server, or standalone server, but if the computer is a standalone server, some functionality will be lost.

2. Choose Start|Programs|Administrative Tools|Routing And Remote Access to open the Routing and Remote Access console.

3. Right-click on the server that needs to have a static IP address pool configured, and choose Properties.

4. On the IP tab, select Static Address Pool, and choose Add.

5. In the New Address Range box, type the starting IP address and the ending IP address. The Number Of Addresses box will be filled in automatically. Choose OK.

Using DHCP

To configure a remote access server to use DHCP to automatically obtain IP addresses and lease them to clients, perform the following steps:

1. As an administrator, log on to a computer running Windows 2000 Server and acting as a remote access server.

2. Choose Start|Programs|Administrative Tools|Routing And Remote Access to open the Routing and Remote Access console.

3. Right-click on the server that needs to be configured to use a Dynamic Host Configuration Protocol (DHCP) server, and choose Properties.

4. On the IP tab, select DHCP.

Enabling Multilink and BAP

As you know, Multilink and BAP can be used to combine multiple ISDN, telephone, or other lines together when additional bandwidth is needed on the network. To configure Multilink and BAP, perform the following steps:

1. As an administrator, log on to a computer running Windows 2000 Server and acting as a remote access server.

2. Choose Start|Programs|Administrative Tools|Routing And Remote Access to open the Routing and Remote Access console.

3. Right-click on the name of the server where Multilink will be configured, and choose Properties.

4. On the PPP tab, check Multilink Connections, and check Dynamic Bandwidth Control Using BAP Or BACP.

Using Smart Cards

To configure smart card authentication for remote access clients, perform the following steps:

1. As an administrator, log on to a computer running Windows 2000 Server and acting as a remote access server.

2. Choose Start|Programs|Administrative Tools|Routing And Remote Access to open the Routing and Remote Access console.

3. Right-click on the remote access server, and choose Properties.

4. On the Security tab, select Authentication Methods.

5. In the Authentication Methods box, select the Extensible Authentication Protocol (EAP) checkbox, and choose OK twice.

6. In the left pane, expand the RRAS name, and then expand the Remote Access Policies folder.

7. In the right pane, double-click on the remote access policy that your smart card remote access clients will use, and choose Edit Profile.

Note: *Edit and Edit Profile are different. Make sure you choose Edit Profile at the bottom of the screen.*

8. On the Authentication tab, select Extensible Authentication Protocol.

9. Make sure that Smart Card Or Other Certificate is showing in the drop-down list box, as shown in Figure 12.4, and choose Configure.

10. In the Smart Card Or Other Certificate dialog box, select the certificate to use, and choose OK.

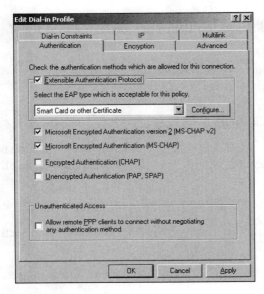

Figure 12.4
Smart card configuration.

Configuring DNIS and ANI/CLI

The Dialed Number Identification Service (DNIS) is used to approve connections by the telephone number the user dials. DNIS sends this number to the hardware that receives these calls. You can configure a single telephone number to forward calls to multiple dial-in hardware components on the network. Automatic Number Identification/Calling Line Identification (ANI/CLI) is used to incorporate the number from which the user dials as part of the user's credentials. This is similar to caller ID. The user's phone number can be configured as his or her logon identity instead of sending a username and password, as with caller ID.

To configure the remote access server to use DNIS, perform the following steps:

1. As an administrator, log on to a computer running Windows 2000 Server and acting as a remote access server.

2. Choose Start|Programs|Administrative Tools|Routing And Remote Access to open the Routing and Remote Access console.

3. Right-click on the remote access server, and choose Properties.

4. On the Security tab, select the Authentication Methods option.

5. Check the Allow Remote System To Connect Without Authentication checkbox. Choose OK to close all of these dialog boxes.

6. Expand the tree in the left pane, and right-click on Remote Access Policies. Select New Remote Access Policy. The Remote Access Policy Wizard begins.

7. On the first page, type a name for the policy.

8. On the next page, choose Add, and then select Called-Station ID from the list of attribute types. Choose Add again.

9. Set the Called-Station ID condition to the connection device's phone number.

10. On the Permissions page, select Grant Remote Access Permission.

11. On the User Profile page, select Edit Profile.

12. From the Edit Dial-in Profile page, set dial-in constraints, authentication, encryption, Multilink, and IP information as needed. When you're finished, choose OK, and the wizard closes.

To configure the remote access server to use ANI/CLI, perform the following steps:

1. As an administrator, log on to a computer running Windows 2000 Server and acting as a remote access server.

2. Choose Start|Programs|Administrative Tools|Routing And Remote Access to open the Routing and Remote Access console.

3. Right-click on the remote access server, and choose Properties.

4. On the Security tab, select the Authentication Methods option.

5. Check the Allow Remote System To Connect Without Authentication checkbox. Choose OK twice.

6. Expand the tree in the left pane, and right-click on Remote Access Policies. Select New Remote Access Policy. The Remote Access Policy Wizard begins.

7. On the first page, type a name for the policy.

8. On the Conditions page, select Add. Choose Called-Station ID, and choose Add.

9. Type in the connection device's phone number, and choose Add.

10. On the Permissions page, select Grant Remote Access Permission.

11. On the User Profile page, select Edit Profile.

12. On this page, set dial-in constraints, authentication, encryption, Multilink, and IP information as needed. When you're finished, choose OK, and the wizard closes.

13. To make this work, you'll need to create user accounts for the phone numbers that will dial up and be authenticated. Set the user account name to the phone number from which the user will be calling. For more information on creating user accounts, refer to Chapter 7.

14. Finally, set the following Registry setting to 31 on the server that will be authenticating the dial-in users: HKEY_LOCAL_MACHINE\System\CurrentControlSet\Services\RasMan\ppp\ControlProtocols\Builtin\UserIdentityAttribute. This value is used when the remote client sends no other username besides the phone number.

    To specify for this server that the calling number configured here will always be used instead of the username, set the following Registry key to 1: HKEY_LOCAL_MACHINE\System\CurrentControlSet\Services\RemoteAccessPolicy\Override User Name.

Warning! *Do not configure both of these Registry settings; configure only one. If both are set, only ANI/CLI authentication can be used for this remote access server. As you know, editing the Registry incorrectly can disable a system immediately and cause it to have to be reinstalled. Always back up the server before making any Registry changes.*

Configuring Different Protocols

All of the protocols described earlier can be configured in the same place. MS-CHAP v2, EAP, MS-CHAP, CHAP, SPAP, PAP, MD5-Challenge, Smart Cards, Certificates, and connecting without authentication can all be configured by performing the following steps:

1. As an administrator, log on to a computer running Windows 2000 Server and acting as a remote access server.

2. Choose Start|Programs|Administrative Tools|Routing And Remote Access to open the Routing and Remote Access console.

3. Right-click on the server that needs to be configured to use a DHCP server, and choose Properties.

4. On the Security tab, choose Authentication Methods.

5. To configure Smart Card or MD5-Challenge, select EAP Methods. For any other protocol, place a check in the appropriate checkbox(es).

Configuring a Guest Account

The Guest account is disabled by default and poses a security risk to the network, but this account can be useful if a user needs to be allowed to access the network and that user doesn't have specific credentials configured. This is the perfect solution when clients need to log on but the phone number they are dialing from isn't known, or when you don't want to create accounts for dial-in users who may be calling from different locations daily. However, enabling the Guest account allows any user who dials into the server to access the network with Guest permissions and privileges. Instead of configuring the guest account, it would be better to create a new account and configure that account as described here. It is best to leave the Guest account disabled, so be careful with this account, and use it only if no other solutions can be found for these clients.

To configure the Guest account, (or preferably a new account instead of the Guest account), follow these steps:

1. As an administrator, log on to a computer running Windows 2000 Server and acting as a remote access server.

2. Choose Start|Programs|Administrative Tools|Routing And Remote Access to open the Routing and Remote Access console.

3. Right-click on the server that needs to be configured to use a DHCP server, and choose Properties.

4. On the Security tab, choose Authentication Methods.

5. In the Authentication Methods box, check the Allow Remote Systems To Connect Without Authentication checkbox. Close the Authentications box and the Server Properties box.

6. Double-click on Remote Access Policies in the left pane. In the right pane, select an existing remote access policy to modify, or right-click in a blank area of the screen and choose New Remote Access Policy. (In this example, I'll choose New Remote Access Policy.) The Remote Access Policy Wizard begins.

7. Type in a name for the new policy, perhaps "Guest Policy."

8. On the Conditions page, choose Add, then Service Type, then Add again.

9. In the Service Type box, choose Login, Add, then OK.

10. On the Permissions page, select Grant Remote Access Permission.

11. On the User Profile page, select Edit Profile.

12. In the Edit Profile screen, on the Authentication tab, check the Allow Remote PPP Clients To Connect Without Negotiating Any Authentication Method checkbox. (To view the help files on this subject, choose OK in the dialog box that appears.) Choose Finish to close the wizard.

13. Choose Start|Programs|Administrative Tools|Active Directory Users And Computers.

14. In the Active Directory Users And Computers console, expand the domain tree, and open the Users folder.

15. If using the Guest account, right-click on it, and choose Enable Account. If using a new account, perform the same operation on it.

16. Once the account is enabled, right-click again and choose Properties.

17. On the Dial-In tab, select Allow Access or Control Access Through Remote Access Policy. Choose OK.

Warning! *Again, let me state that enabling the Guest account opens up large security holes for the network. All a hacker has to do is dial in and guess the password. You might consider creating a separate user account and leaving the Guest account disabled.*

Configuring a Dial-Up Connection

A dial-up connection can be configured for a client who has a modem and a connection to the Internet so that the user can connect to a private network when away from the office. Once the client is set up, the server needs to be configured to handle demand-dial routing and accept incoming calls. A user account needs to be created if the user is not going to log on with the Guest account, as described and configured earlier. Depending on previous remote-access-server configurations, some of these steps may already have been completed, but for the purpose of putting it all together, all of these topics will be covered here.

Configuring the Client

Before configuring a client, make sure that the client meets the minimum requirements for accessing a remote access server. Any of the following clients can be configured:

- Windows 2000

- Windows NT 3.1, 3.5, 3.51, 4

- Windows 9X

- Macintosh

- Windows for Workgroups

- MS-DOS

- LAN Manager

- PPP clients

To set up a dial-up connection for a Windows 2000 client, perform the following steps:

1. As an administrator, log on to a Windows 2000 computer that needs to be configured to dial-up a private network. The computer must have a modem or other dial-up adapter and be capable of dialing a remote computer.

2. Right-click on My Network Places, and choose Properties.

3. Select Make New Connection, and choose Next to start the Network Connection Wizard.

4. Select Dial-Up To Private Network from the list of options shown in Figure 12.5.

5. On the Phone Number To Dial page, type the number that the computer should dial, and configure any additional dialing rules.

6. On the Connection Availability page, choose either Create The Connection For All Users or Create This Connection Only For Myself.

7. Type in the name of the connection, and choose Finish.

8. In the Connect Dial-Up box, type in the user name and password for this user.

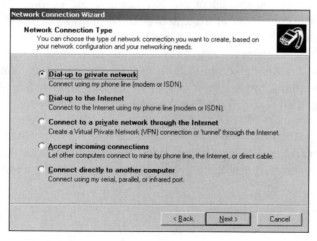

Figure 12.5
Selecting a network connection type.

Configuring the Server

After performing the previous steps for configuring a dial-up client to access a private network, you should test the client computer for connectivity. The computer will most likely dial but will not get registered on the network. To configure the server so this user can log on from a dial-up connection, perform the following steps:

1. As an administrator, log on locally to the remote access server.

2. Choose Start|Programs|Administrative Tools|Routing And Remote Access to open the Routing and Remote Access console.

3. Right-click on the server, and choose Properties.

4. On the General tab, make sure there is a check in the LAN And Demand-Dial Routing checkbox and the Remote Access Server checkbox. Choose OK.

Also, the client must have an account on the network, or the Guest account must be enabled, as described earlier. To create a user account for the new dial-in user, perform the following steps:

1. As an administrator, log on locally to the remote access server.

2. Choose Start|Programs|Administrative Tools|Active Directory Users And Computers.

3. In the Active Directory Users And Computers console, expand the domain tree, and open the Users folder.

4. Right-click in the right pane, and choose New|User. Type the first name, last name, and user logon name in the New Object-User dialog box.

5. Type in a password, and configure password options in the next screen. Choose Next, then Finish.

6. Right-click on the new user account, and choose Properties.

7. On the Dial-In tab, select Control Access Through Remote Access Policy.

After the user account has been created, perform the following steps to configure the user account with a remote access policy and to enable the computer to accept the user's dial-in requests:

1. As an administrator, log on locally to the remote access server.

2. Choose Start|Programs|Administrative Tools|Routing And Remote Access to open the Routing and Remote Access console.

3. Open the Remote Access Policies folder.

4. Either right-click on an existing policy and choose Properties, or right-click in a blank area of the right pane and choose New Remote Access Policy. (Because I've already created policies in this chapter, I'll edit an existing policy.)

12

5. On the Settings tab, make sure that Grant Remote Access Permission is selected, and then choose Add.

6. At this point, one of two things can be configured. You can choose Called-Station-ID and type in the phone number the user will dial, or you can choose Calling-Station-ID and type in the number where the call originated. Make the appropriate configuration choice for your specific scenario, and then continue.

7. On the Settings tab, choose Edit Profile.

8. On the Authentication tab, check Allow Remote PPP Clients To Connect Without Negotiating Any Authentication Method. Choose OK twice.

The user will now be able to log in successfully. Figure 12.6 shows a successful remote access logon and connection from the Routing and Remote Access console for a user called dialup user.

Note: The remote access server can handle as many inbound connections as the hardware on the server allows. A Windows Professional machine allows up to three incoming calls, one of each of these types: dial-up, one VPN, and one direct connection at any given time.

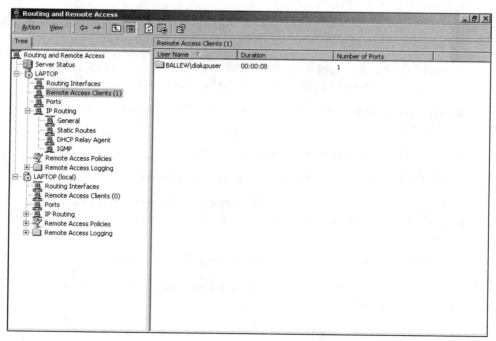

Figure 12.6
A successful remote access logon by a dial-up user.

Configuring Routing

In previous sections, you learned how to create a router by using the Routing and Remote Access console. In this section, you'll learn how to configure the router to function effectively. You'll learn about managing routing interfaces, protocols, static routes, the routers themselves, and more.

Managing Routing Protocols

Routing protocols were described earlier and include Routing Information Protocol (RIP) for IP, Open Shortest Path First (OSPF), DHCP Relay Agent, IP multicast routing, RIP for Service Advertisement Protocol (SAP) for IPX, AppleTalk routing, and Network Address Translation. Protocols can be added and deleted, and their order of preference can be changed.

To add a protocol, perform the following steps:

1. As an administrator, log on locally to the remote access server.

2. Choose Start|Programs|Administrative Tools|Routing And Remote Access to open the Routing and Remote Access console.

3. Expand the IP Routing tree, and right-click on General.

4. Choose New Routing Protocol.

5. In the New Routing Protocol dialog box, select the protocol to add.

To delete a routing protocol, perform the following steps:

1. As an administrator, log on locally to the remote access server.

2. Choose Start|Programs|Administrative Tools|Routing And Remote Access to open the Routing and Remote Access console.

3. Expand the IP Routing tree, and highlight General under IP Routing.

4. In the right pane, select the protocol to delete. Right-click on it, and choose Delete.

To change the preference level of a protocol and the route it takes, perform the following steps:

1. As an administrator, log on locally to the remote access server.

2. Choose Start|Programs|Administrative Tools|Routing And Remote Access to open the Routing and Remote Access console.

3. Under IP Routing, right-click on General, and choose Properties.

4. On the Preference Levels tab, highlight the route or protocol to move, and select Move Up or Move Down.

You would change these routes in dynamic routing environments when multiple routing protocols are being used in a single intranet. If the hop count of a specific route is 7, and the hop count of another route to the same destination is only 3, then it would be better to move the route with hop count 3 up the list on the Preference Levels tab.

Managing Routing Interfaces

An interface is a physical or logical connection used in a network to connect to a router. If a router has two NICS, then it has two interfaces. There are three types of interfaces:

- LAN
- Demand-dial
- IP-in-IP

The LAN interface is a NIC or other similar adapter, but WAN adapters are sometimes shown as LAN adapters. These adapters represent networks such as Ethernet or Token Ring and are always active. NICS usually do not require authentication to be used.

The demand-dial interface is a connection such as two modems and a phone line, two routers connected by a phone line, or a logical connection over a VPN. These connections can be connected all the time (called a *persistent connection*) or only when needed (*demand-dial*). Demand-dial interfaces usually require authentication before the connection is established.

The IP-in-IP tunnel interface is generally used for transmitting multicast traffic across routers where it isn't supported, and authentication is not generally necessary.

To add a new routing interface, perform the following steps:

1. As an administrator, log on locally to the remote access server.

2. Choose Start|Programs|Administrative Tools|Routing And Remote Access to open the Routing and Remote Access console.

3. Expand IP Routing, and right-click on General.

4. Choose New Interface.

5. Select the interface you want to add, and then supply any other requested information.

Note: *When you're adding IPX, the interface will automatically be added to the existing IPX protocols. However, if you add IP, you'll have to add the interface to each IP routing protocol manually. To do this, simply right-click on the protocol and choose New Interface.*

To install a new demand-dial interface, perform the following steps:

1. As an administrator, log on locally to the remote access server.

2. Choose Start|Programs|Administrative Tools|Routing And Remote Access to open the Routing and Remote Access console.

3. Expand the RRAS tree, and right-click on Routing Interfaces.

4. Choose New Demand-Dial Interface.

5. The Demand-Dial Wizard appears. Work through the wizard, supplying the necessary information. The wizard is similar to other wizards already described in this chapter and is easy to use.

To add an IP-in-IP tunnel, perform the following steps:

1. As an administrator, log on locally to the remote access server.

2. Choose Start|Programs|Administrative Tools|Routing And Remote Access to open the Routing and Remote Access console.

3. Expand the RRAS console tree, and right-click on Routing Interfaces.

4. Choose New IP Tunnel.

5. Type in a name for the new interface, and choose OK.

6. In the console tree, right-click on General under IP Routing, and choose New Interface.

7. Highlight the new IP-in-IP tunnel, and choose OK.

8. On the Tunnel tab, type the IP address of the router in the Local Address text box.

9. On the same tab, type the IP address of the tunnel endpoint in the Remote Address text box, and choose OK.

Note: *Interfaces can be deleted simply by right-clicking on them and pressing the Delete key.*

Connecting the Internal Network to the Internet

You can connect the internal network to the Internet by using a modem, an ISDN line, a T-carrier line, or Frame Relay. The first example will describe the steps involved when a modem is used for connecting.

To connect the internal network to the Internet by using a modem, perform the following steps:

1. As an administrator, log on locally to the remote access server.

2. Make sure the modem is installed on the computer according to the modem manufacturer's instructions.

3. Open Control Panel, and double-click Phone And Modem Options.

4. On the Modems tab, make sure the modem is shown. If it isn't, choose Add and install the modem.

5. Choose Start|Programs|Administrative Tools|Routing And Remote Access to open the Routing and Remote Access console.

6. Expand the RRAS tree, and highlight Ports. You should see the modem in the right pane.

7. Right-click on Ports, and choose Properties.

8. In the Port Properties dialog box, make sure the modem is highlighted, and choose Configure.

9. Check the Demand-Dial Routing Connections (Inbound And Outbound) checkbox, and choose OK.

10. Right-click Routing Interfaces in the left pane, and choose New Demand-Dial Interface.

11. Add a default route that will use the newly created interface.

To connect the internal network to the Internet by using an ISDN device, perform the following steps:

1. As an administrator, log on locally to the remote access server.

2. Make sure the ISDN adapter is properly installed.

3. Choose Start|Programs|Administrative Tools|Routing And Remote Access to open the Routing and Remote Access console.

4. Expand the RRAS tree, and highlight Ports. You should see the adapter in the right pane.

5. Right-click on Ports, and choose Properties.

6. In the Port Properties dialog box, make sure the adapter is highlighted, and choose Configure.

7. Check the Demand-Dial Routing Connections (Inbound And Outbound) checkbox, and choose OK.

8. Right-click on Routing Interfaces in the left pane, and choose New Demand-Dial Interface.

9. Add a default route that will use the newly created interface.

To connect the internal network to the Internet by using a T1 line or Frame Relay, perform the following steps:

1. As an administrator, log on locally to the remote access server.

2. Make sure the T-carrier adapter is properly installed and is configured with the IP address given to you by your ISP.

3. Choose Start|Programs|Administrative Tools|Routing And Remote Access to open the Routing and Remote Access console.

4. Expand the RRAS tree, and highlight Routing Interfaces. The T-carrier adapter should be shown in the right pane.

5. Add a default network router that uses this interface.

Using and Managing RIP

If you've decided to use RIP on your network's remote access server, you can use and manage RIP through the RRAS console. To install RIP as a RAS protocol and manage it using the RRAS console, perform the following steps:

1. As an administrator, log on locally to the remote access server.

2. Choose Start|Programs|Administrative Tools|Routing And Remote Access to open the Routing and Remote Access console.

3. Expand the RRAS tree, and right-click on General under IP Routing.

4. Choose New Routing Protocol.

5. From the New Routing Protocol dialog box, choose RIP Version 2 for Internet Protocol and choose OK.

6. Notice a new icon for RIP under IP Routing. Right-click on RIP, and choose Properties.

7. In the RIP Properties dialog box, the following items can be configured:

   • The maximum delay (in seconds) that the router will wait before it sends a triggered update.

   • The type of event logging: log errors only; log errors and warnings; log the maximum amount of information; or disable event logging.

   • How to process announcements from other routers: accept from listed routers only, accept from all routers, or ignore announcements from listed routers.

8. Right-click on RIP again and choose New Interface.

9. Highlight the interface to use for RIP, and choose OK from the Interfaces dialog box.

10. Configure the properties for RIP from the four tabs described next. Choose OK when you're finished.

Four tabs are available for RIP configuration options. To configure RIP correctly, you need to understand what each of the options means and what certain options do.

In the Interfaces dialog box, the General tab provides the following options:

• *Operation Mode*—Two modes for updating RIP information are available: periodic update and auto-static update. Use auto-static update for demand-dial interfaces, and use periodic updates for LAN interfaces.

- *Outgoing Packet Protocol*—Four choices are available for outgoing protocols:

  - *RIP Version 1 Broadcast*—Choose this option if you're using only RIP v1 routers.

  - *RIP Version 2 Broadcast*—Choose this option if you're using both RIP v1 and RIP v2 routers.

  - *RIP Version 2 Multicast*—Choose this option if all neighboring routers support and run RIP v2.

  - *Silent RIP*—Choose this option if the router should listen for RIP announcements from other routers but should not broadcast its own routing table.

- *Incoming Packet Protocol*—Four choices are available for incoming packet protocols:

  - *Ignore Incoming Packets*—Choose this option to configure the router to only announce its own routes and ignore any routes announced by other routers.

  - *RIP Version 1 And 2*—Choose this option if both versions of RIP routers exist on the network.

  - *RIP Version 1 Only*—Choose this option if your network has only RIP v1 routers on it or if you want this router to accept announcements from only RIP v1 routers.

  - *RIP Version 2 Only*—Choose this option if the network has only RIP v2 routers on it or if you want this router to listen for only RIP v2 announcements.

- *Added Cost For Routes*—The default added cost to any route is 1 plus the number of hops it takes to get from point A to point B through the router. If several routes are available and one is more costly than another, you can increase the added cost for routes so that particular route won't be used as often. If multiple routes to a destination address exist, the route with the lowest cost associated with it (least number of hops) will be chosen. The maximum hop count for any route is 15.

- *Tag For Announced Routes*—Used only with RIP v2, this option attaches a number that identifies this route on this interface.

- *Activate Authentication*—Choose this option if you want to include a password with all RIP v2 packets. All routers that use this interface will need to use the same password. The password doesn't provide any authentication, though, only identification. It is not a security feature.

In the Interfaces dialog box, the Security tab provides the following options from the Action drop down list for both incoming and outgoing routes (each is configured separately):

- *Accept All Routes*—This option allows either incoming or outgoing routes to accept all routes from RIP routers.

- *Accept All Routers In The Ranges Listed*—This option allows you to specify a range of routes that will be accepted by the RIP router for incoming or outgoing routes or both.

- *Ignore All Routes In The Ranges Listed*—This option allows you to specify a range of routes that will not be accepted by the RIP router for incoming or outgoing routes or both.

In the Interfaces dialog box, the Neighbors tab provides the following options to specify how this RIP router will interact with neighboring RIP routers:

- *Use Broadcast Or Multicast Only*—Choose this option when all RIP announcements will be sent using the outgoing packet protocol specified on the General tab. (This is the default.)

- *Use Neighbors In Addition To Broadcast Or Multicast*—Choose this option when RIP announcements are sent to specific routers and with the outgoing packet protocol specified on the General tab.

- *Use Neighbors Instead Of Broadcast Or Multicast*—Choose this option when RIP announcements are sent to only neighboring routers. Packets will not be sent using the outgoing packet protocol specified on the General tab. You should select this option if you are using Frame Relay and want to route between specific routers only.

In the Interfaces dialog box, the Advanced tab provides several options for configuration. Some are self-explanatory, but most are not. For instance, Enable Poison-Reverse Processing isn't extremely intuitive. In the following list, I'll introduce the majority of the options that are available and when and why you should use them:

- *Periodic Announcement Interval*—If periodic updates are used, then this number—specifying the amount of time that passes between router updates—can be set anywhere from 15 seconds to 24 hours. The default is 30 seconds. If updates are not important and routes rarely change, this number should be raised, and for routes that change often, the number can be lowered.

- *Time Before Routes Expire (Seconds)*—If periodic updates are used, this number can be set. The default is 180 seconds, but this option can be set anywhere from 15 seconds to 72 hours. The route must be updated before time expires, or it will be considered an invalid route and will eventually be removed.

- *Time Before Route Is Removed*—The default is 120 seconds, but this option can be set anywhere from 15 seconds to 72 hours. This number determines how long an expired route will stay in the routing table before being removed. This option is valid only if periodic updates are used.

- *Enable Split-Horizon Processing*—This option prevents routers from announcing routes learned on the network back to the same network. Split-horizon processing is enabled by default.

12

- *Enable Poison-Reverse Processing*—This option is used to announce routes learned on a network with a metric of 16, meaning that they are unreachable. This prevents problems associated with bad routes from being circulated back to the network where they were originally learned. This option is set by default and should be checked when split-horizon processing is chosen.

- *Enable Triggered Updates*—This option sends changes from this router to others immediately after a change, instead of waiting for the periodic announcement interval.

- *Send Clean-Up Updates When Stopping*—If this RIP router is stopped, the router will send an update to neighboring routers to notify them that certain destinations will now be unreachable. This option allows the neighboring routers to immediately update their routing tables instead of waiting for their information to time out of their own routing tables.

The Advanced tab provides five other options. These options are used to specify whether host routes received in RIP announcements will be accepted or ignored, whether host routes will be included in RIP announcements, whether default routes received in RIP announcements will be accepted, whether default routes are included in RIP announcements, and whether subnet routes will be summarized in the network ID when announced on a network that is not a subnet of the network ID. The default settings are usually fine for these options and will not be detailed further here.

Using and Managing OSPF

If you've decided to use Open Shortest Path First (OSPF) on your network's remote access server, you can use and manage OSPF through the RRAS console. To install OSPF as a RAS protocol and manage it using the RRAS console, perform the following steps:

1. As an administrator, log on locally to the remote access server.

2. Choose Start|Programs|Administrative Tools|Routing And Remote Access to open the Routing and Remote Access console.

3. Expand the RRAS tree, and right-click on General under IP Routing.

4. Choose New Routing Protocol.

5. In the New Routing Protocol dialog box, choose Open Shortest Path First (OSPF) and choose OK.

6. Notice a new icon for OSPF under IP Routing. Right-click on OSPF, and choose New Interface.

7. In the Interfaces dialog box, highlight the interface that OSPF will run on, and choose OK.

After you add the new interface, the OSPF Properties dialog box appears. There are three tabs: General, NMBA Neighbors, and Advanced. To configure the router correctly, you'll need to understand the options in this dialog box.

In the OSPF Properties dialog box, the General tab provides the following options:

- *Enable OSPF For This Address*—This option lists the available IP addresses of the router being configured. Place a check here to enable OSPF for a particular IP address.

- *Area ID*—This option lists which areas are available for this interface. Every interface can have only one area, but if multiple interfaces exist, multiple areas can be chosen.

- *Router Priority*—The higher the number, the higher the priority of the router. If two or more routers exist on a network and are vying for the role of designated router, the router with the higher number wins.

- *Cost*—The lower the cost, the more often the route gets used. To denote an expensive link and configure it so it won't be used as often as other links, increase the number in this window. Do not increase the number past 15.

- *Password*—By default, the password is enabled and is "12345678." This password is used only for identification and not for security purposes. When a password is used, all interfaces in the same area of a network must have identical passwords.

- *Network Type*—Here, you can select broadcast, point-to-point (PPP), or non-broadcast multiple access (NBMA). If broadcast is chosen, then multiple routers can be added to the network, and all routers will be part of a multiple-access broadcast network. These networks can be Ethernet, Token Ring, and FDDI. If PPP is chosen, then the connection is configured between only two routers. This option would be chosen for routers such as T1, T3, and other dial-up links, such as DSL, cable, or ISDN. The NBMA choice is for networks using X.25, Frame Relay, ATM, and so on. NMBA neighbors can also be configured if this option is chosen.

In the OSPF Properties dialog box, the NBMA Neighbors tab (available only if NBMA network type is chosen on the General tab) provides the following options:

- *IP Address*—This specifies where the IP address of the interface is listed. If there are multiple interfaces, multiple IP addresses will be listed here.

- *Neighboring IP Address*—This specifies where the IP address of a neighboring router is added.

- *Router Priority*—This specifies where router priority is configured for the neighbor. This number must be one or greater.

In the OSPF Properties dialog box, the Advanced tab provides the following options:

- *IP Address*—This option specifies the IP address of the interface. If more than one interface is available, multiple IP addresses will be available.

- *Transit Delay*—This is the amount of time that it should take for an update packet to be transmitted over this interface to another router on the network. The default is one second.

- *Retransmit Interval (Seconds)*—This is the number of seconds between advertisements from this interface. For slower lines, the number should be increased, but a number that's too low will result in retransmissions that are not required. The number should not be less than the length of time a transmission would take between any two routers on the network.

- *Hello Interval (Seconds)*—When a router sends a hello message, the router is announcing that it has changes. This number must be the same for all routers on the network. For a LAN, a good number is 10 seconds, and on an X.25 network, it can be as high as 30 to 40 seconds. A shorter interval will cause more traffic on the network than will a longer interval, so the setting should be chosen with care.

- *Dead Interval (Seconds)*—This number represents how many seconds other routers will wait for hello packets before considering the router to be down. If the hello packet interval is set for 10 seconds, and the dead interval is set for 40 seconds, then when a neighboring router has not received four hello messages in a row, the router is considered to be down. The dead interval must be the same for all routers on the network and should be four times the hello interval number.

- *Poll Interval (Seconds)*—When a router is considered to be down due to a dead interval being met, that router still needs to be polled occasionally so that other routers will know when it is running again. The poll interval signifies that amount of time, and it is usually twice as long as the dead interval.

- *Maximum Transmission Unit (MTU) Size (Bytes)*—On an Ethernet network, the default maximum size of an IP packet carrying routing information is 1,500 bytes. For 100MB FDDI, that number is 4,352 bytes.

By right-clicking on the RIP icon under IP Routing and choosing Properties, you open the IP Routing dialog box. This provides four tabs for configuration: General, Areas, Virtual Interfaces, and External Routing.

In the IP Routing dialog box, the General tab provides the following options:

- *Router Identification*—This is where you enter the IP address of the OSPF router.

- *Enable Autonomous System Boundary Router*—This is where you configure this router as an autonomous system (AS) boundary router. An AS router advertises external routing information from other routers and is often connected to the backbone of the network.

- *Event Logging*—This option logs events in Event Viewer. You can select one of the following options:

  - Log Errors Only

  - Log Errors And Warnings

  - Log The Maximum Amount Of Information

  - Disable Event Logging

On the Areas tab of the IP Routing dialog box, you can add, edit, or remove OSPF areas. An *OSPF area* is a subdivision of the network, and a single router can have multiple areas. The maximum number of areas for a single router is 16.

On the Virtual Interfaces tab of the IP Routing dialog box, you can add, edit, or remove OSPF virtual interfaces. *Virtual interfaces* are similar to physical connections but are actually only logical connections. These virtual interfaces connect border routers and backbone routers.

On the External Routing tab of the IP Routing dialog box, you can accept routes from all route sources except specific routes selected, or you can ignore routes from all route sources except those selected. The route source options are available only if Enable Autonomous System Boundary Router is chosen on the General tab. The routing options are:

- AutoStatic Routes
- Local Routes
- RIP Version 2 for Internet Protocol
- SNMP Routes
- Static (Non Demand Dial) Routes
- Static Routes

You can also configure route filters for ignoring or accepting specific listed routes.

Managing Static Routes

Static routes are sometimes necessary and are useful in small networks. These routes can be added, deleted, and configured to perform auto-static updates. These routes must be manually added by an administrator. When static routes are created, the administrator has to update them constantly as new routers or routes are added, so static routes are inappropriate for medium-sized or larger networks. Static routes don't do anything dynamically; they don't discover new routes, detect down routers, or have any expiration limits. However, in some instances with small networks, perhaps with only two routers, a few clients, and minimal topology changes, static routes can be useful. For instance, in a small office or network in which the route paths to resources or other offices do not change, configuring a static route over a low bandwidth WAN link will ensure that all traffic is routed correctly and with no additional traffic since no routing protocol needs to be run across that link.

To add a static route, perform the following steps:

1. As an administrator, log on locally to the remote access server.

2. Choose Start|Programs|Administrative Tools|Routing And Remote Access to open the Routing and Remote Access console.

3. Expand the RRAS tree and IP Routing, and right-click on Static Routes.

4. For an IP route, choose New Static Route; for an IPX route, choose New Route.

5. From the Interface drop-down list, choose from Internal, IP Tunnel 2, or Local Area Connection.

6. Type in the destination IP address, the subnet (network) mask, the gateway, and the metric. Choose OK.

Note: To create a default static route, configure the destination and network mask as 0.0.0.0. If the interface is a demand-dial interface, select Use The Route To Initiate Demand-Dial Connections. If the interface is for a LAN connection, type the IP address of the router that is on the same network segment as the LAN interface.

Deleting a route is as simple as right-clicking on the route and choosing Delete.

To update a demand-dial interface, right-click on the route and choose Update Routes. To update routes dynamically, use Task Scheduler.

Managing Routing Tables

Sometimes, you'll need to manage the router and view the routing tables. A routing table has several parts: Destination, Network Mask, Gateway, Interface, Metric, and Protocol. See Figure 12.7 for a routing table as shown through the Routing and Remote Access console, and see Figure 12.8 for a routing table as shown using the **route print** command at a command prompt.

Because everything revolves around these routing tables, it is imperative to know what each category represents and how to read these tables. The following list describes each part of the routing table shown in the Routing and Remote Access console:

- *Destination*—Specifies the destination host, subnet address, network address, or default route.

- *Network Mask*—Distinguishes between the destination IP address, the host ID address, and the network portion of the address. The routing table uses this information to determine which route is used and when.

LAPTOP - IP Routing Table

Destination	Network mask	Gateway	Interface	Metric	Protocol
127.0.0.0	255.0.0.0	127.0.0.1	Loopback	1	Local
127.0.0.1	255.255.255.255	127.0.0.1	Loopback	1	Local
192.168.0.0	255.255.255.0	192.168.0.42	Local Area C...	1	Local
192.168.0.12	255.255.255.255	127.0.0.1	Loopback	1	Local
192.168.0.42	255.255.255.255	127.0.0.1	Loopback	1	Local
192.168.0.255	255.255.255.255	192.168.0.12	Internal	1	Local
224.0.0.0	240.0.0.0	192.168.0.42	Local Area C...	1	Local
224.0.0.0	240.0.0.0	192.168.0.12	Internal	1	Local
255.255.255.255	255.255.255.255	192.168.0.42	Local Area C...	1	Local
255.255.255.255	255.255.255.255	192.168.0.12	Internal	1	Local

Figure 12.7
Routing table from the Routing and Remote Access console.

Figure 12.8
Routing table from the **route print** command.

- *Gateway*—Specifies the IP address of the gateway that the client must use to get the data out of its network and off to another. This might be a router, a computer, or a local NIC, and this option is not configurable for a demand-dial interface.

- *Interface*—Specifies the address of the NIC that is used to send the packet out of the local network. This is generally a LAN or demand-dial interface used for reaching the next router.

- *Metric*—Specifies the number of hops (routers) to a destination. This number is used by the router to determine the best route to a destination, and the route is generally chosen based on the lowest number of hops to a particular destination.

- *Protocol*—Shows how a particular route was learned; this can be OSPF, RIP, or a number of others. *Local* means that the route was learned locally, not from another source like a neighboring router. This category is shown only in the console and not at the command prompt.

Connection Services

Two components can be used to assist in managing multiple remote access clients on a Windows 2000 network: Connection Point Services (CPS) and Connection Manager with the Connection Manager Administration Kit (CMAK). CPS enables an administrator to create phone books for clients and to automatically distribute and update them as needed. Clients, when out of the office, can use these phone books to dial up remote access servers, ISPs, or Internet access points. Clients do not have to manually configure any dial-up parameters because all options and configurations are already installed and configured automatically using CPS.

Connection Manager and the CMAK Wizard are used to provide an installation package that can be delivered to all of your clients so that their Connection Manager settings relate specifically to the organization and network they belong to. CMAK can be used to build custom service profiles and to customize features and support for remote access clients. The Connection Manager is used by the client to hold predefined dialing information.

The next two sections explain these two services, including requirements, installation, configuration, and management.

Connection Point Services

CPS has two components that need to be configured before you install and use the Connection Manager. These two components are the Phone Book Service (PBS) and the Phone Book Administrator (PBA). PBS provides phone book files to clients, and PBA is used to create and maintain the phone book files. If you use PBA to maintain these files, then as clients log on to the network, they can be configured to download new phone book information automatically. Automating this process for clients can help reduce calls to help desks and technical support personnel because users always have the most up-to-date information about dial-up lines and configurations.

The first step in using Connection Services is to install and configure CPS. Before installing CPS though, make sure the server has met the following requirements:

- IIS 5 must be installed on the computer acting as the CPS server. IIS can be installed from Windows Components within Add/Remove Programs in Control Panel.

- Both FTP and WWW services must be present, although FTP can be disabled when you're not publishing new phone books. Uninstalling FTP will uninstall PBS.

- Consider the load on the new CPS server, and consider making it a dedicated CPS server.

- If multiple servers will run PBS, determine ahead of time how and when those servers will be replicated.

Installing Phone Book Service and Phone Book Administrator

Installing these components is as simple as selecting the appropriate component from the Windows Component Wizard, accessed from Add/Remove Programs in Control Panel. To install CPS, perform the following steps:

1. As an administrator, log on to the server to be used as a CPS server.

2. Open Control Panel and choose Add/Remove Programs.

3. Click on Add/Remove Windows Components.

4. Highlight Management And Monitoring Tools, and click on the Details button.

5. Check the Connection Manager Components checkbox, and choose OK. When prompted, choose Finish.

To install PBA, perform the following steps:

1. As an administrator, log on to the server to be used as a CPS server.

2. From the Windows 2000 Server CD, open the Value Add folder, then the MSFT folder, then the PBA folder.

3. Double-click on pbainst.exe, and choose Yes to verify that you want to install PBA.

4. Restart the computer when the installation is complete.

Using Phone Book Service and Phone Book Administrator

To use PBS, you'll first create a phone book and then publish it. In this section, you'll learn to do both. To create a phone book, perform the following steps:

1. Log on to the CPS server as an administrator.

2. Choose Start|Programs|Administrative Tools|Phone Book Administrator. See Figure 12.9.

3. Choose File|New Phone Book and type in the name of the phone book you're creating.

4. Highlight the new phone book, and choose Tools|Options.

5. Type in the server address, plus a user name and password that will be used to manage the phone book.

6. Choose Edit|Add POP. (POP stands for point-of-presence and represents an access point to the Internet.)

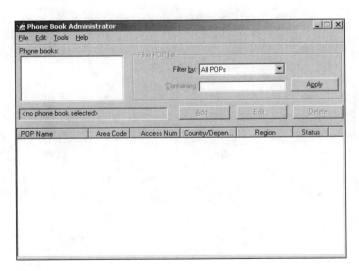

Figure 12.9
Phone Book Administrator.

7. On the Access Information tab, type the POP name, the country, the region, the area code, the access number, and the status.

8. On the Settings tab, select the POP settings. These might not need to be changed. By default, Sign On, Modem, ISDN, and Multicast are checked. Other options include Sign Up, Surcharge, and Custom 1 and 2. You can also set the minimum and maximum analog speeds and add a Dial-Up Networking entry. Choose OK.

Securing the Server

Before publishing the new phone book, you should secure the server. Make sure the following precautions and settings are configured:

- For the C:\Program Files\Phone Book Service and C:\Program Files\PBA files, make sure that only administrators and the appropriate groups have access. Also, remove the check from the checkbox Allow Inheritable Permissions From Parent To Propagate To This Object.

- In Internet Services Manager, accessed through Administrative Tools, enable Write access to the FTP virtual directory that will be used for Phone Book Services. You might want to enable Write access while you're publishing a phone book and then remove it again after you've completed the procedure. Figure 12.10 shows the PBSData Properties dialog box, accessed by right-clicking on PBSData under the Default FTP Site folder.

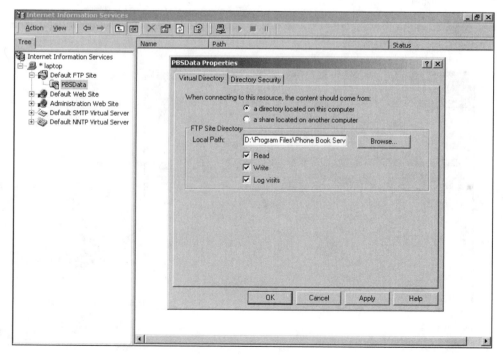

Figure 12.10
The PBSData Properties dialog box.

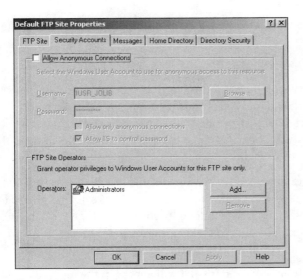

Figure 12.11
The Default FTP Site Properties dialog box.

- From Internet Services Manager, right-click on the Default FTP Site folder, and choose Properties. Figure 12.11 shows the Default FTP Site Properties dialog box. On the Security Accounts tab, uncheck Allow Anonymous Connections. Choose Yes to verify this action. This allows access for users who need to publish phone books to this server.

Publishing a Phone Book

Before you publish a phone book, make sure you've configured the security settings mentioned in the previous section; the PBSData FTP directory must have Write access. Then, to publish a phone book, perform the following steps:

1. Log on to the CPS server as an administrator.

2. Choose Start|Programs|Administrative Tools|Phone Book Administrator.

3. Choose Tools|Publish Phone Book.

4. Browse to where the phone book files will be stored, or specify a location.

5. Choose Create and then Post.

Connection Manager

Connection Manager is a software utility that works with CPS and is used for managing clients and their connections to your servers or the Internet. The Connection Manager, which comes with Connection Manager Administration Kit (CMAK), can be used to build service profiles for clients, to customize the logon messages and graphics users see when they connect using Connection Manager, to simplify distribution of the profiles and customizations, and to provide custom phone books for users who dial in. The distribution of these files can be integrated with a distribution of Internet Explorer for even more functionality.

CMAK Wizard Components

When running the CMAK Wizard, you'll need to provide lots of information. It is best to understand what will be required and make decisions regarding those items before starting the wizard. While you're reading through the following list, make notes or obtain the required information to make the installation go more smoothly. Following are the items you'll need to configure in the wizard:

- *Service Profile Source*—You can create a new service profile or edit an existing one, and you can create as many profiles as you need. You might want to create one profile for mobile users, one for home users, one for Windows 9x clients, and one for Windows NT or Windows 2000 clients. If you need only to make minor changes to a profile for a different group of users, you can edit a similar profile instead of creating a new one.

- *Service and File Names*—The service name is what will appear in the logon dialog box, the Connection Manager title bar, the taskbar, and other locations, so an appropriate service name should be chosen. It can be about 40 characters long, depending on capitalization, punctuation, and the like. The file name is used by the wizard to identify the file, and it must follow the 8.3 rule for file naming. You can't use special characters such as ! , ; = / \ : ' " < or > or extended character sets. Both names can be the same if all rules are followed.

- *Merged Service Profiles*—If any other service profiles exist, their information can be merged into this profile. Merging another profile allows this (referencing) profile to include other (merged) profiles while appearing as a single profile to users. This option allows you to support a wide range of users and to combine local area profiles with remote access profiles for certain users on the network that use both.

- *Support Information*—When users log on, they do so using a Logon dialog box. You can personalize this Logon box with a phone number for customer service or tech support. This information can be about 50 characters long.

- *Realm Name*—You can specify a realm name if your service requires it and if you don't want your users to type it in. This name can be an IAS or RADIUS server (described later in this chapter). You do not always have to type in a realm name.

- *Dial-Up Networking Entries*—On this wizard page, you can add phone book and dial-up networking entries that correspond to previous PBA entries. You can also configure these entries to correspond to specific DNS or WINS servers, or run a dial-up networking script. By default, the entry will allow the server to assign those addresses. When you're adding these entries, the name of each entry must be exactly like the entry in the phone book, including capitalization and spelling.

- *VPN Support*—If you want to include support for VPN connections for either this profile or a merged one, you can select the box from the VPN Support page. This is not required, but if you choose to add support, you'll see another configuration page, the VPN Connection page:

- *VPN Connection*—Here, you can type in the server address of the VPN server and choose to allow the server to assign an address to the client, or you can configure DNS and WINS addresses for this profile manually. To simplify the process for dial-up clients, you can also check the checkbox Use The Same User Name And Password For A VPN Connection As For A Dial-Up Connection.

- *Connect Actions*—You can configure certain actions to occur during the logon process; you can select pre-connect actions, pre-tunnel actions, post-connect actions, or disconnect actions. The pre-tunnel and post-connect actions are for VPN connections such as downloading new phone book entries or running certain programs. These settings can be configured for dial-up or direct connections and can be included in the service profile for these users. All four action types are checked by default. If all four are left checked, four other screens follow, one for each connect action. Actions can be added from each screen; programs can be found by browsing to them; and programs can be configured to run for dial-up clients, direct-connect clients, or both. In the Post-Connect Actions screen, Automatically Download Phone-Book Entries is checked by default.

- *Auto-Applications*—After the connection has been established between the client and the server, auto-applications can be run. These applications are run every time a client connects to the service, and when the application is closed, the connection to the service is terminated. This type of auto-application can be used for email clients and database connections. The programs are not mandatory.

- *Custom Graphics*—When clients log on, they access the network through the Logon dialog box. By default, this Logon box uses the default Windows bitmap. You can change this bitmap by browsing to the one you want. The recommended size of the new bitmap is 330×141 pixels because this is the size at which it will be displayed in the Logon box. These bitmaps must also be 256-color. Phone book bitmaps can also be customized; they must be 114×304 pixels for best results and use 256 colors. You might want to choose a company logo or similar bitmap for these options.

- *Phone Book*—On the Phone Book page, you can specify a phone book file and specify text that should appear when clients choose numbers from the More Access Numbers box. See Figure 12.12.

- *Phone-Book Updates*—If a phone book isn't specified on the Phone Book page, you'll have to specify one that will be downloaded when clients log on. If a phone book is specified on the Phone Book page, you can still type in the name of the server that will hold downloadable phone book files for users. These files can be downloaded automatically each time a user logs on.

- *Icons*—You can use the default icon for the profile, title bar, and status-area screens, or you can add your own. Icons should be close to the suggested bitmap size, or distortion will occur when they're used.

12

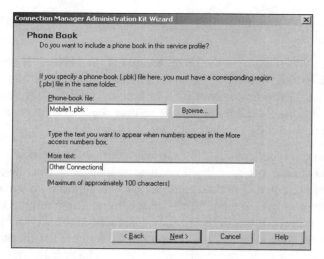

Figure 12.12
The Phone Book page of the CMAK Wizard.

- *Status-Area-Icon Menu*—You can configure what users will see when they right-click on the status-area icon while logged on to the service. If you choose Add here, you can type in the command name and specify how it will appear on the shortcut menu, specify the path to the program to run, and specify any necessary parameters. You can also choose to include this program in the service profile. See Figure 12.13 for this page.

- *Help File*—For larger organizations with an extensive technical support department, a high need for technical support for clients, and multiple in-house help files, you can configure a custom help file for clients. This help file may contain FAQs, links to Web sites, support phone numbers, or documentation of problems. By default, the built-in Connection Manager help files are used.

- *Connection Manager Software*—If users are not currently set up with Connection Manager 1.2 and don't yet have it installed, check the box to include the Connection Manager 1.2 software.

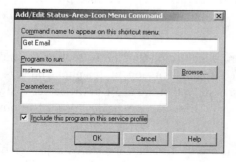

Figure 12.13
The Add/Edit Status-Area-Icon Menu Command dialog box.

- *License Agreement*—If you are creating this profile for users of a service provided by an ISP or other commercial entity, you can add a license agreement to this profile. Users will have to accept the terms of the agreement before the installation is performed. This option is not required.

- *Additional Files*—You can include any other files, software, documentation, or programs that you want included in this profile. This might be your company's logo for background wallpaper, a software package for email or the Internet, or a program for creating company documents.

Using the CMAK Wizard

In this section, you'll learn how to create a profile by using the CMAK Wizard, create dial-up networking entries, create custom graphics for users, and more. Working through the wizard is a lengthy and sometimes complex process, and it requires lots of configuration information. Make sure you have the required information and the time to complete the wizard before starting.

To use the CMAK Wizard, perform the following steps:

1. As an administrator, log on to the computer that will serve as the CPS server.

2. Open Control Panel, and choose Add/Remove Programs.

3. Choose Add/Remove Windows Components, select Management And Monitoring Tools, and check Connection Manager Components if it isn't already checked. Choose Next and then Finish. (If the Management And Monitoring Tools component is already installed, choose Cancel.)

4. Choose Start|Programs|Administrative Tools|Connection Manager Administration Kit. The CMAK Wizard begins.

5. Work through the wizard, and refer to the previous section if you need more information on any particular component. When the wizard finishes, you'll see a screen, shown in Figure 12.14, that displays the service profile's file name and location.

Setting Up the Clients

Now that a phone book and a service profile have been created, you can set up the clients. In this section, I'll explain how to do this manually, but there are other options, especially when using CMAK with Internet Explorer Administration Kit.

To set up clients, perform the following steps:

1. Log on to the CPS server as an administrator.

2. Locate the service profile created in the previous section. The default is C:\Program Files\CMAK\Profiles\<name of profile>\<name of profile>.exe. Share the Profiles folder or the <name of profile> folder.

Figure 12.14
CMAK Wizard completion.

3. From the client computer, open My Network Places and choose Add Network Place.

4. Browse to the shared folder containing the profile; this will be the CMAK folder. Choose Next and then Finish to complete the wizard.

5. From the CMAK folder, double-click on the executable profile, and verify that you want to install the profile.

6. From the first configuration screen, choose to make this connection available for all users or only one user. Place a checkmark in the Add A Shortcut checkbox to add a shortcut to the desktop for this user. See Figure 12.15.

7. From the Profile dialog box, shown in Figure 12.16, test the connection by typing in a user name, password, and domain.

Figure 12.15
Client configuration.

Figure 12.16
Client logon setup.

Advanced Remote Access

Although it seems like RRAS has been fairly complex and complete up to this point, there are some additional components and advanced features that can be configured. In small networks with only three or four client computers, Internet Connection Sharing can be configured. In small offices with TCP/IP clients, Network Address Translation can be used to allow private networks using an internal TCP/IP addressing scheme to access the Internet by using a valid IP address. In larger networks, RADIUS servers can be configured to authenticate dial-up users, and Internet Authentication Service can be used to authenticate dial-up users and demand-dial clients.

In this section, you'll learn how to configure these components and advanced features. In large networks with multiple offices and physical locations, a combination of these components might be used.

Internet Connection Sharing

Internet Connection Sharing (ICS) is an easy way to configure a small home office with only a few computers to share a single Internet connection. ICS not only allows users to share an Internet connection but also dynamically allocates IP addresses to those clients. Name resolution is also automatically configured, and the Windows 2000 computer that is acting as the ICS computer is the network's gateway to the Internet. There are two ways to set up ICS: by creating a new connection or editing an existing one.

Configuring ICS

To create a new connection and configure ICS on a small network, perform the following steps:

1. As an administrator, log on to the computer that has an Internet connection to be shared with others.

2. Choose Start|Settings|Network And Dial-Up Connections|Make New Connection, and choose Next to start the Network Connection Wizard.

3. Work through the wizard, creating the connection to your ISP. When the wizard finishes, test the connection by logging on.

4. Choose Start|Settings|Network And Dial-Up Connections|<connection name>, and choose Properties.

5. On the Sharing tab, check the Enable Internet Connection Sharing For This Connection checkbox, and check Enable On-Demand Dialing if necessary for your clients. See Figure 12.17.

Note: *You can edit an existing connection for ICS by performing Steps 4 and 5.*

If you decide later that certain applications aren't working properly over the shared connection, you can add those applications by using the Settings button shown in Figure 12.17. From here, you can add the name of the application, the remote server port number, and the incoming response ports. Doing this will improve the applications and their functionality.

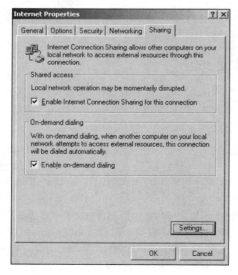

Figure 12.17
Configuring ICS.

ICS Limitations

ICS can be used successfully for only the smallest networks. There are several reasons for this, and those reasons are generally related to how ICS assigns internal TCP/IP addresses. When you're deciding if ICS is right for your network or if another solution would be better, consider the following:

- You must be logged on as an administrator to enable ICS.

- ICS should not be used on a network with more than one domain controller.

- ICS should not be used on a network using DHCP or DNS.

- ICS should not be used if any computers on the network have a static IP address.

- The ICS computer needs two interfaces: a connection to the Internet (generally a modem), and a connection to the LAN (generally a network adapter).

- The ICS computer becomes the DHCP server for the network.

- The DHCP allocator cannot be modified, nor can the range of private IP addresses used.

- The DNS proxy cannot be disabled.

- The range of IP addresses allocated to clients on the home network is in the range of 192.168.x.y with a subnet mask of 255.255.255.0.

- The ICS computer's internal interface will be given a static TCP/IP address of 192.168.0.1. Any previous static address will be overwritten, causing problems if that IP address was used for connecting to other computers before ICS was enabled.

- Only one IP address can be configured for connecting to the Internet.

If any of these limitations prohibits you from using ICS on your local network, consider using Network Address Translation instead. NAT does not have most of the limitations listed here, and it can usually be used when ICS can't be.

Network Address Translation

Network Address Translation (NAT) is most often used to connect small home offices to the Internet. To connect to the Internet, a client (or network) needs at least one unique and valid IP address assigned by an Internet authority such as InterNIC. In a smaller network, the user's ISP usually assigns this IP address. In a small network, the IP addresses used privately are generally not valid on the Internet; they are not assigned by an Internet authority and cannot be used legally. NAT enables these clients to access the Internet when necessary and offers a valid IP address while they are accessing the World Wide Web. Once the user is back on the private network, his or her private IP address is used. NAT is basically a translator of private addresses to globally unique IP addresses when users of a small network need to access the Internet.

Before deciding to implement NAT on a small network, consider the following:

- DHCP and NAT cannot be used together. NAT has addressing components similar to DHCP, and clients cannot distinguish between the two.

- DHCP Relay Agent cannot be used for the same reasons.

- IPSec does not work with NAT, but PPTP VPN does. Clients who use IPSec and L2TP cannot also use NAT because of issues with protocol packets and how they are translated by NAT.

- If NAT is configured to perform name resolution services, then WINS and DNS cannot also be used.

To configure the network to use NAT and a dial-up connection to the Internet through an ISP, you need to configure both the server and the clients. To configure the server, perform the following steps:

Note: The following procedure assumes that the Routing and Remote Access Service has already been enabled. If RRAS hasn't been enabled yet, and you want to set up NAT, use the RRAS Setup Wizard to set up an Internet connection server, and choose NAT. The wizard will walk you through the steps:

1. As an administrator, log on locally to the remote access server.

2. Right-click on My Network Places, choose Properties, and then right-click on the connection for the internal network.

3. Highlight TCP/IP, and choose Properties.

4. For the internal network interface, configure the NIC with an IP address of 192.168.0.1 and a subnet mask of 255.255.255.0. Do not configure a gateway.

Note: This IP address is based on 192.168.x.y, and any IP address in that range can be used. For this example, I'll use 192.168.0.1.

5. Choose Start|Programs|Administrative Tools|Routing And Remote Access to open the Routing and Remote Access console.

6. Expand the RRAS tree and IP routing, and right-click on Ports. Choose Properties.

7. On the Devices tab, highlight the device to configure, and choose Configure.

8. In the Configure Device dialog box, choose Demand-Dial Routing Connections (Inbound And Outbound), and choose OK.

9. In the RRAS tree, right-click on Routing Interfaces, and choose New Demand-Dial Interface. When the Demand Dial Interface Wizard starts, choose Next.

10. Type the interface name. The default name is Remote Router.

11. Choose the connection type: modem, ISDN adapter, or other physical device; or virtual private networking.

12. Select all of the transports and security options needed.

13. Depending on what you chose on the previous page, fill in the required information for the users, protocols, etc., and complete the wizard.

14. In the RRAS tree, right-click on Static Routes, and choose New Static Route. See Figure 12.18.

15. In the Interface drop-down list, choose the interface to use for the default route.

16. In the Destination And Network Mask text box, type "0.0.0.0".

17. If the interface is a demand-dial interface, select Use The Route To Initiate Demand-Dial Connections. If the interface is for a LAN connection, type the IP address of the router that is on the same network segment as the LAN interface.

18. In the Metric drop down list, choose 1. Click OK.

19. Under IP Routing, right-click on General, and choose New Routing Protocol.

20. Select Network Address Translation (NAT), and choose OK.

21. Right-click on NAT and choose New Interface. Click OK.

22. Highlight the interface to add, and choose OK. See Figure 12.19.

    - If this interface connects to the Internet, then select the General tab, and choose Public Interface Connected To The Internet and Translate TCP/UDP Headers (Recommended).

    - If this interface connects to the internal network, then select the General tab, and choose Private Interface Connected To Private Network.

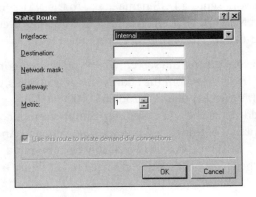

Figure 12.18
Static Route.

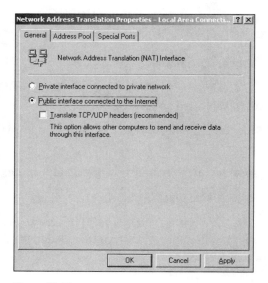

Figure 12.19
Private and public interfaces.

Note: Both interfaces must be available and configured for NAT to work properly.

23. In the left pane of the RRAS tree, right-click on NAT, and choose Properties.

24. On the Address Assignment tab, check Automatically Assign IP Addresses By Using DHCP.

25. If necessary, configure the range of IP addresses to allocate in the IP Address, Exclude, and Mask areas.

26. To enable name resolution, select the Name Resolution tab and check Clients Using Domain Name System, DNS. If you want the connection to the Internet to be initiated when a host on the private network sends a DNS name query to the NAT computer, check Connect To The Public Network When A Name Needs To Be Resolved, and choose the appropriate demand-dial interface from the drop-down list.

Configuring clients is much easier than configuring the server. When you're configuring clients, just make sure that they use an IP address from the address range 192.168.x.y and that it is unique. The subnet mask for the clients is 255.255.255.0. The default gateway and DNS server both use the address of the NAT computer. Simply configuring the clients to use DHCP will configure all of this on a Windows 2000 network. Any client using Windows 2000, Windows NT, or Windows 9x will probably be configured automatically to use DHCP, so there is the chance that you won't need to configure the clients' settings.

Internet Authentication Service

The Internet Authentication Service (IAS) in Windows 2000 allows administrators to create a RADIUS (Remote Authentication Dial-In User Service) server, also called an IAS server, to authenticate forwarded requests from other network servers for the purpose of logging clients on to the network and managing those users. IAS uses the RADIUS protocol to provide centralized authentication, authorization, auditing, and accounting in conjunction with Windows 2000 RRAS servers. When more than one RRAS server exists, or if multiple dial-in clients need to be centrally managed and authenticated, an IAS server can be used to maintain, in a central location, a place to manage all of these entities.

Corporate networks use IAS servers for centralized management of users and accounts; ISPs also use IAS. The IAS server has access to all user information, can check credentials, can audit time used by clients, and can keep detailed records for billing purposes. Clients do not connect directly to the IAS server, though; instead, they connect to a server such as a Network Access Server, a Windows 2000 RAS server, or a Windows 2000 domain controller, all of which can forward requests to the IAS server. The IAS server then authenticates the client, manages the client's time, and sends information back to the forwarding server to send on to the client.

Using an IAS server provides the benefits of centralized administration of multiple RRAS servers and forwarders, and provides the auditing and accounting benefits of maintaining all of the information in one place. Here are some other reasons to use IAS servers:

- RADIUS is fault tolerant, and multiple IAS servers can be configured to serve as backup servers as necessary.

- Remote access policies can be integrated with accounting and authentication to provide one location that contains all required information for users who log on to the network.

- IAS supports PPP and can be used in many environments.

- IAS can authenticate users with a range of methods, from using clear text passwords to using smart cards.

- IAS supports AppleTalk Remote Access Protocol (ARAP).

- Some of the accounting features include logging successes, rejections, lockouts, and attempts to access the network illegally.

Installing an IAS Server

To install an IAS server, perform the following steps:

1. As an administrator, log on to the server that will act as the IAS server.

2. Open Control Panel, and choose Add/Remove Programs.

3. Choose Add/Remove Windows Components.

4. Highlight Networking Services, and click on Details.

5. Check the Internet Authentication Service checkbox, and choose OK, Next, and Finish.

6. Choose Start|Programs|Administrative Tools|Internet Authentication Service to start IAS. See Figure 12.20.

7. Choose Action|Register Service In Active Directory.

Configuring the IAS Server

With IAS installed, you can begin configuring the server. To configure the IAS server, perform the following steps:

1. As an administrator, log on to the IAS server.

2. Choose Start|Programs|Administrative Tools|Internet Authentication Service to start IAS.

3. Right-click on Internet Authentication Service (Local), and choose Properties.

4. On the Service tab, type a description of the server. Accept the defaults to log rejected or discarded authentication requests and to log successful authentication requests.

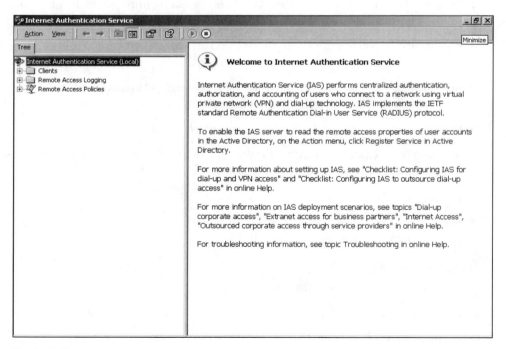

Figure 12.20
Welcome to Internet Authentication Service.

5. On the RADIUS tab, provide the UDP ports that should be used for accounting and authentication. There are two for each by default, and these are usually sufficient. Different ISPs or vendors of network access servers might require a different number here; if so, provide those numbers as necessary.

6. On the Realms tab, you can specify rules for processing user names in all requests. By choosing Add, you can type in text you want to find in a user name and replace it with something else. The realm name is used to identify where the request should go and is used with the user name. If realm names are used, then realm name replacement must be configured. Choose OK when you're finished.

7. Right-click on the Clients folder, and choose New Client.

8. In the Add Client dialog box, type a friendly name for the client, and choose a proto-col. Remember, this is not a user; it is a network access server that will forward requests to the IAS server. The RADIUS protocol is selected by default.

9. In the Client Information box, type the IP or DNS address of the client. If the client should always send the signature attribute in its request, check the checkbox. Type in a shared secret and confirm it. Choose Finish.

10. Highlight the Remote Access Logging folder. Right-click on Local File in the right pane, and choose Properties.

11. On the Settings tab, choose the events to log. Remember, logging takes its toll on a server and should be configured conservatively. This tab provides three logging options:

    • *Log Accounting Requests*—Accounting starts and stops (recommended)

    • *Log Authentication Requests*—Access accepts and rejects (recommended)

    • *Log Periodic Status*—Interim accounting requests

12. On the Local File tab, specify the log file format (database-compatible or IAS), and specify how often to log events (daily, weekly, monthly, unlimited file size, or when the file reaches a certain size). If you need to change the log file directory, you can do that here also. Choose OK.

13. Highlight the Remote Access Policies folder in the left pane. In the right pane, notice the configured policies. You can configure remote access policies for the IAS server as needed from this folder.

Monitoring and Optimization

There's a lot more to running a remote access server than just installing it and configur-ing clients. The day-to-day activities for managing RRAS are the same as for managing a Windows 2000 domain controller. Clients have to be managed, the server has to be monitored, and logging and auditing have to be used appropriately. You'll also need a good remote access group policy, and you'll need to know what tools are available to troubleshoot and manage routing. In this section, all of these monitoring and optimization options will be covered in detail.

Managing Remote Access Clients

To manage remote access clients, you'll need to be able to see who's connected, disconnect clients if necessary, and send messages to those clients.

Figure 12.21 shows the options available for managing clients through the Routing and Remote Access console. Managing clients through this console is as simple as right-clicking on them and choosing the appropriate command. To disconnect a client, choose Disconnect; to see the status of a client, choose Status.

To send a message to one client or to all remote access clients, choose the Send Message command or the Send To All command. Figures 12.22 and 12.23 show the Send Message dialog box from the remote access server and how the message looks when received by the remote access client. The message box for the client is placed on top of any running application.

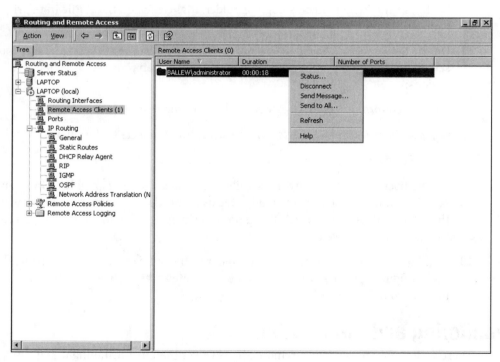

Figure 12.21
Client management.

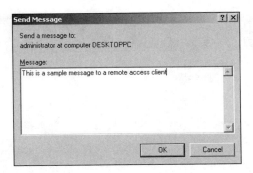

Figure 12.22
Sending a message from a remote access server.

Figure 12.23
Receiving a message at the remote access client.

Using Computer Management and the RRAS Snap-In

You don't have to use the RRAS console for administration of your remote access server and clients. There are two other options. The first option is to administer RRAS through the Computer Management console, and the second is to add the RRAS snap-in to an individualized MMC.

To open RRAS through the Computer Management console, choose Start|Programs|Administrative Tools|Computer Management. You'll have to expand the Services And Applications tree and choose Routing And Remote Access. This is my favorite console because just about everything I need is already located here. Figure 12.24 shows this console and the Routing And Remote Access folder.

Notice also that Event Viewer is available, as are System Information, Performance Logs And Alerts, Device Manager, DHCP, DNS, and many other utilities you'll need to access when you're monitoring and optimizing the RRAS server. Some of these options, as they relate to RRAS, will be discussed later in this section.

Using the Counters in the Performance Console

Another way to optimize the remote access server is to monitor it by using the Performance console. The data that is collected can be compiled in many forms, including reports, logs, or graphs, and it can be configured to sound alerts when certain thresholds are met. (For more information on the Performance console, see Chapter 8.)

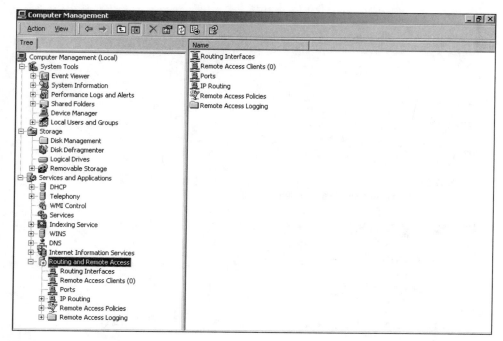

Figure 12.24
Computer Management.

The Performance console provides several counters that relate to the routing and remote access server, IAS clients and servers, and RAS ports. Although listing all of the counters and their uses here would be informative, there are way too many to list and describe effectively. In this section, I'll list the counters I've used to monitor and optimize my RRAS server and describe what I've used those counters for.

Note: *Generally these counters are used to create baselines and to monitor routing and remote access activity. Baselines and cutoffs for many of these counters are specific to individual networks. The best way to use Performance Monitor with the RRAS service is to know how the remote access server reacts under stress and how it reacts when the load is light. From there, you'll be able to judge when problems occur by comparing current counters to established baselines.*

Network Segment

Network segment counters are generally used to monitor WAN utilization on a network and are available only if the Network Monitor driver has been installed. The network segment counters most often used include the following:

- *% Network Utilization*—This is the percentage of network bandwidth in use on a network segment at any given time. If the percentage is above 40, collisions may begin to cause problems.

- *Broadcast Frames Received/Second*—This is used to develop a baseline over a monitored period of time. High numbers of broadcasts cause performance problems, but these numbers are individual for every network.

- *Total Frames Received/Second*—Thresholds depend on the particular network, but high numbers generally mean that routers and bridges might be overloaded.

Network Interface

The network interface counters are used to determine how well the network interfaces are working. In Figure 12.25, notice the choices under Select Instances From List. In this example, there are four network interfaces: the USB to Ethernet Converter, the internal loopback interface for a 127.0.0 network, the internal RAS interface for dial-in clients, and the IP-in-IP (Tunnel) interface. You can choose to monitor all instances or only specific ones. The network interface counters I use most often are listed next, and their thresholds depend on the type of network being monitored and the physical interfaces to those networks.

Here are the network interface counters I use most often:

- *Bytes Total/Sec*—The rate at which bytes—including the framing characters—are sent and received on the interface(s) selected.

- *Current Bandwidth*—An estimate of the interface's current bandwidth, measured in bits per second.

- *Packets Outbound Errors*—The number of outbound packets that could not be transmitted due to errors in the packets.

- *Packets Received Errors*—The number of inbound packets that could not be received due to errors in the packets.

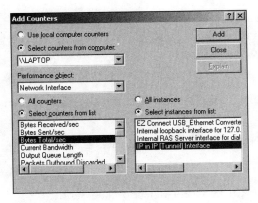

Figure 12.25
Adding network interface counters.

IAS Accounting Server

The IAS accounting server counters are available only if IAS has been installed on the server. There are more than 25 counters for this one performance object, and only a few would ever be used at any given time. Listed next are a few of those counters and their characteristics:

- *Server Up Time*—The time elapsed since the server was started.

- *Accounting Requests/Sec*—The rate at which packets are received on the accounting port.

- *Accounting Responses/Sec*—The rate at which RADIUS packets are sent to the client.

- *Bad Authenticators*—The number of packets sent to the server with invalid Signature attributes.

- *Dropped Packets*—The number of packets that were dropped due to reasons other than having bad authenticators, having unknown types, or being malformed.

- *Invalid Requests*—The number of packets that were received from unknown users or addresses.

- *Malformed Packets*—The number of malformed packets received at the server. Malformed packets are unexpected packets; they can be the result of incorrectly configured vendor-specific attributes.

- *Packets Received*—The total number of packets received.

- *Packets Sent*—The total number of packets sent.

- *Unknown Type*—The total number of packets of unknown origin.

IAS Accounting Clients

Counters for the most-often-used IAS accounting client objects are the same as the counters listed previously for IAS accounting servers. The only difference in the most-used list is that the client object does not contain a Server Up Time counter.

IAS Authentication Server

There are more than 25 counters available for the IAS authentication server. Some of the most-used counters are:

- *Access Accepts*—The total number of RADIUS Accept-Accept packets sent.

- *Access Challenges*—The total number of RADIUS Accept-Challenge packets sent.

- *Access Rejects*—The total number of RADIUS Accept-Reject packets sent.

- *Access Requests*—The total number of packets received on this port.

Note: *For more information on how IAS authenticates users and on the processes involved, consult the Microsoft online help.*

- *Bad Authenticators*—The number of packets that contained invalid Signature attributes.

- *Dropped Packets*—The number of incoming packets that were discarded for reasons other than being malformed, having bad authenticators, or having unknown types.

- *Invalid Requests*—The number of packets received from unknown addresses.

- *Malformed Packets*—The number of malformed packets received that were not bad authenticators or unknown types.

- *Packets Received*—The total number of packets received.

- *Packets Sent*—The total number of packets sent.

- *Server Up Time*—The amount of time that has elapsed since the server was started.

- *Unknown Type*—The number of packets of unknown type which were received.

IAS Authentication Clients

Counters for the most-often-used IAS authentication client objects are the same as the counters listed previously for IAS authentication servers. The only difference in the most-used list is that the client object does not contain a Server Up Time counter.

RAS Port

In a RAS server, there are devices and ports. Devices are physical cards, such as network interface cards, and those devices contain ports so that point-to-point connections can be made with remote access clients. Each port allows a single connection. Ports can be configured to accept inbound remote access connections, or both inbound and outbound demand-dial routing connections. When configuring the device, you can add a phone number and set a maximum number of ports. Figure 12.26 shows the Ports Properties dialog box, which you can open by right-clicking on the Ports folder in the Routing and Remote Access console. Figure 12.27 shows the ports available from inside Performance Console.

In Figure 12.27, notice that several ports are listed, and many are VPN ports. You can monitor all ports or only selected ones. When you're monitoring ports, several counters can be used. The following list does not contain all of the available counters; it contains only the most-used ones:

- *Alignment Errors*—The total number of errors that occurred due to bytes being received that weren't expected.

- *Buffer Overrun Errors*—The total number of errors that occurred due to data being received faster than it could be handled. This is a software-related problem.

- *Bytes Received*—The total number of bytes received for this connection.

- *Bytes Transmitted*—The total number of bytes transmitted on this connection.

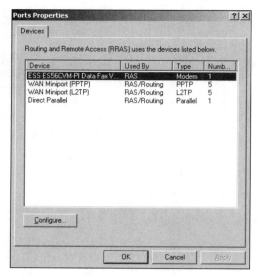

Figure 12.26
Ports available in the Routing and Remote Access console.

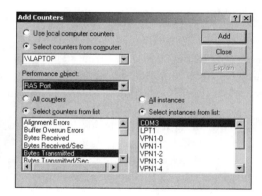

Figure 12.27
Ports available in the Performance console.

- *CRC Errors*—The total number of CRC (cyclical redundancy check) errors for this connection. These errors occur because a frame contains bad data.

- *Serial Overrun Errors*—Similar to buffer overrun errors, except that serial overrun errors occur when the hardware cannot handle the load placed on it and cannot handle the rate at which data is received.

- *Timeout Errors*—The total number of errors that occurred due to expected packets not being received on time.

- *Total Errors*—The total number of CRC, timeout, serial overrun, and buffer overrun errors for a connection.

RAS Total

RAS total counters are the counters I use most often to get a quick glance at how the RAS server is performing. Giving totals of all of the most-used counters in a single place, RAS total counters can be monitored to determine the general health of the RAS network. The following list contains all of the counters available, and all of the counters listed represent totals for the RAS server (all of these counters have been described in previous sections or are self-explanatory):

- Alignment Errors

- Buffer Overrun Errors

- Bytes Received

- Bytes Received/Sec

- Bytes Transmitted

- Bytes Transmitted/Sec

- CRC Errors

- Frames Received

- Frames Received/Sec

- Frames Transmitted

- Frames Transmitted/Sec

- Percent Compression In (see the following Note)

- Percent Compression Out (see the following Note)

- Serial Overrun Errors

- Timeout Errors

- Total Connections

- Total Errors

- Total Errors/Sec

Note: *When bytes are sent or received, they can be compressed. These counters are used to monitor this activity.*

The Performance Logs And Alerts Snap-In

The Performance Logs And Alerts snap-in can be used to create counter logs, trace logs, and alerts. Performance Logs And Alerts is located underneath System Monitor in the Performance console. For more information on Performance Logs And Alerts, see Chapter 8.

To configure a counter log for your RRAS server, open the Performance console, highlight Performance Logs And Alerts, and right-click on Counter Logs. Choose to create New Log Settings, and type in a name for the log. In the New Log dialog box, choose Add to add counters to this log. Add the counters you need from the Select Counters dialog box, and base your decisions on your needs and on the previously supplied information about those counters. This process is detailed in Chapter 8, but it is the same for creating trace logs and alerts. You can save these logs and view them in Notepad.

Alerts can also be configured for RAS events in general or for troubleshooting. Figure 12.28 shows an example of a new alert that will send a network message to an administrator when certain thresholds have been met.

Network Monitor

Network Monitor is a packet-sniffing utility that can be used to capture packets from the RAS server and bring them to a computer that is connecting with it. These captures contain lots of information about the connection. Although this version of Network Monitor is very basic, the information can still be useful. To read more about Network Monitor, see Chapter 8.

Figure 12.29 shows a capture from a remote access client to the remote access server. Notice that utilization is high while the client logs on and retrieves files from the remote access server.

Take a look at all of the information received during this capture. Many items are captured, including percent network utilization, frames per second, bytes per second, and

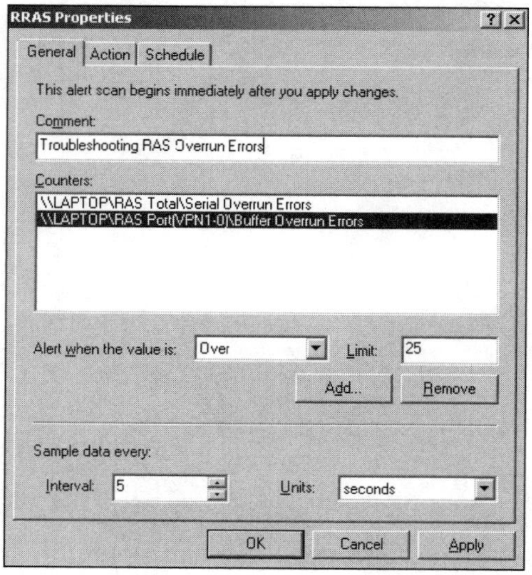

Figure 12.28
Creating an alert.

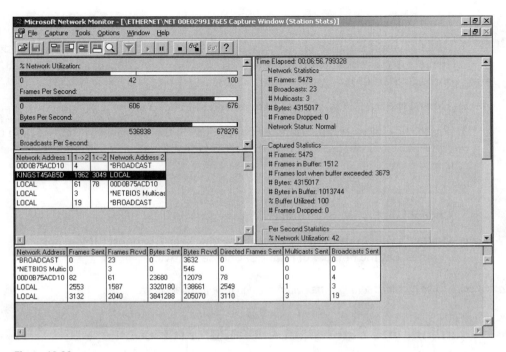

Figure 12.29
A Network Monitor capture.

broadcasts per second. There is also information about the network addresses, frames sent and received, bytes sent and received, and multicasts and broadcasts sent. Finally, network statistics—including number of frames, buffer sizes, errors, and MAC statistics—are included. Having these statistics can prove quite useful when you're troubleshooting specific connections and packet transmissions between the server and its clients.

RAS Idle Disconnect

When remote users dial into a network, a remote policy should be in place that disconnects those users automatically after a predefined period of idle time. Although this is configured in a remote access policy, which has been discussed previously, the RAS Idle Disconnect property needs a section all its own.

The RAS Idle Disconnect property prevents a logged-on user from leaving the computer for a long period of time while remaining connected to the network. An unattended remote access connection not only wastes bandwidth and costs network connection time over public or private lines, but also leaves the computer open to hackers while unattended. Using remote access policies, you can configure these connections to automatically disconnect after a certain period of idle time. Although 10 to 15 minutes seems like an appropriate length of time, making users reconnect unnecessarily isn't a good idea, either. For most users, 30 to 35 minutes is appropriate.

To configure the RAS Idle Disconnect property, perform the following steps:

1. As an administrator, log on to the remote access server, and access the Routing and Remote Access console through Computer Management, through a custom MMC, or through Start|Programs|Administrative Tools|Routing And Remote Access.

2. Expand the tree, and highlight Remote Access Policies in the left pane.

3. Right-click on an existing remote access policy in the left pane, or right-click in the right pane, and choose New Remote Access Policy. Create a policy if necessary before continuing.

4. Right-click on the policy, and choose Properties.

5. Choose Edit Profile in the Properties dialog box.

6. On the Dial-In Constraints tab, check the checkbox Disconnect If Idle For ___ Minutes. Set the number of minutes. Choose OK twice.

Tip: *You might also consider setting a maximum session time for clients here.*

Multilink and Bandwidth Allocation Protocol

As you know, Multilink and BAP are used together to combine multiple physical links to form a single logical link to enhance bandwidth and transmissions. For Multilink to be used, both the sender and the receiver must support it. Also, because Multilink uses several lines at once, callback isn't supported most of the time; callback can be configured with only one number, and Multilink can have several.

BAP can be used with Multilink to dynamically add or drop links as necessary. BAP supports PPP. BAP provides dial-up clients with additional phone numbers when extra bandwidth is needed and sends those numbers in messages to the users.

To configure the server to use Multilink and BAP, perform the following steps:

1. As an administrator, log on to the remote access server, and access the Routing and Remote Access console through Computer Management, through a custom MMC, or through Start|Programs|Administrative Tools|Routing And Remote Access.

2. Right-click on the server name, and choose Properties.

3. On the PPP tab, check the Multilink Connections checkbox and the Dynamic Bandwidth Control Using BAP Or BACP checkbox. Choose OK.

To configure a remote access policy that allows users to use Multilink and BAP, perform the following steps:

1. As an administrator, log on to the remote access server, and access the Routing and Remote Access console through Computer Management, through a custom MMC, or through Start|Programs|Administrative Tools|Routing And Remote Access.

2. Expand the tree, and highlight Remote Access Policies in the left pane.

3. Right-click on an existing remote access policy in the left pane, or right-click in the right pane, and choose New Remote Access Policy. Create a policy if necessary before continuing.

4. Right-click on the policy, and choose Properties.

5. Choose Edit Profile in the Properties dialog box.

6. On the Multilink tab, choose the Allow Multilink option.

7. In Limit Maximum Ports, accept the default of 2.

8. In the Bandwidth Allocation Protocol (BAP) Settings area, accept the defaults of reducing the multilink connection by one line if the lines fall below 50 percent for a period of 2 minutes. Both of these numbers can be changed as required.

9. To require BAP for dynamic Multilink requests, check this checkbox. Choose OK twice.

Note: *More advanced remote access policies will be discussed later in this section.*

Configuring Remote Access Logging

If you've configured an IAS server, you've already seen the logging options that will be discussed here. RRAS supports logging of authentication and accounting information for PPP connections when authentication or accounting is enabled. This information can be used to determine who is accessing the remote access server and to troubleshoot remote access problems and policy issues. To configure logging for the remote access server, perform the following steps:

1. As an administrator, log on to the remote access server, and access the Routing and Remote Access console through Computer Management, through a custom MMC, or through Start|Programs|Administrative Tools|Routing And Remote Access.

2. Expand the tree, and highlight Remote Access Logging in the left pane.

3. In the right pane, right-click on Local File and choose Properties.

4. On the Settings tab, choose the events to log. Remember, logging takes its toll on a server and should be configured conservatively. This tab provides three logging options:

   • *Log Accounting Requests*—Accounting starts and stops (recommended)

   • *Log Authentication Requests*—Access accepts and rejects (recommended)

   • *Log Periodic Status*—Interim accounting requests

5. On the Local File tab, specify the log file format (database-compatible or IAS), and specify how often to log events (daily, weekly, monthly, unlimited file size, or when

the file reaches a certain size). If you need to change the log file directory, you can do that here. Choose OK.

You can view the log files by browsing to C:\Winnt\System32\LogFiles\iaslog.log. Listing 12.1 shows parts of a log file from a remote access user, who is an administrator, accessing a remote access server with all three of the log options checked. Keep in mind that there is quite a bit of information in these logs, but Listing 12.1 only shows a few of the entries in the log.

Listing 12.1   A sample iaslog.log file.

```
192.168.0.42,administrator,05/02/2001,
15:58:16,RAS,LAPTOP,6,2,7,1,5,11,61,0,77,
0x0D0A434F4E4E45435420323838303000D0A,4108,
192.168.0.42,0,,4147,311,4148,MSRASV5.00,4129,

BALLEW\administrator,25,311 1 192.168.0.42
04/30/2001 19:19:41 5,4130,Ballew.com/Users/Administrator,
4127,4,4136,1,4142,0
192.168.0.42,

administrator,05/02/2001,15:58:16,
RAS,LAPTOP,25,311 1 192.168.0.42 04/30/2001
19:19:41 5,4130,Ballew.com/Users/Administrator,
6,2,7,1,4149,Allow access if dial-in permission is
enabled,4127,4,4120,0x0042414C4C4557,4129,

BALLEW\administrator,4136,2,4142,0
192.168.0.42,administrator,05/02/2001,
15:58:16,RAS,LAPTOP,6,2,7,1,5,11,61,0,77,
0x0D0A434F4E4E45435420323838303000D0A,
25,311 1 192.168.0.42 04/30/2001
19:19:41 5,44,15,8,192.168.0.6,12,
1500,13,1,50,9,51,1,55,988837096,45,2,40,1,4108,
192.168.0.42,0,,4147,311,4148,MSRASV5.00,4120,
0x0042414C4C4557,4294967206,0,4136,4,4142,0
192.168.0.42,

"LAPTOP","RAS",05/02/2001,16:07:48,1,
"administrator","Ballew.com/Users/Administrator",,,,,,
"192.168.0.42",11,,"192.168.0.42",,,,0,
"0x0D0A434F4E4E45435420323838303000D0A",
1,2,4,,0,"311 1 192.168.0.42 04/30/2001 19:19:41
6",,,,,,,,,,,,,,,,,,,,,,,,,"MSRASV5.00",311,,,,
```

Although this log looks a bit scary, you can configure Microsoft Access or another database program to format it in a more readable layout. Each database works differently, though, and you'll need to configure your database to accept these logs so they will be easier to read than this type of layout.

The IAS log file includes a great deal of information, including the following (this is not a complete list):

- Computer name

- Service name

- Record date

- Record time

- Packet type

- Username

- Fully qualified username

- Called-station ID

- Calling-station ID

- Callback number

- Framed-IP address

- Client IP address

- Network access server (NAS) IP address

- Event type

As you can tell, logging can provide many answers when you're troubleshooting remote access servers and clients or solving remote access policy problems. However, much of the information shown in Listing 12.1 is useful only to Microsoft Support Personnel or professional troubleshooters.

Router Logging

You can configure the router to log errors as well as authentication and accounting for the routing and remote access server. Four levels of logging are available:

- *Log errors only*—Logs errors only in Event Viewer.

- *Log errors and warnings*—Logs errors and warnings in Event Viewer and is enabled by default.

- *Log the maximum amount of information*—Logs the maximum amount of information possible in Event Viewer. This option should be used only for troubleshooting and should be disabled after the problem has been solved.

- *Disable event logging*—Logs no events in Event Viewer.

To enable Event Logging, perform the following steps:

1. As an administrator, log on to the remote access server, and access the Routing and Remote Access console through Computer Management, through a custom MMC, or through Start|Programs|Administrative Tools|Routing And Remote Access.

2. Right-click on the server, and choose Properties.

3. On the Event Logging tab, select what should be logged. Choose OK.

To view the system log in Event Viewer, open Event Viewer from Administrative Tools and highlight the system log. Figure 12.30 shows a sample Event Viewer system log.

Creating a Remote Access Policy

Although you've already configured a few specific remote access policies to allow a user to dial in from a specific phone number and to configure the RAS Idle Disconnect property, the actual processes involved and the available options have not yet been discussed. When you're creating a policy, you'll use several options from the Conditions page, such as day and time restrictions for users, protocol options, and service types. In this section, you'll learn about the options, and you'll learn how to configure any type of remote access policy, what happens when a user tries to log on to a remote access server, and how policies are applied.

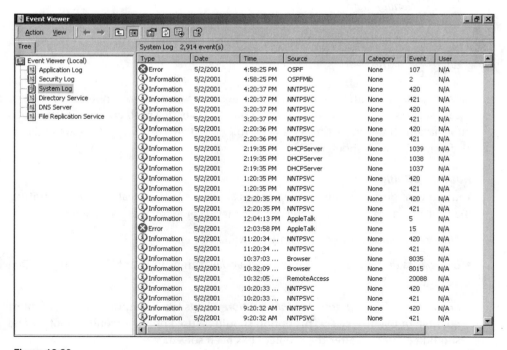

Figure 12.30
Event Viewer and a sample system log.

Conditions and Attributes

When you're creating a remote access policy from the Routing and Remote Access console, several conditions can be added. You are already familiar with a couple of these. At least one condition must be added to create a remote access policy.

Note: Some of these conditions work by pattern matching, which means that the character strings of the client and the server must match exactly. When a match is made, authentication procedures are begun.

The conditions are:

- *Called-Station-ID*—This is the number of the network access server. For this condition to work, all of the components of the connection must support caller ID, including the phone line, the hardware, and the hardware drivers. When prompted, simply type in the phone number of the NAS (network access server). This condition works using pattern matching.

- *Calling-Station-ID*—This is the phone number from where the remote access client is calling. For this condition to work, all of the components of the connection must support caller ID, including the phone line, the hardware, and the hardware drivers. When prompted, simply type in the phone number where the client will be calling from. This condition works using pattern matching.

- *Client-Friendly-Name*—This is the name of the RADIUS client computer that is requesting authentication. This string is for RADIUS (IAS) clients only. This condition works using pattern matching.

- *Client-IP-Address*—This is the IP address of the RADIUS client, a NAS server, and this condition works using pattern matching. This condition works for RADIUS (IAS) clients only.

- *Client-Vendor*—This is the vendor name of the NAS that is requesting authentication as a RADIUS client to an IAS server. Using this condition, you can create separate policies for different vendor machines, enhancing transmission, security, and throughput.

- *Day-And-Time-Restrictions*—This condition is used to specify on what days and times a user can be authenticated and allowed to connect to the server.

- *Framed-Protocol*—There are 12 available protocols—including PPP, SLIP, X.25, and AppleTalk Remote Access—that can be chosen for framing incoming packets. As many as are necessary can be chosen.

- *NAS-Identifier*—This is used to identify the NAS that originated a request. This condition is used for IAS clients only. This condition works using pattern matching.

- *NAS-IP-Address*—This is the IP address of the NAS. This condition works using pattern matching.

12

- *NAS-Port-Type*—This is used to specify what type of port the caller will be using. Choices include ADSL, Ethernet, ISDN, CPN, and X.25.

- *Service-Type*—This is used to specify what type of service the client has requested. Choices include Administrative, Callback, Framed, Login, Outbound, and Call Check.

- *Tunnel-Type*—This is used to specify what type of tunnel the client has requested. Choices include L2TP, IP-in-IP, and PPTP. Encryption and authentication can be further defined in these specific policy settings.

- *Windows-Groups*—This is used to represent the Windows groups that a user belongs to who is attempting to log on. No conditions exist for specific usernames, so group membership is very useful. Nested and universal groups can be used to simplify administration.

Creating a Remote Access Policy

To create a remote access policy, perform the following steps:

1. As an administrator, log on to the remote access server, and access the Routing and Remote Access console through Computer Management, through a custom MMC, or through Start|Programs|Administrative Tools|Routing And Remote Access.

2. Expand the IP Routing tree, and right-click on Remote Access Policies.

3. Choose New Remote Access Policy. The Remote Access Policy Wizard begins.

4. Type in a friendly name for the policy.

5. On the Conditions page, choose Add.

6. On the Select Attribute page, choose an attribute to configure, and choose Add.

7. In the resulting dialog box, type the character string to be matched exactly by the client and the server. Choose OK.

8. Continue to add conditions and attributes as necessary, and when you're finished, choose Next.

9. On the Permissions page, select Grant Remote Access Permissions or Deny Remote Access Permissions as needed for this configuration. Choose Next.

10. On the User Profile page, choose Edit Profile.

11. In the Edit Dial-In Profile dialog box, configure the following items as needed:

    - *Dial-In Constraints tab*—Idle disconnect time, maximum sessions, day and time logon restrictions, specific phone number and dial-in restrictions, and dial-in media restrictions (ADSL, Ethernet, CPN, and so on).

    - *IP tab*—Who will provide the IP address and how IP packet filters will be applied from the client and to the client during this connection.

- *Multilink tab*—Whether Multilink will be enabled for this connection and, if so, how many ports are available. Also, specify how BAP settings will be configured and at what capacity, and whether BAP is required for all dynamic Multilink requests.

- *Authentication tab*—Whether EAP will be used and what EAP type will be configured, which protocols are used (including MS-CHAP, MS-CHAP v2, CHAP, PAP, and SPAP), and whether remote PPP clients can connect without negotiating any authentication method.

- *Encryption tab*—The encryption for this profile (No Encryption, Basic, or Strong). These settings apply only to Windows 2000 Routing and Remote Access.

- *Advanced tab*—Additional attributes for this connection. Many attributes can be configured that weren't offered in the initial conditions configuration. Most of these attributes are vendor specific, and some of them are shown in Figure 12.31.

12. Choose Add and then Finish to complete the setup of the remote access policy.

How Policies Work

When clients attempt to be authorized on a remote access server, the client configuration must match at least one of the remote access policies. This match can be a phone number, an IP address, a friendly name, or any other number of things. When one of these matches is made, authentication processes begin. If no matches are made, authentication fails even if the client's account is configured to allow remote access.

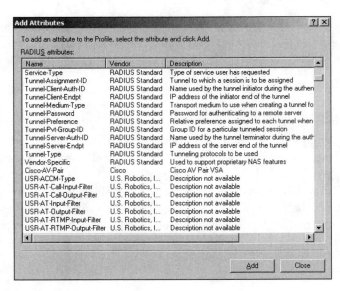

Figure 12.31
Additional attributes.

Following are the steps involved in the policy application process:

1. When a client first dials into a remote access server, the remote access server checks the policy list. If no policies exist, the request is rejected.

2. If policies do exist, they are checked one by one.

3. If the remote client does not match every condition in the first policy, the second policy is checked. This process continues until a matching policy is found or until there are no more policies to check.

4. If all policies are checked and no exact match is found, the request for authentication is rejected.

5. If a policy is found that matches, the remote client's access permissions are examined. If there is a Deny permission for remote access, for this server, or for this network, the request is denied; otherwise, authentication begins.

6. If authentication begins, the remote access server compares the remote user's configuration settings against the matching profile properties. If these conditions match, authentication continues; otherwise, authentication ends unsuccessfully.

7. If the remote access server has Control access set, the remote access server then checks its own permissions to see if it is configured to Grant remote access or Deny remote access. If the server is set to Control access, and that access is set to Deny remote access, the request is rejected. Otherwise, authentication continues.

8. If authentication continues, the remote access server compares the user's account permissions and properties to the profile's properties. If a match is found, authentication is completed; otherwise, authentication fails.

Decision Tree 12.1 shows this process in flowchart form.

Using Routing Tools

Some command-line routing tools may be helpful when you're troubleshooting or managing routers. Pathping, a combination of both PING and Tracert, can be used in troubleshooting routing problems. Mrinfo can be used to display the configuration of a multicast router on a Windows 2000 network. Scheduled tasks can be used to automatically perform tasks such as updating demand-dial routers and other maintenance tasks related to RRAS. Finally, the NetShell (netsh) tool can be used to configure protocols, routes, interfaces, and more from a command line. All of these routing tools will be discussed in this section.

Pathping

The **ping** command is used to communicate with a single host to determine if packets are being delivered and received in a timely manner. The **tracert** command is used to follow a route to a particular host, with the routers listed at each stop along the way. The **pathping**

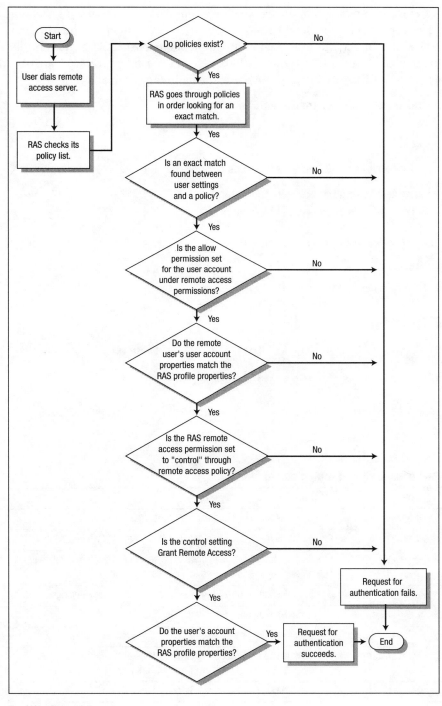

Decision Tree 12.1
Policy application.

command is a combination of the two previous commands, displaying information about packet loss at every router along the way to a particular destination. The **pathping** command offers much more detailed information about a packet loss and routing. This information can be used to determine where network reliability problems are occurring and why. Listing 12.2 is an example of using the **pathping** command.

The syntax for the **pathping** command is:

```
pathping [-n] [-h] [-g] [-p] [-q] [-w] destination
```

Table 12.1 describes what each switch does (or doesn't do).

Listing 12.2   Example of using the pathping command.

```
C:\>pathping -p 5 -h 5 -w 200 www.straydog.org

Tracing route to www.straydog.org [216.71.62.114]
over a maximum of 5 hops:

0  DesktopPC.Ballew.com [208.228.171.78]
1  ...
Computing statistics for 0 seconds...

Source to Here This Node/Link Hop RTT Lost/Sent = Pct Lost/Sent = Pct Address 0

DesktopPC.Ballew.com [208.228.171.78] 100/ 100 =100%    |

1  --    100/ 100 =100%    0/ 100 =  0%  DesktopPC.Ballew.com [0.0.0.0]

Trace complete.
```

Table 12.1   Switches for the pathping command.

Switch	Name	Purpose
-n	Hostnames	Does not resolve IP addresses to hostnames.
-h	Maximum Hops	Specifies the maximum number of hops searched when looking for a destination.
-g	Host-List	Allows consecutive computers to be separated by intermediate gateways. These gateways are also referred to as loose source routes.
-p	Period	Specifies the number of milliseconds to wait in between pings.
-q	Num_Queries	Specifies the number of queries per hop.
-w	Timeout	Specifies how long to wait (in milliseconds) for each reply.
-T	Layer 2 tag	Used to test for QoS connectivity, attaches a layer-2 priority tag to all of its packets, and sends it to all of the network devices in the path.
-R	RSVP test	Used to see if each hop is RSVP capable.

Mrinfo

This command-line tool works well if you are using multicast routing; it displays the configuration of Windows 2000 multicast routers on the network. The **mrinfo** command contacts specified multicast routers by using an Internet Group Management Protocol (IGMP) message. Information in the message includes a version number, interfaces, and neighbors of the router. Also included are the TTL thresholds and flags.

The syntax for the **mrinfo** command is as follows:

```
mrinfo [-n] [-?] [-I] [-t] [-r] destination
```

Table 12.2 describes what the switches are used for.

Listing 12.3 shows a basic **mrinfo** command listing.

Listing 12.3   A basic mrinfo command listing.

```
C:\>mrinfo 192.168.0.42
192.168.0.42 (laptop.ballew) [version 21.68,mtrace,snmp]
192.168.0.42 --> 0.0.0.0 (local) [1/1]
192.168.0.12 --> 0.0.0.0 (local) [1/1/querier]
```

Scheduled Tasks

You can configure tasks to be performed automatically through Scheduled Tasks in Control Panel. As shown in Figure 12.32, Routing and Remote Access tasks can be scheduled using the Scheduled Task Wizard. Almost anything can be configured to run, including tasks for administering dial-up, virtual private networking, and internetwork connections. These tasks can be scheduled to run at any time or any number of times. Certain tasks—such as updating demand-dial routers or updating phone book files—may need to be run weekly. Other tasks—such as running scripts or disk cleaning operations—can be run daily. The programs can be found by browsing to them from the Program Files folder, the PBA folder, the Support Tools folder, and more.

Table 12.2   Switches for the mrinfo command.

Switch	Name	Purpose
-n	-	Displays IP addresses in numeric format.
-I	Address	Specifies the IP address of the interface from which you want to send the mrinfo query. This is determined by default by the IP routing table.
-r	Retries	Specifies how many times an SNMP query will be re-sent. The default value is three.
-t	Seconds	Specifies how long **mrinfo** will wait for a reply. The default value is four seconds.

Figure 12.32
Scheduling RRAS tasks.

NetShell

The NetShell command-line tool, known as Netsh, is the most powerful routing command-line tool available. Netsh can be used to configure interfaces, protocols, routes, filters, and remote access services, but it can also be used to support RRAS scripts for scripting RRAS functions. Those scripts can then be configured to run at specific times with Task Scheduler, mentioned previously. Netsh can also be used to create a backup of the information in the routing table. Netsh can be used only with Windows 2000 computers.

Typing **netsh** at a command prompt is like changing directories at a DOS prompt. At the Netsh command prompt, Netsh can be further separated into six areas called *contexts*. Those contexts are:

- Routing
- Interface
- RAS
- DHCP
- WINS
- AAAA

In this section, we'll be mostly concerned with the routing, interface, and RAS contexts. Figure 12.33 shows how these contexts look when you're switching between them at a command prompt.

*Note: This last section is included for those readers who like to use scripts and work with command-line tools. It is not necessary to know how to use the **netsh** command, but it's included here so that more experienced script programmers can benefit from its utilities.*

Figure 12.33
Using the **netsh** command.

Several global commands can be used with Netsh. Table 12.3 lists these global commands and their uses.

12

Table 12.3   Global commands for Netsh.

Command	Description
..	Moves up one level
?	Display help
add alias	Adds an alias to an existing command
add helper	Adds a Netsh help DLL
cmd	Creates a Windows 2000 command window
commit	Commits changes made in offline mode
delete alias	Deletes an alias from an existing command
delete helper	Deletes a Netsh help DLL
dump	Writes routing configuration to a text file for backing up router information; Listing 12.4 shows a partial **netsh** dump
exec	Executes a script file that contains **netsh** commands
flush	Discards changes made in offline mode
offline	Sets the mode to offline
online	Sets the mode to online
popd	A script command that pops a context from the stack
pushd	A script command that pushes the current context on the stack
set audit-logging	Turns on or off the logging utility
set loglevel	Sets the logging information level
set machine	Configures the computer on which the **netsh** commands are run
set mode	Sets the current mode to either offline or online
show alias	Displays all defined aliases
show audit-logging	Displays the current audit-logging settings

(continued)

Table 12.3   Global commands for Netsh (continued).

Command	Description
show helper	Displays the installed Netsh helper DLLs
show loglevel	Displays the logging information level
show machine	Displays the machine on which the **netsh** commands are run
show mode	Displays the current mode
show netdlls	Displays the current version of Netsh helper DLLs
show version	Displays the current version of the Netsh utility
quit or **bye** or **exit**	Exits the utility

Tip: To move to another context—such as RAS, routing, interface, DHCP, WINS, or AAAA—simply type in the name at whatever prompt is available in the Netsh shell.

Listing 12.4   Partial dump from a netsh command.

```
add multilink type = MULTI
add multilink type = BACP

set user name = Administrator dialin = policy cbpolicy = none
set user name = Guest dialin = policy cbpolicy = none
set user name = JBallew dialin = policy cbpolicy = none
set user name = Joli dialin = policy cbpolicy = none
set user name = Joli Ballew MCSE MCT dialin = policy cbpolicy = none
set user name = Mary Anne dialin = policy cbpolicy = none
set tracing component = * state = disabled
popd
# End of RAS configuration.

# ----------------------------------------
# RAS IP Configuration
# ----------------------------------------
pushd ras ip
delete pool
set negotiation mode = allow
set access mode = all
set addrreq mode = deny
set addrassign method = auto
popd
# End of RAS IP configuration.

*
*
*
```

```
# Routing configuration
pushd routing
reset
popd
# IP configuration
pushd routing ip
reset
set loglevel error
add preferenceforprotocol proto=LOCAL preflevel=1
add preferenceforprotocol proto=NetMgmt preflevel=10
add preferenceforprotocol proto=STATIC preflevel=3
add preferenceforprotocol proto=NONDOD preflevel=5
add preferenceforprotocol proto=AUTOSTATIC preflevel=7
add preferenceforprotocol proto=OSPF preflevel=110
add preferenceforprotocol proto=RIP preflevel=120
add interface name="Local Area Connection" state=enable
set filter name="Local Area Connection" fragcheck=disable
add interface name="Internal" state=enable
set filter name="Internal" fragcheck=disable
add interface name="Loopback" state=enable
set filter name="Loopback" fragcheck=disable
popd
# End of IP configuration
```

Table 12.4 lists RAS context commands and their uses. RAS commands are a subcontext of the Netsh context.

Tip: *For more information on any of these commands, type the command name followed by the* ? *switch.*

Table 12.5 lists routing context commands and their uses.

Table 12.6 lists interface context commands and their uses.

Table 12.4   RAS commands for Netsh.

Command	Description
? or **help**	Displays help
add	Adds an entry to a table
appletalk	Changes to the RAS AppleTalk context
delete	Deletes an entry from a table
dump	Displays RAS configuration information (including authentication type, link type, Multilink type, and some user information)
ip	Changes to RAS IP context
ipx	Changes to RAS IPX context

(continued)

Table 12.4   RAS commands for Netsh *(continued)*.

Command	Description
netbeui	Changes to RAS NetBEUI context
set	Sets configuration information
show	Displays information

Table 12.5   Routing commands for Netsh.

Command	Description
dump	Prints routing configurations to the screen for saving and backing up
? or help	Displays help
ip	Changes to the routing IP context
ipx	Changes to the routing IPX context
reset	Resets IP routing to a fresh state
show	Displays information
unalias	Deletes an alias

Table 12.6   Interface commands for Netsh.

Command	Description
? or help	Displays help
add	Adds an entry to a table
delete	Deletes an entry from a table
dump	Writes configuration information to the screen
ip	Changes to interface IP context
reset	Resets the information to a fresh state
set	Sets configuration information
show	Displays information

Configuring Auto-Static Updates by Using the Netsh Command

As an example of how Netsh scripts can be used with Task Scheduler, you can configure an auto-static update using RIP for IP. Perform the following steps:

1. As an administrator, log on to the remote access server.

2. Choose Start|Programs|Accessories|Command Prompt.

3. At the command prompt, enter the following commands:

   - **netsh interface set interface name =** *Demand Dial Interface Name* **connect= connected**

- **netsh routing ip rip update *Demand Dial Interface Name***

- **netsh interface set interface name= *Demand Dial Interface Name* connect= disconnected**

4. Save the script as demand.scp.

5. Run the command by entering **netsh –f demand.scp**.

You can also run the script from Task Scheduler and configure it to run daily, weekly, or as needed.

Summary

The routing and remote access components included in the Routing and Remote Access console in Windows 2000 Server can be used to enable network users to telecommute, to access their files and folders while on the road, and to retrieve email from the network servers when away from the office. RRAS can also be used in small home offices to allow the owner or proprietor to easily configure a computer as a dial-up server for only a few people, or to allow server-to-server communications using dial-on-demand configurations in larger organizations.

This chapter discussed all aspects of routing and remote access, including the components of a remote access server and router, which protocols can be used with both, and how to install and configure the remote access server and clients. There are many ways to set up the server and clients, including using the server as a dial-up server, using it as a virtual private network, using it for Internet Connection Sharing, and using it with Network Address Translation. Each of these installations and configurations were addressed in this chapter.

After the remote access server was set up, configured, and in use, monitoring and optimizing the remote access server became the focus. You can use the Performance console, Network Monitor, logging, auditing, and routing tools to manage and optimize the server on a day-to-day basis.

This chapter also discussed creating and managing the user accounts and their policies. You learned how to configure servers to log off users after a certain amount of idle time and how to configure day and time restrictions, Multilink, and more.

Finally, I introduced some of the routing tools, which can be used for scripting routing batch files and running them through Task Scheduler.

The Next Step

Well, that about does it. I hope that this book helped you successfully create a Windows 2000 network, or migrate an existing Windows NT network to Windows 2000, and that the network is running smoothly. I hope also that you have incorporated DHCP and are using DNS to its fullest extent, and that you have a couple of remote servers set up for your traveling clients. If you need a little more information, or if you've had any problems, there are a couple of appendixes that will assist you in solving those difficulties.

Also in the appendixes is information on setting up printers and common printing problems, FAQs, troubleshooting tips and tricks, and general problems that arise during installation and configuration.

Appendix A

Windows 2000 Printing

Installing printers has gotten fairly intuitive over the past few years, and many printers virtually configure themselves. With Windows 2000 Server supporting Plug and Play, printers are easier than ever to get up and running, and with Active Directory integration, they are even easier to manage.

In this appendix, you'll learn about printing terminology, printing requirements, installation of the printer itself and its drivers, network printing, printer management, and the role of Active Directory. Following that, printing problems and their solutions will be discussed.

Terminology

Before attempting to install network or shared printers, you need to understand some related terminology. In this section, I'll introduce terminology that is important to understanding any discussion about printers.

To begin, here is the general terminology used when you're installing or connecting to a printer:

- *Creating a printer* means that you are installing the printer software. This print device can be of any type, including as a network printer, a shared printer, or a local printer for one specific computer. Creating a printer can be done using the Add Printer Wizard in Windows 2000.

- *Connecting to a printer* means that a client is accessing a printer that has already been installed and configured. A client who is connecting to a printer for the first time can use the Add Printer Wizard in Windows 2000 to set up that printer for his or her workstation. If the printer driver for the client exists on the print server, it will be downloaded automatically to the client's machine if the client computer uses a Microsoft Windows operating system such as Windows 9x, NT, or 2000. If that is not the case, the client will need to install the printer driver manually.

- *Network printing* means that a print server exists or that the printers that are used are configured with their own adapter cards and TCP/IP addresses. (A *print server*, described later, is a computer for which the printers are installed and configured by an administrator for the purpose of centralizing the management of printing tasks.) Network printing allows clients on the network to print to any printer they have permissions for, such as a printer in their office, a branch office, or even a printer accessed through the Internet.

Some other general printing terms that should be understood include the following:

- *Print device*—The print device is the physical printer. It is not the software, the driver, or the client interface, but the actual hardware that produces the printed documents. There are two types of print devices: local and network.

- *Local print device*—A local print device is a print device that is physically connected to the print server or to a local machine. Such devices connect through a physical port similar to how a desktop PC is connected to a local printer. These ports can be the familiar RS-232/422/IRDS, USB, SCSI, or other similar connecting devices.

- *Network print device*—This print device is connected via a network and not via a physical port. Network print devices have their own TCP/IP addresses and adapter cards that connect them to the network. Network print devices are considered nodes the same way workstations are. Network print devices can also be attached to external network adapters.

- *Printer*—A printer isn't a print device; a printer is the software that the operating system uses to connect to the print device. The printer (software) offers information about the print device, such as whether it is a network printer, a local printer, or attached to a print server. Printing can also be configured to print to a file instead of to a physical printer. The printer (software) also handles other printing tasks such as determining how printing will be handled and which print device (if more than one exists) will be used. A printer is sometimes referred to as a *logical printer*.

- *Print server*—Print devices are physically connected to print servers. Print servers are computers that receive and process clients' printing requests. Shared network printers are configured on print servers.

- *Printer driver*—A printer driver is a collection of files that allows the operating system to convert print commands into something the computer can understand. A printer driver is specific to the printer, and printer drivers cannot be interchanged between different printer manufacturers. Without the proper printer driver installed, the printer will not function.

- *Print job*—When a client sends a request to any printer, a print job has been created. Print jobs can be managed by pausing, deleting, canceling, and resuming if a user has the appropriate permissions.

- *Printer pool*—A printer pool is created when a print server has multiple, identical print devices attached to it. For instance, a print server might have five LPT ports, each with an identical printer attached to it. Because these printers are identical, they use the same printer driver. This being the case, a printer pool can be configured to allow users to simply choose one printer, and then the print server will forward that print request to a print device that isn't busy. This lessens the amount of time that users have to wait for their jobs to print. Make sure the print devices are placed in the same physical location, though, or users won't know where to find their printed documents.

Here are some more printing terms you should know:

- *Queue*—When clients send print jobs to a print device, those jobs wait in line to be printed based on the order of print jobs received and their priority. The queue is the list of print jobs waiting to be printed.

- *Pause*—Pausing a printer doesn't delete any of the documents; it stops the printing process while problems are solved or troubleshooting takes place. You might need to pause the printer to check connectivity, replace a print cartridge, replace paper, or add toner.

- *Resume*—After the printer has been paused, it can be resumed. This is done after the problem has been solved with the print device.

- *Cancel*—This command can be used to cancel all documents in the queue. The documents will be deleted from the print queue. You might use this command if there are multiple documents in the queue that do not need to be printed, if the same documents were sent to be printed multiple times, or if the print queue has hung and needs to be cleared.

- *Offline*—If the printer is deliberately or accidentally taken offline, the documents in the queue remain in the queue. This is a safety measure and provides some fault tolerance for the printers on the network.

- *Redirection*—If a printer goes offline or is not working properly, the documents in that printer's queue can be sent to another printer on the network. This printer must use the same printer driver, however, and the redirection must be completed manually.

- *Notification*—When a print job is completed, the owner of the document is informed via a pop-up box on his or her computer screen or by other, similar means. A different person can be chosen to receive this notification; usually, this person is in charge of picking up the documents from the printer.

- *Priority*—In some instances, certain users or company personnel should have their documents printed before everyone else's; that person might be the president, CEO, or other higher-up. To allow a specific user's documents to print before others and not wait in the print queue, you can set the priority of those documents. Obviously, not all users should have this option available to them; give it to only those users who print critical documents. The priority range is from 1 to 99, with 99 being the highest priority and 1 being the lowest. Priority can also be set for printers. One printer can have a priority of 50, for example, and another can have a priority of 99. Setting priorities for both documents and printers will be discussed in more depth later in this appendix.

- *PrintQueue object*—When Active Directory stores a shared printer, it is stored as a **PrintQueue** object. This object contains information about the printer, and when any of the information changes in the printer's configuration, that information is immediately updated.

- *PostScript*—PostScript is a page description language that sets rules for the appearance of the page being printed. It is the industry standard, and it supports both Type 1 and TrueType fonts. This language was developed by Adobe Systems Inc. in 1985.

Requirements

There are two sets of requirements for setting up printers: the printer must be on Microsoft's Hardware Compatibility List (HCL), and printer drivers must be available for Windows 2000. You can check printer compatibility at this Microsoft Web page: **www.microsoft.com/windows2000/server/howtobuy/upgrading/compat/search/devices.asp**, shown in Figure A.1. You can use this search page by typing in the name and/or model number of a printer or by just searching for all printers for a complete list of compatible hardware.

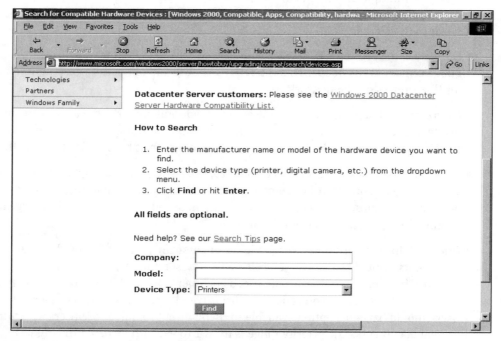

Figure A.1
Searching for hardware devices in Microsoft's HCL.

For network printing, additional requirements include the following:

- The network must have a print server for network printing to work properly and efficiently. This can be a dedicated print server if print traffic is heavy, and the server should run Windows 2000 Server for a large number of connections. Windows 2000 Professional can be used if only 10 or fewer connections are required.

- The print server should have enough RAM to process the documents that are sent to it. The amount of RAM necessary is determined by the load expected on the print server, the number of printers connected, and other factors.

- The print server should have enough hard disk space to hold documents until they can be printed. The server has to hold not only the documents themselves but also the print data that is sent with them. Disk space is necessary when large documents such as databases, spreadsheets, or accounting files are sent to the print server. Some of these documents might be scheduled to print at night, when print traffic is low, to enhance print performance. Spooled documents are stored on the hard disk until they are printed. If users try to print and there is no more available disk space, they'll get a print error message.

- The network must have enough printers to handle the print load. In an office where sales receipts are printed continuously for customer purchases, for example, there should be enough printers installed and configured so neither the employees or the customers have to wait an unacceptable amount of time for their printouts.

- Printers designed for home users or single workstations should not be configured as network printers. These printers cannot handle the printing requirements of network clients and will not be a solid return on the investment. Purchase printers that are designed to be network printers and that meet the needs of your organization's network.

- Print devices should be located strategically in the office and around the network. Print servers and their associated print devices should be located on the subnet that the printing clients are located on, and they should be easily accessible. If a printer pool is not being used, printers should be scattered; if a printer pool is used, printers should all be placed in the same physical location.

- A print administrator should be hired or designated if a security plan or a group policy is used or if multiple printers exist. The print administrator should be responsible for all aspects of the print process, including installing new printers, upgrading drivers, getting clients connected, and enforcing policies. The administrator should also be well versed in troubleshooting printing problems.

Installation

There are several phases to installing a printer. The first phase is the physical installation: actually connecting the printer to the computer. The second phase is installing the printer driver, and occasionally, printer drivers will need to be downloaded from the

Internet. The third phase is configuring the printer (if necessary) as a network printer. You can configure network printing by using the Add Printer Wizard for clients or servers or during installation. In this section, you'll learn about all phases of printer installation.

Physical Installation

To physically install a printer, perform the following steps:

1. Make sure the printer you want to install is on Microsoft's HCL. If it isn't, you might still be able to install it.

2. Make sure that a driver is available for Windows 2000 Server. Check by accessing the manufacturer's Web site or by reading the printer documentation.

3. If necessary, download new drivers for the printer.

4. Make sure you have the appropriate permissions to add a printer and shut down the machine.

5. Shut down the computer. The computer can be a print server or a local workstation.

6. Attach the printer cable to both the printer and the computer to which it will be connected. This cable can be USB, SCSI, RS-232, or a number of other types. Generally, the printer plugs into an LPT1 port, a USB port, a SCSI port, or another type of printer interface.

7. Connect the printer's power supply to the computer, and plug it in. Turn the printer on.

8. Turn on the computer.

9. After the computer boots, one of two things will happen. If the printer is plug-and-play-compatible, Windows 2000 will detect the printer and the plug-and-play installation will begin. If the printer is not plug-and-play-compatible, or if for some other reason Windows 2000 does not recognize it immediately, the printer installation will have to be completed manually. Plug-and-play printer installation is described in the first example, "Installing Plug-and-Play Printers." For manually installing a printer, skip to the next example, "Installing Non-Plug-and-Play Printers." Figure A.2 shows the Found New Hardware screen that is displayed when the printer is detected automatically by Windows 2000.

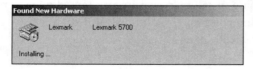

Figure A.2
The message displayed when Windows has found new hardware.

Installing Plug-and-Play Printers

If you see a screen similar to Figure A.2, then your printer has been detected and is plug-and-play-compatible. If that is the case, perform the following steps (these steps are subject to change for different printers and printer manufacturers):

1. In the Found New Hardware Wizard that appears automatically when a plug-and-play printer is detected, choose Next to start the wizard.

2. On the Install Hardware Device Drivers page, select what you'd like the wizard to do when it's looking for and installing the driver that should be used with this device. You can have the wizard either search for a suitable driver (the default option) or display a list of the known drivers for the device so that you can choose a specific driver.

   Select the first option, Search For A Suitable Driver For My Device (Recommended), and choose Next.

3. On the Locate Driver Files page, select any of the following options, depending on driver availability:

   • Floppy Disk Drives

   • CD-ROM Drives

   • Specify A Location

   • Microsoft Windows Update

   Choose Next.

4. On the Driver Files Search Results page, you'll see Windows 2000 looking for drivers for your printer from the hard drive and all of the locations specified. If a suitable driver is found, the wizard will ask you to verify this driver and install it. If a suitable driver is not found, you'll see the screen shown in Figure A.3. If a driver is not found, select Skip Driver Installation Of This Device. Skip the rest of these steps, and move on to the section "Installing Non-Plug-and-Play Printers."

5. If a suitable driver was found, you'll see a screen similar to Figure A.4. Choose Next.

6. The wizard will continue and will vary depending on the printer model and the manufacturer. If the driver you are using works for more than one type of printer, you'll be prompted to select the printer you have. If this is the case, select the printer and choose Next.

7. On the Name Your Printer page, enter a descriptive name for the printer being installed, and decide if you want this printer to be the default printer. Choose Next.

8. On the Printer Sharing page, select one of the following:

   • Do Not Share This Printer

   • Share As

   Because I'll be setting up a network printer later, I'll choose the default of Share As.

A

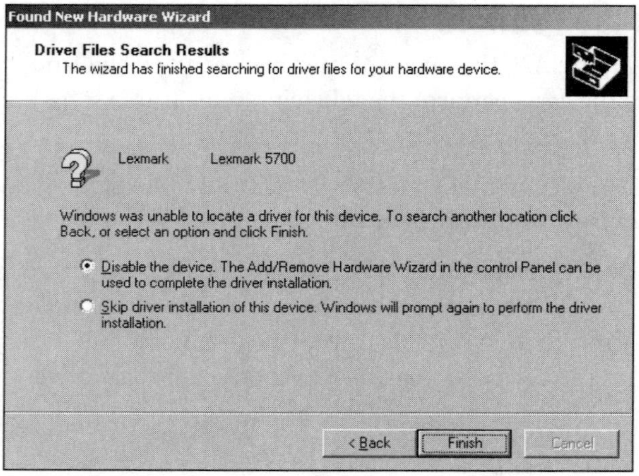

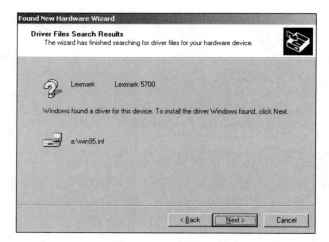

Figure A.3
Driver not found.

Figure A.4
Driver found.

9. On the Location And Comment page type in the location of the printer, and type any applicable comments.

10. On the Print Test Page wizard page, choose Yes to print a test page.

That's it. The final page of the Add Printer Wizard appears so you can verify that all of the information is correct. Figure A.8, shown later in this section, shows this screen.

Installing Non-Plug-and-Play Printers

If you did not see anything like what is shown in Figure A.2, then the printer you want to install probably isn't plug and play or isn't yet supported by Windows 2000. This doesn't necessarily mean that the printer won't function; it means that the printer has to be installed manually.

To install a printer manually, perform the following steps:

1. The printer should be physically installed, and you should have appropriate permissions to add a printer to the local machine.

2. Choose Start|Settings|Printers. Choose Add Printer.

3. The first page of the Add Printer Wizard appears; choose Next.

4. On the Local Or Network Printer page, for simplicity, choose Local Printer. Make sure there is a check in the checkbox Automatically Detect And Install My Plug And Play Printer.

5. If the printer isn't plug and play, you'll see the screen shown in Figure A.5. Choose Next to manually install the printer.

6. On the Select The Printer Port page, choose the port that the printer is physically connected to. Most times, this is LPT1.

7. On the Add Printer page, you have four choices:

   • If you can highlight the printer manufacturer in the left pane and the model number in the right pane, do so and choose Next.

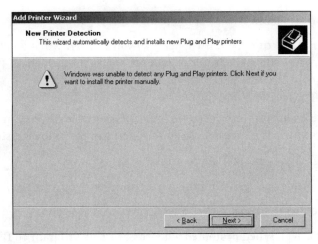

Figure A.5
New Printer Detection.

- If either the printer manufacturer or the printer model isn't listed here, choose Have Disk, and place the driver disk in the floppy drive or CD-ROM drive. If the driver has been downloaded from the Internet, choose Browse to locate the driver on the hard drive or in another location.

- If the printer manufacturer and model number aren't listed here, and you don't have a driver disk, connect to the Internet and choose Windows Update.

- If the printer manufacturer and model number aren't listed here, you don't have a driver installation disk, and there is no information on the Windows Update site, choose Cancel. Then try to download a new driver from the manufacturer's Web site as described in the section "More on Printer Drivers."

8. If you were able to get past Step 7, and if the driver you are using works for more than one type of printer, you'll be prompted to select the printer you have. If this is the case, select the printer and choose Next.

9. On the Name Your Printer page, enter a descriptive name for the printer being installed, and decide if you want this printer to be the default printer. Choose Next.

10. On the Printer Sharing page, select one of the following:

- Do Not Share This Printer

- Share As

Because I'll be setting up a network printer later, I'll choose the default of Share As.

11. On the Location And Comment page, type the location of the printer, and type any applicable comments.

12. On the Print Test Page wizard page, choose Yes to print a test page.

That's it. The final page of the Add Printer Wizard appears so you can verify that all of the information is correct. Figure A.8, shown later in this section, shows this screen.

More on Printer Drivers

If you've been unable to install your printer because of a lack of a suitable driver, you'll have to download a new driver from the Internet. To do this, perform the following steps:

1. Log on to the Internet, and go to the site of the printer manufacturer.

2. Look for links that offer printer drivers. Find the model number of your printer.

3. Select the operating system—in this case, Windows 2000.

4. Choose to download the driver. When prompted, choose Save This Program To Disk, as shown in Figure A.6. Choose OK.

5. Select a location in which to save the file. This can be a floppy disk if the file is small enough, a Zip disk or other hardware device, or the hard drive itself.

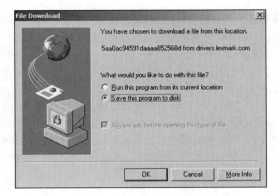

Figure A.6
Downloading a printer driver.

Figure A.7
Expanding a self-extracting driver file.

6. After the driver is downloaded, you might have to find it and expand it before using it with the Add Printer Wizard. See Figure A.7 and Figure A.8.

7. Return to the previous section, "Installing Non-Plug-and-Play Printers." When prompted in Step 7, browse to the location of the new driver.

Figure A.8
Completing the Add Printer Wizard.

Installing Print Cartridges and Toner Cartridges

Once the printer has been installed, you might need to install printer cartridges or other printer hardware to initially get the printer up and running. To install a print cartridge, all you usually have to do is open the top printer cover and pop out the old cartridge or put in a new one. Some printers have programs that can be used to align print cartridge heads, clean the heads, or otherwise maintain the printers. Additionally, some printers show how much ink is available, have see-through paper trays, or have easy-to-install toner cartridges. In most instances, though, for network printers that are expensive and difficult to maintain, an outside entity is responsible for this type of maintenance.

Network Printing

If a printer is already installed on a network and will be accessed by others on the network, the printer must first be shared. This section covers sharing a previously unshared printer. Following that is a brief discussion about how network printers are installed when they need to be configured with their own TCP/IP addresses.

Sharing the Printer

To share a previously unshared printer, perform the following steps:

1. With appropriate permissions to share a printer, log on to the machine that contains the local printer.

2. Choose Start|Settings|Printers to open the Printers window.

3. Right-click on the printer to share, and choose Sharing.

4. On the Sharing tab of the printer's Properties dialog, check the Shared As checkbox and the List In The Directory checkbox.

5. On the Sharing tab, choose the Additional Drivers button.

6. In the Additional Drivers dialog box, check the checkboxes for the additional clients who will need support. These may be Windows 9x, Windows NT, Alpha, PowerPC, or MIPS. If prompted, put in the Windows 2000 Server CD.

Connecting a Client through My Network Places

From the client computer, you use My Network Places to access a previously shared printer. To do this, perform the following steps:

1. With permissions to add a printer, log on to the machine that needs to be configured to access the newly shared printer.

2. Open My Network Places, and choose Add Network Place.

3. In the Add Network Place dialog box, choose Browse.

4. Browse to the printer or type in the path to the printer. The path name is in the form \\Print Server Name\Print Device Name.

5. Type a name for the printer. This name is what the client will see when accessing the printer. Choose Finish.

You will now see a new network place in the My Network Places folder for the printer. The first time you try to print from an application, you might still be prompted to install the printer. If this happens, simply perform the steps described earlier, and type in the path of the network printer. You can configure the printer to act as the default printer at this time as well.

Connecting a Client through the Add Printer Wizard

Another way to add a network printer is through the Add Printer Wizard. To add a printer by using the wizard, perform the following steps:

1. With appropriate permissions to add a printer, log on to the computer for which the printer should be added.

2. Choose Start|Settings|Printers to open the Printers window.

3. Double click on the Add Printer icon, and when the wizard starts, choose Next.

4. On the Local Or Network Printer page, select Network Printer.

5. Choose Type The Printer Name, or choose Next to browse for a printer.

6. If prompted, supply any other information as needed. The new printer will be added to the Printers folder when the wizard is completed.

Network Print Devices

When a printer is connected directly to the network, as is the case with a network print device, that device will use TCP/IP and have a network address. Printers such as these are accessed faster than shared printers and are more efficient. Installing network print devices is similar to installing a local printer (described in previous sections), but for a network print device, an additional port must be configured. You can add this port by using the Add Standard TCP/IP Printer Port Wizard, which is accessed from the Add Printer Wizard described earlier.

Figures A.9 and A.10 show the screens related to adding a network printer; otherwise, the installation is almost exactly the same. In Figure A.9, notice that the Create A New Port option is chosen. Choosing Next now will launch the Add Standard TCP/IP Printer Port Wizard (see Figure A.10).

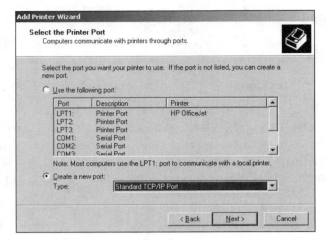

Figure A.9
Creating a TCP/IP port.

Figure A.10
The Add Standard TCP/IP Printer Port Wizard.

Management

Managing printers is also a full-time job. Managing printers includes configuring the printer with separator pages, setting document priorities, setting printer priorities, redirecting the printer, setting notification, and scheduling print times. In this section, I'll introduce all of these tasks.

Separator Pages

Different print devices speak different print languages and print in different modes. Some of these printers can switch between modes automatically, and some printers use separator pages. Separator pages can also be used to separate documents sent to the printer by different users. Custom separator pages can be created by editing a .sep file that comes with Windows 2000 or by creating your own.

Windows 2000 provides four separator page files, located in the %Systemroot%\System32 folder:

- *Pcl.sep*—Uses the PCL (Printer Control Language) when HP print devices are used, and prints a separator page between print jobs.

- *Pscript*—Uses the PostScript printer description language when PostScript printers are used or when HP print devices are used, and does not print a separator page between print jobs.

- *Sysprint.sep*—Prints a separator page between each document and can be used with any PostScript print device.

- *Sysprtj.sep*—A version of Sysprint.sep that includes Japanese characters.

You can configure a separator page by right-clicking on the printer in the Printers window, choosing Properties, and selecting the Advanced tab. From the Advanced tab, choose Separator Page, and browse to the one you want to use. See Figure A.11.

Printer and Document Priorities

Priorities range from 1 to 99, with 1 being the lowest priority. Priorities can be set for both documents and printers. Higher-priority documents will print first and can be configured by right-clicking on the document and choosing Properties. There is generally a slider tab (or something similar) that allows you to change the priority of the document.

For printers, you can set priorities such that critical documents get sent to a higher-priority printer, while non-critical documents get sent to a lower-priority printer. You can also allow the graphics department to send graphics files to a higher-quality printer, while the accounting department sends its files to a less expensive printer. Printer priorities can be set for multiple printers after they are configured to point to the same port. That port can be physical or logical. Once that is configured, printer priorities can be set from the Properties dialog box, at the Advanced tab. See Figure A.11.

Redirecting Printer Documents

When a printer goes offline, the queue might contain several documents waiting to be printed. Redirecting can be done for all of the documents in the queue but not for only a few specific documents. Also, the printer to which those documents are directed must use the same driver (in essence, be an identical printer) as the original printer to which the documents were sent. If all of these conditions are met, and all of the documents in the queue need to be redirected, perform the following steps:

1. With appropriate permissions to manage a printer, log on to a computer where the printers can be managed.

2. Choose Start|Settings|Printers to open the Printers window.

Figure A.11
Setting printer priorities.

3. Right-click on the printer that holds the documents to be printed or on a printer that isn't working. Choose Properties.

4. From the Ports tab, choose Add Port.

5. This port should point to an existing, working print device. Uncheck the port that isn't working. Choose Apply.

Note: *If the print device is working and documents are currently printing, those documents will not be redirected.*

Setting Notification and Scheduling Print Times

You can control print jobs while they are in the print queue by right-clicking on a document and choosing Properties. One of the items that can be configured is who shall receive notification after a print job has finished. In Figure A.12, notice that the person to receive notification is, by default, the owner of the document. The document's priority can also be set here, as I mentioned earlier. Finally, through the Schedule area of the screen, you can schedule when this document should print.

To see a document's properties, or to change a document's properties for priority, notification, or print times, perform the following steps:

1. With permission to manage print documents, log on to the computer where the Print Documents folder is located.

2. Choose Start|Settings|Printers to open the Printers window.

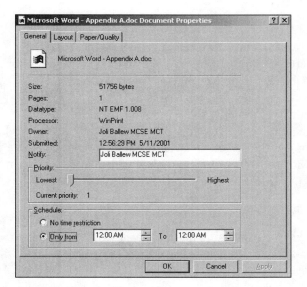

Figure A.12
Document properties.

3. Double-click on the printer you want to manage.

4. In the printer's management screen, notice the print documents in the queue. Right-click on the document to be managed, and choose Properties. (The screen shown in this step may differ depending on the print device and printer software.)

5. From the General tab, make the necessary changes.

Using Printer Pools

Printer pools were discussed earlier, in the section entitled "Terminology." To briefly review, a printer pool is created when a print server has multiple, identical print devices attached to it, and these printers must all use the same printer driver. A printer pool can be configured to allow users to simply choose one printer, and then the print server will forward that print request to a print device that isn't busy. This reduces the amount of time users have to wait for their jobs to print. Once these devices are physically connected, enabling printer pooling is quite easy.

To allow a print port to enable printer pooling, perform the following steps:

1. With appropriate permissions to manage a printer, log on to a computer where the printers can be managed.

2. Choose Start|Settings|Printers to open the Printers window.

3. Right-click on the printer you want to manage, and choose Properties.

4. On the Ports tab, select Enable Printer Pooling.

Active Directory

You can manage printers in Active Directory; tasks you can do here include finding a printer, changing printer properties, sharing printers, and assigning permissions to printers. Printers can also be published in Active Directory so others can find them easily on the network and use them when needed. You can search across a domain for a printer that meets certain standards, such as the ability to print double-sided or to staple documents after printing. In general, Active Directory performs most of the tasks related to administering printers, as long as the default behavior of the printer is acceptable. In fact, printing is so integrated with Active Directory and Windows 2000 that there isn't even a Printers folder in the Active Directory Users And Computers console.

Publishing Printers

Any printer that has been shared by a print server on the network and that has the List In The Directory option selected on the Sharing tab of the printer's Properties dialog will be automatically published in Active Directory. The print server automatically updates Active Directory when the printer's properties change, and each print server is responsible for these updates.

Viewing Printers in Active Directory

As mentioned previously, there is no Printers folder in the Active Directory Users And Computers console. To view the printers installed and shared on the network and registered in Active Directory, perform the following steps:

1. Log on to a computer running Active Directory.

2. Choose Start|Programs|Administrative Tools, and open Active Directory Users And Computers.

3. Highlight the domain name, and choose Action|Find.

4. In the Find box, choose Printers, as shown in Figure A.13. Choose Find Now.

Finding Printers Based on Characteristics

In the Find Printers dialog box, shown in Figure A.13, you can search for printers based on their properties by selecting the Features tab or the Advanced tab. Some of the print features that can be searched for, provided that the print administrator has properly installed and configured the printers and has listed their properties, are listed next:

- Prints double-sided

- Prints in color

- Staples printouts

- Prints at a specific resolution

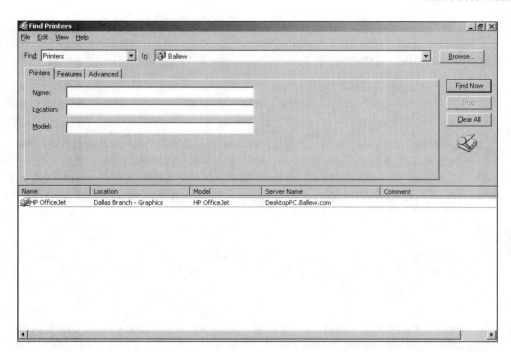

Figure A.13
Finding printers in Active Directory.

- Prints at a specific speed

- Prints on a specific type of paper

- Supports collation

- Supports a specific printer language

- Is located in a specific physical place

- Is a specific model of printer

Group Policies for Printing

Several settings are available for printing and group policies. Those options are listed next with a brief description of each. Following these descriptions are instructions for configuring a group policy for printing. None of these options is configured by default, and enabling the policy and leaving it *not configured* are the same in almost all instances. Disabling any of these policies will cause them not to work.

Here are the options for printing and group policies.

Note: You can access these policies through Active Directory Users and Computers by configuring a group policy for the domain as described later in this section.

- *Allow Printers To Be Published*—The List In The Directory option allows shared printers to be listed in Active Directory. If the Allow Printers To Be Published option is disabled, the List In The Directory option will not apply and will be ignored.

- *Automatically Publish New Printers In Active Directory*—This option determines whether the Add Printer Wizard automatically publishes the shared printers in Active Directory.

Note: *Pruning, coming up next, is the process that Windows 2000 Active Directory uses to keep its printer information up-to-date. If a printer is removed from a print server on the network, then the reference to that printer is removed in Active Directory. By default, the object is pruned if the printer has not been detected two times in a row at 8-hour intervals. Pruning and its related policy settings might need to be configured in some instances, such as when a print server is intentionally taken offline for repair.*

- *Allow Pruning Of Published Printers*—This option determines whether Active Directory can prune the printers published by the computer. By default, the pruning service does prune orphaned printers.

- *Printer Browsing*—By default, shared printers are announced to the browse master server when Active Directory is available. If this policy is enabled, the print spooler announces shared printers to a browse master server that is responsible for keeping track of the printers on the network, and those printers appear in the domain list of the Add Printer Wizard. If this option is disabled, shared printers are not announced at all.

- *Prune Printers That Are Not Automatically Republished*—When deleted printer objects rejoin the network, they are detected and republished in Active Directory. Non-Windows 2000 computers and computers in other domains cannot republish printers in Active Directory automatically, so the system never prunes their printer objects. This policy can be changed from the default to prune non-republishing printers Never, Only If A Print Server Is Found, or Whenever A Printer Is Not Found.

- *Directory Pruning Interval*—Used only on domain controllers, this policy allows an administrator to change the default pruning interval of eight hours. Other choices range from Immediately to Seven Weeks to Never.

- *Directory Pruning Retry*—This option determines the number of times the pruner will attempt to contact the print server before considering the printer orphaned and deleting it. The range is from No Retry to six retries.

- *Directory Pruning Priority*—This option sets the priority of the pruner, which runs only on domain controllers. The range of options includes Lowest, Below Normal, Normal, Above Normal, and Highest. Normal is the default.

- *Check Published State*—By default, Windows 2000 verifies published printers when it starts up. If you want to configure Active Directory to verify the system state at various intervals as it is running, you can configure it here. The options are Never, 30 minutes, 1 hour, 4 hours, 8 hours, 12 hours, and 1 day. The default is Never.

- *Web-Based Printing*—This option allows or disallows Web printing from this server. By default, Internet printing is enabled and supported.

- *Custom Support URL In The Printers Folder's Left Pane*—This option is used to add a custom Web-page link to the left pane of the Printers folder. Web view must be enabled for you to see the changes, however.

- *Computer Location*—A component of the next policy, this option allows a default location to be specified and used when users are searching for printers. This policy can be used to direct users to a specific printer or printers in specific locations.

- *Pre-populate Printer Search Location Text*—This option enables the physical Location Tracking feature. This tracking feature lets administrators assign printers (and computers) to specific locations. This policy overrides the default policy for locating printers by using TCP/IP addresses and subnet masks, and instead locates printers based on their location in the general location scheme configured for the network.

To configure any of these printer options and create a printer group policy, perform the following steps:

1. Log on as an administrator.

2. Choose Start|Programs|Administrative Tools|Active Directory Users And Computers.

3. In the Active Directory Users And Computers console, right-click on the domain name, and choose Properties.

4. On the Group Policy tab, either edit an existing policy by highlighting it and choosing Edit, or choose New to create a new group policy. (I'll choose New.)

5. If you are creating a new group policy, name it "Printing Policy" or something similar. Highlight the policy, and choose Edit.

6. Under the Computer Configuration tree, expand Administrative Templates.

7. Open the Printers folder.

8. In the right pane, right-click on any policy to configure, and choose Properties. Configure as many policies as necessary.

Common Printer Problems and Solutions

Several problems can occur with print devices, and these problems generally relate to a client's inability to print and/or the client's inability to communicate with the printer. In my experience, if a printer has been operational for some time and has developed problems, the printing problems occur for two main reasons: either the print device driver is bad, or there is a problem with the printer's hardware.

Besides bad or corrupt device drivers, hardware problems, and user error, you need to deal with the many requirements for network printing. If any of these requirements haven't been met, problems can occur. In this last section, I'll discuss these and other common printing problems and how to solve them.

Printer Drivers

An incorrect, corrupt, or missing printer driver can cause any of the problems listed next. To correct any of these problems, try reinstalling the printer driver first, and if that doesn't work, delete the printer from the Printers folder and reinstall it. If the problem still isn't solved, try other techniques mentioned later in this appendix.

An incorrect, corrupt, or missing printer driver can cause any of the following problems:

- The printer doesn't print.

- Printer pages come out distorted or unreadable.

- Users cannot print because an error message prevents them, asking them to install a new printer driver.

- The print server can print, but some or all of the clients can't. (Install client operating system support—drivers for the client—on the print server or the client machine.)

- The print server can't print.

Communicating with the Printer

If problems are occurring because some clients can access the printer and print successfully while others can't, there is probably a problem related to those clients communicating with the printer. If this is the case, check the following items:

- Verify all of the physical connections from the client to the print server, personal printer, or network printer.

- If the printer has its own TCP/IP address, verify that the subnet mask and IP address are correct on those clients. Sometimes, problems occur when clients or printers have been moved.

- If the printer has been installed but a test page won't print, check port settings or the computer's network address.

- Make sure the client is connected to the correct printer if more than one printer exists.

- Check the user's rights for the printer.

- Check the protocols installed on the client computer.

- Check the printer share name on the client computer.

- Check the printer availability time on the client computer.

- Check available disk space on the client computer.

Printing Requirements

As I mentioned previously, there are certain requirements for installing and configuring network printers. If any of these requirements are not met or are lacking in resources, problems can occur. If the previous techniques for solving your printer problems have not been successful, check the following items:

- A dedicated print server should be used if print traffic is heavy, and the server should run Windows 2000 Server for a large number of connections.

- Windows 2000 Professional can be used if only 10 or fewer connections are required.

- The print server should have enough RAM to process the documents that are sent to it. Problems can occur when excessive spooling to the hard drive takes place or if thrashing occurs.

- The print server should have enough hard disk space to hold documents until they can be printed. This space includes not only the documents themselves, but also the print data that is sent with them. Lack of hard drive space can prevent users from printing to the print server.

- The network must have enough printers to handle the print load.

- Printers designed for home users or single workstations should not be configured as network printers. These printers cannot handle the printing requirements of network clients and will not be a solid return on the investment.

- Print devices should be located strategically in the office and around the network if a printer pool is used. Printers should all be located in the same place.

- If a printer pool is not being used, printers should be scattered.

- A print administrator should be hired or designated if a security plan or a group policy is used or if multiple printers exist. The print administrator should be responsible for all aspects of the print process, including installing new printers, upgrading drivers, getting clients connected, and enforcing policies.

- Users must have appropriate permissions to access and print to printers on the network. Print administrators must have appropriate permissions to configure or install printers.

- Printer pools must use the same driver, and print devices must be similar. If the devices are not alike in the printer pool, some of the printers will function correctly while others won't.

- If printing priority is used, make sure the correct priorities are set.

A

Printer Hardware

Lots of things can go wrong with printer hardware, especially laser printers and expensive network printers. In all of the places I've worked, an outside technician services these devices weekly or monthly. However, in some organizations, the print administrator can be responsible for some of these tasks. Several things can go wrong with a print device, and the best advice I can give here is to purchase a good A+ book and perhaps even become A+ certified. But as a start, here are some simple and fixable problems that relate to different types of printers and their hardware.

Laser Printers

Laser printers are commonly used in network settings. Common problems and their solutions include the following:

- *Paper jams*—Paper jams usually occur where paper is drawn into the printer, but they also occur at any point throughout the paper's path. Most of the time, the paper can be gently removed from this area without much of a problem. The causes of paper jams range from too many pages being drawn into the printer (a worn roller, perhaps), to paper that is too heavy, thick, or coated, to obstructions in the paper path, such as small bits of paper or other buildup.

- *No power*—Laser printers have their own power supply, internal fuses, main motor, high voltage corona wires, and gear trains. Any of these can cause the printer to appear dead. Because laser printers have high voltage and high temperatures inside, a certified technician should repair any problems related to power. However, you can certainly check to make sure the printer is properly plugged in (to a working outlet) and that the power cable is good.

- *Missing or defective print on the page*—Because the toner is written to the laser printer's drum, and that image is placed on the page, any problems related to the printing on the page is related to the corona wire, the drum assembly, the toner, the control board, or other parts of the laser printer. Simply replacing the toner cartridge or setting the contrast on the printed page can sometimes correct problems. If this does not work, the corona wire could be defective, the drum assembly could be broken, or the fusing unit could need replacing. If replacing the toner cartridge doesn't work, call a certified technician.

Ink Jet Printers

Ink jet printers are also very common in networks, especially in small home offices or small branch offices of larger networks. Ink jet printer problems include the following:

- *No power*—There must be power to the printer. If the printer doesn't turn on, check the outlet first and then the printer's power supply. An ink jet printer's power supply is replaced and tested similarly to a computer's power supply. All of the usual precautions should be taken when you're working with any type of electrical power source. When troubleshooting power, make sure that any fuses on the circuit board haven't blown.

- *Printing is faint*—Most likely, the print cartridges need to be replaced. These are usually snap-in cartridges and can be installed easily.

- *No printing*—If the printer hasn't been used for a while or if the print cartridges are full, the print jets might be clogged, preventing the ink from getting from the cartridge to the internal printer parts. Clean the ink jets according to the manufacturer's instructions.

Dot Matrix Printers

Dot matrix printers are still in use today and must be maintained regularly. Because there aren't as many parts in a dot matrix printer as with other types of printers, problems are usually easily solved. Here are common ones:

- *Missing or defective print on the page*—The print head might be too far away from the platen, and if this is the case, the tension should be reset. The print head positioning belt should be checked occasionally to make sure it is aligned properly. In addition, the printer's roller surfaces should be cleaned regularly.

- *Build-up inside the printer*—Build-up inside the printer can cause general printer problems and can be avoided by properly cleaning the printer occasionally. Besides cleaning the dot-matrix print head, you should also clean the area where the paper is handled, along with the gear train. The gear train and the carriage assembly can be oiled occasionally.

- *No power*—There must be power to the printer. If the printer doesn't turn on, check the outlet first and then the printer's power supply. A dot matrix printer's power supply is replaced and tested similarly to a computer's power supply. All of the usual precautions should be taken when you're working with any type of electrical power source. Some dot matrix printers may also have fuses that have blown, and this can be checked as well.

- *Print is faint*—Most likely, the ribbon cartridge needs to be replaced. This is usually just a snap-in ribbon similar to a new print cartridge or toner cartridge.

Tip: Any problems that occur while the printer is under warranty should be repaired by the manufacturer's technicians or returned and replaced. Messing around inside a printer can void the warranty. Also, if the printer still isn't working after you've tried all of the techniques mentioned in this section, it is best to hire a certified technician to fix the printer instead of trying to repair it yourself.

Appendix B

Windows 2000 Troubleshooting

No matter how adept you are at installing, configuring, and managing a Windows 2000 network, you'll no doubt run into problems eventually. In this appendix, I'll cover some of the most common problems that occur with Windows 2000 components and services, including Active Directory, DNS, DHCP, dial-up networking, group policies, installation, routing and remote access, system policy, TCP/IP, and WINS. These components and services are the most used and often cause the majority of problems. Keep in mind, however, at the start of any troubleshooting procedure, that you need to check a few things before getting too involved. These things include connectivity, power to the resource, permissions to the resource, and the hardware belonging to the resource. You will only waste valuable time if you go through an entire process for troubleshooting a remote access problem, only to discover that the client's NIC is bad or that a connection to the server isn't working. The majority of problems I've encountered revolve around connectivity issues, bad hardware, or permissions problems.

Active Directory

Several problems can occur when you're using Active Directory. Common problems and their causes are as follows:

- *If you cannot add or remove domains*—The domain naming master is unavailable, and this is most likely a connectivity problem. If the computer that serves as the domain naming master is working, check all connections to it. If the computer isn't working, make another computer the domain naming master, or replace the non-functioning computer. It may be necessary to seize the domain naming master role. Another reason why you would not be able to add or remove domains is if the DNS server that is authoritative for the zone is unavailable or offline.

- *If you cannot create Active Directory objects*—The relative ID master is unavailable, and this is most likely a connectivity problem. If the computer that serves as the relative ID master is working, check all connections to it. If the computer isn't working, make another computer the relative ID master, or replace the non-functioning computer. It may be necessary to seize the relative ID master role.

- *If you cannot make changes to Active Directory or group membership won't commence*—The infrastructure master is unavailable, and this is most likely a connectivity problem. If the computer that serves as the infrastructure master is working, check all connections to it. If the computer isn't working, make another computer the infrastructure master, or replace the non-functioning computer. It may be necessary to seize the infrastructure master role.

- *If you cannot change the schema*—The schema master is unavailable, and this is most likely a connectivity problem. If the computer that serves as the schema master is working, check all connections to it. If the computer isn't working, make another computer the schema master, or replace the non-functioning computer. It may be necessary to seize the schema master role. Before making any major changes, however, make sure that the person trying to make the change to the schema is a schema admin.

- *If some clients cannot log on*—If the clients do not have Active Directory client software installed, the PDC emulator might not be available, and this is most likely a connectivity problem. If the computer that serves as the master for the PDC emulator is working, check all connections to it. If the computer isn't working, make another computer the PDC emulator master, or replace the non-functioning computer. It may be necessary to seize the primary domain controller emulator master role.

- *If resources in other domains cannot be reached by any client in the domain*—Verify that all trusts are working properly, and reestablish trusts if necessary. When all clients in a domain can't reach other domains, trusts are most likely the cause. Other causes might be DNS or name resolution problems, discussed later in this appendix.

DNS

The best tools for troubleshooting DNS errors are the NSLookup utility and the event log. In addition to these tools, error messages also indicate specific problems. Both NSLookup commands and the event logs were discussed at length throughout the book, so in this section, I'll look at specific error messages:

- *Name not found*—This message generally indicates that the DNS client computer does not have a valid TCP/IP address, subnet mask, or DNS server IP address. IPConfig can be used to verify this information. Other problems that can cause this error include the inability of the client to contact the DNS server for reasons other than IP address issues, including lost connectivity or the DNS server being offline.

- *Timed out*—The DNS server did not respond during the time allowed for the communication. Again, general connectivity problems, downed DNS servers, and misconfigured gateways, subnet masks, and IP addresses can cause the timeout problem. PING and IPConfig can be used to verify a client's TCP/IP information and determine connectivity problems. The event log can be scoured for information about other types of problems.

- *No response from server*—The server contacted isn't running the DNS server service because it is down or isn't started. Either start the server, or configure the client to access another DNS server until the service has been started.

- *No records*—The DNS server contacted doesn't have any records of the requested type. Use the DNS console to see what types of records are available, and ensure that the DNS database files are in the %systemroot%\System32\Dns directory. Check the event log for other errors.

- *Nonexistent domain*—The computer or DNS domain name does not exist. Check the spelling of the domain, check connectivity to the domain, and use PING and IPConfig to view the TCP/IP properties and the availability of the requested servers.

- *Connection refused (or) Network unreachable*—A connection to the DNS server could not be made, most likely due to connectivity problems or a downed DNS server. Use IPConfig, PING, and Tracert to determine the problem.

- *Server failure*—There is a problem with the DNS server's internal files. These problems are generally typographical errors having to do with names and IP addresses. If the DNS server could not return a valid answer to the client query, check the DNS server's internal files for inconsistencies.

- *Refused*—The DNS name server refused to service the request; this probably occurred because the request was sent to the wrong DNS interface. Check the DNS server for interface requirements for client queries, and configure the client appropriately.

- *Format error*—The query or client request sent a request packet that was not in the proper format, and an error occurred. This could be due to packet corruption on the network or to an error in NSLookup.

DHCP

Because DHCP automatically assigns TCP/IP addresses to clients, only a few problems commonly occur with DHCP. Either the DHCP server isn't providing clients with addresses, there appears to be corrupt data on the server, or the clients have network configuration problems. Listed next are some common problems and their causes and/or solutions:

- *DHCP clients aren't getting addresses from the DHCP server*—There are many causes for this, but one obvious thing to check is whether the DHCP server's IP address has changed. If this has happened, clients will not be able to access the server. Clients also won't be able to access the DHCP server if it is located across a router that doesn't forward DHCP requests (is a DHCP relay agent). Finally, if more than one DHCP server exists on the LAN, make sure that they are not configured with overlapping scopes. Occasionally, overlapping scopes can cause problems such as this one.

- *A DHCP client has an IP address in a different range than other IP addresses on the network*—The DHCP client could not find a DHCP server and used APIPA to automatically assign itself one. You should ping the server from the client and repair the broken connection, or bring the DHCP server online.

- *The DHCP Server service has stopped*—Check that the DHCP server is authorized on the network and that configuration data is correct on the server, and check the audit log for DHCP errors. Most times, the problem that caused the DHCP service to stop is written in the event logs.

- *The DHCP server isn't servicing client requests for IP addresses*—This is sometimes the first and only sign that something has gone awry with the DHCP server service. This behavior has many causes, including the following: one of the DHCP server's NICs isn't working; scopes haven't been properly activated; the server is located on the wrong subnet; or the scope has a problem, such as retirement, incorrect exclusions of ranges, or corrupt DHCP databases. In the case of corruption, you can use the DHCP server data-recovery options. In all other cases, proper configuration should be attempted first.

Dial-Up Networking

Dial-up networking errors often have more to do with hardware failures than with software failures, and related error message numbers range from 600 to 781. Some of the more common error messages are described in this section, and following that are some common hardware problems and their solutions. Of course, not all problems are hardware related, but those that aren't are most likely user errors such as incorrect phone numbers, usernames, passwords, and the like. Some of the more common user errors will also be included.

Error Messages

There are 181 error messages related to dial-up networking; the most common are listed here. To see the rest, and a description of each, open Microsoft Help and type in "dial-up errors." Here are the common errors for dial-up networking:

- *602*—The COM port that the network connection needs to use is already open and in use by another program or user. That port will have to be opened before a connection can be made.

- *604*—The remote access phone-book file and the dial-up configuration are inconsistent and do not contain the same information. Reconfigure the connection.

- *628*—The connection has been closed and should be redialed or reconnected. This might happen with modems if the speed isn't set correctly.

- *629*—The connection was closed by the remote computer due to a noisy line, a phone line error, disconnection by the administrator, or failure to negotiate with the remote access server at an appropriate speed.

- *630*—The connection was terminated because of a hardware error (such as with a modem), a problem with a phone line, or an unrecoverable error.

- *634*—The user could not be registered on the network because of a protocol error or because the address was already in use on the network.

- *646*—The client is not allowed to log on at this time of the day.

- *647*—The account is disabled due to lockout, a disabled account, or security reasons.

- *648*—The password for the account has expired.

- *677*—A modem did not answer the phone; a person or an answering machine did.

- *721*—The remote computer is not responding.

Common Problems

Hardware problems are generally easy to fix and can involve replacing the hardware device or installing a different driver. Occasionally, the device might need power or is turned off. With modems, this is usually the case, and most modem problems are caused by an incompatible modem or incorrect settings on the modem. Other problems can occur if the hardware device isn't installed properly. The same is true of all other physical connecting devices. Once a connection has been made, though, intermittent problems with hardware can include the following:

- *Inability to connect to the remote access server*—This is generally due to user errors, such as incorrect entry of user credentials or passwords, and administrative errors such as incorrect phone book entries or improperly configured address books. However, if this is not the case, other possible reasons include the following: the remote access server is down; the user account isn't valid; the modem isn't compatible with the server; the telephone line isn't working; there is too much static on the phone line; or there is another type of physical connectivity problem such as a broken cable or incorrectly installed modem.

- *Connections to the remote access server keep getting disconnected*—Problems with connections being dropped intermittently might be caused by periods of inactivity, call waiting, someone breaking the connection by picking up a phone in another room, or incorrect modem settings.

- *Connection errors using PPTP, X.25, ISDN, or other dial-up hardware*—These can be caused by improper TCP/IP addresses, improperly configured software, and PAD configuration problems.

Group Policies

Problems with group policies can be harder to trace than other types of problems because group policies are software, and policy configuration problems are usually created by administrators and users. Other problems occur when policies aren't taking effect for users or computers or aren't taking effect locally. The following list describes some of the more common problems (for more problems and solutions, go to Microsoft's Web site or Microsoft Help):

- *Users cannot log on locally to a domain controller*—By default, users can't log on locally to a domain controller. If you want users to log on locally, this capability will have to be specifically configured in a group policy.

- *Auditing isn't working*—Auditing must be enabled in a group policy for any auditing to take place in Active Directory.

- *Group policies aren't being applied to security groups*—This is default behavior. Group policies affect only sites, domains, and OUs, not security groups.

- *Local, site, or domain policies aren't taking effect for users and computers*—When multiple policies exist, they are applied in this order: local, site, domain, OU. If any higher-order policy exists, the lower-level policy is ignored. Also, if No Override is set at any level, policies can be blocked at any level.

- *Local policies aren't working properly*—Because local policies are the lowest type of policy in the hierarchy, any other policy can override them. This is most likely the cause.

Installation

Installation problems do happen, and there are several ways to deal with installation attempts gone bad. In this section, I'll assume that the installation has broken down at some point, and I will walk you through some of the installation repair options.

Frozen Installation

One of the best ways to repair an installation is to use Microsoft Server's Repair option. This is necessary if there has been a loss of power during the installation or if the computer has frozen up and won't continue. You'll need to boot the server with the Setup disks and wait for the R=Repair option to appear on the status bar. After you press R, instructions are offered for repairing the previous installation. The first step in this option is to use the emergency repair disk (ERD) to attempt the repair. If you don't have one, other options are available, but it is best to use the ERD.

Note: If the ERD doesn't exist, and Windows 2000 will boot, then open the Backup program, and on the Welcome tab, choose Emergency Repair Disk. If the server won't boot, and you don't have an ERD on hand, this won't be an option.

Hardware Problems

Other problems that can occur throughout the installation process include the following:

- *Media errors*—A bad CD-ROM drive or a bad CD can cause an installation to fail or not to start. Make sure the CD-ROM drive is compatible and that the CD is free of scratches and fingerprints. You can request a replacement CD from Microsoft if you think the CD is the culprit. If it is the CD-ROM drive that is not working, you can either replace the drive or install over the network.

- *Insufficient disk space*—If there isn't enough disk space on the computer for the Windows 2000 Server files, you'll see this error. You can either install a larger drive or use the Windows 2000 installation to create new partitions, delete old ones, and format partitions as necessary.

- *Other hardware errors*—Windows 2000 Server installation can hang or cause STOP messages to appear if the hardware in the computer isn't on Microsoft's HCL. If incompatible hardware is the problem, replace the hardware before continuing.

Installation Errors

Occasionally, an installation will stop and specific STOP messages will be shown. Here are a couple of them:

- *Incompatible disk hardware*—This error is shown when Windows 2000 doesn't recognize the hard disk. Pressing F6 during the installation and installing the hard disk's driver before continuing with the installation usually solves this.

- *Hardware malfunction*—These types of messages are usually caused by hardware problems that need to be dealt with by a certified technician. This problem has more to do with the physical computer than with the installation process.

Domains and DNS Problems

Another common problem with the installation of Windows 2000 Server is the DNS configuration and the process of joining a domain. In my experience, if there is going to be a problem, it will most likely have to do with one of these two things. Here are some common problems:

- *Can't connect to the domain controller*—Occasionally, the domain name is spelled incorrectly, but more often than not, the problem is something far more complex. Before panicking, verify that the domain controller is up, and if it isn't, choose to join a workgroup during installation, and then configure the domain information after installation is complete. Usually, the problem is with an incorrectly configured or installed NIC, an incompatible NIC driver, or incorrect protocol settings. In my experience, the problem's cause has occasionally even been as obscure as a bad hub, bad cables, or faulty cable connections.

- *Can't find the DNS server*—This is the same as the previous problem and is equally hard to troubleshoot. Occasionally, the DNS name is spelled incorrectly, but more often than not, it is something far more complex. Verify that the DNS server is up, and if it isn't, choose to configure the DNS information after installation is complete. Usually, the problem is with an incorrectly configured or installed NIC, an incompatible NIC driver, or incorrect protocol settings. In my experience, the problem's cause has occasionally even been as obscure as a bad hub, bad cables, or faulty cable connections. The DNS server connection can be configured after installation has finished. General troubleshooting techniques, including using command-line TCP/IP utilities, can be useful in finding the problem.

- *Failure of a dependency service to start*—Again, the NIC or protocol is usually the culprit. Make sure that the adapter has the correct settings, including the type of NIC, and make sure the computer name is unique on the network.

- *Failure of Windows 2000 Server to start after installation*—This is usually a hardware problem. Replace any hardware not on Microsoft's HCL, and check for newer drivers. Try to boot the server in Safe mode, or use the Repair option.

Remote Access

Remote access problems are usually caused when a client can't access a remote access server. Most of the time, this is due to such user errors as incorrectly typed usernames, logon names, passwords, phone numbers, or address book entries. After user error, the next most common reason for remote access failures has to do with connectivity. Make sure that the user can ping the remote access server and that the server is online and working properly. With that out of the way, consider these other possible causes:

- The client or server modem isn't working properly, or the two are incompatible.

- The Routing and Remote Access Service has been stopped, has not been enabled, or has failed on the remote access server.

- Dial-in, PPTP, or L2TP are not enabled for inbound connections on the remote access server.

- The protocols on the remote access server are not configured for all of the types of clients trying to dial in.

- All remote access ports are currently in use, and no ports are available.

- The client and server can't agree on an authentication method, modem speed, encryption algorithm, or other configuration choice.

- The appropriate permissions for the client are not configured, or a group policy prevents it.

- The remote access server is out of TCP/IP addresses in its address pool.

- The remote access server is unable to reach an Active Directory computer for verification.

If the client can connect but cannot access resources, consider the following:

- IP routing might not be enabled, and clients cannot reach needed resources beyond a router on the network.

- Look at packet filters in the remote access policy, and make sure that filters haven't been configured that will prevent certain traffic from entering the remote access server.

Routing

Several things can go wrong with routing, and the most common problems are listed here. Routing problems occur because traffic and data are not being sent from one network or network segment to the next. If you are having routing problems, consider the following fixes:

- Make sure the Routing and Remote Access Service is started and enabled on the RRAS server.

- Make sure that routing is enabled for all protocols in use on the network. If both IP and AppleTalk are used, both protocols must have IP routing enabled. Also check that the routing protocols are installed and configured for the right interface.

- Look at the routing table, and make sure it is receiving routes from other routers on the network.

- Make sure that the router is configured with the correct subnet mask, IP address, and default gateway, and that the router is capable of communicating with its neighboring routers. Check the default route as well, and make sure it is not missing or incorrect.

- If the DHCP relay agent is not working, make sure it is enabled on the correct interface, that the IP address has been entered correctly, that it is working properly and can connect to servers on the network, and that the packet filters are set correctly.

- If RIP for IP is being used, make sure that the routing table entries are correct. The tables might be incorrect because an incorrect version of RIP is in use, there are incorrect subnet configurations on the network, the router is using an incorrect password, packet filters are too restrictive, neighboring routers are incorrectly configured, or default routes might not be propagated.

- If IP Multicast isn't working properly, but other routing tasks are, the NIC might not support multicast promiscuous mode. To determine if this is the problem, check the system event log in Event Viewer.

- If problems are occurring due to OSPF, make sure it is enabled on the interface, that neighboring routers are reachable, that the settings are correct on both this router and neighboring routers, and that a designated router exists.

B

- If problems are occurring with demand-dial routing, make sure RRAS is started, that demand-dial routing is enabled on both the server and the client, and on all interfaces, that demand-dial protocols are installed and configured correctly, that there are enough free ports for clients to dial into, that both the client and the server are using the same protocols, and that the user account is properly configured for the client.

- If problems are occurring with RIP for SAP for IPX, make sure the RRAS is running and that the correct routing protocol is configured for both the interface and the client and server. Also, make sure that the router's IPX network number is correct and that packet filters aren't too restrictive.

TCP/IP

Chapter 10 introduced many tools for troubleshooting TCP/IP and resulting connections. These tools include PING, Tracert, Netstat, ARP, Nbtstat, and NSLookup. Besides the command-line tools that were introduced in that chapter, other TCP/IP troubleshooting techniques are available. When you're trying to solve a connectivity problem on a network, it is best to start with the hardware and the physical connection, and work up through the layers of the OSI model.

General Troubleshooting

The first step in TCP/IP troubleshooting starts with checking the network cable and the connection. Many problems are caused by faulty cables or loose NICs and can be solved easily. If the link light on the NIC isn't green, it isn't working. There would be no reason to check the TCP/IP configuration on a computer if the NIC isn't functioning properly.

If the light is green on the NIC, and the cable is working properly, see if you can browse the network. If you can see other computers in My Network Places, then you can be certain the cable and NIC are working well. If you can't, you might want to double-check the hardware before moving on. This can be done through Device Manager or by replacing the network cable.

The next step in TCP/IP troubleshooting is to check the configuration of TCP/IP properties, making sure that the domain and the computer name are correct. You should make sure you are trying to log on to the correct domain and that the computer name is unique on the network. These are fairly simple tests.

Before doing any pinging, make sure that the network card's drivers are installed, that bindings are configured appropriately, and that services necessary for communication are started. After hardware has been ruled out, and you know TCP/IP is installed and configured correctly, including the DHCP server address, DNS server address, local computer address, subnet mask, gateway, and whatever else is needed, perform the following tests:

1. Ping the loopback address: 127.0.0.1. If this doesn't pass and a reply is not sent back, reinstall and reconfigure TCP/IP on the local computer.

2. Ping a computer on the local subnet. If this fails, recheck the subnet mask and IP address of the local computer, and double-check the status of the cable connecting the local computer to the network.

3. Ping the gateway address. If this fails, check the gateway address configuration of the local computer and then of the computer or router acting as the gateway. Make sure the gateway is working and is configured correctly. Use the **ipconfig /all** command for this task.

4. Ping a computer on a remote subnet or another network. If this fails, you might have a routing problem.

5. Use Tracert to see the path a packet takes from the local computer to a remote computer.

Most of the time, a problem exists because the TCP/IP addresses are incorrect or the subnet mask or gateway has been improperly configured. Most times, these problems can be fixed by using the **ipconfig /all** command and PING to determine the problem. For more complex problems, such as routers gone awry or bad routing paths, see the "Routing" section, earlier in this chapter, or obtain help from Microsoft's Web site.

B

WINS

WINS resolves NetBIOS names into IP addresses for clients on a network. If problems arise with WINS, they do so generally because of an inability of the server to resolve names or the inability of the client to access the WINS server. Following are some of these problems and their solutions:

- If a server cannot resolve names for clients, the cause might be any of the following: configuration of the WINS server is incorrect; the WINS service might not be running; the WINS database could be corrupt; replication might not be occurring between WINS servers; or other replication problems may exist.

- If a client cannot resolve names with a WINS server, this problem might be related to connectivity with the server, the WINS server could be down, the client might not be configured correctly, or the type of name resolution might not be appropriate. NetBIOS names are 15 characters or fewer.

- Consider what name is not being resolved. It might be a DNS problem and not a WINS problem if the name to be resolved is a URL or FQDN.

- If WINS backups are failing, it can be due to the fact that WINS can back up its database to only a local disk and not to a remote drive. Make sure the disk is a local one.

- If the WINS database is corrupt or suspected to be, it can be deleted and rebuilt.

- If replications with other WINS servers are failing, make sure that any router involved is working properly, and if so, ping the other servers to determine connectivity. Also make sure that the appropriate push-pull relationships are configured.

Tips and Tricks

Several tips and tricks can be employed to make configuring and managing Windows 2000 Server components easier. Some of the tips and tricks listed here are also considered Microsoft's "Best Practices," and some stem from personal experience and learning the hard way. Any time a component can be made easier to manage, or be made to run with less administrator interaction, it is well worth the initial effort to do so. This section provides some tips for making Windows 2000 management a little easier.

Active Directory

Following are some tips for managing Active Directory and the Active Directory schema:

- When modifying the schema, be extremely careful and do not make changes lightly. Modifying the schema is best left in the hands of experienced programmers. For more information, visit Microsoft's Web site and search for *The Active Directory Programmer's Guide*.

- If you do modify the schema, make a backup of the system state first, and then make sure that it's offline and that the schema operations master is removed from the network. Before bringing the changes back online, fully test the changes in a test network similar to the organization's network.

- Do not always log on as an administrator, especially when tasks can be done by logging on as a print operator, server operator, power user, or other group member. When you're logged on as an administrator, certain viruses have a better opportunity to attack parts of the system not available to other group members.

- When logged on as a power user or other group member, you can use the Run As command to run programs (*.exe) as an administrator. This prevents you from having to log on as an administrator, and run the program as an administrator. This command restricts only that the program be run as administrator, while the logon of the user itself has not been changed. You can access the Run As command by using Windows Explorer to locate the program to run and then right-clicking while holding down the Shift key. You'll see the dialog box shown in Figure B.1. You'll have to know the administrator's password to run the program.

DNS

Following are some tips for managing DNS:

- You can enhance DNS performance on the network by adding secondary servers where needed. These servers can be used to balance DNS traffic, while the primary servers can be reserved for clients who use dynamic registrations of their A and PTR resource records.

- To simplify deployment and troubleshooting, use Active Directory and Active Directory-integrated zones where possible.

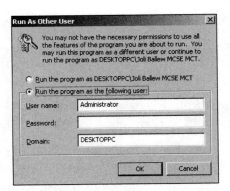

Figure B.1
The Run As dialog box.

- If clients are running Windows 2000 Professional, make sure they are configured to perform automatic dynamic updates of their resource records.

- Have some sort of DNS backup, be it two DNS servers or one primary and one secondary server, for every zone on the network.

- Don't randomly add CNAME records when they aren't needed to alias a hostname in an A resource record. Manually managing CNAME records can become quite tiresome.

- For all zones in the network, make sure that email addresses are configured on the DNS server for the administrator(s) for that zone. Email messages can be sent to administrators for a variety of reasons, including query errors and other DNS problems.

- Use the DNS console to change the DNS configuration. Even though you can use command-line utilities or text files, the console is less complex and will prevent mistakes.

DHCP

Following are some tips for managing DHCP:

- Use the 80/20 rule when using DHCP. Let one DHCP server use 80% of the scope of available addresses, and let a second have 20%. This setup provides fault tolerance and some load balancing.

- Do not deactivate scopes unless they are going to be permanently removed from the DHCP server. When a scope is deactivated, current leases are no longer serviced. To temporarily deactivate a scope, edit the exclusion ranges instead.

- If you must use DHCP conflict detection to check IP addresses before they are leased, make sure you choose to ping the address only one or two times. Any more than that will cause unnecessary network traffic and will slow down DHCP lease tasks.

- Because DHCP is resource-intensive, make sure the DHCP server is capable of handling the DHCP traffic and activity.

- Keep DHCP audit logging enabled so DHCP errors can be found quickly through Event Viewer and system logs.

- Do not change the default DHCP settings on clients or servers until such a need arises. Generally, the default settings are appropriate and work well for most organizations.

- If you are using routers, make sure they can act as DHCP relay agents or that they can forward BOOTP requests.

- Reduce or increase the length of DHCP leases to clients as necessary. For large, unchanging networks, longer leases will work fine as long as there are plenty of available addresses in the scope. For networks with lots of remote access clients, mobile users, or computers that are moved often, require shorter lease times.

Dial-Up Networking

Following are some tips for managing dial-up networking:

- Make sure all hardware related to dial-up networking is not only on Microsoft's HCL but also is compatible with the server's hardware.

- Before getting into protocols and connectivity with the server when troubleshooting, use the modem or other device's self-diagnostics to make sure it is working properly. Additionally, make sure the maximum port speed is set correctly on the device.

- Use automatic IP addressing for clients whenever possible. DHCP is enabled by default and is the easiest way to manage dial-up clients.

- Some clients will have multiple adapters or local area connections and will have multiple dial-up configurations. Make sure these connection options in My Network Places have intuitive names and are not easily confused. For instance, names could be "Dallas office," "Dial-up to Dallas," "Dial-up to Sacramento," or "ISP."

- For protocols, do not install unnecessary ones. There is no need to install IPX/SPX if only TCP/IP is used.

Group Policies

Following are some tips for managing group policies:

- Don't go overboard with No Override and Block Policy settings. Although these settings can be useful, using them too often can make permission and group policy problems difficult to pinpoint.

- The more group policy objects are configured, the longer they take to be processed, and the longer it takes clients to log on.

- You can disable parts of a group policy that are all configured as "not configured"; simply right-click on the console root, choose Properties, and then choose Disable User Configuration Settings. Even policies that are not configured must still be processed, and disabling them keeps them from going through the processing procedure.

- If group policy information is stored in another domain and must be processed from there, client logons will take longer.

- Users with laptops should, in almost all circumstances, have client-side caching enabled.

Installation

Following are some tips for managing Windows 2000 installation:

- Make sure that all hardware is on Microsoft's HCL and that the computer meets minimum requirements. Preferably, the computer should exceed minimum requirements.

- Before starting, have all of the required information written down—including the domain name, DNS name, server name, IP address, subnet mask, and gateway—so that installation can move smoothly through those areas.

- Know what type of licensing you will choose and why. Remember, choose Per Server if you aren't sure.

- Know what types of partitions and file systems you want to use and why.

- Don't install a multiboot configuration for a server unless there are compelling reasons to do so.

- Create a hard-to-guess administrator password, but remember what it is or you won't be able to log on and you'll have to reinstall.

- Practice remote installations and custom installations in a test lab prior to a rollout on the network. These types of installations can have various problems and should be thoroughly tested first to avoid lengthy network downtime.

Remote Access

Following are some tips for managing remote access:

- If at all possible, use DHCP for clients calling in and using remote access. This makes management simpler and less problematic. If DHCP isn't used, configure the remote access server with a static IP address pool from which addresses can be drawn.

- Use strong authentication, including passwords longer than eight characters and containing both numbers and upper- and lowercase letters, and make sure those passwords don't spell out words or names of users' pets or the like. Use the strongest authentication protocol that can be negotiated between clients and servers, such as MS-CHAP 2 instead of MS-CHAP, or EAP-TLS with smart card logons.

- A single remote user should have only one remote access policy, not multiple policies.

- If encryption can be used, use it. Encryption can be used with VPNs to make hacking passwords or other data more difficult.

- Enable account lockout so that after a certain number of bad password and logon attempts, the user is prevented from logging on for a specified amount of time. Also, set time restrictions when applicable.

- For demand-dial clients, you should configure dial-out hours and demand-dial filters to defray excessive costs and line charges as needed.

- Consider controlling remote access for clients through a remote access policy. This way, groups of remote access users can be managed together.

Routing

Following are some tips for managing routing:

- When you're creating a static routed IP environment, keep it small and limit it to a single path. Small is defined as 2 to 10 networks, and single path means that there is only one path that a data packet can take from one point to another on the network. Any other type of statically routed configuration will be too difficult to manage.

- Statically routed environments are good for small businesses and home offices or for branch offices with a single network. Remember that, with static networks, there is no fault tolerance because static routers do not update their route tables automatically.

- For statically routed networks, physically secure the routers so they cannot be tampered with, and give only a few trusted administrators rights to run the Routing and Remote Access Service.

- RIP for IP is best suited for small to medium-sized networks made up of 10 to 50 networks. These networks can have multiple paths for packets to take when moving from point A to point B. Because there are multiple links, the information in the routing tables changes dynamically.

- RIP for IP networks using Windows 2000 RIP routers have a maximum of 14 routers.

- OSPF routed environments are best suited to large and very large networks that contain more than 50 networks. These environments are generally corporations, campuses, or worldwide networks. As with RIP for IP, multiple paths exist for data to take. Even though OSPF was originally designed for the largest of networks, it can still be configured for very small ones. The single network uses 0.0.0.0 as the backbone.

- NAT networks should be configured with the default IP addressing schemes offered. The scheme used by default is the private network ID of 192.168.0.0 and subnet mask 255.255.255.0.

- In a NAT network, to enable Internet users to access resources on your private network, you'll need to configure a static IP address on the resource server, a subnet mask, a default gateway, and a DNS server. You must also exclude the IP address that is used by the resource computer from the range of IP addresses being allocated by the NAT computer. Finally, you must configure a unique port that is a static mapping of a public address and a port number to a private address and a port number.

- For a NAT network to access a private intranet using a VPN connection, you should use PPTP and create a VPN connection from the host to the private intranet server.

- For demand-dial networks, understand the cost of the line charges before deciding if the connection will be configured as persistent or on-demand. If the line is charging by the minute, then choose on-demand. If the line simply charges a monthly fee, perhaps persistent will work.

- If on-demand dialing has been chosen, use static routing. For persistent connections, it is best to use dynamic routing.

- The Windows 2000 Resource Kit includes the Rasmon utility, which can be used to view remote access connection information, including connection statistics, device errors, and line speed.

- When using demand-dial routing, use the strongest authentication encryption possible.

TCP/IP

Following are some tips for managing TCP/IP:

- Multihomed computers and devices need an IP address for each adapter that is installed.

- All TCP/IP resources on the same network segment should have the same subnet mask.

- You can configure multiple default gateways for a client, and if the first default gateway fails, the next gateway in the list will be tried.

- Enable TCP/IP filtering to limit what kind of TCP/IP traffic can be processed.

- In smaller networks, use APIPA if possible to avoid the overhead of administrating a TCP/IP network.

- Disable NetBIOS over TCP/IP for computers that use only DNS for name resolution. Some proxy servers can be configured this way because NetBT support is not required.

B

- Several TCP/IP utilities are available for connectivity, diagnostic, and server-based software. The connectivity utilities are Ftp, Lpr, Rcp, Rexec, Rsh, Telnet, and Tftp. The diagnostic utilities include Arp, Hostname, IPConfig, Lpq, Nbtstat, Netstat, NSLookup, PING, Route, Tracert, and Pathping. The server-based software utilities include TCP/IP printing services, IIS, and Peer Web Services. To get all you can out of TCP/IP and Windows 2000 Server, you should become familiar with these utilities. You can get more information on all of these from the "TCP/IP Utilities" topic in Microsoft Help.

- Of the three TCP/IP configuration options—automatic, dynamic, and manual— automatic is the easiest to set up and manage. However, APIPA is good only for small, non-routed networks. Dynamic addressing using DHCP is the next in line, offering support for any size network with easy administration and few problems. Manual addressing is OK for small networks but requires a lot of administrative overhead. Manual addressing is needed for certain computers and printers, but it should generally be avoided when DHCP or APIPA can be used in its place.

- TCP/IP should be integrated to work with DNS, WINS, IPSec policies, and TCP/IP filtering whenever possible.

WINS

Following are some tips for managing WINS:

- WINS default settings work for most organizations. Unless there is a reason to change these settings, don't.

- Static WINS entries cause administrative overhead and should be configured only if it's absolutely necessary. If you must use static entries temporarily, make sure you keep Migrate On selected; for permanent static entries, do not use Migrate On.

- When checking the WINS database for corruption or inconsistency, do so at non-peak times such as at night or on the weekend.

- When configuring WINS replication, use the Push/Pull choice.

- Don't install too many WINS servers; install only what you need. For WINS servers, more is not necessarily better.

- Make sure you back up and compact the WINS database regularly.

- Configure each WINS server to point to itself.

FAQs

There are several questions that I see regularly in my In box, and several that network administrators frequently ask me. In this last section, I'll list those questions along with the answers.

How can I get technical support from Microsoft, what does it cost, and what information do I need when I call or contact them?

There are several places to look for and get help with Windows 2000 Server. Listed here are some of those places and the order in which they should be accessed.

- Check the Windows 2000 Help files on the server itself first. There is quite a bit of information there.

- Try Microsoft's Web site and search for technical articles and the Microsoft Knowledge Base.

- Finally, consider assisted support. This support is available as both no-charge and paid assisted support, and it's available on the Web or over the telephone. (I've even gotten help through email, but I think I was just lucky.)

About Assisted Support

Free support is available if you purchased a retail copy of Windows 2000 Server and have a product ID number. With this, you are entitled to 90 days of support starting with the first time you contact a Microsoft Product Support Technician. The paid support runs currently at $195 U.S. for Web support and $245 U.S. for phone support. You can use most major credit cards, and the phone number is 1-(888)-456-5570 in the U.S. and Canada. Web support is available from Microsoft's Web site. This support is available 24 hours a day, 7 days a week.

Before you call, make sure you have written down the version of the product, the hardware that is installed, the computer type, the operating system version, the exact error message(s), and what you were doing when the problem occurred. If you've tried to solve the problem yourself before contacting Microsoft, you'll also need a full explanation of what you've tried already.

What are Requests for Comments (RFCs), and where can I read them?

RFCs are notes and technical solutions that are collected by the RFC editors (currently a very small group of people). RFCs contain information about the Internet and discuss many aspects of computer communication, focusing on networking protocols, procedures, programs, and concepts. These notes are located at **www.rfc-editor.org/**, and anyone can search for information on official Internet protocol standards or any other information regarding computers and connectivity. Often, you'll be prompted to read a specific RFC by Microsoft Help or by technical support to solve a specific problem or to gain more information about a particular component.

What are STOP errors, and where can I find out what they mean and how to fix them?

STOP errors are caused when a problem occurs with the processor, operating system, or installed hardware, and Windows 2000 Server cannot recover. There are several types of STOP errors, including general errors caused by unknown problems from which Windows cannot recover, specific errors caused by known problems from which Windows cannot recover, and hardware-related errors from which Windows cannot recover. Microsoft suggests that with any STOP error, one should try restarting the computer to see if the operating system can recover on its own. If this doesn't solve the problem, go here for more information: **www.microsoft.com/technet/win2000/win2kpro/manuals/progs/ pgsappb.asp**.

Where can I find out what specific error messages mean and how to solve the problems that cause those messages?

Error messages don't mean much to most people, especially if there isn't anything in the Microsoft Help file regarding the message or the message number. The Microsoft Web site now offers a place to type in the specific message and get a specific answer. This site is accessed at **www.microsoft.com/windows2000/support/search/default.asp**.

Are there any specific guidelines for Windows 2000 disaster recovery that I should follow before or when disaster strikes?

Yes, there certainly are. These guidelines start with developing a strategy before the disaster, understanding and using Backup and Restore recovery options, and restoring and reconciling server services. To download the documents for developing your own disaster recovery plan, go here: **www.microsoft.com/technet/win2000/recovery.asp**.

Where can I learn about the latest hot fixes and service packs, and how can I obtain them?

Again, Microsoft's Web site has an area just for this purpose at **www.microsoft.com/ technet/security/default.asp**. Here, you can obtain the latest hot fixes and service packs. Currently, SP2 is available as a download or for purchase on a CD. Also, information and articles related to viruses, security patches, and the latest hot topics are available.

Where can I find out about technical chats?

Microsoft holds many technical chats throughout the year that anyone can join. They are detailed at **www.microsoft.com/technet/chats/default.asp**. Microsoft will even send you an email reminder about the chat, and you can join in anytime you'd like. You can also send requests for technical chat issues to **technet@Microsoft.com**, and view transcripts of previous chats at **www.microsoft.com/technet/chats/trans.asp**.

What can I download from Microsoft for Windows 2000 Server?

Several downloads are available, and they change often. You can view the current available downloads for Windows 2000 Server here: **www.microsoft.com/technet/win2000/win2ksrv/downld.asp**. These downloads generally consist of the following types of programs or tools:

- Service packs

- Security bulletins

- Evaluation editions

- Migration tools such as the Active Directory Migration Tool

- Customer support diagnostics

- Free Resource Kit tools

- Help files

What types of newsgroups should I belong to, and where can I find them?

You can find newsgroups on any subject imaginable simply by typing "newsgroups" in any Web browser search field. Microsoft offers its own newsgroups at **www.microsoft.com/technet/newsgroups/default.asp?URL=/technet/newsgroups/NodePages/win2k.asp**. These newsgroups are vital to any administrator's arsenal of troubleshooting weapons. Newsgroup participants share information, problems, and solutions, and support each other by assisting in answering others' questions. In the Windows 2000 Server Networking newsgroup, you can currently view information about new service packs, intermittent network failures, logging in on multiple domains, and more.

Glossary

Accessibility Wizard—A Windows wizard used to provide accessibility options, including keyboard enhancements (such as sticky keys, filter keys, and toggle keys), sound enhancements (such as Sound Sentry), display options (such as high contrast), and mouse options (such as using mouse keys).

Account lockout policies—Policies that can be set for account lockout duration, threshold, and lockout reset counters. If too many failed logon attempts are made, the user will be unable to log on for a specific amount of time.

Account policies—A set of policies that includes password policies, lockout policies, and Kerberos policies. Account policies can be used to secure the network against unauthorized attempts at access and user actions that threaten security.

ACE (access control entry)—An entry in a discretionary access control list or in an object's system access control list. This entry contains information about a specific user's permissions or about an object's or user's auditing information, respectively. If a user wants to access a file and read it, the ACL must have an ACE for that user. If no ACE exists for that user, or if the entry doesn't match what the user wants to do, then that particular type of access is denied. If a user has Read permission in the ACE but not Write permission, the user can only read the file.

ACL (access control list)—A list that is used to keep track of which users and groups can access which files or folders and to what degree. ACLs contain access control entries (ACEs).

Active Directory—A directory service that logically stores all objects in a network and makes those objects manageable from a single machine. Active Directory services store information about objects and make this information available to the users on the network. Active Directory is the "glue" that holds all of the information, resources, objects, and users together on a network. Active Directory is what allows information to be readily available to users and clients, and it's a major part of what makes Windows 2000 such a successful operating system for networks. Active Directory offers a single point of administration for all resources, including files, printers, hosts, databases, users, services, Web access, scanners, fax servers, print servers, and thousands of additional resources.

Active partition—The partition the computer boots from. It must be a primary partition when you're using a basic disk. The active partition and the system partition can be the same if Windows 2000 is used and if the computer does not dual-boot.

APIPA (Automatic Private IP Addressing)—A feature that automatically assigns IP addresses to users on a network whether or not DHCP is used. APIPA can be used for automatic IP addressing on networks smaller than 200 clients in a small office. If DHCP is used, APIPA steps in to allow users on a network to communicate when the DHCP server is down. Because the IP addresses offered by APIPA are in the 169.254.y.z range, clients will be able to see only those clients on their own subnet, and APIPA can be used only as a quick and temporary fix when a DHCP server on the network goes down.

Assigned applications—Applications or upgrades that are installed automatically and the users have no choice in whether these applications are installed. Users cannot delete these applications once they are installed.

Asynchronous processing—A setting that allows users to log on before configured logon scripts have finished running.

Auditing—An option that can be set for logon events, account management, directory service access, object access, policy change, privilege use, process tracking, and system events for the purpose of monitoring a network while looking for potential problems or security flaws.

Author mode—MMCs can be run in this mode when a user or administrator needs to create a new console or modify an existing one.

Basic disk—A basic disk can contain primary partitions, extended partitions, and logical drives. It is created by default and is commonly used because it is backward-compatible with Windows NT volume sets, striped sets, mirrored volumes, and disk striping with parity. All versions of Windows, including 9x and NT, can use basic storage because it is the industry standard. Basic disks can be converted to dynamic disks without data loss.

Block Policy Inheritance—An option available for group policy inheritance that can be configured in a domain or an OU only. Administrators of OUs or nested OUs can block policy inheritance from the other levels processed before them. Because policies are inherited and are changed by the lower level only if there is a conflict, some inherited policies may be undesirable even though they do not conflict with an existing policy. If this is the case, administrators can block all policy inheritance from these upper levels. This setting can be configured in the Group Policy Editor.

Boot logging—A log used to debug boot errors. This log is created by the computer that is booting, is named Ntbtlog.txt, and is saved in the systemroot directory. A portion of the log shows the drivers that have been loaded and indicates whether they were loaded successfully.

Certificate Authority—A trusted third party that verifies that people and things are who they say they are. Certificates securely bind public keys to entities that hold the related private keys. These certificates are digitally signed and show that the data is reliable and has not been tampered with before its acceptance.

Certificate Services—A Windows 2000 component that provides an extra measure of security by creating a reliable way to exchange information on nonsecure networks; this is done by providing a standard for establishing the validity of and creating trust between networks that exchange data. The Certificate Services component provides a way to offer secure email, smart card authentication, and Web-based authentication. Components are additional utilities, programs, services, and support that you can add after basic installation to enhance what the server can do.

Certified applications—Applications (programs) that are fully tested by Microsoft and an independent testing organization and that are guaranteed to run on Windows 2000 Server without any problem at all.

COM+ (Component Object Model Enhanced)—A technology that was created to assist programmers in the development of objects and application programs. The Component Object Model (COM) provides an interface between objects on a network. Component Services, which are part of the software architecture, can process requests, such as determining the type of certificate that a particular server issues or intercepting system requests for the purpose of ensuring security. You can think of COM+ Services as creating an interface between objects, the same way the clipboard can be used to move a particular piece of information from one program to another.

Compatible applications—Microsoft's second highest ranking for applications. This ranking guarantees that the independent certified vendor has fully tested the application to run with Windows 2000 products and will provide Windows-2000-related support.

Cryptography—A mathematical technique that allows transmitted data to be encrypted (encoded) on one end and decrypted (decoded) on the other end to ensure that unwanted readers cannot interpret it.

DDNS (Dynamic DNS)—An extension of DNS that allows the integration of the DHCP server with the DNS server for automatic updating of IP addresses and domain names.

De facto standards—Standards that weren't stated as company policy or by any community or organization but were adopted over time by users, the public, or management.

Decentralized network—A network that is managed by multiple administrators or administrative teams. These administrators or teams might be located in different geographical areas or perform differing and incompatible business functions.

DHCP (Dynamic Host Configuration Protocol)—The DHCP server automatically assigns its clients their TCP/IP addresses so that an administrator doesn't have to manually install the individual machines with those addresses.

Glossary

Digital certificate—A set of data, used in public key encryption that completely identifies an entity, much like a birth certificate would when combined with a Social Security card and a driver's license.

Disk imaging—An installation option provided by the Microsoft System Preparation tool (Sysprep.exe). This option can be used when multiple client installations are needed and those computers have the same hardware. This type of installation offers the clients new security IDs and is fully customizable; however, like RIS, it can perform only clean installations of Windows 2000 Professional.

Disk quotas—Settings that are used to limit the amount of space that clients can have on the server's hard disk.

Distribution groups—Groups created solely for the purpose of email distribution. These groups do not enhance security in any way.

DNS (Domain Name System)—A service that resolves hostnames to IP addresses for clients on the current network. DNS is what allows a user to type **www.microsoft.com** instead of the TCP/IP address, which would be difficult to remember.

Domain GPOs—The third type of group policy object (GPO) processed. Domain GPOs override any site and local GPOs that have been configured. If more than one domain GPO exists for a network, those policies are processed in the order specified by the administrator of that domain.

Domain local groups—A type of group in Active Directory; these are most often used to provide the member user accounts with appropriate access to resources in the local domain. Domain local groups in a mixed-mode environment can contain user accounts, computers, and global groups. The domain local groups in a native-mode environment can consist of those objects plus other domain local groups from the same domain.

Domain namespace—A database structure that is used to locate objects on the network and to provide name resolution on the network. The domain namespace is used by DNS to provide name resolution for network clients.

Domain naming master—The domain controller where you can make changes such as adding or deleting domains in the forest. There can be only one domain naming master in any forest at any time.

Domain—A group of computers that are part of a network and share a common directory database. Each domain in a Windows 2000 network has its own Active Directory database and therefore creates a security boundary around itself. For other domains to be accessed, or for users in other domains to access resources in yours, appropriate trusts must be created. A domain consists of a Windows 2000 server acting as a domain controller, plus network resources such as other computers, printers, and files. Unlike Windows NT, a Windows 2000 network has no primary or backup domain controllers; it has only member servers and domain controllers.

Dynamic disks—Disks that can contain only dynamic volumes and cannot contain logical drives. Dynamic disks cannot be accessed by MS-DOS and cannot be converted to basic disks without data loss. Dynamic disks can be configured only for NTFS partitions and cannot be configured on laptops or dual-boot systems where access is needed to other partitions.

Extended partition—The part of a basic disk that can contain logical drives. If you want to configure more than four volumes on the basic disk, you can make one an extended partition with logical drives.

FAT permissions—Also known as Share permissions, these permissions can be placed only on folders, not on files, and because of this, there are fewer security options available for shares, and there is less control over files in shared folders. Users who are not supposed to access the share can do so if they are sitting at the machine where the share resides. Share permissions are Read, Change, and Full Control and are applied cumulatively.

File permissions—Permissions that can be placed on files. File permissions—which include Read, Read And Execute, Write, Modify, and Full Control—can be set only on NTFS drives.

Folder permissions—Permissions that can be placed on folders. NTFS folder permissions are List Folder Contents, Read, Read And Execute, Write, Modify, and Full Control. FAT folder permissions include Full Control, Change, and Read.

Folder Redirection—An option that lets administrators redirect a folder from a client's user profile to a specified location on the network for centralized management. The folders that can be redirected to these network shares include Application Data, Desktop, My Documents, My Pictures, and Start Menu. For instance, when a client saves a file to their My Documents folder, that file is actually saved to the network server and not the local machine.

Forests—Created from multiple trees, forests contain one or more Windows 2000 domains that share a common schema, configuration, and global catalog and that are connected by a two-way transitive trust.

Global catalog—The global catalog holds a replica of every object in Active Directory, and this list contains information about each object in the domain. The global catalog performs two main functions: providing information about universal group membership to the domain controllers; and allowing users to search Active Directory for information on any object in the domain. The global catalog does not replicate all of the information across these domains; instead, it keeps information on certain objects that are important to the global community.

GPOs (group policy objects)—Objects that hold group policy settings. GPOs are essentially documents that are created by the Group Policy snap-in. GPOs are stored at the domain level and affect all domain users.

GPT (Group Policy Template)—A container that stores information in Active Directory and is located in the Sysvol folder on a domain controller. The GPT stores information about security settings, applications for software installation, administrative templates, and script file locations. GPTs are created automatically when a group policy object is created, and they are named based on the GUID (globally unique identifier) of the GPO they are associated with.

Group policies—Policies that are used for the main purpose of securing the user's desktop. Applying a group policy is the best way to ensure that a user's environment is secure and to enable a corporate or company-wide desktop policy.

HCL (Hardware Compatibility List)—A list, available at **www.microsoft.com/hcl/default**, that is used to check the existing hardware for compatibility with Microsoft Windows 2000. This list allows an administrator to determine if the hardware about to be installed is compatible with Microsoft products. At the site, you can search for specific devices by type and, with the inventory list in hand, verify which hardware devices will work, will need to be retired, or will need to be replaced.

Home directories or **home folders**—Folders that can be configured not only for the local machine but also on a network server. Creating a user's home folder on a network server—rather than allowing the user's personal documents to be stored on the local machine—offers many advantages, such as centralized backup procedures and plenty of disk space.

IAS (Internet Authentication Service)—A service used to authenticate dial-in users on a network. IAS also supports the RADIUS protocol (Remote Authentication Dial-In User Service), which is a security protocol widely used by Internet service providers (ISPs) and which is the most popular type of authentication to date.

IIS (Internet Information Services)—Services used to turn a specific network server into a machine that can support the creation, management, and configuration of Web sites, support File Transfer Protocol (FTP), and support Simple Mail Transfer Protocol (SMTP).

ILS (Site Server Internet Locator Service)—A service used to keep user information current in network directories by scanning the TCP/IP stack and updating those directories. This service also provides support for telephony applications that allow users to access such options as caller ID, video conferencing, and faxing.

Indexing Service—A service that offers full-text searching of files. This service is installed by default during the Windows 2000 Server setup but is set to manual startup. The Indexing Service is processor-intensive, so before using this service, make sure that your server has the necessary resources.

Infrastructure master—A domain controller responsible for updating group member lists when group members are renamed or moved. The infrastructure master becomes involved only if a user from one domain is added or moved to a group in another domain.

IPSec (Internet Protocol Security)—An open standard for securing communications over the Internet. IPSec allows and ensures private and secure communications by using cryptographic services.

IPX/SPX (Internetwork Packet Exchange/Sequenced Packet Exchange)—A protocol stack that is used primarily in Novell networks, is relatively small and fast, and is fully supported by Windows 2000.

Kerberos Version 5—The network authentication protocol that is used by default on a computer with Windows 2000. Kerberos offers many benefits over other network authentication protocols. For instance, Kerberos allows the client to obtain credentials once from a server on the network and to then use those credentials to log on to any other server in the network. Kerberos also provides simplified trust management, offering two-way and transitive trusts between security authorities for available domains.

LDAP (Lightweight Directory Access Protocol)—A protocol used to identify objects through Active Directory and to let users view and handle information in Active Directory. LDAP is what allows a user to ask for specific components or objects on a network over a TCP connection. LDAP is designed around five models: Data, Organizational, Security, Functional, and Topological. These models define an object's attributes and class, how the objects are organized in the directory, how the objects are manipulated, where the supporting secure connections are, and how the information will be obtained for the clients.

Glossary

LKGC (last known good configuration)—An option that allows the computer to boot to the state it was in the last time it booted successfully. By starting the system with the LKGC, you can erase any device drivers, new adapters, and new services that were installed and that modified the Registry since the last boot-up.

Local GPO—Found on every Windows 2000 computer, the local GPO (group policy object) is configured for a computer even if it doesn't belong to any network and isn't part of any Active Directory domain. Local GPOs are the least powerful GPOs and are overridden by every other GPO that can be created. In a non-networked environment, local GPOs can be very powerful, but for the discussion at hand, they are the lowest in the group policy hierarchy and are thus loaded first.

Loopback policy setting—An option that allows an administrator to attach a set of user restrictions to the user portion of a GPO that holds the computer objects. There are two settings for Loopback: Replace and Merge. Replace simply ignores the user's own GPO list and replaces it with the GPO for the computer that the user is logged onto. In Merge mode, the user's policies are applied first, the new GPO is applied second, and the user's own GPO policies are overridden if necessary.

Message Queuing—A Windows 2000 component that provides services associated with the transfer of information that distributed applications need to function reliably even if a computer is offline. This service also allows these applications to function reliably in heterogeneous networks, and it provides loosely knit communication services.

Mixed-mode domains—Domains containing Windows 2000 domain controllers coexisting with Windows NT servers. Windows 2000 servers default to mixed-mode domains automatically when Windows 2000 Server is installed.

MMC (Microsoft Management Console)—A structure for holding various administrative tools (consoles). MMC provides a graphical interface for using these tools. The console's left pane usually holds a console tree, and the right pane is usually a detail pane. You can customize and extend your MMC by adding snap-ins.

Multi-master replication—A model that represents the concept of having multiple domain controllers instead of a primary domain controller (PDC) and multiple backup domain controllers (BDCs). In the multi-master replication model, replication traffic is not bothersome to clients on a network because replication can take place through a series of replications throughout the network and can occur at different intervals. If one server goes down, the others simply continue to offer network services, and this technology is transparent to the general users on a network.

NAT (Network Address Translation)—The process of converting internal IP addresses to external addresses for small networks. NAT can be used when clients need access to the Internet or an outside network only occasionally or if only one or two public IP addresses are owned by the company or organization.

Native mode—An operating-system mode in which all of the domain controllers in a domain are running Windows 2000 Server.

No Override option—A setting in Group Policy that allows administrators at higher levels of the Active Directory hierarchy to make sure that their policies are enforced at the lower levels. No Override should be used sparingly because it makes troubleshooting permissions problems more difficult.

NT LAN Manager (NTLM) authentication—The Kerberos of Windows NT. NTLM was the authentication protocol of choice for a Windows NT network, was based on a challenge/response technique, and is currently used in a Windows 2000 network when users need to access resources on a Windows NT 4 server.

NTFS permissions—Permissions that are used only on NTFS volumes and are not available for configuration on FAT or FAT32 volumes. NTFS permissions not only affect resources over a network, but also protect resources locally. Files and folders can have dissimilar permissions assigned as well. The ability of NTFS permissions to work locally and to allow the administrator to place permissions on files as well as on folders is another good reason to use the NTFS file system instead of FAT. See *File permissions* and *Folder permissions*.

NTVDM (Windows Virtual DOS Machine)—A utility that allows the 16-bit, MS-DOS, and other legacy applications to run in their own address spaces. The ability to have private address spaces is a main factor in reducing blue screens in Windows 2000 products.

Object—A logical representation of a resource on a network. The object contains information about the resource it represents. An object's attributes include such information as where the object is located, what type of resource it is, and other attributes.

OU (organizational unit)—An Active Directory container object used within domains. An administrator can divvy up the duties of a single domain among multiple departments without the tedium of creating trusts or using additional hardware. The OU can be used to group objects together by department, location, function, type, or just about any other category you can think of. An effective OU forms a meaningful, logical hierarchy that defines organizational structure and separates administrative tasks or services, defines the physical locations or functions of an organization, and/or delegates tasks of a network. An OU is the smallest scope to which a group policy can be applied.

OU GPO—Organizational unit GPOs are group policy objects that are processed in the following order for an entire organizational unit: root, child, grandchild, user, and computer GPOs.

Glossary

Pagefile—On the hard disk of a Windows 2000 server, an area that is used to hold information previously stored in RAM.

Parity—Information that is generally used in error checking to make sure that data was transferred correctly from one place to another. When it is used in RAID systems, parity creates an additional binary digit so data can be reconstructed if a single disk in the array fails. This parity information (binary digit) is stored on its own volume and provides fault tolerance. If one of the disks fails, the missing data is re-created using this parity information.

Partition—A portion of a disk that acts like it is its own physical disk. Partitions can be created on basic disks.

Password policies—Policies that are set for password history, age, length, complexity, and encryption for the purpose of securing the network against password attacks and other security holes.

PDC emulator—An emulator that is used mainly to act as a Windows NT PDC when Windows NT BDCs or down-level clients are on the network. Technically, the PDC emulator is the entity responsible for replicating updates to the existing BDCs. The PDC emulator also handles password changes and is the primary password authority on the network.

PKI (Public Key Infrastructure)—A set of rules, policies, and standards that allow the verification of all parties in an electronic transaction. PKI consists of digital certificates, Certification Authorities, and various third-party certificate signers. PKI allows a network to protect itself against unwanted attacks and lapses in security by using new authentication techniques based on the cryptography of user names and hostnames, thus ensuring that critical data cannot be stolen from the wire. Cryptography is a mathematical technique that allows the transmitted data to be encrypted on one end and decrypted on the other end to ensure that it cannot be interpreted by unwanted readers.

PnP (Plug and Play)—Technologies that are incorporated into Windows 2000 Server to allow plug-and-play peripherals to be automatically installed. These devices can be disk drives, printers, or NICs, or any other type of applicable device. Windows NT 4 didn't provide any real support for PnP, and installing additional peripherals was usually trying. Windows 2000 solves this problem by offering a much easier way to install these newer devices.

Primary partition—On a basic disk, this is a volume from which the computer boots. You can have one, two, three, or four primary partitions on a basic disk, or three primary partitions and one extended partition.

Process—A program or a piece of a program.

Publishing applications—A way of providing applications that allows the users to decide if they want to install the applications offered to them or not. Users can also remove any applications installed at a later date. These applications are installed through the user's Add/Remove Programs icon in the Control Panel.

Quality of Service (QoS) Admission Control—A component, new in Windows 2000 products, that sets standards for the quality of data transmission. Using QoS services, you can specify the quality of each network connection for every subnet on the network.

RAID (Redundant Array of Independent Disks)—A data storage method in which data is distributed among two or more hard disks in order to improve performance and reliability. Also a method of classifying various types of arrays. Windows 2000 supports three RAID levels: 0, 1, and 5.

RAID 0—A RAID level that is used when multiple disks are installed and data is to be striped across the disks. For instance, if a disk array contains five disks, then a 20MB file will (theoretically) be broken up into five pieces, and each piece will then be written to each of those disks in order. When this happens, disk read and write time is improved because the data can be written across multiple disks faster than to a single disk.

RAID 1—An array that uses a mirrored volume. This scheme provides fault tolerance by writing all of the data to two physical disks instead of one. If one of the disks fails, it can be replaced, and the data from the other disk (the mirror) can be copied back to it.

RAID 5—Usually referred to as disk striping with parity. RAID 5 is similar to RAID 0 in that multiple disks are used, and data is broken up into pieces that are written to those disks in a specific order. Although there are major differences between these two RAID types, the main difference is that RAID 5 contains an additional disk to hold parity information.

Recovery Console—A powerful tool that allows an administrator to log on to a machine and troubleshoot it when it won't boot with safe mode. Troublesome drivers, a corrupt Master Boot Record, Registry corruption, and many other catastrophic events can be repaired using this method. An administrator can use this tool to access root and system directories and to perform repairs.

Remote storage—A utility that is used to monitor the disk space that is available on the company's server(s). This utility can be used to move data off the server if the data has been successfully saved to another location. This movement takes place when the amount of available storage space drops below a specific level or threshold. With Remote Storage, you can also make a server's disk space more efficient by making magnetic tape devices and other removable media more accessible.

Rights—Access rules that can be set for a number of events, such as allowing specific users to access this computer from the network, act as part of the operating system, add workstations to a domain, back up files and directories, change the system time, create a pagefile, debug programs, and more. Rights and permissions work together to secure the network.

RIS (Remote Installation Services)—This feature allows a client to connect (with the appropriate hardware) to a RIS server to obtain an image of an installation; this image can be configured to produce clean installations for clients. For RIS to work properly, the service must run on Windows 2000 Server, have access to an Active Directory DHCP server and a DNS server, and perform only clean installations of Windows 2000 Professional on its clients. RIS is an exceptional service that can be used to remotely install Windows 2000 Professional clients without having to physically visit each desk and install those clients manually. By using the Remote Installation Client Wizard, a DHCP server, a DNS server, and a RIS server, you can perform hundreds of remote installations quickly and efficiently across different physical locations.

Glossary

Safe mode—A boot option in which only essential drivers are loaded. Often, a new driver will be installed on a computer, and when the computer is rebooted, it will blue-screen. Using safe mode allows the computer to boot without unnecessary drivers, and problems can then be addressed.

Security Accounts Manager (SAM) database—A Windows database that includes information on users, local and group accounts, computer accounts, security principals, and existing trusts. The SAM is consulted when users log on to the network.

Schema—The set of rules that defines Active Directory objects and their attributes. Windows NT did not offer this type of manipulation. The schema is extensible, which means that within the Active Directory structure, new attributes and information can be stored. For instance, you can add a user's phone number, member ID number, or other information to personalize the schema to suit the organization's needs. The information in the schema is universal to all domains in the domain or forest.

Schema master—The domain controller that holds a writable copy of the schema. Because the schema is extensible and can be edited, this information must be stored in a central location, available to all domains in the forest.

Script debugger—A component that is installed automatically during the Windows 2000 Server installation. This component is used to identify errors in script programs that run on the server. These scripts may be written in VBScript, JavaScript, or other scripting languages. Script Debugger offers client and server tools for finding and solving script errors.

Scripts—Batch (.bat) and command (.cmd) files that are used to automate tasks that are run when the computer is started up or shut down or when a user logs on or logs off. Scripts have many configuration choices, including whether the scripts should be run synchronously or asynchronously, whether they are visible or hidden, and what the maximum timeout period for a script can be.

Security groups—Groups used to assemble resources into manageable units and to assign permissions to resources through those units.

Shared distribution folder—A folder created for unattended installations. When you do a network installation, the client must be able to connect to the server that contains the installation files. The shared distribution folder contains these files.

Simple volume—A volume that contains disk space from a single dynamic disk. When a basic disk is converted to a dynamic disk, it is first configured as a simple volume. You can extend this volume with space from the same disk or from other physical disks. If it is extended to other physical disks, it becomes a spanned volume. Simple volumes can be mirrored, but spanned volumes cannot.

Site GPOs—Group policy objects that are linked to sites to make the settings apply to them. A site GPO overrides a local GPO.

Site structure—The representation of the physical environment that is part of the Active Directory and is represented there. In order to identify the physical organization of your network, you must construct at least one site object in Active Directory.

Slipstreaming—A process that allows Windows 2000 service packs to be installed only once instead of the multiple times required by Windows NT. After new components are added to a system, the service pack does not have to be reinstalled. This saves time and money in a variety of ways.

Smart card—Essentially, a computer on a credit card. The card can be swiped through a reader, and the user can be authenticated using the information on the card.

SMP (symmetric multiprocessing)—The ability to use multiple processors such that the processors' tasks can be distributed evenly across multiple processors in the machine.

Spanned volume—A simple volume that has been extended to multiple physical dynamic disks. These volumes cannot be mirrored. Spanned volumes do not have to be the same size because when data is written to the volumes, it is written until the disk is full and then continued on the next disk.

SSL (Secure Sockets Layer)—A protocol that allows encryption for outbound connections and that provides authentication and privacy by using public key technology.

SSO (Single Sign-On)—A process that allows a user to have one set of credentials for logging on to a network. Windows 2000 supports SSO.

Standardizing—Agreeing on a set of specifications, methods, or technologies. Standardization has many benefits, and a major one is the ability to reduce TCO (Total Cost of Ownership) for a company. For example, standardizing applications will require less training for the employees. This standardization also reduces the number of help desk calls, especially if users will not be allowed to install their own programs.

Striped volume—A volume that stores data on more than one physical dynamic disk. The data that is written to the disks is divided into data blocks that are evenly distributed to the disks; this is called "striping." These volumes cannot be mirrored or extended. Striped volumes offer good read/write performance because the data is written to multiple disks simultaneously. RAID 5 is a type of striped volume.

Subnets—Subnetworks, used to separate a network into physical entities. Separating the network into subnets reduces network traffic by transforming one large network into smaller ones that are more easily administered.

Glossary

Swapping—The process of transferring information between RAM and the hard disk.

Synchronous processing—A processing method in which the desktop does not load until after the logon script has finished running. Consequently, users cannot log on until all logon scripts have finished running.

Task Scheduler—A tool, located in the Control Panel, that can be used to schedule programs or batch files to run at specified times or intervals or to run only once. These programs can be maintenance utilities, scripts, or even specific documents.

TCP/IP (Transmission Control Protocol/Internet Protocol)—The protocol suite that is used to power the Internet and for which Microsoft Windows 2000 products have full built-in support. An industry-supported suite of protocols, TCP/IP provides routable access to the networks of all types and resources.

Templates—Registry-based policies that are used to require certain Registry settings that establish the behavior and appearance of the desktop, including components, applications, and settings for printers, disk quotas, and file protection. The templates for users also contain settings for the Start menu, the taskbar, and the desktop. More than 400 settings are available for the user's environment.

Terminal Services—Windows services that are used the way older mainframes were used: the client doesn't have any software, so to speak, and instead accesses everything from the terminal server. The terminal server has all of the programs and applications, and Terminal Services is a utility that allows the Windows 2000 server to act as a mainframe for "thin" clients. The server can be configured to hold all applications and data, and the clients are configured to log on to this server and use its resources. Because clients can access the applications on the server, no applications need to be installed on their machines. In addition, data is stored on the server instead of on the client machines, making backups more efficient and secure.

Thin clients—Sometimes called "terminal server clients," these clients can access applications stored on a server that they cannot host on their own computers.

Thrashing—The problem of having excessive swapping and page faults on a hard disk.

Thread—A process that contains specific commands inside a program.

Transitive trusts—Two-way trusts that work like this: If domain A trusts domain B, and domain B trusts domain C, then domain A trusts domain C.

UDF (uniqueness database file)—A file used when more than one computer is to be installed and machine-specific information needs to be entered. This data might be multiple usernames or computer names, and it is used with the answer file to provide the ability to install more than one machine at a time. The UDF has a .udf extension.

Universal groups—New to Windows 2000, they can be used only when the domain is in native mode. Universal groups are used to assign permissions for users to access resources forest-wide.

User mode—The mode to choose when you want to use an MMC or assign an MMC to a user, and you don't want the user to be able to change or modify the MMC.

User profile—A collection of settings created through the Active Directory Users And Computers console to provide a desktop environment that contains the user's personal data, folders, Start menu parameters, and application settings. User profiles can be local, roaming, or mandatory, and they can be configured to affect the appearance of users' desktops no matter what computer they log onto. User profiles are stored in the C:\Documents And Settings\<user logon name> folder.

Volume—A portion of a disk that acts like it is its own physical disk. Volumes look like "C:" and "D:" in Disk Management and My Computer.

Windows Media Services component—A component that enables you to stream multi-media content from the server to the network users. It also allows a network to use Advanced Streaming Format (ASF) over the Internet or a local intranet. Windows Media Services can be used to offer training programs or other network-wide broadcasts to all users on the network.

WINS (Windows Internet Naming Service)—A service that's similar to DNS except that WINS is used to resolve NetBIOS names to IP addresses for clients on the network, and is used mainly with down-level clients, such as Windows NT 4 and earlier. Again, this service allows a user to type a familiar name instead of a hard-to-remember IP address.

Index

B

What's on the CD-ROM

What's on the CD-ROM

The Windows 2000 Server On Site companion CD-ROM contains elements specifically selected to enhance the usefulness of this book, including:

- Planning worksheets included for account and user policies, active directory, cost estimates, and topology.
- Design worksheets for OUs, trees, forests, and sites.
- Design worksheets for determining current standards, improving standards, and maintaining standards.
- Migration worksheets for project committees, migration methods, making the plan work, and pilot and rollout.
- DNS and DHCP server worksheets to ensure a smooth transition.
- A sample PDF chapter from the *Microsoft Project Black Book*. The book focuses on installing and implementing Project 2000 and includes project planning strategies.

System Requirements

Software

- Your operating system must be Windows 98, NT 4, or Windows 2000. For example: Your operating system must be Windows 98, NT 4, or 2000.
- Microsoft Excel is required to view and edit the worksheets included in the CD-ROM. See the following examples:
- Adobe Acrobat Reader is needed to view the Bonus Software.
- A Web browser such as Netscape Navigator or Internet Explorer is needed to access The Coriolis Group's Web Site or to email for support.

Hardware

- An Intel (or equivalent) Pentium 100MHz processor is the minimum platform required; an Intel (or equivalent) Pentium 133MHz processor is recommended.
- 32MB of RAM is the minimum requirement. For example: 32MB of RAM is the minimum requirement.